INTRODUCTION TO INDUSTRIAL/ ORGANIZATIONAL PSYCHOLOGY

SIXTH EDITION

Ronald E. Riggio

Kravis Leadership Institute
Claremont McKenna College

CONSULTING EDITOR

Lyman W. Porter

University of California, Irvine

PEARSON

Boston   Columbus   Indianapolis   New York   San Francisco   Upper Saddle River   Amsterdam
Cape Town   Dubai   London   Madrid   Milan   Munich   Paris   Montréal   Toronto   Delhi
Mexico City   São Paulo   Sydney   Hong Kong   Seoul   Singapore   Taipei   Tokyo

To my students—past, present, and future.

Editorial Director: Craig Campanella
Editor in Chief: Jessica Mosher
Executive Editor: Susan Hartman
Editorial Assistant: Shiva Ramachandran
Marketing Manager: Wendy Albert
Managing Editor: Denise Forlow
Project Manager: Sherry Lewis
Sr. Manufacturing and Operations Manager for Arts and Sciences: Mary Fischer
Senior Operations Specialist: Diane Peirano
Cover Design Manager: Jayne Conte

Cover Designer: Suzanne Duda
Cover Photo: Shutterstock/79582930
Digital Media Director: Brian Hyland
Digital Media Editor: Michael Halas
Digital Media Project Manager: Pamela Weldin
Full-Service Project Management: Anand Natarajan, Integra
Composition: Integra
Printer/Binder: Edwards Brothers Malloy
Cover Printer: Lehigh-Phoenix Color
Text Font: 10.5/12, ITC New Baskerville Std

Credits and acknowledgments borrowed from other sources and reproduced, with permission, in this textbook appear on appropriate page within text (or on page 502).

Library of Congress Cataloging-in-Publication Data
Riggio, Ronald E.
    Introduction to industrial/organizational psychology/Ronald E. Riggio.—6th ed.
        p. cm.
    Includes bibliographical references and index.
    ISBN-13: 978-0-205-25499-6 (alk. paper)
    ISBN-10: 0-205-25499-3 (alk. paper)
    1. Psychology, Industrial.   2. Organizational change.   I. Title.
    HF5548.8.R475 2013
    158.7—dc23

                                                2012011017

10 9 8 7 6 5 4 3 2 1

Student Edition
ISBN 10: 0-205-25499-3
ISBN 13: 978-0-205-25499-6

Instructor's Review Copy
ISBN 10: 0-205-92822-6
ISBN 13: 978-0-205-92822-4

BRIEF CONTENTS

PART ONE   Introduction

In this first section, we discuss the field of industrial/organizational psychology, learn what it is, and examine its history. The second chapter is an overview of social scientific research methods, and how this methodology is used by I/O psychologists. This section sets the groundwork for what is to come.

PART TWO   Personnel Issues

In these five chapters, we will take a "tour" of personnel functions in organizations. We will examine how jobs are analyzed, how workers are recruited and selected for jobs, how workers' job performance is evaluated, and finally, how workers are trained.

PART THREE   Worker Issues

These three chapters will examine important psychological states that influence employee work behavior: the motivation to work, the satisfaction one gets from a job, and the stress that occurs because of job demands. These three states represent the vital issues of why people work and what happens to them internally because of work rewards and demands.

PART FOUR   Work Group and Organizational Issues

In the next five chapters, we will examine how workers interact in the formation of work groups and larger work organizations. The study of this interaction of workers and work groups comprises a good part of the area within I/O psychology known as organizational psychology. In reviewing organizational issues, we will start small, looking at communication between two workers, and finish big, examining how large work organizations are designed and structured.

CONTENTS

PART TWO   Personnel Issues

CHAPTER THREE   Job Analysis

CHAPTER FOUR   Employee Recruitment, Selection, and Placement

PREFACE

Introduction to Industrial/Organizational Psychology provides an inviting and comprehensive introduction to the field of industrial/organizational (I/O) psychology. Two important themes guided the writing of this textbook. First, because I/O psychology is a field with both a strong scientific base and an applied orientation, the book demonstrates the connection between psychological theory and application: Theoretical concepts are shown to lead to useful interventions. Second, this book was designed and written with the student in mind. Whenever possible, the text draws on examples and illustrations from the world of work that students understand. For instance, many work-setting examples include service industries, such as retail chains and fast-food restaurants, and Web-based organizations rather than concentrating solely on traditional office or factory work settings.

Introduction to Industrial/Organizational Psychology is an introductory textbook that appeals to a wide range of students with varying academic backgrounds. It is designed for use in undergraduate survey courses in I/O psychology or in psychology of work behavior courses and is suited for courses that contain a mix of psychology majors and nonmajors. The text is appropriate for courses at four-year colleges and universities, as well as at two-year, community colleges. Although the book is written at a level that makes the material accessible to students who are relatively new to the field of psychology, the coverage of topics is comprehensive. The text includes "classic" theories and research along with the latest developments and innovations to make this a thorough and challenging overview of the field. Instructors will find this the most thoroughly referenced I/O psychology text on the market!

What's New: The Sixth Edition

It is surprising how much the world of work and work technology continues to change and evolve. It has only been a few years since the last edition, but much has changed and evolved in the I/O psychology world. As a result, there are several new topics in this edition. One major change has been the separation of the employee screening, testing, and selection process into two chapters: one focusing on recruitment, screening and placement (Chapter 4) and another devoted to methods of assessing and selecting employees (Chapter 5).

The final chapter from the last edition focused on areas related to I/O psychology, specifically human factors and occupational health psychology. I/O psychology is broad enough without taking students (and faculty) too far afield, so those topics have been omitted in this new edition.

As in previous editions, this edition is designed to be a resource for both the teacher and the student—a resource that gives a comprehensive overview but can also be used as a starting point for advanced investigations into the field of I/O psychology.

Aside from the new arrangement of chapters, the major changes and additions in this edition are as follows:

- A focus on the broader construct of job engagement, with job satisfaction, organizational commitment, and other positive employee attitudes and behaviors as components of engagement.
- More student-oriented features.
- New and expanded coverage of international issues.
- Cutting edge topics such as workplace bullying, virtual teams and organizations, and web-based training and assessment.
- Thoroughly updated. The latest research on each key topic has been included. There are more than 250 new references in this edition, most published within the last 5 years. Again, students will find this an excellent resource for term papers and in their future coursework.
- Expanded instructor's manual and ancillaries. The instructor's manual and test bank has been expanded and updated and includes exercises and additional material.

Text Structure

Introduction to Industrial/Organizational Psychology is divided into four parts. Part One provides an introduction to the field and an overview of research methods used by I/O psychologists. Part Two covers employee and personnel issues, including separate chapters on job analysis, employee selection and placement, assessing potential employees, evaluating employee performance, and employee training. Part Three is called "Worker Issues" and deals with processes that are worker centered: worker motivation, positive work attitudes and behaviors, and negative work attitudes and behaviors. Part Four covers organizational topics that are group oriented: communication, group processes, leadership, organizational power and politics, organizational structure, and culture and development.

Special features included in each chapter of *Introduction to Industrial/ Organizational Psychology* complement the text narrative and provide further illustrations and examples of I/O psychology in the "real world." One of these features, Applying I/O Psychology, takes some of the theoretical and research material presented in the chapter and shows how I/O psychologists apply this knowledge to make positive changes in actual work settings. A second feature, Up Close (which is particularly student oriented), provides students with practical information concerning how I/O psychology can increase understanding of everyday work situations. A third feature, On the Cutting Edge, highlights more current areas of research or practice in I/O psychology. Inside Tips, found at the beginning of each chapter, is designed to connect chapters and help students see the "big picture" of the field of I/O psychology, as well as to provide specific study tips.

The chapters are designed to facilitate learning. Each chapter begins with an outline of the topics and ends with a chapter summary and a series of study questions/exercises that help students review and think about the chapter material. Stop and Review questions are strategically placed in the margins. These questions are designed to allow the student to "self-test" whether she or he has retained important material just read or studied. A glossary of key terms also appears throughout the chapters, with a more complete alphabetical glossary at the end of the book.

The text is complemented by instructor's resource materials prepared by Heidi Riggio, Amber Garcia, and me. We have worked hard to make this ancillary package the best available. It includes detailed outlines, suggestions for lectures, discussion questions, in-class exercises, audiovisual resources, and other special features.

Supplements

Instructor's Manual with tests (0-205-87311-1): Written by Professor Heidi Riggio, Professor Amber Garcia, and the author of the text, Professor Ron Riggio, the instructor's manual is a wonderful tool for classroom preparation and management. Corresponding to the chapters in the text, each of the manual's chapters contains a brief overview of the chapter with suggestions on how to present the material, sample lecture outlines, classrooms activities and discussion topics, ideas for in-class and out-of-class projects, and recommended outside readings. The test bank contains multiple choice, short answer and essay questions, each referencing the relevant page in the text.

Pearson MyTest Computerized Test Bank (0-205-94800-6) (www.pearson mytest.com): The Test Bank comes with Pearson MyTest, a powerful assessment-generation program that helps instructors easily create and print quizzes and exams. You can do this online, allowing flexibility and the ability to efficiently manage assessments at any time. You can easily access existing questions and edit, create, and store questions using the simple drag-and-drop and Wordlike controls. Each question comes with information on its level of difficulty and related page number in the text. For more information, go to HYPERLINK "http://www.PearsonMyTest.com"www.PearsonMyTest.com.

MySearchLab (0-205-90113-1): MySearchLab provides engaging experiences that personalize learning, and comes from a trusted partner with educational expertise and a deep commitment to helping students and instructors achieve their goals. Features include the ability to highlight and add notes to the eText online or download changes straight to the iPad. Chapter quizzes and flashcards offer immediate feedback and report directly to the grade book. A wide range of writing, grammar, and research.

Acknowledgments

I would like to thank the many adopters of the previous editions of the text. Many of you have provided important feedback that has helped in revisions. I would also like to thank the many reviewers whose valuable input helped shape the six editions of the text. They have become too numerous to list, but special thanks to John F. Binning, Illinois State University, and Chris Cozby, California State University, Fullerton.

Special thanks go to my research assistants through the years, but particular thanks to Masakatsu (Bob) Ono for his work on this edition. I welcome all comments, criticisms, and suggestions. Please contact me at:

Ron Riggio, Ph.D.
Kravis Leadership Institute
Claremont McKenna College
888 Columbia Avenue
Claremont, CA 91711
e-mail: ron.riggio@cmc.edu

Follow me on Twitter: http://twitter.com/#!/ronriggio

To the Student (Please don't skip this. It will help.)

This book was written for you. When I decided to write the first edition of this text in 1987, I did so because my students complained about the texts I had been using. I was not happy with them either. They simply weren't accessible. They were too technical and not "student friendly." So, when I wrote this book (and subsequent editions), I have tried to keep my students in mind every step of the way. I have tried to keep the book current, readable, and relevant to students' current and future working lives. There are special features, such as the Stop and Review questions, that were created to help you determine if you are retaining the material you are reading and studying.

This text is set up to cover the broad-ranging field of I/O psychology, and I've tried to keep it interesting and lively. In addition, the text is designed not only to maximize learning but also to be a resource book for continued explorations of the field of I/O psychology. For instance, there is career and educational information about the field, and the book is very thoroughly referenced. Although some students may find it distracting to have points referenced with "(Author, year)" throughout, these references will be extremely useful in finding starting points for term papers or future exploration. I hope that you will find this text an important, permanent addition to your personal library. It is a book that can be used in future scholarly work, and you will find it a useful reference in your later career.

I would like to thank the student readers of previous editions for their valuable input, suggestions, and comments about the text. Please let me hear from you, as well.

How to Read and Study This Book

This book is set up to maximize your learning about industrial/organizational psychology. Key terms are set in boldface type when they are first discussed, and brief definitions of these terms appear in the adjacent margins (longer definitions are at the end in a glossary). You should look over the key terms before you begin reading a chapter and then alert yourself to them as you read. As you move along, you can test yourself by using the margin definitions. Of course, the key terms deal only with major points in each chapter, for there is much more to mastering the material. Not only should you be able to define important terms and concepts, but you should also know how they apply to work behavior. As you learn the important points made throughout the book, stop occasionally and ask yourself such questions as, "How does this apply to the working world that I know?" "Have I seen examples of this concept before?" "How can the material that I am learning be applied in my own working life?" "How can this new information help me to see work and work behavior in a new way?"

Also located in the margins are brief Stop and Review questions. Their purpose is to stop you at certain points in your reading/studying so that you can go back and review the material just covered. Often, students find that they get caught up in the reading, and they forget to retain or "encode" the material for later recall. The review questions are intended to help you check if you are retaining important pieces of information.

Three other chapter features are also set off from the text. The first, Applying I/O Psychology, deals with specific applications of I/O psychology theories or concepts. The Up Close feature offers helpful research-based information that can further your understanding of your past, present, or future world of work. These usually take a how-to approach to some common issue or problem at work. Finally, On the Cutting Edge offers some of the latest developments in the field.

At the beginning of each chapter is another learning aid called Inside Tips. This aid will help you understand how the various chapters and topic areas fit together. They may also offer suggestions on how to study the information in the chapter.

At the end of each chapter is a brief summary of the central concepts. There are also study questions and exercises designed to make you think a little more about the topics presented and to review and apply what you have learned. Finally, there are suggestions for additional reading. These usually include at least one reference book related to the general theme of the chapter (useful as a starting point for research papers) and a couple of topical readings—books or journal review articles on a specific topic. Welcome to I/O psychology.

PART ONE

CHAPTER

1

Introduction:
Definitions and History

Inside Tips
UNDERSTANDING INDUSTRIAL/ORGANIZATIONAL PSYCHOLOGY

This first chapter is intended to define I/O psychology and to give you a feel for what the field is all about and what I/O psychologists do. The examples drawn from the early history of I/O psychology and the discussion of current and future trends show how far the field has progressed over time.

Because industrial/organizational psychology is so broad in its scope, it is not easy to gain a good understanding of the entire field by simply learning definitions or studying some of its historical roots; to actually comprehend the scope of I/O psychology you need to get through this entire textbook. Each chapter, from Chapters 3 through 15, presents a general topic and several specialties that I/O psychologists study. As you go through the book, step back and try to see how the various topics fit together. You will then begin to find the threads that hold the field of I/O psychology together.

Like it or not, you and I will spend a big part of our waking lives working. Not only does work take up a large chunk of the day, it also often governs where we live, how we live, and the kinds of people with whom we associate. It makes sense, then, that we should want to learn more about the world of work and our own work behavior.

Have you ever wondered what motivates people to work, what makes someone a good manager or leader, or why some people are competent, loyal workers, whereas others are untrustworthy and unreliable? Have you ever considered the ways a particular job might be redesigned to make it more efficient or the processes by which large organizations make decisions? Have you noticed that work can sometimes be very engaging and a great source of satisfaction, but it can also be terribly stressful at times? Industrial/organizational psychologists have studied all these and other questions and issues.

In this chapter, we will define the field of industrial/organizational psychology, look at some of the specialty areas within the discipline, and learn a bit about what industrial/organizational psychologists do. We will also look briefly at the history of industrial/organizational psychology, focusing on some of the important early developments in the field. Finally, we will consider industrial/organizational psychology today to see how the field is progressing, and we will examine some of the important trends now and for the near future.

What Is Industrial/Organizational Psychology?

psychology
the study of behavior and mental processes

Psychology is the scientific study of behavior and mental processes. Psychologists use systematic scientific methods in an effort to understand more about the hows and whys of behavior and human thought processes. Within the broad field of psychology are many specialty areas, each of which focuses on a different aspect of behavior. For instance, developmental psychology focuses on developmental behavior over the life span, cognitive psychology studies human thinking (cognition) and how the mind works, and social psychology studies human social behavior.

industrial/ organizational (I/O) psychology
the branch of psychology that is concerned with the study of behavior in work settings and the application of psychology principles to change work behavior

Industrial/organizational (I/O) psychology is that specialty area within the broad field of psychology that studies human behavior in work settings. As you might imagine, the study of human behavior in work settings is a large undertaking. Most jobs are quite complicated, requiring the use of a wide range of mental and motor skills. Work organizations are often large and complex entities made up of hundreds or even thousands of workers who must interact and coordinate activities to produce some product, service, or information. More and more often, workers are physically distant from one another, working in different parts of the country or the world, coordinating their work activities through online networks and other communication technologies.

Some I/O psychologists study the basic personnel functions within organizations, such as the way workers are recruited and selected, how employees are trained and developed, and the measurement of employee job performance. Other I/O psychologists study the psychological processes underlying work behavior, such as the motivation to work, and worker feelings of job satisfaction and stress. Still other I/O psychologists focus on group processes in the workplace, including the relationships between workplace supervisors and subordinates, and how groups of workers coordinate to get the job done. Finally, some psychologists and other social scientists study the broader picture, including the structure of work organizations, and how the physical, social, and psychological environments affect worker behavior. The structure of this textbook will parallel these various areas of subspecialization in I/O psychology and related areas.

The Science and Practice of Industrial/Organizational Psychology

I/O psychology has two objectives: first, to conduct research in an effort to increase our knowledge and understanding of human work behavior; and second, to apply that knowledge to improve the work behavior, the work environment, and the psychological conditions of workers. Thus, I/O psychologists are trained to be both scientists and practitioners, in what is referred to as the scientist–practitioner model. Although some I/O psychologists may operate primarily as either scientists or practitioners, most I/O psychologists believe that the best practitioners are strongly based in the science of I/O psychology (Anderson, Herriot, & Hodgkinson, 2001; Katzell & Austin, 1992). There have been many calls for I/O scholars and practitioners to work more closely together (Cascio & Aguinis, 2008).

The scientific objective of I/O psychology involves the study and understanding of all aspects of behavior at work. As scientists, I/O psychologists conduct research and publish the results of these efforts in professional journals such as those listed in Table 1.1. The information published in these journals helps inform the practice of I/O psychology (Latham, 2001). We will discuss the scientific objective in great depth in Chapter 2.

It is important to realize, however, that the study of work behavior is a multidisciplinary, cooperative venture. Industrial/organizational psychologists are not the only professionals who study work behavior. Researchers in the fields of management, sociology, political science, organizational communication, economics, and several other social sciences contribute to what we know and understand about the worker and work organizations. Because this research takes place on many fronts, I/O psychologists need to be aware of recent developments in other fields. A quick look at the titles of journals that publish research of interest to I/O psychologists illustrates the multidisciplinary nature of the study of work behavior, including such terms as *management, business, personnel,* and the related area of *ergonomics* (see Table 1.1).

The multidisciplinary nature of the study of work behavior may be illustrated by current research on virtual work teams. Greater numbers of workers are physically distant from one another. Yet, these workers must collaborate and work together in teams. In studying virtual work teams, an information scientist might be concerned with the issue of improving the information technology so that the team members can coordinate activities efficiently. An organizational communication specialist might be concerned with understanding how the loss of the nonverbal cues present in face-to-face work teams might adversely affect the development of good working relationships among team members. A cognitive scientist might want to study the processes by which virtual teams

TABLE 1.1

Journals Publishing Research in Industrial/Organizational Psychology and Related Areas

Academy of Management Journal	Ergonomics
International Journal of Selection and Assessment	The Leadership Quarterly
Academy of Management Learning and Education	Group Dynamics
International Review of I/O Psychology	Organization Science
Academy of Management Perspectives	Group and Organization Management
Journal of Applied Psychology	Organizational Behavior and Human Decision Processes
Academy of Management Review	
Journal of Applied Social Psychology	Human Factors
Administrative Science Quarterly	Organizational Dynamics
Journal of Business and Psychology	Human Performance
American Psychologist	Journal of Leadership and Organizational Psychology
Journal of Business Research	
Consulting Psychology Journal	Personnel
Annual Review of Psychology	Human Relations
Journal of Management	Leadership
European Journal of Work and Organizational Psychology	Personnel Psychology
	The Industrial-Organizational Psychologist (newsletter of the Society for Industrial and Organizational Psychology)
Journal of Occupational and Organizational Psychology	
Applied Psychological Measurement	Training and Development Journal
Journal of Organizational Behavior	Work & Stress

generate ideas and make decisions. A management expert could be primarily concerned with how to lead and manage virtual work teams, whereas an economist might concentrate on the costs and benefits of virtual organizations. Many work issues are similarly complex and need to be examined from a variety of perspectives. Most important, we need to keep an open mind and stay in touch with what other disciplines are doing if we are going to truly understand the working world and human work behavior.

The applied objective of I/O psychology involves the application of psychological principles, and of knowledge gleaned from psychological research, to work behavior. As practitioners, I/O psychologists may be called on to deal with specific work-related problems or issues. For example, an I/O psychologist might evaluate an employee testing program or conduct an employee attitude survey or some type of employee training program.

The Roots and Early History of Industrial/ Organizational Psychology

To understand the impact that I/O psychology has had on the world of work, it is important to know a little bit about the history of the field. We will examine historical periods in I/O psychology's past and focus on a significant event or important phenomenon in each time period. We will later look at the present and future of I/O psychology.

THE BEGINNINGS

Around the turn of the 20th century, when the field of psychology was still in its infancy, a few early psychologists dabbled in the study of work behavior. For example, Hugo Munsterberg was an experimental psychologist who became interested in the design of work and personnel selection for jobs such as streetcar operator (Munsterberg, 1913). Another experimental psychologist who pioneered the field of industrial psychology (the broader label, "industrial/organizational psychology," was not used extensively until the 1970s) was Walter Dill Scott, who was interested in studying salespersons and the psychology of advertising (Scott, 1908). Scott went on to become the first professor in this new field and also started a consulting company to practice what was being learned from research.

Another early spark that helped ignite the field of I/O psychology was provided not by a psychologist, but by an engineer named Frederick W. Taylor. Taylor believed that scientific principles could be applied to the study of work behavior to help increase worker efficiency and productivity. He felt that there was "one best method" for performing a particular job. By breaking the job down scientifically into measurable component movements and recording the time needed to perform each movement, Taylor believed that he could develop the fastest, most efficient way of performing any task. He was quite successful in applying his methods, which became known as time-and-motion studies. These time-and-motion procedures often doubled, tripled, and even quadruped laborer output! Taylor's system for applying scientific principles to increase work efficiency and productivity eventually became known as scientific management. In addition to applying time-and-motion procedures, Taylor also incorporated into his system of scientific management other considerations, such as selection of workers based on abilities and the use of proper tools (Taylor, 1911).

Taylor and his followers, including the husband-and-wife team of Frank and Lillian Gilbreth (Lillian Gilbreth was one of the earliest women I/O psychologists), implemented the principles of scientific management and revolutionized several physical labor jobs by making the accepted work procedures more efficient and productive (Gilbreth, 1916). For example, scientific management principles and procedures such as time-and-motion studies greatly improved the efficiency of a wide variety of typical types of jobs, including cabinetmaking, clerical filing, lumber sawing, and the making of reinforced concrete slabs (increased from 80 to 425 slabs per day!) (Lowry, Maynard, & Stegemerten, 1940).

Unfortunately, Taylor's philosophy was quite narrow and limited. In his day, many jobs involved manual labor and were thus easily broken down and made more efficient through the application of principles of scientific management. Today, jobs are much more complex and often require sophisticated problem-solving skills or the use of creative thinking. Fewer and fewer people engage in physical labor. Many of these "higher-level" tasks are not amenable to time-and-motion studies. In other words, there is probably not one best method for creating computer software, developing an advertising campaign, or managing people.

Frederick W. Taylor was the founder of the scientific management movement.

time-and-motion studies
procedures in which work tasks are broken down into simple component movements and the movements timed to develop a more efficient method for performing the tasks

scientific management
begun by Frederick Taylor, a method of using scientific principles to improve the efficiency and productivity of jobs

UP CLOSE   What Does an I/O Psychologist Really Do?

One of the most common questions asked by students in I/O psychology courses is, "What does an I/O psychologist do, really?" The answer to this question is not simple for a couple of reasons. First, many undergraduate students and laypersons have not had much exposure to I/O psychologists either face-to-face or in the media. Unlike clinical psychologists, who are frequently depicted in films, interviewed on news shows, and stereotyped in cartoons and on TV, most people have never seen an I/O psychologist. A second and more important reason why it is difficult to understand what I/O psychologists do is because I/O psychologists do so many different kinds of things. I/O psychology is a broad field encompassing a large number of specialty areas, many of which are quite unrelated to one another. Consequently, it is next to impossible to talk about a "typical" I/O psychologist.

In addition to performing a variety of jobs and tasks, I/O psychologist researchers and practitioners (Ph.D.-level) are employed in a variety of settings, with about 40% employed in colleges and universities, about 20% working in research or consulting firms, about 20% working for businesses and industries, and about 10% employed in federal, state, or local government (Khanna & Medsker, 2010; Medsker, Katkowski, & Furr, 2005). The majority of individuals with master's degrees in I/O psychology are working in the private sector or in government positions. What's more, I/O psychology is a "hot" and growing field. The U.S. Department of Labor predicts that employment for I/O psychologists will grow by 26% through 2018.

I/O psychologists work for a variety of major U.S. and international corporations, including Dow Chemical, Ford Motor Company, IBM, Toyota, Disney, Standard Oil, Xerox Corporation, Unisys, United Airlines, and Pepsi. They can hold job titles such as Director of Human Resources, Personnel Research Psychologist, Vice President of Employee Development, Manager of Employee Relations, Senior Employment Specialist, Testing Specialist, Quality Performance Manager, Consultant, and Staff Industrial Psychologist.

To help you better understand what I/O psychologists do, as well as help you understand the diverse areas of specialization within I/O psychology, let's look at some brief profiles of actual I/O psychologists.

Dr. M is an I/O psychologist working for a large aerospace firm. Her main area of expertise is sophisticated robot systems, and she has helped design and test several sophisticated robotlike systems for use in outer space. Dr. M maintains that her training in research methods, which allows her to approach work problems systematically, was the most valuable part of her academic education.

Dr. C received his Ph.D. in I/O psychology in the 1970s. His first job was conducting research for the General Telephone and Electronics Laboratories on the organizational processes in some of the company's operational units, including assessing job satisfaction, facilitating communication, and helping to resolve conflicts. Some years later, Dr. C joined a large consulting firm, and he currently is employed by an international consulting company where he conducts survey feedback and other organizational development programs for a variety of businesses and organizations.

Dr. H was originally an I/O psychologist in the United States Navy. His responsibilities there included developing and researching placement systems for certain Navy personnel. He currently works for the U.S. government as a grant officer helping to determine funding decisions for psychological research projects.

Dr. R is an I/O psychologist who owns a private consulting practice in a small Midwestern city. Before becoming an independent consultant, Dr. R worked for a large consulting firm in a metropolitan area, where he conducted job analyses and ran training seminars for businesses. His decision to move to a less urban area was primarily responsible for his decision to start an independent practice. Dr. R specializes in personnel selection, job analysis, and the design of training and development programs, although he occasionally engages in other activities such as conducting attitude and marketing surveys and serving as an expert witness in labor-related legal cases. In a sense, he has had to become an industrial/organizational "jack-of-all-trades," because he is one of the few I/O psychologists in his region. Dr. R claims that the most valuable training he received was in statistics, psychology, and the business courses that he took after receiving his Ph.D., so that he could become more knowledgeable about various business operations and learn business terminology.

Ms. O received a master's degree in industrial/organizational psychology just a few years ago. She is an assistant director of marketing research for a national chain of fast-food restaurants. Her duties include researching the sites for new restaurants and designing

UP CLOSE *(continued)*

and organizing customer satisfaction surveys. Ms. O also teaches I/O psychology and marketing courses at a local community college.

Dr. P, an I/O psychologist, is a professor in the school of management in a large state university. He previously held academic positions in university psychology departments. Dr. P is quite well known and respected for his research in I/O psychology. In addition to his research and teaching, Dr. P has served as a consultant for several large corporations, including many Fortune 500 companies.

Mr. K, who has a master's degree in organizational psychology, is the director of human resources for a biomedical company, which means that he is responsible for the administration of all facets of human resources for his

organization. Mr. K oversees payroll, benefits, compensation, and personnel activities such as the development of job descriptions, employee selection, and personnel training. He also has an active internship program that uses undergraduate and graduate students as interns who help set up special human resource programs for his employees.

After a successful career in the finance industry, Dr. A went back to graduate school and received her Ph.D. in industrial/organizational psychology. She has worked in the human resources department at AT&T and has published books and research articles on a variety of topics in I/O psychology. She is currently president of a consulting organization and is quite active in research and professional affairs in the field.

It is important to emphasize that scientific management and I/O psychology are not directly connected, although the principles of scientific management did have an influence on the development of I/O psychology. Today, industrial engineers carry on the tradition of scientific management in efforts to improve the efficiency of jobs. Although work efficiency and increased productivity are certainly important to I/O psychologists, I/O psychology looks beyond efficiency to examine the impact of work procedures and conditions on the working person.

Stop & Review

Describe in detail the two objectives of I/O psychology.

WORLD WAR I AND THE 1920s

At the outbreak of World War I, Robert Yerkes, who was president of the American Psychological Association, and a group of psychologists worked with the U.S. Army to create intelligence tests for the placement of Army recruits. The Army Alpha and Beta tests (the Alpha test was used for those who could read; the Beta test for nonliterate recruits) represented the first mass testing efforts and set the stage for future testing efforts. Even today, employee testing and selection is an important area of I/O psychology. Following World War I, psychologists began to be involved in the screening and placement of personnel in industry. Throughout the 1920s, while the United States was experiencing tremendous industrial growth, industrial psychology began to take hold: The first doctoral degree in industrial psychology was awarded in 1921, and psychologists worked directly with industries as consultants and researchers (Katzell & Austin, 1992).

Lillian Gilbreth was an influential early I/O psychologist.

It was also in the 1920s that the first psychological consulting organizations began. Walter Dill Scott opened a short-lived personnel consulting firm in 1919, and the Psychological Corporation was founded by James McKeen Cattell in 1921 (Vinchur & Koppes, 2011). Today, consulting organizations offering consulting services to business and industry are thriving and are a major place of employment for I/O psychologists.

The Great Depression Years and World War II

As the U.S. economy slumped during the 1930s, there was less opportunity for industrial psychologists to work with industries and businesses. Although industrial psychology continued to grow at a slower pace, an important development came out of this period from a group of Harvard psychologists who were conducting a series of experiments at a manufacturing plant of the Western Electric Company in Hawthorne, Illinois. Researcher Elton Mayo and his colleagues wanted to study the effects of the physical work environment on worker productivity.

In the most famous of the experiments, Mayo explored the effects of lighting on worker productivity. Focusing on a group of women who were assembling electrical relay-switching devices, he systematically varied the level of illumination in the room. He expected to be able to determine the optimal level of lighting for performing the task. However, the results were surprising and dramatically changed psychologists' views of the worker from then on. No matter what level the lighting was set at, productivity increased! When lighting was increased, worker output went up. Further increase to very bright illumination resulted in further improvement. Turning the lights down (even to such low levels that it appeared that the women were working in moonlight) also led to increases in productivity. There was a steady increase in workers' output following any change in lighting. In other studies, Mayo systematically varied the length and timing of work breaks. Longer breaks, shorter breaks, and more or fewer breaks, all resulted in a steady increase in worker output (Mayo, 1933).

Mayo knew that every change in the work environment could not possibly be causing the steady rises in worker productivity. Something else had to be affecting output. Upon closer examination, he concluded that the workers were being affected not by the changes in the physical environment but by the simple fact that they knew they were being observed. According to Mayo, these workers believed that the studies were being conducted in an effort to improve work procedures, and their positive expectations, coupled with their knowledge of the observations, seemed to Mayo to determine their consistent increases in productivity, a phenomenon that has been labeled the Hawthorne effect. Although in the first example discovered by Mayo the "Hawthorne effect" was positive, resulting in increased productivity, this was not always the case. In another of his studies, work group productivity fell following the introduction of changes in the work environment. Because these workers believed that the results of the studies would lead to more demanding production quotas, they restricted output whenever they were being observed, thus producing a "negative" Hawthorne effect (Roethlisberger & Dickson, 1939).

Although researchers have noted a number of serious flaws in the methods Mayo used to conduct the Hawthorne experiments (see Chapter 2), the general conclusions reached by Mayo and his colleagues resulted in the development of the human relations movement, which recognized the importance of social factors and something called "worker morale" in influencing work productivity. In fact, this movement stated that a harmonious work environment, with good interpersonal relationships among coworkers, should be a productive work environment, particularly when the work itself is boring or monotonous. According to Mayo,

Hawthorne effect
changes in behavior occurring as a function of participants' knowledge that they are being observed and their expectations concerning their role as research participants

human relations movement
a movement based on the studies of Elton Mayo that emphasizes the importance of social factors in influencing work performance

workers in repetitive or low-level positions—jobs that do not themselves provide satisfaction—will turn to the social environment of the work setting for motivation.

World War II also contributed greatly to the growth of I/O psychology. First, the tremendous need for state-of-the-art machinery, and the increasing complexity of that machinery, was an important impetus for human factors psychology, and for training soldiers to operate the equipment. Second, I/O psychologists were called on to improve selection and placement of military personnel, continuing the work that psychologists had begun during World War I.

The *Army General Classification Test,* a group-administered, pencil-and-paper test, was developed to separate recruits into categories based on their abilities to learn military duties and responsibilities. Screening tests were also created to select candidates for officer training. In addition, psychologists helped the U.S. Office of Strategic Services (OSS)—the forerunner of today's CIA—develop intensive assessment strategies for selecting candidates for dangerous espionage positions. Some of these techniques included "hands-on" situational tests in which candidates had to perform some tasks under difficult and near impossible conditions. The aim was to assess their ability to deal with stressful and frustrating circumstances, which is very important for soldiers involved in military espionage.

THE POSTWAR YEARS AND THE MODERN ERA

It was after World War II that industrial/organizational psychology truly began to blossom, and specialty areas began to emerge. A distinct focus on personnel issues, such as testing, selection, and the evaluation of employees, was helped in part by the publication of a new journal, *Personnel Psychology,* in 1948. During the Cold War years of the 1950s and 1960s, the growth of the defense industry further spurred the development of a specialty area called engineering psychology (today referred to as human factors psychology, or ergonomics; this has become a separate discipline, but shares roots with I/O psychology). Engineering psychologists were called in to help design control systems that were both sensible and easy to operate. In addition, the contributions of sociologists and social psychologists who began studying and performing extensive research in work organizations helped create a subspecialty area of organizational psychology.

The 1960s through the early 1990s was a time when research and practice in I/O psychology flourished. Many of the topics currently associated with I/O psychology were developed and explored in depth during this period, particularly topics such as motivation and goal setting, job attitudes, organizational stress, group processes, organizational power and politics, and organizational development. We will examine a great deal of this work throughout this book.

One historical event during this time period that had a major impact on I/O psychology was civil rights legislation. One portion of the sweeping Civil Rights Act of 1964, Title VII, banned discrimination in employment practices. Designed to protect underrepresented groups such as ethnic minorities from being unfairly discriminated against in work-related decisions, this legislation forced organizations to take a closer look at the ways people were selected for jobs. Particular attention was given to the fairness of employment selection tests and personnel decisions such as promotions, compensation, and firings. Subsequent civil rights legislation protected other groups from discrimination, including older people (Age Discrimination in Employment Act, 1967 and 1978) and people with disabilities (Americans with Disabilities Act, 1990). As a result, I/O psychologists have played an important part in helping to establish and implement fair employment standards. We will discuss these matters further in Part II.

Industrial/Organizational Psychology Today and in the Future

Today, industrial/organizational psychology is one of the fastest growing areas of psychology. I/O psychologists are in the forefront of those professionals who are satisfying the huge demand for information leading to greater understanding of the worker, the work environment, and work behavior. They are involved in nearly every aspect of business and industry, and as we will see, the range of topics they research and the varieties of tasks they perform are extensive.

Perhaps the mission of the Society for Industrial and Organizational Psychology (SIOP), the professional organization for I/O psychology, most clearly defines this field (and reflects aspirations for the future):

> [T]o enhance human well-being and performance in organizational and work settings by promoting the science, practice, and teaching of I-O Psychology.

Although the efforts of I/O psychologists have helped improve behavior at work, other developments in the working world and in the world at large have in turn influenced the field of I/O psychology. We will examine four key trends in the world of work that are important today and in the future of I/O psychology.

First trend: The changing nature of work

Jobs and organizations are rapidly changing and evolving. Organizations are becoming flatter, with fewer levels in the hierarchy, and they are being broken up into smaller subunits with greater emphasis on work teams. With telecommuting, advanced communication systems, and sophisticated networking, people can work in almost any location, with team members who are quite remote. This will have important implications for how work is done, and I/O psychologists will be very involved in helping workers adapt to technological and structural changes (Craiger, 1997; Huber, 2011). In addition, I/O psychologists will assist organizations in redesigning jobs for greater efficiency, in creating new and more flexible organizational structures and work teams, and in helping workers become more engaged, motivated, and better able to deal with stresses that result from all the changes.

Many jobs are becoming increasingly complex due to technological advancements, and they are more demanding, requiring workers to process more and more information and to make more decisions (Ones & Viswesvaran, 1998a). In addition, organizations worldwide are reducing their workforces. Organizational downsizing is a strategy of reducing an organization's workforce to improve organizational efficiency, productivity, and/or competitiveness (Mentzer, 2005; Molinsky & Margolis, 2006). Organizations are downsizing

Stop & Review

Name three pre–World War II events that had a significant impact on I/O psychology.

---

organizational downsizing
a strategy of reducing an organization's workforce to improve organizational efficiency and/or competitiveness

because of technological advancements such as robotic and computer-assisted manufacturing that eliminate workers' jobs, because of increased efficiency in jobs and the elimination of overlapping worker functions, and because of a general reduction in middle-level managers (De Meuse, Marks, & Dai, 2011; Murphy, 1998). In addition, economic downturns, such as the economic meltdown in 2007–2008, tend to increase the number of laid-off workers. Moreover, catastrophic events can affect certain industries, such as the September 11, 2001, terrorist hijackings and airliner crashes that caused the immediate downsizing of nearly all U.S. commercial airlines. Downsizing requires organizations to "do more with less" to survive—including the fact that fewer workers are doing more work (Cascio & Wynn, 2004; DeWitt, 1993). Research evidence shows that some of the changes in the nature of work, such as telecommuting, increased mobility of U.S. workers, and organizational downsizing, have led to decreased levels of worker loyalty and commitment to organizations (e.g., Allen et al., 2001).

Another trend is **outsourcing** of work—contracting with an external organization to accomplish tasks that were previously done, or could be done, within the organization (Davis-Blake & Broschak, 2009). Outsourcing is used to increase output and can reduce overhead costs associated with the personnel needed to do the tasks in-house. I/O psychologists are involved in helping to understand the effects that the increased use of outsourcing is having on variables such as the way jobs are conducted, group processes, structure and design of organizations, employee commitment, motivation, and other factors.

outsourcing
contracting with an external organization to accomplish work tasks

Second trend: Expanding focus on human resources

The increasing concern with the management and maintenance of an organization's human resources that began with Mayo and the human relations movement continues to be important. Organizations have become more and more concerned about and responsive to the needs of workers. At the same time, organizations are realizing that skilled and creative workers are the keys to success. The term "talent management" is a frequent buzzword heard in organizations—important because it reflects the emphasis on the value of the worker and the need to select, care for, and develop workers' talents. This will become even more important in the future (Cascio & Aguinis, 2008; Losey, Ulrich, & Meisinger, 2005).

The technological age of the past few decades has seen a tight labor market for truly skilled workers, particularly in high-tech industries. This means that organizations will have to compete ferociously to attract and keep the best workers (Goldsmith & Carter, 2010; Turban, 2001). Greater emphasis will need to be given to such areas as employee recruitment and selection procedures. Companies will also have to offer more enticing benefit programs to attract and retain the best workers—including "family friendly" policies such as employer-sponsored childcare and extended family leaves (Grandey, 2001; Halpern & Murphy, 2005). In addition, continuing advancements in work technology and the ever-increasing body of knowledge needed by workers to perform their jobs mean that older workers will be retrained often to remain contributing members of the workforce. In addition, the United States and much of Europe is facing an increasingly aging workforce, and relatively fewer young people entering the workforce (Hedge, Borman, & Lammlein, 2006). All of this suggests the need

APPLYING I/O PSYCHOLOGY

Exploring Training and Careers in Industrial/Organizational Psychology

The usual professional degree in industrial/organizational psychology, as in all areas of psychology, is the doctorate (Ph.D.). However, a growing number of programs offer master's degrees in psychology with an emphasis in I/O psychology, and a handful of college programs even offer a bachelor's degree with a major in I/O psychology (Trahan & McAllister, 2002). The master's degree (M.A. or M.S.) can also qualify one as a practitioner of psychology, although licensing requirements may vary from state to state. In recent years, the employment picture for I/O psychologists, particularly those with a Ph.D., has been very good, with salaries among the highest in the field of psychology.

To explore graduate training in I/O psychology:

- Talk to your psychology advisor in depth about the process of applying to graduate programs, including the alternatives available, the requirements for admission, the deadlines, letters of recommendations, and the like.
- Find out additional information about graduate programs and the application process by contacting the following professional organizations:

  - The Society for Industrial and Organizational Psychology, Inc. (SIOP) is the U.S.-based professional organization for I/O psychologists. They maintain a Web site (www.siop.org) and have detailed information available about I/O psychology graduate programs at both the Ph.D. and master's levels.
    - The European Association for Work and Organizational Psychology (EAWOP) is the European counterpart of SIOP (www.eawop.org). (Many countries have national associations for I/O psychology.)
  - The American Psychological Association (APA) is the largest professional organization for psychologists. They maintain a Web site (www.apa.org) with detailed, step-by-step information for exploring and applying to graduate programs (including a "Guide to Getting into Graduate School").

- The Association for Psychological Science has some relevant information about scientific careers in psychology (www.psychologicalscience.org).

To explore a possible career in industrial/organizational psychology:

- Go to your university's career guidance office and to the psychology department advisor to find out what information is available on careers in I/O psychology.
- Both APA and SIOP have career information available at their respective Web sites.
- Arrange a short "information interview" with a practicing I/O psychologist in your area. Ask for a few minutes of the professional's time to find out first-hand what she or he does for a living. You might talk to several such professionals, because individuals' job duties can vary greatly. Again, the career guidance office may be able to help you locate practicing I/O psychologists.
- Read beyond the textbook. Examine some of the suggested readings at the end of each chapter. Go to the library and scan through some of the journals that publish research in I/O psychology. (There is a list of these journals in Table 1.1.) If you are really serious, you can join SIOP as a student member, with a SIOP professional member's sponsorship (your professor may be a SIOP member).

Regardless of whether you choose a career in I/O psychology, the topics studied by I/O psychologists pertain to just about any job in any work setting. A good knowledge of principles of industrial/organizational psychology can help facilitate understanding of human behavior and organizational processes occurring in the work place.

Note: All three professional organizations offer student affiliate memberships that you can join to receive regular correspondence.

for greater focus on personnel issues, such as recruiting, screening, and testing potential workers, and on employee training, development, and compensation programs, all of which are specialties of I/O psychologists.

While the skilled labor force is dwindling, the number of low-skilled jobs in the service industry is growing, as is the population of low and unskilled workers. A human resources challenge for the future is to help provide meaningful and rewarding work experiences in these positions and to help transition workers from the unskilled to the skilled labor force.

Finally, research in I/O psychology is beginning to focus more broadly, seeing the worker as a "whole person" rather than just a working being. I/O psychology is looking more and more at individual development, addressing topics such as the processes by which workers become engaged in their work, how they cope with stress and adapt to changes, and understanding the role of emotions in the workplace (Ashkanasy & Cooper, 2008; Härtel, Ashkanasy, & Zerbe, 2005). I/O psychology has also recognized the "overlap" between employees' work life and home life—that issues at home can spill over into the workplace, and vice versa (Pitt-Catsouphes, Kossek, & Sweet, 2006; Poelmans, 2005).

Third trend: Increasing diversity and globalization of the workforce

The increasing number of women and ethnic minorities entering the organizational workforce has led to greater and greater workplace diversity. This diversity will increase in the future. Women and ethnic minorities—who have been targets of employment discrimination—now make up the majority of the U.S. workforce, and there are similar trends worldwide. Moreover, the diversity of cultures in workplaces will also increase as workers become more internationally mobile. Existing workforces will consist of members from a greater number and variety of cultures. In addition, it has been suggested that there are many different layers or levels examining cultures and cultural differences (Erez & Gati, 2004).

Although increased diversity presents challenges to organizations and managers, this increased workforce diversity also represents a tremendous strength and opportunity. An obvious advantage of increased workforce diversity is the opportunity for different viewpoints and perspectives that will lead to organizational creativity and innovation (Jackson & Joshi, 2011). Increased workforce diversity can also help an organization in understanding and reaching new markets for products or services. An organization's commitment to diversity can also help in recruiting and retaining the best workers. For instance, cutting-edge companies that value workforce diversity not only attract the most qualified workers, but also the valuing of diversity permeates the entire organizational culture, leading to reduced organizational conflict, greater cooperation among workers, and increased flexibility and innovation (Cascio, 2009; Jackson, 1994; Loden & Rosener, 1991).

Industrial/organizational psychologists will have to assist organizations in dealing with the challenges increasing diversity will bring (Ivancevich & Gilbert, 2000; Jackson & Joshi, 2011). Although diversity has benefits, demographic and cultural differences can, if not carefully managed, create great difficulties in the functioning of work teams—increasing destructive conflict, inhibiting team cooperation, and impeding performance (van Knippenberg, DeDreu, &

Many organizations today are international with offices around the globe

Homan, 2004; Williams & O'Reilly, 1998). The key to dealing successfully with diversity will involve getting beyond the "surface" issues that divide people, and getting at the "deeper" benefits that diversity brings (Cascio, 2009; Härtel, 1998).

In the past several decades, there has been a rapid, continuing shift toward a more global economy. Businesses and industries worldwide are focusing more and more on the global marketplace (Erez, 2011). Companies that were formerly concerned only with domestic markets and competition must now consider the international picture. As more and more organizations go international, there is an increasing need for workers to be trained for working in or with organizations located in other countries (Stroh, Black, Mendenhall, & Gregersen, 2005). The successful executive or manager of the future must be globally aware, knowledgeable and respectful of other cultures, and capable of working with people from a wide variety of backgrounds (Teagarden, 2007).

Fourth trend: Increasing relevance of I/O psychology in policy and practice

Although I/O psychology has had an important impact in how we select, train, develop, and motivate employees, there is huge potential for I/O psychology to play an even bigger part in helping to improve work performance and make the conditions for workers better, more rewarding, and more "healthy." It has been suggested that I/O psychology could have a tremendous future impact on the workplace and that it is critical that research in I/O psychology be directly relevant to the practice of I/O psychology. Cascio and Aguinus (2008) suggest a number of workplace and social issues and questions that should be addressed by I/O psychology in the future. These include:

- Selecting and developing better organizational leaders—including leaders who are ethical and socially responsible.
- Improving the lot of workers through fair compensation, flexible work policies (including work–family issues), and reducing discrimination in the workplace.
- Leveraging workforce diversity and globalization in optimal ways.
- Improving performance through optimal management and development of talent.
- Helping organizations (and the people in them) to embrace positive change and be more innovative.

Stop & Review

Describe three current and future trends in I/O psychology.

Summary

Industrial/organizational psychology is the branch of *psychology* that deals with the study of work behavior. I/O psychologists are concerned with both the science and practice of industrial/organizational psychology. The scientific goal is to increase our knowledge and understanding of work behavior, whereas the practical goal is to use that knowledge to improve the psychological well-being of workers. The study of work behavior is a multidisciplinary, cooperative venture. Because I/O psychologists are not the only professionals who study work behavior, they combine their research with that of other social sciences.

Important historical contributions that led to the development of the field of I/O psychology include the work of Frederick Taylor, who founded the school of *scientific management*, which held that work behavior could be studied by systematically breaking down a job into its components and recording the time needed to perform each. The application of such *time-and-motion studies* increased the efficiency of many manual labor jobs. During both World War I and World War II, psychologists became involved in the psychological testing of military recruits to determine work assignments. This first large-scale testing program was the beginning of formalized personnel testing, which is still an important part of I/O psychology. Elton Mayo and his *human relations movement* emphasized the role that social factors play in determining worker behavior. Through a series of studies, he demonstrated the importance of worker morale or satisfaction in determining performance. Mayo also discovered the *Hawthorne effect*, or the notion that subjects' behavior could be affected by the mere fact that they knew they were being observed and by the expectations they associated with being participants in an experiment. Following World War II, there was tremendous growth and specialization in I/O psychology, including specialties within the field that focus on how work groups and organizations function and on how technology and workers interface.

Today, industrial/organizational psychology is a rapidly growing field. Several important trends present challenges to I/O psychology and represent cutting-edge areas of research in the field. These include the changing nature of work and the rapidly expanding nature of jobs, partly caused by a reduction in workforce due to *organizational downsizing* and *outsourcing* for efficiency; an expanding focus on human resources; increasing diversity in the workforce that presents both challenges and opportunities, including the increasing globalization of business. Finally, I/O psychologists are having a bigger impact on shaping policies and practices regarding the workplace and issues regarding workers and the workforce.

Study Questions and Exercises

1. Although I/O psychology is a distinct specialty area in the larger field of psychology, consider how the topics studied by I/O psychologists might benefit from other psychology specialty areas. For example, what contributions have social psychology, educational psychology, cognitive psychology, and other areas made to I/O psychology?

2. Consider the historical advancements made by scientific management, human relations, and the army's intelligence testing programs.

How has each of these influenced what we know about work and about workers today?

3. Consider the important trends in I/O psychology today. Are there any ways that these trends have affected or will affect your life as a worker?

4. Imagine that you chose a career path in I/O psychology. What research questions or practice issues interest you? How might these interests affect your choice of training in I/O psychology and the job title you might hold?

Web Links

www.apa.org

American Psychological Association—publisher of journals with information about careers and graduate programs.

www.siop.org

Society for Industrial and Organizational Psychology—excellent information on graduate training in I/O psychology.

http://www.psychologicalscience.org

Association for Psychological Science—includes many links to other psychology Web sites. Click on "psychology links."

http://www.siop.org/psychatwork.aspx

What do I/O psychologists *really* do? This is a link to the SIOP site that profiles the careers of I/O psychologists.

http://www.siop.org/gtp/GTPapply.aspx

SIOP Web site on preparing for and applying to a graduate program.

http://www.psychologydegree.net/

A resource for students exploring graduate education in Psychology, including I/O Psychology.

Suggested Readings

Rogelberg, S. G. (Ed.). (2007). *Encyclopedia of industrial and organizational psychology*. Thousand Oaks, CA: Sage. *This two-volume encyclopedia is a good starting place for understanding basic I/O psychology terms and concepts.*

Zedeck, S. (Ed.). (2011). *APA handbook of industrial and organizational psychology*. Washington, DC: American Psychological Association. *This three-volume set goes into great detail on all areas of I/O psychology. It is an excellent, and up-to-date resource for the serious study of the field.*

Koppes, L. L. (Ed.). (2006). *Historical perspectives in industrial and organizational psychology*. Mahwah, NJ: Lawrence Erlbaum Associates. *This excellent edited book provides an excellent history of the*

early days of the field of I/O psychology. There are two particularly interesting chapters: one looking at the history of I/O psychology in the United States and another looking at the non-U.S. history of I/O psychology.

Society for Industrial and Organizational Psychology, Inc. (SIOP), Division 14 of the American Psychological Association. www.siop.org. *The Industrial-Organizational Psychologist. The official newsletter of the largest U.S. organization of I/O psychologists. Although it is actually SIOP's newsletter, it looks more like a journal and contains current information about the field, timely articles, and reviews, as well as job announcements. Students can become SIOP members and get a subscription.*

CHAPTER

2

Research Methods in Industrial/Organizational Psychology

CHAPTER OUTLINE

Inside Tips
UNDERSTANDING THE BASICS OF RESEARCH METHODS AND DESIGN

This chapter presents a general overview of selected research methods topics and their use in general and specifically in I/O psychology. Although it is intended to be a general introduction to research methods, some of the material can be quite complicated, particularly if you have not had a course that has introduced you to these concepts. If this is the case, you might want to devote some extra time to this chapter and consider looking at an introductory research methods textbook, such as the one listed in the Suggested Readings.

Many of the concepts discussed in this chapter will be used throughout the book when presenting and discussing theories, interpreting research results, and studying the effectiveness of various interventions used by I/O practitioners. Because this chapter introduces a number of important terms, you should plan to spend some time studying their definitions and understanding how they are used. In summary, this is an important chapter that serves as a foundation for what is to come.

Imagine that you want to find the answer to a work-related question, such as what qualities make a person an effective manager. How would you go about answering this question? You might ask people you know, but what if you get conflicting answers? Your father might say that a good manager must have a thorough knowledge of the task and of work procedures. A friend might believe that the most important quality is skill in relating to people. Your boss might answer that the situation determines which type of manager works best. Three people, three answers. Who is correct?

You might then try another strategy: observing some good managers to see for yourself which qualities make someone an effective work group leader. But how do you know who is a "good" manager? Moreover, how will you determine which characteristics make the good manager effective? The only sound procedure for answering the question of what makes a good manager is to use systematic, scientific research methods. Scientific research methods rely not on hunches or beliefs, but on the systematic collection and analysis of data.

How would you approach the problem in a more systematic, scientific fashion? First, to determine the most important characteristics of a successful work group manager, you would need to define "success." Is a successful manager one who leads a productive work group, one who is well liked and respected by subordinates, or one who leads a work group that is both productive and satisfied? Once you have defined your criteria for managerial success, the next step is to figure out how you will measure such success. It is important that the measurement be accurate and precise so that a clear distinction between truly successful and unsuccessful managers can be made. Next, you must isolate the specific characteristics that you believe are related to success as a work group manager. From your experience or reading, you may have some informed ideas about the kinds of knowledge, abilities, or personality that make a successful manager, but you must test these ideas in some systematic fashion. This is the purpose of research methods in psychology. Research methodology is a set of procedures that allow us to investigate the hows and whys of human behavior and to predict when certain behavior will and will not occur.

In this chapter we will study the basic social science research methods used by I/O psychologists to study work behavior. We will learn why the research process is important for industrial/organizational psychology and examine the goals of social science research methods. We will review the step-by-step procedures used in social science research and conclude with a discussion of how research results are interpreted and applied to increase our understanding of actual work behavior.

Social Science Research Methods

One of the prime purposes of the social science research methods used by I/O psychologists is to enable the researcher to step back from any personal feelings or biases to study a specific issue objectively. Objectivity is the overarching theme of scientific research methods in general, and of social science research methods in particular. It is this objectivity, accomplished via the social scientific process, that distinguishes how a social scientist approaches a work-related problem or issue and how a nonscientist practitioner might approach the same problem or issue. Research methodology is simply a system of guidelines and procedures designed to assist the researcher in obtaining a more accurate and unbiased analysis of the problem at hand. Similarly, statistical analysis is nothing more or less than procedures for testing the repeated objective observations that a researcher has collected.

objectivity
the unbiased approach to observation and interpretations of behavior

GOALS OF SOCIAL SCIENCE RESEARCH METHODS

Because I/O psychology is a science, it shares the same basic goals of any science: to describe, explain, and predict phenomena (Kaplan, 1964). Because I/O psychology is the science of behavior at work, its goals are to describe, explain, and predict *work* behavior. For example, an I/O psychologist might attempt to satisfy the first goal by describing the production levels of a company, the rates of employee absenteeism and turnover, and the number and type of interactions between supervisors and workers for the purpose of arriving at a more accurate picture of the organization under study. The goal of explaining phenomena is achieved when the I/O psychologist attempts to discover why certain work behaviors occur. Finding out that a company's employee turnover rates are high because of employee dissatisfaction with the levels of pay and benefits would be one example. The goal of prediction would be addressed when a researcher attempts to use the scores from certain psychological tests to predict which employee would be the best candidate for a management position, or when a researcher uses a theory of motivation to predict how employees will respond to different types of incentive programs.

I/O psychology is also an applied science and therefore has the additional goal of attempting to control or alter behavior to obtain desired outcomes.

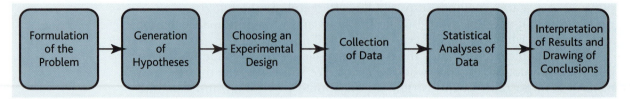

FIGURE 2.1
Steps in the Research Process

Using the results of previous research, an I/O psychologist can attempt to alter some aspect of work behavior. For example, some long-standing evidence indicates a connection between employee participation in organizational decision making and levels of job satisfaction (Argyris, 1964; Locke & Schweiger, 1979). Knowing this, an I/O psychologist might implement a program of increased employee participation in company policy decision making in an effort to improve levels of employee job satisfaction.

STEPS IN THE RESEARCH PROCESS

The process of conducting research typically follows a series of steps (see Figure 2.1). The first step is the formulation of a problem or issue for study. The second step is the generation of hypotheses. The third step is designing the research, which includes selecting the appropriate research method or design. The fourth step is the actual collection of data, which is governed by the particular research design used. The fifth step involves analyses of the collected data. This leads to the final step, which involves the interpretation of results and the drawing of conclusions based on the results.

Formulation of the problem or issue

The first step in conducting research is to specify the problem or issue to be studied. Sometimes, a researcher develops an issue because of his or her interests in a particular area. For example, an I/O psychologist might be interested in the relationships between worker job satisfaction and employee loyalty to the organization, or between worker productivity and the length of time that employees stay with a particular organization. Often, the selection of a research problem is influenced by previous research. On the other hand, a client company that has a particular problem that needs to be alleviated, such as an extraordinarily high level of employee absenteeism, may provide the practicing I/O psychologist–consultant with an issue. Similarly, large organizations may have I/O psychologists on staff whose job is to study problems using social science methods to better understand the problem or to help solve it.

variables
the elements measured in research investigations

Generation of hypotheses

hypotheses
statements about the supposed relationships between or among variables

The next step in the research process involves taking those elements that the researcher intends to measure, known as **variables**, and generating statements concerning the supposed relationships between or among variables. These statements are known as **hypotheses**. In the examples of research issues given

TABLE 2.1
Examples of Hypotheses in I/O Psychology Research

- Greater employee participation in organizational decision making is related to higher levels of job satisfaction (Locke & Schweiger, 1979).
- High rates of pay are related to high job satisfaction [this study found only a marginal relationship between pay and satisfaction] (Judge et al., 2010).
- Use of tests of mechanical ability increases the effectiveness of selecting employees for mechanical and engineering positions (Muchinsky, 1993).
- Applicants who are characterized by a higher degree of conscientiousness will exhibit higher levels of job performance (Barrick & Mount, 1991).
- Employees with high job demands and fewer resources to do their job are more likely to experience job burnout (Nahrgang, Morgeson, & Hofmann, 2011).
- As employee age increases, voluntary absenteeism decreases (Hackett, 1990).
- Increasing employees' sense of control over the work environment is related to reductions in work stress (Jackson, 1983).

earlier, job satisfaction, worker productivity, employee loyalty, employment tenure, and absenteeism are all variables. The hypotheses will later be tested through the analysis of the collected, systematic observations of variables, better known as the collection and analysis of research data (see Table 2.1).

By testing hypotheses through the collection of systematic observations of behavior, a researcher may eventually develop a theory or model, which is an organization of beliefs that enables us to understand behavior more completely. In social science, models are representations of the complexity of factors that affect behavior. In I/O psychology, models are representations of the factors that affect work behavior.

theory/model
the organization of beliefs into a representation of the factors that affect behavior

We have all seen architects' cardboard and plaster models of buildings and the plastic models of aircraft that can be purchased in hobby shops. These are concrete models that represent the physical appearance of the actual building or aircraft. The models used in I/O psychology research are abstract representations of the factors influencing work behavior. Developing a theory and diagramming that theory are convenient ways to organize our thinking and our understanding of complex behavioral processes.

Many people who do not have an understanding of scientific research methodology have misconceptions about theories. Either they believe that theories represent the personal views of scientists, or they believe that theories represent proven facts. Neither is wholly true. Theories are important because they help us to represent the complex and often intangible forces that influence human behavior. By using a theory as a guide, I/O psychologists can develop strategies for conducting research to find support for, or against, the theory. A theory is the starting point for understanding and influencing behavior, and theories can be used as guides to improve the work world for all concerned.

Although I/O psychologists use research models to guide their investigations, models of human work behavior are also the products of research. The researcher may use an existing theory or model to develop certain hypotheses about aspects of work behavior and then test those hypotheses through research. These results may then be used to refine the model or to create a new, "improved" model. It is through the creation, testing, and refinement of theories that advances are made in the science of I/O psychology.

Selecting the research design

Once hypotheses are generated, the researcher chooses a research design that will guide the investigation. The type of design selected depends on such things as the research setting and the degree of control that the researcher has over the research setting. For instance, a researcher may decide that he or she will conduct a study of workers' task performance by observing workers in the actual work setting during normal working hours, in order to make the setting as "natural" as possible. Alternatively, the researcher may decide instead that it would be less disruptive to bring workers into a laboratory room where the work tasks could be simulated. Different settings may require different research designs.

The researcher may also be constrained in the selection of a research design by the amount of control the researcher has over the work setting and the workers. The company may not allow the researcher to interfere with normal work activities, forcing the researcher to use observational measurement of behavior or to use existing data that the organization has already collected. We shall discuss specific research designs shortly.

Collection of data

The next step in the research process involves the testing of hypotheses through data collection. The collection of data is governed by the particular research design used. However, an important concern in data collection is sampling, or selecting a representative group from a larger population for study. In most research, it is impossible to investigate all members of a particular population. For example, in pre-election polls of preferences, all potential voters cannot be surveyed. Instead, a sample is selected, and the results obtained from this subgroup are generalized to the larger population. In a large company there may be offices scattered throughout the country, so a researcher may select only certain sites to participate due to travel costs or may sample a smaller number of employees from each of several sites. The process of selection must follow strict guidelines to ensure that the sample is indeed representative of the larger population from which it is drawn. Two such sampling techniques are random sampling and stratified sampling.

With random sampling, research participants are chosen from a specified population in such a way that each individual has an equal probability of being selected. For example, to choose a random sample of 20 workers from a company employing 200 workers, we would begin with a list of all workers, and using a table of random numbers or a computer program that generates random numbers, randomly select 20 workers. The concept of sampling also applies to studying behaviors from certain individuals or groups of individuals. For example, if we wanted a random sampling of a particular employee's typical work behavior, we might study different, random 5-minute time periods throughout a typical workday or week.

sampling
the selection of a representative group from a larger population for study

random sampling
the selection of research participants from a population so that each individual has an equal probability of being chosen

Stratified sampling begins with the designation of important variables that divide a population into subgroups, or strata. For example, we might want to consider male and female employees and management and nonmanagement personnel as different strata. We then randomly select a specified number of employees in such a way that our research sample mirrors the actual breakdown of these groups in the total population. For example, assume that 40% of the individuals in our total worker population are female and 60% are male, while 25% are management and 75% are nonmanagement. We would want to choose a sample that represented these percentages. Forty percent of the individuals in our selected sample should be female, and 25% should be management personnel. We may also want to ensure that the percentages of male and female managers and nonmanagers in our sample are representative of the larger population.

Both of these sampling techniques help ensure that the sample is representative of the population from which it is drawn. The random selection procedure also protects against any sorts of biases in the choice of participants for study.

stratified sampling
the selection of research participants based on categories that represent important distinguishing characteristics of a population

Analyses of research data

Once data are gathered, they are subjected to some form of analysis for interpretation. Most often, this involves statistical analyses of quantitative data (i.e., data with numerical values), although data can be analyzed using qualitative data analysis techniques (not based on the numerical values of the data). Statistical analysis of data requires that the research observations be quantified in some way. Statistics are simply tools used by the researcher to help make sense out of the observations that have been collected. Some statistical analyses are very simple and are used to help describe and classify the data. Other statistical techniques are quite complex and help the researcher make detailed inferences. For example, some statistics allow the researcher to determine the causes of certain observed outcomes. A brief discussion of certain statistical analysis techniques is presented in the Appendix at the end of this chapter.

Interpretation of research results

The final step in the research process is interpretation of the results. Here the researcher draws conclusions about the meaning of the findings and their relevance to actual work behavior as well as their possible limitations. For example, imagine that a researcher decides to study the effects on work group productivity of two managerial styles: a directive style, whereby the manager closely supervises workers, telling them what they should be doing and how they should be doing it, and a nondirective, participative style, whereby the manager allows the workers a great deal of freedom in deciding how they will get the work task done. The researcher conducts the study on groups of directive and nondirective frontline managers who are employed at several factories that manufacture jet aircraft parts. By collecting and analyzing data, the researcher concludes that directive managers lead more productive groups. However, the researcher might want to set some limits for the use of these findings. The researcher might caution that these results may only apply to managers who are

A researcher who studied management styles in a restaurant would need to be cautious in interpreting data. Would the same kind of supervision produce the same results in a retail store? In a law firm?

supervising factory work groups and might not pertain to managers of service organizations, such as hospitals or restaurants, or to managers of salespersons. The researcher might also mention that although a directive management style appears to be related to productivity, it is not known whether it is related to other important variables, such as employee satisfaction or work quality.

In the next few sections, we will examine in depth some of the steps in the research process. First, we will examine the various research designs used to govern the collection of research data. Second, we will briefly discuss how research variables are measured. Next, we will discuss some of the problems and limitations of conducting research in I/O psychology and will consider the ways that research results and theories can be applied to the practice of I/O psychology. Finally, we will discuss rules of conduct for researchers who are studying people and their work behavior. Research methods are obviously important to practicing I/O psychologists. See the Up Close feature to learn how a knowledge of research methods can help you in your working life.

Major Research Designs

When testing theories and collecting data, researchers use specific research designs. Two of the most common designs are the experimental design and the correlational design, although other methodologies can be used. We will begin by looking at each of these two general research designs. Another method of conducting research is called meta-analysis. This is a method that allows researchers to "combine" results from different studies. Finally, researchers will occasionally conduct an in-depth, descriptive investigation of a particular issue, which is known as a case study. Each of these research designs will be explored.

THE EXPERIMENTAL METHOD

The experimental method is most commonly associated with research conducted in a laboratory, although it can also be applied in an actual work setting, in which case it is known as a field experiment. The experimental method is designed to give the researcher a very high degree of control over the research setting. In a laboratory experiment the researcher has a great deal of control, which is a major advantage of conducting research in a laboratory. In a field experiment, the researcher typically has less control than in the laboratory, but the researcher must still maintain control over the situation in a field experiment to draw strong conclusions.

experimental method
a research design characterized by a high degree of control over the research setting to allow for the determination of cause-and-effect relationships among variables

---

UP CLOSE   How to Use Research Methods in Your Own Life

Although a thorough knowledge of social science research methods is critical for an I/O psychologist, how might this knowledge apply to the life of the typical working person?

Perhaps the greatest value of social science research methods is that the general principles of trying to take an objective (unbiased) perspective, using caution concerning cause-and-effect interpretations, and basing interpretations on repeated observations can be extremely useful as guidelines for decision making. Rather than basing important work-related decisions on hunches, previous experience, or personal preferences, approach the problems as a scientist would. Step back from your own biases. Try to collect some objective data to clarify the problems, and base your decisions on the data.

For example, a student approached me about her part-time job, which had been a source of grief to her and to others who worked with her at the customer service desk of a large department store. The problem was that the manager never seemed to schedule hours in a way that satisfied all the employees. Some employees seemed to get the "better" hours, whereas others were complaining that they consistently had to work the "bad" shifts. The student believed that she had the perfect solution: The employees would all submit their ideal work schedules and possible alternatives, and the manager would arrange them in a way that was satisfactory to everyone.

I suggested that rather than assuming that she had reached a workable solution, she should go back and approach the problem from a research perspective. First, I recommended that she determine the magnitude and scope of the problem. She developed a brief survey that she gave to all the department employees, asking about their satisfaction with the current work scheduling. The results indicated that the majority of the workers did indeed have difficulties with the scheduling. She next approached the manager to see whether she would be open to suggestions for change, which she was. Rather than relying on just her solution, the student then solicited suggestions for dealing with the difficulties from all the employees. When a new strategy was eventually selected (they did try a variation of her suggestion), it was implemented on a trial basis, with careful assessment of its effects on employee attitudes and on difficulties related to scheduling conflicts. By following this systematic method of relying on data, the workers were thus able to improve their situation.

A sound background in research methods can also assist in the evaluation of new work techniques or management strategies. Whenever you hear of some revolutionary strategy for increasing work performance or efficiency, do what a good social scientist would do: Go directly to the primary source. Find out what research evidence (if any) supports the technique and read those reports with a critical eye. See if there are serious flaws in the ways that the technique was tested, flaws that might make you doubt whether it really works.

independent variable
in the experimental method, the variable that is manipulated by the researcher

dependent variable
in the experimental method, the variable that is acted on by the independent variable; the outcome variable

treatment group
the group in an experimental investigation that is subjected to the change in the independent variable

control group
a comparison group in an experimental investigation that receives no treatment

Stop & Review

Describe the six steps in the research process.

extraneous variables
variables other than the independent variable that may influence the dependent variable

In the experimental method, the researcher systematically manipulates levels of one variable, called the independent variable, and measures its effect on another variable, called the dependent variable. The dependent variable is the outcome variable, or the behavior that is of primary interest to the investigator. In the experimental method, other variables in the setting are presumed to be held constant. That is, no elements except the independent variable are allowed to vary. As a result, any change in the dependent variable is presumed to have been caused by the independent variable. The primary advantage of the experimental method is that it allows us to determine cause-and-effect relationships among variables.

To determine whether the manipulation of an independent variable produces any significant change in a dependent variable, following the experimental method researchers often compare the results of two groups of participants. One group, called the experimental group, or treatment group, is subjected to the change in the independent variable. The second group, called the control group, receives no change. In other words, the second group is not subjected to the treatment. This comparison of treatment and control groups allows the researcher to determine the magnitude of the effect produced by the manipulation of the independent variable (the treatment). Measuring the dependent variable of the control group allows the researcher to rule out any normal fluctuations that might have occurred naturally in the absence of the treatment. The comparison of treatment and control groups gives the researcher greater confidence that the treatment was (or was not) effective.

For example, imagine that a researcher wants to test the effectiveness of a new training program for sales skills. A number of salespersons are randomly assigned to the treatment group and attend the training session. Other salespersons are randomly assigned to the control group and do not receive the training content. (In a good experimental design the control group should also attend "a session," but one that does not have the training content; this allows the researcher to control for any effects that may result from participants' simply attending a program.) A comparison of the subsequent sales records of the two groups allows the researcher to determine the effectiveness of the program. In this case, the independent variable is whether the salespersons did or did not receive the training content; the dependent variable would be the amount of sales. It is also possible to expand the experimental method to include a number of different treatment groups—for example, different types of sales training programs—and to compare the effectiveness of these various treatments with one another and with a control group. Of course, the experimental method is not used only for comparing treatment and control groups. Any variable that can be broken into distinct categories or levels can serve as an independent variable in an experimental design. For instance, we might examine differences between male and female workers, or among "high," "medium," and "low" producing workers (as determined by productivity measures).

Aside from the specified independent variables, other variables that may be affecting the dependent variable are termed extraneous variables. It is these variables that increase the difficulty of conducting research, because they can be any factors other than the independent variables that influence the dependent variable. Consider, for example, the Hawthorne studies discussed in Chapter 1. In these studies of the influence of lighting and other work conditions on assembly line productivity (the independent variables), the attention paid to the workers by the researchers was an extraneous variable that affected productivity (the dependent variable).

The key to the success of the experimental method is to hold all extraneous variables constant. For example, observing all research participants, treatment and control groups, at the same time of day, using the same methods, same equipment, and so forth. This is of course much easier to do in a laboratory setting than in an actual work setting. Sometimes extraneous variables result from systematic differences in the individuals being studied. For example, if participants are given the opportunity to volunteer to participate in a particular treatment group (with the nonvolunteers serving as a control group), there may be some motivational differences in the treatment volunteers that might act as a moderating or confounding variable, thus affecting the results. That is, participants in the treatment group might be more energetic and "helpful" than those in the control group, and it would thus be impossible to tell whether any differences between the two groups resulted from the treatment or from these inherent motivational differences. Many potential extraneous variables can be controlled through the random assignment of participants to the experimental and control groups. Random assignment ensures that any motivational differences or other individual characteristics show up in equivalent proportions in both groups. In other words, assigning participants randomly to treatment and control groups serves to control for the effects of extraneous variables.

random assignment
a method of assigning subjects to groups by chance to control for the effects of extraneous variables

One of the major drawbacks of the experimental method is its artificiality. A researcher who controls the experimental setting may create a situation that is quite different from the actual work setting. There may thus be some concern about whether the results will apply or generalize to real settings. In field experiments, there is less concern about the generalizability of findings, because the participants and the setting are usually representative of those that can be affected by the results. However, any time that a researcher creates an experimental situation, he or she runs the risk of generating artificial conditions that would not exist in the usual work setting.

Two examples of the experimental method: A laboratory and a field experiment

One experimental study was designed to determine which of two decision-making styles was most effective when individuals were working under high stress conditions (Johnston, Driskell, & Salas, 1997). In this laboratory experiment, 90 U.S. Navy–enlisted personnel volunteered and were required to take part in a simulation, where they would be working as a ship's radar screen operator. The participants were randomly assigned to one of two training groups. The first group learned a "vigilant" decision-making style. Vigilant decision making is where the decision maker scans and considers all information in an orderly, sequential fashion, taking into account all information, and reviewing all alternatives before making a decision. Participants in the second group were trained in "hypervigilant" decision making. In hypervigilant decision making, the decision maker scans only the information that is needed in a particular circumstance, and scanning of information does not follow a systematic, ordered sequence. The type of training participants received constituted the independent variable. Stress was created by having distracting radio communications played and by an experimenter who told the participants to "hurry up" and "perform better" at regular intervals.

The participants were seated at a computer screen that presented a simulation of a ship's radar screen that systematically presented images representing approaching ships, submarines, and aircraft. Participants had to identify each object, determine if it was a "friendly" or enemy craft, and engage the enemy crafts. The dependent variable in this study consisted of the number of objects that were correctly identified and dealt with appropriately. The results of the study confirmed the researchers' hypothesis that hypervigilant decision making was best under high stress conditions, primarily because it is quicker, more efficient, and provides less of a cognitive "load" on the radar operator.

Our second example of the experimental method is a field experiment designed to test the effects on safe driving behavior of worker participation in setting safety-related goals (Ludwig & Geller, 1997). The study participants were 324 college-aged pizza deliverers from three pizza stores. Observation of the drivers showed that they often did not stop completely at a stop sign as they headed out on deliveries. Pizza deliverers were randomly assigned to one of two types of safety meetings focusing on the importance of making a full and safe stop. In one condition, driving-related safety goals were set by store managers. In the other condition, the deliverers participated in setting their driving safety goals. The type of goal setting constituted the independent variable. At certain intervals, the managers observed stopping behaviors as the drivers exited the stores' parking lots and headed down the road on their deliveries. During the posttraining period, managers posted the rates of safe stopping for the drivers to see. Also recorded were other safety behaviors, such as whether or not the drivers wore their seat belts and used their turn signals when turning onto the highway. Each of these safe driving behaviors constituted the study's dependent variables.

The results showed that both groups, those who helped set their own safety goals and those whose goals were set by managers, engaged in safer stopping behavior during the time period when their managers were watching and providing feedback. But only the group who had set their own stopping safety goals showed increased use of turn signals and seat belt use. In other words, the safe stopping behavior "generalized" to other safety behaviors, but only for the group that participated in setting its own goals.

Although both of these studies were fairly well designed and executed and produced some useful knowledge, both have limitations. The laboratory investigation used navy-enlisted personnel, not actual ship radar operators, which raises the question of whether the results would generalize to actual radar operators or to other similar workers, such as air traffic controllers. As presented, the dependent variables in the studies are fairly limited. (Both studies were presented in simplified format. Additional variables were measured in each.) For example, although the safety study found that drivers increased seat belt usage and the use of their turn signals, we don't know if other driving behaviors (e.g., speeding) were similarly affected. Although the results of studies such as these may answer some questions, additional questions might arise. For example, from the results of these experiments, we still don't know for sure why one particular decision-making style was better, or exactly why setting your own safety goals had better effects on safe driving.

This is the research process. Results of one study may stimulate subsequent research in the same area. Scientific research builds on the results of previous studies, adding and refining, to increase our knowledge of the behavior in question.

QUASI-EXPERIMENTS

In many cases, a researcher does not have the control over the situation needed to run a true experiment. As a result, a quasi-experiment is used, which is a design that follows the experimental method but lacks features such as random assignment of participants to groups and manipulation of the independent variable. For example, a researcher might compare one group of workers who have undergone a particular training program with another group of workers who will not receive the training, but because they were not randomly assigned to the groups, the groups are not equivalent. As a result, cause-and-effect relationships cannot be determined. For example, one study examined the effectiveness of a management coaching program and compared managers in the coaching programs to other managers not receiving coaching, but who were matched on age, years of experience, and salary (Evers, Brouwers, & Tomic, 2006).

Quasi-experiments are quite common in I/O psychology because of the difficulties in controlling extraneous variables and, often, the unit of analysis is groups or organizations, rather than individuals. Quasi-experiments can be used, for example, to compare departments or organizations on some variables of interest. It is important in making these comparisons, however, that the groups be as equivalent as possible. Moreover, in quasi-experimental designs, researchers often try to measure as many possible extraneous variables as they can in order to statistically control for their effects. This helps strengthen the results obtained in quasi-experiments. As mentioned, many of the studies we will explore in this book are quasi-experimental designs, and they are quite frequent in I/O psychology.

> **quasi-experiment**
> follows the experimental design but lacks random assignment and/or manipulation of independent variable

THE CORRELATIONAL METHOD

The second major method for data collection, the correlational method (also referred to as the observational method), looks at the relationships between or among variables as they occur naturally. When the correlational method is used, in contrast to the experimental method, there is no manipulation of variables by the experimenter. A researcher simply measures two or more variables and then examines their statistical relationship to one another. Because the correlational method does not involve the manipulation of independent variables, distinctions between independent and dependent variables are not nearly as important as they are in the experimental method. Because the correlational

> **correlational method**
> a research design that examines the relationship among or between variables as they naturally occur

method does not require the rigid control over variables associated with the experimental method, it is easy to use in actual work settings. In addition, correlational research can be conducted with archival data—data that an organization has already collected. For example, an organization might use data on employee absenteeism and look at the relationship between number of sick days and ratings on a job satisfaction survey that was administered to employees. Because of its ease of use, a great deal of the research on work behavior thus uses the correlational method. The major drawback of this method is that we cannot determine cause-and-effect relationships. A very common problem is the tendency of people to try to make causal statements from correlations, which leads to many misconceptions and faulty interpretations of data. Many students of statistics quickly learn that correlation does not necessarily imply causality.

Considerable caution must be exercised when interpreting the results of correlational research. For example, suppose that a researcher finds a relationship between workers' attitudes about their employer and the amount of money they invest in a company stock program. Employees with very positive attitudes tend to use a greater portion of their income to purchase stock. It could be that their favorable attitudes cause them to demonstrate their support for (and faith in) the company by buying stock, but the cause-and-effect relationship could also go the other way: employees who purchase stock at bargain prices may develop more positive attitudes about the company because they now have an investment in it. On the other hand, a third variable (an extraneous variable), such as the length of time employees have worked for the company, may actually be the cause of the observed correlation between employee attitudes and stock purchases. Employees with a long tenure may generally have more favorable attitudes about the company than newcomers (over time those with negative attitudes usually leave the organization). These employees are also older and may be able to invest a larger proportion of their incomes in stock options than younger workers, who may be raising families and purchasing first homes. Length of time on the job may thus influence both of the other two variables. The simple correlation between employee attitudes and stock purchases therefore does not lead us to any firm cause-and-effect conclusions.

Two examples of the correlational method

Two researchers studied the ability of certain tests and other assessment methods to predict future managerial success. The participants were more than 1,000 entry-level women managers, all of whom took part in a two-day testing program at an assessment center. The assessment techniques included an interview, some standardized tests, and several scored exercises. (We will discuss assessment centers and employee assessment techniques in Chapters 4 & 5.) At the end of the assessment, each woman was rated on a four-point scale of "middle-management potential," with endpoints ranging from *not acceptable* to *more than acceptable*. Seven years later, measures of the women's "management progress" were obtained. Results indicated "a sizable correlation between predictions made by the assessment staff and subsequent progress seven years later" (Ritchie & Moses, 1983, p. 229).

In a study of secretaries and managers in seven German companies, researchers examined the relationship between the time it took for these office workers to deal with computer errors and the workers' "negative emotional reactions," such as voicing frustration or outbursts of anger (Brodbeck, Zapf, Prumper, & Frese, 1993). This study was an observational field study because the researchers observed the workers as they went through their normal daily routine at work. The observers merely recorded the errors workers made while working at computers, noted the time that it took workers to deal with the computer errors, and noted their emotional reactions. As you might expect, there was a significant positive relationship (a positive correlation) between the length of time workers spent trying to solve computer errors and their reactions of frustration and anger. In other words, the more time the workers spent trying to solve computer errors, the more angry and frustrated they became.

As mentioned, each of the methods, experimental and correlational, has its own strengths and weaknesses. Sometimes researchers might use both methods in a large-scale investigation. Although the experimental method is most commonly associated with laboratory studies, and correlational research is most often associated with field research, either method can be used in either setting. The key to using the experimental method in a field investigation is gaining control over the environment by manipulating levels of the independent variable and holding extraneous variables constant. Because the correlational method looks at the relationships among variables as they naturally exist, a correlational design may often be easier to implement, particularly in actual work settings, as the study of German office workers demonstrates.

COMPLEX CORRELATIONAL DESIGNS

Although simple correlational designs do not allow the determination of cause-and-effect relationships, most correlational designs in modern I/O psychology research involve complex statistical analyses that allow for combining predictor variables, statistically controlling for possible extraneous variables, and methods that allow for inferring the likelihood of cause and effect.

A multiple regression design allows a researcher to examine the relationship between a particular outcome variable and multiple predictors. This allows the researcher to determine how a number of variables correlate with a certain outcome. For example, a researcher might be interested in how ability in combination with motivation together predict job performance. For example, a study of nurses might use a measure of technical nursing skills and motivation to predict the nurses' on-the-job performance evaluations. The simple correlations between technical skills and performance and motivation and performance can be examined, but through multiple regression (we will learn more about this in the Appendix at the end of the chapter), the researcher can see how skills and motivation in combination predict performance.

The multiple regression design also allows a researcher to control for possible extraneous variables and examine the effect of one variable on

multiple regression design
examines the relationship between a particular outcome variable and multiple predictors

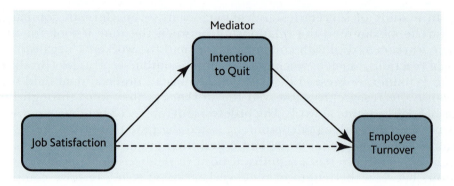

FIGURE 2.2
A Mediation Model for the Job Satisfaction-Employee Turnover Relationship

another, after controlling for (or "holding constant") the effects of extraneous variables. In the study of nurses, for example, the researcher might measure and control for possible extraneous variables such as the age and years of experience of the nurses in examining how skills and motivation affect performance.

Certain complex designs can also be used to infer causality. One example that is quite common in the I/O psychology literature is the use of a *mediation model*. In a mediation model the relationship between two variables is hypothesized to be explained by, or mediated by, a third variable—the *mediator variable* (see Figure 2.2). For example, the relationship between job satisfaction and employee turnover (assuming that less satisfied employees are more likely to quit their jobs) is mediated by a third variable—the intention to quit.

META-ANALYSIS

As we have seen, the results of a single research study provide some answers, but often raise other questions. Moreover, different research investigations of the same topic or issue may reach inconsistent, and sometimes totally contradictory, conclusions. For example, one study may find strong support for a given hypothesis, a second study may find only weak support, and a third study may have results that are opposite those of the first study. Students who are just beginning to explore research in I/O psychology or other social sciences seem to get particularly frustrated by such inconsistencies. How can any conclusions be drawn from the varying and often conflicting results of several independent research investigations?

meta-analysis
a technique that allows results from several different research studies to be combined and summarized

The answer is found in a methodological technique called **meta-analysis**, which allows the results of a number of studies to be combined and analyzed together to draw a summary conclusion (Rosenthal, 1991; F. Wolf, 1986). Meta-analyses are usually conducted when there are 20 or more separate studies of a given hypothesis or topic. Meta-analysis may be used for several purposes, including summarizing the relationship between variables examined in each of a set of studies and determining other factors

that are associated with increases or decreases in the magnitude of relationships between variables of interest (these "other factors" are often referred
to as moderating variables). Although it depends on the research question
and the types of studies and their specific research designs, meta-analysis will
typically use an indicator of effect size from each examined study. Effect size
refers to an estimate of the magnitude of the relationship between any variable *X* and any variable *Y* (in a correlational design), or the size of the effect
of an independent variable on a dependent variable (in an experimental
design). One measure of effect size is the correlation coefficient, which is
provided in many studies to describe relationships between variables (see
the Appendix at the end of the chapter for more information on correlation
coefficients).

Meta-analysis is used to compare and combine data from all of the
examined studies, taking into account the effect sizes and the number of participants in each of the independent studies. Typically, meta-analytic techniques
yield a summary statistic that tells us something about the overall relationship
between the variables examined in each of the studies and whether the results
from the independent studies are significantly different from each other in
meaningful ways. For example, different studies examining the relationship
between job satisfaction and employee absenteeism have produced different
results, with some studies reporting higher levels of job satisfaction associated
with lower rates of absenteeism (e.g., Ostroff, 1993b), and others reporting no
association between the two factors (Ilgen & Hollenback, 1977; see Chapter 9
for more information). Meta-analytic procedures may suggest that different
studies yield different results because each uses a different measure of absenteeism or job satisfaction or because the participants in studies were different.
Meta-analyses have been used to summarize the research results from many
studies of the absenteeism–job satisfaction relationship and have found that
the two factors are indeed related—low satisfaction is related to higher rates
of absenteeism—but the relationship is not as strong as most people believe
(e.g., Scott & Taylor, 1985).

Meta-analytic studies have become quite popular, particularly in I/O
psychology and other fields studying work behavior (Steiner, Lane, Dobbins,
Schnur, & McConnell, 1991). These analyses have addressed such issues as the
effectiveness of employment tests (Hunter & Hunter, 1984), college grade point
average in predicting job performance (Roth, BeVier, Switzer, & Schippman,
1996), the relationship between age and work motivation (Kooij et al., 2011),
the effectiveness of managerial training programs (Burke & Day, 1986; Powell
& Yalcin, 2010), and the validity of certain leadership theories (Gerstner & Day,
1997; Judge & Piccolo, 2004).

One meta-analysis confirmed the widely held view that more physically
demanding jobs, such as hazardous jobs with high risk for injury, were related
to workers becoming stressed and "burned out." (Nahrgang, Morgeson,
& Hofmann, 2011). In another meta-analysis, of 55 studies investigating
the relationship between workers' personalities, positive job attitudes, and
organizational citizenship behaviors—pro-company behaviors by employees—it

effect size
an estimate of the
magnitude of a
relationship or effect
found in a research
investigation

was found that positive job attitudes were a better predictor of organizational citizenship behaviors than were workers' personalities (Organ & Ryan, 1995).

THE CASE STUDY METHOD

We have stated that there are difficulties in conducting controlled research in actual work settings. Often a researcher or scientist–practitioner will have the opportunity to conduct research in a business or industry, but will find it impossible to follow either the experimental or the correlational method. The study may involve a one-time-only assessment of behavior, or the application of an intervention to only a single group, department, or organization. Such research is known as a case study. The results of a single case study, even if the study involves the application of some highly researched intervention strategy, do not allow us to draw any firm conclusions. A case study is really little more than a descriptive investigation. We are unable to test hypotheses or to determine cause-and-effect relationships from a case study because it is like conducting research with only one participant. What may have seemed to work in this one instance may not work in a second or third case. However, this does not mean that the case study method is not valuable, and in fact, many exploratory studies follow this method. Case studies can provide rich, descriptive information about certain work behaviors and situations. In some topic areas, where it has been impossible to conduct controlled experimental studies, the results of case studies may be the only evidence that exists. Moreover, such results might inspire the development of hypotheses that will later be tested with experimental or correlational studies (Dunnette, 1990).

case study
a research investigation involving a one-time assessment of behavior

In one example of the case study method, a psychologist found that company picnics, games, and other social activities increased employees' loyalty to the organization.

Measurement of Variables

One of the more difficult aspects of research is the measurement of variables. A variable must be operationalized, that is, brought down from the abstract level to a more concrete level and clearly defined so that it can be measured or manipulated. In the first example of the correlational method outlined earlier, the variable "middle-management potential" was operationalized as a rating on a four-point scale. In the experimental study of pizza delivery drivers, "safe driving behavior" was operationalized as wearing a seat belt, using a turn signal, and coming to a full stop at an intersection. Both variables could be considered as operational definitions of the more general variable of "performance."

During the process of operationalizing a variable, a particular technique for measuring the variable is usually selected. We will examine two of the general categories of techniques used to measure variables in I/O psychology: observational techniques and self-report techniques.

OBSERVATIONAL TECHNIQUES

One procedure for measuring research variables is through direct, systematic observation. This involves the researchers themselves recording certain behaviors that they have defined as the operationalized variables. For example, a researcher might consider the number of items manufactured as a measure of productivity or may look for certain defined supervisory behaviors, such as demonstrating work techniques to subordinates, giving direct orders, and setting specific work quotas, to assess whether a manager has a "task-oriented" supervisory style.

The measurement of variables through direct observation can be either obtrusive or unobtrusive. With obtrusive observation the researcher is visible to the persons being observed. The primary disadvantage of this technique is that the participants may behave differently because they know that they are a part of a research investigation. This is exactly what happened in the original Hawthorne experiments. Researchers engaging in obtrusive observation must always consider how their presence will affect participants' behavior, and thus the results of the study.

Unobtrusive observation also involves direct observation of behavior, but in this case participants are unaware of the researcher's presence and do not know that their behavior is being studied. The primary advantage of unobtrusive observation is that the researcher can be fairly confident that the recorded behavior is typical. The major drawback to unobtrusive observation lies in ethical concerns about protecting the privacy of the participants.

SELF-REPORT TECHNIQUES

Direct observational measurement techniques are often costly and difficult to obtain, requiring the assistance of trained observers. More commonly, researchers measure variables through self-report techniques, which include a variety of methods for assessing behavior from the responses of the research participants

operationalized
clearly defining a research variable so that it can be measured

🕑 Stop & Review
Describe and contrast the experimental and correlational methods.

obtrusive observation
research observation in which the presence of the observer is known to the participants

unobtrusive observation
research observation in which the presence of the observer is not known to the participants

self-report techniques
measurement methods relying on research participants' reports of their own behavior or attitudes

themselves. One of the most popular self-report techniques is surveys. Surveys can be used to measure any number of aspects of the work situation, including workers' attitudes about their jobs, their perceptions of the amount and quality of the work that they perform, and the specific problems they encounter on the job. Most typically, surveys take the form of pencil-and-paper measures that the participants can complete either in a group session or on their own time. However, surveys can also involve face-to-face or telephone interviews.

The most obvious problem with surveys is the possibility of distortion or bias of responses (either intentional or unintentional). If the survey is not conducted in a way that protects respondents' anonymity, particularly when it deals with sensitive issues or problems, workers may feel that their answers can be traced back to them and possibly result in retribution by management. In these cases, workers may temper their responses and give "socially desirable" answers to survey questions.

Self-report techniques are also used in I/O psychology research to assess workers' personalities, occupational interests, and management or supervisory style; to obtain evaluations of job candidates; or to elicit supervisors' ratings of worker performance. Compared to observational techniques, self-reports allow the researcher to collect massive amounts of data relatively inexpensively. However, developing sound self-report tools and interpreting the results are not easy tasks and require thorough knowledge of measurement theory as well as research methods and statistics. Many I/O psychologist researchers and practitioners use self-report measures extensively in their work.

Key Issues in Measuring Variables: Reliability and Validity

When measuring any variable in social science research, there are certain measurement standards that need to be considered. Two critically important in measurement are reliability and validity. Reliability refers to the stability of a measure over time or the consistency of the measure. For example, if we administer a test to a job applicant, we would expect to get essentially the same score on the test if it is taken at two different points of time (and the applicant did not do anything to improve test performance in between). Reliability also refers to the agreement between two or more assessments made of the same event or behavior, such as when two observers may independently rate the on-the-job performance of a call center operator. In other words, a measurement process is said to possess "reliability" if we can "rely" on the scores or measurements to be stable, consistent, and free of random error.

One way to think about the reliability of a measurement instrument is to think of the simple thermometer used to take body temperature. That might be a device that goes in your ear or in your mouth, but as you take your body temperature, you might occasionally get slightly different readings: the first time your temperature is 99.1, the second time you get 99.2, the third time it's 99.1 again, but we know that the thermometer is a highly reliable measure—we would be surprised to get a 110-degree reading. Measurement instruments used in I/O psychology are much less reliable, on average, than a thermometer. Imagine a scale that requires an employee to rate her job satisfaction on a 9 point scale each month. The ratings might vary from month to month, but we would be able to look across the months, and across many different employees, and calculate the reliability of the job satisfaction rating instrument, but as you might imagine, it would not be as reliable as a body temperature measure.

Validity refers to the accuracy of inferences or projections we draw from measurements. Validity refers to whether a set of measurements allows accurate inferences or projections about "something else." That "something else" can be an assessment of the stress of a worker, a job applicant's standing on some characteristic or ability, or it can be whether an employee is meeting performance standards.

validity
the accuracy of inferences drawn from a measurement

We can also discuss (and will later) the issue of the validity of a research study, which concerns whether the study itself is actually assessing the constructs and concepts that the researcher wants to measure. This sort of validity relates to the rigor of the study—did it follow good social science practices, was it well designed, and did the researcher draw appropriate conclusions.

We will explore the constructs of reliability and validity in more detail later, and in Chapter 5, when we discuss the use of employee-screening methods used in making hiring decisions.

Measuring Work Outcomes: The Bottom Line

There are a tremendous number of potential independent variables in I/O psychology research. I/O psychologists have examined how characteristics of workers such as personality, attitudes, and education affect work behavior. As we saw in Chapter 1, factors in the physical and social work environment can be manipulated to see how they affect worker performance and satisfaction and engagement with their work. Other variables, such as the amount and frequency of compensation, styles of supervision, work schedules, and incentive programs, also serve as independent variables in research on work behavior.

Many dependent variables are also studied in I/O research. However, a great deal of research in I/O psychology focuses on dependent variables such as productivity, work quality, employee turnover, employee absenteeism, and employee satisfaction/engagement. These key dependent variables represent work outcomes—what often translates to the "bottom line" in work organizations. Most commonly, changes in these important variables result in financial losses or gains for businesses.

Of these important dependent variables, the first two, work productivity and quality, are usually theoretically linked, because a company's goals should be to produce as much as possible while ensuring that the output is of high quality. However, although these variables are linked, they are typically considered separately by many businesses. For example, in many manufacturing plants the departments responsible for production volume and for quality control are often separate.

On the surface, it may seem that the measurement of a variable like productivity is relatively simple and accurate. This may be true if the task involves production of concrete objects, such as the number of hamburgers sold or the number of books printed. However, for companies that deal with more abstract products, such as services, information, or ideas, the measurement of productivity is not as easy, nor as precise.

The accurate measurement of quality is often more difficult (Hoffman, Nathan, & Holden, 1991). For example, in a department store, productivity may be assessed by the dollar amount of sales, which is a fairly reasonable and simple assessment. However, the quality of the salespersons' performance might involve factors such as the friendliness, courteousness, and promptness of their service, which are usually more difficult to measure. Similarly, a writer's productivity might be defined as the number of books or articles the author produced (a straightforward assessment), although the quality of the writing may be more difficult to measure. Thus, quality is often quite difficult to define operationally. We will deal with the measurement of worker productivity and worker performance in more detail in upcoming chapters, particularly in Chapter 6.

Although they are distinct variables, employee absenteeism, turnover, and satisfaction/engagement are also theoretically tied to one another (Vroom, 1964). In Chapter 1 we saw that Mayo believed that there was a strong relationship between employee satisfaction and productivity. However, this is not always the case; the happy worker is not necessarily the productive worker. There may, however, be a relationship between employee satisfaction and a tendency to show up for work and stay with the job. Specifically, it is thought that higher satisfaction leads to lower absenteeism and turnover. However, these long-standing notions about the interrelatedness of job satisfaction, absenteeism, and turnover have come under question, primarily because of problems in the accurate measurement of absenteeism and turnover (see Hollenbeck & Williams, 1986; Porter & Steers, 1973; Tharenou, 1993). Some forms of absenteeism and turnover are inevitable, due to circumstances beyond the employees' control, such as severe illness or a move dictated by a spouse's job transfer. These types of absenteeism and turnover are not likely to be affected by job satisfaction, whereas voluntary absenteeism—playing "hooky" from work—may be caused by low levels of job satisfaction. We will discuss this issue in detail in Chapter 9.

In any case, the interrelationships between job satisfaction, absenteeism, and turnover are important. If negative relationships do indeed exist between employee satisfaction and rates of absenteeism and turnover (they are negative relationships because higher satisfaction would be associated with lower absenteeism and lower turnover), it is important that companies strive to keep workers satisfied. Happy workers may be less likely to be absent from their jobs voluntarily or to look for work elsewhere. Reduced rates of absenteeism and turnover can translate into tremendous savings for the company.

Turnover and absenteeism can be measured fairly easily, but the assessment of worker satisfaction is much less precise, because attitudes about a wide range of elements in the work environment must be considered. Moreover, the worker attitude-behavior relationship needs to be studied in depth. A more complex construct is replacing the simple notion of job satisfaction, and that is the notion of *employee engagement*, which involves not only employee attitudes about their jobs, but also their broader attitudes about the organization, and their commitment to it. We will deal more deeply with these issues in Chapter 9.

Although these key variables are most commonly considered dependent variables, this does not preclude the possibility that any one of them could be used as an independent variable. For example, we might classify workers into those who are "good attenders" with very few absences and "poor attenders" who have regular absences. We could then see whether there are differences in the good and poor attenders' performance levels or in their attitudes about their jobs. However, certain variables, such as productivity, absenteeism, and turnover, represent the bottom-line variables that translate into profits or losses for the company, whereas job satisfaction tends to be the bottom-line variable for the employee. These bottom-line variables are most often considered dependent variables.

Interpreting and Using Research Results

When a researcher conducts a study and obtains research results, it is the researcher's task to make sense of the results. To interpret research data accurately, an I/O psychologist must be very knowledgeable about methods of data collection and statistical analysis and be aware of potential research problems and the strengths and limitations of the methods that have been used.

When interpreting results, it is important to consider the limitations of the findings. One concern is the extent to which we are successful in eliminating extraneous or "confounding" variables. This is called internal validity. In an experiment, internal validity deals with how confident we are that the change in a dependent variable was actually caused by the independent variable, as opposed to extraneous variables. A second concern is the external validity of the research results, that is, whether the results obtained will generalize to other work settings. In other words, how well do the findings apply to other workers, jobs, and/or environments? For example, say that the results of research on patterns of interactions in workers in an insurance claims office indicate a significant positive relationship between the amount of supervisor–supervisee contact and worker productivity: As supervisors and workers interact more, more work is completed. Can these results be generalized to other settings? Maybe, maybe not. These findings might be particular to these workers, related to their specific characteristics. The participants may be the kind of workers who need a lot of supervision to keep them on task. Other groups of workers might view interactions with supervisors negatively, and the resulting dissatisfaction might lead to a restriction of output. Alternatively, the results might be specific to the type of tasks in which workers are engaged.

internal validity
the extent to which extraneous or confounding variables are removed

external validity
whether research results obtained in one setting will apply to another setting

Because insurance claims often need to be approved by supervisors, a worker must interact with the supervisor to complete the job. As a result, increased supervisor–supervisee contact may be a sign of increased efficiency. For assembly line workers, however, supervisor–supervisee interactions might be a distraction that reduces productivity, or they might have little effect on output. To know whether research results will generalize to a variety of work settings, results must be replicated with different groups of workers in different work settings. Eventually, further research may discover the moderating variables that determine when and where supervisor–subordinate contacts have beneficial effects on work productivity.

External validity is especially important for research conducted under tightly controlled circumstances, such as a laboratory investigation, where the conditions of the research setting may not be very similar to actual work conditions. One solution is to combine the strength of experimental research—well-controlled conditions—with the advantage of real-world conditions by conducting experimental research in actual work settings.

So far, we have been discussing only one objective of research in I/O psychology: the scientific objective of conducting research to understand work behavior more completely. As you recall, in Chapter 1 we mentioned that there are two goals in industrial/organizational psychology: the scientific and the practical, whereby new knowledge is applied toward improving work conditions and outcomes. Although some research in I/O psychology is conducted merely to increase the base of knowledge about work behavior, and some I/O practitioners (and practicing managers) use strategies to affect work behavior that are based on hunches or intuition rather than on sound research evidence, the two facets of I/O psychology should work together. To be effective, the applications used by I/O practitioners to improve work behavior must be built on a strong foundation of research. Through sound research and the testing of hypotheses and theories, better applications develop. Moreover, the effectiveness of applications can be demonstrated conclusively only through additional evaluation and research (see the Box "Applying I/O Psychology").

Stop & Review
List the five common work outcomes that are often measured in I/O psychology.

Ethical Issues in Research and Practice in I/O Psychology

It is very important in conducting any type of psychological research involving human beings that the researcher, student or professional, adhere to ethical principles and standards. The American Psychological Association (APA) lists several core principles that should guide the ethical conduct of research in psychology, including I/O psychology (APA, 2002). These guiding principles include: striving to benefit the persons with whom the psychologist is working and taking care to do no harm; being honest and accurate in the science, teaching, and practice of psychology; and respecting the rights of people to privacy and confidentiality.

Although the ethical issues pertaining to I/O psychologists are complex, we will review a few of the key elements for research and practice of I/O psychology.

APPLYING I/O PSYCHOLOGY

The Hawthorne Effect: A Case Study in Flawed Research Methods

The initial Hawthorne studies clearly followed the experimental method because Mayo and his colleagues manipulated levels of lighting and the duration of work breaks. Furthermore, because the studies were conducted in the actual work setting, they were also field experiments. The result, particularly the discovery of the Hawthorne effect, is a classic in the field of I/O psychology. In fact, this effect is studied in other areas of psychology and social science.

Although the original Hawthorne studies were set up in the experimental method, the discovery of the Hawthorne effect actually resulted from a breakdown in research procedures. The changes observed in the dependent variable (productivity) were caused not by the independent variable (lighting), but by an extraneous variable that was not controlled by the researchers: the attention the workers received from the observers. Although Mayo and his colleagues eventually became aware of this unanticipated variable, which led to the discovery of the Hawthorne effect, the design and implementation of the studies had other methodological problems.

In the 1970s, researchers reexamined the data from the original Hawthorne experiments, combing through the records and diaries kept by Mayo and his colleagues. These investigators found a series of very serious methodological problems that cast doubt on the original conclusions drawn from the Hawthorne studies. These re-analyses indicated difficulties with the number of participants (one of the studies used only five participants), the experimenters' "contamination" of the participant population (two of the five participants were replaced because they were not working hard enough), the lack of control or comparison groups, and the absence of appropriate statistical analyses of data (Franke & Kaul, 1978; Parsons, 1974). The I/O psychologist Parsons discovered not only serious flaws in the published reports of the Hawthorne experiments but also a number of extraneous variables that were not considered, further confounding the conclusions. For example:

> [U]nlike the big open floor of the relay assembly department, the test room was separate, smaller, and quieter…and the supervisors were friendly, tolerant observers, not the usual authoritarian foremen… Back in their relay-assembly department, the women had been paid a fixed hourly wage plus a collective piecework rate based on the department's total output. In the test room, the collective piecework rate was based on the output of only the five workers, so that individual performance had a much more significant impact on weekly pay. The monetary reward for increased individual effort thus became much more evident and perhaps more effective than in the department setting. (Rice, 1982, pp. 70–74).

All in all, there are significant flaws in the research design and execution of the Hawthorne experiments. Of course, this does not mean that a Hawthorne effect cannot exist, because we do know that the presence of others can affect behavior. What it does mean is that the original Hawthorne studies were too methodologically muddled to enable researchers to draw any firm conclusions from them. On the one hand, we must forgive Mayo and his associates on some of these issues because their studies were conducted before many of the advancements in research methodology and design were made. On the other hand, some of the errors in data collection were obvious. In many ways, the Hawthorne studies illustrate some of the difficulties of conducting research and the dangers of drawing conclusions based on flawed research methods. The moral is that conducting research is a complex but important endeavor. Researchers and users of research must display caution in both the application of methods and the interpretation of results to avoid errors and misinformation.

informed consent
a research participant is fully informed of the nature of the experiment and has the right to not participate

The researcher must obtain participants' **informed consent**—a sort of "full disclosure." That is, participants must be told in advance the purposes, duration, and general procedures involved in the research, and they have the right to decline participation at any point. At the end of the research, participants should be fully debriefed, and the researcher should ensure that no harm has been caused. Researchers must also protect the privacy of research participants by either collecting data anonymously or keeping the data confidential—with identities known only to the researchers for purposes of accurate recordkeeping.

The same general principles apply to the practice of I/O psychology. In addition, practicing I/O psychologists should not misrepresent their areas of expertise and be honest, forthright, and fair in their dealings with clients and client organizations. An excellent case reader deals specifically with ethical issues for the practicing I/O psychologist, entitled *The Ethical Practice of Psychology in Organizations* (Lowman, 2006). Another resource is the book *Decoding the Ethic Code: A Practical Guide for Psychologists* (Fisher, 2009).

Summary

The goals of I/O psychology are to describe, explain, predict, and then alter work behavior. Research methods are important tools for I/O psychologists because they provide a systematic means for investigating and changing work behavior. *Objectivity* is the overriding theme of the social scientific method used to study work behavior.

The first step in conducting research involves the formulation of the problem or issue. The second step is the generation of *hypotheses*, which are simply statements about the supposed relationships among variables. It is through the systematic collection of observations of behavior that a researcher may develop a set of hypotheses into a more general *theory*, or *model*, which are ways of representing the complex relationships among a number of variables related to actual work behavior. The third step in conducting research is choosing a particular design to guide the actual collection of data (the fourth step). The data collection stage includes sampling, the methods by which participants are selected for study. The final steps in the process are the analyses of research data and the interpretation of research results.

I/O psychologists use two basic types of research designs. In the *experimental method*, the researcher manipulates one variable, labeled the *independent variable*, and measures its effect on the *dependent variable*. In an experimental design, any change in the dependent variable is presumed to be caused by the manipulation of the independent variable. Typically, the experimental method involves the use of a *treatment group* and a *control group*. The treatment group is subjected to the manipulation of the independent variable, while the control group serves as a comparison by not receiving the treatment. Variables that are not of principal concern to the researchers, but that may affect the results of the research, are termed *extraneous variables*. In the experimental method, the researcher attempts to control for extraneous variables through the *random assignment* of participants to the treatment and control groups, in order to ensure that any extraneous variables will be distributed evenly between the groups. The strength of the experimental method is the high level of control that the researcher has over the setting, which allows the investigator to determine cause-and-effect relationships. The weakness of the method is that the controlled conditions may be artificial and may not generalize to actual, uncontrolled work settings. *Quasi-experiments* follow the experimental method, but do not involve random assignment or manipulation of the independent variable. The other type of research method, the *correlational method* (sometimes called the observational method), looks at the relationships among measured variables as they naturally occur, without the intervention of the experimenter and without strict experimental controls. The strength of this design is that it may be more easily conducted in actual settings. However, the correlational method does not allow the specification of cause-and-effect relationships.

Meta-analysis is a method that allows the results of a number of studies to be combined and analyzed together to draw an overall summary or conclusion. Meta-analysis may also be used to determine if the results of different studies of the same factors are significantly different from each other.

The *case study* is a commonly used descriptive investigation that lacks the controls and repeated observations of the experimental and correlational methodologies. The case study can provide important information, but does not allow the testing of hypotheses.

An important part of the research process involves the measurement of variables. The term *operationalization* refers to the process of defining variables so that they can be measured

for research purposes. I/O psychology researchers use a variety of measurement techniques. Researchers may measure variables through the direct obtrusive or unobtrusive observation of behavior. In *obtrusive observation*, the researcher is visible to the research participants, who know that they are being studied. *Unobtrusive observation* involves observing participants' behavior without their knowledge. Another measurement strategy is *self-report techniques*, which yield information about participants' behavior from their own reports. One of the most widely used self-report techniques is the *survey*.

Key issues in the measurement of variables are *reliability*, which refers to the stability or consistency of the measurement, and *validity*, which is the accuracy of the inferences drawn from the measurement.

When interpreting research results, attention must be given to *internal validity*, whether extraneous variables have been accounted for in the research, as well as the *external validity* of the findings, that is, whether they will generalize to other settings. A critical concern to I/O psychologists is the interrelation of the science and practice of industrial/organizational psychology and adhering to ethical principles and guidelines that govern research and practice in I/O psychology.

Study Questions and Exercises

1. Consider the steps in the research process. What are some of the major problems that are likely to be encountered at each step in the research process?

2. What are the strengths and weaknesses of the experimental and the correlational methods? Under what circumstances would you use each?

3. Consider the various measurement techniques used by I/O psychologists. Why are many of the variables used in I/O psychology difficult to measure?

4. Choose some aspect of work behavior and develop a research hypothesis. Now try to

design a study that would test the hypothesis. Consider what your variables are and how you will operationalize them. Choose a research design for the collection of data. Consider who your participants will be and how they will be selected. How might the hypothesis be tested statistically?

5. Using the study that you designed earlier, what are some of the ethical considerations in conducting the research? What information would you include in an informed consent form for that study's participants?

Web Links

http://methods.fullerton.edu
A research methods Web site designed to accompany Cozby's textbook (see Suggested Readings).

http://www.apa.org/ethics/code/index.aspx
APA site for ethics in conducting research.

Suggested Readings

Aron, A., Coups, E., & Aron, E. N. (2010). *Statistics for psychology* (5th ed.). Upper Saddle River, NJ: Prentice Hall. *This straightforward text examines basic methods students in the social and behavioral sciences need to analyze data and test hypotheses.*

Cozby, P. C., & Bates, S. C. (2012). *Methods in behavioral research* (11th ed.). Boston, MA: McGraw-Hill. *An excellent and very readable introduction to research methods.*

Rogelberg, S. G. (Ed.). (2002). *Handbook of research methods in industrial and organizational psychology.* Malden, MA: Blackwell. *A very detailed "encyclopedia" of all topics related to methodology in I/O Psychology. A professional-oriented guidebook, but worth investigating.*

Appendix: Statistical Analyses of Research Data

Although a comprehensive treatment of research methods and statistics is beyond the scope of this text, it is important to emphasize that the science and practice of industrial/organizational psychology require a thorough knowledge of research methods and statistics and some experience using them. More important for our present concerns, it is impossible to gain a true understanding of the methods used by I/O psychologists without some discussion of the statistical analyses of research data.

As mentioned earlier in this chapter, research methods are merely procedures or tools used by I/O psychologists to study work behavior. Statistics, which are arithmetical procedures designed to help summarize and interpret data, are also important research tools. The results of statistical analyses help us to understand relationships between or among variables. In any research investigation there are two main questions: (1) is there a statistically significant relationship between or among the variables of interest? And (2) what is the strength of that relationship? For example, does the independent variable have a strong, moderate, or weak effect on the dependent variable (e.g., What is the effect size?)? Statistics provide the answers to these questions.

There are many types of statistical analyses, and which is most appropriate in a given study depends on such factors as the variables of interest, the way these variables are measured, the design of the study, and the research questions. Concerning the measurement of variables, it is important to point out that variables can be described as being either *quantitative* or *qualitative* in nature. Quantitative data (also known as *measurement* data) refers to a numerical representation of a variable, such as an individual's weight provided by a scale, a score on a cognitive ability test, a student's grade point average, and so on. In all cases, some sort of measurement instrument has been used to measure some quantity. Qualitative data (also referred to as *categorical* or *frequency* data) refers to numbers that are used as labels to categorize people or things; the data provide frequencies for each category. When data collection involves methods like discussion or focus groups, for example, the data are likely to be qualitative and expressed in such statements as, "Twelve people were categorized as 'highly favorable' to changes in work schedules, 20 as 'moderately favorable,' and 9 as 'not favorable.'" Here, we are categorizing participants into groups, and the data represent the frequency of each category. In contrast, if instead of categorizing participants into high, moderate, and low favorability, we assigned each of them a score based on some continuous scale of favorability (scale from 1 to 10), the data would be measurement data, consisting of scores for each participant on that variable. Independent variables are often qualitative, involving categories, although they may also involve quantitative measurement, whereas dependent variables are generally quantitative. Different types of statistical techniques are used to analyze quantitative and qualitative data. Because they tend to be more frequently used in I/O psychology, our discussion will focus on procedures used to analyze quantitative, or measurement, data.

We will discuss two types of statistics: (1) *descriptive statistics*, used to summarize recorded observations of behavior, and (2) *inferential statistics*, used to test hypotheses about research data.

DESCRIPTIVE STATISTICS

The simplest way to represent research data is to use descriptive statistics, which describe data in ways that give the researcher a general idea of the results. Suppose we have collected data on the job performance ratings of 60 employees. The rating scale ranges from 1 to 9, with 9 representing outstanding performance. As you can see in Table A.1, it is difficult to make sense out of the raw data. A frequency distribution, which is a descriptive statistical technique that presents data in a useful format, arranges the performance scores by category, so that we can see at a glance how many employees received each numerical rating. The frequency distribution in Figure A.1 is in the form of a bar graph or histogram.

Other important descriptive statistics include measures of central tendency and variability. Measures of central tendency present the center point of a distribution of scores. This is useful in summarizing the distribution in terms of the middle or average score. The most common measure of central tendency is the mean, or average, which is calculated by adding all the scores and dividing by the number of scores. In our performance data, the sum of the scores

quantitative (measurement) data
data that measure some numerical quantity

qualitative (categorical or frequency) data
data that measure some category or measurement quality

descriptive statistics
arithmetical formulas for summarizing and describing research data

frequency distribution
a descriptive statistical technique that arranges scores by categories

measures of central tendency
present the center point in a distribution of scores

mean
a measure of central tendency; also known as the average

TABLE A.1

Performance Rating Scores of 60 Employees

Employee	Score	Employee	Score	Employee	Score
Adams	5	Alva	6	Ang	6
Bates	4	Bender	1	Berra	7
Brown	6	Cadiz	5	Camus	8
Chow	7	Cisneros	4	Crow	5
Davis	8	Dawes	7	DeRios	4
Driver	4	Dudley	6	Evans	6
Ewing	5	Exner	4	Fang	2
Farris	3	Fernal	5	Ford	9
Frank	5	Gant	3	Ghent	5
Gower	3	Grant	6	Gwynne	2
Hall	6	Hawkes	7	Horner	4
Hull	4	Hu	8	Jacobs	6
Justin	3	Kee	5	Kubiak	9
Lang	5	Lantz	7	Leong	5
Mayes	5	Mertz	3	Mio	4
Murphy	4	Nguyen	5	Page	5
Pierce	2	Rabago	6	Richards	3
Sherrod	7	Simpson	8	Suls	6
Taylor	3	Tucker	2	Tran	4
Woll	5	Young	6	Zapf	5

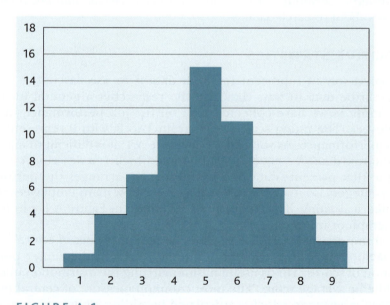

FIGURE A.1

Frequency Distribution (Histogram) of 60 Employee Performance Rating Scores

is 303 and the number of scores is 60. As a result, the mean of our frequency distribution is 5.05. Another measure of central tendency is the median, or the midpoint of the distribution, such that 50% of the scores (in this example, 50% would be 30 of the 60 scores) fall below the median, and 50% fall above the median. In this distribution of scores, the median is in the center rating category of 5.

Measures of variability show how scores are dispersed in a frequency distribution. If scores are widely dispersed across a large number of categories, variability will be high. If scores are closely clustered in a few categories, variability will be low. The most commonly used measure of distribution variability is the standard deviation. In a frequency distribution, the standard deviation indicates how closely the scores spread out around the mean. The more widely dispersed the scores, the greater the standard deviation. The more closely bunched the scores, the smaller the standard deviation. For example, imagine that two managers each rate 15 subordinates on a 5-point performance scale, and the mean (average) ratings given by each manager are the same: 2.8 on the 5-point scale. However, manager A's ratings have a large standard deviation, whereas manager B's ratings have a very small standard deviation. What does this tell you? It means that manager A gave more varied ratings of subordinate performance than did manager B, because the standard deviation represents the variance of the distribution of scores. In contrast, manager B gave similar ratings for all 15 subordinates, such that all the ratings are close in numerical value to the average and do not vary across a wide numerical range. Both the mean and the standard deviation are important to more sophisticated inferential statistics.

INFERENTIAL STATISTICS

Although descriptive statistics are helpful in representing and organizing data, inferential statistics are used to test hypotheses. For example, assume that we wanted to test the hypothesis that a certain safety program effectively reduced rates of industrial accidents. One group of workers is subjected to the safety program, whereas another (the control group) is not. Accident rates before and after the program are then measured. Inferential statistics would tell us whether or not differences in accident rates between the two groups were meaningful. Depending on the research design, different sorts of inferential statistics will typically be used.

When inferential statistics are used to analyze data, we are concerned about whether a result is meaningful, or statistically significant. The concept of statistical significance is based on theories of probability. A research result is statistically significant if its probability of occurrence by chance is very low. Typically, a research result is statistically significant if its probability of occurrence by chance is less than 5 out of 100 (in research terminology, the probability, or p, is less than 0.05; $p < 0.05$). For example, say we find that a group of telephone salespersons who have undergone training in sales techniques have average (mean) sales of 250 units per month, whereas salespersons who did not receive the training have mean sales of 242 units. Based on the difference in the two means and the

---

median
a measure of central tendency; the midpoint of a distribution of scores

variability
estimates the distribution of scores around the middle or average score

standard deviation
a measure of variability of scores in a frequency distribution

inferential statistics
statistical techniques used for analyzing data to test hypotheses

statistical significance
the probability of a particular result occurring by chance, used to determine the meaning of research outcomes

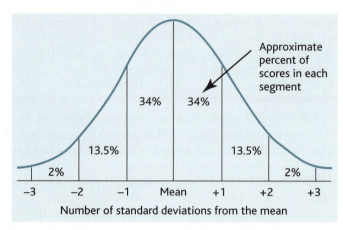

FIGURE A.2
A Normal Distribution

variability (standard deviations) of the two groups, a statistical test will determine whether the difference in the two groups is statistically significant (and thus if the training program actually increases sales).

normal distribution (bell-shaped curve)

a distribution of scores along a continuum with known properties

The concept of the normal distribution of variables is also important for the use of inferential statistics. It is assumed that many psychological variables, especially human characteristics such as intelligence, motivation, or personality constructs, are normally distributed. That is, scores on these variables in the general population are presumed to vary along a continuum, with the greatest proportion clustering around the midpoint and proportions dropping off toward the endpoints of the continuum. A normal distribution of scores is symbolized visually by the bell-shaped curve. The bell-shaped curve, or normal distribution, is a representative distribution of known mathematical properties that can be used as a standard for statistical analyses. The mathematical properties of the normal distribution are represented in Figure A.2. The exact midpoint score, or median, of the normal distribution is the same as its mean. In a normal distribution, 50% of the scores lie above the midpoint and 50% below. The normal distribution is also divided in terms of standard deviations from the midpoint. In a normal distribution, approximately 68% of all scores lie within one standard deviation above or below the midpoint or mean. Approximately 95% of all scores in a normal distribution lie within two standard deviations above or below the midpoint. Now that you know the properties of the bell-shaped, or normal, curve, go back to the frequency distribution in Figure A.1. You should notice that this distribution closely approximates the bell-shaped, normal distribution.

STATISTICAL ANALYSIS OF EXPERIMENTAL METHOD DATA

As mentioned, depending on the research design, different inferential statistics may be used to analyze data. Typically, one set of statistical techniques is used to test hypotheses from data collected in experimental methods, and another set is used to analyze data from correlational research.

The simplest type of experimental design would have a treatment group, a control group, and a single dependent variable. Whether or not a group receives the treatment represents levels of the independent variable. The most common statistical technique for this type of study is the *t*-**test**, which examines the difference between the means on the dependent variable for the two groups, taking into account the variability of scores in each group. In the example of trained and untrained salespersons used earlier, a *t*-test would determine whether the difference in the two means (250 units vs. 242 units) is statistically significant, that is, not due to chance fluctuations. If the difference is significant, the researcher may conclude that the training program did have a positive effect on sales.

When an experimental design moves beyond two group comparisons, a statistical method called *analysis of variance*, or ANOVA, is often used. Analysis of variance looks at differences among more than two groups on a single dependent variable. For example, if we wanted to examine differences in sales performance between a group of salespersons exposed to 2 weeks of "sales influence tactic training," a group exposed to 2 days of training, and a group with no training, analysis of variance would be the appropriate technique. In this instance, we still have one dependent variable and one independent variable as in the two-group case; however, the independent variable has three, rather than two, levels. Whenever a research design involves a single independent variable with more than two levels and one dependent variable, the typical statistical technique is referred to as a one-way analysis of variance (it is called a "one-way" because there is a single independent variable). The one-way ANOVA would tell us whether our three groups differed in any meaningful way in sales performance.

When a research design involves more than one independent variable, which is very common, the technique that is typically used is the factorial analysis of variance. For example, we may wish to examine the effect of the three levels of our influence training program on sales performance for a group of salespersons that receives a sales commission compared to one that does not. This design involves a single dependent variable (sales performance) and two independent variables, one with three levels (training) and one with two levels (commission vs. no commission). The number of different groups in a research study is determined by the number of independent variables and their levels. In this case, our design would result in six groups of salespersons ($2 \times 3 = 6$), and the analysis would involve a 2×3 factorial analysis of variance.

There is a major advantage to examining more than one independent variable in a research study, and it involves the types of effects that may be detected. Suppose that in our study we find that influence tactic sales training significantly increases sales performance. This change in the dependent variable due to the independent variable of training is called a *main effect*. Similarly, we may find a main effect of the sales commission variable, such that salespersons who receive a commission have significantly higher sales performance than those who do not. This type of effect could not be detected if we were examining either independent variable alone. However, by examining both independent variables at the same time, we may detect a different type of effect called an *interaction*.

t-test
a statistical test for examining the difference between the means of two groups

Stop & Review

How would a researcher use descriptive and inferential statistics?

Two variables are said to interact when the effect of one independent variable on the dependent variable differs, depending on the level of the second independent variable. In our study, an interaction between influence tactic sales training and sales commission would be indicated if our training program only increased the sales performance of salespersons who received a commission and did not affect the performance of salespersons who did not receive commissions.

An even more sophisticated technique, *multivariate analysis of variance (MANOVA)*, examines data from multiple groups with multiple dependent variables. The logic of MANOVA is similar to that of ANOVA, but there is more than one dependent variable investigated at a time. For instance, we may want to investigate the effects of training or receiving a sales commission (or both) on sales performance and worker job satisfaction. MANOVA procedures would tell us about differences between our groups on each of these dependent variables. Understanding how these complex statistical techniques work and how they are calculated is not important for our discussion. These terms are presented only to familiarize you with some of the statistics that you might encounter in research reports in I/O psychology or in other types of social science research and to increase your understanding of the purposes of such procedures.

STATISTICAL ANALYSIS OF CORRELATIONAL METHOD DATA

When a research design is correlational, a different set of statistical techniques is usually used to test hypotheses about presumed relationships among variables. As mentioned earlier, the distinction between independent and dependent variables in a correlational design is not as important as in the experimental method. In a correlational design, the independent variable is usually called the predictor, and the dependent variable is often referred to as the criterion. In a simple correlational design with two variables, the usual statistical analysis technique is the correlation coefficient, which measures the strength of the relationship between the predictor and the criterion. The correlation coefficient ranges from +1.00 to −1.00. The closer the coefficient is to either +1.00 or −1.00, the stronger the linear relationship between the two variables. The closer the correlation coefficient is to 0, the weaker the linear relationship. A positive correlation coefficient means that there is a positive linear relationship between the two variables, where an increase in one variable is associated with an increase in the other variable.

Assume that a researcher studying the relationship between the commuting distance of workers and work tardiness obtains a positive correlation coefficient of .75. This figure indicates that the greater the commuting distance of employees, the greater the likelihood that they will be late for work. A negative correlation coefficient indicates a negative relationship: An increase in one variable is associated with a decrease in the other. For example, a researcher studying workers who cut out patterns in a clothing factory hypothesizes that there is a relationship between workers' job experience and the amount of waste produced. Statistical analysis indicates a negative correlation coefficient of −.68: The more experience workers have, the less waste they produce. A correlation coefficient of 0 indicates that there is no relationship between the two

correlation coefficient
a statistical technique used to determine the strength of a relationship between two variables

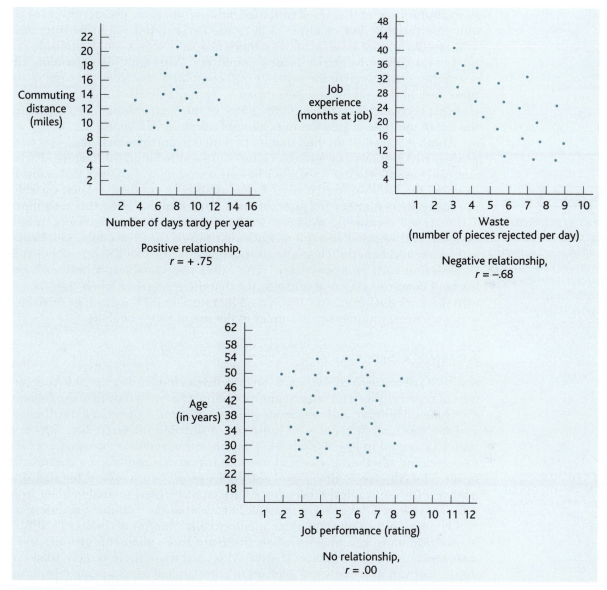

FIGURE A.3

Plots of Scores for Positive, Negative, and Zero Correlations

variables. For example, a researcher measuring the relationship between the age of factory workers and their job performance finds a correlation coefficient of approximately .00, which shows that there is no relationship between age and performance. (These relationships are presented graphically in Figure A.3.)

Whereas the simple correlation coefficient is used to examine the relationship between two variables in a correlational study, the *multiple regression* technique allows a researcher to assess the relationship between a single criterion and multiple predictors. Multiple regression would allow a researcher to examine how well several variables, in combination, predict levels of an outcome variable. For example, a personnel researcher might be interested in how educational level, years of experience, and scores on an aptitude test predict the job performance of new employees. With multiple regression, the researcher could analyze the separate and combined predictive strength of the three variables in predicting performance. Again, a detailed understanding of multiple regression is far beyond the scope of this text, although we will discuss the use of multiple regression in personnel selection in Chapter 4.

Another statistical method that is often used in correlational designs is *factor analysis*, which shows how variables cluster to form meaningful "factors." Factor analysis is useful when a researcher has measured many variables and wants to examine the underlying structure of the variables or combine related variables to reduce their number for later analysis. For example, using this technique, a researcher measuring workers' satisfaction with their supervisors, salary, benefits, and working conditions finds that two of these variables, satisfaction with salary and benefits, cluster to form a single factor that the researcher calls "satisfaction with compensation." The other two variables, supervisors and working conditions, form a single factor that the researcher labels "satisfaction with the work environment." If you read literature in I/O psychology or related social sciences, you may see examples of the use of factor analysis.

Stop & Review

Describe a statistical test that would be used in an experimental research design and one that would be used in a correlational research design.

APPENDIX SUMMARY

Statistics are research tools used to analyze research data. *Descriptive statistics* are ways of representing data to assist interpretation. One such statistic is the *frequency distribution*. The *mean* and *median* are *measures of central tendency* in a distribution, and the *standard deviation* is an indicator of distribution variability. *Inferential statistics* are used to test hypotheses. The concept of *statistical significance* is used to determine whether a statistical test of a hypothesis produced a meaningful result. The concept of the *normal distribution* provides a standard for statistical analyses. Different inferential statistics are typically used to analyze data from different research designs. For example, a *t-test* is used to examine the difference between two groups on some dependent variable. *Analysis of variance* (ANOVA) is used for statistical analyses when there are more than two groups, and a *multivariate analysis of variance* (MANOVA) is used when there is more than one dependent variable. Statistical analyses of correlational method data rely on the *correlation coefficient*, a statistic that measures the strength and direction of a relationship between two variables. *Multiple regression* involves correlational research with more than two variables. *Factor analysis* allows for statistical clustering of variables to form meaningful factors or groupings of variables.

PART TWO

CHAPTER

3 | Job Analysis

Inside Tips

JOB ANALYSIS: ESTABLISHING A FOUNDATION
FOR PERSONNEL PSYCHOLOGY

The topic of this chapter, job analysis, is the foundation of nearly all personnel activities. To appraise employee performance, hire the right person for a job, train someone to perform a job, or change or redesign a job, we need to know exactly what the job is. This is the purpose of job analysis. Many of the topics we will discuss in the next several chapters rest on this foundation. For example, when we discuss the recruitment, screening, testing, and selection of applicants for a job (in the next two chapters), we determine what knowledge, skills, abilities, and other characteristics (KSAOs) are required to perform the job before we hire someone. When we discuss evaluating job performance (Chapter 6), we need to know what the job consists of before we can tell if someone is doing it well or poorly.

In addition, the analysis of jobs draws heavily on the research methods and measurement issues studied in Chapter 2. In job analysis, we strive to be as objective and precise as possible. Measurement methods and techniques of observing and recording data are critical issues in analyzing jobs.

The topic of job analysis also relates to some of the issues discussed in Chapter 1. For example, when Taylor was applying time-and-motion methods to the study of a job, he was in effect conducting a job analysis. Additionally, one of the job analysis methods we will discuss in this chapter examines the specific processes by which a job gets done. These are the same types of processes Taylor studied in his scientific management methods. Making connections such as these will help you to see how the various topics that we will be discussing fit together.

I magine that graduation is on the horizon, and you want to find out about the sorts of jobs for which you might be qualified and what sorts of companies or organizations you might work for. In all likelihood, you would turn to some source of information that deals with personnel, or human resources, issues. You might visit your campus's career center or begin with a Web-based search. You need to know about careers and jobs, and the requirements needed to succeed in them.

In the next five chapters, we will be examining the specialty of industrial/organizational psychology referred to as personnel psychology. **Personnel psychology** is concerned with the creation, care, and maintenance of a workforce, which includes the recruitment, placement, training, and development of workers; the measurement and evaluation of their performance; and the concern with worker productivity and well-being. In short, the goal of personnel psychology is to take care of an organization's human resources (the organization's *personnel*).

personnel psychology
the specialty area of I/O psychology focusing on an organization's human resources

In organizations, human resources departments are responsible for most personnel matters. In addition to maintaining employee records—tabulating attendance, handling payroll, and keeping retirement records—human resources departments deal with numerous issues relating to the company's most valuable assets: its human workers. I/O psychologists who specialize in personnel psychology are involved in activities such as employee recruitment and selection, the measurement of employee performance and the establishment of good performance review procedures, the development of employee training and development programs, and the formulation of criteria for promotion, firing, and disciplinary action. They also need to be well-versed in employment laws and regulations to ensure that their organizations are in compliance with federal and state laws and guidelines. I/O psychologists may also establish effective programs for employee compensation and benefits, create incentive programs, and design and implement programs to protect employee health and well-being.

Job Analysis

One of the most basic personnel functions is job analysis, or the systematic study of the tasks, duties, and responsibilities of a job and the knowledge, skills, and abilities needed to perform it. Job analysis is the starting point for nearly all personnel functions, and job analysis is critically important for developing the means for assessing personnel (Wheaton & Whetzel, 1997). Before a worker can be hired or trained and before a worker's performance can be evaluated, it is critical to understand exactly what the worker's job entails. Such analyses should also be conducted on a periodic basis to ensure that the information on jobs is up to date. In other words, it needs to reflect the work actually being performed. For example, as time goes by, an administrative assistant in a small organization might assume additional tasks and responsibilities that did not exist earlier. If the company has to replace this person, but does not have an up-to-date job analysis for the position, it is doubtful that the company would be able to hire an individual with all the knowledge, skills, abilities, and other characteristics needed to perform the job as it currently exists.

Because most jobs consist of a variety of tasks and duties, gaining a full understanding of a job is not always easy. Therefore, job analysis methods need to be comprehensive and precise. Indeed, large organizations have specialists whose primary responsibilities are to analyze the various jobs in the company and develop extensive and current descriptions for each.

Most jobs are quite complex and require workers to possess certain types of knowledge and skills to perform a variety of different tasks. Workers may need to operate complex machinery to perform their jobs or they might need to possess a great deal of information about a particular product or service. Jobs might also require workers to interact effectively with different types of people, or a single job might require a worker to possess all these important skills and knowledge. As jobs become more and more complex, the need for effective and comprehensive job analyses becomes increasingly important. It must be emphasized, however, that although job analysis provides us with a greater understanding of what a particular job entails, in today's complex and ever-changing, ever-evolving jobs, job analysis should not be a limiting process. Analyses of jobs should allow for flexibility and creativity in many jobs, rather than being used to tell people how to do their work.

To perform a good job analysis, the job analyst must be well trained in the basic research methods we discussed in Chapter 2. Job analysis typically involves the objective measurement of work behavior performed by actual workers. Therefore, a job analyst must be an expert in objective measurement techniques to perform an accurate job analysis. In fact, a review of research on job analysis suggests that experience and training in job analysis methods are critical for effective job analysis (Landy, 1993; Voskuijl & van Sliedregt, 2002).

A job analysis leads directly to the development of several other important personnel "products": a job description, a job specification, a job evaluation, and performance criteria. A job description is a detailed accounting of the tasks,

job analysis
the systematic study of the tasks, duties, and responsibilities of a job and the qualities needed to perform it

job description
a detailed description of job tasks, procedures, and responsibilities; the tools and equipment used; and the end product or service

TABLE 3.1

Examples of a Job Description and a Job Specification

Partial job description for Human Resources Assistant

Job summary: Supports human resources processes by administering employment tests, scheduling appointments, conducting employee orientation, maintaining personnel records and information.

Job tasks and results: Schedules and coordinates appointments for testing; administers and scores employment tests; conducts new employee orientation programs; maintains personnel databases, involving assembling, preparing, and analyzing employment data; must maintain technical knowledge by attending educational workshops and reviewing publications; must maintain strict confidentiality of HR information.

Partial job specification for Human Resources Assistant

Minimum of two years experience in human resources operations. Bachelor's degree in business, psychology, social sciences, or related area; Master's degree in HR-related discipline desired; Proficiency in database management programs and statistical analysis software; good interpersonal skills, with training and presentation experience.

Adapted from: Plachy, R. J., & Plachy S. J. (1998). *More results-oriented job descriptions.* New York: AMACOM.

job specification
a statement of the human characteristics required to perform a job

job evaluation
an assessment of the relative value of a job to determine appropriate compensation

procedures, and responsibilities required of the worker; the machines, tools, and equipment used to perform the job; and the job output (end product or service). Workers are most familiar with job descriptions. Often new workers are provided with descriptions of their jobs during initial orientation and training. Human resources departments may also make job descriptions for various jobs accessible to employees. For instance, you can sometimes see job descriptions posted on bulletin boards or on e-mail listservs as part of announcements for company job openings.

A job analysis also leads to a **job specification**, which provides information about the human characteristics required to perform the job, such as physical and personal traits, work experience, and education. Usually, job specifications give the minimum acceptable qualifications that an employee needs to perform a given job. A sample job description and job specification are presented in Table 3.1. A third personnel "product," **job evaluation**, is the assessment of the relative value or worth of a job to an organization to determine appropriate compensation, or wages. We will discuss job evaluation in much more depth later in this chapter.

Finally, a job analysis helps outline performance criteria, which are the means for appraising worker success in performing a job. Performance criteria and performance appraisals will be the topics of Chapter 6.

These products of job analysis are important because they provide the detailed information needed for other personnel activities, such as planning, recruitment and selection programs, and performance appraisal systems (see Figure 3.1). Job analyses and their products are also valuable because of legal decisions that make organizations more responsible for personnel actions as part of the movement toward greater legal rights for the worker. Foremost

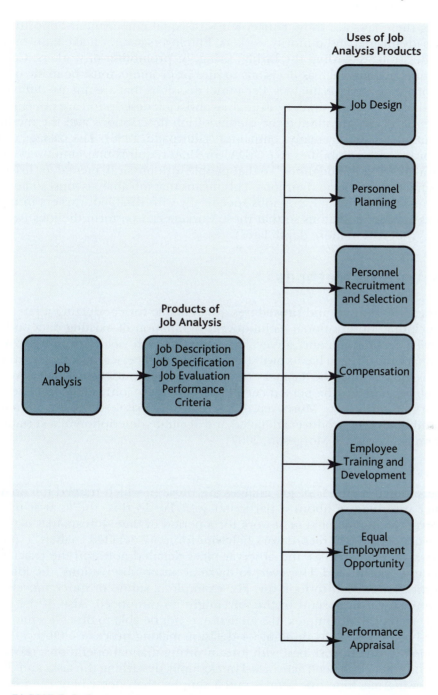

FIGURE 3.1

Links Between Job Analysis and Personnel Functions

Source: Based on Ghorpade, J. V. (1988). *Job analysis: A handbook for the human resource director* (p. 6). Englewood Cliffs, NJ: Prentice Hall.

among these laws are those concerned with equal employment opportunities for disadvantaged and minority workers. Employers cannot make hasty or arbitrary decisions regarding the hiring, firing, or promotion of workers. Certain personnel actions, such as decisions to hire or promote, must be made on the basis of a thorough job analysis. Personnel decisions that are not are difficult to defend in court. Sometimes a job analysis and a job description are not enough. Courts have also questioned the quality of job descriptions and the methods used in job analysis by many companies (Ghorpade, 1988). The passage of the Americans with Disabilities Act (ADA) in 1990 requires that employers make "reasonable accommodations" so that people with physical, mental, or learning disabilities can perform their jobs. This means that job analysts must sometimes be concerned with analyzing jobs specifically with disabled workers in mind, to make accommodations so that those workers can perform the jobs (we will discuss the ADA in more depth later).

Job Analysis Methods

A variety of methods and procedures are available for conducting a job analysis, including observational techniques, examination of existing data on jobs, interview techniques, and surveys. Each method will yield a different type of information, and each has its own strengths and weaknesses. In certain methods, such as interviewing, the data may be obtained from a variety of sources, such as the job incumbent (the person currently holding the job), supervisory personnel, or outside experts. Moreover, different job analysis methods are often used in combination to produce a detailed and accurate description of a certain job (Brannick, Levine, & Morgeson, 2007).

Observations

Observational methods of job analysis are those in which trained job analysts gather information about a particular job. To do this, the analyst usually observes the job incumbent at work for a period of time. Job analysts may also make use of videos to record work behavior for more detailed analysis. Typically in observational analysis, the observer takes detailed notes on the exact tasks and duties performed. However, to make accurate observations, the job analyst must know what to look for. For example, a subtle or quick movement, but one that is important to the job, might go unnoticed. Also, if the job is highly technical or complex, the analyst may not be able to observe some of its critical aspects, such as thinking or decision-making processes. Observational techniques usually work best with jobs involving manual operations, repetitive tasks, or other easily seen activities. For example, describing the tasks and duties of a sewing machine operator is much simpler than describing the job of a computer technician, because much of the computer technician's job involves cognitive processes involved in troubleshooting computer problems.

With observational techniques, it is important that the times selected for observation are representative of the worker's routine, especially if the job requires that the worker be engaged in different tasks during different times of

🕑 Stop & Review

List and define three products of a job analysis.

This job analyst uses observational methods to analyze this machinist's job

the day, week, or year. For example, an accounting clerk may deal with payroll vouchers on Thursdays, may spend most of Fridays updating sales figures, and may be almost completely occupied with preparing a company's tax records during the month of January.

One concern regarding observational methods is whether the presence of the observer in some way influences workers' performance. There is always the chance that workers will perform their jobs differently simply because they know that they are being watched (recall the Hawthorne effect discussed in Chapter 1).

Participation

In some instances, a job analyst may want to actually perform a particular job or job operation to get a firsthand understanding of how the job is performed. For example, several years ago, I was involved in conducting a job analysis of workers performing delicate microassembly operations. These microassemblers were working with fitting together extremely tiny electrical components. The only way to gain a true understanding of (and appreciation for) the fine hand–eye coordination required to perform the job was to attempt the task myself.

Existing data

Most large, established organizations usually have some information or records that can be used in the job analysis, such as a previous job analysis for the position or an analysis of a related job. Such data might also be borrowed from another organization that has conducted analyses of similar jobs. Human resources professionals often exchange such information with professionals at other organizations. Existing data should always be checked to make sure it conforms to the job as it is currently being performed and also to determine if the existing data accounts for the inclusion of new technology in the job.

Interviews

Interviews are another method of job analysis. They can be open-ended ("Tell me all about what you do on the job"), or they can involve structured or standardized questions. Because any one source of information can be biased, the job analyst may want to get more than one perspective by interviewing the job incumbent, the incumbent's supervisor, and, if the job is a supervisory one, the incumbent's subordinates. The job analyst might also interview several job incumbents within a single organization to get a more reliable representation of the job and to see whether various people holding the same job title in a company actually perform similar tasks.

Surveys

Survey methods of job analysis usually involve the administration of a pencil-and-paper questionnaire that the respondent completes and returns to the job analyst. Surveys can consist of open-ended questions ("What abilities or skills are required to perform this job?"); closed-ended questions ("Which of the following classifications best fits your position? (a) supervisory, (b) technical, (c) line, (d) clerical"); or checklists ("Check all of the following tasks that you perform in your job.").

The survey method has two advantages over the interview method. First, the survey allows the collection of information from a number of workers simultaneously. This can be helpful and very cost effective when the analyst needs to study several positions. Second, because the survey can be anonymous, there may be less distortion or withholding of information than in a face-to-face interview. One of the drawbacks of the survey, however, is that the information obtained is limited by the questions asked. Unlike an interview, a survey cannot probe for additional information or for clarification of a response.

Often in conducting job analyses, job incumbents or knowledgeable supervisors of job incumbents are referred to as **subject matter experts (or SMEs)**. Subject matter experts can provide job analysis information via interviews or through survey methods.

subject matter expert (SME)
an individual who has detailed knowledge about a particular job

Job diaries

Another method for job analysis is to have job incumbents record their daily activities in a diary. An advantage of the job diary is that it provides a detailed, hour-by-hour, day-by-day account of the worker's job. One difficulty of diary methods, however, is that it is quite time consuming, both for the worker who is keeping the diary and for the job analyst who has the task of analyzing the large amount of information contained in the diary.

An important concern in all the preceding methods of job analysis is potential errors and inaccuracies that occur simply because job analysts, job incumbents, and subject matter experts are all human beings. In one review, Morgeson and Campion (1997) outlined 16 potential sources of inaccuracy in job analysis, ranging from mere carelessness and poor job analyst training to biases such as overestimating or underestimating the importance of certain tasks and jobs to information overload stemming from the complexity of some jobs. As you recall from our discussion of research methods, an important theme for I/O psychologists is to take steps to ensure that proper methods are used in all sorts of organizational analyses. Nowhere is this more important than in conducting job analyses.

Specific Job Analysis Techniques

In addition to these various general methods for conducting job analyses, there are also a number of specific, standardized analysis techniques. These techniques have not only been widely used but have also generated a considerable amount of research on their effectiveness. We will consider four of these specific techniques: the job element method, the functional job analysis, the Position Analysis Questionnaire, and the critical incidents technique.

JOB ELEMENT METHOD

job element method

a job analysis method that analyzes jobs in terms of the knowledge, skills, abilities, and other characteristics (KSAOs) required to perform the jobs

The **job element method** of job analysis looks at the basic knowledge, skills, abilities, or other characteristics—KSAOs—that are required to perform a particular job (Primoff, 1975). These KSAOs constitute the basic job elements.

In the job element method the job analyst relies on "experts" (subject matter experts, or SMEs) who are informed about the job to identify the job elements (KSAOs) required for a given job. The experts then rate or rank the different elements in terms of their importance for performing the job. The job element method is "person oriented" in that it focuses on the characteristics of the individual who is performing the job. This method has been used most often in jobs in the federal government. Because of its limited scope, the job element method is often combined with other job analysis methods outlined next (Bemis, Belenky, & Soder, 1983).

CRITICAL INCIDENTS TECHNIQUE

critical incidents technique (CIT)

a job analysis technique that relies on instances of especially successful or unsuccessful job performance

The **critical incidents technique (CIT)** of job analysis records the specific worker behaviors that have led to particularly successful or unsuccessful job performance (Flanagan, 1954). For example, some critical incidents for the job of clerical assistant might include: "Possess knowledge of word processing programs"; "Notices an item in a letter or report that doesn't appear to be right, checks it, and corrects it"; "Misfiles charts, letters, etc., on a regular basis"; and "Produces a manuscript with good margins, making it look like a professional document." All of these behaviors presumably contribute to the success or failure of the clerical assistant. Research indicates that information is best provided by experts on the job and that careful qualitative analysis methods should be used (Butterfield, Borgen, Amundson, & Asa-Sophia, 2005; Mullins & Kimbrough, 1988). Therefore, information on such incidents is obtained by questioning, either through interviews or questionnaires, job incumbents, job supervisors, or other knowledgeable individuals. Through the collection of hundreds of critical incidents, the job analyst can arrive at a very good picture of what a particular job—and its successful performance—is all about. An example of a critical incidents interview form is presented in Figure 3.2.

The real value of the CIT is in helping to determine the particular knowledge, skills, and abilities that a worker needs to perform a job successfully. For example, from the critical incidents given for the clerical assistant position, we know that the successful worker will need to know how to file, use a word processing program, check basic grammar and sentence structure, and set up a typed manuscript page. The CIT technique is also useful in developing appraisal systems for certain jobs, by helping to identify the critical components of successful performance. In fact, recently the results of CIT analyses have been used to teach "best practices" in professions such as medicine, counseling, and customer service (e.g., Rademacher, Simpson, & Marcdante, 2010).

The following is an example of an interview question designed to elicit critical incidents for a particular job. This question focuses on an incident where a subordinate was behaving in a "helpful" way. Another question might try to elicit when workers are not being helpful; in other words, when they may be hurting group productivity.

"Think of the last time you saw one of your subordinates do something that was very helpful to your group in meeting their production schedule." (Pause until the respondent has such an incident in mind.) "Did the subordinate's action result in an increase in production of as much as one percent for that day?–or some similar period?"
(If the answer is "no," say) "I wonder if you could think of the last time that someone did something that did have this much of an effect in increasing production." (When respondent indicates he/she has such a situation in mind, say) "What were the general circumstances leading up to this incident?"

"Tell me exactly what this person did that was so helpful at that time."
"Why was this so helpful in getting your group's job done?"
"When did this incident happen?"
"What was this person's job?"
"How long has the person been on this job?"

Another example of a question designed to elicit critical incidents may be as simple and general as, "Think of the best (worst) subordinate you have known. Tell me about a time that shows why this person was the best (worst)."

FIGURE 3.2
Critical Incidents Interview Form
Source: Adapted from Flanagan, J. C. (1954). The Critical Incidents Technique. *Psychological Bulletin, 51,* 342.

POSITION ANALYSIS QUESTIONNAIRE

One of the most widely researched job analysis instruments is the Position Analysis Questionnaire (PAQ) (McCormick, Jeanneret, & Mecham, 1969), which is a structured questionnaire that analyzes various jobs in terms of 187 job elements that are arranged into six categories, or divisions, as follows:

Position Analysis Questionnaire (PAQ)
a job analysis technique that uses a structured questionnaire to analyze jobs according to 187 job statements, grouped into six categories

Information input—Where and how the worker obtains the information needed to perform the job. For example, a newspaper reporter may be required to use published, written materials as well as interviews with informants to write a news story. A clothing inspector's information input may involve fine visual discriminations of garment seams.

Mental processes—The kinds of thinking, reasoning, and decision making required to perform the job. For example, an air traffic controller must make many decisions about when it is safe for jets to land and take off.

Work output—The tasks the worker must perform and the tools or machines needed. For example, a word processor must enter text using keyboard devices.

Relationships with other persons—The kinds of relationships and contacts with others required to do the job. For example, a teacher instructs others, and a store clerk has contact with customers by providing information and ringing up purchases.

Job context—The physical and/or social contexts in which the work is performed. Examples of job context elements would be working under high temperatures or dealing with many conflict situations.

Other job characteristics—Other relevant activities, conditions, or characteristics necessary to do the job.

Each of these job elements is individually rated using six categories: extent of use, importance to the job, amount of time, applicability, possibility of occurrence, and a special code for miscellaneous job elements. The standard elements are rated on a scale from 1, for minor applicability, to 5, for extreme applicability. There is an additional rating for "does not apply" (McCormick, 1979). A sample page from the PAQ is shown in Figure 3.3.

INFORMATION INPUT

1. INFORMATION INPUT

1.1 Sources of Job Information

Rate each of the following items in terms of the extent to which it is used by the worker as a source of information in performing his job.

Code	Extent of Use (U)
N	Does not apply
1	Nominal/very infrequent
2	Occasional
3	Moderate
4	Considerable
5	Very substantial

1 _____ Written materials (books, reports, office notes, articles, job instructions, signs, etc.).

2 _____ Quantitative materials (materials which deal with quantities or amounts, such as graphs, accounts, specifications, tables of numbers, etc.).

3 _____ Pictorial materials (pictures or picturelike materials used as **sources** of information, for example, drawings, blueprints, diagrams, maps, tracings, photographic films, x-ray films, TV pictures, etc.).

4 _____ Patterns/related devices (templates, stencils, patterns, etc., used as **sources** of information when **observed** during use; do **not** include here materials described in item 3 above).

5 _____ Visual displays (dials, gauges, signal lights, radarscopes, speedometers, clocks, etc.).

6 _____ Measuring devices (rulers, calipers, tire pressure gauges, scales, thickness gauges, pipettes, thermometers, protractors, etc., used to obtain visual information about physical measurements; do **not** include here devices described in item 5 above).

7 _____ Mechanical devices (tools, equipment, machinery, and other mechanical devices which are **sources** of information when observed during use or operation).

8 _____ Materials in process (parts, materials, objects, etc., which are **sources** of information when being modified, worked on, or otherwise processed, such as bread dough being mixed, workpiece being turned in a lathe, fabric being cut, shoe being resoled, etc.).

9 _____ Materials **not** in process (parts, materials, objects, etc., not in the process of being changed or modified, which are sources of information when being inspected, handled, packaged, distributed, or selected, etc., such as items or materials in inventory, storage, or distribution channels, items being inspected, etc.).

10 _____ Features of nature (landscapes, fields, geological samples, vegetation, cloud formations, and other features of nature which are observed or inspected to provide information).

11 _____ Constructed features of environment (structures, buildings, dams, highways, bridges, docks, railroads, and other "man made" or altered aspects of the indoor or outdoor environment which are **observed** or **inspected** to provide job information; do not consider equipment, machines, etc., that an individual uses in work, as covered by item 7).

FIGURE 3.3

Sample Page from the Position Analysis Questionnaire (PAQ)

Source: McCormick, E. J., Jeanneret, P. R., & Mecham, R. C. (1969). *Position Analysis Questionnaire* (p. 4). West Lafayette, IN: Occupational Research Center, Purdue University.

The PAQ results produce a very detailed profile of a particular job that can be used to compare jobs within a company or similar positions in different organizations. Because the PAQ is a standardized instrument, two analysts surveying the same job should come up with very similar profiles. This might not be the case with interview techniques, where the line of questioning and interpersonal skills specific to the interviewer could greatly affect the job profile.

As mentioned, the PAQ has historically been one of the most widely used and thoroughly researched methods of job analysis (Hyland & Muchinsky, 1991; Peterson & Jeanneret, 1997). In one interesting study, the PAQ was used to analyze the job of a homemaker. It was found that a homemaker's job is most similar to the jobs of police officer, firefighter, and airport maintenance chief (Arvey & Begalla, 1975).

FUNCTIONAL JOB ANALYSIS

Functional job analysis (FJA) has been used extensively by organizations in both the public and private sectors (Fine & Cronshaw, 1999; Fine & Getkate, 1995; Fine & Wiley, 1971). It was developed in part to assist the U.S. Department of Labor in the construction of a comprehensive job classification system and to help create the *Dictionary of Occupational Titles (DOT)* (U.S. Department of Labor, 1991). The *DOT* was a reference guide that classified and gave general descriptions for over 40,000 different jobs. The *DOT* has been replaced by the online O*NET system that we will discuss shortly.

Functional Job Analysis uses three broad categories representing the job's typical interaction with data, people, and things. *Data* is information, knowledge, and conceptions. Jobs are evaluated with an eye to the amount and type of interaction the person performing the job has with data—numbers, words, symbols, and other abstract elements. *People* refers to the amount of contact with others that a job requires. These people can be coworkers, supervisors, customers, or others. *Things* refers to the worker's interaction with inanimate objects such as tools, machines, equipment, and tangible work products. Within each of these categories there is a hierarchy of work functions that ranges from the most involved and complex functions (given the numerical value of "0") to the least involved and least complex (the highest digit in the category; see Table 3.2). For example, using FJA, the job of industrial/organizational psychologist requires "coordinating" data (value of "1"), "mentoring/leading" people (the highest value of "0"), and "handling" things (relatively low value of "7"). For the occupation of job analyst, the corresponding numbers are 2, 6, and 7, meaning that this job involves "analyzing" data, "exchanging information" with people, and "handling" things.

As mentioned, the DOT has been replaced by O*NET—the Occupational Information Network (www.onetcenter.org). The O*NET database contains information about job categories, job KSAOs, as well as information about wages and salaries, job training and licensing requirements for particular jobs,

Functional job analysis (FJA)
a structured job analysis technique that examines the sequence of tasks in a job and the processes by which they are completed

Dictionary of Occupational Titles (DOT)
a reference guide that classifies and describes over 40,000 jobs

O*NET
The U.S. Department of Labor's Web site that provides comprehensive information about jobs and careers

TABLE 3.2		
Hierarchy of Work Functions Used in Functional Job Analysis		
Data	People	Things
0 Synthesizing	0 Mentoring, Leading	0 Setting up
1 Coordinating, Innovating	1 Negotiating	1 Precision working
2 Analyzing	2 Instructing, Consulting	2 Operating-controlling
3 Compiling	3 Supervising	3 Driving-operating
4 Computing	4 Diverting	4 Manipulating
5 Copying	5 Persuading	5 Tending, Data processing
6 Comparing	6 Exchanging information	6 Feeding, Off bearing
	7 Serving	7 Handling
	8 Taking instructions, Helping	

Source: U.S. Department of Labor. (1991). *Dictionary of Occupational Titles* (Rev. 4th ed.). Washington, DC: Government Printing Office. Fine & Cronshaw. (1999).

and much, much more. Table 3.3 presents only a small portion of the summary report for the job of industrial/organizational psychologist.

Today, using functional job analysis, the job analyst may begin with the general job description provided by O*NET. The analyst will then use interviewing and/or observational techniques to conduct a more detailed study of a certain job. FJA is especially helpful when the job analyst must create job descriptions for a large number of positions. It is also quite popular because it is cost effective and because it uses job descriptions based on national databases, which are often considered satisfactory by federal employment enforcement agencies (Mathis & Jackson, 1985). FJA has also proven useful in research designed to gain insight into how workers are performing their jobs. For instance, in a study of over 200 nursing assistants in nursing homes, functional job analysis discovered that nursing assistants were spending too little time dealing with the people aspects of their jobs (e.g., giving attention to elderly residents) and a disproportionately large amount of time dealing with data (e.g., reports) and things, such as changing bedding (Brannon, Streit, & Smyer, 1992).

COMPARING THE DIFFERENT JOB ANALYSIS TECHNIQUES

Several comparison studies of the various job analysis techniques have been conducted. A series of investigations by Levine and his associates (Levine, Ash, & Bennett, 1980; Levine, Ash, Hall, & Sistrunk, 1983) compared various techniques in terms of their accuracy, level of detail, and cost effectiveness. They found that functional job analysis, the critical incidents technique, and the Position Analysis Questionnaire were all reasonably effective job analysis

TABLE 3.3

O*NET Summary Report for Occupation: Industrial-Organizational Psychologists (greatly abbreviated)

Sample of reported job titles: Consultant, I/O Psychologist, Consulting Psychologist, Management Consultant, Research Scientist ...

Tasks

Develop and implement employee selection and placement programs.
Analyze job requirements and content ... for classification, selection, training....
Identify training and developmental needs
Assess employee performance

Knowledge

Personnel and Human Resources
Psychology
Customer and Personal Service
Education and Training
Administration and Management
Law and Government
Communications and Media
Mathematics
Sales and Marketing

Skills

Critical Thinking
Active Listening
Complex Problem Solving
Service Orientation
Speaking

Abilities

Oral and Written Comprehension and Expression
Problem Sensitivity
Deductive and Inductive Reasoning
Originality

Work Activities

Getting information and interpreting its meaning for others
Organizing, planning, prioritizing work
Analyzing data
Making decisions and problem solving
Providing consultation and advice to others
Interacting with computers, etc.

[Other information includes: Interests, Work Styles, Work Values, Related Occupations, and Wages & Employment Trends (2004 median wages are over $74,000 per year, by the way, with good growth prospects. 2011 median wages are over +$94,000 per year.)]

According to functional job analysis, the job of restaurant cook involves
compiling data, speaking to people, and doing precision work with things.

methods. Whereas FJA and the CIT provided detailed, comprehensive types of
analyses, the PAQ yielded more limited information, probably because it uses
the same general instrument to analyze all types of jobs. The FJA and CIT, by
contrast, are tailored to analyze specific jobs, and CIT is particularly suited to
analyzing complex jobs (Anderson & Wilson, 1997). However, the PAQ was
found to be more cost effective and easier to use than the other methods.

Regardless of the specific instrument used, when job analysis is used to compare different types of jobs, the job analyst must use caution in the interpretation
of numerical scale values. For example, both a marketing director and a head
janitor could conceivably be rated on the behavior of "negotiation with others"
as the same value on a rating scale. Even though these jobs may be similar in the
amount of time spent in negotiations, it would be erroneous to conclude that
the negotiations have equal weight, that they are equally demanding, or that
they require an equal level of skill. One suggested solution to this problem is to
rate the "relative importance" (RI) of tasks, including the RI between jobs and
the RI within similar jobs, and also to evaluate the tasks "qualitatively," rather
than relying solely on quantitative evaluation (Harvey, 1991).

Overall, no one method or technique of job analysis has emerged as superior to all others. It may be that a trained analyst could conduct very good job
analyses using any of several methods (Muchinsky, 1987). Obviously, a combination of methods should lead to a more detailed, more reliable, and "better"
analysis than the use of any one technique alone.

O*NET: A USEFUL TOOL FOR UNDERSTANDING JOBS

O*NET is the U.S. Department of Labor's Web-based site that is intended to be
the primary source of information about occupations. O*NET is a downloadable
database of information about jobs. In addition to the database that replaces

CLOSE   **What do you want to do for a living?—Using O*NET for your career search**

"My Next Move" (http://www.mynextmove.org/) is a useful online tool for your career search. It is managed by the National Center for O*NET Development, and it lists over 900 different careers from the O*NET Database. There are three ways to use this Web site depending upon your answer to the question: *What do you want to do for a living?* Think about it for a moment.

1. *"I want to be a…"*

   If you have a clear idea about what you want to do for a living, you can search careers using key words. In this case, the Web site asks you to describe your dream career in a few words. For instance, you can type "doctor." Then, it directs you to a list of career options (e.g., physician assistants, optometrists, surgeons). Once you click a career option, it directs you to the page that summarizes the required knowledge, skills, abilities, tasks, and responsibilities in your chosen job. It also displays the appropriate educational training and personality for the job, together with a job outlook on the average salary and likelihood of new job opportunities.

2. *"I'll know it when I see it."*

   If you think you will know when you actually see some career options, you can browse careers by industry. Over 900 career options are organized by

21 different industries (e.g., arts & entertainment, construction, education, government, and health & counseling). You can look for a list of career options based on your choice of industries.

3. *"I'm not really sure."*

   If you are not quite sure about your career, you can tell the Web site what you like to do by answering questions regarding the type of work you might enjoy. Based on your answers, it will suggest potential career options that meet your interests and training. The questions constitute a self-assessment tool for career exploration called the O*NET Interest Profiler (http://www.onetcenter.org/IP.html). O*NET Interest Profiler gives you scores for six broad occupational interest areas: realistic, investigative, artistic, social, enterprising, and conventional. Once you have scores for each area, follow the instructions on the O*NET Interest Profiler page to discover your career options.

   In addition to scores for interest areas, you will be asked to specify one among five job zones. Each of the five job zones corresponds to a level of preparation (from "little or no preparation" to "extensive preparation") required for the job in terms of experience, education, and training. You can also specify your job zone based on your plans for preparation. The Web site will then present careers that fit your interests and preparation level.

Sample Result:

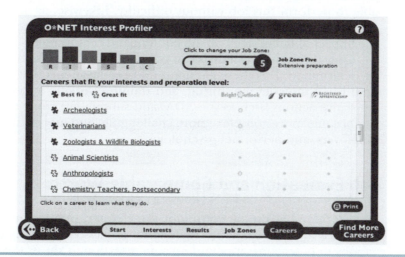

the *Dictionary of Occupational Titles* (DOT), O*NET has career exploration tools to assist individuals in evaluating their career interests, information on the job-related skills and training needed for particular jobs, consumer guides that explain personnel testing and assessment, and a clearinghouse for information for I/O psychologists, human resources professionals, and career and vocational counselors. The Department of Labor intends to make the ever-evolving O*NET the central source for information about jobs, careers, and the world of work.

Job Analysis and the ADA

In 1990, passage of the Americans with Disabilities Act (ADA) presented a new challenge to job analysts. Title I of the ADA stated that "in employment matters it is illegal to discriminate against a qualified person with a disability: Such an individual is one who can perform the essential functions of a job with or without reasonable accommodation." Implementation of the ADA also requires that employers (with 15 or more employees) prevent employment discrimination against disabled persons, and they must also make reasonable accommodations that will allow disabled persons to perform essential job duties. For example, an employer may need to construct a different type of workstation or provide a voice-activated computer for a quadriplegic worker in a wheelchair.

⏱ Stop & Review

Define the three dimensions used in Functional Job Analysis.

Although the ADA does not require employers to conduct formal job analyses (Esposito, 1992), you might imagine the difficulties involved in trying to adapt or alter a job for a disabled employee without having conducted a thorough analysis of it. Moreover, compliance with the ADA requires employers to understand the "essential elements" (e.g., functions), or content, of a job (Greenlaw & Kohl, 1993; Mitchell, Alliger, Morfopoulos, 1997). It is imperative that requirements for a particular job be reviewed and updated. For example, an old job specification for a warehouse stocker might require heavy lifting, yet because the position involves operating a forklift, there may be little or no manual lifting required. Therefore, a person with a serious disability might be able to perform this job without difficulty. Likewise, as more and more tasks become automated, job analyses need to be kept up to date so that they reflect the impact of technology on job content and requirements.

Only through job analysis can essential job elements and job requirements be determined. It is these elements and requirements that need to be considered when interviewing, hiring, and training workers with disabilities. Due to legislative actions such as the ADA, and subsequent court rulings, job analysis has become more complex, more challenging, and more critical to job analysts, employers, and personnel psychologists.

Job Evaluation and Comparable Worth

As mentioned at the beginning of the chapter, one of the products of a job analysis is a job evaluation, which is the process of assessing the relative value of jobs to determine appropriate compensation. That is, the wages paid for a particular job should be related to the knowledge, skills, abilities, and other characteristics it requires. However, a number of other variables, such as the supply of potential workers, the perceived value of the job to the company, and the job's history, can also influence its rate of compensation.

Detailed job evaluations typically examine jobs on a number of dimensions called **compensable factors**. Examples of compensable factors might be the physical demands of a job, the amount of training or experience required, the working conditions associated with the job, and the amount of responsibility the job carries. Each job may be given a score or weighting on each factor. The summed total of the weighted compensable factors indicates the value of the job, which is then translated into the dollar amount of compensation. Bear in mind that a compensable factors analysis of a job determines rates of compensation based solely on the training, responsibility, and conditions associated with a job. It does not take into account market conditions, such as the supply and demand for workers for a certain job. Therefore, because these market factors are not considered, a compensable factors analysis would show that a brain surgeon should be paid more than a major league baseball left-handed relief pitcher or a professional sports' goalkeeper. Market factors, including the scarcity of top professional athletes, are what cause the average pitcher's or goalkeeper's salaries to be much higher than the surgeon's.

> **compensable factors**
> the job elements that are used to determine appropriate compensation for a job

For decades, the issue of how jobs are compensated has been a source of controversy. Specifically, there has been a great deal of concern over discrimination in compensation, particularly wage discrepancies for men and women. Two pieces of federal legislation address this issue. The Equal Pay Act of 1963 mandates that men and women performing equal work receive equal pay. Further, a U.S. Supreme Court ruling made defense of pay differentials by employers more difficult than it has been in the past (Greenlaw & Kohl, 1993). Title VII of the Civil Rights Act of 1964 prohibits discrimination in employment practices based on race, color, religion, sex, and national origin. Despite these laws, however, there is considerable evidence that women receive lower wages than men performing the same or equivalent work (Blau & Kahn, 2007; Crampton, Hodge, & Mishra, 1997). In fact, although the most recent research shows that pay for women is catching up to the wages paid men, these gains are slow in coming. For example, in 1980, women were paid about 68% of the wages paid men for comparable work (Perlman & Pike, 1994), improving by only about 2 to 3% per decade, to 72% in 1990, 75% in 2000, and 77% in 2010.

Two issues bear directly on the "gender gap" in wages. The first concerns access to higher-paying jobs (Wittig & Berman, 1992). Traditionally, many such jobs were primarily held by men, but throughout the 1960s and 1970s, the women's rights movement helped increase the access of women to these positions. However, although women are now found in nearly every type of job, there is still considerable sex stereotyping of jobs, which means that many relatively high-paying jobs and professions are still filled mainly by men. For example, men are found in large numbers in skilled craft jobs that receive higher wages than clerical jobs, which are filled mainly by women. In corporations, men fill more finance positions and women are overrepresented in lower paying human resources posts.

Women workers have made some small advances in the wages "gender gap" since this cartoon came out.

comparable worth
the notion that jobs that require equivalent KSAOs should be compensated equally

The second issue deals with the fact that women are often paid far less than men for performing equivalent tasks. In the 1980s, this gender-based pay disparity gave birth to the concept of comparable worth, or equal pay for equal work. For example, the job of human resources clerk, a traditionally "female" job, and the position of records manager in the production department, a job usually filled by men, both require workers to perform similar tasks, such as keeping records and managing data files. Because of the similarity in duties, both positions should be paid equal wages. However, the job of records manager typically pays higher wages than the position of HR clerk.

Because of its focus on evaluating the worth of work tasks, the issue of comparable worth is tied to the ability of organizations to conduct valid and fair job evaluations, which should reveal instances of equal jobs receiving unequal compensation. However, opponents of the comparable worth movement argue that job evaluation methods may be inaccurate because they do not account for factors like the oversupply of female applicants for certain jobs, such as teachers and airline attendants, the lower levels of education and work experience of women relative to men, and women's preferences for certain types of "safe" jobs with "pleasant working conditions." Advocates of the comparable worth movement argue that even these factors do not account for the considerable disparity in pay for men and women (Judd & Gomez-Mejia, 1987; Pinzler & Ellis, 1989; Thacker & Wayne, 1995). For a number of reasons, women are simply not paid the same wages for the same level of work. One argument is that society does not value the type of work required by many jobs that are filled primarily by women, such as secretarial, clerical, teaching, and nursing positions. Alternatively, certain jobs that are filled primarily by men may be compensated at higher levels because more value is ascribed to them (Sorensen, 1994).

exceptioning
the practice of ignoring pay discrepancies between particular jobs possessing equivalent duties and responsibilities

Another reason for gender-based pay disparity is the practice of exceptioning, whereby a job evaluation reveals that two jobs, with equivalent duties and responsibilities, receive very different rates of pay, yet no steps are taken to rectify the inequality. In other words, an "exception" is made because it is too costly or too difficult to raise the wages of the lower-paid job. An example of exceptioning is the pay rates for physicians and nurses. The average salary of a physician is three to five times that of a nurse, yet the two jobs have many comparable duties and responsibilities. Although the imbalance in salaries is known to exist, hospitals are financially unable to pay nurses what they are worth, so an exception is made.

The issue of comparable worth has been hotly debated by both business and government officials. Certain cases of sex discrimination in employee compensation have reached the courts, highlighting the issue of comparable worth. For example, in *AFSCME v. State of Washington* (1983), a job evaluation of state employee positions found that women's job classes were paid approximately 20% less than comparable men's classes. It was recommended that women state employees should be paid an additional $38 million annually. Because the state of Washington did not act on the recommendation, the women employees' union sued. The court ruled that the state was discriminating against its women employees and awarded them nearly $1 billion. In a very controversial decision, the U.S. Supreme Court would not allow the largest gender discrimination case, involving 1.5 million women employees of Wal Mart to go forward, even though there was evidence that the women were paid less than men in comparable positions.

If the comparable worth movement goes forward and the government decides to take steps to correct pay inequalities, the impact on workers and work organizations will be tremendous. First, job evaluations will have to be conducted for nearly all jobs in the country—a staggering and expensive task. Second, because it is unlikely that workers and unions will allow the wages of

Stop & Review
Explain the Americans with Disabilities Act (ADA).

Stop & Review
What two issues are involved in the wage gender gap?

glass ceiling
limitations placed on women and minorities preventing them from advancing into top-level positions in organizations

ON THE *CUTTING* EDGE

Glass Ceiling or Labyrinth: Which Better Describes Gender Inequities in the Workplace?

The term glass ceiling has been used to refer to the limitations placed on women (and ethnic minorities) that prevent them from advancing into top management positions. Although discrimination in employment practices is illegal, biases and stereotypes still influence decisions as to who is and who is not qualified to hold a position (Fagenson & Jackson, 1993). For example, one common stereotype holds that women have a management style that is different (and therefore less effective) than men, although studies have shown no substantial differences in the styles of male and female managers (Eagly, 2007; Lester, 1993).

Although we have seen that women are making some small gains in achieving equality in pay and level of positions, there is still a wide gender gap in top-level positions. For example, only 6% of the highest paid executives of Fortune 500 companies (e.g., chairman, president, chief financial officer) are women, and only 2% of the CEOs are women (comparable figures for top European Union corporations are 11% and 4%, respectively—slightly, but not appreciably, better; Eagly & Carli, 2007). Moreover, women in top management positions are paid less than their male counterparts (Bertrand, 2000). Rather than simply being shut out of promotion to top-level positions (i.e., a metaphor of glass ceiling), there is evidence that the career progression of women and ethnic minorities is slower than that of white males, so that it takes longer to get to the top (Eagly & Carli, 2007; Powell & Butterfield,

ON THE *CUTTING* EDGE (*continued*)

1994, 1997). In other words, routes to top leadership do exist for women, but they are full of twists and turns like those in a labyrinth. In order to pass through it, women need to be persistent, be aware of their progress, and carefully analyze their situations (Eagly & Carli, 2007).

Sadly, the glass ceiling or the labyrinth seems to be a worldwide phenomenon. Women represent less than 10% of senior management in all industrialized countries, ranging from a high of 8% in Belgium to a low of .3% in Japan (Adler, 1993). In a study of workers in the United States, the United Kingdom, Africa, Australia, and Papua New Guinea, glass ceilings existed for all "nondominant" groups in the companies surveyed. The "nondominant" groups varied from country to country, but in each case members of these groups were underutilized, were underrepresented in high-level positions, and followed different career paths than members of the dominant group (Stamp, 1990). A more recent study of 43 different countries revealed that there was increasing variability in this phenomenon (Terjesen & Singh, 2008). The results showed, on average, female workers held about 29% of

all leadership positions and it varied from 6% in Turkey to 46% in the United States. It appears that more women are breaking the glass ceiling or passing through the labyrinth in some countries than in others.

What can be done to break the glass ceiling? First, in the United States, the Civil Rights Act of 1991 created a Glass Ceiling Commission and gave women the right to sue on the basis of discrimination (Tavakolian, 1993). The U.S. Office of Federal Contract Compliance Programs (OFCCP) also began examining the recruitment and promotion policies at upper management levels, focusing on possible discrimination against women in upper-level positions (Brown, 1991). Such laws and attention from federal governments will obviously help protect women and minorities from blatant discrimination. However, much of the "gender gap" may not result from blatant discrimination, but from the devaluing of certain occupations, such as teaching or nursing—occupations that are dominated by women (Sorensen, 1994). Whether we call it the glass ceiling or the labyrinth, an unsettling bias toward women (and minorities) seems to continue to be an issue to be dealt with in the workplace.

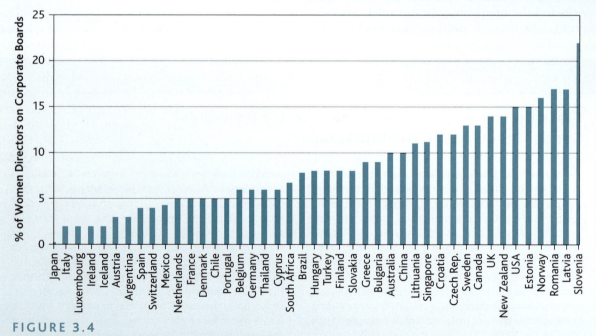

FIGURE 3.4

Women Are Underrepresented on Corporate Boards of Directors in All Countries in the World

Source: Terjesen, S., & Singh, V. (2008). Female presence on corporate boards: A multicountry study of environmental context. *Journal of Business Ethics, 83,* 55–63.

higher-paid workers to be cut, the salaries of the lower-paid workers will have to be raised—also an enormous expense. Regardless of what takes place in the next few years, the issue of comparable worth has focused greater attention on job evaluations and job evaluation procedures. It is thus likely that greater attention will be given to improving such procedures in the near future (Lowe & Wittig, 1989; Perlman & Pike, 1994).

Stop & Review

What is a compensable factors analysis?

Summary

Job analysis is the systematic study of a job's tasks, duties, and responsibilities and the knowledge, skills, and abilities needed to perform the job. The job analysis, which is the important starting point for many personnel functions, yields several products: a *job description*, which is a detailed accounting of job tasks, procedures, responsibilities, and output; a *job specification*, which consists of information about the physical, educational, and experiential qualities required to perform the job; a *job evaluation*, which is an assessment of the relative value of jobs for determining compensation; and performance criteria, which serve as a basis for appraising successful job performance.

Job analysis methods include observation, use of existing data, interviews, and surveys. One structured job analysis technique is the *job element approach*, a broad approach to job analysis that focuses on the knowledge, skills, abilities, and other characteristics (KSAOs) required to perform a particular job. The *critical incidents technique* of job analysis involves the collection of particularly successful or unsuccessful instances of job performance. Through the collection of hundreds of these incidents, a very detailed profile of a job emerges. Another structured job analysis technique, the *Position Analysis Questionnaire* (PAQ), uses a questionnaire that analyzes jobs in terms of 187 job elements arranged into six categories. *Functional job analysis* (FJA) is a method that has

been used to classify jobs in terms of the worker's interaction with data, people, and things. FJA uses the *Dictionary of Occupational Titles* (DOT), a reference book listing general job descriptions for thousands of jobs (since replaced by the U.S. Labor Department's O*NET database), and examines the sequence of tasks required to complete the job as well as the process by which the job is completed. Research has determined that all these specific, standardized methods are effective.

Job analysis yields a *job evaluation* or an assessment of the relative value of jobs used to determine appropriate compensation. These evaluations usually examine jobs on dimensions that are called *compensable factors*, which are given values that signify the relative worth of the job and translate into levels of compensation.

An important topic in the area of job evaluation concerns the "gender gap" in wages. Evidence indicates that women are paid far less than men for comparable work. This inequity has given rise to the comparable worth movement, which argues for equal pay for equal work. This issue is controversial because of the difficulty and costs of making compensation for comparable jobs equitable. Research has also suggested that women and ethnic minorities are affected by a *glass ceiling*, or *labyrinth*, which creates difficulties for members of minority groups in rising to the highest-level positions in organizations.

Study Questions and Exercises

1. Consider each of the products of a job analysis. How do these products affect other organizational outcomes?

2. Compare and contrast the four specific, structured methods of job analysis: the functional job analysis, the job element method,

the Position Analysis Questionnaire, and the critical incidents technique. Make a table listing their respective strengths and weaknesses.

3. Consider your current job, or a job that you or a friend had in the past. How would you begin to conduct a job analysis of that position? What methods would you use? What are the important components of the job?

4. Using the preceding job, go to O*NET and find the code for that job title using the "Occupational listings," sorted by title (www. onetcenter.org/occupations.html). Using the code, look up the online job using the occupational title (http://online.onetcenter.org/find/) and find the information for that job [or you can put in the code for I/O psychologist (19-3032.00)].

5. List some of the reasons why women are paid less for comparable work performed by men. Think of some stereotypically "female" jobs and comparable jobs that are stereotypically held by men. Are there inequities in compensation between the "male" and "female" jobs? Why or why not?

Web Links

www.onetcenter.org
  The U.S. Department of Labor's "one-stop" site for job career information.

www.job-analysis.net
  An interesting site, part of a larger human resources site, with detailed information and links on job analysis methods and practice.

Suggested Readings

Brannick, M. T., Levine, E., & Morgeson, F. P. (2007). *Job and work analysis: Methods, research, and applications for human resource management.* Thousand Oaks, CA: Sage. *A more scholarly review of research and methods of job analysis.*

Eagly, A. H., & Carli, L. L. (2007). *Through the labyrinth: The truth about how women become leaders.* Cambridge, MA: Harvard Business School Press. *This book introduces the metaphor of the labyrinth to describe the special "twists and turns" and dead ends that women have to face in making it to top leadership positions.*

Prien, E. P., Goodstein, L. D., Goodstein, J., & Gamble, L. G. (2009). *A practical guide to job analysis.* San Francisco: Pfeiffer. *A guide to job analysis for human resources professionals. Provides all of the "nuts and bolts" of job analysis.*

4 Employee Recruitment, Selection, and Placement

Inside Tips
UNDERSTANDING EMPLOYMENT ISSUES AND PROCESSES

In the next two chapters you will be able to apply more of the methodological issues from Chapter 2. Effective employee staffing, screening, testing, and selection require grounding in research and measurement issues, particularly reliability and validity. In addition, the foundation for employee selection is job analysis (Chapter 3).

When considering the steps in the employee selection process, it is important that one note the influence exerted by federal legislation and court decisions. Federal guidelines developed to prevent employment discrimination have, in a sense, required employers to take a hard look at the quality of the methods used to recruit, screen, and select employees. This has led to the greater involvement of I/O psychologists in the development of more accurate and fairer employee screening, selection, and placement procedures.

Because employee issues deal with the care and nurturing of an organization's human resources and because psychology often has a similar concern with human potential, there is a natural link between psychology and personnel work. As a result, many students trained in psychology and other social sciences are drawn to careers in human resources.

You have completed your background research and have chosen an exciting (and what will hopefully be a rewarding) position. Armed with your new knowledge, and a highly polished resume, you take to the streets (or more likely, the information highway) to begin the process of finding the right position in the right organization. At the same time, organizations are out looking for you—recruiting new, promising employees through ads, Web sites, and on-campus visits.

In Chapter 3, we saw how job analysis is the basic foundation of personnel psychology. Job analysis leads to a thorough understanding of jobs. Once there is a good understanding of the various jobs within an organization, companies are better able to find persons who can fill those jobs and excel at performing them. We will look now at how organizations find and hire persons to perform jobs.

Organizations spend a tremendous amount of time, money, and energy trying to recruit and select a qualified, capable, and productive workforce. Although there are always significant numbers of unemployed workers in the population, the market for truly skilled workers is tight. Organizations continue to compete with one another for the most skilled and productive employees. More and more, companies are realizing the importance of developing comprehensive programs for employee recruitment, screening, testing, and selection. They are also becoming more forward-thinking—planning ahead several years to try to predict their future human resources needs. Moreover, they are beginning to understand that the costs of hiring the wrong types of workers greatly outweigh the investment of developing good recruitment and screening programs. Depending on the job level, the costs of recruiting, selecting, training, and then releasing a single employee can range from a few thousand dollars to several hundreds of thousands of dollars, depending on the level of the position—it has been estimated that the hiring costs are approximately three times the person's annual salary (Cascio, 2003; Wanous, 1992).

In this chapter, we will follow the progression of personnel functions involved in the planning for recruitment, selection, and placement of workers. We will begin with an examination of how organizations determine their human resource needs. We will then focus on employee recruitment and discuss how employers use the information obtained from job applicants to make their selection decisions. We will look at how organizations place workers in appropriate jobs, and we will discuss the legal issues in staffing, selection, and placement. In Chapter 5, we will focus specifically on the methods used for assessing employees in the selection process, which includes assessment of resumes, employment tests, references and recommendations, and other means used for evaluating and selecting employees.

Human Resource Planning

The best organizations continually evaluate their human resource needs and plan their hiring and staffing in order to meet their companies' business goals. Human resource planning (HR planning) begins with the strategic goals of the organization. For example, imagine an Internet-based marketing company that provides marketing services for small businesses. This company has recently branched out and now provides clients with Web sites that the clients can control themselves. The marketing company will need Web site experts to build and maintain the infrastructure for the sites, and will need to provide customer support services to help clients maintain their own Web sites. This will mean that the company needs to hire a certain number of web design experts and customer service agents with web knowledge to staff the customer help lines.

Human resources professionals need to consider a number of factors in HR planning: What are the organization's goals and strategic objectives? What are the staffing needs required for the organization to accomplish its goals? What are the current human resource capacities and existing employee skills in the organization? Which additional positions are needed to meet the staffing needs (sometimes referred to as a "gap analysis," i.e., what is the gap between the HR capacities the company has and what it needs)?

Staffing today's organizations requires that companies take into account a number of critical issues, such as the changing nature of work and the workforce (e.g., greater need for experienced, "knowledge" workers), increased competition for the best workers, assuring that there is good "fit" between workers and organizations, and increasing workforce diversity (Ployhart, 2006).

Human resources planning also considers the short- and long-term time-frames, and begins to ask the broader HR questions: what are the training needs of employees going to be in the future? How can we competitively recruit the highest potential employees? How competitive are we in our compensation and benefit programs? How can we find employees who are a "good fit" for our company and its culture?

One model of human resource planning suggests that companies need to focus on four interrelated processes (Cascio, 2003). These are:

Talent Inventory. An assessment of the current KSAOs (knowledge, skills, abilities, and other characteristics) of current employees and how they are used.

Workforce forecast. A plan for future HR requirements (i.e., the number of positions forecasted, the skills those positions will require, and some sense of what the market is for those workers).

Action plans. Development of a plan to guide the recruitment, selection, training, and compensation of the future hires.

Control and evaluation. Having a system of feedback to assess how well the HR system is working, and how well the company met its HR plan (you will find that evaluation is critical for all HR functions—we need to constantly evaluate I/O programs and interventions to determine their effectiveness).

Steps in the Employee Selection Process

To understand how organizations select employees for jobs, we will look at each of the steps in the process, from the recruitment of applicants, to the various employee screening and testing procedures, to selection decisions and placement of employees in appropriate jobs. Throughout this discussion, keep in mind that the goal is straightforward—to try to gather information that will predict who, from the pool of applicants, will be the "best" employees.

An Example of Workforce Planning: CEO Succession at Corporate Giants

Before former CEO of GE, Jack Welch, retired the company went through extensive succession planning.

One area of workforce planning that is very important, and also gets a lot of attention, is the planning for a successor to a company's chief executive officer (CEO). One famous example was the search for the successor to GE's (formerly General Electric, but now an enormous worldwide corporate giant) legendary CEO, Jack Welch.

It was thought that GE engaged in some good and some bad practices in planning for and finding Jack Welch's successor. On the positive side, GE did not look for a "clone" of Welch. They had an eye toward the future, and realized that the new CEO would have to move the company forward in an increasingly fast-paced and changing world. In fact, Jack Welch himself said that the future GE CEO would be nothing like him, and emphasized the need for someone with more international experience.

On the negative side, GE identified three potential successors—high-level executives within GE—and pitted them against one another in what was called a "dysfunctional horserace." The ensuing conflict and bad feelings caused the two "losers" to leave GE following the selection of the "winner," Jeffrey Immelt, which led to a loss of talent within the company. GE was also criticized for not considering external candidates.

Anne Mulcahy, former CEO of Xerox Corporation, discussed the succession plan for her successor, and used this successful process to outline suggested steps for CEO succession (Mulcahy, 2010):

1. Begin planning early. Mulcahy was replaced in 2008, but the succession planning began in 2001.
2. Clear guidelines and timelines need to be developed.
3. Avoid pitting candidates against one another, and search broadly.
4. The front-running candidate should have contact with the sitting CEO, who can help orient and develop him or her.
5. Limit CEO terms to no more than a decade, so that the CEO does not become too entrenched in the position.

Employee Recruitment

Employee recruitment is the process by which organizations attract potential workers to apply for jobs. Greater numbers of organizations are developing strategic programs for recruitment. The starting point for a good recruitment program is an understanding of the job and what kinds of worker characteristics are required to perform the job. Here, the recruiter relies on the products of job analysis—job descriptions and job specifications (see Chapter 3).

One of the primary objectives of a successful program is to attract a large pool of qualified applicants. A wide variety of recruitment techniques and tactics can be used, including job advertisements on Internet sites (e.g., Monster.com, careerbuilder.com), newspapers and trade magazines and on television, radio, or billboards; the use of employment agencies (including executive search firms—i.e., "headhunters"—for high-level positions); and referrals by current employees. College students are most familiar with on-campus recruitment programs and web-based career sites that post openings as well as allowing applicants and employers to "connect" online, through professional social networking sites (e.g., LinkedIn.com, Plaxo.com).

Research has assessed the effectiveness of the various recruitment methods by examining both the quality of newly hired workers and the rate of turnover in new workers. Early evidence suggested that employee referrals and applicant-initiated contacts (that is, "walk-ins") yielded higher-quality workers and workers who were more likely to remain with the company than newspaper ads or employment agency placement (Breaugh, 1981; Breaugh, Greising, Taggart, & Chen, 2003; Saks, 1994). There are important reasons why employee referrals and walk-ins lead to better workers: First, employees are unlikely to recommend friends and acquaintances who are not good potential workers in order to save themselves from embarrassment. Thus, the referring employees essentially do an informal "screening" that ends up benefiting the company. Applicants who directly apply for a position in a company ("walk-ins") have typically researched the company and/or position and that may suggest that they are more motivated "self-starters" than those applicants responding to ads.

Like many things, the Internet has changed employee recruitment. The larger Internet job sites, such as monster.com and hotjobs.com, have millions of registered job seekers and employers, allowing a potential applicant to search hundreds of jobs in minutes, post a resume, and get career advice. The downside of Internet recruitment, however, is the large number of potential applicants who need to be sifted through. As one researcher puts it, you have to kiss a lot of "frogs" to find the "princes" (Bartram, 2000). Recently, there have been attempts to provide detailed information about what sort of applicants might best fit the positions and the organization and jobs on companies' Web sites. It has been suggested that an interactive company Web site that would provide feedback about the applicant's fit could help reduce the number of mismatched applicants (Breaugh, 2008; Hu, Su, & Chen, 2007).

employee recruitment
the process by which companies attract qualified applicants

🕑 Stop & Review

What are the four processes in a model of human resource planning?

Recruitment is a two-way process: While the recruiting organization is attempting to attract and later evaluate prospective employees, job applicants are evaluating various potential employers (Turban, Forret, & Hendrickson, 1998). Research shows that a majority of young job applicants prefer larger, multinational firms, with a smaller subset preferring working for small organizations (Barber, Wesson, Roberson, & Taylor, 1999; Lievens, Decaesteker, Coetsier, & Geirnaert, 2001). In addition, job seekers are influenced by the type of industry, the profitability of the company, the company's reputation, the opportunities for employee development and advancement, and the company's organizational culture (Cable & Graham, 2000; Cable & Turban, 2003; Cober, Brown, Levy, Cober, & Keeping, 2003). There is also considerable evidence that the characteristics of an organization's recruitment program and of recruiters can influence applicants' decisions to accept or reject offers of employment (Maurer, Howe, & Lee, 1992; Rynes, 1993; Stevens, 1997). In other words, it is important for organizations to make a favorable impression on a prospective employee to encourage the individual to want to take the job offer (Cable & Turban, 2001). A meta-analysis by Chapman et al. (2005) found that recruiters who were viewed by applicants as personable, trustworthy, competent, and informative led to more positive impressions by applicants. Recruiters play an important part in helping applicants decide if there is a good fit between themselves and the position and organization (Breaugh, 2008).

In their efforts to attract applicants, however, many companies will "oversell" a particular job or their organization. Advertisements may say that "this is a great place to work," or that the position is "challenging" and offers "tremendous potential for advancement." This is not a problem if such statements are true, but if the job and the organization are presented in a misleading, overly positive manner, the strategy will eventually backfire. Although the recruitment process may attract applicants, the new employees will quickly discover that they were fooled and may look for work elsewhere or become dissatisfied and unmotivated. An important factor in the recruitment process that may help alleviate potential misperceptions is the realistic job preview (RJP), which is an accurate description of the duties and responsibilities of a particular job. Realistic job previews can take the form of an oral presentation from a recruiter, supervisor, or job incumbent; a visit to the job site; or a discussion in a brochure, manual, video, or company Web site (Breaugh, 2008; Wanous, 1989). However, research indicates that face-to-face RJPs may be more effective than written ones (Saks & Cronshaw, 1990). Another type of RJP that has not received much attention is a work simulation (Breaugh, 2008). We will learn more about work simulations in Chapter 5 in our discussion of employee screening methods.

Historically, research has shown that realistic job previews are important in increasing job commitment and satisfaction and in decreasing initial turnover of new employees (Hom, Griffeth, Palich, & Bracker, 1998; McEvoy & Cascio, 1985; Premack & Wanous, 1985). Some of the positive effects of RJPs are caused by the applicant's process of self-selection. Presented with a realistic view of what the job will be like, the applicant can make an informed decision about whether the job is appropriate. RJPs may also be effective because they lower

realistic job preview (RJP)

an accurate presentation of the prospective job and organization made to applicants

unrealistically high expectations about the job and may provide an applicant with information that will later be useful in dealing with work-related problems and stress (Caligiuri & Phillips, 2003; Wanous, 1992). The implementation of realistic job previews often requires recruiting more applicants for job openings, because a greater proportion of applicants presented with the RJP will decline the job offer than when no preview is given. However, the usual result is a better match between the position and the worker hired and a more satisfied new worker.

One recruitment issue that has gotten increasing attention is the unrealistic expectations that many applicants, particularly young or inexperienced workers, sometimes have about certain jobs and careers. It has been shown that realistic job previews need to be coupled with *expectation lowering procedures* that work to dispel misconceptions about certain jobs (Morse & Popovich, 2009). For example, many people are drawn to careers in consulting, or to certain health care professions, because the jobs seem important, interesting, and exciting. However, savvy recruiters work to lower expectations among inexperienced applicants, by also focusing, in a realistic way, on the not-so-pleasant aspects of these jobs.

Another important goal for any recruitment program is to avoid intentional or unintentional discrimination. Employment discrimination against underrepresented groups such as women, ethnic minorities, the elderly, and the disabled, intentional or unintentional, is illegal. In order to avoid unintentional discrimination, employers should take steps to attract applicants from underrepresented groups in proportion to their numbers in the population from which the company's workforce is drawn. In other words, if a company is in an area where the population within a 10- to 20-mile radius is 40% white, 30% African American, 10% Asian American, and 10% Hispanic, the recruitment program should draw applicants in roughly those proportions to avoid unintentionally discriminating against any group.

Not only is it important to be able to attract underrepresented applicants, it is also important to be able to get them to accept job offers. If an organization is perceived as not welcoming to members of minority groups, it will be difficult to get candidates to accept jobs. For example, research has shown that qualified members of minority groups lost enthusiasm for jobs in organizations that had few minority group members, and few minorities in higher level positions (Avery & McKay, 2006; McKay & Avery, 2006). We will discuss the topics of employment discrimination, equal employment opportunity, and affirmative action later in this chapter.

Due to the competitive nature of recruiting the very best employees, companies need to give greater consideration to recruitment methods and processes. Some researchers have specifically looked at recruitment efforts that target specific groups of potential employees, such as college students. For example, many innovative organizations, particularly those creating web-based innovations (e.g., Google, Facebook, Zynga) are competing hard to recruit high-potential college graduates. Retail giants, such as Wal-Mart, have actively targeted seniors, through associations such as the American Association for Retired Persons (AARP).

CLOSE   Using Social Network Sites in Pre-Screening Job Applicants

The use of social network sites (SNS), such as Facebook and LinkedIn, has become so common that many hiring managers are now searching their job applicants' comments, pictures, and profiles on SNS. According to a survey conducted by CareerBuilder.com, 45% of hiring managers reported that they searched applicants on SNS. The same report also revealed that 35% of employers decided not to hire certain applicants because they found unfavorable comments or pictures of the applicants on the Internet. However, the survey also found that information on a more professional SNS (e.g., LinkedIn) could help strengthen a candidate's likelihood of getting hired.

Are you a potential job applicant? Activity on SNS has both pros and cons. You can now share your life with many friends. You can also join a community to share similar interests or enhance professional skills. Occasionally, however, you may accidentally share information that you did not intend to share or you may post comments that would be considered unacceptable in a professional situation.

One study found that the information on SNS can reveal an individual's personality, work ethics, behavior, and tendencies (Back et al., 2010). Therefore, investigating job applicants' daily behaviors on SNS to see if candidates are suitable for positions may seem to make sense to many employers (Brown & Vaughn, 2011). Nevertheless, organizations need to be cautious when using the information found on SNS for their hiring decisions. For their selection processes to be legally defensible, the information they obtain and utilize should be relevant to job requirements (i.e., ensuring the validity of such information). The use of SNS allows employers to unearth a variety of information about job applicants, including age, marital status, or religious affiliation. The discovery of such information is prohibited in traditional job application and interview processes. Moreover, contrary to the common perception that SNS reveals undisclosed information about a person, these sites are places where people may present themselves in a socially desirable manner. As a result, employers may end up with inaccurate assessments of job applicants. In addition, there is no consistency in the type of information employers can find, since SNS users can edit privacy settings and customize their profiles. This leads to inconsistent assessment across different job applicants.

Despite these limitations in using information from SNS, such information does have some impact on hiring decisions. If you are an SNS user, you may want to reconsider how and why you use certain SNS. Ultimately, acting more professionally in the "bare-all" online world is advisable.

Employee Screening

employee screening
the process of reviewing information about job applicants used to select workers

Stop & Review

List three goals of an employee recruitment program.

Employee screening is the process of reviewing information about job applicants to select individuals for jobs. A wide variety of data sources, such as resumes, job applications, letters of recommendation, employment tests, and hiring interviews, can be used in screening and selecting potential employees. If you have ever applied for a job, you have had firsthand experience with some of these. We will consider all of these specific screening methods in Chapter 5 because they are quite complex and represent an important area where the expertise of I/O psychologists is especially important.

Employee Selection and Placement

Employee selection is the actual process of choosing people for employment from a pool of applicants. In employee selection, all the information gained from screening procedures, such as application forms, resumes, test scores, and hiring interview evaluations, is combined in some manner to make actual selection decisions.

employee selection
the process of choosing applicants for employment

A MODEL FOR EMPLOYEE SELECTION

The model for recruiting and hiring effective and productive employees is actually quite simple. It consists of two categories of variables: criteria and predictors. Criteria (or the singular, criterion) are measures of success. The most common way to think of success on the job is in terms of performance criteria. A performance criterion for a cable TV installer may be the number of units installed. For a salesperson, dollar sales figures may be a performance criterion (we will discuss performance criteria in more depth in Chapter 6). Yet, when it comes to hiring good employees, we may want to go beyond these rather simple and straightforward performance criteria. The general criterion of "success" for an employee may be a constellation of many factors, including performance, loyalty, and commitment to the organization, a good work attendance record, ability to get along with supervisors and coworkers, and ability to learn and grow on the job. Thus, for the purpose of hiring workers we might want to think of "success on the job" as the ultimate criterion—a criterion we aspire to measure, but something that we may never actually be able to capture with our limited measurement capabilities.

criteria
measures of job success typically related to performance

Predictors are any pieces of information that we are able to measure about job applicants that are related to (predictive of) the criterion. In employee selection, we measure predictors, such as job-related knowledge and expertise, education, and skills, in an effort to predict who will be successful in a given job. Figure 4.1 (see page 86) illustrates this model for employee selection. Through evaluation of resumes and hiring interview performance, and from the results of employment tests, applicants are measured on a number of predictors. These predictor variables are then used to select applicants for jobs. Evaluation of the success of an employee selection program involves demonstrating that the predictors do indeed predict the criterion of success on the job (see Smith, 1994).

predictors
variables about applicants that are related to (predictive of) the criteria

MAKING EMPLOYEE SELECTION DECISIONS

Once employers have gathered information about job applicants, they can combine that information in various ways to make selection decisions. Primary goals in this process are to maximize the probability of accurate decisions in selecting job applicants and to assure that the decisions are made in a way that is free from both intentional and unintentional discrimination against

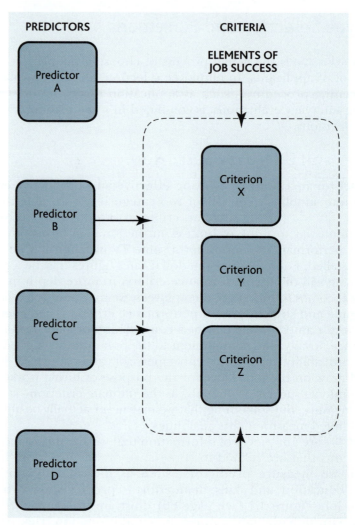

FIGURE 4.1
A Model for Employee Selection

these applicants. In an ideal situation, we want to employ applicants who will be successful and reject those who will not be successful in the job. In reality, however, errors are involved.

There are two types of decision errors in employee selection. When we erroneously accept applicants who would have been unsuccessful on the job, we are making false-positive errors (see Figure 4.2). On the other hand, when we erroneously reject applicants who would have been successful in the job, we are making false-negative errors. Although both errors are problematic to the organization, it is more difficult to identify false-negative errors than false-positive errors. We cannot eliminate these errors entirely, but we can minimize them by using more objective decision strategies.

false-positive errors
erroneously accepting applicants who would have been unsuccessful

false-negative errors
erroneously rejecting applicants who would have been successful

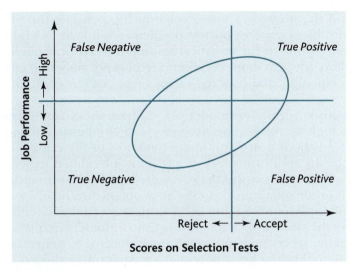

FIGURE 4.2
Accuracy of Prediction in Employee Screening
Source: Millsap & Kwok (2004)

All too often employee selection decisions are made subjectively, using what is often referred to as the clinical approach. In this approach, a decision maker simply combines the sources of information in whatever fashion seems appropriate to obtain some general impression about applicants. Based on experience and beliefs about which types of information are more or less important, a decision is made. Although some good selection decisions may be made by experienced decision makers, subjective, clinical decisions are error prone and often inaccurate (see Meehl, 1954). The alternative is to use a statistical decision-making model, which combines information for the selection of applicants in an objective, predetermined fashion. Each piece of information about job applicants is given some optimal weight that indicates its strength in predicting future job performance. It makes sense that an objective decision-making model will be superior to clinical decisions, because human beings, in most cases, are incapable of accurately processing all the information gathered from a number of job applicants. Statistical models are able to process all of this information without human limitations.

One statistical approach to personnel decision making is the multiple regression model, an extension of the correlation coefficient (see Chapter 2 Statistical Appendix). As you recall, the correlation coefficient examines the strength of a relationship between a single predictor, such as a test score, and a criterion, such as a measure of job performance. However, rather than having only one predictor of job performance, as in the correlation coefficient or bivariate regression model, multiple regression analysis uses several predictors. Typically, this approach combines the various predictors in an additive, linear fashion. In employee selection, this means that the ability of each of the predictors to predict job performance can be added

multiple regression model

an employee selection method that combines separate predictors of job success in a statistical procedure

Stop & Review

Define and discuss the concepts of predictors and criteria

together and that there is a linear relationship between the predictors and the criterion; higher scores on the predictors will lead to higher scores on the criterion. Although the statistical assumptions and calculations on which the multiple regression model is based are beyond the scope of this text, the result is an equation that uses the various types of screening information in combination.

The multiple regression model is a compensatory type of model, which means that high scores on one predictor can compensate for low scores on another. This is both a strength and a weakness of the regression approach. For example, an applicant's lack of previous job-related experience can be compensated for by test scores that show great potential for mastering the job. However, in other situations this may be problematic. Take, for example, the screening of applicants for a job as an inspector of microcircuitry, a position that requires the visual inspection of very tiny computer circuits under a microscope. From her scores on a test of cognitive ability (i.e., general intelligence), an applicant might show great potential for performing the job. However, the applicant might have an uncorrectable visual problem that leads her to score poorly on a test of visual acuity. Here, the compensatory regression model would not lead to a good prediction, for the visual problem would mean that the applicant would fail, regardless of her potential for handling the cognitive aspects of the job.

A second type of selection strategy, one that is not compensatory, is the **multiple cutoff model**, which uses a minimum cutoff score on each of the predictors. An applicant must obtain a score above the cutoff on each of the predictors to be hired. Scoring below the cutoff on any one predictor automatically disqualifies the applicant, regardless of the scores on the other screening variables. For example, a school district may decide to hire only those probationary high school teachers who have completed a specified number of graduate units and who have scored above the cutoff on a national teacher's examination. The main advantage of the multiple cutoff strategy is that it ensures that all eligible applicants have some minimal amount of ability on all dimensions that are believed to be predictive of job success.

multiple cutoff model
an employee selection method using a minimum cutoff score on each of the various predictors of job performance

Cutoff scores are most commonly used in public-sector organizations that give employment tests to large numbers of applicants (Truxillo, Donahue, & Sulzer, 1996). The setting of cutoff scores is an important and often controversial decision, because of the legal issues involved. Particular care needs to be taken by I/O psychologists to set cutoff scores that distinguish the best candidates for jobs, but cutoffs that do not unfairly discriminate against members of certain ethnic minority groups, women, or older workers (see Cascio, Alexander, & Barrett, 1988).

The multiple regression and multiple cutoff methods can be used in combination. If this is done, applicants would be eligible for hire only if their regression scores are high and if they are above the cutoff score on each of the predictor dimensions. Of course, using both strategies at the same time greatly restricts the number of eligible applicants, so they are used together only when the pool of applicants is very large.

Another type of selection decision-making method is the **multiple hurdle model**. This strategy uses an ordered sequence of screening devices. At each stage in the sequence, a decision is made either to reject an applicant or to allow the applicant to proceed to the next stage. An example of the multiple hurdle model used for hiring police officers is presented in Figure 4.3. In this example, the first stage or hurdle is receiving a passing score on a civil service exam. If a passing score is obtained, the applicant's application blank is evaluated. An applicant who does not pass the exam is no longer considered for the job. Typically, all applicants who pass all the hurdles are then selected for jobs.

One advantage of the multiple hurdle strategy is that unqualified persons do not have to go through the entire evaluation program before they are rejected. Also, because evaluation takes place at many times on many levels, the employer can be quite confident that the applicants who are selected do indeed have the potential to be successful on the job. Because multiple hurdle selection programs are expensive and time consuming, they are usually only used for jobs that are central to the operation of the organization.

multiple hurdle model an employee selection strategy that requires that an acceptance or rejection decision be made at each of several stages in a screening process

Employee Placement

Whereas employee selection deals with how people are hired for jobs, **employee placement** is the process of deciding to which job hired workers should be assigned. Employee placement typically only takes place when there are two or more openings that a newly hired worker could fill. Placement also becomes important when large organizations close departments or offices, and the company does not want to lay off the workers from the closed sites, but instead wants to reassign these workers to other positions within the organization. Although placement is a different personnel function, many of the methods used in placement are the same as those used in employee selection. The main difference is that in placement the worker has already been hired. Therefore, the personnel specialist's job is to find the best possible "fit" between the worker's attributes (KSAOs) and the requirements of the job openings.

Personnel specialists are looking more broadly at the issue of employee selection and placement. Rather than just focusing on fitting potential employees into the right job, researchers and practitioners are concerned with how particular individuals might fit with a particular work group or team and with a specific organization (Van Vianen, 2000; Werbel & Gilliland, 1999). Assuring that there is good fit between individuals and their work organizations and work environments allows organizations not only to predict who will be the better performers, but also helps to increase well-being among the selected employees (Arthur, Bell, Villado, & Doverspike, 2006).

employee placement the process of assigning workers to appropriate jobs

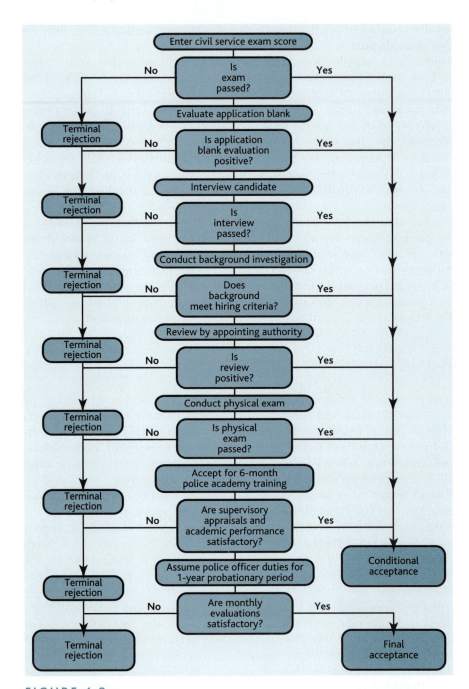

FIGURE 4.3

Multiple Hurdle Model for Police Officer Selection

Source: Cascio, W. E. (1987). *Applied psychology in personnel Management* (p. 282). Englewood Cliffs, NJ: Prentice-Hall.

In today's global environment, many organizations are multinational, with offices around the world. As a result, attention is being paid to employees selected for international assignments. Researchers have suggested that cultural sensitivity and ability to adapt to different situations and surroundings are important for employees working in other countries and cultures (Caligiuri, Tarique, & Jacobs, 2009; Offerman & Phan, 2002). Importantly, it has been suggested that selecting and placing the right employees for global assignments is not enough. Attention must be paid to the ongoing development and training for workers going abroad (Mesmer-Magnus & Viswesvaran, 2007; Teagarden, 2007). We will discuss this further in Chapter 7, which focuses on employee training and development.

EQUAL EMPLOYMENT OPPORTUNITY IN EMPLOYEE SELECTION AND PLACEMENT

In 1964 the Civil Rights Act was passed. A section of this major piece of federal legislation, Title VII, was intended to protect against discrimination (i.e., an unfair advantage or disadvantage) in employment on the basis of race, ethnic background, gender, or religious preference. All companies in the United States with more than 15 employees are subject to Title VII. Additional laws have since helped protect against age discrimination and discrimination against disabled persons (see Table 4.1). This antidiscrimination legislation has led to massive changes in personnel procedures and decision making.

As a result of the Civil Rights Act, a federal agency, the **Equal Employment Opportunity Commission (EEOC)**, was created to ensure that employers' employee selection and placement procedures complied with the antidiscrimination laws. The EEOC's authority entails the investigation of discrimination claims filed against employers. In an investigation, their role is to conduct a fair and accurate assessment of the allegations. In the 1970s the EEOC developed the Uniform Guidelines on Employee Selection Procedures (1974, 1978), which serve as the standards for complying with antidiscrimination laws. Three concepts are important for understanding the Guidelines and their impact on employee selection procedures.

The first of these concepts is the notion of **protected groups**, which include women, African-Americans, Native Americans, Asian-Americans, and Latinos. In addition, Title VII of the Civil Rights Act protects individuals based on their nation of origin and religious affiliation. Later legislation extended protected class status to older and disabled workers. Employers must keep separate personnel records, including information on all actions such as recruitment, selection, promotions, and firings, for each of these groups and for majority group workers. If some action is found to discriminate against one or more of these groups, the second concept, adverse impact, comes into play. Discrimination can be either intentional (unequal treatment of employees based on protected status) or unintentional. **Adverse impact** is when members of a protected group are treated unfairly, either intentionally or unintentionally, by an employer's personnel action. For instance, the Guidelines state that if any personnel decision causes a disproportionate

🕑 **Stop** & **Review**
Define and give examples of four employee selection methods.

Equal Employment Opportunity Commission (EEOC)
the federal agency created to protect against discrimination in employment

protected groups
groups including women and certain ethnic and racial minorities that have been identified as previous targets of employment discrimination

adverse impact
when members of a protected group are treated unfairly by an employer's personnel action

TABLE 4.1

Federal Laws and Key Court Cases Affecting Employment

Civil Rights Act of 1964

Protects against employment discrimination on the basis of "race, color, religion, sex, or national origin." Led to the establishment of the Equal Employment Opportunity Commission (EEOC), the federal body that enforces the law.

Age Discrimination in Employment Act (passed in 1967, amended in 1978)

Protects against employment discrimination on the basis of age. Specifically targeted toward workers between 40 and 70 years of age.

Griggs v. Duke Power Company (1971)

This Supreme Court ruling said that if hiring procedures led to adverse impact, the employer has the burden of proof to show that the hiring procedures are valid.

Albermarle Paper Company v. Moody (1975)

A Supreme Court ruling that required employers to adhere to the Uniform Guidelines, including demonstrating that selection procedures are valid.

EEOC Uniform Guidelines (1974, 1978)

Established rules for fair employment practices. Established the notion of adverse impact and the four-fifths rule.

Americans with Disabilities Act (1990)

Protects against employment discrimination for qualified individuals with a physical or mental disability. Says that employers must provide "reasonable accommodations" to help the individual perform the job.

Civil Rights Act of 1991

Upheld the concepts set forth in *Griggs v. Duke* and allows workers who claim discrimination to have a jury trial and seek both compensatory and punitive damages against employers.

Family and Medical Leave Act of 1993

Allows employees in organizations of 50 or more workers to take up to 12 weeks of unpaid leave each year for family or medical reasons.

percentage of people in a particular group to be hired in comparison to another group, adverse impact exists. As we will see in more detail in Chapter 5, even if it is unintentional, if we were to use a test or other selection tool that was inherently discriminating against certain protected group members, the use of the test is not legally defensible. The Guidelines led to the establishment of the four-fifths rule, which states that a hiring procedure has adverse impact when the selection rate for any protected group is 4/5, or 80%, of the group with the highest hiring rate. If the four-fifths rule demonstrates adverse impact, the employer must show that the hiring procedures used are valid. In a classic legal decision, *Griggs v. Duke Power Company* (1971), the Supreme Court ruled that the burden of proof on whether an employment selection test is fair rests with the employer. This means that it is up to employers to show that their screening tests and other selection methods are valid indicators of future job performance. The Civil Rights Act of 1991 reaffirmed the *Griggs v. Duke* concepts. Therefore, it is wise for organizations to validate any and all of their employee screening instruments to ensure against possible instances of discrimination.

We have already seen in Chapter 3 that the Americans with Disabilities Act protects against discrimination for disabled workers, and requires employers to make reasonable accommodations for disabled workers to perform jobs. In relation to employee selection, applicants with disabilities may encounter difficulties with certain types of employee screening and selection tests, if their disability interferes with test performance. For instance, a vision-impaired applicant may need to be presented with a large-print version of a pencil-and-paper test, or if vision is severely impaired, an audio test may need to be administered. Any written test might be inappropriate for testing a dyslexic applicant. A difficulty then arises in comparing the test results of the disabled applicant, who received a different version of the test, or who was administered the test in a different format, with applicants completing the regular version of the test (Ingate, 1992). Yet, the disability may not hinder the individual's ability to do the job. Therefore, personnel specialists must offer reasonable accommodations so that an applicant's disability does not interfere with test performance.

The passage of the Americans with Disabilities Act (ADA) has sparked a great deal of debate about whether or not disabled applicants whose disability interferes with test taking should or should not be tested (Arnold & Thiemann, 1992). It seems the solution lies not in the test scores themselves, but in the judicious interpretation of the scores (Ingate, 1992). An even more fundamental issue is determining if an applicant even has a disability because it is illegal to ask applicants about disabilities.

The Age Discrimination in Employment Act (1967) protects against discrimination in personnel decisions, including hiring, promotion, and layoffs, for workers aged 40 years and older. The Family Medical Leave Act of 1993 protects employees having children from employment discrimination, and allows for up to 12 weeks of unpaid leave for family or medical emergencies. This means that parents caring for a newborn or for an ill family member are protected against being fired or discriminated against because of the need to take extended time from work for family care.

The final important concept from the Uniform Guidelines is **affirmative action**, the voluntary development of organizational policies that attempt to ensure that jobs are made available to qualified persons regardless of sex, age, or ethnic background. In general, affirmative action programs will hire or promote a member of a protected group over an individual from the

affirmative action
the voluntary development of policies that try to ensure that jobs are made available to qualified individuals regardless of sex, age, or ethnic background

majority group if the two are determined to be equally qualified. However, if the protected group member is less qualified than a majority group applicant—usually a white male—the organization is under no obligation to hire the less-qualified applicant. Affirmative action programs typically deal with all personnel functions, including recruitment, screening, selection, job placements, and promotions.

bona fide occupational qualifications (BFOQ)
real and valid occupational needs required for a particular job

There are certain exceptions to Title VII coverage, such as in cases where a particular position requires the workers to be of only one class. The term that is used is that the position has **Bona fide occupational qualifications (BFOQs)**, or real occupational needs. For example, a fashion designer is allowed to hire only female models for showing her line of women's clothing, or a sports club is allowed to hire only male or female locker room attendants for their respective locker rooms. Keep in mind, however, that the courts have allowed only very few exceptions to Title VII based on BFOQs. In particular, restaurants that have hired only female waitpersons, or airlines hiring with policies of hiring only female flight attendants, have not been allowed by the courts to continue this practice.

Stop & Review

Define and discuss the concepts of protected groups, adverse impact, and affirmative action.

Summary

Human resource planning is the process of hiring and staffing an organization. It involves thinking forward to the positions that need to be filled, the talent needed to fill them, and the process of how the organization will fill these positions.

Employee recruitment is the process of attracting potential workers to apply for jobs. There are a variety of employee recruitment methods, such as advertisements, college recruitment programs, employment agencies, and employee referrals. An important element of the recruitment process is presenting applicants with an accurate picture of the job through the use of *realistic job previews* (*RJPs*), which help increase satisfaction and decrease turnover of new employees. *Employee screening* is the process of reviewing information about job applicants to select individuals for jobs, and will be covered in depth in Chapter 5.

Once the screening information has been obtained, a selection decision must be made.

All too often, subjective decision-making processes are used. Statistical models of decision making include the *multiple regression model*, an approach that allows predictors to be combined statistically; the *multiple cutoff* strategy, a method of setting minimum cutoff scores for each predictor; and the *multiple hurdle* approach, a stringent method that uses an ordered sequence of screening devices. *Employee placement* involves assigning selected employees to jobs to which they are best suited.

Regardless of the screening and selection procedures used, an overarching concern in all personnel decisions is to protect against discrimination in employment. The federal *Equal Employment Opportunity Commission* (*EEOC*) has established guidelines to prevent discrimination against ethnic minorities and other *protected groups*. To take preventive steps to avoid employment discrimination, many organizations have adopted *affirmative action* plans to ensure that jobs are made available to members of protected groups.

Study Questions and Exercises

1. What are some of the key concerns that organizations should consider in human resource planning?

2. What factors need to be considered in employee recruitment on the part of the employer? On the part of the applicant?

3. In what ways has antidiscrimination legislation affected how personnel professionals recruit, screen, and select people for jobs?

List some ways that employers can try to avoid discrimination in personnel decision making.

4. Consider the different employee selection methods: multiple regression, multiple cutoff, and multiple hurdle. For each, develop a list of jobs or occupations that would probably require that particular method.

Web Links

www.hr-guide.com

Contains many useful resources relating to all aspects of HR. The personnel selection section is particularly good.

Suggested Readings

Reynolds, D. H., & Weiner, J. A. (2009). *Online recruiting and selection: Innovations in talent acquisition.* New York: Wiley. *A guide for recruiters that discusses on-line recruiting processes and procedures. An interesting read if you are going on the job market.*

Schuler, R. S., & Jackson, S. E. (2007). *Strategic human resource management.* New York: Wiley. *A textbook on HR management by two leading researchers in the field.*

Personnel and *Personnel Journal.* These journals have many informative and readable articles discussing issues related to recruitment, screening, and selection.*

5 | Methods for Assessing
and Selecting Employees

Inside Tips
UNDERSTANDING THE HIRING AND ASSESSMENT PROCESS

In this chapter we will continue our look at how employees are selected into organizations, by focusing directly on assessment techniques used in hiring. As mentioned earlier, we will be applying some of the research and measurement methods discussed in Chapter 2.

A study hint for organizing and understanding the many screening and testing procedures presented in this chapter is to consider those processes in the context of some of the methodological issues discussed previously. In other words, much of the strength or weakness of any particular employment method or process is determined by its ability to predict important work outcomes, which is usually defined as "job performance." The ability to predict future employee performance accurately from the results of employment tests or from other employee screening procedures is critical. However, other important considerations for screening methods concern their cost and ease of use, or in other words, their utility. Hiring interviews, for example, are considered to be relatively easy to use, whereas testing programs are thought (rightly or wrongly) to be costly and difficult to implement. Often, our own experiences in applying for jobs give us only a limited picture of the variety of employee screening methods.

You have found what you consider to be the perfect job. You polish up your resume (and hopefully have some friends, and perhaps your career services counselor, read it over and make suggestions) and spend a lot of time crafting a dynamic cover letter. You then begin the online application process. A week later, you receive an e-mail scheduling you for an "employment testing session and interview." You begin to wonder (and worry) about what the testing session and interview will be about.

In this chapter, we will focus on the methods used in assessing and screening applicants for jobs. This is an area where I/O psychologists have been greatly involved—in the development of employment tests, work simulations, hiring interview protocols, and other methods used to predict who, among a large pool of applicants, might be best suited for success in a particular job.

Employee Screening and Assessment

As we saw in Chapter 4, *Employee screening* is the process of reviewing information about job applicants to select individuals for jobs. A wide variety of data sources, such as resumes, job applications, letters of recommendation, employment tests, and hiring interviews, can be used in screening and selecting potential employees. If you have ever applied for a job, you have had firsthand experience with some of these. We will consider all these screening methods in this section, except for employment tests and interviews. Because of the variety and complexity of tests used in employee screening and selection, we will consider employment testing and hiring interviews in a separate section.

EVALUATION OF WRITTEN MATERIALS

The first step in the screening process involves the evaluation of written materials, such as applications and resumes. Usually, standard application forms are used for screening lower-level positions in an organization, with resumes used to provide biographical data and other background information for higher-level jobs, although many companies require all applicants to complete an application form. The main purpose of the application and resume is to collect biographical information such as education, work experience, and outstanding work or school accomplishments. Often, these applications are submitted online. Such data are believed to be among the best predictors of future job performance (Feldman & Klich, 1991; Knouse, 1994; Owens, 1976). However, it is often difficult to assess constructs such as work experience to use it in employee screening and selection. Researchers have suggested that work experience can be measured in both quantitative (e.g., time in a position; number of times performing a task) and qualitative (e.g., level of complexity or challenge in a job) terms (Quinones, 2004; Quiñones, Ford, & Teachout, 1995; Tesluk & Jacobs, 1998).

It is also important to mention, however, that first impressions play a big role in selection decisions. Because written materials are usually the first contact a potential employer has with a job candidate, the impressions of an applicant's credentials received from a resume or application are very important. In fact, research has shown that impressions of qualifications from written applications influenced impressions of applicants in their subsequent interviews (Macan & Dipboye, 1994).

Most companies use a standard application form, completed online or as a hard copy (see the sample application form in Figure 5.1). As with all employment screening devices, the application form should collect only information that has been determined to be job related. Questions that are not job related, and especially those that may lead to job discrimination (as we discussed in Chapter 4), such as inquiries about age, ethnic background, religious affiliation, marital status, or finances, should not be included.

From the employer's perspective, the difficulty with application forms is in evaluating and interpreting the information obtained to determine the most qualified applicants. For example, it may be difficult to choose between an applicant with little education but ample work experience and an educated person with no work experience.

There have been attempts to quantify the biographical information obtained from application forms through the use of either weighted application forms or biographical information blanks (BIBs). **Weighted application forms** assign different weights to each piece of information on the form. The weights are determined through detailed research, conducted by the organization, to determine the relationship between specific bits of biographical data, often referred to as *biodata*, and criteria of success on the job (Breaugh, 2009; Mael, 1991, Stokes, Mumford, & Owen, 1992). We will discuss the use of biodata in more detail in the section on employment tests.

Another type of information from job applicants is a work sample. Often a work sample consists of a written sample (e.g., a report or document), but artists, architects, and software developers might submit a "portfolio" of work products/samples. Research suggests that work samples can be valuable in predicting future job performance (Jackson, Harris, Ashton, McCarthy, & Tremblay, 2000; Lance, Johnson, Douthitt, Bennett, & Harville, 2000; Roth, Bobko, & McFarland, 2005). Work samples can also be developed into standardized tests, and we will discuss these later in the chapter.

weighted application forms forms that assign different weights to the various pieces of information provided on a job application

APPLICATION FOR EMPLOYMENT
FOR THE POSITION OF

Job Title _____   Job Number _____

1. INSTRUCTIONS

Print in dark ink or type

Applicants failing to complete all sections of this form will be disqualified from consideration for positions

2. NAME, ADDRESS AND TELEPHONE

Name: Last, First, Middle Initial

Address: Number, Street, Apartment or Space Number

City, State, Zip Code

Telephone Number

Area Code

Home ( )
Work ( )
Message ( )
Ask for

3. EMPLOYMENT HISTORY

Please show all employment within the last ten years plus other related experience. Include military or volunteer experience. Begin with your current employer.
A resume may be attached, but will not be accepted in lieu of completion of any section of this form.

Firm Name (Department)	From: Mo/Yr	Title
Street	To: Mo/Yr	Duties
City, State, Zip Code	Total: Yrs & Mos	
Telephone (include area code)	Starting salary	
Supervisor's Name	Final Salary	
Supervisor's Title	Hrs Worked per Week	Reason for Wanting to Leave
Firm Name (Department)	From: Mo/Yr	Title
Street	To: Mo/Yr	Duties
City, State, Zip Code	Total: Yrs & Mos	
Telephone (include area code)	Starting salary	
Supervisor's Name	Final Salary	
Supervisor's Title	Hrs Worked per Week	Reason for Wanting to Leave
Firm Name (Department)	From: Mo/Yr	Title
Street	To: Mo/Yr	Duties
City, State, Zip Code	Total: Yrs & Mos	
Telephone (include area code)	Starting salary	
Supervisor's Name	Final Salary	
Supervisor's Title	Hrs Worked per Week	Reason for Wanting to Leave

Name: Last, First, Middle Initial

Job Title:

Job Number:

4. EDUCATION AND TRAINING

Circle highest level completed   9   10   11   12   GED   College: 1   2   3   4   5   6   7   8

Institutions of higher education, trade, vocational, or professional schools attended (other than high school):

School	Dates Attended	Major/Concentration	Degree/Certificate

5. SKILLS, LICENSES, AND CERTIFICATES

Please list all skills related to this position. For licenses and certificates, list the type, class, state, level and expiration date.

6. GENERAL INFORMATION

1. Have you ever been employed under any other name? No ☐   Yes ☐

   If yes, please indicate name(s): _____
   (This information will be used to facilitate verification of work records.)

2. May we contact your current employer? ☐ Yes ☐ No   Previous employers? ☐ Yes ☐ No

3. Please describe in detail how your experience, knowledge, and abilities qualify you for this position.

4. Check all appropriate boxes which indicate your interest:
   ☐ Full-Time   ☐ Part-Time   ☐ Permanent   ☐ Temporary

5. How soon are you available for employment? _____

7. CLERICAL AND SECRETARIAL APPLICANTS ONLY

Indicate which of the following you are skilled in using:

☐ Typewriter _____ (cwpm) ☐ Shorthand _____ (wpm) ☐ Wordprocessor ☐ Dictating machine
☐ Other _____

FIGURE 5.1
A Sample Application Form

REFERENCES AND LETTERS OF RECOMMENDATION

Two other sources of information used in employee screening and selection are references and letters of recommendation. Historically, very little research has examined their validity as selection tools (Muchinsky, 1979). Typically, reference checks and letters of recommendation can provide four types of information: (1) employment and educational history, (2) evaluations of the applicant's character, (3) evaluations of the applicant's job performance, and (4) recommender's willingness to rehire the applicant (Cascio, 1987).

There are important reasons that references and letters of recommendation may have limited importance in employee selection. First, because applicants can usually choose their own sources for references and recommendations, it is unlikely that they will supply the names of persons who will give bad recommendations. Therefore, letters of recommendation tend to be distorted in a very positive direction, so positive that they may be useless in distinguishing among applicants. One interesting study found that both longer reference letters and letters written by persons with more positive dispositions tended to be more favorably evaluated than either short letters or those written by less "positive" authors (Judge & Higgins, 1998). In addition, because of increased litigation against individuals and former employers who provide negative recommendations, many companies are refusing to provide any kind of reference for former employees except for job title and dates of employment. Thus, some organizations are simply foregoing the use of reference checks and letters of recommendation.

Letters of recommendation are still widely used, however, in applications to graduate schools and in certain professional positions. One study examined the use of reference letters by academics and personnel professionals in selection. As expected, letters of reference are used more frequently for selection of graduate students than for selection of employees, although both groups did not rely heavily on reference letters, primarily because most letters tend to be so positively inflated that they are considered somewhat useless in distinguishing among applicants (Nicklin & Roch, 2009).

In many graduate programs steps have been taken to improve the effectiveness of these letters as a screening and selection tool by including forms that ask the recommender to rate the applicant on a variety of dimensions, such as academic ability, motivation/drive, oral and written communication skills, and initiative. These rating forms often use graphic rating scales to help quantify the recommendation for comparison with other applicants. They also attempt to improve the accuracy of the reference by protecting the recommender from possible retaliation by having the applicants waive their rights to see the letter of reference.

The use of background checks for past criminal activity has been on the rise, and has fueled an industry for companies providing this service. Although more common for applicants for positions in law enforcement, jobs working with children and other vulnerable populations, and positions in government agencies, many companies are routinely conducting background checks on most or all candidates for jobs before hire, in an attempt to protect employers from litigation (Blumstein & Nakamura, 2009). Interestingly, although background checks are becoming commonplace, there has been very little research examining the impact on organizations.

EMPLOYMENT TESTING

After the evaluation of the biographical information available from resumes, application forms, or other sources, the next step in comprehensive employee screening programs is employment testing. As we saw in Chapter 1, the history of personnel testing in I/O psychology goes back to World War I, when intelligence testing of armed forces recruits was used for employee placement. Today, the use of tests for employment screening and placement has expanded greatly. A considerable percentage of large companies and most government agencies routinely use some form of employment tests to measure a wide range of characteristics that are predictive of successful job performance. For example, some tests measure specific skills or abilities required by a job, whereas others assess more general cognitive skills as a means of determining if one has the aptitude believed to be needed for the successful performance of a certain job. Still other tests measure personality dimensions that are believed to be important for particular occupations. Before we discuss specific types of screening tests, however, it is important to consider some issues and guidelines for the development and use of tests and other screening methods.

CONSIDERATIONS IN THE DEVELOPMENT AND USE OF PERSONNEL SCREENING AND TESTING METHODS

Any type of measurement instrument used in industrial/organizational psychology, including those used in employee screening and selection, must meet certain measurement standards. Two critically important concepts in measurement (that were introduced in Chapter 2) are reliability and validity. Reliability refers to the stability of a measure over time or the consistency of the measure. For example, if we administer a test to a job applicant, we would expect to get essentially the same score on the test if it is taken at two different points of time (and the applicant did not do anything to improve test performance in between). Reliability also refers to the agreement between two or more assessments made of the same event or behavior, such as when two interviewers independently evaluate the appropriateness of a job candidate for a particular position. In other words, a measurement process is said to possess "reliability" if we can "rely" on the scores or measurements to be stable, consistent, and free of random error.

reliability
the consistency of a measurement instrument or its stability over time

A variety of methods are used for estimating the reliability of a screening instrument. One method is called test–retest reliability. Here, a particular test or other measurement instrument is administered to the same individual at two different times, usually involving a one- to two-week interval between testing sessions. Scores on the first test are then correlated with those on the second test. If the correlation is high (a correlation coefficient approaching +1.0), evidence of reliability (at least stability over time) is empirically established. Of course, the assumption is made that nothing has happened during the administration of the two tests that would cause the scores to change drastically.

test–retest reliability
a method of determining the stability of a measurement instrument by administering the same measure to the same people at two different times and then correlating the scores

parallel forms
a method of establishing the reliability of a measurement instrument by correlating scores on two different but equivalent versions of the same instrument

internal consistency
a common method of establishing a measurement instrument's reliability by examining how the various items of the instrument intercorrelate

validity
a concept referring to the accuracy of a measurement instrument and its ability to make accurate inferences about a criterion

content validity
the ability of the items in a measurement instrument to measure adequately the various characteristics needed to perform a job

A second method of estimating the reliability of an employment screening measure is the parallel forms method. Here two equivalent tests are constructed, each of which presumably measures the same construct but using different items or questions. Test-takers are administered both forms of the instrument. Reliability is empirically established if the correlation between the two scores is high. Of course, the major drawbacks to this method are the time and difficulty involved in creating two equivalent tests.

Another way to estimate the reliability of a test instrument is by estimating its internal consistency. If a test is reliable, each item should measure the same general construct, and thus performance on one item should be consistent with performance on all other items. Two specific methods are used to determine internal consistency. The first is to divide the test items into two equal parts and correlate the summed score on the first half of the items with that on the second half. This is referred to as split-half reliability. A second method, which involves numerous calculations (and which is more commonly used), is to determine the average intercorrelation among all items of the test. The resulting coefficient, referred to as *Cronbach's alpha*, is an estimate of the test's internal consistency. In summary, reliability refers to whether we can "depend" on a set of measurements to be stable and consistent, and several types of empirical evidence (e.g., test–retest, equivalent forms, and internal consistency) reflect different aspects of this stability.

Validity refers to the accuracy of inferences or projections we draw from measurements. Validity refers to whether a set of measurements allows accurate inferences or projections about "something else." That "something else" can be a job applicant's standing on some characteristic or ability, it can be future job success, or it can be whether an employee is meeting performance standards. In the context of employee screening, the term *validity* most often refers to whether scores on a particular test or screening procedure accurately project future job performance. For example, in employee screening, validity refers to whether a score on an employment test, a judgment made from a hiring interview, or a conclusion drawn from the review of information from a job application does indeed lead to a representative evaluation of an applicant's qualifications for a job, and whether the specific measure (e.g., test, interview judgment) leads to accurate inferences about the applicant's criterion status (which is usually, but not always, job performance). Validity refers to the quality of specific inferences or projections; therefore, validity for a specific measurement process (e.g., a specific employment test) can vary depending on what criterion is being predicted. Therefore, an employment test might be a valid predictor of job performance, but not a valid predictor of another criterion such as rate of absenteeism.

Similar to our discussion of reliability, validity is a unitary concept, but there are three important facets of, or types of evidence for, determining the validity of a predictor used in employee selection (see Binning & Barrett, 1989; Schultz, Riggs, & Kottke, 1999). A predictor can be said to yield valid inferences about future performance based on a careful scrutiny of its content. This is referred to as content validity. Content validity refers to whether a predictor measurement process (e.g., test items or interview questions) adequately sample important job behaviors and elements involved in performing a job. Typically, content validity is established by having experts such as job incumbents or supervisors judge the appropriateness of the test items, taking into account information from the job analysis (Hughes & Prien, 1989). Ideally, the experts should determine that the test does indeed sample the job content in a representative way. It is common for organizations constructing their own screening tests for specific jobs to rely heavily on this content-based evidence of validity. As you can guess, content validity is closely linked to job analysis.

A second type of validity evidence is called construct validity, which refers to whether a predictor test, such as a pencil-and-paper test of mechanical ability used to screen school bus mechanics, actually measures what it is supposed to measure—(a) the abstract construct of "mechanical ability" and (b) whether these measurements yield accurate predictions of job performance. Think of it this way: most applicants to college take a predictor test of "scholastic aptitude," such as the SAT (Scholastic Aptitude Test). Construct validity of the SAT deals with whether this test does indeed measure a person's aptitude for schoolwork, and whether it allows accurate inferences about future academic success. (Students taking the SAT may agree or disagree with how accurately the SAT measures their personal scholastic aptitude—likely related to their scores on the test.) There are two common forms of empirical evidence about construct validity. Well-validated instruments such as the SAT, and standardized employment tests, have established construct validity by demonstrating that these tests correlate positively with the results of other tests of the same construct. This is referred to as *convergent validity*. In other words, a test of mechanical ability should correlate (converge) with another, different test of mechanical ability. In addition, a pencil-and-paper test of mechanical ability should correlate with a performance-based test of mechanical ability. In establishing a test's construct validity, researchers are also concerned with *divergent*, or *discriminant*, *validity*—the test should not correlate with tests or measures of constructs that are totally unrelated to mechanical ability. Similarly to content validity, credible judgments about a test's construct validity require sound professional judgments about patterns of convergent and discriminant validity

Criterion-related validity is a third type of validity evidence and is empirically demonstrated by the relationship between test scores and some measurable criterion of job success, such as a measure of work output or quality. There are two common ways that predictor–criterion correlations can be empirically generated. The first is the *follow-up method* (often referred to as *predictive validity*). Here, the screening test is administered to applicants without interpreting the scores and without using them to select among applicants. Once the applicants become employees, criterion measures such as job performance assessments are collected. If the test instrument is valid, the test scores should correlate with the criterion measure. Once there is evidence of the predictive validity of the instrument, test scores are used to select the applicants for jobs. The obvious advantage of the predictive validity method is that it demonstrates how scores on the screening instrument actually relate to future job performance. The major drawback to this approach is the time that it takes to establish validity. During this validation period, applicants are tested, but are not hired based on their test scores.

construct validity
refers to whether an employment test measures what it is supposed to measure

criterion-related validity
the accuracy of a measurement instrument in determining the relationship between scores on the instrument and some criterion of job success

In the second approach, known as the *present-employee method* (also termed *concurrent validity*), the test is given to current employees, and their scores are correlated with some criterion of their current performance. Again, a relationship between test scores and criterion scores supports the measure's validity. Once there is evidence of concurrent validity, a comparison of applicants' test scores with the incumbents' scores is possible. Although the concurrent validity method leads to a quicker estimate of validity, it may not be as accurate an assessment of criterion-related validity as the predictive method, because the job incumbents represent a select group, and their test performance is likely to be high, with a restricted range of scores. In other words, there are no test scores for the "poor" job performers, such as workers who were fired or quit their jobs, or applicants who were not chosen for jobs. Interestingly, available research suggests that the estimates of validity derived from both methods are generally comparable (Barrett, Phillips, & Alexander, 1981).

All predictors used in employee selection, whether they are evaluations of application materials, employment tests, or judgments made in hiring interviews, must be reliable and valid. Standardized and commercially available psychological tests have typically demonstrated evidence of reliability and validity for use in certain circumstances. However, even with widely used standardized tests, it is critical that their ability to predict job success be established for the particular positions in question and for the specific criterion. It is especially necessary to assure the reliability and validity of nonstandardized screening methods, such as a weighted application form or a test constructed for a specific job.

TYPES OF EMPLOYEE SCREENING TESTS

The majority of employee screening and selection instruments are standardized tests that have been subjected to research aimed at demonstrating their validity and reliability. Most also contain information to ensure that they are administered, scored, and interpreted in a uniform manner. The alternative to the use of standardized tests is for the organization to construct a test for a particular job or class of jobs, and conduct its own studies of the test's reliability and validity. However, because this is a costly and time-consuming procedure, most employers use standardized screening tests. While many of these tests are published in the research literature, there has been quite a bit of growth in consulting organizations that assist companies in testing and screening. These organizations employ I/O psychologists to create screening tests and other assessments that are proprietary and used in their consulting work. More and more, companies are outsourcing their personnel testing work to these consulting firms.

Stop & Review

What are three facets of validation that are important for employee screening tests?

Test formats

Test formats, or the ways in which tests are administered, can vary greatly. Several distinctions are important when categorizing employment tests.

Individual versus group tests—Individual tests are administered to only one person at a time. In individual tests, the test administrator is usually more involved than in group tests. Typically, tests that require some kind of sophisticated apparatus, such as a driving simulator, or tests that require constant supervision are administered individually, as are certain intelligence and personality tests. Group tests are designed to be given simultaneously to more than one person, with the administrator usually serving as only a test monitor. The obvious advantage to group tests is the reduced cost for administrator time. More and more, tests of all types are being administered online, so the distinction between individual and group testing are becoming blurred, as many applicants can complete screening instruments online simultaneously.

Speed versus power tests—Speed tests have a fixed time limit. An important focus of a speed test is the number of items completed in the time period provided. A typing test and many of the scholastic achievement tests are examples of speed tests. A power test allows the test-taker sufficient time to complete all items. Typically, power tests have difficult items, with a focus on the percentage of items answered correctly.

Paper-and-pencil versus performance tests—"Paper-and-pencil tests" refers to both paper versions of tests and online tests, which require some form of written reply, in either a forced choice or an open-ended, "essay" format. Many employee screening tests, and nearly all tests in schools, are of this format. Performance tests, such as typing tests and tests of manual dexterity or grip strength, usually involve the manipulation of physical objects.

As mentioned, many written-type tests are now administered via computer (usually Web-based), which allows greater flexibility in how a test can

Some employment tests involve sophisticated technology, such as this flight simulator used to train and test airline pilots.

be administered. Certain performance-based tests can also be administered via computer simulations (see box "On the Cutting Edge," p. 116).

Although the format of an employment test is significant, the most important way of classifying the instruments is in terms of the characteristics or attributes they measure such as biographical information (biodata instruments), cognitive abilities, mechanical abilities, motor and sensory abilities, job skills and knowledge, or personality traits (see Table 5.1 for examples of these various tests).

TABLE 5.1
Some Standardized and Well-Researched Tests Used in Employee Screening and Selection

Cognitive Ability Tests

Comprehensive Ability Battery (Hakstian & Cattell, 1975–82): Features 20 tests, each designed to measure a single primary cognitive ability, many of which are important in industrial settings. Among the tests are those assessing verbal ability, numerical ability, clerical speed and accuracy, and ability to organize and produce ideas, as well as several memory scales.

Wonderlic Cognitive Ability Test (formerly the *Wonderlic Personnel Test*) (Wonderlic, 1983): A 50-item, pencil-and-paper test measuring the level of mental ability for employment, which is advertised as the most widely used test of cognitive abilities by employers.

Wechsler Adult Intelligence Scale-Revised or *WAIS-R* (Wechsler, 1981): A comprehensive group of 11 subtests measuring general levels of intellectual functioning. The WAIS-R is administered individually and takes more than an hour to complete.

Mechanical Ability Tests

Bennett Mechanical Comprehension Test (Bennett, 1980): A 68-item, pencil-and-paper test of ability to understand the physical and mechanical principles in practical situations. Can be group administered; comes in two equivalent forms.

Mechanical Ability Test (Morrisby, 1955): A 35-item, multiple-choice instrument that measures natural mechanical aptitude. Used to predict potential in engineering, assembly work, carpentry, and building trades.

Motor and Sensory Ability Tests

Hand-Tool Dexterity Test (Bennett, 1981): Using a wooden frame, wrenches, and screwdrivers, the test-taker takes apart 12 bolts in a prescribed sequence and reassembles them in another position. This speed test measures manipulative skills important in factory jobs and in jobs servicing mechanical equipment and automobiles.

O'Connor Finger Dexterity Test (O'Connor, 1977): A timed performance test measuring fine motor dexterity needed for fine assembly work and other jobs requiring manipulation of small objects. Test-taker is given a board with symmetrical rows of holes and a cup of pins. The task is to place three pins in each hole as quickly as possible.

Job Skills and Knowledge Tests

Minnesota Clerical Assessment Battery or *MCAB* (Vale & Prestwood, 1987): A self-administered battery of six subtests measuring the skills and knowledge necessary for clerical and secretarial work. Testing is completely computer-administered. Included are tests of typing, proofreading, filing, business vocabulary, business math, and clerical knowledge.

TABLE 5.1

Some Standardized and Well-Researched Tests Used in Employee Screening and Selection (continued)

Purdue Blueprint Reading Test (Owen & Arnold, 1958): A multiple-choice test assessing the ability to read standard blueprints.

Various Tests of Software Skills. Includes knowledge-based and performance-based tests of basic computer operations, word processing, and spreadsheet use.

Personality Tests

California Psychological Inventory or *CPI* (Gough, 1987): A 480-item, pencil-and-paper inventory of 20 personality dimensions. Has been used in selecting managers, sales personnel, and leadership positions.

Hogan Personnel Selection Series (Hogan & Hogan, 1985): These pencil-and-paper tests assess personality dimensions of applicants and compares their profiles to patterns of successful job incumbents in clerical, sales, and managerial positions. Consists of four inventories: the prospective employee potential inventory, the clerical potential inventory, the sales potential inventory, and the managerial potential inventory.

Sixteen Personality Factors Questionnaire or *16 PF* (Cattell, 1986): Similar to the CPI, this test measures 16 basic personality dimensions, some of which are related to successful job performance in certain positions. This general personality inventory has been used extensively in employee screening and selection.

Revised NEO Personality Inventory or *NEO-PI-R* (Costa & McCrae, 1992). A very popular personality inventory used in employee screening and selection. This inventory measures the five "core" personality constructs of Neuroticism (N), Extraversion (E), Openness (O), Agreeableness (A), and Conscientiousness (C).

Bar-On Emotional Quotient Inventory (*EQ-I*; Bar-On, 1997) and the Mayer–Salovey–Caruso Emotional Intelligence Test (MSCEIT) (Mayer, Caruso, & Salovey, 1999). Two measures of emotional intelligence.

Biodata instruments

As mentioned earlier, biodata refers to background information and personal characteristics that can be used in a systematic fashion to select employees. Developing biodata instruments typically involves taking information that would appear on application forms and other items about background, personal interests, and behavior and using that information to develop a form of forced-choice employment test. Along with items designed to measure basic biographical information, such as education and work history, the biodata instrument might also involve questions of a more personal nature, probing the applicant's attitudes, values, likes, and dislikes (Breaugh, 2009; Stokes, Mumford, & Owens, 1994). Biodata instruments are unlike the other test instruments we will discuss because there are no standardized biodata instruments. Instead, biodata instruments take a great deal of research to develop and validate. Because biodata instruments are typically designed to screen applicants for one specific job, they are most likely to be used only for higher-level positions. Research indicates that biodata instruments can be effective screening and placement tools (Dean, 2004; Mount, Witt, & Barrick, 2000;

biodata
background information and personal characteristics that can be used in employee selection

How successful were your teachers in arousing your academic interests'?
a. Extremely successful
b. Very successful
c. Somewhat successful
d. Not at all successful

What is your usual state of health?
a. Never ill
b. Never seriously ill
c. About average
d. Feel poorly from time to time
e. Often feel "under the weather"

On the average, how many hours of homework did you do a week in high school?
a. 20 or more
b. 10–20
c. 5–10
d. Less than 5

Which one of the following seems most important to you?
a. A pleasant home and family life
b. A challenging and exciting job
c. Getting ahead in the world
d. Being active and accepted in community affairs
e. Making the most of your particular ability

Do you generally do your best:
a. At whatever job you are doing
b. Only in what you are interested
c. Only when it is demanded of you

FIGURE 5.2
Sample Biodata Items

Ployhart, Schneider, & Schmitt, 2006). Comprehensive biodata instruments can give a very detailed description and classification of an applicant's behavioral history—a very good predictor of future behavior (sample biodata items are given in Figure 5.2). One potential problem in the use of biodata instruments concerns the personal nature of many of the questions and the possibility of unintentional discrimination against minority groups because of items regarding age, financial circumstances, and the like (Mael, Connerly, & Morath, 1996). Thus, biodata instruments should only be developed and administered by professionals trained in test use and validation. It has been suggested that given the success of biodata in employee selection, it is surprising that biodata instruments are not more widely used (Breaugh, 2009).

Cognitive ability tests

Tests of cognitive ability range from tests of general intellectual ability to tests of specific cognitive skills. Group-administered, pencil-and-paper tests of general intelligence have been used in employee screening for some time. Two such widely used older instruments are the Otis Self-Administering Test of

Mental Ability (Otis, 1929) and the Wonderlic Personnel Test (now called the Wonderlic Cognitive Ability Test; Wonderlic, 1983). Both are fairly short and assess basic verbal and numerical abilities. Designed to measure the ability to learn simple jobs, to follow instructions, and to solve work-related problems and difficulties, these tests are used to screen applicants for positions as office clerks, assembly workers, machine operators, and certain frontline supervisors.

One criticism of using general intelligence tests for employee selection is that they measure cognitive abilities that are too general to be effective predictors of specific job-related cognitive skills. However, research indicates that such general tests are reasonably good predictors of job performance (Barrett & Depinet, 1991; Gottfredson, 1986; Hunter & Hunter, 1984). In fact, it has been argued that general intelligence is the most consistent predictor of performance, across all types and categories of jobs (Carretta & Ree, 2000; Schmidt & Ones, 1992). One meta-analysis of workers in the United Kingdom found that tests of cognitive abilities predicted both job performance and the success of employee training efforts (Bertua, Anderson, & Salgado, 2005; Salgado et al., 2003).

Historically, there has been some reluctance on the part of employers to use general intelligence tests for screening job applicants. Because there is some evidence that scores on some general intelligence tests may favor the economically and educationally advantaged, there are fears that general intelligence tests might discriminate against certain ethnic minorities, who tend to be overrepresented among the economically disadvantaged. It has been argued that general intelligence tests may underestimate the intellectual abilities and potentials of members of certain ethnic minorities. It has also been suggested that cognitive test performance may be affected by ethnic differences in test-taking motivation, such that members of ethnic minority groups may have less positive expectations and more aversion to taking tests than members of the white majority group (Chan, Schmitt, DeShon, Clause, & Delbridge, 1997; Ployhart, Ziegert, & McFarland, 2003). In certain instances, this may lead to unfair discrimination in employee selection, a concern we will discuss in the section on legal issues later in this chapter. However, a series of meta-analyses concluded that cognitive abilities tests are valid for employment screening, that they are predictive of job performance, and that they do not underpredict the job performance of minority group members (Sackett, Borneman, & Connelly, 2008).

Mechanical ability tests

Standardized tests have also been developed to measure abilities in identifying, recognizing, and applying mechanical principles. These tests are particularly effective in screening applicants for positions that require operating or repairing machinery, for construction jobs, and for certain engineering positions. The Bennett Mechanical Comprehension Test, or BMCT (Bennett, 1980), is one such commonly used instrument. The BMCT consists of 68 items, each of which requires the application of a physical law or a mechanical operation (for examples, see Figure 5.3). One study using the BMCT and several other

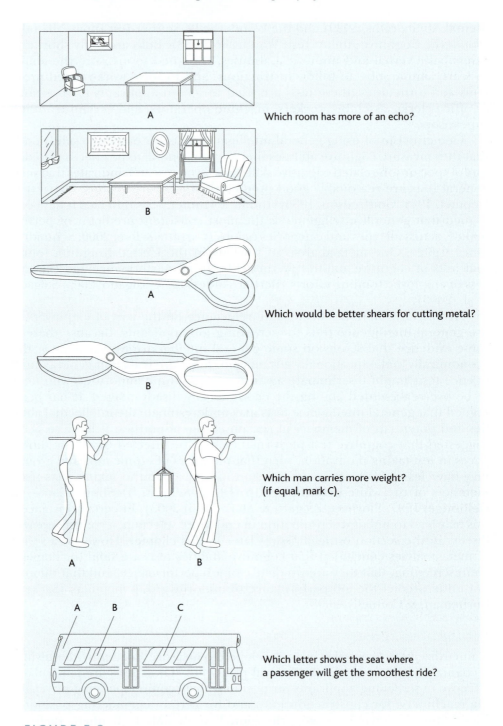

Which room has more of an echo?

Which would be better shears for cutting metal?

Which man carries more weight?
(if equal, mark C).

Which letter shows the seat where
a passenger will get the smoothest ride?

FIGURE 5.3

Sample Items from the Bennett Mechanical ComprehensionTest.

Source: Bennett, G. K. (1940). *Test of Mechanical Comprehension.* New York: Psychological Corporation.

instruments determined that the BMCT was the best single predictor of job performance for a group of employees manufacturing electromechanical components (Muchinsky, 1993). A U.K. military study also found that a mechanical comprehension test predicted recruits' abilities to handle weapons (Munnoch & Bridger, 2008).

Motor and sensory ability tests

A number of tests measure specific motor skills or sensory abilities. Tests such as the Crawford Small Parts Dexterity Test (Crawford, 1981) and the Purdue Pegboard (Tiffin, 1968) are timed performance instruments (speed tests) that require the manipulation of small parts to measure the fine motor dexterity in hands and fingers required in jobs such as assembling computer components and soldering electrical equipment. For example, the Crawford test uses boards with small holes into which tiny pins must be placed using a pair of tweezers. The second part of the test requires screwing small screws into threaded holes with a screwdriver. Sensory ability tests include tests of hearing, visual acuity, and perceptual discrimination. The most common test of visual acuity is the Snellen Eye Chart, which consists of rows of letters that become increasingly smaller. Various electronic instruments are used to measure hearing acuity. No doubt you have taken one or more of these in school or in a doctor's office. In employment settings, they are used in basic screening for positions such as inspectors or bus drivers who require fine audio or visual discrimination.

Job skills and knowledge tests

Various standardized tests also assess specific job skills or domains of job knowledge. Examples of job skill tests for clerical workers would be a standardized typing test or tests of other specific clerical skills such as proofreading, alphabetical filing, or correction of spelling or grammatical errors, as well as the use of software. For example, the Judd Tests (Simmons, 1993) are a series of tests designed to assess competency in several areas of computer competence, including word processing, spreadsheet programs, and database management.

A special sort of job skill test involves the use of **work sample tests**, which measure applicants' abilities to perform brief examples of some of the critical tasks that the job requires. The sample tasks are constructed as tests, administered under standard testing conditions, and scored on some predetermined scale. Their obvious advantage is that they are clearly job-related. In fact, work sample tests can serve as a realistic job preview, allowing applicants to determine their own suitability (and capabilities) for performing a job (Callinan & Robertson, 2000). A drawback is that work samples are usually rather expensive to develop and take a great deal of time to administer.

One example of a work sample test was developed for applicants for the job of concession stand attendant at a city park's snack bar. The test required applicants to use the cash register, make change, fill out a report,

work sample tests
used in job skill tests to measure applicants' abilities to perform brief examples of important job tasks

page someone over a loudspeaker, and react to an "irate customer" who was arguing about receiving the wrong change. In addition to being an effective screening device, this work sample also served as a realistic job preview, providing applicants with a good idea of what the job was all about (Cascio & Phillips, 1979). Research suggests that work sample tests can be a very good predictor of job performance (Roth, Bobko, & McFarland, 2005; Schmidt & Hunter, 1998).

Job knowledge tests are instruments that assess specific types of knowledge required to perform certain jobs. For example, a job knowledge test for nurses or paramedics might contain questions asking about appropriate emergency medical procedures. A job knowledge test for a financial examiner might include questions about regulations governing financial transactions and securities regulations. Research has demonstrated good predictive validity for job knowledge tests (Ones & Viswesvaran, 2007).

Personality tests

personality tests
instruments that measure psychological characteristics of individuals

Personality tests are designed to measure certain psychological characteristics of workers. A wide variety of these tests are used in employee screening and selection in an attempt to match the personality characteristics of job applicants with those of workers who have performed the job successfully in the past. During the 1960s and 1970s, there was some controversy over the use of such tests because of evidence that the connection between general personality dimensions and the performance of specific work tasks was not very strong or direct (Ghiselli, 1973; Guion & Gottier, 1965). However, in the 1990s meta-analytic reviews of research suggested that certain work-related personality characteristics can be quite good predictors of job performance, particularly when the personality dimensions assessed are derived from a thorough analysis of the requirements for the job (Robertson & Kinder, 1993; Tett, Jackson, & Rothstein, 1991).

General personality inventories, such as the Minnesota Multiphasic Personality Inventory, or MMPI (Hathaway & McKinley, 1970), are also used to screen out applicants who possess some psychopathology that might hinder the performance of sensitive jobs, such as police officer, airline pilot, or nuclear power plant operator. However, most of the time, personality tests are used to assess the "normal" characteristics that are deemed to be important for the performance of certain jobs. For example, personality dimensions such as achievement motivation or persistence might be used to screen applicants for positions in sales jobs, and tests for traits of responsibility and service orientation may be administered to applicants for bank teller positions.

In the past several decades, there has been a trend toward developing personality tests that more specifically measure job-relevant aspects of personality. For example, Gough (1984, 1985) has derived work orientation and managerial potential scales from the California Psychological Inventory (CPI), a general personality inventory that measures 20 personality

> If you *agree* with a statement, or feel that it is true about you, answer TRUE. If you *disagree* with a statement, or feel that it is not true about you, answer FALSE.
>
> _____People often expect too much of me.
>
> _____The idea of doing research appeals to me.
>
> _____It is hard for me to just sit still and relax.
>
> _____I enjoy hearing lectures on world affairs.
>
> _____I read at least ten books a year.
>
> _____I like parties and socials.

FIGURE 5.4

From *California Psychological Inventory™ Instrument* by Harrison G. Gough, Ph.D., Copyright 1987 by CPP, Inc., Mountain View, CA 94303. All rights reserved. Further reproduction is prohibited without the Publisher's written consent. California Psychological Inventory is a trademark of CPP, Inc.

Modified and reproduced by special permission of the Publisher CPP, Inc., Mountain View, CA 94043, from California Psychological Inventory Form-434 by Harrison G. Gough, Ph.D. Copyright 1995 by CPP, Inc. All rights reserved. Further reproduction is prohibited without the Publisher's written consent

dimensions (Gough, 1987) (see Figure 5.4). The work orientation scale of the CPI is a predictor of employee performance across positions, whereas the managerial potential scale is used in screening and selecting candidates for management and supervisory positions. Hogan and Hogan (1985) and others have developed a series of personality scales to measure personality characteristics predictive of employee success in general job categories such as sales, management, and clerical work. The use of personality tests in employee screening and selection is on the rise (Salgado, Viswesvaran, & Ones, 2001). It is critically important, however, that the personality tests be carefully selected to match the requirements of the job (Murphy & Dzieweczynski, 2005).

Research examining the use of personality tests in employee screening has found that certain personality characteristics, such as "conscientiousness" and "dependability," are good predictors of both job performance and work attendance (Barrick & Mount, 1991; Barrick, Mount, & Strauss, 1994), but may not be predictive of managerial success (Robertson, Baron, Gibbons, MacIver, & Nyfield, 2000). The personality traits of "dominance" and "extraversion" are good predictors of success as a manager and of career success (Barrick & Mount, 1993; Megargee & Carbonell, 1988; Seibert & Kraimer, 2001). We will examine the role that personality variables play in contributing to managerial performance more fully in Chapter 13, when we discuss leadership.

A relatively new construct that has begun to capture the attention of I/O psychologists interested in the selection of employees is that of emotional intelligence. Emotional intelligence involves knowledge, understanding, and regulation of emotions, ability to communicate emotionally, and using

emotional intelligence
ability to understand, regulate, and communicate emotions and to use them to inform thinking

Much employment testing today is computer administered.

polygraphs
instruments that measure physiological reactions presumed to accompany deception; also known as lie detectors

integrity tests
measures of honest or dishonest attitudes and/or behaviors

emotions to facilitate thinking (Mayer & Salovey, 1997; Salovey & Mayer, 1990). As such, emotional intelligence is partly personality, partly an ability, and partly a form of intelligence, so it does not fit neatly into any of our categories of tests. However, it is easy to see how this interesting construct might be related to performance as a supervisor or workplace leader who needs to inspire followers and be aware of their feelings, and ability to regulate emotions in a positive way might be beneficial for any worker, particularly when facing interpersonal problems or conflicts with other employees, or when under stress. Researchers are just beginning to explore the use of measures of emotional intelligence in employee selection (Christiansen, Janovics, & Siers, 2010; Urch Druskat, Sala, & Mount, 2006).

Honesty and integrity tests

In the past, polygraphs, or lie detectors—instruments designed to measure physiological reactions presumably associated with lying such as respiration, blood pressure, or perspiration—were used in employee selection. Most often polygraphs were used to screen out "dishonest" applicants for positions in which they would have to handle cash or expensive merchandise, although they had also been used by a wide number of organizations to screen and select employees for almost any position. Research, much of it conducted by industrial/organizational psychologists, called into question the validity of polygraphs. A major problem concerned the rate of "false positive" errors, or innocent persons who are incorrectly scored as lying. Because of this questionable validity and the potential harm that invalid results could cause innocent people, the federal government passed legislation in 1988 that severely restricted the use of polygraphs in general employment screening. However, polygraphs are still allowed for the testing of employees about specific incidents, such as thefts, and for screening applicants for public health and safety jobs and for sensitive government positions (Camara, 1988).

Since the establishment of restrictions on the use of polygraphs, many employers have turned to using paper-and-pencil measures of honesty, referred to as integrity tests. Typically, these tests ask about past honest/dishonest behavior or about attitudes condoning dishonest behavior. Typical questions might ask, "What is the total value of cash and merchandise you have taken from your employer in the past year?" or "An employer who pays people poorly has it coming when employees steal. Do you agree or disagree with this statement?" Like polygraphs, these tests also raise the important issue of "false positives," or honest persons who are judged to be dishonest by the instruments (Murphy, 1993). On the other hand, meta-analyses of validity studies of integrity tests indicate that they are somewhat valid predictors of employee dishonesty and "counterproductive behaviors," such as chronic tardiness, taking extended work breaks, and "goldbricking" (ignoring or passing off assigned work tasks), but are less related to employee productivity (Ones & Viswesvaran, 1998b; Van Iddekinge, Roth, Raymark, & Odle-Dusseau, 2011). It has also been suggested that integrity tests might predict productive employee behaviors because integrity overlaps with work-related personality constructs such as conscientiousness and emotional stability (Sackett & Wanek, 1996). Wanek (1999) suggested that integrity tests should never be the sole basis for a hiring decision and that they are best used in combination with other valid predictors.

Other employee screening tests

In addition to the categories of employee tests we have discussed, there are other types of tests that do not fit neatly into any of the categories. For example, many employers concerned about both safety issues and poor work performance screen applicants for drug use, usually through analysis of urine, hair, or saliva samples. Unfortunately, current laboratory tests are not 100% accurate. Interestingly, the problem with drug testing is unlike the problem with polygraphs because drug-testing inaccuracies are more likely to be false negatives—failing to detect the presence of drugs—rather than false positives (Normand, Salyards, & Mahoney, 1990). Unlike the polygraph, however, today there are few restrictions on drug testing in work settings. Moreover, such testing is on the rise, with 84% of HR professionals saying in 2006 that their organizations conduct preemployment drug testing. In addition to testing for the presence of drugs in applicants, pencil-and-paper tests have been developed to screen employees who have attitudes that are related to drug use (Marcoulides, Mills, & Unterbrink, 1993).

A very questionable screening "test" is handwriting analysis, or graphology. In graphology, a person trained in handwriting analysis makes judgments about an applicant's job potential by examining the personality characteristics that are supposedly revealed in the shape, size, and slant of the letters in a sample of handwriting. Although used by some companies to screen applicants, the validity of handwriting analysis in assessing performance potential is highly questionable (Bar-Hillel & Ben-Shakhar, 2000; Ben-Shakhar et al., 1986; Bushnell, 1996; Driver, Buckley, & Frink, 1996).

THE EFFECTIVENESS OF EMPLOYEE SCREENING TESTS

The effectiveness of using standardized tests for screening potential employees remains a controversial issue. Critics of testing cite the low validity coefficients (approximately 0.20) of certain employment tests. (As the model at the beginning of Chapter 4 illustrates, the validity coefficient is the correlation coefficient between the predictor, or the test score, and the criterion, usually a measure of subsequent job performance). However, supporters believe that a comparison of all screening methods—tests, biographical information, and hiring interviews—across the full spectrum of jobs reveals that employment tests are the best predictors of job performance (Hunter & Hunter, 1984). Obviously, the ability of a test to predict performance in a specific job depends on how well it can capture and measure the particular skills, knowledge, or abilities required. For example, tests of word processing and other clerical skills are good predictors of success in clerical positions because they do a good job of assessing the skills and knowledge needed to be a successful clerical assistant.

ON THE *CUTTING* EDGE

The Future of Employment Testing: "Smart" Tests and Performance-based Simulations

Most companies today use computer-based testing (CBT) or Web-based programs to administer pencil-and-paper employment tests (Burke, 1992; Gibby & McCloy, 2011; Wainer, 2000). In CBT, applicants complete the test instruments on a PC or online. Computers can then immediately score the tests, record the results in databanks, and provide the test-taker with feedback if appropriate. Besides being cost-effective, meta-analytic research has shown that for most uses, there are no significant differences in test results between tests administered in computerized versus pencil-and-paper format (Mead & Drasgow, 1993; Wang, Jiao, Young, Brooks, & Olson, 2007).

A more sophisticated development is the use of computer-adaptive testing (CAT). Despite its prevalent usage in educational and governmental institutions, it is relatively recent that organizations have started to adopt CAT for preemployment testing purposes (Kantrowitz, Dawson, & Fezter, 2011). In computer-adaptive tests (often referred to as "smart" tests), the computer program "adjusts" the difficulty of test items to the level of the person being tested. For example, if a test-taker misses several questions, the computer will adjust the level of test difficulty by asking easier questions. If the test-taker is getting several answers correct, the computer will present more difficult questions. Although CAT is typically only used with knowledge-based tests where there are right and wrong answers, it has also been applied to personality

tests (Kantrowitz et al., 2011). Computer-adaptive testing is usually quicker and more efficient than traditional testing because by adjusting the test's difficulty to fit the test-taker, the computer can get an accurate assessment using fewer questions. You may soon encounter a CAT program because many of the standardized graduate school entrance exams are now available in CAT form.

Traditional employment tests, whether they be on paper or computer administered, are limited by the fact that they present only written information. A novel approach to testing makes use of either computer-based or interactive video-computer technology. In interactive video testing, an applicant views a videotaped example of a simulated work setting. The video scene usually presents a realistic, work-related problem situation. The applicant is then asked to respond with an appropriate solution. In effect, through video-computer technology, the applicant is "transported" into the work situation and required to "perform" work-related tasks and make work-related decisions (Kleinmann & Strauss, 1998). In addition to testing an applicant's work-related knowledge and decision making, such interactive testing provides applicants with a realistic job preview of the job. The major drawback to interactive computer-video testing is the cost of development of such testing programs. However, with the rapid advancements in computer technology, and in testing generally, interactive testing should become more common in the near future.

---

test battery
a combination of employment tests used to increase the ability to predict future job performance

The most effective use of screening tests occurs when a number of instruments are used in combination to predict effective job performance. Because most jobs are complex, involving a wide range of tasks, it is unlikely that successful performance is due to just one particular type of knowledge or skill. Therefore, any single test will only be able to predict one aspect of a total job. Employment screening tests are usually grouped together into a test battery. Scores on the various tests in the battery are used in combination to help select the best possible candidates for the job (see Ackerman & Kanfer, 1993). For example, one study showed that a combination of tests, such as a personality test and an ability test, are a better predictor of job performance than either test used alone (Mount, Barrick, & Strauss, 1999). In a study of call center workers, a combination of a cognitive ability test, a personality inventory, and a biodata inventory predicted worker performance better than any one predictor alone (Konradt, Hertel, & Joder, 2003).

We have seen that standardized tests can be reliable and valid screening devices for many jobs. However, two important issues regarding this use of tests must be considered: validity generalization and test utility. The validity generalization of a screening test refers to its validity in predicting performance in a job or setting different from the one in which the test was validated. For example, a standardized test of managerial potential is found to be valid in selecting successful managers in a manufacturing industry. If the test is also helpful in choosing managers in a service organization, its validity has generalized from one organization to another. Similarly, validity generalization would exist if a test of clerical abilities is successful in selecting applicants for both secretarial and receptionist positions. Of course, the more similar the jobs and organizations involved in the validity studies are to the jobs and organizations that subsequently use the screening tests, the more likely it is that validity will generalize from one situation to another.

High validity generalization of a standardized test will greatly increase its usefulness—and reduce the workload of I/O psychologists—because the instrument may not need to be validated for use with each and every position and organization. Some I/O psychologists, such as Schmidt and his colleagues, argued that the validity generalization of most standardized employee screening procedures is quite high, which means that they can be used successfully in a variety of employment settings and job classifications (Schmidt & Hunter, 1977, 1981; Schmidt, Hunter, Outerbridge, & Trattner, 1986; Schmidt et al., 1993). At the other extreme is the view that the ability of tests to predict future job success is situation-specific, and validity should be established for each use of a screening instrument. Although few I/O psychologists believe that the validity of test instruments is completely situation-specific, there is some disagreement over how well their validity generalizes.

From an international perspective, some types of tests may generalize better across countries and cultures. For example, tests of cognitive abilities should be important for many jobs throughout the world, and evidence suggests they are less prone to cultural effects (Salgado, Anderson, Moscoso, Bertua, & de Fruyt, 2003), whereas personality tests, for example, may be more susceptible to cultural effects.

Test utility is the value of a screening test in helping to affect important organizational outcomes. In other words, test utility determines the success of a test in terms of dollars gained by the company through the increased performance and productivity of workers selected based on test scores. For example, in one organization a valid screening test was used to select applicants for 600 jobs as computer programmers (Schmidt, Hunter, McKenzie, & Muldrow, 1979). The estimated money gained in one year from the increased speed and efficiency of the chosen workers was more than $97 million. The initial cost of the screening tests was only $10 per applicant, a very good return on investment.

All in all, utility analyses of standardized employee testing programs indicate that such tests are usually cost effective. Hunter and Schmidt (1982)

validity generalization
the ability of a screening instrument to predict performance in a job or setting different from the one in which the test was validated

Stop & Review

Define five categories of employment tests.

test utility
the value of a screening test in determining important outcomes, such as dollars gained by the company through its use

went so far as to estimate that the U.S. gross national product would be increased by tens of billions of dollars per year if improved employee screening and selection procedures, including screening tests, were routinely implemented. Utility analyses allow the employer to determine the financial gains of a testing program and then compare them to the costs of developing and implementing the program.

Another important issue in testing is the importance of ethics in the administration and use of employment testing, including the protection of the privacy of persons being tested. I/O psychologists are very concerned about ethical issues in testing. In fact, the Society for Industrial and Organizational Psychology (SIOP) published a fourth edition of its *Principles* for the Validation and Use of Personnel Selection Procedures (SIOP, 2003). This publication outlines important ethical concerns for employment testing.

faking
purposely distorting one's responses to a test to try to "beat" the test

A final issue concerning testing is the issue of faking. Faking is trying to "beat" the test by distorting responses to the test in an effort to present oneself in a positive, socially desirable way. Faking is a particular concern for personality and integrity tests (Ryan & Sackett, 1987). Laypersons tend to believe that employment tests are easily faked, but this is not the case: First, many tests have subscales designed to determine if a test-taker is trying to fake the test. Second, it is often difficult for the test-taker to determine exactly which responses are the correct (desired) responses. Finally, there is evidence that personality and integrity tests are quite robust, still validly measuring their intended constructs even when test-takers are trying to fake (Furnham, 1997; Hough, 1998; Ones & Viswesvaren, 1998c).

ASSESSMENT CENTERS

assessment center
a detailed, structured evaluation of job applicants using a variety of instruments and techniques

One of the most detailed forms of employment screening and selection takes place in an assessment center, which offers a detailed, structured evaluation of applicants on a wide range of job-related knowledge, skills, and abilities. Specific managerial skills and characteristics an assessment center attempts to measure include oral and written communication skills, behavioral flexibility, creativity, tolerance of uncertainty, and skills in organization, planning, and decision making. Because a variety of instruments are used to assess participants, the assessment center often makes use of large test batteries. As we saw in Chapter 1, the assessment center approach was developed during World War II by the U.S. Office of Strategic Services (the forerunner of the CIA) for the selection of spies. Today, they are used primarily to select managers, but they are also being used extensively for managerial development purposes—to provide feedback to managers concerning their job performance–related strengths and weaknesses (Lievens & Klimoski, 2001; Thornton & Rupp, 2006). We will discuss this use of assessment centers in the chapter on employee training (Chapter 7).

In assessment centers, applicants are evaluated on a number of job-related variables using a variety of techniques, such as personality and ability tests that are considered to be valid predictors of managerial success. Applicants also

Instructions:

You are now Mr. C. D. Evans, Plant Superintendent of the East District in Division A of the Green Area of the Eastern Telephone Company. You have just arrived in your new job. Mr. I. W. Prior, your predecessor, died suddenly of a heart attack last Wednesday, March 28. You were notified Friday at 4 p.m. of your new appointment, but you could not get here until today, Sunday, April 1.

Today is your first day on your new job and here is what your secretary has left for you. Since it is Sunday, no one else is around and you cannot reach anyone on the telephone. You must leave in exactly three hours to catch a plane for an important meeting connected with your previous assignment...In the large envelope in front of you, you will find three packets. One contains an organization chart, a map of the district and the division, a copy of the management guide, and a copy of the union contract. The second packet contains the materials your secretary has left on your desk for your attention. These materials include letters, reports, memoranda, etc. Your secretary has attached materials from the files to some of the documents. The third packet contains... office forms, memo pads, pencils, and paper. You can use these materials to write letters, memos, notes to yourself, etc. (Bray, Campbell, & Grant, 1974, pp. 24–25)

The second packet on the hypothetical desk contained twenty-five problems that the participants had to address.

FIGURE 5.5
Example of an Assessment Center In-basket Exercise

take part in a number of situational exercises, which are attempts to approximate certain aspects of the managerial job. These exercises are related to work samples, except that they are approximations rather than actual examples of work tasks (see Howard, 1997; Streufert, Pogash, & Piasecki, 1988). Sometimes, these situational exercises are used independently in employment screening as a situational test (Weekley & Jones, 1997, 1999). Situational tests can be written, live tests, or be presented via video (Lievens & Sackett, 2006). One popular situational exercise is the in-basket test (Fredericksen, 1962), which requires the applicant to deal with a stack of memos, letters, and other materials that have supposedly collected in the "in-basket" of a manager (see Figure 5.5). The applicant is given some background information about the job and then must actually take care of the work in the in-basket by answering correspondence, preparing agendas for meetings, making decisions, and the like. A group of observers considers how each applicant deals with the various tasks and assigns a performance score. Despite the obvious "face validity" of the in-basket exercise, some research has been critical of the in-basket exercise as a selection tool (Schippman, Prien, & Katz, 1990). Much of the criticism, however, deals with the fact that in-basket exercises are difficult to score and interpret because they are attempting to assess a variety of complex skills and knowledge bases.

Another situational exercise is the leaderless group discussion (Bass, 1954). Here, applicants are put together in a small group to discuss some work-related

situational exercise assessment tools that require the performance of tasks that approximate actual work tasks

In the assessment center, applicants are assessed as they play the role of a marketing manager—writing memos, answering e-mail messages, making decisions—as part of a computerized in-basket exercise.

topic. The goal is to see how each applicant handles the situation and who emerges as a discussion leader. Other assessment center exercises might require the assessee to make a presentation, role-play an encounter with a supervisee, or engage in a team exercise with other assessees (Bobrow & Leonards, 1997). Trained observers rate each applicant's performance on each exercise. Because evaluation of assessment center exercises is made by human observers/assessors, to avoid systematic biases and to ensure that assessors are in agreement on ratings of assessees (in other words, that there is reliability in the ratings), training of assessors is critical (Lievens, 1998; Schleicher, Day, Mayes, & Riggio, 2002; Woehr & Arthur, 2003).

The result of testing at the assessment center is a very detailed profile of each applicant, as well as some index of how a particular applicant rated in comparison to others. Although research has indicated that assessment centers are relatively good predictors of managerial success (Gaugler, Rosenthal, Thornton, & Bentson, 1987; Hermelin, Lievens, & Robertson, 2007; Tziner, Ronen, & Hacohen, 1993), the reasons why assessment centers work are less clear (Kleinmann, 1993; Klimoski & Brickner, 1987). Of course, the major drawback is the huge investment of time and resources they require, which is the major reason that assessment centers are usually only used by larger organizations and for the selection of candidates for higher-level management positions. However, recent innovations using videotape and computerized assessment of participants has led to a recent renewal of interest in assessment centers, both in managerial selection and in other forms of evaluation (see box "Applying I/O Psychology").

APPLYING I/O PSYCHOLOGY

The Use of Assessment Center Methodology for Assessing Employability of College Graduates

Since the early 1990s, the use of assessment centers and assessment center methods has grown. There has been an increase in the use of assessment centers in managerial selection, and assessment centers are also being used as a means of training and "brushing up" managers' skills (Hollenbeck, 1990; Thornton & Rupp, 2006). Assessment center methods are also being expanded to facilitate screening and orientation of entry-level employees. In colleges and universities, assessment center methodologies are being used to evaluate new students or in outcome evaluation—measuring the managerial skills and potential "employability" of students as they graduate.

For instance, in one university's master's-level program in industrial/organizational psychology, first-year master's students are put through an assessment center evaluation, with second-year master's students serving as evaluators (Kottke & Schultz, 1997). This not only allows for an assessment of student skills, but also provides students with direct, hands-on experience with assessment. In another project, all graduates of a state university's business school underwent a "mini" assessment center, including completing a computerized in-basket test that assessed both managerial skills and skills in operating computer software, participation in a leaderless group discussion, mock hiring interview, and formal presentation (Riggio, Aguirre, Mayes, Belloli, & Kubiak, 1997; Riggio, Mayes, & Schleicher, 2003). The goal was to evaluate the "managerial potential" of business school graduates

and to track them during their early careers as a way of determining if the knowledge and skills measured in the assessment center are indeed predictive of future career success. A follow-up study did indeed demonstrate that college assessment center ratings of leadership potential correlated with later ratings of leadership made by the former college students' work supervisors (Schleicher et al., 2002). In another student assessment center, assessment center ratings were related to early career progress of the alumni (Waldman & Korbar, 2004).

Why the surge of interest in assessment centers? There are several reasons. First, the assessment center methodology makes sense. It offers a detailed, multimodal assessment of a wide range of knowledge, skills, abilities, and psychological characteristics. This is the test battery approach we discussed earlier. Second, much of the measurement in assessment centers is "performance based," and there is a trend in assessment away from pencil-and-paper assessment and toward more behavior- or performance-based assessment. Third, assessment centers are easier to conduct today. With computer and video technology, it is easy to conduct an assessment center and store the participants' performance data for later, more convenient, evaluation (Lievens, 2001). Finally, evidence indicates that assessment centers serve a dual purpose by assessing participants and also helping them to develop managerial skills by undergoing the assessment center exercises (Englebrecht & Fischer, 1995; Howard, 1997).

HIRING INTERVIEWS

To obtain almost any job in the United States, an applicant must go through at least one hiring interview, which is the most widely used employee screening and selection device. Despite its widespread use, if not conducted properly, the hiring interview can be a very poor predictor of future job performance (Arvey & Campion, 1982; Harris, 1989; Huffcutt & Arthur, 1994).

I/O psychologists have contributed greatly to our understanding of the effectiveness of interviews as a hiring tool. Care must be taken to ensure the reliability and validity of judgments of applicants made in hiring interviews (see box "Up Close"). Part of the problem with the validity of interviews is that many interviews are conducted haphazardly, with little structure to them

(Wright, Lichtenfels, & Pursell, 1989). You may have experienced one of these poor interviews that seemed to be nothing more than a casual conversation, or you may have been involved in a job interview in which the interviewer did nearly all of the talking. Although you might have learned a lot about the company, the interviewer learned little about your experience and qualifications. In these cases it is obvious that little concern has been given to the fact that, just like a psychological test, the hiring interview is actually a measurement tool and employment decisions derived from interviews should be held to the same standards of reliability, validity, and predictability as tests (Dipboye, 1989).

A number of variations on the traditional interview format have been developed to try to improve the effectiveness of interviews as a selection tool. One variation is the situational interview, which asks interviewees how they would deal with specific job-related, hypothetical situations (Dipboye, Wooten, & Halverson, 2004; Motowidlo, Dunnette, & Carter, 1990). Another variation has been referred to as the behavior description interview (Janz, 1982) or structured behavioral interview, which asks interviewees to draw on past job incidents and behaviors to deal with hypothetical future work situations (Motowidlo et al., 1992). A meta-analysis suggests that asking about past behaviors is better than asking about hypothetical situations (Taylor & Small, 2002), although the additional structure and focusing provided by these variations to traditional interviews are effective in improving the success of hiring interviews as selection devices (Maurer & Faye, 1988; Moscoso, 2000; Weekley & Gier, 1987).

There has been increased use of videoconference technology to conduct hiring interviews. This can be done either via a live videoconference or via a computer–video interface. I/O psychologists have only begun studying videoconference interviews. One interesting finding is that interviewers tend to

The hiring interview should maintain high standards of measurement, the same as other screening methods.

make more favorable evaluations of videoconference applicants than in face-to-face interviews, likely because there are some nonverbal cues, particularly cues that reveal anxiety and discomfort, absent in videoconference interviews (Chapman & Rowe, 2001).

When used correctly as part of an employee screening and selection program, the hiring interview should have three major objectives. First, the interview should be used to help fill in gaps in the information obtained from the applicant's resume and application form and from employment tests, and to measure the kinds of factors that are only available in a face-to-face encounter, such as poise and oral communication skills (Huffcutt, Conway, Roth, & Stone, 2001). Second, the hiring interview should provide applicants with realistic job previews, which help them decide whether they really want the job and offer an initial orientation to the organization (Rynes, 1989). Finally, because the hiring interview is one way that an organization interacts directly with a portion of the general public, it can serve an important public relations function for the company (Cascio, 1987, 2003).

There are serious concerns about the accuracy of judgments made from hiring interviews, because unlike screening tests or application forms, which ask for specific, quantifiable information, hiring interviews are typically more free-wheeling affairs (Lievens & DePaepe, 2004). Interviewers may ask completely different questions of different applicants, which makes it very difficult to compare responses. Although hiring interviews are supposed to be opportunities for gathering information about the applicant, at times the interviewer may do the majority of the talking. These interviews certainly yield very little information about the applicant and probably no valid assessment of the person's qualifications.

The reliability of interviewer judgments is also problematic. Different interviewers may arrive at completely different evaluations of the same applicant, even when evaluating the same interview (Arvey & Campion, 1982; Riggio & Throckmorton, 1988). Also, because of nervousness, fatigue, or some other reason, the same applicant might not perform as well in one interview as in another, which further contributes to low reliability.

Perhaps the greatest source of problems affecting hiring interview validity is interviewer biases. Interviewers may allow factors such as an applicant's gender, race, physical disability, physical attractiveness, appearance, or assertiveness to influence their judgments (Forsythe, Drake, & Cox, 1985; Gallois, Callan, & Palmer, 1992; Heilman & Saruwatari, 1979; Van Vianen & Van Schie, 1995; Wright & Multon, 1995). There may also be a tendency for an interviewer to make a snap judgment, arriving at an overall evaluation of the applicant in the first few moments of the interview. The interviewer may then spend the remainder of the time trying to confirm that first impression, selectively attending to only the information that is consistent with the initial evaluation. Another potential source of bias is the *contrast effect*, which can occur after the interview of a particularly good or bad applicant. All subsequent applicants may then be evaluated either very negatively or very positively in contrast to this person.

In general, the hiring interview may fail to predict job success accurately because of a mismatch between the selection instrument and the information

⏱ Stop *&* Review

Define and describe an assessment center.

snap judgment
arriving at a premature, early overall evaluation of an applicant in a hiring interview

"WHOEVER YOU ARE, YOU'RE HIRED."

One problem with hiring interviews is the tendency for interviewers to make snap decisions based on first impressions or limited information.

it obtains, and the requirements of most jobs. Receiving a positive evaluation in an interview is related to applicants' abilities to present themselves in a positive manner and to carry on a one-on-one conversation (Guion & Gibson, 1988; Hanson & Balestreri-Spero, 1985; Kacmar, Delery, & Ferris, 1992). In other words, evaluations of interviewees may be strongly affected by their level of communication or social skills. Therefore, for some jobs, such as those that involve primarily technical skills, performance in the interview is in no way related to performance on the job, because the types of skills required to do well in the interview are not the same as those required in the job. Researchers have also found a relationship between general cognitive ability and interview performance—suggesting that more intellectually gifted persons receive more positive interview evaluations (Huffcutt, Roth, & McDaniel, 1996). Despite this relationship, research suggests that interview performance from a well-conducted, structured interview can predict job performance above and beyond the effects of cognitive ability (Cortina, Goldstein, Payne, Davison, & Gilliland, 2000).

Stop & Review

Name and define four potential biases in hiring interviews.

UP CLOSE   How to Conduct More Effective Hiring Interviews

A great deal of research indicates that typical hiring interviews, although widely used, are not always effective predictors of job performance. There are, however, ways to improve their reliability and validity, some of which are outlined here:

Use structured interviews. Structured interviewing, in which the same basic questions are asked of all applicants, is nearly always more effective than unstructured interviewing, because it allows for comparisons among applicants (Campion, Palmer, & Campion, 1998; Dipboye, 1994; Wiesner & Cronshaw, 1988). The use of structured questions also helps prevent the interview from wandering off course and assists in keeping interview lengths consistent.

Make sure that interview questions are job related. Interview questions must be developed from a detailed job analysis to ensure that they are job related (Goodale, 1989). Some researchers have developed situational interview questions (Latham et al., 1980), which are derived from critical incidents job analysis techniques that ask applicants how they would behave in a given job situation. Evidence indicates that situational interviews predict job success more accurately than the traditional interview format (Latham, 1989; Latham & Saari, 1984).

Provide for some rating or scoring of applicant responses. To interpret the applicant responses objectively, it is important to develop some scoring system (Goodale, 1989; Graves & Karren, 1996). Experts could determine beforehand what would characterize good and poor answers. Another approach is to develop a scale for rating the quality of the responses. It may also be beneficial to make some record of responses to review later and to substantiate employment decisions rather than relying on memory. Huffcutt and Arthur (1994) emphasized that it is important that interviewers have both structured interview questions and structured criteria (e.g., rating scales) for evaluating applicants.

Limit prompting and follow-up questioning. These are prone to bias. The interviewer can lead the applicant to the "right" (or "wrong") response through follow-up questions (Campion et al., 1998).

Use trained interviewers. Interviewer training improves the quality of hiring interview decisions (Campion et al., 1998; Huffcutt & Woehr, 1999). There is also some evidence that interviewers may get better with experience (Arvey, Miller, Gould, & Burch, 1987). Interviewers can be instructed in proper procedures and techniques and trained to try to avoid systematic biases (Howard & Dailey, 1979). Training is also important because of the public relations function of hiring interviews (e.g., the interviewer is representing the organization to a segment of the public; Stevens, 1998).

Consider using panel or multiple interviews. Because of personal idiosyncrasies, any one interviewer's judgment of an applicant may be inaccurate. One way to increase interview reliability is to have a group of evaluators assembled in a panel (Arvey & Campion, 1982; Roth & Campion, 1992). Although panel interviews may improve reliability, they may still have validity problems if all interviewers are incorrect in their interpretations or share some biases or stereotypes. Also, the use of panel interviews is costly. Using multiple (separate) interviews is another way to increase the reliability of judgments made in hiring interviews (Conway, Jako, & Goodman, 1995). However, there is evidence that different interviewers may not share information adequately to come up with a good hiring decision (Dose, 2003).

Use the interview time efficiently. Many times, interviewers waste much of the time asking for information that was already obtained from the application form and resume. In one study it was found that previewing the applicant's written materials yielded more information in the hiring interview (Dipboye, Fontenelle, & Garner, 1984). However, information obtained from the written materials should not be allowed to bias the processing of information received during the interview (Dipboye, 1982).

One study used a highly structured interview with many of the preceding properties, including questions

UP CLOSE   (continued)

based on job analysis, consistent questions and struc-ture for all interviews, rating scales with examples and illustrations to assist in scoring answers, and an interview panel. The results indicated high agreement on decisions made by different interviewers on the same applicants, indicating good reliability of interview evaluations and good prediction of subsequent job performance of applicants hired for entry-level positions in a paper mill (Campion, Pursell, & Brown, 1988).

It is interesting to note that in a review of court cases involving allegations of discrimination in hiring, judges also valued good measurement properties in hiring inter-views—ruling more favorably for the organization if the interviews were objective, job related, structured, and based on multiple interviewers' evaluations (Williamson, Campion, Malos, Roehling, & Campion, 1997).

Monitor the effectiveness of interviews. A hiring interview needs to meet the same standards as any screen-ing instrument, such as an employment test. Therefore, it is very important to collect data on the effectiveness of hiring interview procedures to ensure that the interview process is indeed working (Graves & Karren, 1996).

Summary

The first step is the evaluation of written mate-rials such as applications and resumes. Basic background information can be translated into numerical values to compare the qualifications of applicants through the use of *weighted appli-cation forms.* Employee screening also involves methods such as references and letters of recom-mendation. However, the use of these methods is on the decline because they tend to be overly positive and are often uninformative.

The second step in screening is employee testing, which typically uses standardized instru-ments to measure characteristics that are pre-dictive of job performance. Any screening test or method must demonstrate that it is a reli-able and valid predictor of job performance. Three methods for establishing reliability are *test–retest reliability, parallel forms,* and *internal consistency.* The three forms of validity that are most important for the development and use of screening tests are *content validity,* or whether the test content adequately samples the knowl-edge, skills, and abilities required by the job, *construct validity,* which refers to whether a test measures what it is supposed to measure, and *criterion-related validity,* or the relationship between screening test scores and some criterion of job success.

Employee screening tests vary greatly both in their format and in the characteristics that they measure. Categories of such tests include *biodata* instruments, cognitive ability tests, mechanical ability tests, motor and sensory ability tests, job skills and knowledge tests, *per-sonality tests,* and miscellaneous instruments such as *integrity tests.* For the most part, the standardized tests are among the best predic-tors of job performance. Often they are used in combination—in *test batteries*— to help select the best qualified candidates. An important issue regarding the effectiveness of employee screen-ing tests is *validity generalization,* or a test's ability to predict job performance in settings different from the one in which it was validated. Another concern is *test utility,* an estimate of the dollars gained in increased productivity and efficiency because of the use of screening tests. *Faking* is trying to beat an employment test by distorting responses. *Assessment centers* use the test battery approach to offer a detailed, structured assess-ment of applicants' employment potential, most often for high-level managerial positions.

Employment screening for most jobs includes at least one hiring interview. Just like any other selection method, the interview is a measurement tool. Unfortunately, research indicates that the hiring interview, as it is typically used, generally has low levels of reliability and validity. Used correctly, the interview should help supply information that cannot be obtained from applications, resumes, or tests and should present the applicant with a realistic job preview. However, most interviews are not conducted with this in mind. One of the greatest sources of problems with hiring interviews stems from interviewer biases.

Study Questions and Exercises

1. Imagine that you were in charge of hiring new employees for a particular job that you are familiar with. Which screening methods would you choose, and why?

2. Search for a detailed job advertisement or a job description. What are the KSAOs that the job seems to require? Suggest which sorts of tests or other screening procedures might best measure the KSAOs associated with the job.

3. Consider the last job you applied for. What kinds of screening procedures did you encounter? What were their strengths and weaknesses? How could they have been improved?

4. It is clear that in much of the hiring that takes place, subjective evaluations of applicants are often the basis for the decisions. Why is this the case? What are some reasons that more objective—and more valid—hiring procedures are often ignored by employers?

Web Links

www.ipac.org

Site for the International Personnel Assessment Council, an organization devoted to personnel testing and assessment.

www.wonderlic.com

Test publisher sites where you can look at some of the employment tests available

www.cpp.com
http://www.siop.org/workplace/employment%20testing/testtypes.aspx

SIOP provides a list of categories of employment screening tests listing advantages and disadvantages of each type: http://www.siop.org/workplace/employment%20testing/testtypes.aspx

Suggested Readings

Farr, J. L., & Tippins, N. T. (Eds.). (2010). *Handbook of employee selection.* New York: Routledge. *A detailed and scholarly edited handbook on all aspects of employee selection. Good starting point for scholarly paper.*

Guion, R. M. (2011). *Assessment, measurement, and prediction for personnel decisions.* (2nd ed.). New York: Routledge. *An advanced-level textbook that provides a scholarly overview of issues in selection, with particular focus on legal and ethical issues.*

Society for Industrial and Organizational Psychology. (2003). *Principles for the validation and use of personnel selection procedures* (4th ed.). College Park, MD: Society for Industrial and Organizational Psychology. *This handbook is a statement of the principles, adopted by the Society for Industrial and Organizational Psychology, of "good practice in the choice, development, evaluation and use of personnel selection procedures."*

Inside Tips
EMPLOYEE PERFORMANCE: A CRITERION FOR SUCCESS

This chapter looks at how employees' job performance is measured and appraised in organizations. Often, measures of performance are the criteria used to determine the effectiveness of an employee testing or screening program as discussed in the previous chapter. Because job performance is such an important outcome variable in I/O psychology, it is important to understand the measurement issues concerning this factor. For example, when reviewing studies that discuss influences on job performance, you should investigate how performance was operationally defined and measured. Were objective or subjective criteria used? How accurate or inaccurate might the assessments of performance be? How can performance assessments and appraisals be improved?

Job Performance and Performance Appraisals

From the first few days on the job, you have wondered, "How am I doing?" Are you performing at an acceptable (or better) level? How are you performing in comparison to others in a similar position, or compared to what your supervisor expects? You wait for some assessment of your job performance, with a mixture of eager anticipation and trepidation.

The evaluation of employees' job performance is a vital personnel function and of critical importance to the organization. In this chapter, we will consider the very important variable of job performance in the context of assessments and evaluations. We will discuss the importance of performance appraisals, procedures for appraising performance, and the difficulties encountered in attempting to appraise performance. We will also look at research on performance appraisals and assessment and discuss the legal concerns in performance appraisals.

It is important to note, as we saw in Chapter 4, that the measurement of job performance serves as our criterion measure to determine if employee screening and selection procedures are working. In other words, by assessing new workers' performance at some point after they are hired, organizations can determine if the predictors of job performance do indeed predict success on the job. Measurement of performance is also important in determining the effectiveness of employee training programs as we will see in Chapter 7. In addition to training programs, performance assessments can also serve as a basis for evaluating the effectiveness of other organizational programs or changes, such as changes in work design or systems, supervisors, or working conditions.

In work organizations, measurement of performance typically takes place in the context of formalized performance appraisals, which measure worker performance in comparison to certain predetermined standards. Performance appraisals serve many purposes for the individual worker, for the worker's supervisor, and for the organization as a whole (Cleveland, Murphy, & Williams, 1989).

For the worker, performance appraisals are linked to career advancement. Performance appraisals function as the foundation for pay increases and promotions, provide feedback to help improve performance and recognize weaknesses, and offer information about the attainment of work goals. Work supervisors use

performance appraisals
the formalized means of assessing worker performance in comparison to certain established organizational standards

TABLE 6.1
The Many Purposes of Performance Appraisals

For the Worker:

means of reinforcement (praise, pay raises)
career advancement (promotions, increased responsibility)
information about work goal attainment
source of feedback to improve performance

For the Supervisor:

basis for making personnel decisions (promotions, firings, etc.)
assessment of workers' goal attainment
opportunity to provide constructive feedback to workers
opportunity to interact with subordinates

For the Organization:

assessment of productivity of individuals and work units
validation of personnel selection and placement methods
means for recognizing and motivating workers
source of information for personnel training needs
evaluation of the effectiveness of organizational interventions (e.g., training programs, system changes, etc.)

performance appraisals to make personnel decisions such as promotions, demotions, pay raises, and firings and to give workers constructive feedback to improve work performance. Moreover, the formal performance appraisal procedure facilitates organizational communication by helping to encourage interaction between workers and supervisors. Research has shown that employees who receive regular performance appraisals that are characterized as "helpful" to the performance of their job show stronger commitment to their jobs and organizations (Kuvaas, 2011). For the organization, performance appraisals provide a means of assessing the productivity of individuals and work units (see Table 6.1).

The Measurement of Job Performance

As we have seen, job performance is one of the most important work outcomes. It is the variable in organizations that is most often measured and that is given the most attention. This makes sense, because the success or failure of an organization depends on the performance of its employees.

There are many ways to measure job performance. Yet, as we saw in our discussion of personnel selection in Chapter 4, I/O psychologists typically refer to measures of job performance as performance criteria (Austin & Villanova, 1992). Performance criteria are the means of determining successful or unsuccessful performance. As we saw in Chapter 3, performance criteria are one of the products that arise from a detailed job analysis, for once the specific

performance criteria measures used to determine successful and unsuccessful job performance

elements of a job are known, it is easier to develop the means to assess levels of successful or unsuccessful performance.

OBJECTIVE VERSUS SUBJECTIVE PERFORMANCE CRITERIA

One important categorization of job performance assessments is to distinguish between objective and subjective measures of job performance. Objective and subjective performance criteria are also sometimes referred to as "hard" and "soft" performance criteria, respectively (Smith, 1976; Viswesvaran, 2001). Objective performance criteria involve the measurement of some easily quantifiable aspects of job performance, such as the number of units produced, the dollar amount of sales, or the time needed to process some information. For example, an objective criterion for an assembly-line worker might be the number of products assembled. For an insurance claims adjuster, the average amount of time it takes to process a claim might be an objective measure of performance (see Table 6.2). Such criteria are often referred to as measures of productivity.

Subjective performance criteria consist of judgments or ratings made by some knowledgeable individual, such as a worker's supervisor or coworker. These criteria are often used when objective criteria are unavailable, difficult to assess, or inappropriate. For example, it is usually inappropriate to use objective performance criteria to assess a manager's job, because it is

objective performance criteria

measures of job performance that are easily quantified

subjective performance criteria

measures of job performance that typically consist of ratings or judgments of performance

---

TABLE 6.2

Examples of Objective Job Performance Criteria

Job Title	Measure
Typist	Lines per week
Logger	Cords (of wood) cut; weight of wood legally hauled
Keypuncher	Number of characters; number of errors
Service representative	Errors in processing customer orders
Toll collector	Dollar accuracy; axle accuracy
Clerk	Errors per 100 documents checked; number of documents processed
Wood harvester	Number of cords delivered
Tree planter	Bags of tree seedlings planted
Skateboard maker	Number produced; number rejected
Sewing machine operator	Minutes per operation
Dentist	Errors in reading radiographs
Inspector	Errors detected in finished product
Tool/die maker	Dies produced
Helicopter pilot	Deviations from proper instrument readings
Bank teller	Number of shortages; number of overages
Air traffic controller	Speed of movement of aircraft through the system; correction of pilot error; errors in positioning aircraft for final approach; errors in aircraft separation

Source: Table from *The measurement of work performance: Methods, theory, and applications* by F. J. Landy and J. L. Farr. Copyright 1983, Elsevier Science (USA), reproduced with permission from the publisher.

difficult to specify the exact behaviors that indicate successful managerial performance. Instead subjective criteria, such as subordinate or superior ratings, are used.

Objective performance criteria offer two main advantages. First, because objective criteria typically involve counts of output or the timing of tasks, they are less prone to bias and distortion than subjective performance ratings. Second, objective criteria are usually more directly tied to "bottom-line" assessments of an organization's success, such as the number of products assembled or dollar sales figures. It is often more difficult to determine the links between subjective criteria and bottom-line outcomes.

Stop & Review
Describe nine purposes of performance appraisals.

As mentioned, it is often difficult, if not impossible, to obtain objective performance criteria for certain jobs, such as graphic artist, software developer, and executive vice president. Jobs such as these may best be assessed through ratings or judgments. Another drawback of objective assessments is that they may focus too much on specific, quantifiable outcomes. Because many jobs are complex, looking at only one or two objective measures of performance may not capture the total picture of performance. Some aspects of job performance such as work quality, worker initiative, and work effort are difficult to assess objectively. For example, a salesperson might have high dollar sales figures, but may be so pushy and manipulative that customers are unlikely to return to the store. Likewise, a research analyst may have relatively low output rates because he spends a great deal of time teaching new workers valuable work techniques and helping coworkers solve problems. It is important to emphasize that comprehensive evaluation of employee performance might include both very positive, outside-of-the-job-description activities, such as helping other workers, as well as counterproductive behaviors, such as "goofing off," substance abuse on the job, or disrupting the work team (Viswesvaran & Ones, 2000).

In many cases, collecting objective performance data is time consuming and costly (although see "On the Cutting Edge"). By contrast, subjective performance criteria are usually easy and relatively inexpensive to obtain and thus may be the preferred method of assessment for many organizations. Moreover, subjective performance criteria can be used to assess variables that could not be measured objectively, such as employee motivation or "team spirit."

Regardless of the criteria used to evaluate performance of a job, a number of important criterion concerns or issues have implications for conducting accurate performance appraisals (Bernardin & Beatty, 1984). A primary issue is whether the criteria identified in the job analysis relate to the true nature of the job. A particular concern here is criterion relevance: the notion that the means of appraising performance is indeed pertinent to job success, as identified in the job analysis. A performance appraisal should cover only the specific KSAOs needed to perform a job successfully. For example, the performance criteria for a bookkeeper should deal with knowledge of accounting procedures, mathematical skills, and producing work that is neat and error-free, not with personal appearance or oral communication skills—factors that are clearly not relevant to the effective performance of a bookkeeper's job. However, for a public relations representative, personal appearance and communication skills may be relevant performance criteria.

criterion relevance
the extent to which the means of appraising performance is pertinent to job success

ON THE *CUTTING* EDGE

The Boss Is Watching: Electronic Monitoring of Employee Performance

"Your call may be monitored in an effort to improve our customer service." How many times have you heard that when calling a helpline? Probably most of the time. Workers in call centers, as well as many employees who work on-line or on company computer networks, can have their performance monitored electronically. For example, employees in the collections department of a credit card company must maintain computerized records of phone calls, correspondence, and other activity for all accounts. The computerized monitoring system allows supervisors to note the number and length of calls to each account as well as the amount of money collected. Supervisors receive a detailed weekly report of employee computer activities that give a good indication of how the workers spent their time. A hard measure of employee performance is obtained from the amount of money collected from each account. Estimates are that about 80% of employers use some sort of electronic surveillance of employee performance (Alge, 2001).

Although electronic performance monitoring can lead to more objective assessments of employee performance, workers have raised certain objections. Some have argued that computer monitoring focuses only on those behaviors that are easily quantified, such as time engaged in a particular activity or dollar sales figures, but ignores measures of quality (Brewer & Ridgway, 1998). Another important consideration is the protection of employees'

rights to privacy (Ambrose, Alder, & Noel, 1998). There is some question as to when employer monitoring of work activities begins to infringe on the employees' freedom to conduct work activities in a manner they see fit (Chalykoff & Kochan, 1989; Zweig & Scott, 2007; Zweig & Webster, 2002). Another concern is whether employees view electronic monitoring as being a "fair" supervisory practice (McNall & Roch, 2009). A related problem is that employee creativity and innovation in work methods may be stifled if the workers know that work activities are being monitored.

Research has investigated the effects of computerized monitoring on employee performance with controlled experiments (e.g., Aiello & Kolb, 1995; Stanton & Barnes-Farrell, 1996; Stanton & Julian, 2002). Much of this research suggests that giving employees feedback about the performance monitoring and allowing workers a "voice" in the performance monitoring program through having workers participate in setting their performance goals alleviates many of the "negatives" associated with computerized monitoring (Ambrose & Alder, 2000; Nebeker & Tatum, 1993). In any case, computerized monitoring is here to stay and, as systems become more sophisticated, is likely to increase even more in the future. The challenge for I/O psychologists is to understand the effects of electronic performance monitoring on employees' behaviors, motivation, and satisfaction with the job and organization (Stanton, 2000).

A related concern is criterion contamination: the extent to which performance appraisals contain elements that detract from the accurate assessment of job effectiveness—elements that should not be included in the performance assessment. A common source of criterion contamination stems from appraiser biases. For example, a supervisor may give an employee an overly positive performance appraisal because the employee has a reputation of past work success or because the employee was a graduate of a prestigious university. Criterion contamination can also result from extraneous factors that contribute to a worker's apparent success or failure in a job. For instance, a sales manager may receive a poor performance appraisal because of low sales levels, even though the poor sales actually result from the fact that the manager supervises a young, inexperienced sales force.

criterion contamination
the extent to which performance appraisals contain elements that detract from the accurate assessment of job effectiveness

criterion deficiency
the degree to which a criterion falls short of measuring job performance

criterion usefulness
the extent to which a performance criterion is usable in appraising a particular job

It is unlikely that any criterion will capture job performance perfectly; every criterion of job performance may fall short of measuring performance to some extent. Criterion deficiency describes the degree to which a criterion falls short of measuring job performance perfectly. Criterion deficiency occurs when the measurement of the performance criteria is incomplete. An important goal of performance appraisals is to choose criteria that optimize the assessment of job success, thereby keeping criterion deficiency to a minimum.

A final concern is criterion usefulness, or the extent to which a performance criterion is usable in appraising a particular job in an organization. To be useful, a criterion should be relatively easy and cost effective to measure and should be seen as relevant by the appraiser, the employee whose performance is being appraised and the management of the organization.

SOURCES OF PERFORMANCE RATINGS

Stop & Review

Compare and contrast objective and subjective performance criteria and give examples of each.

Because performance ratings play such an important role in performance assessment in organizations, a great deal of personnel research has focused on the process and methods of rating performance. Before we examine the various methods of rating job performance, we need to consider who is doing the rating. In the vast majority of cases, it is the immediate supervisor who rates the performance of direct reports (Jacobs, 1986). However, performance appraisals can also be made by a worker's peers, by subordinates, by the worker himself/herself, or even by customers evaluating the performance of a service worker. The obvious advantage of getting these different perspectives on performance assessment is that each type of appraiser—supervisor, self, peer, subordinate, and customer—may see a different aspect of the worker's performance and thus may offer unique perspectives (Conway, Lombardo, & Sanders, 2001). Moreover, multiple-perspective performance appraisals can have increased reliability (there are more raters evaluating the same performance behaviors) and an increased sense of fairness and greater acceptance by the worker being evaluated (Harris & Schaubroeck, 1988).

Supervisor appraisals

By far, most performance appraisals are performed by supervisors. In fact, conducting regular appraisals of employee performance is considered one of the most important supervisory functions. Supervisor performance appraisals are so common because supervisors are usually quite knowledgeable about the job requirements, are often in a position to provide rewards for effective performance (and suggestions for improvement for substandard performance), and typically have a great deal of contact with supervisees. This is probably why research has consistently demonstrated that supervisory ratings have higher reliability than either peer or subordinate ratings of performance (Viswesvaran, Ones, & Schmidt, 1996). In addition, the test-retest reliability of supervisor ratings is quite high (Salgado, Moscoso, & Lado, 2003). Still, supervisors may have a limited perspective on employees' performance, so in addition to supervisor appraisals, other organizational member appraisals are important.

How would the performance of this artisan best be assessed?

Self-appraisals

Self-appraisals of performance have been used by many companies, usually in conjunction with supervisor appraisals. Although there is evidence that self-appraisals correlate slightly with supervisor performance appraisals, self-appraisals tend to be more lenient and focus more on effort exerted rather than on performance accomplishments (Heidemeier & Moser, 2009; Wohlers, Hall, & London, 1993; Wohlers & London, 1989). Quite often, there are large discrepancies between how supervisors rate performance and the worker's self-rating (Furnham & Stringfield, 1994). It has been suggested that part of the discrepancy between self- and supervisor appraisals can be overcome if both the worker and the supervisor are thoroughly trained to understand how the performance rating system works (Schrader & Steiner, 1996; Williams & Levy, 1992) and when workers receive more frequent, regular performance feedback from supervisors (Williams & Johnson, 2000). One advantage of appraisal discrepancies, however, may be that they highlight differences in supervisor and worker perceptions and can lead to an open dialogue between supervisor and supervisee (Campbell & Lee, 1988). Self-appraisals of performance are also useful in encouraging workers to be more committed to performance-related goals (Riggio & Cole, 1992).

Although studies of U.S. workers have found that self-appraisals tend to be more lenient than supervisor performance ratings, a study of Chinese workers found that their appraisals showed a "modesty bias." That is, Chinese workers gave themselves lower ratings of job performance than did their supervisors (Farh, Dobbins, & Cheng, 1991). This may also occur in other countries and cultures where employees are less "self-oriented" than Americans (Barron & Sackett, 2008; Korsgaard, Meglino, & Lester, 2004). In comparison to U.S. workers, the self-appraisals of Chinese workers were substantially lower on average, indicating that the accuracy of self-appraisals and their discrepancy from supervisor ratings may need to be evaluated with culture taken into account.

Peer appraisals

Although once rare, the use of peer ratings of performance is on the rise (Dierdorff & Surface, 2007). Research evidence indicates that there is good agreement between performance ratings made by peers and those made by supervisors (Conway & Huffcutt, 1996; Harris & Schaubroeck, 1988; Vance, MacCallum, Coovert, & Hedge, 1988). This makes sense because both supervisors and peers have the opportunity to directly observe workers on the job. One obvious problem with peer ratings of performance is the potential for conflict among employees who are evaluating each other, a particular problem when peers are competing for scarce job rewards (DeNisi, Randolph, & Blencoe, 1983; McEvoy & Buller, 1987).

With the increased emphasis on coordinated work teams, peer appraisals of performance may be of greater importance now and in the future. We will consider team performance appraisals in depth later in this chapter. Moreover, research shows that supervisors tend to give some weight to peer appraisals and will incorporate them into their own supervisory appraisals (Makiney & Levy, 1997).

Stop & Review

Define four important criterion concerns in performance appraisals.

Subordinate appraisals

Subordinate ratings are most commonly used to assess the effectiveness of persons in supervisory or leadership positions. Research on subordinate appraisals indicates considerable agreement with supervisor ratings (Mount, 1984; Riggio & Cole, 1992). Subordinate ratings may be particularly important because they provide a different, meaningful perspective on a supervisor's performance—the perspective of the persons being supervised—and because there is evidence that ratings of supervisors may be associated with subordinate job satisfaction. Importantly, a meta-analysis demonstrated that both subordinate and peer ratings of performance correlated significantly with objective measures of job performance (Conway et al., 2001).

In general, supervisors and managers have been found to support the use of subordinate appraisals. In one study, it was found that supervisors were supportive of subordinate appraisals as a useful and positive source of data, except in situations when they are used as a basis for determining salary (Bernardin, Dahmus, & Redmon, 1993). The most positive attitudes expressed toward subordinate appraisals were from supervisory employees who received appraisal feedback from both subordinates and supervisors at the same time. Attitudes toward the use of subordinate appraisals were less positive and more cautious, however, when subordinate appraisal feedback was given to supervisors with no other sources of appraisal data. More recently, it was found that supervisors who discussed the ratings with their direct reports improved their performance more than supervisors who did not discuss the feedback with supervisees (Walker & Smither, 1999). Thus, these findings suggest that how subordinate appraisals are used influences their effectiveness.

Customer appraisals

Another form of performance rating for employees working in customer service positions is ratings made by customers. Although customer ratings are not usually considered a method of performance appraisal, they can offer an interesting perspective on whether certain types of workers (salespersons, waitpersons, telephone operators) are doing a good job. Customer evaluations of an individual employee's performance are most appropriate when the employee and customer have a significant, ongoing relationship, such as customers evaluating a supplier, a sales representative, a real estate agent, a stockbroker, or the like. Interestingly, there is evidence that organizations that strongly encourage customer service, and those that train their employees in customer service delivery, tend to receive more favorable evaluations from customers (Johnson, 1996; Schneider & Bowen, 1995).

360-degree feedback

360-degree feedback
a method of gathering performance appraisals from a worker's supervisors, subordinates, peers, customers, and other relevant parties

A comprehensive form of performance appraisal gathers ratings from all levels in what is commonly called 360-degree feedback (London & Beatty, 1993; Waldman, Atwater, & Antonioni, 1998). In 360-degree feedback programs (sometimes referred to as multi-rater feedback), performance ratings are gathered from supervisors, subordinates, peers, customers, and suppliers (if applicable). The obvious advantages of 360-degree feedback include improved reliability of measurement because of the multiple evaluations, the inclusion of more diverse perspectives on the employee's performance, the involvement of more organizational members in the evaluation and feedback process, and improved organizational communication. Although 360-degree feedback programs may have distinct advantages, including enhanced development and improved performance of employees (London & Smither, 1995; Tornow, 1993), the costs of such detailed assessments of worker performance may be prohibitive. In addition, there have been calls for more research to demonstrate the advantages of 360-degree evaluations over less comprehensive and costly performance appraisal programs (Borman, 1998; Dunnette, 1993; Greguras & Robie, 1997). Recent research has also suggested that there may be cultural differences in how employees are rated by others, so multi-rater systems may yield different results in different countries or cultures (Eckert, Ekelund, Gentry, & Dawson, 2010).

For the most part, 360-degree feedback programs are being used as a management development tool, rather than being used only as a performance appraisal system. Therefore, we will discuss 360-degree feedback more fully in the next chapter on employee training.

Methods of Rating Performance

When it comes to subjectively evaluating employee performance, a variety of rating methods can be used. We will review some of the more common methods. These methods can be classified into two general categories, those that can be termed "comparative methods" and those that can be labeled "individual methods."

COMPARATIVE METHODS

Comparative methods of performance appraisal involve some form of comparison of one worker's performance with the performance of others. These procedures are relatively easy to implement in work organizations and include *rankings*, *paired comparisons*, and *forced distributions*.

Rankings

The comparative method of rankings requires supervisors to rank their direct reports from best to worst on specific performance dimensions, or to give an overall comparative ranking on job performance. Although this is a simple and easy technique that supervisors are not likely to find difficult or time consuming, it has several limitations. First, although ranking separates the best workers from the worst, there are no absolute standards of performance. This is a problem if few or none of the entire group of workers are performing at "acceptable" levels. In this case, being ranked 2nd or 3rd in a group of 15 is misleading,

comparative methods
performance appraisal methods involving comparisons of one worker's performance against that of other workers

rankings
performance appraisal methods involving the ranking of supervisees from best to worst

because even the highest-ranking workers are performing at substandard levels. Conversely, in a group of exceptional workers, those ranked low may actually be outstanding performers in comparison to other employees in the organization or workers in other companies.

Paired comparisons

paired comparison
performance appraisal method in which the rater compares each worker with each other worker in the group

Another comparative method of performance appraisal uses paired comparisons, in which the rater compares each worker with every other worker in the group and then simply has to decide who is the better performer. Of course, this technique becomes unwieldy when the number of group members being evaluated becomes large (for instance, there are 6 possible paired comparisons for a group of 4 workers, but 28 paired comparisons for a 7-member group). Each person's final rank consists of the number of times that individual was chosen as the better of a pair. The drawbacks of this technique are similar to those of the ranking method. However, both these comparative techniques have the advantage of being simple to use and of being applicable to a variety of jobs. One possible use for this technique might be to decide which team member(s) to eliminate when downsizing.

Forced distributions

forced distributions
assigning workers to established categories of poor to good performance with fixed limitations on how many employees can be assigned to each category

In the comparative method known as forced distributions, the rater assigns workers to established categories ranging from poor to outstanding on the basis of comparison with all other workers in the group. Usually, the percentage of employees who can be assigned to any particular category is controlled to obtain a fixed distribution of workers along the performance dimension. Most often the distribution is set up to represent a normal distribution (see Figure 6.1). This forced distribution evaluation technique is similar to the procedure used by an instructor who grades on a so-called "normal curve," with preassigned percentages of A, B, C, D, and F grades. One large U.S. company established a policy of placing all employees in a performance distribution with the bottom 10% of performers fired each year in an effort to continually upgrade the performance level of the entire workforce.

One possible problem with the forced distribution occurs when there is an abundance of either very good or very poor workers in a supervisor's work group. This can create a situation where a supervisor might artificially raise or lower some employees' evaluations to fit them into the predetermined distribution.

Information comparing the performance of one employee to that of others can be used in conjunction with other performance appraisal methods. For example, a study by Farh and Dobbins (1989) found that when subordinates were presented with information comparing their job performance with that of their peers, their self-ratings of performance were more accurate and there was greater agreement between self-appraisals and appraisals made by supervisors. Thus, although comparative methods may sometimes yield misleading results, the use of comparative information may increase the accuracy and quality of self-appraisals of performance.

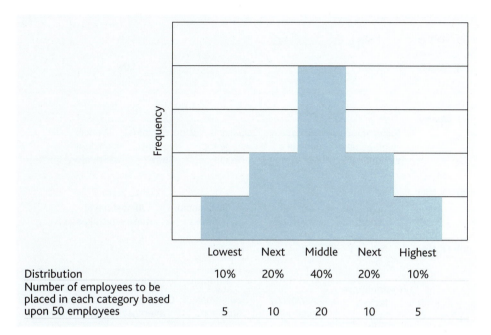

	Lowest	Next	Middle	Next	Highest
Distribution	10%	20%	40%	20%	10%
Number of employees to be placed in each category based upon 50 employees	5	10	20	10	5

FIGURE 6.1
A Forced Distribution Performance Rating Using Five Categories with a Sample of 50 Employees

INDIVIDUAL METHODS

It is more common for employees to be evaluated using what could be termed "individual methods." Individual methods involve evaluating an employee by himself/herself. However, even though ratings are made individually, appraisals using individual methods may still make comparisons of one individual employee's rating with individual ratings of other employees. We will begin our discussion of individual methods with the most widely used method of performance rating: graphic rating scales.

individual methods
performance appraisal methods that evaluate an employee by himself or herself, without explicit reference to other workers

Graphic rating scales

The vast majority of performance appraisals use graphic rating scales, which offer predetermined scales to rate the worker on a number of important aspects of the job, such as quality of work, dependability, and ability to get along with coworkers. A graphic rating scale typically has a number of points with either numerical or verbal labels, or both. The verbal labels can be simple, one-word descriptors, or they can be quite lengthy and specific (see Figure 6.2). Some graphic rating scales use only verbal endpoints, or anchors, with numbered rating points between the two anchors.

When graphic rating scales are used in performance assessment, appraisals are usually made on anywhere from 7 to 12 key job dimensions, which are derived from the job analysis. Better graphic rating scales define the dimensions and the particular rating categories very clearly and precisely. In other words, it

graphic rating scales
performance appraisal methods using a predetermined scale to rate the worker on important job dimensions

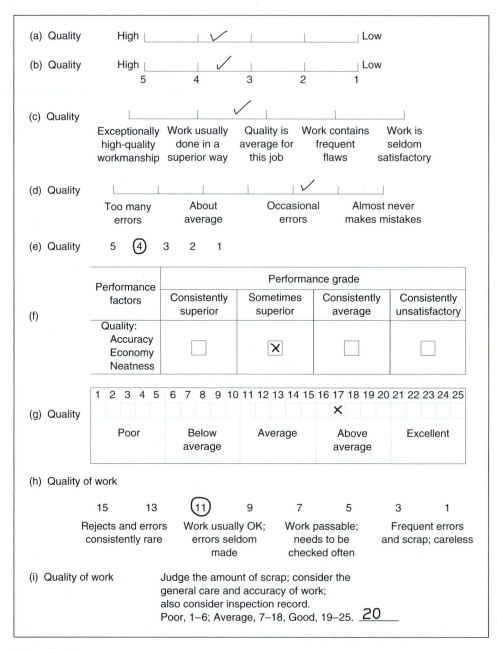

FIGURE 6.2
Examples of Graphic Rating Scale
Source: Guion, R. M. (1965). *Personnel testing.* New York: McGraw-Hill.

is important that the rater know exactly what aspect of the job is being rated and what the verbal labels mean. For instance, in Figure 6.2 examples *f* and *i* define the job dimension, whereas example *h* defines the rating categories.

Although good graphic rating scales take some time to develop, often the same basic scales can be used for a number of different jobs by simply switching the relevant job dimensions. However, a common mistake made by many organizations is attempting to develop a "generic" set of performance rating scales for use with all persons and all jobs within the company. Because the relevant job dimensions change drastically from job to job, it is critical that the dimensions being rated are those that actually assess performance of the particular job. The major weakness of graphic rating scales is that they may be prone to certain biased response patterns, such as the tendency to give everyone "good" or "average" ratings. Also, limiting ratings to only a few job dimensions may constrain the appraiser and may not produce a total picture of the worker's job performance.

Behaviorally anchored rating scales

An outgrowth of the critical incidents method of job analysis is the development of behaviorally anchored rating scales (BARS), which attempt to clearly define the scale labels and anchors used in performance ratings (Smith & Kendall, 1963). Rather than having scale labels such as poor, average, or good, BARS have examples of behavioral incidents that reflect poor, average, and good performance in relation to a specific dimension.

behaviorally anchored rating scales (BARS) performance appraisal technique using rating scales with labels reflecting examples of poor, average, and good behavioral incidents

Figure 6.3 presents a behaviorally anchored rating scale for appraising the job of Navy recruiter on the dimension of salesmanship skills. Note first the very detailed definition of the job dimension at the top of the scale. On the left are the rating points ranging from 8 to 1. The verbal descriptors to the right of each category give examples of behavioral incidents that would differentiate a recruiter's sales skills, from highest levels to lowest.

As you might imagine, the development of BARS is a lengthy and tedious process. The result, however, is a rating instrument that focuses clearly on performance behaviors relevant to a particular job. An appraiser is forced to spend a great deal of time just thinking about what adequate or inadequate performance of a certain job dimension entails, particularly if the rater had a hand in developing the scale. This increased attention to job behaviors helps to overcome some of the general biases and stereotyping that may occur in other performance ratings, for a worker cannot be summarily judged without consideration of how the person's past behavior supports the rating.

Behavioral observation scales

A performance assessment technique related to the BARS is behavioral observation scales (BOS). With this method, raters indicate how often the worker has been observed performing key work-related behaviors (Latham & Wexley, 1977). Whereas BARS focus on expectations that a worker would be able to perform specific behaviors that are typical of certain performance levels, behavioral observation scales concentrate on critical behaviors that were actually performed. Bear in mind that behavioral observation scales do not involve the direct observation and assessment of performance behaviors, but rather the recollections of the observers, who may be biased or selective in

behavioral observation scales (BOS) performance appraisal methods that require appraisers to recall how often a worker has been observed performing key work behaviors

Job: Navy Recruiter
Job dimension: Salesmanship skills

Skillfully persuading prospects to join the Navy, using Navy benefits and opportunities effectively to sell the Navy; closing skills; adapting selling techniques appropriately to different prospects; effectively overcoming objections to joining the Navy.

8 A prospect stated he wanted the nuclear power program or he would not sign up. When he did not qualify, the recruiter did not give up; instead, he talked the young man into electronics by emphasizing the technical training he would receive.

7 The recruiter treats objections to join the Navy seriously; he works hard to counter the objections with relevant, positive arguments for a Navy career.

6 When talking to a high school senior, the recruiter mentions names of other seniors from that school who have already enlisted.

5 When an applicant qualifies for only one program, the recruiter tries to convey to the applicant that it is a desirable program.

4 When a prospect is deciding on which service to enlist in, the recruiter tries to sell the Navy by describing Navy life at sea and adventures in port.

3 During an interview, the recruiter said to the applicant, "I'll try to get you the school you want, but frankly it probably won't be open for another three months, so why don't you take your second choice and leave now."

2 The recruiter insisted on showing more brochures and films even though the applicant told him he wanted to sign up right now.

1 When a prospect states an objection to being in the Navy, the recruiter ends the conversation because he thinks the prospect must not be interested.

FIGURE 6.3

A Behaviorally Anchored Rating Scale (BARS)

Source: Borman, W. C. (1987). Behavior-based rating scales. In R. A. Berk (Ed.), *Performance assessment: Methods and applications* (p. 103). Baltimore: The Johns Hopkins University Press.

what they remember. Studies have compared behavioral observation scale and graphic rating scale assessments of performance and showed that employees preferred the BOS method (Tziner, Joanis, & Murphy, 2000; Tziner, Kopelman, & Joanis, 1997).

Checklists

checklists

performance appraisal methods using a series of statements about job performance

Another individual method of performance rating is the use of checklists, which consist of a series of statements about performance in a particular job. The statements are derived from a job analysis and can reflect either positive or negative aspects of performance (see Figure 6.4). The rater's task is to check off the statements that apply to the worker being evaluated. Each of the statements is given a numerical value reflecting the degree of effective performance associated with it. The numerical values assigned to the checked items are then summed to give an overall appraisal of the worker's performance.

A variation of checklist rating is the forced-choice scale, developed in an attempt to overcome the rater's tendency to give generally positive or negative performance appraisals. While using the forced-choice technique, the rater is unaware of how positive an appraisal is being made. This format presents

Instructions: Below you will find a list of behavioral items. Read each item and decide whether it describes the person being evaluated. If you feel the item does describe the person, place a check mark in the space provided. If the item does not describe the person, leave the space next to the item blank.

1   Regularly sets vague and unrealistic program goals
2   Is concerned only with the immediate problems of the day and sees very little beyond the day-to-day
3   Develops work schedules that allow for completion of projects provided no major problems are encountered
4   Is aware of needs and trends in area of responsibility and plans accordingly
5   Follows up on projects to ensure that intermediate goals are achieved
6   Looks for new markets and studies potential declines in current markets
7   Anticipates and plans for replacement of key personnel in the event of corporate relocation

FIGURE 6.4

A Checklist Rating Scale for a Project Manager

Source: Jacobs, R. R. (1987). Numerical rating scales. In R. A. Berk (Ed.), *Performance assessments: Methods and applications* (pp. 82–99). Baltimore: The Johns Hopkins University Press.

Note: This is only a portion of the checklist. Scores are derived based on the number of items checked and the scale values of those items.

groups of descriptive statements from which the rater must select the one that is either most or least descriptive of the worker. The statements carry different values that are later added to form the overall performance appraisal.

Although checklists are easy to use and provide detailed appraisals of performance that are focused on job-related behaviors, they do have some drawbacks. The development of such techniques is expensive and time consuming, requiring the generation of applicable work-related statements and the assignment of accurate performance values. Also, checklists may limit the focus of a performance appraisal, because the rater must choose among a finite set of statements that might not capture all aspects of an individual's performance of a particular job.

Narratives

A relatively simple form of individual performance evaluation is the use of narratives, which are open-ended, written accounts of the worker's performance or listings of specific examples of performance strengths and weaknesses. The advantage of narratives is that appraisers have the freedom to describe performance in their own words and to emphasize elements that they feel are important. Their major drawback is that they offer no quantification of performance, which makes it very difficult to compare workers' performance. An additional problem with narratives is that the worker may misinterpret the meaning of the report. For example, an appraiser may write that the worker is doing a "fair job," meaning that some improvement is needed, but the worker may interpret the word "fair" to mean "adequate" or "good," and may thus believe that no improvement is necessary.

Stop & Review

List and define three comparative methods of performance appraisal.

narratives
open-ended written accounts of a worker's performance used in performance appraisals

We have seen that there are quite a number of methods for rating employee job performance, but what works best? All forms of ratings suffer from the same limitation: They are subjective, and thus prone to the unique perspective and biases of the person doing the rating. No one method of rating performance has emerged as superior to the others. However, a key issue is the focus of the rater's attention on actual job performance (see DeNisi & Peters, 1996). Therefore, methods that focus raters on performance-related job behaviors—the BARS and BOS methods—should theoretically improve rater accuracy.

Problems and Pitfalls in Performance Appraisals

Despite the various performance appraisal tools designed to help obtain more objective assessments, the appraisal evaluation process remains very subjective. Because appraisers selectively observe on-the-job performance and rate what they believe to be an individual's performance level, their judgments are prone to a number of systematic biases and distortions. A great deal of research has helped uncover some of these problems. Understanding these potential errors in the performance appraisal process can make it easier to develop the means to combat them and to produce better appraisals of work performance. We will consider several types of such systematic problems, including leniency/severity errors, halo effects, recency effects, causal attribution errors, and personal biases.

Leniency/severity errors

leniency error
the tendency to give all workers very positive performance appraisals

A leniency error in performance ratings occurs when an appraiser tends to judge all workers leniently, routinely giving them very positive appraisals (Hauenstein, 1992). A severity error is the exact opposite and arises when an appraiser tends to rate employees on the low end of performance scales, giving generally negative appraisals. For the rater making a severity error, no performance ever seems good enough. There is also a central tendency error, whereby the appraiser tends always to use the midpoint of the rating scale. All three of these errors lead to the same problem: a short-circuiting of the appraisal process because the rater's tendency to use only one area of the performance scale does not actually discriminate among poor, fair, and outstanding workers (Houston, Raymond, & Svec, 1991). In statistical terms, the ratings show little variance. As shown, some techniques, such as the various comparative methods, help combat such response tendency errors.

severity error
the tendency to give all workers very negative performance appraisals

central tendency error
the tendency to give all workers the midpoint rating in performance appraisals

Halo effects

halo effect
an overall positive evaluation of a worker based on one known positive characteristic or action

A halo effect in performance appraisal occurs when appraisers make overall positive appraisals of workers on the basis of one known positive characteristic or action (Nisbett & Wilson, 1977; Viswesvaran, Schmidt, & Ones, 2005). If a particular worker did an outstanding job on a particular task, the supervisor assumes that all of this person's work is also outstanding, regardless of whether it really is. Certain personal characteristics such as physical attractiveness or

Using multiple evaluators increases the reliability of performance ratings.

being labeled a "rising star" may also lead to halo effects (Landy & Sigall, 1974). Research indicates that halo effects occur because raters use the one salient characteristic as the basis for forming an overall, generally positive or negative, impression of the worker's performance (Lance, LaPointe, & Fisicaro, 1994). There is also a "reverse" halo effect, sometimes called the "rusty halo" or "horns" effect (Baron, 1986), in which an overall negative performance appraisal is made on the basis of one instance of failure or one negative characteristic.

Because halo effects are such a common source of bias in performance appraisals, a number of rater training programs have been developed to try to control for them (Ivancevich, 1979; McIntyre, Smith, & Hassett, 1984; Pulakos, 1984). Many of these training programs involve simply making raters more aware of the phenomenon of halo effects and helping them to focus on behavioral dimensions of job performance.

Recency effects

Another potential error in performance appraisals is the tendency to give greater weight to recent performance and lesser value to earlier performance; this can be referred to as the recency effect. Because performance assessments usually rely on the appraiser's memory of a worker's past performance, there are bound to be problems related to accurate recall. In general, the greater the delay between the performance and the appraisal of work behaviors, the less accurate the appraisal will be (Heneman & Wexley, 1983; Murphy & Balzer, 1986). The lesser value given to earlier performance because of the recency effect may not always be detrimental to accurate performance appraisals, however. Earlier performance by a relatively new employee may reflect the

recency effect
the tendency to give greater weight to recent performance and lesser weight to earlier performance

employee's learning period, where mistakes may be more numerous, whereas later performance may reflect the employee's performance once he or she has more completely learned about the job.

Causal attribution errors

causal attribution
the process by which people assign cause to events or behaviors

The process by which people ascribe cause to events or behaviors is known as causal attribution. Research has uncovered a number of systematic biases in causal attribution that have important implications for the accuracy of performance appraisals. Two of these attributional biases are particularly relevant to performance appraisals. The first is the tendency for appraisers to give more extreme appraisals if they believe that the cause of a worker's performance is rooted in effort rather than ability (Knowlton & Mitchell, 1980; Struthers, Wiener, & Allred, 1998). That is, if an appraiser feels that particularly high levels of performance were the result of great effort on the part of a worker, that worker will receive a more positive performance appraisal than one whose high levels of performance were perceived as resulting from possession of natural ability or talent. Similarly, a performance failure due to a lack of sufficient effort will be judged more harshly than a failure believed to be caused by lack of ability.

actor–observer bias
the tendency for observers to overattribute cause to characteristics of the actor and the tendency for the actor to overattribute cause to situational characteristics

The second pertinent bias in causal attribution is called the actor–observer bias (Jones & Nisbett, 1972). This bias is founded in the notion that in any event there is an actor—the person performing a behavior—and an observer—the person watching and appraising the event and the actor's behavior. In performance appraisals the worker is the actor and the appraiser is the observer. The bias in causal attribution occurs when the actor and observer are each asked to state the cause of the particular event. In the case of performance appraisals, the event could be a particularly successful or unsuccessful work outcome. The actor tends to overemphasize the role that situational factors, such as luck, task difficulty, and the work environment, played in the result. In contrast, the observer has a tendency to attribute cause to dispositional factors, or personal characteristics of the actor such as ability, effort, and personality. This means that the performance appraiser tends to believe that performance is due primarily to qualities in the worker and tends to neglect the role that situational factors played in the performance outcome. Therefore, in certain situations of poor work performance, the supervisor may blame the worker, when the failure was actually due to circumstances beyond the control of the worker. On the other side, the worker is prone to overemphasizing situational factors and, in cases of failure, will try to lay the blame elsewhere, for example, by faulting the working conditions or coworkers. The actor–observer bias not only leads to inaccurate perceptions of work performance but is also one of the main reasons that supervisors and supervisees do not always see eye to eye when it comes to performance appraisals (see "Applying I/O Psychology"). Interestingly, in one study it was found that actors, but not observers, were aware of the actor–observer bias in specific rating situations, suggesting that workers may realize that supervisors are being biased, but may not be able to make their supervisors aware of it (Krueger, Ham, & Linford, 1996).

Personal biases

In addition to the biases and errors that can afflict any appraiser of work performance, the personal biases of any particular appraiser can also distort the accuracy of assessments. The most common personal biases are those based on the worker's sex, race, age, and physical characteristics, including disabilities (Kraiger & Ford, 1985; Stauffer & Buckley, 2005; Wilson, 2010; Woehr & Roch, 1996). It even has been found that pregnancy can be a source of negative bias in performance appraisals (Halpert, Wilson, & Hickman, 1993). It is no secret that women, ethnic minorities, older people, and people with disabilities are sometimes discriminated against in performance appraisals, despite legislation specifically designed to ensure fairness. However, reviews of research on racial and gender bias in performance appraisal concluded that such bias may be less of a problem than commonly believed (Arvey & Murphy, 1998; Bowen, Swim, & Jacobs, 2000). On the other hand, having a close personal relationship with a supervisee, or mere liking for that individual over others, could bias appraisals in a favorable direction (Lefkowitz, 2000).

There is also evidence that certain types of individuals are more prone to bias in performance appraisals. For example, in an interesting review of research, it was found that supervisors who have high levels of power over those they are evaluating tended to make more negative performance evaluations than supervisors who did not have as much power over supervisees (Georgesen & Harris, 1998). One explanation is that powerful individuals attend more to negative stereotypic information about their subordinates, such as being particularly harsh in an evaluation when an inexperienced, young worker makes a mistake (Rodriguez-Bailon, Moya, & Yzerbyt, 2000).

Certain personal biases may be deeply ingrained in individuals and are therefore difficult to overcome. As with other biases, one way to deal with personal biases is to make appraisers more aware of them. Because discrimination in personnel procedures has been outlawed through federal civil rights legislation, most organizations and managers are on the lookout to prevent such biases from leading to discrimination. Ironically, programs designed to protect against personal biases and subsequent discrimination may lead to instances of reverse discrimination, a bias toward favoring a member of a particular underrepresented group over members of the majority group.

Cross-Cultural and International Issues

The individual focus of performance appraisals, where a single worker is the focus of the evaluation, is, in many ways, a Western/U.S. view of evaluating performance (Fletcher & Perry, 2001). In many non-U.S. cultures, the focus is on the work group, or collective, instead of on individual performance. For instance, Japanese and Russian workers may prefer receiving performance feedback at the group, rather than the individual, level (Elenkov, 1998; Erez, 1994). There may also be cultural norms regarding how direct and "blunt" feedback can be (Fletcher & Perry, 2001). Because of the personal nature of traditional performance appraisals, it is important that cultural norms and expectations be considered in the development and delivery of a performance appraisal system.

Stop & Review

Describe five sources or types of error/ bias in performance appraisals.

APPLYING I/O PSYCHOLOGY

Combating the Actor–Observer Bias in Performance Appraisals

The actor–observer bias, or the tendency for actors to make situational attributions and for observers to make dispositional attributions, is a particular problem in performance appraisals that can lead to inaccurate assessments and cause rifts between the evaluating supervisor and subordinates. How can this bias be overcome?

One way to try to combat this problem is to create performance rating forms that require the evaluator to take into account the various situational factors that may have hampered the employee's performance (Bernardin, Hagan, Kane, & Villanova, 1998). Although this strategy can avoid some of the observer bias, there may still be some tendencies toward overattributing cause to dispositional characteristics of the worker. An even better remedy is to change the perspective of the observers/ evaluators by providing them with direct experience with the actor's job. Because much of the actor–observer bias is the result of the differing perspectives of the actor and the observer, putting the observer/appraiser "in the shoes" of the actor/worker can help the observer see conditions as the actor sees them (Mitchell & Kalb, 1982).

A large savings and loan organization has done just that. All supervisors who are responsible for conducting the performance appraisals of customer service representatives—tellers and loan officers—must spend one week during each appraisal period working in customer service. The belief is that because many of these supervisors are far removed from the customer service situation, they are unable to evaluate objectively the pressures that the workers have to deal with, such as difficult or irate customers. Providing appraisers with this direct experience helps them take into account the situational variables that affect employees' performance, thus leading to more accurate assessments.

A common misconception is that the actor–observer bias will be overcome if both supervisor performance appraisals and workers' self-appraisals are obtained. However, if the actor–observer bias is operating, all this will produce is two very discrepant performance appraisals: one from the supervisor, blaming the worker for poor performance, and one from the worker, blaming the situation. Peer evaluations likewise will not be of much help, because coworkers are also subject to the actor–observer bias. Peer evaluations will also over attribute cause to characteristics of the person being appraised, because the coworker is also an observer.

The Performance Appraisal Process

In the past two decades, research on performance appraisals has focused more on the cognitive processes underlying performance appraisal decisions—how an evaluator arrives at an overall evaluation of a worker's performance (Bretz, Milkovich, & Read, 1992; Feldman, 1981; Kravitz & Balzer, 1992). This research views performance appraisal as a complex, decision-making process, looking at: (a) how information about the worker's performance is acquired; (b) how the evaluator organizes and stores information about a worker's performance behaviors; and (c) how the evaluator retrieves and translates the stored information in making the actual performance appraisal (Ilgen, Barnes-Farrell, & McKellin, 1993; Judge & Ferris, 1993).

The results of several studies suggest that evaluators form ongoing, or "on-line," evaluations of others (Murphy, Philbin, & Adams, 1989; Woehr, 1992). That is, evaluators form opinions as they observe behavior day-to-day, rather than just waiting until the time a formal performance rating is required and then forming an opinion based solely on memory. Because evaluation of performance is an ongoing, information-processing task, evaluators should be presented with the performance appraisal rating instruments up front, so that they can familiarize themselves with the rating dimensions before they begin to observe and evaluate performance (Woehr, 1992). Having this knowledge of rating dimensions beforehand has been shown to increase the agreement between supervisor ratings and self-ratings of workers' performance (Williams & Levy, 1992). In addition, it may be helpful for evaluators to keep diaries or daily records of individual employee performance. It has been found that using diaries as a means for structuring information in memory increases the accuracy of evaluators' recall. In research, evaluators who used diaries to record performance information were more accurate in their recall and were also more accurate in their appraisals of worker performance (DeNisi & Peters, 1996; DeNisi, Robbins, & Cafferty, 1989).

The performance appraisal process involves more than just the process of evaluating and rating worker performance. A good performance appraisal should consist of two parts. The first is the performance assessment, or the means of measuring a worker's performance to make personnel decisions. This part we have discussed at length. The second part is performance feedback, which is the process of providing information to a worker regarding performance level with suggestions for improving future performance (Boswell & Boudreau, 2002). Performance feedback typically occurs in the context of the performance appraisal interview. Here, the supervisor typically sits down face-to-face with the worker and provides a detailed analysis of the worker's performance, giving positive, constructive criticism and suggestions and guidelines for improvement. Guidelines for effective feedback are given in Table 6.3.

performance feedback
the process of giving information to a worker about performance level with suggestions for future improvement

TABLE 6.3

Guidelines for Effective Performance Feedback

1. Feedback should be descriptive rather than evaluative.
2. Feedback should be specific rather than general.
3. Feedback should be appropriate, taking into account the needs of the employer, the worker, and the situation.
4. Feedback should be directed toward behavior that the worker can do something about or is able to change.
5. Feedback should be well timed. More immediate feedback is usually more effective.
6. Feedback should be honest rather than manipulative or self-serving.
7. Feedback should be understood by both parties. If necessary, additional input should be sought to enhance and clarify the feedback process.
8. Feedback should be proactive and coactive. When change in past behavior is required, specific directions for change should be provided. Both parties should agree on the need for change and the remedy.
9. Feedback should not be used as an opportunity to criticize or to find fault with the worker. It should be a natural process in the ongoing superior-subordinate relationship.

Source: Harris, T. E. (1993). *Applied organizational communication: Perspectives, principles, and pragmatics.* Hillsdale, NJ: Erlbaum.

Although constructive feedback is critical to a good performance appraisal, more "informal" feedback from supervisor to subordinate should take place regularly, on a day-to-day basis (Farr, 1993).

Because of the importance of performance appraisals, the appraisal process is likely to have some psychological and emotional effects on the worker. It is crucial that the supervisor be aware of this potential impact of the procedure and be equipped to deal with the worker's possible reactions (Kinicki, Prussia, Wu, & McKee-Ryan, 2004). Whether the worker perceives the performance appraisal process positively or negatively, and how the worker acts on the information provided in the feedback session, are in large part determined by how the information is presented by the supervisor (Ilgen, Fisher, & Taylor, 1979; Kluger & DeNisi, 1996). Research has shown that if the appraiser demonstrates support for the worker and welcomes the worker's input and participation in the assessment process, the performance appraisal is usually more effective (Cederblom, 1982; Wexley, 1986). For example, in one study, workers participated in the construction of behaviorally anchored rating scales to appraise their performance. These workers had more favorable perceptions of the appraisal process and were more motivated to try to improve their performance than were workers who did not have a hand in developing their rating instruments (Silverman & Wexley, 1984). Research has also indicated that training programs for appraisers that include training in providing feedback and in dealing with workers' possible reactions to that feedback are effective in improving the entire performance appraisal process (Ivancevich, 1982) (see "Up Close" for suggestions on how to improve performance appraisals, and Table 6.4, which provides suggestions for appraiser training programs).

One model suggests that performance appraisal are effective depending on the extent to which the performance ratings are measured accurately, free of bias and systematic errors, and how positively the appraisal process is viewed by the participants (Levy & Williams, 2004). Critically important is the employees' perceptions of the fairness of the appraisal process (Flint, 1999; Nurse, 2005).

TABLE 6.4

Suggestions for a Good Appraiser Training Program

Hauenstein (1998) suggests that a good training program for performance appraisers should have the following:

1. Familiarizing appraisers with the performance dimensions used in the evaluation system.
2. Providing appraisers with opportunities for practice and feedback (using written or videotaped examples).
3. Appraisers should be informed about common rating biases and trained to reduce these biases.
4. Appraisers should be trained to improve their observational skills and use notes and behavioral diaries.
5. Training should improve appraiser's self-confidence in conducting performance appraisals.
6. Appraisers should be trained to provide good feedback, to be sensitive to employees' reactions to evaluations, and to involve employees in the process as much as possible.

UP CLOSE   How to Improve Performance Appraisals

Given the pervasiveness of biases and errors in performance appraisals, how can the appraisal process be improved? Research suggests several ways to improve the process.

1. *Improve performance appraisal techniques*— Generally, the more time and energy devoted to the development of detailed, valid instruments for measuring performance, the better the overall quality of the performance appraisal. This means creating different performance appraisal instruments for different job classifications. (You can't, for example, use the same generic rating form for both frontline workers and managerial personnel.) These measures of performance must evolve from detailed job analyses and should involve relatively straightforward and unambiguous procedures (Yammarino & Waldman, 1993).

2. *Train the appraisers*—Because conducting good performance appraisals is a difficult process, prone to error and potential bias, it is imperative that appraisers be adequately trained. They must be taught how to use the various appraisal instruments and should be instructed to avoid possible errors, such as halo effects and leniency/severity errors (Bernardin & Bulkley, 1981; Hedge & Kavanagh, 1988; Woehr & Huffcutt, 1994). Moreover, evidence suggests that appraisers should be knowledgeable of the performance appraisal methods and procedures up front, before they begin observing workers' performance (Woehr, 1994).

3. *Obtain multiple evaluations*—One way to increase the reliability of performance appraisals is to use multiple ratings, such as more than one supervisor rating or a combination of supervisor ratings, self-appraisals, and peer appraisals. If the results of the multiple appraisals agree with one another, and if all the appraisers are not influenced by a common bias, it is likely that the result will be a very accurate assessment of performance.

4. *Appraise appraisers*—Unfortunately, in many organizations supervisors detest conducting performance appraisals because they view the assessments as a difficult and thankless task—extra work piled onto an already heavy workload. To get supervisors to take performance appraisals seriously, it is important that the task of conducting assessments be considered an integral part of their job. This means that the quality of the supervisors' performance appraisals should be assessed and that the supervisors should also receive feedback about their performance of this crucial task. High-quality appraisals need to be rewarded.

5. *Conduct performance appraisals regularly and often*—Performance appraisals serve not only as tools to assist in personnel decisions, but also as a source of feedback for the worker. Frequent and regular assessments are one of the best ways to help workers learn to overcome problems and improve performance (Cummings & Schwab, 1978).

6. *Review and revise performance appraisals*—As jobs change because of technological innovations and organizational restructuring, performance appraisal systems must be constantly updated to deal with the changing nature of the jobs being evaluated.

Legal Concerns in Performance Appraisals

Because performance appraisals are tied to personnel actions such as promotions, demotions, and raises, they are carefully scrutinized in terms of fair employment legislation (Malos, 1998; Martin, Bartol, & Kehoe, 2000). Under these legal guidelines, any performance appraisal must be valid. Historically, court cases have ruled that to be considered "valid," appraisals must be based on a job analysis and must be validated against the job duties that the workers actually perform (*Albemarle Paper v. Moody*, 1975; *United States v. City of Chicago*, 1976). Moreover, performance appraisals need to be administered and scored under controlled and standardized conditions (*Brito v. Zia Company*, 1973).

Specifically, court cases have ruled that appraisers must receive training, or at least written instructions, on how to conduct performance appraisals, that assessments must focus on performance-related behaviors rather than on performance-related personality traits or other dispositional variables, and that appraisals must be reviewed with the employees (Barrett & Kernan, 1987; Feild & Holley, 1982). In addition, just as the ADA requires that employers make reasonable accommodations for disabled workers in performing their jobs, performance appraisals of these workers need to also take into account both the disability and the accommodations to avoid discrimination in the appraisal.

Historically, employers in the United States have had the right to terminate an employee, with or without cause, in what is called "employment-at-will" rights. With increased employment litigation, however, this right to fire at will has been challenged. Most often discharged employees have argued that there was an "implied employment contract," such as promises made by an employer. For example, before deregulation of provision of utilities (e.g., electricity), many utility employees were led to believe that they had "lifetime employment," because workers were rarely fired or laid off. However, in the more competitive postderegulation environment, utility companies needed to downsize, causing many of the laid-off workers to seek legal recourse. To prevent problems in this area, employers should be careful to fully inform new employees about employment-at-will and should avoid making any sort of real or implied "contracts" or promises regarding future employment. This is also another reason why performance appraisals need to be accurate, frequent, and backed up with good recordkeeping. For instance, if an employee had a record of mediocre or substandard performance, and the person is one of the first to be let go during a workforce reduction, having accurate records of the employee's performance will reduce the company's exposure should the employee seek legal recourse.

Team Appraisals and the Future of Performance Appraisals

The increase in team-based work groups has important implications for the use of performance appraisals. It has been argued that true work teams, where workers complete highly interdependent tasks, with shared team goals, should be appraised as a team, rather than using traditional individual appraisals (Delery, Gupta, Jenkins, & Walker, 1998; Wildman, Bedwell, Salas, & Smith-Jentsch, 2011). One model suggests that a good appraisal of team performance should assess team members' competencies (knowledge, skills), their team behaviors (effective communication, collaboration, decision making), and the total team performance (output, quality) (Reilly & McGourty, 1998). Often, team performance appraisals may require team members to evaluate one another, as well as an evaluation by the supervisor or team leader of the team as a unit.

The shift toward team approaches, as well as the fact that the nature and structure of many jobs change quickly over time, present special challenges to performance appraisal. Performance appraisal systems, therefore, need to be subject to constant review and revision. Smither (1998) argued that performance appraisal should not be an end product, but should be integrated into day-to-day performance, employee development, and the greater goals of the organization. Employees need to be active participants in the appraisal process, if they are to perceive it as fair and have a positive, constructive reaction to the appraisals (Gilliland & Langdon, 1998; Greenberg, 1986).

Stop & Review

Outline five techniques for improving performance appraisals.

Summary

A thorough job analysis is the starting point for measuring and evaluating actual job performance. *Performance appraisals* involve the assessment of worker performance on the basis of predetermined organizational standards. Performance appraisals serve many important purposes, including being the basis for personnel decisions and a means of assessing performance. One way to categorize performance is in terms of objective and subjective criteria. *Objective performance criteria* are more quantifiable measurements of performance, such as the number of units produced or dollar sales. *Subjective performance criteria* typically involve judgments or ratings of performance. Concerns for a performance criterion include whether it is relevant to job success, called *criterion relevance*; whether the criterion contains elements that detract from the "pure" assessment of performance, termed *criterion contamination*; whether the degree to which a criterion falls short of perfect assessment of job performance, called *criterion deficiency*; and whether the criterion is usable, called *criterion usefulness*.

Research on ratings of job performance has examined who is making performance ratings. Self-appraisals are ratings or evaluations made by the workers themselves. Peer appraisals involve coworkers rating each other's performance. In some instances, subordinates may rate the performance of their supervisors. Most common, of course, are supervisory ratings of subordinates' performance. *360-degree feedback* involves getting multiple performance evaluations, from supervisors, peers, subordinates, and customers.

There are a variety of methods for rating performance. *Comparative methods* of appraisal, such as the paired comparison and forced distribution techniques, directly compare one worker's performance with that of another worker's. *Individual methods* of appraisal do not make direct comparisons with other workers. Individual methods include *checklists* and forced choice scales and are easy-to-use methods of appraisal that require the evaluator simply to check off statements characteristic or uncharacteristic of a particular worker's job performance. The most common method of individual performance appraisal involves the use of *graphic rating scales*, whereby an appraiser uses a standardized rating instrument to make a numerical and/or verbal rating of various dimensions of job performance. A specific type of rating technique, the *behaviorally anchored rating scale* (BARS), uses examples of good and poor behavioral incidents as substitutes for the scale anchors found in traditional rating instruments.

A major problem in rating job performance is caused by systematic biases and errors. Response tendency errors, such as *leniency/severity* or *central tendency errors*, lead to consistently good, bad, or average ratings, respectively. *Halo effects* occur when appraisers make overall positive (or negative) performance appraisals because of one known outstanding characteristic or action. There are also errors caused by giving greater weight to more recent performance, known as *recency effects*, and various attribution errors, including the *actor–observer bias*. The latter may lead an appraiser to place greater emphasis on dispositional factors and lesser emphasis on situational factors that may have affected performance.

A good performance appraisal consists of two parts: the performance assessment and *performance feedback*. The feedback should occur in a face-to-face situation in which the supervisor provides constructive information, encouragement, and guidelines for the improvement of the worker's future performance.

Because performance appraisals are important to the worker's livelihood and career advancement, there are considerable legal overtones to the appraisal process. Performance appraisals must be valid procedures, resulting from job analysis, that do not unfairly discriminate against any group of workers.

Because of the proliferation of work teams, organizations are developing team appraisals—evaluating an interdependent group of workers as a unit. The changing nature of work means that performance appraisal systems need to be constantly reviewed and revised to keep up with changes in jobs.

Study Questions and Exercises

1. Think of a job you have had in the past or talk to someone you know about his or her job. Using what you know about the position, try to determine what the relevant performance criteria would be for the job. Develop methods for assessing the performance criteria. Would you measure these criteria objectively or subjectively?

2. Using the job from question 1, design a performance appraisal system for the position. What does it consist of? Who will do the evaluations?

3. What are the advantages and disadvantages of using graphic rating scales versus comparative methods of performance appraisals?

4. In some organizations, performance appraisals are taken too lightly; they receive little attention and are conducted irregularly and infrequently, and there is little motivation for appraisers to do a good job. Why might this occur? Imagine that your task is to convince the management of one of these organizations to improve its performance appraisal system. What would you say to convince the management? What components of a good performance appraisal system would you suggest be implemented?

Web Links

www.performance-appraisal.com
This site maintained by Archer North Consultants has some interesting information on performance appraisals.

http://performance-appraisals.org
This site has a wealth of resources to help understand performance appraisals, including many suggested books and a Q&A area.

Suggested Readings

Bennett, W., Lance, C. E., & Woehr, D. J. (Eds.). (2006). *Performance measurement: Current perspectives and future challenges.* Mahwah, NJ: Lawrence Erlbaum. *This scholarly edited collection reviews many state-of-the-art approaches to measuring worker performance.*

DelPo, A. (2007). *The performance appraisal handbook: Legal & practical rules for managers* (2nd ed.). Berkeley, CA: Nolo Press. *This very interesting guide, written by an attorney, gives practical and legal advice to managers.*

Wildman, J. L., Bedwell, W. L., Salas, E., & Smith-Jentsch, K. A. (2011). Performance measurement at work: A multilevel perspective (pp. 303–341). In S. Zedeck (Ed.), *APA handbook of industrial and organizational psychology* (Vol. 1). Washington, DC: American Psychological Association. *A very good overview of issues regarding types and forms of performance appraisals, with a thorough review of research.*

CHAPTER OUTLINE

Inside Tips

This chapter concludes the focus on personnel processes by looking at how employees are trained and developed over their careers. We will also touch on topics that were introduced in several of the earlier chapters. We return to methodological issues (particularly experimental design issues) when considering the evaluation of training programs. The section on assessing training needs is in some ways related to the discussion of job analysis procedures in Chapter 3, except that now we are assessing what knowledge, skills, abilities, and other characteristics (KSAOs) workers need to perform their jobs rather than analyzing the jobs themselves. Analyses of employee performance data (Chapter 6) can also assist in training needs analysis. Because training relates to many personnel decisions, some of the legal concerns regarding equal employment opportunity that we looked at in Chapters 5 and 6 are relevant here too. It is important to consider how employee training ties in with the other personnel and employee issues studied previously.

You have just graduated from college. You went through the arduous process of applying for jobs, being screened, interviewed, and "courted" to some extent by your employer. You are anxious to get to work—to show them what you can do and to make your mark on the company. However, before you are able to get started, the company sends you to a training center where you will learn the basics of the job, learn company policies and procedures, and learn about the culture of your new organization.

Employee training is a planned effort by an organization to facilitate employees' learning, retention, and transfer of job-related behavior. In most organizations, training is not limited to new employees, as various types of training and development programs are offered at all stages of an employee's career.

employee training
planned organizational efforts to help employees learn job-related knowledge, skills, and other characteristics

In this chapter we will begin by examining areas of employee training. We will also examine the fundamentals of the learning process and how learning applies to employee training and development. We will then look at factors that affect the success of training programs. Next, we will look at how employee training needs are assessed and study general training methods. Finally, we will examine how training programs are evaluated.

Areas of Employee Training

Training, like learning, is a lifelong process. Organizations need to provide for the wide variety of training needs of workers to stay competitive. We will briefly examine some of these specific focuses of employee training and development programs.

New employee orientation and training

Orientation programs are typically designed to introduce employees to the organization and its goals, philosophy, policies, and procedures. They can also acquaint workers with both the physical structure and the personnel structure of the organization, such as the chain of supervisory command and the various relevant departments and divisions. During orientation new employees also learn about compensation, benefits, and safety rules and procedures. In short, initial training should provide enough information so that new employees can quickly become productive members of the organization's workforce. In fact, there is some evidence that when it comes to employee orientation and early training, more is better (Saks, 1996). An additional function of an orientation program is to help newcomers deal with the stresses of adjusting to a new work environment (Wanous, 1993; Waung, 1995).

BEFORE YOU START
- ☐ Return a signed contract
- ☐ Complete New Employee Packet
- ☐ Sign up for health insurance etc.

DURING YOUR FIRST TWO WEEKS
- ☐ Obtain Employee identification card
- ☐ Obtain access key card
- ☐ Complete benefits worksheet etc.

AFTER YOUR FIRST THREE MONTHS, YOU SHOULD KNOW…

ABOUT YOUR JOB
- ☐ Department's goals and mission
- ☐ Department organization and personnel
- ☐ Your reporting lines
- ☐ Your duties and responsibilities etc.

ABOUT YOUR WORK ENVIRONMENT
- ☐ your work area and office
- ☐ your colleagues and their job functions
- ☐ how to use email and phones
- ☐ how to obtain/order office supplies and resources etc.

ABOUT YOUR PAY
- ☐ your pay rate
- ☐ overtime policies and regulations
- ☐ travel reimbursement procedures
- ☐ accrual policies for sick and vacation days etc.

ABOUT YOUR RIGHTS AND RESPONSIBILITIES
- ☐ benefits available to you and your family
- ☐ organizational policies on equal employment opportunities, sexual harassment, etc.
- ☐ formal training available to you
- ☐ policies on discipline and procedures governing your employment etc.

FIGURE 7.1
Example of a New Employee Orientation Checklist (abbreviated)

Although new employee orientation and training are a large part of most organizations' training programs, many do not give sufficient attention or resources to this area, despite its very important role in creating a productive and dedicated workforce. In fact, research shows that new workers are often eager and willing to learn (Morrison, 1993). Moreover, evidence suggests that employees receiving adequate initial training are more satisfied and less likely to quit during the first six months of a job than workers who receive little initial training (Wanous, Poland, Premack, & Davis, 1992; Wanous, Stumpf, & Bedrosian, 1979). It has been suggested that adequate new employee orientation programs can pay huge dividends over time in increased employee productivity and satisfaction with the job and the organization (Hacker, 2004).

It is important to note that initial employee orientation is mainly designed to acquaint new employees with the organization and with basic organizational processes (Wesson & Gogus, 2005). (See Figure 7.1 for an example of an employee orientation program checklist.) A more in-depth process of socializing employees into the organization will be discussed in Chapter 11.

Retraining and continuing education programs

Considerable evidence indicates that a certain amount of the knowledge and skills of workers either erodes or becomes obsolete during their work careers (London & Bassman, 1989). To maintain workers' proficiencies, organizations must encourage and support basic "refresher courses" as well as continuing education programs that provide workers with new information. With rapid technological advancements, it is critical that the skills and knowledge of persons employed in jobs that require the use of advanced technology be constantly updated.

A retirement planning session, or brochure for retirement planning.

Certain professionals, particularly those in licensed health-care professions such as medicine, dentistry, and clinical psychology, require some form of continuing education to continue to work in the field. Other professionals, such as managers, lawyers, engineers, and architects, are also increasingly encouraged to participate in continuing education programs.

Research on employee retraining suggests that older employees may resist retraining efforts due to lack of self-confidence in their ability to learn (Maurer, 2001). It has been suggested that organizations need to provide incentives and support for older workers' participation in retraining programs (Warr & Birdi, 1998).

Retirement planning and preparation

The training departments of many organizations offer employees assistance in planning and preparing for retirement. Research suggests that many workers do not prepare well (or at all) for retirement (Kim & Moen, 2001). Seminars are offered on such topics as making the retirement decision, retirement plans and options, investment and money management, and services and opportunities for retirees and seniors. More general programs aimed at helping retirees adjust to a nonworking lifestyle are also offered. An increase in preretirement training programs reflects a general trend toward more employee training and greater concern for employees' pre- and postretirement welfare. One study found that both pre- and postretirement planning were needed for employees to successfully retire (Donaldson, Earl, & Muratore, 2010).

Employee career development

Organizations are becoming more and more aware of the need for greater attention to the development and planning of employees' careers. Helping workers plan their careers can help lead to a more productive, more satisfied, and more loyal workforce (Gaffney, 2005; Noe, 1996). Many organizations have developed formal career development systems, which benefit all parties involved, including workers, managers, and the organization (see Table 7.1).

Career development systems typically offer a variety of programs, including career counseling, courses in career planning, and workshops that provide tools and techniques for helping employees manage their careers. For example, career counseling programs might help individuals set career goals and develop a plan for getting the type of training and education necessary to meet those goals. They may also assist in finding jobs for employees who are about to be laid off. With increased job mobility and organizational downsizing, research has demonstrated that it is very important today for employees to learn to take responsibility for and "self-manage" their careers (Barnett & Bradley, 2007; Kossek, Roberts, Fisher, & DeMarr, 1998). Moreover, companies that demonstrate they are concerned about employee career advancement are going to be more successful at attracting and retaining employees.

TABLE 7.1		
Benefits of a Career Development System		
For Managers/Supervisors	**For Employees**	**For the Organization**
Increased skill in managing own careers	Helpful assistance with career decisions and changes	Better use of employee skills Increased loyalty
Greater retention of valued employees	Enrichment of present job and increased job satisfaction	Dissemination of information at all organizational levels
Better communication between manager and employee	Better communication between employee and manager	Better communication within organization as a whole
More realistic staff and development planning	More realistic goals and expectations	Greater retention of valued employees
Productive performance appraisal discussions	Better feedback on performance	Expanded public image as a people-developing organization
Increased understanding of the organization	Current information about the organization and future trends	Increased effectiveness of personnel systems and procedures
Enhanced reputation as a people developer	Greater sense of personal responsibility for managing career	
Employee motivation for accepting new responsibilities		
Build talent inventory for special projects		
Clarification of fit between organizational and individual goals		

Source: Leibowitz, Z. B., Farren, C., & Kaye B. I. (1986). *Designing Career Development Systems* (p. 7). San Francisco: Jossey-Bass.

Training workers for international assignments

The increasing globalization of business means that many workers will be required to interface with representatives of organizations based in other nations. In some cases, workers may work for a foreign-based company, or they may spend some time working in a host country. Working in another culture requires specialized training (Shen, 2005; Tung, 1997).

There are many important objectives for programs to train employees for work in international settings. Some of the skills required for working in another culture include foreign language skills, knowledge of the host country's general culture, and knowledge of the country's specific business culture and work rules (Ronen, 1989). Some scholars have suggested that the best workers—those who can easily adjust to different international assignments—are those who possess what has been called "cultural intelligence" (Offerman & Phan, 2002). More recently, it has been suggested that managers who are destined for international assignment should view this sort of cross-cultural training as an ongoing process of development (Teagarden, 2007).

Training in diversity issues, harassment, and ethical behavior

With internationalization and increased access to jobs, work groups are becoming increasingly diverse, with more women and older employees in the workforce, as well as national and cultural diversity. This has prompted organizations to allocate resources to diversity training programs and efforts to prevent harassment, including sexual harassment. Besides helping to fight discrimination against specific groups of employees, diversity training is also aimed at capitalizing on the advantages of diverse work teams, as we saw in Chapter 1.

Most diversity training programs seek to raise employees' awareness of diversity issues, to try to increase understanding of people from other backgrounds and cultures, and to strive to change negative attitudes and behaviors. There is evidence that diversity training can help employees in the implementation of diversity initiatives and making such programs work (Combs & Luthans, 2007). The Hong Kong Bank and the Bank of Montreal have longstanding training programs to deal with issues related to gender, racial, and cultural diversity (Tung, 1997).

Nearly one-fourth of U.S. women report being sexually harassed at work, with more than half reporting they experienced potentially harassing behaviors (Ilies, Hauserman, Schwochau, & Stibal, 2003). As a result, employee sexual harassment training is becoming mandatory in many areas. Research evidence suggests that sexual harassment is affected by the organizational culture and climate (Fitzgerald, Drasgow, Hulin, Gelfand, & Magley, 1997). As a result, a majority of U.S. companies have developed training programs designed to reduce sexual harassment in the workplace. Many of these programs focus on increasing awareness of harassing behavior (e.g., Blakely, Blakely, & Moorman, 1998) and trying to neutralize situations and "cultures" that promote or allow sexual harassment. There is some evidence that sexual harassment training does indeed have positive effects, particularly in helping male employees better understand what sorts of behaviors constitute sexual harassment (Antecol & Cobb-Clark, 2003). In addition, it has been suggested that sexual harassment training needs to focus both at the individual employee level and at the work group or team level (Raver & Gelfand, 2005).

Although health-care workers, lawyers, and other professional workers have had regular training in professional ethics, there has recently been increased attention to ethics training for a broader range of workers. In light of the many high-profile corporate ethical scandals, many organizations have developed ethics training programs for managers and for rank-and-file employees. Moreover, business schools have placed increased emphasis on ethics courses, although there is some concern about the success of ethics training courses (Allen, Bacdayan, Kowalski, & Roy, 2005). There is some preliminary evidence that ethics training in business does have positive effects (Valentine & Fleischman, 2004).

Team training

As organizations rely more and more on work teams, I/O psychologists and HR professionals have begun to realize the importance of training aimed at developing the team as a group, rather than the individual focus that is common to most employee training programs (Hollenbeck, DeRue, & Guzzo, 2004; Stagl, Salas, & Burke, 2007). Team training programs typically have several components: (a) gaining an understanding of the knowledge and skills of each of the individual group members; (b) training in teamwork skills (e.g., how to coordinate activities, how to fairly distribute workload, group problem solving and decision making); and (c) developing shared goals and work procedures (Campbell & Kuncel, 2001). As you might imagine, team training is critical to certain groups, such as airline cockpit crews (Helmreich, Merritt, & Wilhelm, 1999). Cannon-Bowers and Salas (1997) suggested that successful team training should measure both team and individual performance with feedback provided so that team members can learn to diagnose and evaluate their own performance within the team.

Fundamental Issues in Employee Training

Employee training is rooted in basic theories of learning. Designers of good employee training programs are familiar with learning theories and principles. Most relevant theories for employee training are social learning theory and cognitive theories of learning. Social learning theory emphasizes the observational learning of behavior (Bandura, 1977). A key process in social learning theory is modeling. Modeling is imitative learning that occurs through observing and reproducing another person's action, such as when an employee learns to operate a piece of machinery by watching a supervisor work with the equipment and imitating the supervisor's actions. Cognitive theories of learning view workers as information processors, focusing on how new information is stored and retrieved and how that information is used to produce work behavior (Howell & Cooke, 1989; Tannenbaum & Yukl, 1992). Cognitive theories are particularly useful in understanding complex thought processes, such as how workers can go beyond learned information and come up with novel and creative solutions or ideas.

social learning theory
learning theory that emphasizes the observational learning of behavior

modeling
learning that occurs through the observation and imitation of the behavior of others

cognitive theories of learning
learning theories that emphasize that humans are information processors

KEY ISSUES IN THE SUCCESS OF TRAINING PROGRAMS

If employee training programs are to be successful, a number of key issues should be considered. For example, we must take care to see that learning achieved during the training sessions actually transfers to new behaviors at the worksite. We also need to consider the trainees' willingness and readiness to learn. In addition, we need to look at the structure of the training program in terms of when, where, and how training will take place. Let's look more closely at these key training issues.

Transfer of training

An important concern is the transfer of training (Baldwin & Ford, 1988). How well does learning transfer from the training situation to the actual work environment? Because training transfer is influenced by the degree of similarity between the training tasks and the actual job tasks, the most useful training programs directly

transfer of training
concept dealing with whether training is actually applied in the work setting

address the actual tasks that are performed on the job. Positive transfer of learned tasks has been found to be maximized when there are identical stimulus and response elements found in the training and in job situations (Wexley & McCellin, 1987). Transfer of training will also be more likely if the work environment supports the new behaviors that are learned and if the work environment allows the trainee an opportunity to use those newly learned behaviors (Cromwell & Kolb, 2004; Kim, 2004; Tracey, Tannenbaum, & Kavanagh, 1995).

Setting training goals and receiving feedback and reinforcement for achieving training goals also positively affect training transfer (Winters & Latham, 1996). One study found that when trainees set goals for implementing the training strategies and feedback was given concerning the achievement of those goals, the trained behaviors tended to stay in place (Wexley & Baldwin, 1986). Without feedback and reinforcement, learned skills or procedures may deteriorate as workers forget some of their important elements, pick up bad habits that interfere with their application, or lapse into using old work strategies (Marx, 1982). Thus, concern should be given to the maintenance of newly learned work behaviors. It is important that workers see the connection between the learning of new behaviors and how the use of the new learning will enhance their working lives. "Brush-up" or reminder training sessions should follow a few months down the line. In short, training should take place on a regular basis, be thorough, and continue throughout an employee's career. For effective transfer and maintenance of learning, employees must see that learning new work skills helps them to be better, more productive workers, which in turn can lead to promotions and other forms of career advancement.

Trainee readiness

trainee readiness
the individual's potential for successful training

A second consideration is what could be termed **trainee readiness**. A great deal of research indicates that positive employee attitudes toward training programs are critical for training success (Noe, 1986; Warr & Bunce, 1995; Webster & Martocchio, 1993). Is the trainee prepared to learn? Does the trainee feel the need for training and see the usefulness of the material that will be learned? Trainee ability, or "trainability," is another important factor to consider (Kanfer & Ackerman, 1989). For example, does the employee possess the basic prerequisites to be a good candidate for learning these new behaviors? In other words, does the trainee have the aptitude to learn? Finally, if a training program is going to be successful, we must consider the trainee's motivation (Tharenou, 2001). If an individual has no desire to learn new tasks and to take on new responsibilities, it is unlikely that much learning will take place (Baldwin & Magjuka, 1997; Baldwin, Magjuka, & Loher, 1991). Or, if a trainee feels unable to master the material—if he or she feels the material is "beyond reach"—learning will be adversely affected (Mathieu, Martineau, & Tannenbaum, 1993). Moreover, research has indicated that both giving employees a realistic preview of what the training program is about and providing them with the personal and career-related benefits have positive effects on both trainee reactions to the program and their learning (Martocchio, 1993; Smith-Jentsch, Jentsch, Payne, & Salas, 1996; Webster & Martocchio, 1995).

An important issue in some highly-skilled, highly-specialized jobs, such as surgeon or air traffic controller, is the readiness for a trainee to move from working in a simulated environment, to actually performing the job. This sort of trainee readiness has been studied in the medical profession, where simulations are used extensively before the doctor is allowed to practice on an actual patient (McGaghie, Issenberg, Petrusa, & Scalese, 2010).

Training program structure

A third issue concerns the structure of the training program. When and how often does training take place? How long are the training sessions? How much opportunity is there for trainees to practice or apply what they have learned? How much guidance and individual attention does each trainee receive?

The bulk of research evidence does indeed support the old adage that "practice makes perfect." In fact, evidence indicates that practice should continue to the point of overlearning, or where practice continues even after the trainee has established that the material has been learned (Driskell, Willis, & Copper, 1992; McGeehee & Thayer, 1961). Should the practice be continuous, in what is called massed practice, or should practice sessions be spaced over time? Nearly all evidence supports spaced over massed practice, particularly if the practice involves retrieval-type learning (such as a recall test) rather than recognition learning (Schmidt & Bjork, 1992). Students are probably familiar with this. Studying course material in continuous, spaced sessions over the semester beats intense, last-minute "cramming" nearly every time!

Training research has also looked at whether it is better to segment the material into parts, in what is called part learning, or to present the material as a whole (*whole learning*). The research evidence suggests that whole learning is better than *part learning*, particularly when the trainees have high levels of cognitive abilities (Adams, 1987). For example, teaching a worker to operate a bulldozer would be more successful if presented as a whole task, such as learning to manipulate the controls that both drive the vehicle and operate the shovel, as opposed to learning the two tasks separately, particularly because operating a bulldozer requires driving while controlling the shovel simultaneously.

Another critical element is providing trainees with feedback about learning accomplishments. To be effective, feedback must be immediate rather than delayed. More feedback is generally better, although there is a point where too much feedback may only serve to overload and confuse trainees. Finally, research has shown that positive feedback—information about what a trainee has done right—is more effective than negative feedback, which focuses on what the trainee has done wrong (Martocchio & Webster, 1992).

Finally, evidence indicates that to be effective, training programs should be highly structured to increase the meaningfulness of the material to be learned (Fantuzzo, Riggio, Connelly, & Dimeff, 1989; Wexley & Latham, 1991). Adding structure to training programs may involve presenting a general overview of the material to trainees before actual training begins and imposing a logical or orderly sequence on the presentation of the training material. Trainees should also be made aware of the importance and goals of practicing newly learned skills (Cannon-Bowers, Rhodenizer, Salas, & Bowers, 1998).

COMMON PROBLEMS IN EMPLOYEE TRAINING PROGRAMS

Estimates of the cost of personnel training in the United States alone range from the tens of billions to the hundreds of billions of dollars per year. Yet, one problem with many personnel training programs is that although organizations make a major commitment to training in terms of time, money, and other resources, training programs are not as effective as they could be, partly because they do not adequately follow sound learning principles. Another problem is that employee training programs in some companies are not well organized. Perhaps you have even experienced such "haphazard" training in one of your jobs, where you received little formal training and were expected to learn "on-the-job" with little guidance. Or, you may have heard of workers who attend training sessions that seem to have little relevance to the jobs the workers perform (see the Up Close feature).

 **CLOSE** **Why Do Some Organizations Give So Little Attention to New Employee Orientation and Training?**

Traditionally, some organizations have tended to throw new employees into a work situation with only minimal training and orientation, assuming that they will learn the job by observing and doing (Dipboye, 1997). In these instances, there appears to be a strong belief that the really good workers will distinguish themselves by their ability to adapt and survive.

One reason for this "sink-or-swim" treatment of new employees is that employee training and orientation have not been very high priorities for many organizations, particularly smaller businesses and relatively new companies. These organizations are so preoccupied with basic survival—maintaining productivity rates and keeping the size and quality of the workforce constant—that training (along with other personnel considerations, such as a program of regular performance appraisals) is put on the back shelf. When conditions stabilize and the company has grown or matured, these personnel functions may be given greater emphasis.

Another reason for the absence of new employee training programs is the lack of assessment of training needs (Dipboye, 1997). Many organizations are simply unaware of what new employees need (and want) to know. Those who know the most about new employee training needs are probably the frontline supervisors, who observe firsthand the skill and knowledge deficiencies of new workers. For some reason, however, these training needs are not communicated to the upper-level decision makers. Of course, it may not be helpful to ask the new workers about their needs; because they are new, they are usually unaware of their training requirements. New workers may also not readily admit to certain skill or knowledge deficiencies in an effort to appear that they are indeed competent. A related problem arises when there is no sound evaluation of existing training programs, for it is unlikely that additional resources will be allocated unless the benefits of such programs have been demonstrated. Finally, inadequate training and orientation may be rooted in the belief that the best way for new workers to learn is by doing. Although on-the-job training can be effective, organizations need to consider its costs for new employees, such as reduced levels of production and potential damage to the product, the equipment, or the workers. For instance, several years ago at IBM's higher-end computer manufacturing plant, it was estimated that a poorly trained assembly worker's mistake while constructing an expensive computer system could cost between $10,000 and $100,000 worth of damage (DeAngelis, 1994). Unregulated on-the-job training may also cause workers to learn poor work habits rather than the proper ones.

A Model for Successful Training Programs

Theories and principles of learning should be taken into account in the design and implementation of any good employee training program. In addition, to be successful, training programs need to follow a structured, step-by-step model (see Figure 7.2). A successful training program should begin by *assessing training needs*. In other words, the organization must first have some idea of what workers need to know to perform their jobs.

The next step is *establishing training objectives*—goals for what the training is supposed to accomplish. Training objectives need to be specific and related to measurable outcomes because training objectives are used both to set a course for the training program and to help later in determining if the training was indeed successful (Goldstein & Ford, 2002).

The next step in the training program involves the *development and testing of training materials*. A variety of factors must be taken into account in developing training materials, such as the trainees' educational and skill levels, whether the training material focuses on the areas that are directly related to successful job performance, and what training methods will provide the best cost–benefit trade-off. It is also important that training materials be thoroughly tested before they are put into regular use.

The actual *implementation of the training program* is the next step in the training model. Important considerations in implementing the training program include when and how often the training will take place, who will conduct the training, the assignment of trainees to sessions, and where the training will be conducted.

The final step is the *evaluation of the training program* to determine if the training was effective. This step involves a detailed analysis of whether training objectives were met and whether the training translates into trainees using the newly learned behaviors on the job.

Let's look more closely at some of the issues related to successful personnel training programs, starting with a discussion of training needs assessment.

ASSESSING TRAINING NEEDS

A successful training program should begin by assessing training needs. In other words, the organization must have some idea of what workers need to know to perform their jobs. Typically, an assessment of training needs should include analyses on many levels: the organizational level (the needs and goals of the organization), the task level (the requirements for performing the task), and the person level (the skills and knowledge required to do the job). An additional analysis can be done at the demographic level (determining training needs for specific demographic groups).

Organizational analysis

The organizational level of needs analysis considers issues such as the long- and short-term organizational goals and their implications for training, the available training resources, and the general climate for training (that is, the workers'

FIGURE 7.2
A Model for Successful Employee Training Programs

Stop & Review
List and define four key issues that are important in determining the success of training programs.

and supervisors' commitment to participation in the training program). In addition, organizational analysis considers training needs that are the result of internal and external factors affecting the organization. For example, the introduction of a new manufacturing system and technology would require the organization to plan the kinds of technical skills, managerial skills, and support that workers will need to use the new machines and processes (Kozlowski & Salas, 1997; Salas & Cannon-Bowers, 2001). Similarly, a sales organization's decision to provide greater emphasis on customer service might require the development of new training programs. In an organizational analysis, a strategy for assessing training climate might involve surveying employees regarding their perceptions of training needs and their attitudes toward participation in training programs. The organizational level of needs analysis would also want to determine whether managers' expectations regarding training needs were consistent with organizational goals.

Task analysis

The task level of analysis is concerned with the knowledge, skills, and abilities and other characteristics (KSAOs) that a worker requires to perform a specific job effectively. The starting point for obtaining this information is the job description derived from a detailed job analysis. (As you may recall from Chapter 3, a job analysis is the starting point for just about any personnel operation.) The next and most difficult step involves translating the specific task requirements of the job into the basic components of knowledge and skill that can be incorporated into a training program. For example, a job as department store assistant manager might require the worker to handle customer complaints effectively. However, it may be difficult to determine the specific skills required to perform this task to train prospective employees.

Person analysis

The person analysis of employee training needs examines the current capabilities of the workers themselves to determine who needs what sort of training. Person analysis usually relies on worker deficiencies outlined in performance appraisals for incumbent workers and information derived from employee selection data, such as screening tests for new workers. Another important source of information is job incumbents' self-assessments of training needs (Ford & Noe, 1987), which may also help build employee commitment to the training program.

The use of the three levels of training needs analysis—task, organizational, and person analysis—can help determine which workers need training in which areas and provide information to guide the development of specific training techniques. It has been argued that effective training programs should be based on an analysis of training needs on many levels, rather than simply focusing on one level of analysis (Ostroff & Ford, 1989). In addition, the organization must consider the impact of a proposed training program in terms of both the potential benefits, such as increased efficiency and productivity, and the potential costs of the program itself.

Demographic analysis

It has been suggested that training needs analysis may have to be conducted on a fourth level, demographic analysis (Latham, 1988). A demographic analysis involves determining the specific training needs of various demographic groups, such as women and men, certain ethnic minorities, and workers of different age brackets. For example, a study of the perceived training needs of workers 40 years of age and older found that the younger workers (aged 40–49 years) believed that they needed training in management skills, and the middle-aged group (aged 50–59 years) preferred training in technological skills, whereas the oldest group (60 years and older) showed little interest in any type of training, perhaps because they felt that they had little to gain from additional training (Tucker, 1985). We will discuss training for special groups later in the chapter.

ESTABLISHING TRAINING OBJECTIVES

The second step in a successful training program is establishing training objectives. As mentioned earlier, it is important that objectives be specific and that they be associated with measurable outcomes. Training objectives should specify what the trainee should be able to accomplish on completion of the training program (Goldstein & Ford, 2002). For example, objectives for a training program for cashiers might be that the trainee will be able to operate and maintain the cash register and make change on completion of training.

Training objectives are important in guiding the design of the training program and the selection of training techniques and strategies. Moreover, the emphasis on establishing training objectives that are specific and measurable is particularly important in eventually evaluating the effectiveness of the training program (Kraiger, Ford, & Salas, 1993; Kraiger & Jung, 1997).

DEVELOPING AND TESTING OF TRAINING MATERIALS: EMPLOYEE TRAINING METHODS

The next step in our employee training model involves developing and testing the training materials. A wide variety of employee training methods are available, ranging from the relatively simple and straightforward to the fairly complex and sophisticated. In actual practice, most comprehensive training programs utilize a combination of several training methods and techniques.

It is important to pilot test the training materials, perhaps by using a group of workers who can provide their reactions to the materials and the program. This process leads to a refinement of the training materials and improvement in the program. Let's look at some of the more common training materials and methods.

Employee training methods can be grouped into two broad categories: the on-site methods, or those conducted on the job site, and the off-site methods, or those conducted away from the actual workplace.

> ⏱ Stop & Review
>
> What are the five steps in a good employee training program?

On-site methods

On-site training methods may be further divided into several categories, including on-the-job training, apprenticeship, vestibule training, and job rotation.

On-the-job training—One of the oldest and most widely used training methods, on-the-job training consists simply of putting an inexperienced worker in the workplace and having a more experienced worker teach that person about the job. This technique thus relies on principles of modeling, with the experienced worker serving as the role model. Also, because actual hands-on learning is involved, the worker can receive immediate feedback, be reinforced for successful efforts, and have a chance to learn how to correct errors.

The popularity of on-the-job training is obvious because it requires little preparation and has few costs to the organization, aside from the time invested by the experienced worker. Moreover, because the trainee is actually working while learning, certain small levels of output offset the costs of the supervising worker's time. However, problems occur when the organization neglects to consider the abilities and motivations of the experienced workers who serve as trainers. If these trainers do not see the personal benefits of serving as trainers (especially when there are no obvious benefits!), they will not be motivated to do a good job. Also, being a good trainer requires certain qualities, such as patience and an ability to communicate. If the trainer lacks these characteristics, this can interfere with trainees' learning. For example, one study found that experienced trainers often presented ideas abstractly or spoke "over-the-heads" of trainees (Hinds, Patterson, & Pfeffer, 2001). Problems can also arise if the trainer does not know or follow proper work procedures. In this case, the trainer may teach the new worker wrong or inefficient methods.

On-the-job training is best used when the trainers have been carefully selected because of their ability to teach and when they have received systematic training to help them be more effective. Trainers should also receive some type of reward or recognition for performing their training duties. Finally, the organization must accept the fact that during the on-the-job training period, production rates will suffer. It is impossible to expect the trainer–trainee team to do a good job of training while simultaneously maintaining high output rates. It has been suggested that to be effective, on-the-job training should be used with other training methods, including off-site methods such as seminars and programmed instruction (Wexley & Latham, 1991).

Apprenticeship—Skilled trade professions, such as carpentry, printing, masonry, and plumbing, use a very old type of training program called apprenticeship. A typical apprenticeship can last for several years and usually combines some supervised on-the-job training experience (usually at least 2,000 hours) with classroom instruction. The on-the-job experience allows the apprentice to learn the mechanics of the profession, whereas the classroom training usually teaches specific cognitive skills and rules and regulations associated with the

---

on-the-job training
an employee training method of placing a worker in the workplace to learn firsthand about a job

⏱ Stop & Review

Describe the four levels of training needs analysis.

apprenticeship
a training technique, usually lasting several years, that combines on-the-job experience with classroom instruction

profession (Harris, Simons, Willis, & Carden, 2003). For example, an apprentice in the housing construction industry will learn the mechanical skills of building a house while on the job and will learn about building codes and how to read blueprints in the classroom. The obvious advantage of apprenticeship programs is the detailed, long-term nature of the learning process. However, there have been charges from civil rights groups that apprentices are disproportionately chosen from majority groups and that women and members of ethnic minorities have been selectively omitted. However, affirmative action programs in many apprenticed professions have attempted to rectify these problems (Carnevale, Gainer, & Villet, 1990; Wexley & Yukl, 1984).

It is important to mention that the term *apprenticeship* has been used to describe a number of training programs that are quite different from traditional, formal apprenticeship. These informal "apprenticeships" might be better labeled as "mentorships," because they typically do not have the strict combination of hands-on learning and classroom training required by formal apprenticeships. We will discuss mentoring a bit later when we look at the use of mentoring in managerial training.

Vestibule training—Vestibule training is another on-site training method. This method uses a separate training area adjacent to the actual work area to simulate that setting, complete with comparable tools and equipment. In vestibule training, professional trainers teach the new workers all aspects of the job, allowing them hands-on experience in the work simulation area. The main advantage of vestibule training is that there is no disruption of actual production, because trainers rather than experienced workers provide instruction, and the novice workers are not in the actual work setting. The major drawback to this method is its costs in terms of the trainers, space, and equipment needed. In recent years, some large supermarkets have set up vestibule training areas at closed check-out stations to teach prospective checkers how to operate laser scanners and cash registers to ring up goods. Vestibule training is used to eliminate the delays to customers that inevitably occur when using on-the-job training.

vestibule training
training that uses a separate area adjacent to the work area to simulate the actual work setting

Job rotation—A final on-site training method is job rotation, in which workers are rotated among a variety of jobs, spending a certain length of time (usually several weeks to two months) at each. The basic premise behind job rotation is to expose workers to as many areas of the organization as possible so they can gain a good knowledge of its workings and how the various jobs and departments fit together. Job rotation can also be beneficial to the organization because of "cross training" of workers. Thus, if a worker is absent or quits, another worker has already been trained to perform the job. Most commonly, job rotation is used to help entry-level management personnel find the positions for which they are best suited. It can also be used to groom managers for higher-level positions, presumably making them more effective by enabling them to see the organization from a variety of perspectives. Research has shown that job rotation not only increases learning, but it also has positive effects

job rotation
a method of rotating workers among a variety of jobs to increase their breadth of knowledge

on employees' career progression and development (Campion, Cheraskin, & Stevens, 1994; Ortega, 2001). Job rotation has also been used in various team approaches to work task design to increase worker flexibility, eliminate boredom, and increase worker job satisfaction and commitment to the organization (Wexley & Latham, 2001). For example, studies of nurses in Japan found that job rotation allowed the nurses to understand more about their hospitals and their organizations' missions, leading to greater commitment to their jobs and hospitals.

It is important to mention, however, that job rotation does not consist of simply moving workers from task to task with little or no preparation. A careful analysis of training needs should be done for each position to which a worker is rotated. It is also important to orient and train the worker adequately on each task. Finally, an evaluation should be done of the worker's performance at each task, and the effectiveness of the overall job rotation training experience should be conducted.

Off-site methods

Training that takes place in a setting other than the actual workplace uses off-site methods. Because of the greater flexibility and control over the situation they afford, off-site methods are more varied and diverse than the on-site techniques. We will consider several off-site methods: seminars, audiovisual instruction, behavior modeling training, simulation techniques, programmed instruction, and computer-assisted instruction.

seminar
a common training method in which an expert provides job-related information in a classroom-like setting

Seminars—A very common method of employee training, and one that is very familiar to students, is the **seminar**, which typically involves some expert providing job-related information orally in a classroom-like setting. Although this method of training allows a large number of workers to be trained simultaneously at relatively low cost, it has some drawbacks. First, because the seminar is primarily a one-way form of communication, employees may not become highly involved in the learning process. Also, it is unclear whether workers will be able to translate the information they receive from seminars into an actual performance of work behaviors. Finally, the seminar method is often only as good as the presenter. A training program presented by a speaker who is unprepared and speaks in a monotone is unlikely to lead to any significant learning. In fact, one early study found that the seminar was one of the least effective of various employee training methods (Carroll, Paine, & Ivancevich, 1972). On a more positive note, however, seminar methods of instruction have been shown to be an effective learning strategy, particularly when used with more educated workers, such as when seminars are used in managerial and leadership training (Avolio, Reichard, Hannah, Walumbwa, & Chan, 2009; Burke & Day, 1986). Another study found a positive impact of an employee health promotion program on healthful behaviors of employees and reduced absenteeism (Mills, Kessler, Cooper, & Sullivan, 2007). Of course, seminars can be made even more effective if the lecture presentation is combined with question-and-answer periods or audience discussion to encourage a more "active" learning process.

Audiovisual instruction—Audiovisual instruction uses videos to train workers. In effect, audiovisual instruction is a seminar provided in a different format. Although there may be some fairly large initial costs for purchase or development of training materials, the audiovisual method can be even more cost effective than traditional seminar techniques if large numbers of employees are going to be trained.

As in seminars, the quality of audiovisual instruction determines its effectiveness as a training tool. In many instances, a video can be more entertaining than a seminar and may do a better job of attracting the audience's attention. An obvious problem occurs, however, when the informational content is sacrificed for entertainment value.

Audiovisual presentations are especially effective when the information is presented visually rather than verbally. A few minutes of video can visually demonstrate manual operations (with instant replay, stop action, or slow motion) or can expose workers to a number of different locations and settings, both of which would be impossible in a seminar presentation. Moreover, recorded audiovisual programs can ensure uniformity of training by exposing all workers to the same information. For example, one company has prepared a video presentation giving new employees information about company policies, procedures, and employee rights and benefits in a thorough, graphic, and cost-effective manner.

Behavior modeling training—Another employee training technique is behavior modeling training (Decker & Nathan, 1985; Goldstein & Sorcher, 1974). In behavior modeling training, which is based on social learning theory, trainees are

audiovisual instruction the use of films, videotapes, and other electronic media to convey training material

behavior modeling training a training method that exposes trainees to role models performing appropriate and inappropriate work behaviors and their outcomes and then allows trainees to practice modeling the appropriate behaviors

At an insurance company's training facility, claims adjusters are given audiovisual instruction as well as hands-on experience.

exposed to videotaped or live role models displaying both appropriate and inappropriate work behaviors as well as their successful or unsuccessful outcomes. Trainees are then allowed an opportunity to try to replicate and practice the positive work behaviors. Research indicates that behavior modeling training, if used correctly, can effectively improve employee job performance (Mann & Decker, 1984; Meyer & Raich, 1983; Taylor, Russ-Eft, & Chan, 2005). Behavior modeling training was also shown to be effective in computer software training (Gist, Schwoerer, & Rosen, 1989) and in training U.S. government employees for working in Japan (Harrison, 1992). In another interesting study, behavior modeling training was found to be more effective than either seminars or programmed instruction (see later discussion) in training computer operators (Simon & Werner, 1996). Recent research suggests that for learning complex tasks, even behavior modeling training needs to be followed up to ensure that the training transfers to the actual work setting (May & Kahnweiler, 2000). Behavior modeling may be a particularly effective strategy for ethics training, where models can demonstrate complex ethical and moral decision making and actions (Kaptein, 2011).

simulation
training that replicates job conditions without placing the trainee in the actual work setting

Simulation techniques—Simulation training is a method of replicating job conditions to instruct employees in proper work operations without actually putting them in the job setting. Jet pilots, astronauts, and nuclear power plant operators are all subjected to intensive simulation training before they are allowed to control the complex and dangerous machinery that they will operate on the job. Simulation training allows the worker hours of practice under conditions that are quite similar to the actual work setting, without allowing the possibility of damaging the equipment, the product, the environment, or themselves.

Most commonly, simulation training uses replications of complex machinery or equipment, such as jet cockpit flight simulators or mock-ups of the control panels used by nuclear power plant operators. Other simulations may be designed to give trainees exposure to what would normally be very hazardous working conditions. For example, a Southern California police department has constructed a mock city (complete with a bank and a convenience store!) for use in training police personnel in simulated emergency conditions. Police trainees attempt to foil simulated robbery attempts and rescue hostages from terrorists using the mock city and blank ammunition. According to the police authorities, the realism of this simulation has led to better preparation of new officers in dealing with actual life-threatening situations. As you can imagine, simulation training is often very expensive. However, the chance for hands-on experience, immediate feedback, and repeated practice makes it a very effective technique.

Web-based training.   More and more, employee training is being done through Web-based, interactive programs. Webinars (live or recorded) are replacing seminar and audiovisual programs. More than a decade ago, Whalen and Wright (2000) argued that much of future training will be Web-based due to the flexibility and scope of the training programs that can be delivered via the web, the convenience of having training "on demand," when employees need it, and the relatively low cost of Web-based training in comparison to "live" employee training programs. For example, a Web-based health promotion training program was found to have positive effects on employee health, but at a much lower cost than a live training program (Williams & Day, 2011).

Web-based training has incorporated an older form of learning, known as *programmed instruction.*

Programmed instruction involves the use of self-paced individualized training. Each trainee is provided with either printed materials or, more commonly, Web-based content to learn and then answers a series of questions that test how much learning has taken place. When test answers are substantially correct, the trainee is instructed to move on to the next unit. If the questions are answered incorrectly, some review of the previous unit is required. Most of the student study guides that accompany college textbooks are examples of programmed instruction.

programmed instruction
self-paced individualized training in which trainees are provided with training materials and can test how much they have learned

The benefits of programmed instruction are that it is efficient, because individuals proceed at their own paces, and that it provides immediate feedback. In addition, programmed instruction is an "active," involved form of learning. Furthermore, although the development of such programs is time consuming, the initial cost diminishes greatly over time if large numbers of employees are trained. A problem can arise, however, in keeping the programs up-to-date, especially in fields where there are rapid changes in technology or in the types of products produced or services performed, requiring that new instruction programs must be continually created.

Computer-assisted instruction (CAI) is a more sophisticated approach to individualized employee training. Although CAI is actually a form of programmed instruction, CAI systems offer the flexibility to change and update the instructional programs continually. CAI also allows for immediate testing of the trainee's learning because the computer can ask questions and instantly score the correctness of responses, automatically returning the trainee to the earlier lesson if the answers are incorrect, and quickly presenting the next unit when the answers are correct (recall the computer-adaptive and Web-based testing discussed in Chapter 5). Typically, training organizations offer Web-based courses that can also generate detailed data on each trainee's performance across all the lessons. One problem with individualized instruction, such as CAI, is that some employees may not have the self-motivation to learn and may do better in formal, "live" training programs (Brown, 2001).

computer-assisted instruction
programmed instruction delivered by computer that adapts to the trainee's learning rate

A recent development in CAI is computerized, interactive programs that combine audiovisual techniques, programmed instruction, and simulation techniques. With these programs, a trainee may be presented with a video representation of a work situation. The computer then asks questions about which course of action the trainee would like to take. The response is then used to choose the next video segment, where the trainee can see the results of the choice played out. One such program, used for management training, exposes the trainee to a variety of difficult interpersonal and decision-making situations. The trainee is brought into a simulated work situation with actors portraying the roles of coworkers. In one setting, the trainee might need to deal with a subordinate who is angry about having been given a negative performance appraisal. In another situation, the trainee may be asked to play the role of leader of a decision-making group and choose one of several possible courses of action. Choosing the correct management strategies leads to a positive outcome. If an incorrect choice is made, the trainee will view the disastrous results played out in the subsequent scene.

There has also been some use of online gaming platforms to develop teams—putting team members through simulated environments in order to build coordination and cooperation among team members. We will discuss these methods further in Chapter 12.

Management/leadership training methods

Because managers and organizational leaders are considered to play such a central role in administrative functions, coordinating organizational activities and motivating workers, and because managerial skills are abstract and difficult to learn, a large share of training resources go into the training and development of managers. In fact, a variety of special techniques are used almost exclusively in management training.

One common and very popular management training technique is the **problem-solving case study**, which presents trainees with a written description of a real or hypothetical organizational problem. Each trainee is allowed time to study the case individually and come up with a solution. The trainees then meet in small groups to present and critique their solutions and discuss the problem further. One purpose of such studies is to show trainees that there are no single or easy solutions to complex problems (Berger, 1983). Another goal is to help trainees develop skills in diagnosing and dealing with organizational problems. Although the problem-solving case study is a popular management training method, some doubt its effectiveness (Argyris, 1980; Campbell, Dunnette, Lawler, & Weick, 1970), specifically whether the learning from the hypothetical situation transfers well to actual management situations.

An extension of this method is to have trainees engage in role-playing a certain management situation. For example, in a role-playing exercise to develop managers' abilities to handle difficult interpersonal situations, a trainer may play a subordinate who has chronic performance problems. The trainee plays the manager, and the trainer may later offer feedback concerning how the situation was handled. In role-playing the basic idea is that trainees will become more involved in a problem situation if they act it out. Sometimes, participants will reverse roles to gain a different perspective on the problem situation. A beneficial side effect of role-playing may be that management trainees simultaneously learn to develop their presentational and communication skills.

Another management training technique is the use of simulations of organizations or **management games**, which are usually scaled-down enactments of the management of organizations. They are in many ways similar to some of the more complicated board or computer simulation games that people play at home. One example is called "Tinsel Town," where trainees function as the top management team of a fictional movie studio (Devine, Habig, Martin, Bott, & Grayson, 2004). Participants may either play in groups, forming management teams to compete against other teams, or play against one another individually.

problem-solving case study

a management training technique that presents a real or hypothetical organizational problem that trainees attempt to solve

role-playing

a management training exercise that requires trainees to act out problem situations that often occur at work

management games

a management training technique using scaled-down enactments of the operations and managements of organizations

As with case studies, the difficulty is in generalizing learning from the game situation to the actual work setting. Also, participants may become so caught up in the game that they do not comprehend the management principles that are being taught. An early review of research on management games, however, indicated that they are an effective management training technique (Keys & Wolfe, 1990).

Another management training technique is the conference, or group discussion. Conferences usually involve a very unstructured type of training in which participants are brought together to share ideas and information and solve some shared management problems. The basic goal of conferences is for practicing managers to learn effective management techniques that have been used by other managers. Their main advantage is that they encourage individual participation in the learning process. As mentioned, full-scale training programs usually include a number of training methods. This is particularly true in management training, in which trainees may attend workshops lasting several days, with participants exposed to training in a variety of areas, including problem solving, decision making, and interpersonal skills, using a number of techniques.

conference
an unstructured management training technique in which participants share ideas, information, and problems; also called a group discussion

A very complex, involved type of managerial training/development is called action learning. Action learning consists of teams of employees who are assembled to work on a company-related problem or issue (Conger & Toegel, 2003). Rather than being a simulation, action learning has the team working on an actual assignment such as developing a new product or solving an organizational problem (Conger & Xin, 2000). The concept behind action learning is that managers learn by doing, whereas the organization benefits from the results of the action learning team's project. For example, action learning teams at General Electric have been formed to deal with issues as diverse as investigating markets for leasing locomotive engines, developing new applications for plastic in the design of automobile bodies, and developing marketing plans for foreign markets—with the team members, learning as they contribute to expanding GE's businesses (Dotlich & Noel, 1998). Interest in action learning in organizations is on the rise, with an academic journal, *Action Learning: Research & Practice*, devoted to the topic.

action learning
teams assembled to work on a company-related problem or issue to learn by doing

Becoming very popular in management development is the use of *360-degree feedback*—the multisource, multiperspective performance appraisal method that we discussed in Chapter 6. A 360-degree feedback can be an effective management development tool, but only if the manager is open to and accepting of the potentially critical feedback (Waldman & Bowen, 1998). Atwater, Brett, and Waldman (2003) suggest that 360-degree feedback will be most successful when participants are trained in the technique, when feedback is honest and constructive, when the feedback is combined with other training efforts so that the manager can see how to improve performance, and when there is careful follow-up monitoring and feedback. As in all types of training, there are individual differences. Some managers may react favorably to 360-degree feedback, but others may not benefit and may have a negative reaction (Atwater, Waldman, Atwater, & Cartier, 2000). A longitudinal study of managers who received 360-degree feedback suggested that the technique led to improved managerial competence over time (Bailey & Fletcher, 2002).

mentoring

a training program in which an inexperienced worker develops a relationship with an experienced worker who serves as an advisor

An increasingly popular training program for new managers that combines elements of on-the-job training and a sort of informal "apprenticeship" is mentoring, a process by which an inexperienced worker develops a relationship with an experienced worker to promote the former's career development (Allen & Eby, 2007). Much of the learning that takes place in these relationships involves the protégé attempting to imitate the mentor's work and interpersonal style. Modeling thus appears to be one key learning process in mentoring. Mentoring among managers in large organizations is becoming more and more common as young, inexperienced workers typically look to older, more experienced workers to help them to "learn the ropes" of the job (Kram & Hall, 1989; Ragins, Cotton, & Miller, 2000). It has even been suggested that women executives will have difficulty moving up the corporate ladder unless they receive some mentoring from higher-ups (Ragins, 1999).

Since its appearance as a formal training strategy in the late 1970s (Roche, 1979), there has been extensive research, as well as popular interest, in mentoring as a management training and development technique. For the most part, there are many positive results of good mentoring relationships. For instance, protégés generally advance more quickly in their careers, have greater job and career satisfaction, and have lower turnover than workers without mentors (Ragins, 1999). Of course, a mentoring program is only going to be successful if there are good relationships between mentors and protégés (Young & Perrewé, 2000), and mentoring programs using more "powerful," senior mentors seem to be more effective than peer mentoring programs (Ensher, Thomas, & Murphy, 2001). Research, however, suggests that mentoring relationships that develop on their own, informally, are typically more successful than formal, assigned mentoring relationships (Raabe & Beehr, 2003; Scandura & Williams, 2001). Research has also indicated that a number of factors may influence workers' willingness to serve as mentors. For instance, managers are more willing to mentor newer workers if those workers show greater promise and if they are more similar to the mentor in terms of factors such as educational background (Burke, McKeen, & McKenna, 1993; Olian, Carroll, & Giannantonio, 1993). Gender may also play a part in willingness to mentor (Ragins & Cotton, 1993), with women less likely than men to volunteer as mentors, particularly if the protégé is a man.

Mentoring as a management development technique is quite popular in organizations today. Although the benefits of mentorship to protégés are obvious, there are also some payoffs for the mentor and for the organization (Fagenson, 1989). The mentor, who may be at a midlife career standstill, may become energized by the chance to assist in the development of an eager young worker's career. The organization also benefits, because mentoring leads to a more well-trained and satisfied young workforce. On the other hand, mentors may find mentoring time consuming and burdensome (Ragins, 1989; Ragins & Scandura, 1993). Protégés may also react negatively if they feel forced into participating in mentorship programs (Chao, Walz, & Gardner, 1992; Gunn, 1995; Ragins & Cotton, 1999). Recently, Ensher and Murphy (2005) looked at various alternatives to formal mentoring programs, including "virtual mentoring" and the use of multiple individuals as mentoring role models.

Formal mentoring programs are very common in organizations today.

One management development technique that is becoming wildly popular with high-level executive leaders is "executive coaching" (McKenna & Davis, 2009). Coaching is typically a one-on-one relationship between a consultant and a key executive/manager that is designed to help develop and improve the executive's professional performance (Kilburg, 2000). Although coaches use a wide range of techniques, perhaps their most important function is providing frank feedback to managers and executives and helping in setting developmental goals. There is very limited research on the effectiveness of coaching, but its use is on the rise, and a few studies suggest that it is effective (e.g., Kampa-Kokesch & Anderson, 2001), although it has not been rigorously evaluated (Peterson, 2011). Given the "counseling" nature of executive coaching, issues regarding the ethics of psychological practice are extremely important.

coaching
a one-on-one relation-ship where a consultant helps an executive improve performance

IMPLEMENTATION OF THE TRAINING PROGRAM

Once the training materials and methods have been selected and pilot tested, the next step in the training model is the implementation of the training program. When implementing the training program, factors such as trainee readiness, trainee expectations, and the climate for training—whether the employees and the organization feel positively about the training and encourage it—need to be considered. It is also important to provide trainees with a "rationale" for training—to let them know how the training will benefit them and the organization (Quiñones, 1997). As training progresses, it is important that trainees be given feedback about their learning and opportunities to practice newly learned techniques or behaviors.

Stop & Review

Give three examples each of off-site and on-site employee training methods.

EVALUATION OF THE TRAINING PROGRAM

A crucial component of any employee training program is the evaluation of training effectiveness, for there is no use in investing money and resources in training programs unless they do indeed work. Despite its importance, however, relatively few programs are actually subjected to rigorous evaluation (Birati & Tziner, 1999; Goldstein & Ford, 2002).

The evaluation of a training program should first outline the criteria that indicate the program's success and develop the means for measuring these criteria. One very useful framework suggests that there are four types of criteria for evaluating a program's effectiveness (Kirkpatrick, 1959–1960; Latham & Saari, 1979; Warr, Allan, & Birdi, 1999):

1. *Reaction criteria*—measures of the impressions of trainees, including their assessments of the program's value, the amount of learning they received, and their enjoyment of the program. Reaction criteria are usually assessed via training evaluation rating surveys given to trainees immediately after training sessions or workshops. It is important to note that reaction criteria do not measure whether any learning has taken place. Rather, they assess trainees' opinions about the training and their learning.

2. *Learning criteria*—measures of the amount of learning that has taken place. Typically, these take the form of some sort of tests assessing the amount of information retained from the program.

3. *Behavioral criteria*—measures of the amount of newly learned skills displayed once the trainee has returned to the job. Observational methods of measurement are typically used to assess behavioral criteria, with supervisors recording the use of newly learned behaviors.

4. *Results criteria*—measures the outcomes that are important to the organization, such as increased trainee work output as expressed by production rates, dollar sales figures, or quality of work. Using the results criteria, a cost–benefit analysis can be performed by comparing the costs of the program to the dollar value of the results. This is usually the most important evaluation of a program's effectiveness. However, it is sometimes difficult to translate training outcomes into dollars and cents. For example, if one of the goals is to improve employee attitudes, it may be very hard to place a dollar value on such results.

The important question in the evaluation of programs is whether any measured changes in criteria are indeed the result of training. The methods used in the proper evaluation of a training program are those used to determine the effectiveness of any other type of program introduced into an organization. For a formal evaluation to demonstrate conclusively that training has caused certain outcomes, it should be based on experimental designs. Unfortunately, many evaluations use what might be called "preexperimental designs," which do not allow for proper assessments (Campbell & Stanley, 1963) (see Figure 7.3).

One example, the posttest-only design simply measures criteria following the completion of a training program. However, this does not tell us anything conclusive about its effectiveness because we have no basis for any sort of comparison.

A pretest–posttest design—measuring behavior before and after training—is also an inadequate experimental design. Although this approach compares the criterion measures collected before and after the training program, we cannot be sure that the differences from pretest to posttest were due to the program. Consider the example of a training program designed to teach bank tellers to be more friendly and attentive to customer needs. With a simple pretest–posttest evaluation, we can never be sure that later observed increases in the quality of customer service were due to training or to other factors, such as a recent pay raise or change in management. Although these limited designs do not allow us to draw clear conclusions, even such limited evaluations are better than no evaluation at all (Sackett & Mullen, 1993).

To be sure of the effectiveness of a training program, one should apply a more sophisticated, true experimental design that uses at least one treatment group, which receives the training, and one control group, which does not undergo any training. The simplest and most common experimental design for evaluation research uses one training group and one control group, both of which are measured before and after the program. To ensure that there are no unexpected differences in members of the training and control groups, employees are randomly assigned to the two groups. The pretest and posttest scores are then compared. This experimental design makes it clear that any positive changes in the criterion measures of the training group, relative to the control group, are most likely due to the training program.

A more sophisticated experimental design is the Solomon four-group design (Solomon, 1949). This method of evaluation uses four groups, two that are trained and two that are not. In the Solomon design, two of the groups are identical to those in the basic experimental design mentioned earlier. That is, one training group and one control group are measured both before and after the training program. However, the additional training and control groups are measured only after the program, which is intended to help rule out the fact that administering a pretraining measure might sensitize employees to what the program is designed to do and might thus produce certain changes in the criterion measures that occur without the benefit of training. For example, if our bank tellers are given a pretraining test of their customer service knowledge, they might realize that management is very interested in this issue, which might cause all tellers to give greater attention to customers, regardless of whether they later receive customer service training. Although the Solomon four-group design is an effective design for evaluating training programs, it is underused, primarily because of the large number of participants and groups required (Braver & Braver, 1988). The Solomon four-group design can be used, however, for more than just evaluation of training programs. One study used the design to evaluate employee reactions to a

posttest-only design
a program evaluation that simply measures training success criterion following completion of the training program

pretest–posttest design
a design for evaluating a training program that makes comparisons of criterion measures collected before and after the introduction of the program

Solomon four-group design
a method of program evaluation using two treatment groups and two control groups

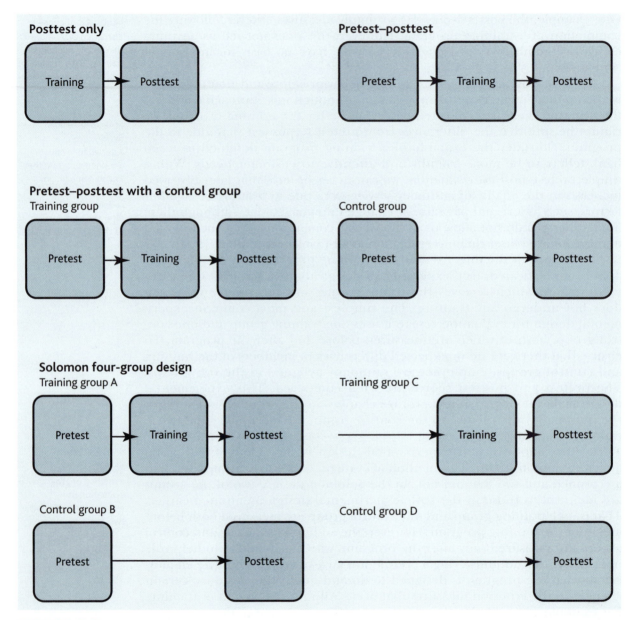

FIGURE 7.3
Four Methods for Evaluation of Training Programs

major organizational restructuring (Probst, 2003). Figure 7.3 summarizes the various evaluation designs.

A comprehensive evaluation of a training program must be well designed and executed to ensure that the training is indeed effective. This means careful consideration must be given to the selection and measurement of criteria, an experimental design with adequate control groups must be used, and the costs versus benefits of the program must be assessed (Arvey, Maxwell, & Salas, 1992; Birati & Tziner, 1999).

An obvious problem in evaluating the effectiveness of training programs is the inability to use a true experimental design due to constraints imposed by the particular work organizations. However, quasi-experimental designs can be used (Campbell & Stanley, 1963; Cook, Campbell, & Peracchio, 1991). As discussed in Chapter 2, quasi-experiments are approximations of experimental designs. One example is the nonequivalent control group design. This design is typically used when it is impossible to assign trainees randomly to experimental and control groups. A nonequivalent control group might consist of similar employees from another company location that is not undergoing the new training program. The training and control groups are "nonequivalent" because they may differ systematically on variables, such as experience, previous training, supervisory methods, or any other factor that would be controlled for via random assignment in a true experimental design.

⏱ Stop & Review

Illustrate the four types of criteria for evaluating employee training programs.

Equal Employment Opportunity Issues in Employee Training

Because training is linked to job performance and can lead to personnel actions such as pay increases, promotions, and terminations, several equal employment opportunity concerns are related to personnel training (Russell, 1984). One such issue deals with educational or training prerequisites for certain jobs. Because members of underprivileged groups are likely to have less education and formal job training than members of more privileged groups, setting certain levels of education or training as job prerequisites may be considered discriminatory. As mentioned in Chapter 4, equal employment opportunity legislation protects against discrimination against specific groups in providing access to jobs. If access to some jobs requires certain training, employers must take steps to guard against any discrimination in this area by providing remedial education or training for groups of workers who lack the educational prerequisites. For example, some employers are supporting agencies that will train chronically unemployed or underemployed individuals in basic job skills either by making financial contributions or by hiring persons who have undergone the training.

The methods used in employee training programs may also create instances of potential discrimination. For example, the lectures offered in many seminar programs may lead to different rates of learning in different groups of trainees. If certain underprivileged groups lack the education needed to process the information and to perform well on any examinations administered, using the results of such training classes to screen or place workers can lead to unintentional discrimination. A similar case occurs in training courses that require certain strenuous activities, such as lifting and carrying heavy materials, in which women may be at some disadvantage. One example was a training course for

Training requirements should not exclude employees on the basis of gender or ethnicity.

firefighters that demanded that trainees lift and carry a 150-pound dummy over their shoulders for several yards or down a flight of stairs to simulate carrying an unconscious person from a burning building. A question arose as to whether this part of the course discriminated against women. Critics stated that firefighters rarely carried a person out of a burning building and that the ability to do this was not a critical requirement for adequate performance of their job. Because of the possibility of discrimination and because the fire department could not prove that this was a necessary skill for the position, the training task was eliminated.

Similarly, organizations that require workers to attend and complete some type of training program to gain a position or a promotion must demonstrate that completion of the program is predictive of success in the jobs that trainees will be holding. If not, there is the possibility that certain disadvantaged groups of trainees may not do as well in the program because of unfamiliarity with the training procedures and format. In other words, because of their lack of experience with the classroom situation, they may not learn as well as members of the majority group, which can lead to discrimination. For example, if being promoted to a frontline supervisory position in a factory requires attending classes in supervisory skills and passing an examination to complete the course, the organization must prove that completion of the training is related to later success as a supervisor and that the program itself does not discriminate in terms of ability to pass the course. In these cases, the training program is just like any other selection tool. It must be shown to be valid, fair, and job related.

ON THE *CUTTING* EDGE

Training for the Twenty-first Century: Adaptability, Creativity, and Proactive Thinking

Today's organizations exist in a rapidly changing environment. Likewise, jobs are constantly changing in terms of structure, technology, and tasks. Your job today might be completely different six months from now. As a result, I/O psychologists and human resources professionals are giving greater attention to training the skills required in ever-changing jobs and work environments.

One model suggests that the skills needed for adaptive performance include *solving problems creatively*, *dealing with uncertain work situations, handling emergencies*, and *being interpersonally* and *culturally adaptable* (Pulakos, Arad, Donovan, & Plamandon, 2000). Other research suggests that effective, adaptable workers need to develop what is called "proactive thinking," which involves a willingness and ability to

take action to change a situation to one's advantage (Kirby, Kirby, & Lewis, 2002). There is evidence that both adaptive performance and proactive thinking can be trained.

Another area that is receiving a great deal of attention is training workers to be more creative. Special attention has been given to developing creative and innovative workers and organizational leaders (Birdi, 2007; Mumford & Licuanan, 2004). A meta-analysis of 70 studies suggests that creativity training is generally effective in getting people to be more creative and innovative in approaching tasks (Scott, Leritz, & Mumford, 2004). In all likelihood, work-related training in the future will focus more on strategies to be creative and adaptive, rather than learning specific tasks and procedures.

Summary

Employee training is a planned effort by an organization to facilitate the learning, retention, and transfer of job-related behavior. Training is not limited to new employees, but often involves various types of training and development programs offered throughout an employee's career. Specific areas of employee training include new employee orientation, employee retraining and continuing education, retirement planning and career development, and worker training for international assignments, for diversity, to reduce sexual harassment, and to increase ethical behavior at work.

An understanding of learning theories is fundamental in the design of employee training programs. For example, the concept of *modeling*, which is imitative of learning, is expressed in *social learning theory*. If training programs are to be successful, a number of key issues will affect their effectiveness. For example, *transfer of training*, or how the learning translates into use of

the newly learned behaviors, and the job characteristics of the trainees, such as *trainee readiness*, must be taken into account. Finally, concern must be given to how training programs are structured and how they are conducted.

The first step in a successful employee training program is assessing training needs, which occurs on several levels. Organizational analysis considers the organization's goals, resources, and the climate for training; task analysis evaluates the specific knowledge, skills, and abilities that a job requires; and person analysis examines the capabilities and deficiencies of the workers themselves. Training needs may also have to be conducted through demographic analysis, which is targeted toward assessing the training needs of specific groups, such as males versus females or the old versus the young. The second step involves establishing training objectives, whereas the third step focuses on employee training methods. The various training methods

can be broken down into two general categories: on-site methods and off-site methods. Of
on-site methods, *on-the-job training* is the most
widely used, consisting of putting inexperienced
workers into the work site under the direction of
an experienced teacher–worker. *Apprenticeship*
is a much more long-term on-site method,
combining classroom training with supervised
on-the-job training. *Vestibule training* sets up a
model training area adjacent to the actual work
site, using professional trainers and hands-on
experience. *Job rotation* is a training technique
designed to broaden workers' experience by
rotating employees among various jobs.

Off-site methods include the common *seminar* method and *audiovisual instruction* that provides graphic depictions of work activities, and
Web-based training (webinars). A technique
that uses aspects of both audiovisual technology
and concepts of social learning theory is *behavior
modeling training*, a method of exposing trainees
to videotapes of models engaged in appropriate
work behaviors and then having them practice
the observed behaviors. *Simulation techniques*
involve classroom replications of actual work-
stations. *Programmed instruction* is a form of self-
paced training in which workers can learn at
their own pace. A sophisticated version of programmed instruction is *computer-assisted instruction (CAI)*.

Several specific methods and techniques
used in management training include *problem-
solving case studies*, *role-playing*, and *management
games*, which all involve simulations of actual
management situations. *Action learning* is a
complicated form of training in which teams
are formed to perform a special project or
assignment that benefits the organization, while
the team members learn and develop managerial skills. A 360-degree feedback is also used
as a management development tool. *Mentoring*
is a management training program in which an
inexperienced worker is assigned to an experienced mentor who serves as a role model.
Coaching is where a consultant advises an executive to improve performance.

Once training programs have been implemented, the evaluation of their effectiveness is
very important. The first step in evaluation is
to determine criteria of training effectiveness.
Four types are typically used: reaction criteria,
learning criteria, behavioral criteria, and results
criteria. Once the criteria are established, basic
research methods and design should be used
to evaluate the training programs. The *pretest–
posttest* design is a common but inadequate
means of assessing a program in which measures
of criteria are collected both before and after a
training intervention, allowing for a comparison of changes in learning or work behaviors.
However, this method is inadequate because
of the lack of a good comparison group. Better
evaluation designs use both a training group
and a comparison, or control, group that is not
subjected to the training program. A very complex and sophisticated evaluation design is the
Solomon four-group design, which uses two training
groups and two control groups.

Finally, certain legal issues must be considered in the design and implementation of
training programs. Training or educational
prerequisites and the training programs themselves must not unfairly discriminate on the
basis of ethnicity, age, sex, or disability.

Study Questions and Exercises

1. Consider how learning takes place in work
organizations. How does employee training relate to learning in college classrooms?
What are the similar methods and underlying theories/concepts of learning?

2. Consider a work organization that you have
had some contact with, either one in which
you were employed or in which a friend or
relative is working. Based on your knowledge, how might a training needs assessment

be conducted? Consider all four levels of assessment: organizational, task, person, and demographic analysis.

3. Compare and contrast the advantages and disadvantages of on-site versus off-site training methods.

4. Consider the various designs for evaluating employee training programs. Although the more complex and sophisticated designs usually provide better evaluation, what are some of the difficulties of conducting an assessment in actual work organizations?

5. Review the discussion of EEO issues in personnel training. What are the various ways that training programs could discriminate against members of protected groups (ethnic minorities, women, people with disabilities, or the elderly)?

Web Links

www.astd.org
The American Society for Training and Development is a professional organization devoted to employee training.

www.eeoc.gov
Site for the federal agency dealing with employment discrimination issues.

Suggested Readings

Boud, D., & Garrick, J. (Eds.). (2000). *Understanding learning at work*. London: Routledge. *An interesting edited book that looks at the underlying learning theory in employee training programs, taking into account the recent advancements in training technology and the changing nature of work.*

Noe, R.A. (2010). *Employee training & development.* (5th ed.). New York: McGraw-Hill/Irwin. *A textbook containing just about everything you would want to know about personnel training.*

Sessa, V. I., & London, M. (2006). *Continuous learning in organizations: Individual, group, and organizational perspectives.* Mahwah, NJ: Erlbaum. *This book takes a very broad look at how to turn organizations into learning systems.*

PART THREE

CHAPTER

8 | Motivation

CHAPTER OUTLINE

Inside Tips

MOTIVATION WITHIN THE CONTEXT OF INDUSTRIAL/
ORGANIZATIONAL PSYCHOLOGY

Two areas of I/O psychology involve a tremendous amount of theorizing: motivation and leadership (the topic of leadership will be discussed in Chapter 12). Because both motivation and leadership are extremely complex and important topics in the work world, they have historically been given a great deal of attention by I/O psychologists. This chapter introduces a variety of theories of motivation. Rather than viewing these as isolated models, consider the ways in which they are similar. Some of these similarities are reflected in the grouping of theories into categories, such as need theories and job design theories, as shown in the chapter outline. Other similarities can also help draw related concepts together. For example, the need theories emphasize the satisfaction of basic human needs as a key to motivation, whereas reinforcement theory argues that motivation is caused by work-related rewards, or reinforcers. However, the satisfaction of human needs can also be seen as the experience of a reward. By understanding similarities such as these, you can begin to synthesize what at first appears to be an overwhelming mass of abstract and unrelated theories.

Besides looking for similarities among motivation theories and noticing topics that were previously discussed, pay close attention to the last section of the chapter, which emphasizes that motivation is only one of the many variables that can affect work outcomes. This is an important point because it reminds us to consider the "total picture"—the interrelationships among many organizational variables—when studying work behavior.

I t's still the first month of your new job. You have noticed that some of your colleagues seem to put lots of energy and drive into their work. Others try to get by with minimal effort. Why is this the case? When we begin to infer some underlying processes of effort, energy, or drive, we are trying to capture the elusive construct of motivation. If you surveyed managers and asked them to list the most difficult aspects of their jobs, odds are that the majority would mention difficulties in motivating workers as a particular problem.

Motivation is complex and elusive and has historically been of great interest to the wider field of psychology. As a result, work motivation is one of the most widely researched topics in I/O psychology.

In this chapter, we will begin by defining motivation. Next, we will examine the various theories of work motivation and see how some of them have been applied in attempts to increase worker motivation. Finally, we will look at how work motivation relates to work performance.

Defining Motivation

According to one definition (Steers & Porter, 1991), motivation is a force that serves three functions: It energizes, or causes people to act; it directs behavior toward the attainment of specific goals; and it sustains the effort expended in reaching those goals.

motivation
the force that energizes, directs, and sustains behavior

Because motivation cannot be observed directly, it is very difficult to study. We can only infer motives either by observing goal-directed behavior or by using some psychological measurement technique. Throughout its history, I/O psychology has offered many theories of work motivation (Diefendorff & Chandler, 2011). We have already touched on the simplistic models put forth by scientific management and the human relations movement (Chapter 1). According to Frederick Taylor, workers are motivated by money and material gains, whereas Elton Mayo stressed the role that interpersonal needs play in motivating workers. Since these early days, more sophisticated theories of motivation have been developed. Some stress the importance of specific needs in determining motivation. Other theories emphasize the connection between work behaviors and outcomes—the influence of attaining rewards and achieving goals. Other theories focus on the role of job design in affecting motivation. Still another category of theories argues that motivation is a cognitive process and that workers rationally weigh the advantages and disadvantages of expending work energy. We will review examples of each of these categories of work motivation theories.

Need Theories of Motivation

needs
physiological or psychological deficiencies that an organism is compelled to fulfill

Several motivation theories assert that people have certain needs that are important in determining motivation. Needs involve specific physiological or psychological deficiencies that the organism is driven to satisfy. The need for food and the drive of hunger is a physiological need and drive inherent in all living organisms; the need for human contact is a psychological need. Need theories of motivation propose that motivation is the process of the interaction among various needs and the drives to satisfy those needs. We will first look at some basic need theories and then examine one need theory, McClelland's achievement motivation theory, in more depth.

BASIC NEED THEORIES

need hierarchy theory
a motivation theory, proposed by Maslow, that arranges needs in a hierarchy from lower, more basic needs to higher-order needs

Two basic need theories are those proposed by Abraham Maslow and Clayton Alderfer. Both of these theories maintain that several different types or categories of needs play a role in human motivation. Maslow's theory, called the need hierarchy theory, proposes five categories of needs, which form a hierarchy from the more basic human needs to more complex, higher-order needs (Maslow, 1965, 1970). See Table 8.1 for a description of these needs.

According to Maslow, the lower-order needs (physiological needs, safety needs, and social needs)—what Maslow called "deficiency needs"—must be satisfied in a step-by-step fashion before an individual can move on to higher-order needs (esteem and self-actualization needs)—what Maslow referred to as "growth needs." Because higher-order needs are unlikely to be

---

TABLE 8.1

Maslow's Hierarchy of Needs (arranged from lowest- to highest-order needs)

1. *Physiological needs:* the basic survival needs of food, water, air, sleep, and sex
2. *Safety needs:* the needs for physical safety (need for shelter) and needs related to psychological security
3. *Social needs:* the need to be accepted by others and needs for love, affection, and friendship
4. *Esteem needs:* the needs to be recognized for accomplishments and to be admired and respected by peers
5. *Self-actualization needs:* the needs to reach one's highest potential and to attain a sense of fulfillment; the highest level of needs

satisfied in the typical worker, there is also a constant upward striving that explains why, for example, even successful, high-level executives continue to exhibit considerable motivation. In other words, they are no longer motivated by money to provide for subsistence needs, but by a need for esteem, recognition, or self-growth.

Building in part on Maslow's theory is Clayton Alderfer's (1972) ERG theory, which collapses Maslow's five categories of needs into three: existence needs, which are similar to Maslow's basic physiological and safety needs; relatedness needs, which stem from social interaction and are analogous to the social needs in Maslow's hierarchy; and growth needs, which are the highest-order needs, dealing with needs to develop fully and realize one's potential. Alderfer made predictions similar to Maslow's, that as each level of need becomes satisfied, the next higher level becomes a strong motivator.

ERG theory
Alderfer's motivation model that categorizes needs into existence, relatedness, and growth needs

Although both basic need theories have received a great deal of attention from professionals in psychology, business, and other areas, neither theory has led to any type of useful application or strategy for improving work motivation (Miner, 1983). Although both theories do a good job of describing various types of needs and of distinguishing the lower- from the higher-order needs, both theories are quite limited. In particular, the predictions made by both theories about need-driven behavior have not held up (Rauschenberger, Schmitt, & Hunter, 1980; Wahba & Bridwell, 1976).

McClelland's Achievement Motivation Theory

A more comprehensive need theory of motivation, and one that deals specifically with work motivation, is David McClelland's achievement motivation theory (McClelland, 1961, 1975). This theory states that three needs are central to work motivation: the needs for achievement, power, and affiliation. According to McClelland, people are motivated by different patterns of needs, or motives, terms that he uses interchangeably. The factors that lead to work motivation may differ from person to person, depending on their particular pattern of needs. The three key motives, or needs, in his theory are as follows:

achievement motivation theory
McClelland's model of motivation that emphasizes the importance of three needs—achievement, power, and affiliation—in determining worker motivation

1. *Need for achievement*—the compelling drive to succeed and to get the job done. Individuals with a very high need for achievement are those who love the challenge of work. They are motivated by a desire to get ahead in the job, to solve problems, and to be outstanding work performers. Need for achievement is also associated with being task oriented, preferring situations offering moderate levels of risk or difficulty, and desiring feedback about goal attainment.

2. *Need for power*—the need to direct and control the activities of others and to be influential. Individuals with a high need for power are status oriented and are more motivated by the chance to gain influence and prestige than to solve particular problems personally or reach performance goals. McClelland talks about two sides to the need for power: One is personal power that is used toward personal ends and the other is institutional power, or power that is oriented toward organizational objectives (McClelland, 1970).

3. *Need for affiliation*—the desire to be liked and accepted by others. Individuals motivated by affiliation needs strive for friendship. They are greatly concerned with interpersonal relationships on the job and prefer working with others on a task. They are motivated by cooperative rather than competitive work situations.

This approach emphasizes the differences in these basic needs from person to person. According to McClelland, we all possess more or less of each of these motives, although in each individual a particular need (or needs) tends to predominate. In his earlier work, McClelland (1961) emphasized the role of need for achievement in determining work motivation (hence the name, "achievement motivation theory"). However, in later analyses, McClelland (1975) stressed the roles that the needs for power and affiliation also play in worker motivation. His theory can also be related to leadership, for he argued that a leader must be aware of and be responsive to the different needs of subordinates to motivate workers successfully (see Chapter 13).

Thematic Apperception Test (TAT)

a projective test that uses ambiguous pictures to assess psychological motivation

To assess an individual's motivational needs, McClelland used a variation of the Thematic Apperception Test (TAT). Respondents are instructed to study each of a series of fairly ambiguous pictures for a few moments and then "write the story it suggests" (see below Photo) The brief

Sample Item from a Variation of the Thematic Apperception Test (TAT) Used by McClelland

stories are then scored using a standardized procedure that measures the presence of the three basic needs to obtain a "motivational profile" for each respondent. The TAT is known as a projective test; that is, respondents project their inner motivational needs into the content of the story they create. One criticism of McClelland's theory concerns the use of the TAT, for its scoring can sometimes be unreliable, with different scorers possibly interpreting the stories differently. Also, there is a tendency for participants who write longer "stories" to be given higher scores on achievement motivation. It is important to note that other measures of motivational needs exist that do not rely on projective techniques (e.g., Spence & Helmreich, 1983; Steers & Braunstein, 1976). Despite the criticisms of McClelland's version of the TAT and criticisms of the measurement properties of projective tests in general, meta-analysis shows that the TAT is a reasonably good measurement tool (Spangler, 1992). It is important to note that there are alternative, self-report measures of motives, and that these measures also do a good job of assessing basic underlying motivational needs.

The majority of research on McClelland's theory has focused on the need for achievement (McClelland, 1961; McClelland, Atkinson, Clark, & Lowell, 1953). Evidence indicates that individuals with a high need for achievement attain personal success in their jobs, but only if the type of work that they do fosters personal achievement. That is, there must be a match between the types of outcomes a particular job offers and the specific motivational needs of the person. For example, people who have a great need for achievement might do best in a job in which they are allowed to solve problems, such as a scientist or engineer, or in which there is a direct relation between personal efforts and successful job outcomes, such as a salesperson working on commission. For example, need for achievement tends to be positively correlated with workers' incomes—high achievers made more money than those with a low need for achievement (McClelland & Franz, 1993). High need-achievement individuals are also more attracted to and successful in entrepreneurial careers (Collins, Hanges, & Locke, 2004). However, persons high in need for achievement might be less effective in team situations, and they have a tendency to try to accomplish goals by themselves rather than delegate to others or work with them as a unit (a reason why, perhaps, many high-achieving college students prefer individual over group projects and assignments).

Alternatively, those high in the need for affiliation should do best in a job in which they work with others as part of a team. However, research suggests that affiliation-motivated people are only cooperative when they feel secure and safe (Winter, 2002). Finally, persons with a high need for power should thrive in jobs that satisfy their needs to be in charge. In fact, research shows that many successful managers are high in the need for power, presumably because much of their job involves directing the activities of others (McClelland & Boyatzis, 1982; McClelland & Burnham, 1976).

The work of McClelland and his associates has led to several applications of the achievement motivation theory toward improving motivation in work settings. One strategy is a program that matches workers' motivational profiles to the requirements of particular jobs to place individuals in positions that will best allow them to fulfill their predominant needs (McClelland, 1980). A second application, effective in positions that require a strong need for achievement, is an achievement training program in which individuals are taught to be more achievement oriented by role-playing achievement-oriented actions and strategies and developing plans for setting achievement-related goals (Miron & McClelland, 1979). (But see Up Close box for some potential dangers associated with too much need for achievement.) The achievement motivation theory thus not only has been fairly well tested but also has led to these useful intervention strategies (Miner, 1983).

Behavior-Based Theories of Motivation

The next two motivation theories have been categorized as "behavior-based theories," because each theory focuses on behavioral outcomes as critical to affecting work motivation. These two theories are reinforcement theory and goal-setting theory.

REINFORCEMENT THEORY

reinforcement theory
the theory that behavior is motivated by its consequences

positive reinforcers
desirable events that strengthen the tendency to respond

negative reinforcers
events that strengthen a behavior through the avoidance of an existing negative state

punishment
unpleasant consequences that reduce the tendency to respond

Reinforcement theory draws on principles of operant conditioning and states simply that behavior is motivated by its consequences. A consequence that follows a behavior and serves to increase the motivation to perform that behavior again is a reinforcer. These reinforcers can be of two types. Positive reinforcers are events that are in and of themselves desirable to the person. Receiving praise, money, or a pat on the back are all common positive reinforcers. Negative reinforcers are events that lead to the avoidance of an existing negative state or condition. Being allowed to escape the noise and confusion of a busy work area by taking a short break in a quiet employee lounge or working hard at a task to avoid the wrath of a watchful supervisor are negative reinforcement situations. Negative reinforcement increases the motivation to perform the desired behavior again in an effort to keep the aversive negative condition from returning. For example, if a clerical worker feels that being behind schedule is a particularly aversive condition, the individual will be motivated to work hard to avoid the unpleasant state of being behind schedule. It is important to reemphasize that both negative and positive reinforcement can increase the motivation to repeat a behavior.

Punishment is the term used to describe any unpleasant consequence that directly follows the performance of a behavior. The effect of punishment is to weaken the tendency to perform the behavior again. Punishment is applied to behaviors that are deemed inappropriate. Receiving a harsh reprimand from your boss for too much socializing on the job and receiving a demotion because of sloppy work are examples of punishment. Reinforcement theory argues that reinforcement is a much better motivational technique than is punishment, because the goal of punishment is to stop unwanted behaviors, whereas reinforcement is designed to strengthen the motivation to perform a particular desired behavior. In addition, it is important to emphasize that punishment is

UP CLOSE   What Is a Workaholic?

According to McClelland, the need for achievement is a continuum ranging from very low to very high levels of achievement. Typically, we consider a high achievement level to be positive, but can we ever have too much need for achievement? The answer appears to be yes. When an individual's compelling drive to succeed in a job becomes so great that all other areas of life (family, health concerns, and leisure) are given little or no concern, we may label the person a workaholic or "achievement addicted" (Burke, 2006; Porter, 1996, 2001). Spence and Robbins (1992) suggested that although workaholics are highly involved in work, they do not necessarily enjoy working—they experience high levels of stress and may have related psychological and physical health issues (Burke, 2000a). The concept of the workaholic is related in many ways to the hard-driving "Type A," or "coronary-prone," behavior pattern, a topic we will discuss in the chapter on worker stress, Chapter 10.

Based on interviews with workaholics, Machlowitz (1976) derived 15 characteristics common to them. Look over the list and see how you match up to the definition:

1. An ongoing work style
2. A broad view of what a job requires
3. A sense of the scarcity of time
4. The use of lists and time-saving gadgets
5. Long work days
6. Little sleep
7. Quick meals
8. An awareness of what one's own work can accomplish
9. An inability to enjoy idleness
10. Initiative
11. Overlapping of work and leisure
12. A desire to excel
13. A dread of retirement
14. Intense energy
15. An ability to work anywhere (workaholics can always be spotted taking work into the bathroom)

It is interesting to note that many workers and work organizations place a high value on workaholics, and many companies actually encourage workaholism. For example, workaholic bosses may be singled out as role models for younger managers, and workaholic supervisors might encourage and reward similar workaholic behaviors in subordinates. In addition, as more and more companies downsize and eliminate personnel, it may promote workaholism because fewer workers must handle all of the work duties. Recent research suggests that workaholism does not necessarily lead to stress if the workaholic employee is engaged in and enjoys his/her job (van Beek, Taris, & Schaufeli, 2011).

generally a poor managerial strategy for several reasons: First, the chronic use of punishment can create feelings of hostility and resentment in workers and reduce morale and job satisfaction. Second, punished workers may try to retaliate and "get back" at punitive supervisors (de Lara, 2006). Third, punishment tends only to suppress behavior; once the threat of punishment is taken away, the worker may continue to use the undesirable behavior. Fourth, continual use of punishment leads to inefficient supervisors—ones who must spend too much of their time constantly "on watch" to catch workers committing undesirable behaviors and administer the punishment. Finally, there is some evidence that women supervisors who use punishment are evaluated more harshly than their male counterparts, and the women's use of discipline is perceived to be less effective (Atwater, Carey, & Waldman, 2001).

One way to better understand reinforcement theory is to focus on *schedules* of reinforcement. Reinforcement in the work environment typically takes place on a partial or intermittent reinforcement schedule, which can be of either the interval or ratio type. When interval schedules are used, the reinforcement is based on the passage of time, during which the individual is performing the desired behavior. When ratio schedules are used, reinforcement follows the performance

Stop & Review

What are the three needs in McClelland's theory? How are they measured?

of a number of desired behaviors. Both interval and ratio schedules can be either fixed or variable. Thus there are four reinforcement schedules: fixed interval, variable interval, fixed ratio, and variable ratio. Most typically, in work settings we think of these four types of schedules as representing different schedules of pay.

In the fixed-interval schedule, the reinforcement occurs after the passage of a specified amount of time. Employees who are paid an hourly or daily wage or a weekly or monthly salary are being reinforced on this schedule, which has two important characteristics. First, the reinforcement is not contingent on the performance of the desired behavior. Of course, it is assumed that during the intervening time period, people are performing their jobs. However, reinforcement follows regardless of whether the rate of performing job-related behaviors is high or low. Second, the fixed-interval schedule is predictable. People always know when a reinforcement is coming.

A variable-interval schedule is a somewhat rare means of work compensation. On these schedules, reinforcement is also determined by the passage of time, but the interval varies. For example, a worker for a small business might be paid on the average of once a month, but the exact time depends on when the owner does the payroll. Bonuses that are given on the bosses' whims are also on a variable-interval schedule.

In a fixed-ratio schedule, reinforcement depends on the performance of a set number of specified behaviors. Examples include workers who are paid for the number of components assembled, baskets of fruit picked, or reports written. This type of fixed-ratio payment is commonly referred to as "piecework." The strength of such a schedule is that reinforcement is contingent on execution of the desired behavior. Individuals on ratio schedules have high rates of responding in comparison to persons on interval schedules, who are merely "putting in time."

A variable-ratio schedule also involves reinforcement that is contingent on the performance of behaviors, but the number of responses required for a particular reinforcement varies. An example of a variable-ratio schedule is a salesperson on commission, who is required to give a number of sales presentations (the work behavior) to make a sale and receive a commission (the reinforcement). Variable-ratio schedules usually lead to very high levels of motivation because the reinforcement is contingent on performance and because of the "surprise element": You never know when the next reinforcement is coming. Gambling is reinforced on a variable-ratio schedule, which is why it is such an addicting behavior.

Research indicates that different types of schedules lead to various patterns of responding and thus have important implications for the use of reinforcement in motivating workers. Generally, evidence suggests that ratio schedules result in higher levels of motivation and subsequent task performance than do fixed-interval schedules (Pritchard, Hollenback, & DeLeo, 1980; Pritchard, Leonard, Von Bergen, & Kirk, 1976). These findings are important, especially because the majority of U.S. workers are paid on fixed-interval reinforcement schedules.

Obviously, reinforcement principles are used informally on a day-to-day basis to motivate workers through compensation systems and other forms of rewards for work outcomes. However, when reinforcement theory is applied formally as a program to increase worker motivation, it most often takes the form of organizational behavior modification, in which certain target behaviors are

---

fixed-interval schedule

reinforcement that follows the passage of a specified amount of time

variable-interval schedule

reinforcement that follows the passage of a specified amount of time, with exact time of reinforcement varying

fixed-ratio schedule

reinforcement that is contingent on the performance of a fixed number of behaviors

variable-ratio schedule

reinforcement that depends on the performance of a specified but varying number of behaviors

organizational behavior modification

the application of conditioning principles to obtain certain work outcomes specified, measured, and rewarded. For example, one model of organizational behavior modification takes a four-step approach, involving

1. Specifying the desired work behaviors;
2. Measuring desired performance of these behaviors using trained observers;
3. Providing frequent positive reinforcement, including graphs demonstrating individual and group performance of desired behaviors; and
4. Evaluation of the program's effectiveness (Komaki, Coombs, & Schepman, 1991).

Such programs have been used to motivate workers to be more productive, to produce higher-quality work, and to cut down on rates of absenteeism, tardiness, and work accidents by rewarding good performance, attendance, and/or safe work behaviors (e.g., Mawhinney, 1992; Merwin, Thomason, & Sanford, 1989). One study found that simply recognizing employees for improved work attendance led to significant reductions in employee absenteeism (Markham, Scott, & McKee, 2002), although it is important that the employees want the recognition and evaluate the plan favorably.

For example, in one study of roofing crews, roofers were offered monetary incentives (positive reinforcers) for reducing the hours needed to complete roofing jobs, and they were provided with feedback and earned time off (negative reinforcement) if they maintained high safety standards, using a regular checklist evaluation of safe work behaviors. These incentives were very successful in improving both the productivity and the safety behaviors of the work crew (Austin, Kessler, Riccobono, & Bailey, 1996). In general, organizational behavior modification has been a successful strategy for enhancing worker motivation (Hamner & Hamner, 1976; Luthans, Rhee, Luthans & Avey, 2008).

A car salesperson works on a variable-ratio schedule of compensation: Her earnings depend on the number of successful sales pitches she makes.

EXTRINSIC VERSUS INTRINSIC MOTIVATION

One limitation to reinforcement theory is that it emphasizes external, or extrinsic, rewards. That is, persons are motivated to perform a behavior because they receive some extrinsic reward from the environment. Yet, theorists such as Deci and Ryan (1985) emphasize that people are often motivated by internal or intrinsic motivation. Intrinsic rewards are derived from the workers' sense of accomplishment and competence at performing and mastering work tasks and from a sense of autonomy or control over one's own work. According to the notion of intrinsic motivation, workers are motivated by challenges at work, with the reward being the satisfaction of meeting the challenge or of a job well done. You have probably experienced firsthand intrinsic motivation at school or work, when you felt the glow of accomplishment with a particularly challenging assignment. Likewise, people who say they love their work because of its challenge and opportunity to "stretch" their skills and abilities are intrinsically motivated workers.

intrinsic motivation
the notion that people are motivated by internal rewards

According to intrinsic motivation theorists, it is not enough to offer tangible, extrinsic rewards to workers. To motivate workers intrinsically, jobs need to be set up so that they are interesting and challenging and so that they call forth workers' creativity and resourcefulness (Deci, 1992; Gagne & Deci, 2005; Houkes, Janssen, de Jonge, & Bakker, 2004). Moreover, relying heavily on extrinsic rewards tends to decrease intrinsic motivation (parents are told, for example, that giving a child money for good grades will lower the child's intrinsic motivation to work hard at school; Deci, Koestner, & Ryan, 1999). It has been suggested that work organizations overemphasize extrinsic rewards to the detriment of intrinsic motivation (Heath, 1999). Another approach used to promote intrinsic motivation at work is to allow workers some control, or autonomy, in deciding how their work should be planned and conducted (Deci, 1972). As we will see as we discuss additional theories of motivation, many models of motivation focus on intrinsic rewards as critical for work motivation.

Goal-setting Theory

goal-setting theory
the motivational theory that emphasizes the setting of specific and challenging performance goals

Goal-setting theory emphasizes the role of specific, challenging performance goals and workers' commitment to those goals as key determinants of motivation. Typically, goal-setting theory is associated with Edwin Locke (1968; Locke & Latham, 1984, 1990a), although theories concerning the establishment of defined performance goals have been around for some time (see, for example, Drucker, 1954; Lewin, 1935). Goal-setting techniques have also been used in nonwork settings to motivate people to lose weight, to exercise regularly, and to study.

Goal-setting theory states that for employees to be motivated, goals must be clear, specific, attainable, and, whenever possible, quantified. General goals, such as urging employees to do their best or to work as quickly as possible, are not as effective as defined, measurable goals. In addition, goal-setting programs may emphasize taking a large, challenging goal and breaking it down into a series of smaller, more easily attained goals. For example, as I sat down to write this textbook, the task seemed overwhelming. It was much easier (and more motivating) to view the book as a series of chapters, tackle each chapter individually, and feel a sense of accomplishment each time the first draft of a chapter was completed. (You may be faced with something similar as you try to study and master the book. It may be less overwhelming to set smaller study "goals" and take it one chapter or section at a time.) Difficult or challenging goals will also result in greater levels of motivation, if the goals have been accepted by the workers (Locke, Shaw, Saari, & Latham, 1981). For example, there is evidence that if workers participate in goal setting, as opposed to having supervisors set the goals, there is increased motivation as measured by workers setting higher performance goals than those set by supervisors (Erez & Arad, 1986). Of course, goals should not be so high that they are impossible to achieve (Erez & Zidon, 1984).

⏱ Stop & Review
Give examples of the four types of reinforcement schedules. How are punishment and negative reinforcement different?

Research on goal setting has also stressed the importance of getting workers committed to goals, for without such commitment, it is unlikely that goal setting will be motivating (Locke, Latham, & Erez, 1988; Wofford, Goodwin, & Premack, 1992). A number of strategies have been used to influence employees' commitment to performance goals. These include the use of extrinsic rewards (e.g., bonuses), the use of peer pressure via setting both individual and group goals, and the encouragement of intrinsic motivation through providing workers with feedback about goal attainment (Sawyer, Latham, Pritchard, & Bennett, 1999). In addition, providing feedback about what goals other high-performing individuals or groups are achieving can also encourage motivation toward goal attainment (Vigoda-Gadot & Angert, 2007; Weiss, Suckow, & Rakestraw,

1999). In one instance, goal commitment was strengthened through the use of negative reinforcement: Achieving work group goals meant the group would avoid possible layoffs (Latham & Saari, 1982). Similarly, groups will be more committed to achieving goals if lack of goal attainment means losing a possible financial bonus (Guthrie & Hollensbe, 2004).

As you might imagine, goal-setting theory has generated a great deal of research (Latham & Locke, 2007). Several meta-analyses indicate support for the effectiveness of goal setting as a motivational technique (Mento, Steele, & Karren, 1987; Tubbs, 1986; Wofford et al., 1992).

Research has tried to discover reasons why goal setting is an effective motivational technique (e.g., Kernan & Lord, 1990; Vance & Colella, 1990). One study found that the setting of specific, challenging goals may stimulate high-quality planning on the part of workers. This "planning quality" then contributes to better performance in achieving goals (Smith, Locke, & Barry, 1990). Feedback accompanying goal attainment may also enhance a worker's job performance and ability to become more innovative and creative on the job, through a trial-and-error learning process (Locke & Latham, 1990b). In addition, research has looked beyond individual motivation in goal setting, to the effects of setting group goals on group-level or work-team motivation (Crown & Rosse, 1995; Locke & Latham, 2006).

Although goal-setting theory has stimulated a great deal of research, there has been considerable interest from practitioners in applying goal-setting theory to increase worker motivation. A wide variety of motivational techniques and programs, such as incentive programs and management by objectives, or MBO (which we will discuss in Chapter 15), are consistent with goal-setting theory. Because goal setting is a relatively simple motivational strategy to implement, it has become quite popular.

Job Design Theories of Motivation

The need theories emphasize the role that individual differences in certain types of needs play in determining work motivation. The behavior-based theories focus on behavioral outcomes as the key to motivation. By contrast, two job design theories, Herzberg's two-factor theory and the job characteristics model, stress the structure and design of jobs as key factors in motivating workers. They argue that if jobs are well designed, containing all the elements that workers require from their jobs to satisfy physical and psychological needs, employees will be motivated.

HERZBERG'S TWO-FACTOR THEORY

Influenced greatly by the human relations school of thought, Frederick Herzberg developed a theory of motivation that highlighted the role of job satisfaction in determining worker motivation (we will discuss job satisfaction in great depth in Chapter 9, but we are here looking at job satisfaction as one element in the motivation "equation") (Herzberg, 1966; Herzberg, Mausner, & Snyderman, 1959). He stated that the traditional, single-dimension approach to job satisfaction, with its continuum ends ranging from job dissatisfaction to job satisfaction, is wrong, and that job satisfaction and job dissatisfaction are actually two separate and independent dimensions. Herzberg arrived at these conclusions, called the two-factor theory, after analyzing the survey responses of many white-collar, professional workers who were asked to describe what made them feel especially good or bad about their jobs. What he found was that the factors clustered into one of two categories. Certain factors, when present, seemed to cause job satisfaction, and Herzberg labeled them motivators. Other factors, when absent, tended to cause job dissatisfaction, and he called them hygienes. Motivators are factors related to job content; they are inherent in the work itself. The type of work, the level of responsibility associated with the job, and the chances for recognition, advancement, and personal achievement are all motivators. Hygienes are related to the context in which people perform their jobs. Common hygienes include benefits, working conditions (including both physical and social conditions), type of supervision, base salary, and company policies (see Table 8.2).

To illustrate Herzberg's concepts of hygienes and motivators, consider the jobs of high school teacher and paramedic. Neither job is particularly well paid, and the working conditions of the paramedic, with odd hours out in the field working under high pressure to save lives, are not too appealing. In other words, the hygienes in the two jobs are low to moderate. And, as you might expect with reduced hygienes, teachers and paramedics might often voice their dissatisfaction over low pay and poor working conditions. However, the positions of teacher and paramedic have high levels of responsibility, shaping young minds and saving lives, respectively. Moreover, both teachers and paramedics consider themselves to be professionals, doing work that has value to society. These are the motivators that, according to Herzberg, will lead to job satisfaction and keep levels of motivation high for people in these professions.

Herzberg's theory indicates that if managers are to keep workers happy and motivated, two things must be done. First, to eliminate job dissatisfaction, workers must be provided with the basic hygiene factors. That is, they must be compensated appropriately, treated well, and provided with job security. However, furnishing these hygienes will only prevent dissatisfaction; it will not necessarily motivate workers. To get workers to put greater effort and energy into their jobs, motivators must be present. The work must be important, giving the workers a sense of responsibility, and should provide chances for recognition and upward mobility.

two-factor theory
Herzberg's motivational theory that proposes that two factors—motivators and hygienes—are important in determining worker satisfaction and motivation

motivators
elements related to job content that, when present, lead to job satisfaction

hygienes
elements related to job context that, when absent, cause job dissatisfaction

TABLE 8.2
Profile of Herzberg's Motivators and Hygienes

Motivators	Hygienes
Responsibility	Company policy and administration
Achievement	Supervision
Recognition	Interpersonal relations
Content of work	Working conditions
Advancement	Salary
Growth on job	

Unfortunately, research has not been very supportive of Herzberg's theory. In particular, the two-factor theory has been criticized on methodological grounds because subsequent research did not replicate the presence of the two distinct factors (Schneider & Locke, 1971). There also have been difficulties in clearly distinguishing hygienes and motivators. For example, salary, which should be a hygiene because it is external to the work itself, may sometimes act as a motivator because pay can be used to recognize outstanding employees and indicate an individual's status in the organization. It has also been suggested that Herzberg's theory applies more to white-collar than to blue-collar workers (Dunnette, Campbell, & Hakel, 1967). As a result, some scholars do not consider it to be a viable theory of motivation, although it continues to be used as a theory to explain worker motivation in a number of jobs (Lundberg, Gudmundson, & Andersson, 2009; Sachau, 2007; Udechukwu, 2009).

Despite criticisms and a lack of supportive research, Herzberg's theory helped stimulate the development of an innovative strategy used to increase worker motivation known as *job enrichment*. We will discuss job enrichment shortly, but first we must consider our second job design theory of motivation: the job characteristics model.

> **Stop & Review**
>
> Under what conditions is goal setting most effective?

JOB CHARACTERISTICS MODEL

The job characteristics model emphasizes the role of certain aspects or characteristics of jobs in influencing work motivation (Hackman & Oldham, 1976, 1980). According to Hackman and Oldham (1976), employees must experience three important psychological states to be motivated: Workers must perceive their work as meaningful, associate a sense of responsibility with the job, and have some knowledge of the results of their efforts. Five core job characteristics contribute to a worker's experience of the three psychological states:

> **job characteristics model**
>
> a theory that emphasizes the role that certain aspects of jobs play in influencing work motivation

1. *Skill variety*—the degree to which a job requires the worker to use a variety of abilities and skills to perform work-related tasks. A job that demands a range of skills is likely to be perceived as challenging and meaningful.
2. *Task identity*—the degree to which a job requires the completion of an entire job or function. The worker needs to see the observable outcome or product of work efforts.
3. *Task significance*—the degree to which a job has a substantial impact on other people within the organization, such as coworkers, or persons outside of the organization, such as consumers.
4. *Autonomy*—the degree to which the job gives the worker freedom and independence to choose how to schedule and carry out the necessary tasks.
5. *Feedback*—the degree to which the job allows the worker to receive direct and clear information about the effectiveness of performance.

Skill variety, task identity, and task significance all affect the experience of meaningfulness in work; autonomy influences the sense of responsibility associated with the job and with work outcomes; and feedback influences the worker's experience of work results.

These five core job characteristics can be assessed and then combined into a single motivating potential score (MPS) using the following formula:

$$\text{MPS} = \frac{\text{Skill Variety} + \text{Task Identity} + \text{Task Significance}}{3} \times \text{Autonomy} \times \text{Feedback}$$

Hackman and Oldham used this formula to show that motivation is not a simple combination of the five job characteristics. In the formula, skill variety, task identity, and task significance are averaged, which means that jobs can have low levels of one or two of these characteristics, which are compensated for by a high score on the third. This average score is then multiplied by the core characteristics of autonomy and feedback. However, if any of the levels of autonomy, feedback, or skill variety plus task identity plus task significance are zero, the MPS will be zero—no motivating potential! For a job to have any motivating potential, it must have both autonomy and feedback and at least one of the other three characteristics.

To summarize the basic job characteristics model, the five core job characteristics influence the three critical psychological states—meaningfulness, responsibility, and knowledge of results—that in turn lead to motivation and certain work outcomes, such as the motivation to work, improve performance, and grow on the job (Figure 8.1). Actually, the job characteristics model is more complex. According to Hackman and Oldham, certain "moderators" can affect the success of the model in predicting worker motivation. One such moderator is growth need strength, or an individual's need and desire for personal growth and development on the job. In other words, some workers desire jobs that are challenging, responsible, and demanding, whereas others do not. According to the theory, improving the dimensions of the five core job characteristics should have motivating effects only on those workers who are high in growth need strength. Workers low in this moderator are not likely to be motivated by jobs that offer enriched opportunities for responsibility, autonomy, and accountability.

To validate their theory, Hackman and Oldham (1975) developed a questionnaire to measure the five core characteristics, called the Job Diagnostic Survey (JDS). The JDS and alternative tools, such as the Job Characteristics Inventory (Fried, 1991; Sims, Szilagyi, & Keller, 1976), have stimulated a great deal of research on the job characteristics model. Generally, the results have been favorable (see, for example, De Varo, Li, & Brookshire, 2007; Graen, Scandura, & Graen, 1986), although there have been some results that are not supportive of the model (Tiegs, Tetrick, & Fried, 1992). A meta-analysis of nearly 200 studies of the model found general support for its structure and for its effects on job motivation and related work outcomes (Fried & Ferris, 1987). The job characteristics model has been found to predict motivation to come to work, with workers who have enriched, "motivating" jobs having better attendance records than workers whose jobs lack the critical job characteristics (Rentsch & Steel, 1998). Workers in enriched jobs also have greater psychological "well-being" (de Jonge et al., 2001).

growth need strength
the need and desire for personal growth on the job

Job Diagnostic Survey (JDS)
a questionnaire that measures core job characteristics

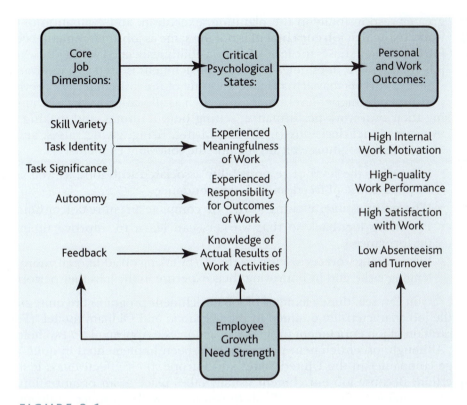

FIGURE 8.1

The Job Characteristics Model of Work Motivation

Source: Hackman, J. R., & Oldham, G. R. (1976). Motivation through the design of work: Test of a theory. *Organizational Behavior and Human Performance,* 16, 256.

One important difficulty with the use of the JDS (and other, similar self-report measures of job characteristics) to test the job characteristics model relates to the old problem with correlation and causality that we discussed in Chapter 2. Research has found a positive correlation between the presence of core job characteristics and employee satisfaction and self-reported motivation. However, because most of this research is based on self-report measures of both job characteristics and job satisfaction/motivation, we cannot be sure of the direction of causality. Is it the presence of motivating job characteristics that causes job satisfaction and motivation, as the job characteristics model predicts, or is it the case that motivated, satisfied workers see their jobs as being rich in key job characteristics? Some researchers have criticized the use of self-report measures of job characteristics, advocating instead the use of job analysis methods to determine if jobs have "motivating" job characteristics (Spector, 1992; Spector & Jex, 1991; Taber & Taylor, 1990).

These two job design theories of motivation—Herzberg's theory and the job characteristics model—have led to the development and refinement of a strategy used to motivate workers through job redesign. This intervention strategy is called job enrichment, and it involves redesigning jobs to give workers

job enrichment

a motivational program that involves redesigning jobs to give workers a greater role in the planning, execution, and evaluation of their work

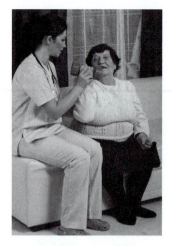

This physical therapist experiences at least two of the psychological states identified by the job characteristics model: She knows her work is meaningful, and she sees the results.

greater responsibility in the planning, execution, and evaluation of their work. (Note that job enrichment is not the same as job enlargement, because job enrichment raises the level of responsibility associated with a job, whereas job enlargement does not.) When job enrichment is used as a motivational strategy, workers may actually take on some of the tasks that were previously performed by higher-level supervisors, such as allocating work tasks, appraising their own work performance, setting output quotas, and making their own personnel decisions (including hiring, firing, giving raises, and the like). These programs typically include the following elements:

- Increasing the level of responsibility associated with jobs, as well as the workers' sense of freedom and independence.
- Wherever possible, allowing workers to complete an entire task or function.
- Providing feedback so that workers can learn to improve their own performance.
- Encouraging workers to learn on the job by taking on additional, more challenging tasks, and by improving their expertise in the jobs they perform.

As you can see, these elements of job enrichment programs are quite similar to the job characteristics outlined in the Hackman and Oldham model. (For an illustration of job enrichment programs in action, see Applying I/O Psychology.)

Although job enrichment programs have been implemented in quite a few large companies in the United States and Europe, their effectiveness is still in question. Because job enrichment usually takes place at an organizational or departmental level, it is very difficult to conduct a well-controlled evaluation of the effectiveness of the program. Specifically, because the unit of analysis—the participant—is usually the organization or department, it is very difficult to compare the success of various job enrichment programs. Most often, support for or against job enrichment is based on the results of a series of case studies. Although many of these case studies find job enrichment programs to be successful, other case studies illustrate failed job enrichment programs. It is clear, however, that some of these failures may be due more to faulty implementation of the program (e.g., management does not support the program; jobs aren't truly enriched) rather than to any weakness in the concept and theory of job enrichment. In addition, the idea from the job characteristics model that workers vary in growth need strength indicates that some workers (those high in growth need) will benefit and be motivated by enriched jobs, and some will not. Thus, levels of growth need strength in the workforce may also play a role in the success or failure of job enrichment. It has also been suggested that job enrichment might help improve motivation and morale for employees who remain following organizational downsizing (Niehoff, Moorman, Blakely, & Fuller, 2001).

Cognitive Theories of Motivation

equity theory
a theory that workers are motivated to reduce perceived inequities between work inputs and outcomes

This category, labeled "cognitive theories of motivation," presents two theories that view workers as rational beings who cognitively assess personal costs and benefits before taking action: equity theory and expectancy theory.

APPLYING I/O PSYCHOLOGY

Job Enrichment in a Manufacturing and a Service Organization

In 1971, a decision was made to implement a job enrichment program in a Volvo automobile assembly plant in Kalmar, Sweden, that was suffering from extremely high levels of absenteeism and turnover. First, the traditional assembly-line workers were separated into teams with 15 to 25 members. In keeping with the general principles of job enrichment, each team was made responsible for an entire auto component or function (for example, upholstery, transmission assembly, or electrical system wiring). Each team was given the freedom to assign members to work tasks, to set their own output rates, to order supplies, and to inspect their own work, all of which had previously been performed by supervisors. To encourage team spirit, each group was given carpeted break rooms, and job rotation (rotating workers periodically from one task to another) was encouraged to alleviate boredom. The results of the program indicated a significant decline in both absenteeism and turnover along with improved product quality, although there was a slight decline in productivity and the costs of implementing the program were great. It was also discovered that some workers did not adapt well to the enriched jobs and preferred the more traditional assembly line (Goldman, 1976). However, management proclaimed the program a success and implemented the strategy in several other plants (Gyllenhammar, 1977; Walton, 1972).

In another job enrichment program, a large U.S. financial institution decided to introduce job enrichment into their credit and collections department, which serviced the company's credit card account activity, collected on overdue accounts, and dealt with any credit-related difficulties experienced by cardholders, such as changes of address, lost cards, and credit inquiries. In the existing situation, each type of work was handled by a specialist, so that an inquiry on a single account might be handled by several workers. This often led to confusion and to frustration on the part of cardholders, who felt as if they were being passed from worker to worker for even simple service requests. On the employee side, jobs were repetitive and monotonous, which led to high rates of absenteeism and turnover.

The job enrichment program involved dividing the department into two distinct operating units, each composed of a number of two-member teams. One unit dealt solely with actions on current accounts and the other unit only with past due accounts. Rather than assigning work based on the type of task that needed to be performed, each team was now given complete responsibility for certain accounts. This restructuring increased the level of responsibility required of each worker and reduced the routine nature of the jobs. Also, workers were able to receive feedback about their work because they dealt with an action on an account from start to finish. Nine months after the implementation of the job enrichment program, productivity had increased without any increase in staff, collection of past due accounts was more efficient, absenteeism was down 33%, and the 9-month turnover rate was zero (Yorks, 1979).

EQUITY THEORY OF MOTIVATION

Equity theory states that workers are motivated by a desire to be treated equitably or fairly. If workers perceive that they are receiving fair treatment, their motivation to work will be maintained, and steady performance can be expected. If, on the other hand, they feel that there is inequitable treatment, their motivation will be channeled into some strategy that will try to reduce the inequity.

Equity theory, first proposed by J. Stacey Adams (1965), has become quite popular. According to this theory, the worker brings inputs to the job, such as experience, education and qualifications, energy, and effort, and expects to receive certain outcomes, such as pay, fringe benefits, recognition, and interesting and challenging work, each in equivalent proportions. To determine whether the situation is equitable, workers make some social

inputs
elements that a worker invests in a job, such as experience and effort

outcomes
those things that a worker expects to receive from a job, such as pay and recognition

comparison others
persons used as a basis for comparison in making judgments of equity/inequity

comparisons between their own input–outcome ratio and those of comparison others, who can be coworkers, people with a similar job or occupation, or the workers' own experiences. It must be stressed that equity theory is based on workers' perceptions of equity/inequity. In certain instances, workers may perceive that an inequity exists when there is not one, but equity theory's predictions are still valid because they operate on worker perceptions.

According to equity theory, lack of motivation is caused by two types of perceived inequity. Underpayment inequity results when workers feel they are receiving fewer outcomes from the job in ratio to inputs. Imagine that you have been working at a particular job for over a year. A new employee has just been hired to do the same type of job. This person is about your age and has about the same background and level of education. However, your new coworker has much less work experience than you. Now imagine that you find out that this new employee is making $1.50 per hour more than you are. Equity theory predicts that you would experience underpayment inequity and would be motivated to try to balance the situation by doing one of the following:

underpayment inequity
worker's perception that inputs are greater than outcomes

⏱ Stop & Review
Define Herzberg's concepts of motivators and hygienes and give examples of each.

- *Increasing outcomes*—You could confront your boss and ask for a raise, or find some other way to get greater outcomes from your job, perhaps even through padding your expense account or taking home office supplies (see Greenberg, 1990).
- *Decreasing inputs*—You might decide that you need to limit your work production or quality of work commensurate with your "poor" pay.
- *Changing the comparison other*—If you find out that the new employee is actually the boss's daughter, she is clearly not a similar comparison other (Werner & Ones, 2000).
- *Leaving the situation*—You might decide that the situation is so inequitable that you are no longer motivated to work there (Van Yperen, Hagedoorn, & Geurts, 1996).

Now imagine that you are on the receiving end of that extra $1.50 per hour. In other words, compared to your comparison others, you are receiving greater outcomes from your average-level inputs. This is referred to as overpayment inequity, which also creates an imbalance. In this case, equity theory predicts that you might try doing one of the following:

overpayment inequity
worker's perception that outcomes are greater than inputs

- *Increasing inputs*—You might work harder to try to even up the input–outcome ratio.
- *Decreasing outcomes*—You might ask for a cut in pay, although this is extremely unlikely.
- *Changing comparison others*—An overpaid worker might change comparison others to persons of higher work status and ability. For example, "Obviously my boss sees my potential. I am paid more because she is grooming me for a management position."
- *Distorting the situation*—A distortion of the perception of inputs or outcomes might occur. For example, "My work is of higher quality and therefore deserves more pay than the work of others."

It is this last outcome, the possibility of psychological distortions of the situation, that weakens the predictive power of this cognitive theory of motivation. Equity theory has difficulty predicting behavior when people act nonrationally, as they sometimes do.

Although most of the research on equity theory has used pay as the primary outcome of a job, other factors may constitute outcomes. For example, one study found that workers would raise their inputs in response to receiving a high-status job title (Greenberg & Ornstein, 1983). In other words, the prestige associated with the title served as compensation, even though there was no raise in pay. There was one catch, however; the workers had to perceive the higher job title as having been earned. An unearned promotion led to feelings of overpayment inequity. Another study looked at Finnish workers who felt inequity because they were putting too much effort and energy into their work compared to the norm. The greater the felt inequity, the more likely these workers reported being emotionally exhausted and stressed (Taris, Kalimo, & Schaufeli, 2002).

Although equity theory has been well researched, the majority of these studies have been conducted in laboratory settings (Greenberg, 1982; Mowday, 1979; although see Bretz & Thomas, 1992; Carrell, 1978; Martin & Peterson, 1987). As you might imagine, there is greater support for equity theory predictions in the underpayment inequity than in the overpayment inequity condition (Campbell & Pritchard, 1976; Pritchard, Dunnette, & Jorgenson, 1972).

Research has also examined the role of individual differences as moderators of equity. In particular, this research has focused on the construct of *equity sensitivity*. It has been suggested that individuals vary in their concern over the equity of input–outcome ratios. In other words, some people are quite sensitive to equity ratios and prefer balance, whereas others may be less concerned with equitable relationships, and still other individuals may prefer to have either an outcome advantage or an input advantage, preferring to be overcompensated or undercompensated for their work (Huseman, Hatfield, & Miles, 1987; Sauley & Bedeian, 2000; see Table 8.3). Obviously, if only certain individuals are motivated by equity, it will limit the theory's ability to predict which employees are influenced through equity.

It has been suggested that there may be cultural differences that can impact equity theory (Bolino & Turnley, 2008). For example, there may be cultural differences in how people evaluate inputs and outcomes, and in whom they choose as comparison others.

Despite the voluminous research, no particular applications have been developed directly from the equity theory. As Miner (1983, p. 48) stated, "The theory has tremendous potential insofar as applications are concerned, but these have not been realized, even though the theory itself has stood the test of research well."

EXPECTANCY (VIE) THEORY OF MOTIVATION

One of the most popular motivation theories is expectancy theory, which is also known as *VIE theory*, referring to three of the theory's core components: valence, instrumentality, and expectancy. Expectancy theory is most often associated with Vroom (1964), although there were some later refinements and modifications of

> ⏱ Stop & Review
>
> According to the MPS, which job characteristics are most important in motivating workers?

expectancy theory
a cognitive theory of motivation that states that workers weigh expected costs and benefits of particular courses before they are motivated to take action

TABLE 8.3

Equity Sensitivity: Three Types of Individuals

Benevolents—These individuals are "givers." They are altruistic and are relatively content with receiving lower outcomes for their inputs.

Entitleds—These individuals are "takers." They are concerned with receiving high outcomes, regardless of their levels of inputs.

Equity Sensitives—These individuals adhere to notions of equity. They become distressed when feeling underpayment inequity, and guilt when overrewarded.

Individual differences in equity sensitivity can be measured via self-report instruments (Huseman, Hatfield, & Miles, 1987; Sauley & Bedeian, 2000). Only the motivation of individuals in the third category, the equity sensitives, should adhere to the predictions made by the equity theory of motivation.

---

valence

the desirability of an outcome to an individual

instrumentality

the perceived relationship between the performance of a particular behavior and the likelihood of receiving a particular outcome

expectancy

the perceived relationship between the individual's effort and performance of a behavior

the theory (Graen, 1969; Porter & Lawler, 1968). Like equity theory, expectancy theory assumes that workers are rational, decision-making persons whose behavior will be guided by an analysis of the potential costs and benefits of a particular course of action. Also like equity theory, expectancy theory focuses on the particular outcomes associated with a job, which refer not only to pay, but also to any number of factors, positive or negative, that are the potential results of work behavior. For example, positive outcomes include benefits, recognition, and job satisfaction, and negative outcomes include reprimands, demotions, and firings.

As mentioned, the three core components of expectancy theory are valence, which refers to the desirability (or undesirability) of a particular outcome to an individual; instrumentality, which is the perceived relationship between the performance of a particular behavior and the likelihood that a certain outcome will result—in other words, the link between one outcome (the worker's behavior) and another outcome (obtaining recognition or a pay raise, for example); and expectancy, which is the perceived relationship between the individual's effort and performance of the behavior. Both the expectancy and the instrumentality components are represented as probabilities (for example, "If I expend X amount of effort, I will probably complete Y amount of work"— the expectancy component; "If I complete Y amount of work, I will likely get promoted"—the instrumentality component). Expectancy theory states that the motivation to perform a particular behavior depends on a number of factors: whether the outcome of the behavior is desirable (valence); whether the individual has the ability, skills, or energy to get the job done (expectancy); and whether the performance of the behavior will indeed lead to the expected outcome (instrumentality). In research and applications of expectancy theory, each of the components is measured, and a complex predictive formula is derived.

Consider as an example the use of expectancy theory in studying how students might be motivated, or not motivated, to perform exceptionally well in college courses. For this student, the particular outcome will be acceptance into a prestigious graduate (Ph.D.) program in I/O psychology. First, consider the valence of the outcome. Although it may be a very desirable outcome for some (positively valent), it is not for others (negative or neutral valence). Therefore, only those students who view being admitted to a graduate program as desirable are going to be motivated to do well in school to achieve this particular outcome. (Note: This does not mean that there are not other reasons for doing well in school, nor that good grades are the only requirements for admission to graduate school.) For those who desire the graduate career, the next component to consider is expectancy. Given what you know about your own abilities, study habits, and effort, what is the probability that you will actually be able to achieve the required grades? Here you might consider your willingness to sacrifice some of your social life to study more, as well as considering your past academic performance. Should you say, "Yes, I have the 'right stuff' to get the job done," it is likely that you will be highly motivated. For those individuals unwilling to expend the time and energy required, motivation will be much less. Finally, what about instrumentality? It is well known that there are many more qualified applicants to graduate programs than there are openings. Therefore, the probability of actually achieving the desired outcome, even if you perform at the required level, is less than certain. It is here that motivation might also potentially break down. Some people might believe that the odds are so poor that working overtime to get good grades is simply not worth it. Others might figure that the odds are not so bad, and thus the force of their motivation, in expectancy theory terms, will remain strong.

At work, expectancy theory might be applied using promotions, the performance of special work projects, or avoidance of a supervisor's displeasure as potential outcomes. For example, if an employee's goal is to avoid her supervisor's criticism (which is negatively valent), she might consider the expectancy ("Can I perform the job flawlessly to avoid my supervisor's displeasure?") and the instrumentality ("Even if I do an error-free job, will my supervisor still voice some displeasure?") of that goal before being motivated even to try to avoid having the boss become displeased. If the supervisor is someone who never believes that an employee's performance is good enough, it is unlikely that the employee will exhibit much motivation to avoid her or his displeasure, because it is perceived as inevitable.

Expectancy theory illustrates the notion that motivation is a complex phenomenon, affected by a number of variables. This theory looks at factors such as individual goals, the links between effort and performance (expectancy), the links between performance and outcomes (instrumentality), and how outcomes serve to satisfy individual goals (valence). It is one of the most complicated yet thorough models of work motivation. The theory has generated a considerable amount of research, with evidence both supporting (Matsui, Kagawa, Nagamatsu, & Ohtsuka, 1977; Muchinsky, 1977a) and criticizing certain aspects of the theory (Pinder, 1984; Stahl & Harrell, 1981; Van Eerde & Thierry, 1996). In addition, researchers have noted problems in the measurement of the VIE components of valence, instrumentality, and expectancy in several studies (Schmidt, 1973; Schwab, Olian-Gottlieb, & Heneman, 1979; Wanous, Keon, & Latack, 1983). Expectancy theory continues to be a popular cognitive model for understanding work motivation. Although there is no single agreed-upon strategy for its application, it does lead to many practical suggestions for guiding managers/leaders in their attempts to motivate workers (e.g., Isaac, Zerbe, & Pitt, 2001), including the following:

- Managers should try to define work outcomes—potential rewards and costs associated with performance—clearly to all workers.

- The relationships between performance and rewards should also be made clear. Workers need to know that if they achieve certain goals, rewards are sure to follow.
- Any performance-related goal should be within the reach of the employee involved.

In sum, both expectancy theory and equity theory are based on cognitive models of motivation. They assume that individuals are constantly aware of important elements in their work environment and that motivation is determined by a conscious processing of the information received. The problem is that some people may simply be more rational than others in their usual approaches to work. The effectiveness of these cognitive models of motivation is also weakened by the fact that in some situations, individuals, regardless of their usual rational approach, may behave in a nonrational manner (for example, when workers become so upset that they impulsively quit their job without considering the implications). Moreover, there is some evidence that even when people are using rational means to evaluate a particular situation, individuals vary in the ways that they process information (see Zedeck, 1977).

Comparing, Contrasting, and Combining the Different Motivation Theories

Work motivation is an important topic. The importance of the construct is reflected in the many theories that have been constructed to try to "capture" motivational processes and predict when workers will and will not be motivated. In reviewing the various motivational models, it is important to examine the ways in which the theories are similar and how they are different. (See Table 8.4 for a summary of the motivation theories we have discussed.)

The early need theories of motivation, those of Maslow and Alderfer, are primarily descriptive models that explain that people's motivation is rooted in different levels of needs. Reinforcement theory, on the other hand, focuses on the role of the environment in "drawing out" a person's motivation. Need theories can be viewed as the "push" from within, whereas reinforcement represents the "pull" from without. Yet, more complex versions of need theories, like McClelland's, go beyond the simple categorization of needs. In McClelland's model, the needs for achievement, power, and affiliation interact with how a worker views the job and the work environment. For example, someone with a high need for achievement will be concerned with how the job can meet her achievement-related goals. Someone with high power needs will seek out ways to direct others' activities. In other words, there is an interaction between needs from within the individual and what the work environment, external to the person, has to offer. Of course, the fact that workers evaluate how their needs can be achieved suggests that rational, cognitive factors also come into play. Thus, there is some overlap between McClelland's need theory and aspects of the cognitive models of motivation.

Similar connections can be made between the behavior-based theories of motivation and the cognitive models. For example, the notion of intrinsic rewards suggests that workers think rationally about their accomplishments,

TABLE 8.4
Summary of Theories of Motivation

Theory	Elements/Components	Applications
Need Theories		
Maslow's Need Hierarchy	Levels of needs arranged in a hierarchy from lower- to higher-order needs	(no direct intervention programs)
Alderfer's ERG Theory	Three levels of needs: existence, relatedness, growth	
Behavior-based Theories		
Reinforcement Theory	Consequences of behavior: reinforcers and punishment	Organizational behavior modification
Goal-setting Theory	Setting of challenging goals and commitment to goals	Various goal-setting programs (e.g., MBO)
Job Design Theories		
Herzberg's Two-factor Theory	Jobs must provide hygienes and motivators	Job enrichment
Job Characteristics Model	Jobs must provide five key job characteristics	Job enrichment
Cognitive Theories		
Equity Theory	Inputs = outcomes; emphasizes drive to reduce inequities	(various applications but no agreed-upon intervention programs)
Expectancy (VIE) Theory	Valence, instrumentality, expectancy	

and the setting and achieving of performance goals is an important component of both goal-setting theories and the expectancy/VIE model of motivation (see Mento, Locke, & Klein, 1992; Tubbs, Boehne, & Dahl, 1993).

Why are there so many different theories of motivation? It has been argued that these different perspectives represent the complexity and the multifaceted nature of human motivation (Locke & Latham, 2004). For example, some elements of motivation come from within the worker, some elements are external to the person, some involve rational, cognitive decision making, and some elements are more emotional (Seo, Feldman Barrett, & Bartunek, 2004). A very interesting experiment found that both equity theory and needs theory explained worker motivation on a tedious task (Lambert, 2011), so it may be that different theories can be applied to predict and explain worker motivation.

The Relationship Between Motivation and Performance

Motivation is central to any discussion of work behavior because it is believed that it has a direct link to good work performance. In other words, it is assumed that the motivated worker is the productive worker.

ON THE *CUTTING* EDGE

Motivating Through Team-based Rewards

Traditionally, organizations reward, through pay and bonuses, the performance of individual workers. However, in keeping with the trend toward greater use of work teams, there has been growing interest in team-based strategies for motivating workers. This involves both making pay contingent on team, rather than individual, performance, as well as payment of bonuses and other financial incentives. Although team-based rewards should, in theory, foster greater cooperation and teamwork, how is individual motivation affected when rewards are based on group rather than individual efforts? Research indicates that team-based rewards can be as motivating as individual rewards in many cases, especially if the work team is not too large (Honeywell-Johnson & Dickinson, 1999; Kim & Gong, 2009). In addition, research suggests that team-based rewards work best when members are committed to the team, when their work is highly interdependent so that they must rely on one another to get the job done, when workers are fully informed about the incentive system and how it works, and when the system is perceived as fair (Blanchard, Poon, Rodgers, & Pinel, 2000; DeMatteo, Eby, & Sundstrom, 1998). Furthermore, team rewards are most appropriate when the group performance is easily identified, but when it is difficult to determine specific individual contributions to the team output. Researchers have also begun exploring team-based rewards in virtual work teams (Bamberger & Levi, 2009; Hertel, Konradt, & Orlikowski, 2004). Despite the growing interest in team-based rewards, they are still the exception rather than the rule in work organizations (McClurg, 2001). In addition, there have been calls for organizations to do more evaluation of the effectiveness of team-based reward systems (Milne, 2007). We will discuss team rewards in more detail in Chapter 9.

Yet this may not always be true because many other factors can affect productivity independent of the effects of worker motivation. Furthermore, having highly motivated workers does not automatically lead to high levels of productivity. The work world is much more complex than that. As mentioned at the beginning of the chapter, many managers consider motivation to be the primary problem when they see low levels of productivity. However, a manager must approach a productivity problem as a social scientist would. Before pointing the finger at worker motivation, a detailed assessment of all the other variables that could affect productivity must first be undertaken. These variables can be divided into four categories: systems and technology variables, individual difference variables, group dynamics variables, and organizational variables.

Systems and technology variables

Regardless of the level of motivation, if workers are forced to work with inadequate work systems, procedures, tools, and equipment, productivity will suffer. Poor tools and systems will affect work productivity independent of employee motivation. This is often seen in the low agricultural production of some developing countries. A common mistake is to assume that these disadvantaged nations suffer from a lack of worker motivation. A more reasonable (and accurate) explanation is that they lack the appropriate agricultural technology to be as productive as other countries.

Stop & Review

Explain the three components of the expectancy theory of motivation.

Lack of technology, not motivational problems, often limits agricultural production in developing countries.

Individual difference variables

A variety of factors within the individual can affect work productivity regardless of motivation. For example, lacking the basic talents or skills to get the job done will hamper productivity, even in the most motivated worker. Perhaps the least-productive workers in any work setting are also the most motivated: new employees. At least initially, the novice employee is energized and determined to make a good impression on the boss. Unfortunately, a total lack of knowledge about the job makes this person relatively inefficient and unproductive, despite high motivation. Other workers, because of a lack of basic abilities or education, or perhaps because of being placed in a job that is incompatible with their own interests and talents, may be particularly unproductive. What may appear on the surface to be a motivational problem is actually a problem of individual abilities. We have already touched on some of these individual factors that affect performance when we looked at employee screening, selection, and placement.

Group dynamics variables

Rather than working by themselves, most workers are a part of a larger unit. For the group to be efficient and productive, individual efforts must be coordinated. Although most members may be highly motivated, group productivity can be poor if one or two key members are not good team workers. In these situations, the influence of motivation on productivity becomes secondary to certain group dynamics variables. We will discuss the group processes that come into play in affecting work performance in Chapter 12.

Organizational variables

The productivity of an organization requires the concerted and coordinated efforts of a number of work units. High levels of motivation and output in one department may be offset by lower levels in another department. Organizational politics and conflict may also affect the coordination among groups, thus lowering productivity despite relatively high levels of motivation in the workforce. We will look at the effects of such variables as organizational politics and conflict in upcoming chapters.

As you can see, the role of motivation in affecting work outcomes is important, but limited. The world of work is extremely complex. Focusing on a single variable, such as motivation, while ignoring others leads to a narrow and limited view of work behavior. Yet, motivation is an important topic, one of the most widely researched in I/O psychology. However, it is only one piece of the puzzle that contributes to our greater understanding of the individual in the workplace.

Summary

Motivation is the force that energizes, directs, and sustains behavior. The many theories of work motivation can be classified as need theories, behavior-based theories, job design theories, and cognitive theories. Maslow's and Alderfer's basic need theories propose that needs are arranged in a hierarchy from the lowest, most basic needs, to higher-order needs such as the need for esteem or self-actualization. McClelland's *achievement motivation theory* proposes that the three needs important in work motivation are needs for achievement, power, and affiliation, which can be measured with a projective test known as the *Thematic Apperception Test*. Unlike Maslow's and Alderfer's need theories, McClelland's theory has been used extensively in work settings to encourage worker motivation.

Behavior-based theories include both reinforcement and goal-setting approaches to motivation. *Reinforcement theory* stresses the role that *reinforcers* and *punishments* play in motivation. Reinforcement theory is evident in the various schedules used to reward workers. The theory is applied to increase motivation through *organizational behavior modification* programs. *Goal-setting theory* emphasizes setting challenging goals for workers and getting workers committed to those goals as the keys to motivation.

Job design theories of motivation stress the structure and design of jobs as key factors in motivating workers. Herzberg's *two-factor theory* focuses on job satisfaction and dissatisfaction as two independent dimensions important in determining motivation. *Motivators* are factors related to job content that, when present, lead to job satisfaction. *Hygienes* are elements related to job context that, when absent, cause job dissatisfaction. According to Herzberg, the presence of hygienes will prevent job dissatisfaction, but motivators are needed for employee job satisfaction and hence, motivation. Hackman and Oldham have proposed the *job characteristics model*, another job design theory of motivation, which states that five core job characteristics influence three critical psychological states that in turn lead to motivation. This model can be affected by certain moderators, including *growth need strength*, the notion that certain workers feel a need to grow on their jobs. Workers must be high in growth need strength if programs such as job enrichment are indeed going to produce motivation. *Job enrichment*, which involves redesigning jobs to give workers greater responsibility in the planning, execution, and evaluation of their work, is the application that grew out of the job design model of motivation.

Cognitive theories of motivation emphasize the role that cognition plays in determining worker motivation. *Equity theory* states that workers are motivated to keep their work *inputs* in proportion to their *outcomes*. According to equity theory, workers are motivated to reduce perceived inequities. This perception of equity/inequity is determined by comparing the worker's *input–outcome* ratio to similar *comparison others*. *Expectancy (VIE) theory* (with its three core components of valence, instrumentality, and expectancy) is a complex model, which states that motivation is dependent on expectations concerning effort–performance–outcome relationships.

Motivation is indeed a complex construct. Yet, despite the importance given to worker motivation in determining work performance, numerous variables related to systems and technology, individual differences, group dynamics, and organizational factors may all affect work performance directly, without regard to worker motivation. Thus, although motivation is important, it is only one determinant of work behavior.

Study Questions and Exercises

1. Motivation is an abstract concept, one that cannot be directly observed. Using your knowledge of research methods, list some of the methodological issues/problems that motivation researchers must face.

2. Some theories of motivation have led to successful strategies for enhancing work motivation, whereas others have not. What are some of the factors that distinguish the more successful theories from the less successful?

3. Apply each of the various theories to describing/explaining your own level of motivation at school or at work. Which model gives the best explanation for your personal motivation?

4. Basic need theories, goal-setting theory, and reinforcement theory are very general models of work motivation. What are the strengths and weaknesses of such general theories?

5. How would you design a program to improve motivation for a group of low-achieving high school students? What would the elements of the program be? What theories would you use?

Web Links

www.accel-team.com/motivation/
This consulting organization's site contains an overview of classic motivation theories.

Suggested Readings

Harder, J. W. (1991). Equity theory versus expectancy theory: The case of major league baseball free agents. *Journal of Applied Psychology, 76,* 458–464. *For you baseball fans, this is an interesting study that applied both equity and expectancy theories to performance of free agent major league baseball players. A nice example of using existing, "real world" data to study motivation.*

Kanfer, R., Chen, G., & Pritchard, R. D. (Eds.). (2008). *Work motivation: Past, present, and future.* New York: Routledge. *An edited book covering all aspects of work motivation in I/O psychology. [This and the next reference would be good starting points for a term paper on work motivation.]*

Latham, G. P. (2012). *Work motivation: History, theory, research, and practice* (2nd ed.). Thousand Oaks, CA: SAGE. *A thorough examination of work motivation from one of the leading scholars in the field.*

Positive Employee
Attitudes and Behaviors

Inside Tips
THE POSITIVE ASPECTS OF WORK

If someone were to ask us about our jobs or careers, we would probably report some positive feelings, as well as indicating some aspects of the job with which we were dissatisfied. This chapter more than any other pulls together a number of issues and topics from I/O psychology. We will look at the positive aspects of jobs—what causes workers to be engaged in their jobs, their organizations, and their careers. We will explore how positive employee attitudes and behaviors are connected to job performance. This is really an issue of motivation, similar to those examined in Chapter 8. This chapter also deals with some measurement issues that were introduced in Chapter 2. The measurement of employee attitudes, for example, presents a number of measurement problems. The connection between attitudes and their ability to predict important behaviors has a long and important history in both social and industrial/organizational psychology.

Y ou are getting settled into your new job. A great deal of effort went into finding the position, making it through the screening process, and landing the job, and in your initial training and orientation. You've learned the ropes and know what to do, but what is going to determine if you stay in this job, with this company, and even in this career path? We work partly out of necessity, but we stay in a job or an organization because of the positive things that come from the job, the company, and the career.

Seventy-five years ago, the only compensation that most workers received from their jobs was a paycheck. As time went on, this changed as workers began to demand and receive more from their jobs. Today's workers receive a variety of forms of compensation, including health care, retirement, and numerous other benefits and programs. However, one thing that the workers of the past and today's workers have in common is that their jobs constitute a major part of their lives and are one of the greatest sources of personal pleasure and pain. Although jobs can be satisfying in some regards, with positive feelings of accomplishment and purpose, they can also be stressful, and the source of negative feelings. Such negative feelings may, in turn, affect worker attitudes and behaviors.

In the next two chapters we will explore the positive and negative effects of jobs on workers. In this chapter we will focus on employee engagement, including job satisfaction, organizational commitment, and positive employee attitudes and behaviors. We will examine how these influence work performance, absenteeism, and turnover. We will also focus on some of the programs and techniques designed to increase employees' engagement in their work and their organizations. We will then focus on positive employee behaviors and how we can encourage the best from workers, for the good of the organization and for improving employee well-being.

Employee Engagement

Employee engagement is a psychological state that is characterized by vigor (energy), dedication, and absorption in one's work and organization (Schaufeli, Salanova, Gonzalez-Roma, & Baker, 2002). Highly engaged employees are enthusiastic about their jobs, committed to their work and the organization, and it is assumed that this state leads them to be more motivated, productive, and more likely to engage in positive work behaviors (Macey & Schneider, 2008). We will use employee engagement as an "umbrella" term to focus on positive employee attitudes, including the related (and much more thoroughly researched) constructs of job satisfaction and organizational commitment.

employee engagement
a psychological state characterized by vigor, dedication, and absorption in one's work/organization

What factors contribute to employee engagement? Saks (2006) suggests that jobs that are high in job characteristics (recall the Job Characteristics Model discussed in Chapter 8) are more meaningful and more likely to engage employees. In addition, if the employees feel that they are supported by their supervisors and their organization, they are more likely to experience high levels of engagement. Finally, being recognized and rewarded for one's accomplishments, and working in an organization that treats people fairly, all contribute to employee engagement.

The construct of employee engagement has received a great deal of attention from consultants and HR professionals, but less attention from researchers. It does, however, represent a more global way of looking at the positive attitudes and feelings of employees about their work and their work organizations. One self-report measure of employee engagement assesses two separate, but related, components, *job engagement* (sample scale items: "Sometimes I am so into my job that I lose track of time" and "I am highly engaged in this job") and *organization engagement* (sample items: "Being a member of this organization is very captivating" and "I am highly engaged in this organization") (Saks, 2006). This research found that employee engagement was positively related to job satisfaction and negatively related to employees' stated intentions to quit their jobs.

Job Satisfaction

While job engagement is a broad construct that refers to how much employees are psychologically and emotionally committed to their jobs and their organizations, it is a relatively new and understudied variable in I/O psychology. A related variable—one that has been extensively studied—is job satisfaction.

job satisfaction
the positive and negative feelings and attitudes about one's job

global approach
views job satisfaction as an overall construct

facet approach
views job satisfaction as made up of individual elements, or facets

Job satisfaction consists of the feelings and attitudes one has about one's job. All aspects of a particular job, good and bad, positive and negative, are likely to contribute to the development of feelings of satisfaction (or dissatisfaction). As seen in Chapter 2, job satisfaction, along with productivity, quality, absenteeism, and turnover, is one of the key dependent variables commonly considered (and measured) in research in I/O psychology. There are two approaches to conceptualizing job satisfaction. The first is the global approach, which considers overall job satisfaction. This way of looking at job satisfaction simply asks if the employee is satisfied overall, using a yes–no response, a single rating scale, or a small group of items that measure global job satisfaction. The second is the facet approach, which considers job satisfaction to be composed of feelings and attitudes about a number of different elements, or facets, of the job. For example, overall satisfaction may be a composite of numerous factors: satisfaction with pay, the type of work itself, working conditions, the type of supervision, company policies and procedures, relations with coworkers, and opportunities for promotion and advancement. The facet approach considers each of these aspects individually, assuming that a particular worker might be quite satisfied with some facet, such as the amount of pay, but unsatisfied with others, such as the quality of supervision and the opportunities for promotion.

There has been considerable discussion over which approach is better (Highhouse & Becker, 1993). Proponents of the global approach argue that it is overall satisfaction with a job that is important and that such complete satisfaction is more than the sum of satisfaction with separate job facets (Scarpello & Campbell, 1983; Schneider, 1985). Moreover, evidence suggests that even single-item measures of job satisfaction work reasonably well for assessing job satisfaction (Wanous, Reichers, & Hudy, 1997). On the other hand, advocates of the facet approach maintain that this view provides better and more detailed assessments of job satisfaction, allowing a researcher insight into how a particular individual feels about the various facets of the job and the work situation. Moreover, there may be tremendous variation in how highly individual workers value certain facets of job satisfaction (Rice, Gentile, & McFarlin, 1991). For example, satisfaction with pay may be an important element of job satisfaction for one worker, but not for another. In addition, some facets may not apply to all types of jobs. For instance, CEOs of companies and self-employed professionals are not affected by opportunities for promotion—a facet that may be an important contributor to job satisfaction of lower-level managers in large organizations.

Proponents of the facet definition argue that it helps to indicate specific areas of dissatisfaction that can be targeted for improvement (Locke, 1976; Smith, Kendall, & Hulin, 1969). Still others believe there are advantages to using both types of measurement approaches based on findings that indicate that each approach offers interesting and important information (Ironson, Smith, Brannick, Gibson, & Paul, 1989). Overall, much of the psychological research on the topic utilizes the facet approach in the measurement of job satisfaction.

THE MEASUREMENT OF JOB SATISFACTION

Regardless of the approach, when considering the measurement of job satisfaction, it is important to bear in mind the difficulties encountered in attempting to define the factors that may influence satisfaction, as well as the difficulties inherent in trying to measure any attitude.

As mentioned earlier, most instruments designed from the facet approach measure satisfaction with such things as pay, working conditions, and relationships with supervisors and coworkers. However, other variables such as preemployment expectations, individual personality characteristics, and the fit between the organization or job and the employee may also affect worker satisfaction (Ostroff, 1993a). Satisfaction with career choice and the employee's career progression can also contribute to job satisfaction (Scarpello & Vandenberg, 1992). Research has suggested that elements of job satisfaction may be deeply rooted in the individual workers. These researchers have suggested that there may be genetic "predispositions" to be satisfied or dissatisfied with one's job (see box On the Cutting Edge).

Although a variety of factors might contribute to job satisfaction for most workers (e.g., working conditions, relationships at work), as mentioned before, the connection between such factors and job satisfaction may not be a direct link. Job satisfaction may be moderated by the perceptions of individual workers (Gardner & Pierce, 1998; Mathieu, Hofmann, & Farr, 1993). This is because different employees may perceive the same job differently, and it is those individual perceptions that determine whether or not an employee is satisfied with the job. For instance, improving the working environment may affect satisfaction for some employees, but not for others, because not everyone is dissatisfied with the environment.

Another major obstacle in the measurement of job satisfaction is the same obstacle encountered in the measurement of any attitude—the necessary

ON THE *CUTTING* EDGE

Personality, Genetics, and Job Satisfaction

Can job satisfaction be a reality for all workers? And, how much can the organization do toward increasing or maintaining job satisfaction for its workers? Although the organization can do much to foster job satisfaction, the factors that cause job satisfaction are not entirely under the control of the organization. Workers can influence their own levels of job satisfaction through such actions as performing their jobs well and maintaining good attendance at work. Even if we could set up the ideal workplace, would this lead all workers to enjoy high levels of job satisfaction? Research on the influences of personality and genetic factors on job satisfaction suggest that the answer is "no."

For example, workers who score high on personal alienation—indicating deep-set tendencies toward feeling isolated, lonely, and powerless—do not seem to be as affected by interventions designed to increase workers' job satisfaction as are workers scoring low on this personality characteristic (Efraty & Sirgy, 1990). Persons high on negative affect/emotions, as well as persons prone to boredom, may also be less likely to feel job satisfaction (Dormann, Fay, Zapf, & Frese, 2006; Kass, Vodanovich, & Callender, 2001). Moreover, personality differences may mean that workers will find different "sources" of job satisfaction in the workplace. For instance, workers with low self-esteem appear to find more satisfaction in jobs in which expectations of performance are clear (e.g., there are clear guidelines for performance), whereas job satisfaction in persons with higher self-esteem is not as affected by knowledge of performance expectations (Pierce, Gardner, Dunham, & Cummings, 1993). Indications are that workers' personalities may vary in terms of the amount of job satisfaction they are able to achieve, and under what conditions

they are best able to achieve it. In fact, it has been argued that dispositional factors may be responsible for the fact that surveys of U.S. workers during both good and bad economic times seem to show approximately the same percentages of satisfied and dissatisfied workers (Staw & Ross, 1985). In other words, although economic conditions fluctuate, the distribution of different personality types in the workforce remains relatively stable.

Perhaps more interesting is the finding that genetic factors present at birth can influence a worker's job satisfaction. Studies examining the genetic and environmental components of job satisfaction using identical twins who were reared apart in different homes found a higher correlation in the twin adults' job satisfaction than would be found between persons in the general population (Arvey, Bouchard, Segal, & Abraham, 1989; Keller, Bouchard, Arvey, Segal, & Dawis, 1992). In other words, despite the fact that the identical twins were raised in totally different environments, and likely were in completely different job environments, the twins' levels of job satisfaction were quite similar. More recent research has discovered some of the genetic markers associated with job satisfaction (Song, Li, & Arvey, 2011).

Of course, such findings do not suggest that organizations have no responsibility in helping workers to achieve job satisfaction. What these findings do suggest is that job satisfaction may not be completely determined by characteristics of the organization or of the job (Dormann & Zapf, 2001). Although organizations must provide an environment where employees can meet their job-related needs, they cannot guarantee that every worker will achieve the same level of satisfaction. Likewise, workers should not place the entire responsibility for their own job satisfaction on the employer.

reliance on respondents' self-reports. Recall that problems with self-report measures include the fact that workers may (intentionally or unintentionally) fail to report their true feelings. Strategies for measuring job satisfaction have included interviews, group meetings, and a variety of structured, survey methods, such as rating scales or questionnaires. The obvious advantages of using a rating scale or questionnaire, instead of a face-to-face meeting, are the reduced time invested in the administration of the instrument and the fact that anonymity of responses can often be maintained (particularly if large numbers of employees are being surveyed). Such anonymity may help to ensure that worker responses are more candid than they might be in a face-to-face interview. That is, some workers, fearing retaliation from management, may not give an accurate representation of their levels of job satisfaction in an interview or a meeting and may try to present an overly positive picture of their feelings.

On the other hand, meetings or interviews can provide richer information because the interviewer can ask follow-up questions or request further elaboration or clarification of an answer. In addition, response biases (e.g., tendencies for all or most employees to give overly positive or negative responses) and ambiguous items that employees may interpret differently may seriously damage the validity of a pencil-and-paper job satisfaction measure. Another problem with survey instruments is context effects (Harrison & McLaughlin, 1993). Context effects occur when a neutral item is responded to negatively or positively, simply because it is grouped with other items that are worded negatively or positively. Finally, even well-designed, standardized instruments may become outdated and require periodic revisions due to changes in technology and work roles (Roznowski, 1989). In summary, no matter which type of measurement is selected, careful thought and planning must go into the development and administration of job satisfaction measures.

Despite the complexities, many organizations develop their own interviews, scales, or surveys that are used to measure employee job satisfaction. Although such in-house techniques can be designed to assess satisfaction with specific issues relevant to each company's employees, their results may be difficult to interpret. First, these measures may not be reliable or valid. To construct measures that are reliable and valid, one must have a rather extensive background in survey development and measurement techniques. Moreover, it takes quite a bit of research to establish the reliability and validity of a job satisfaction measure. Many organizations don't have the employees with the skills needed to construct such measures. Second, it is very difficult to know what a particular rating or score means without being able to compare it to some standard. For example, if employees indicate relatively low levels of satisfaction with salary on some scale, does this mean that they are actually dissatisfied with the money they make? They may merely be stating a desire for more money—a desire shared by most employees of most organizations.

Because of these problems in creating and interpreting in-house job satisfaction measures, many companies are using standardized surveys. Besides being cost-effective, a major advantage of using such standardized measures is that they provide normative data that permit the comparison of ratings with those from similar groups of workers in other companies who have completed

Stop & Review

Describe the two approaches to conceptualizing job satisfaction.

the survey. This allows the organization to know whether the job satisfaction levels of its employees are low, high, or in the "normal" range, as compared to other workers in other organizations. As demonstrated earlier in the comparison of levels of satisfaction with salary, if a company simply assumes its employees' ratings are low (when, in fact, they are average when compared to the norm), management may spend time and resources on a problem that doesn't exist.

The ability to compare scores from standardized job satisfaction measures that have been obtained from different groups of workers in different companies also allows researchers to investigate the various organizational factors that cause job satisfaction and dissatisfaction. In other words, if different questionnaires were used for all studies, researchers could not be sure that the studies were measuring and comparing the same things.

Two of the most widely used standardized surveys of job satisfaction are the *Minnesota Satisfaction Questionnaire (MSQ)* and the *Job Descriptive Index (JDI)*. The Minnesota Satisfaction Questionnaire (Weiss, Dawis, England, & Lofquist, 1967) is a multiple-item rating scale that asks workers to rate their levels of satisfaction/dissatisfaction with 20 job facets, including supervisor's competence, working conditions, compensation, task variety, level of job responsibility, and chances for advancement. Ratings are marked on a scale from "very dissatisfied" to "neutral" to "very satisfied." Sample items from the MSQ are presented in Figure 9.1.

The Job Descriptive Index (Smith et al., 1969) is briefer than the MSQ and measures satisfaction with five job facets: the job itself, supervision, pay, promotions, and coworkers. Within each of the five facets is a list of words or short phrases. Respondents indicate whether the word or phrase describes their job, using the answers "yes," "no," and "undecided." Each of the words or phrases has a numerical value that reflects how well it describes a typically satisfying job. Items checked within each scale are summed, yielding five satisfaction scores that reflect the five facets of job satisfaction. In the past it was suggested that the five scales could be summed into a total score of overall job satisfaction. However, one study indicates that such a total score is not the best overall measure and suggests the use of a global assessment instrument called the Job In General (or JIG scale) as an accompaniment to the five JDI scales (Ironson et al., 1989).

Since its development in the 1960s, the JDI has become the most widely used standardized measure of job satisfaction (Roznowski, 1989). Moreover, the JDI was revised and improved in the mid-1980s by replacing some of the older scale items with improved items (Smith, Kendall, & Hulin, 1987). Figure 9.2 presents sample items from the JDI.

Both the MSQ and the JDI have been widely researched, and both have established relatively high levels of reliability and validity (Kinicki, McKee-Ryan, Schriesheim, & Carson, 2002; Smith et al., 1969, 1987; Weiss et al., 1967). One obvious difference between the two measures is the number of job satisfaction facets measured: The JDI measures 5 facets, the MSQ assesses 20. An important question is how many or how few facets are needed to measure job satisfaction adequately. One study suggested that some of the JDI facets could be split into two parts. For example, the satisfaction with supervision scale could be split into satisfaction with the supervisor's ability and satisfaction with the supervisor's

Minnesota Satisfaction Questionnaire (MSQ)
a self-report measure of job satisfaction that breaks satisfaction down into 20 job facets

Job Descriptive Index (JDI)
a self-report job satisfaction rating scale measuring five job facets

On my present job, this is how I feel about	Very Dissatisfied	Dissatisfied	Neutral	Satisfied	Very Satisfied
1 Being able to keep busy all the time	1	2	3	4	5
2 The chance to work alone on the job	1	2	3	4	5
3 The chance to do different things from time to time	1	2	3	4	5
4 The chance to be somebody in the community	1	2	3	4	5
5 The way my boss handles his/her workers	1	2	3	4	5
6 The competence of my supervisor in making decisions	1	2	3	4	5
7 The way my job provides for steady employment	1	2	3	4	5
8 My pay and the amount of work I do	1	2	3	4	5
9 The chances for advancement on this job	1	2	3	4	5
10 The working conditions	1	2	3	4	5
11 The way my co workers get along with each other	1	2	3	4	5
12 The feeling of accomplishment I get from the job	1	2	3	4	5

FIGURE 9.1

Sample Items from the Minnesota Satisfaction Questionnaire

Source: Adapted from Weiss, D. J., Dawis, R. V., England, G. W., & Lofquist, L. H. (1967). *Manual for the Minnesota satisfaction questionnaire: Minnesota studies in vocational rehabilitation.* Minneapolis, MN: University of Minnesota, Vocational Psychology Research.

interpersonal skills (Yeager, 1981). Other evidence indicates that some of the 20 MSQ scales are highly correlated with one another and thus could be collapsed into fewer facets (Gillet & Schwab, 1975; Wong, Hui, & Law, 1998). One may conclude from these viewpoints that there is no consensus on what constitutes the ideal or best measurement of job satisfaction. However, most researchers do agree that a valid, reliable, and standardized instrument will provide the most accurate assessment.

Think of your present work. What is it like most of the time? In the blank beside each word given below, write

Y   for "Yes" if it describes your work
N   for "No" if it does NOT describe it
?   if you cannot decide

Work on present job

Routine
Satisfying
Good

Think of the pay you get now. How well does each of the following words describe your present pay? In the blank beside each word, put

Y   if it describes your pay
N   if it does NOT describe it
?   if you cannot decide

Present pay

Income adequate for
normal expenses
Insecure
Less that I deserve

Think of the opportunities for promotion that you have now. How well does each of the following words describe these? In the blank beside each word, put

Y   for "Yes" if it describes your opportunities for promotion
N   for "No" if it does NOT describe them
?   if you cannot decide

Opportunities for promotion

Dead-end job
Unfair promotion policy
Regular promotions

Think of the kind of supervision that you get on your job. How well does each of the following words describe this supervision? In the blank beside each word below put

Y   if it describes the supervision you get on your job
N   if it does NOT describe it
?   if you cannot decide

Supervision on present job

Impolite
Praises good work
Doesn't supervise enough

Think of the majority of the people that you work with now or the people you meet in connection with your work. How well does each of the following words describe these people? In the blank beside each word below, put

Y   if it describes the people you work with
N   if it does NOT describe them
?   if you cannot decide

People on your present job

Boring
Responsible
Intelligent

Think of your job in general. All in all, what is it like most of the time? In the blank beside each word below, write

Y   for "Yes" if it describes your job
N   for "No" if it does NOT describe it
?   if you cannot decide

Job in general

Undesirable
Better than most
Rotten

FIGURE 9.2

Sample Items from the Job Descriptive Index, Revised (Each scale is presented on a separate page.)

Source: Smith, P. C., Kendall, L. M., & Hulin, C. L. (1985). Job descriptive index. From *The measurement of satisfaction in work and retirement* (rev. ed.). Bowling Green, OH: Bowling Green State University.

Note: The Job Descriptive Index is copyrighted by Bowling Green State University. The complete forms, scoring key, instructions, and norms can be obtained from Department of Psychology, Bowling Green State University, Bowling Green, OH 43403.

In addition to the MSQ and JDI, a number of job satisfaction scales have been developed for research purposes, such as the *Job Satisfaction Survey* (Spector, 1997a), a briefer facet measure of job satisfaction that has been used sporadically in research. From the practitioner standpoint, numerous consulting firms specialize in job satisfaction/employee satisfaction surveys, although companies need to use caution because many of these surveys have not, like the MSQ and JDI, been subjected to rigorous research evaluation.

UP CLOSE   Job Satisfaction at the International Level

As you read this chapter, you will become more aware of some of the aspects of work that are related to job satisfaction for workers. However, the large majority of these studies are done in the United States. As with research in all areas of psychology, we cannot conclude that the results of studies conducted with workers within the United States will generalize to workers in other countries and cultures. For example, you probably find that good relationships with your coworkers and supervisors add to the satisfaction that you find in your job. Are such personal relationships at work as important to workers throughout the world as they appear to be with American workers? And, what other aspects of work add to job satisfaction for workers outside the United States?

One study conducted in Japan found that supportive supervision, as well as support from coworkers, was positively correlated with workers' job satisfaction (Kumara & Koichi, 1989). According to this study, support from coworkers and supervisors was especially important to employees who did not feel positive about the work they performed (e.g., those who found their jobs unpleasant, very difficult, or stressful). These workers in "unfulfilling" jobs depended on good interpersonal relationships to feel satisfied, similar to findings of studies conducted using U.S. workers.

Along with having good social relationships at work, many U.S. workers prefer to have a variety of tasks to do and to have some autonomy in performing those tasks. Similarly, workers in Australia (Hopkins, 1990), Canada (Baba & Jamal, 1991), and the Netherlands (Efraty & Sirgy, 1990) appear to be more satisfied with jobs that offer diverse tasks and independence. These facets of the job may also account for the findings in the United States and in other developed nations that show that older workers, and those holding higher-level jobs, experience more satisfaction than very young workers and those in blue-collar positions (Gamst & Otten, 1992; Gattiker & Howg, 1990; Kravitz, Linn, & Shapiro, 1990). In fact, one comparison of white-collar workers in the United States and India found remarkable similarity in the factors that contributed to these workers' job satisfaction (Takalkar & Coovert, 1994).

Obviously, the international findings discussed here are mostly based on studies of workers in developed countries, where workers enjoy a certain level of job security, adequate pay, and good working conditions. For example, one study found differences in job satisfaction levels between U.S. workers and workers in the Philippines (Rothausen, Gonzalez, & Griffin, 2009). Another study found differences in job satisfaction among workers from countries in central and eastern Europe (Lange, 2009). Whether or not workers in more underdeveloped nations would look to such things as task variety and autonomy for sources of job satisfaction has not yet been determined (Judge, Parker, Colbert, Heller, & Ilies, 2001). Perhaps workers in underdeveloped nations have different sources of satisfaction, which are possibly related to more basic survival needs (e.g., pay) than workers in more developed nations. However, one would expect that as these nations develop and gain economic strength, workers the world over will look to their jobs to fulfill higher-level needs, such as support from coworkers, recognition, and the opportunity to control their own work behaviors and reach their highest potential.

It is important to mention that cultural factors can affect both how workers define and perceive job satisfaction, and how members of different countries or cultural groups respond to job satisfaction measures. As a result, there have been many attempts to understand job satisfaction globally (see box Up Close: Job Satisfaction at the International Level).

Stop & Review

Compare and contrast the MSQ and the JDI.

JOB SATISFACTION AND JOB PERFORMANCE

As you recall from our discussion of the human relations movement, Mayo and his colleagues proposed that there was a relationship between one aspect of job satisfaction—employee satisfaction with social relationships at work—and work productivity. Moreover, the job design theories of motivation discussed in Chapter 8—Herzberg's two-factor theory and the job characteristics model—are as much theories of job satisfaction as they are of motivation. Both theories emphasize that satisfaction with the job is a key to determining motivation. Is there any truth to this notion that the "happy worker is the productive worker"?

A meta-analysis suggests that there is indeed a moderate correlation between job satisfaction and job performance (Judge, Thoreson, Bono, & Patton, 2001). But what is the causal relationship? Does job satisfaction cause job performance? One early theory of the job satisfaction–performance relationship suggests that it may be the other way around: Good job performance leads to (causes) job satisfaction! (But, of course, it is not that simple, as other factors mediate the relationship.)

This early theory, suggested by Porter and Lawler (1968), clarifies how this process might operate. According to them, job satisfaction and performance are not directly linked. Instead, effective job performance leads to job-related rewards, such as pay increases, promotions, or a sense of accomplishment. If the process for offering these rewards is perceived as fair, receiving these rewards leads to job satisfaction and also to higher and higher levels of performance. This creates a situation in which job satisfaction and job performance are actually independent of one another, but are linked because both are affected by job-related rewards (see Figure 9.3). Interestingly, the Porter–Lawler model builds on the equity theory of motivation discussed in Chapter 8, because notions of equity—fairness in job-related inputs and outcomes—are central to

Porter–Lawler model
a theory where the relationship between job satisfaction and performance is mediated by work-related rewards

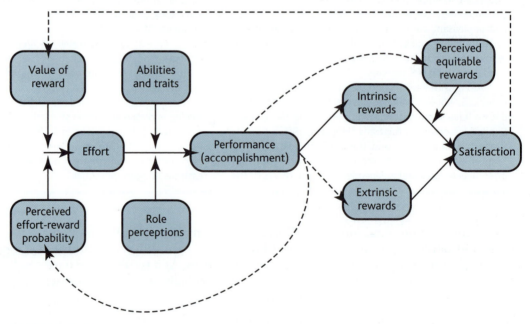

FIGURE 9.3

The Porter–Lawler Model of the Job Performance–Job Satisfaction Relationship

Source: Porter, L. W., & Lawler, E. E. (1968). *Managerial attitudes and performance.* Homewood, IL: Dorsey Press. As adapted by Baron, R. A. (1986). *Behavior in organizations: Understanding and managing the human side of work* (2nd ed.). Boston: Allyn & Bacon.

the argument. Specifically, motivation to perform the job and the satisfaction derived from the job are both caused by the relationship between what an individual puts into the job and what is received from the job in terms of rewards. In other words, both motivation and job satisfaction come from the perceived equitable relationship between the employee's inputs to the job and the job outcomes.

Many other factors could potentially affect the job satisfaction–performance relationship, for example, the types of jobs that people perform. In fact, evidence suggests that job satisfaction might be more strongly related to job performance for individuals in complex jobs, such as managers, scientists, and engineers, than in more structured jobs such as accounting and sales (Judge, Thoresen et al., 2001). Complex jobs, because they require creativity and ingenuity, might offer more opportunity for intrinsic reinforcement, and that may strengthen the connection between satisfaction and performance, in comparison to more routine jobs, where satisfaction may be more affected by the structure or conditions of work, or extrinsic rewards.

Some researchers emphasize that the perception of fairness or justice in pay is the most important part of this link between performance and job satisfaction (Miceli, 1993). That is, "relative deprivation" (a discrepancy between a worker's expectations and rewards) and perceived fairness of pay may mediate the relationship between performance and job satisfaction, regardless of the actual rewards obtained. For example, if highly paid workers do not perceive their pay to be fair, or to meet their expectations, their satisfaction is likely to be negatively affected. This may extend beyond pay. A sense of being fairly treated is a very important determinant of job satisfaction (Clay-Warner, Reynolds, & Roman, 2005).

In summary, both job satisfaction and job performance are important but complex work outcomes. There is some evidence that these two variables are linked, but the relationship is not necessarily direct, influenced by a variety of other variables, such as job-related rewards, job complexity, feelings of equity and justice, and other factors.

Organizational Commitment

Just as there are different operational definitions of job satisfaction, so too are there different definitions of the construct of organizational commitment. For example, is it an attitude, a behavior, or both? Previously, organizational commitment, also referred to as company loyalty, was associated with an acceptance of the organization's goals and values, a willingness to exert effort on behalf of the organization, and a desire to remain with the organization (Porter, Steers, Mowday, & Boulian, 1974). This definition encompasses both attitudes and behaviors. More recently, the concept of organizational commitment has been taken to imply worker attitudes, such as those just mentioned, whereas the concept of organizational citizenship behaviors (OCB) refers to commitment-related behaviors (Organ, 1990). (We will discuss OCB more fully later in this chapter.) For example, there is a negative correlation between the attitude of organizational commitment and the behavior of quitting a job. Organizational commitment is similar to job satisfaction because both involve feelings about the work situation (and both can be seen as components of the "umbrella" construct of employee engagement). However, because organizational commitment deals specifically with workers' attitudes about the organization, it may be more directly linked to employee attendance variables such as absenteeism and turnover than is job satisfaction. A good definition of organizational commitment is that it is the worker's attitudes about the entire work organization.

The most widely used organizational commitment measure is a 15-item self-report instrument called the Organizational Commitment Questionnaire (OCQ), which is presented in Figure 9.4. Another model of organizational commitment views it as composed of three dimensions: *affective commitment,* which is the employee's emotional attachment to the organization; *continuance*

organizational commitment
a worker's feelings and attitudes about the entire work organization

---

Instructions: Listed below are a series of statements that represent possible feelings that individuals might have about the company or organization for which they work. With respect to your own feelings about the particular organization for which you are now working (company name), please indicate the degree of your agreement or disagreement with each statement by checking one of the seven alternatives below each statement.*

1   I am willing to put in a great deal of effort beyond that normally expected in order to help this organization be successful.
2   I talk up this organization to my friends as a great organization to work for.
3   I feel very little loyalty to this organization. (R)
4   I would accept almost any type of job assignment in order to keep working for this organization.
5   I find that my values and the organization's values are very similar.
6   I am proud to tell others that I am part of this organization.
7   I could just as well be working for a different organization as long as the type of work was similar. (R)
8   This organization really inspires the very best in me in the way of job performance.
9   It would take very little change in my present circumstances to cause me to leave this organization. (R)
10 I am extremely glad that I chose this organization to work for over others I was considering at the time I joined.
11 There's not too much to be gained by sticking with this organization indefinitely. (R)
12 Often, I find it difficult to agree with this organization's policies on important matters relating to its employees. (R)
13 I really care about the fate of this organization.
14 For me this is the best of all possible organizations for which to work.
15 Deciding to work for this organization was a definite mistake on my part. (R)

FIGURE 9.4
Organizational Commitment Questionnaire (OCQ)
Source: Mowday, R. T., Steers, R., & Porter, L. W. (1979). The measure of organizational commitment. *Journal of Vocational Behavior, 14,* 228.
Note: *Responses to each item are measured on a 7-point scale with scale point anchors labeled: (1) strongly disagree; (2) moderately disagree; (3) slightly disagree; (4) neither disagree nor agree; (5) slightly agree; (6) moderately agree; (7) strongly agree. An "R" denotes a negatively phrased and reverse-scored item.

commitment, which refers to commitment to continue with the organization because there are costs associating with leaving; and *normative commitment,* which is like a sense of duty or obligation to stay with the company (Meyer & Allen, 1997). Separate scales are used to measure each of these three commitment dimensions (Meyer, Allen, & Smith, 1993). Research has demonstrated that self-report measures of organizational commitment such as these do a good job of measuring the construct (Goffin & Gellatly, 2001).

🕑 Stop & Review

Describe the Porter–
Lawler model.

ORGANIZATIONAL COMMITMENT AND JOB SATISFACTION

The concepts of job satisfaction and organizational commitment are closely related, although distinct. Research indicates a fairly high positive correlation between the two factors (Arnold & Feldman, 1982; O'Driscoll, Ilgen, & Hildreth, 1992; Stumpf & Hartman, 1984). Part of this high positive correlation may be due to the fact that workers may possibly respond positively to both job satisfaction and organizational commitment measures, due to a positive response bias, or workers may have a desire to avoid *cognitive dissonance.* Cognitive dissonance is an unpleasant state of perceived self-inconsistency (Festinger, 1957). Workers thus avoid cognitive dissonance by convincing themselves that they are satisfied simply because they are loyal to the organization ("I have stayed with this company through thick and thin, therefore I must like my job."). Although it is conceivable that a worker could be quite satisfied with a job but have low feelings of commitment to the organization, or vice versa, the feelings tend to be positively related. Studies show mixed results as to the direction of influence between these two constructs. For example, O'Driscoll and colleagues (1992) found that job satisfaction may directly affect organizational commitment, whereas other studies indicate that organizational commitment leads to job satisfaction (Becker & Billings, 1993; Vandenberg & Lance, 1992).

Both organizational commitment and job satisfaction are most likely affected by numerous factors, including the type and variety of work, the autonomy involved in the job, the level of responsibility associated with the job, the quality of the social relationships at work, compensation, and the chances for promotion and advancement in the company. However, there appears to be some consensus that organizational values influence organizational commitment, whereas perceived equity of rewards influences job satisfaction. That is, perceived fairness in rewards influences job satisfaction, whereas perceived congruence between organizational and employee values, and between organizational values and actions, tends to influence organizational commitment (Finegan, 2000; Fritz, Arnett, & Conkel, 1999). Organizational commitment also tends to be weakened by the perceived chances of finding a job with another company (Bateman & Strasser, 1984; Gilbert & Ivancevich, 2000). For instance, if highly skilled worker Carol could easily find a job with another company, but her friend Kim had difficulty finding her current job, Carol will likely have a lower level of organizational commitment than Kim. In addition, there appears to be positive correlations between organizational commitment and age, education, and time on the job, such that older and more educated workers, and those with longer tenure with the company, tend to be more committed to the organization (Becker & Billings, 1993; Lee, Ashford, Walsh, & Mowday, 1992).

As discussed in Chapter 1, beginning in the 1990s and into the financial "meltdown" of the past several years, many organizations have found it necessary to reduce the size of their workforces by laying off or terminating workers. Thousands of people at a time can lose their jobs when a major corporation reduces the number of people it employs. Such actions, called *downsizing* (although some companies have tried to soften this term by relabeling it "rightsizing"), can have an impact on the workers who are retained, as well as on those who lose their jobs. For many of the remaining employees, feelings of organizational commitment and job satisfaction can decline following downsizing, especially if the employees are close to those who were laid off, or if they feel that their own jobs may be in jeopardy. However, studies show that explanations from management giving the reasons for the lay offs and giving remaining employees a sense of control over their future work situations can have positive effects on the remaining workforce (Brockner et al., 2004). There is also some evidence that the overall work effort of employees may actually increase following downsizing (Taylor & Giannantonio, 1993).

As you might imagine, maintaining job satisfaction and organizational commitment is a challenge to both employers and employees—a challenge that becomes even more difficult during trying economic times. Yet, organizations must be concerned with both employee job satisfaction and organizational commitment if they are to maintain a high-quality, loyal workforce.

Employee Attitudes and Employee Attendance

As previously mentioned, employee attendance variables such as absenteeism and turnover are associated with employee engagement, job satisfaction, and organizational commitment. Employees who are engaged, or who have positive feelings about their jobs and work organizations, should be less likely to be absent from work and to leave for a job elsewhere than those who are disengaged and hold negative attitudes about their jobs. However, before considering these relationships, we must consider how employee attendance variables are defined and measured (Hackett & Guion, 1985; Johns, 1994b; Lee, 1989).

Employee Absenteeism

Both absenteeism and turnover can be categorized into voluntary and involuntary forms. Voluntary absenteeism is when employees miss work because they want to do something else. Calling in sick to take a three-day weekend or taking a day off to run errands or to go shopping are examples of voluntary absenteeism. Involuntary absenteeism occurs when the employee has a legitimate excuse for missing work, typically illness. Because involuntary absenteeism is inevitable, the organization must be prepared to accept a certain amount of such absences. It is voluntary absenteeism, however, that the organization would like to eliminate. Of course, it is very difficult to distinguish voluntary from involuntary absenteeism, because most employees are unlikely to admit that they were voluntarily absent (Dalton & Mesch, 1991; Hammer & Landau, 1981). One way that researchers have operationalized the measurement of voluntary and involuntary absenteeism is to use absence frequency (the number of days absent) as a measure of voluntary absenteeism and absence length (the number of consecutive days absent) as an assessment of involuntary absenteeism (Atkin & Goodman, 1984). However, this is a very crude measure. It is important to note that voluntary absenteeism is likely to be more strongly associated with employee job satisfaction; involuntary absenteeism is beyond the control of the employee (Sagie, 1998).

Research examining the relationship between job satisfaction and employee absenteeism has produced conflicting findings. Sometimes, there is a slight negative relationship between the two (with higher levels of job satisfaction associated with lower rates of absenteeism; Ostroff, 1993a), and sometimes no significant relationship at all is found (Ilgen & Hollenback, 1977; Porter & Steers, 1973). A meta-analysis of a number of studies indicates that job satisfaction and absenteeism are indeed negatively correlated but that the relationship between the two is not very strong (Scott & Taylor, 1985). One reason the relationship is not as strong as one might think stems from problems in measuring absenteeism that cause voluntary and involuntary absenteeism to be lumped together in most of these studies. In other words, there may be a significant negative correlation between job satisfaction and voluntary absenteeism, but no significant relationship between job satisfaction and involuntary absenteeism due to illness. According to one study, there is an association between voluntary absence and job satisfaction; however, this study concluded that rather than job satisfaction causing the absenteeism, it was really the absenteeism that was leading to lower job satisfaction (Tharenou, 1993). Perhaps to avoid cognitive dissonance, workers who voluntarily missed work rationalized that if they were choosing to be absent, they must not have been very satisfied with their jobs.

Another problem might be that even though workers are satisfied with their jobs, they may find certain nonwork activities (for example, taking an extra day of vacation or attending a sporting event) more interesting or more important (Youngblood, 1984). Employees may also be absent because of factors beyond their control, such as health, transportation, or child-care problems (Goldberg & Waldman, 2000). Additionally, individual absenteeism may be affected by coworkers' absenteeism rates and by the organization's policy and "climate" toward absenteeism (Gellatly, 1995; Johns, 1994a; Markham & McKee, 1995). For example, if coworkers are frequently absent, or if management has a lenient policy that is tolerant of absences, employees might be inclined to miss work regardless of how satisfied or dissatisfied they are with their jobs (Haccoun & Jeanrie, 1995; Harrison & Martocchio, 1998).

Finally, although the construct of absenteeism may appear quite simple, it, like other behaviors, is probably more complicated than it appears to be on the surface. Some of this complexity may be illustrated by studies indicating a negative correlation between age and voluntary absenteeism, and a positive correlation between age and involuntary absenteeism (Hackett, 1990). In other words, younger workers tend to voluntarily miss work, whereas older workers tend to miss work because they are more frequently ill.

Although it may seem apparent that absenteeism, especially voluntary absenteeism, would be related to turnover (e.g., workers who have a lot of unexcused absences don't last long on the job), researchers hold conflicting views of this relationship. Some researchers have concluded that there is a positive relationship between absenteeism and turnover, whereas others have concluded that no such relationship exists. A meta-analysis of 17 separate studies showed a relationship between absenteeism and turnover. Moreover, the relationship was not mediated by type of absenteeism. In other words, turnover did not appear to be more related to voluntary absenteeism than to involuntary absenteeism (Mitra, Jenkins, & Gupta, 1992).

EMPLOYEE TURNOVER

As with absenteeism, there are difficulties in defining and measuring turnover (Campion, 1991). Involuntary turnover occurs when an employee is fired or laid off. A certain amount of involuntary turnover is likely to be considered inevitable and possibly even beneficial. Firing workers who are not performing at desirable levels can be viewed as a positive, "weeding" process (Mobley, 1982). Layoffs often occur for financial reasons and thus are likely to be beyond the control of management. Most voluntary turnover takes place when a competent and capable employee leaves to work elsewhere. It is this turnover that is costly to the organization, because losing a valued employee means reduced organizational productivity and increased expenses associated with hiring and training a replacement. According to one school of thought, voluntary turnover is likely to be influenced by lack of job satisfaction and organizational commitment, whereas involuntary turnover is not. As with absenteeism, research that does not distinguish between voluntary and involuntary turnover may not find the expected relationships between employee attitudes and turnover simply because the two types of turnover are lumped together. Interestingly, some researchers note that there are also problems in categorizing turnover as either voluntary or involuntary because some poor workers may not be fired but may voluntarily choose to leave the organization, which is likely to be glad to see them go. However, this means that voluntary turnover might be further classified as either dysfunctional or functional, depending on whether it has negative or beneficial outcomes for the organization (Dalton, Krackhardt, & Porter, 1981). More recently, it has been suggested that involuntary turnover caused by downsizing—so-called reduction-in-force turnover—should be treated as a completely different category than either voluntary or involuntary turnover (McElroy, Morrow, & Rude, 2001).

Both job satisfaction and organizational commitment have been investigated as predictors of employee turnover. Meta-analyses indicate that both low levels of job satisfaction and organizational commitment are related to higher rates of turnover (Griffeth, Hom, & Gaertner, 2000). Research has demonstrated that organizational commitment develops from job satisfaction and in turn influences an employee's decision to remain with or leave the organization

(Gaertner, 2000; Williams & Hazer, 1986). However, although organizational commitment appears to be a predictor of turnover, one of the best predictors of employee turnover is absenteeism, particularly the rate of absences in the years immediately before the employee leaves (Griffeth et al., 2000; Mitra et al., 1992).

Researchers have turned their attention to measuring employees' self-reported intentions to leave, or turnover intentions, in an effort to prevent the loss of valuable employees. We have already seen that employee engagement leads to reduced turnover intentions. The obvious problem with measuring turnover intentions is that many workers who report that they intend to quit their jobs may not actually turnover because they lack alternative employment, because they reevaluate the situation, or because they are not risk takers (Allen, Weeks, & Moffitt, 2005; Vandenberg & Barnes-Nelson, 1999). Regardless of the strength of the connection between intentions to turnover and actual turnover, measuring employees' intentions to quit their jobs can be a measure of dissatisfaction with the job or organization and used by employers to try to remedy the situation to prevent costly turnover.

turnover intentions
workers' self-reported intentions to leave their jobs

Because voluntary turnover can be costly to an organization, it is important to understand some of the reasons why good performers may leave their jobs (Lee & Maurer, 1997). It has been found that productive, valuable employees who do not receive work-related rewards, such as promotions and pay raises, are likely candidates for leaving their jobs (Trevor, Gerhardt, & Boudreau, 1997). Simply stated, employees who feel that they are not treated fairly are more prone to leave (Griffeth & Gaertner, 2001). Studies also indicate that perceived lack of influence or power within the organization can cause workers to seek employment elsewhere, especially if they feel positive about the other job opportunities available to them (Buchko, 1992; Lee & Mitchell, 1994; Schminke, 1993). As stated earlier, both job satisfaction and organizational commitment are associated with turnover, and this need for workers to feel that they have some influence within the organization may help explain this association. That is, those workers who have such influence are probably more satisfied with their jobs and thus more committed to the organization (Dwyer & Ganster, 1991). This may also help explain the reason that giving workers a sense of power over their jobs, or allowing them to participate in decision-making processes, is associated with higher levels of job satisfaction, as we shall see later in this chapter.

In summary, when examining the relationships between job satisfaction and other outcome variables such as absenteeism and turnover, it is important to consider the type of absenteeism and turnover being measured. Voluntary absenteeism and turnover are most likely to be affected by employee attitudes. Unfortunately, many studies do not distinguish between voluntary and involuntary absenteeism and turnover, which leads to a possible "watering down" of any observed effects. Moreover, cause-and-effect relationships often cannot be assumed. In fact, some studies indicate that the relationships are reciprocal, with each variable sometimes being the "cause" and at other times being the "effect."

Increasing Employee Engagement, Job Satisfaction, and Organizational Commitment

As we have seen, employee engagement, job satisfaction and organizational commitment are considered important by organizations because they are linked to costly absenteeism and turnover. Job satisfaction is particularly important to the employee because it reflects a critical work outcome: feelings of fulfillment from the job and the work setting. Because of this, organizations have implemented a number of programs and techniques in an effort to increase employees' engagement, satisfaction, and commitment. These programs take many forms. Some change the structure of work, others alter the methods of worker compensation, and still others offer innovative fringe benefit plans and packages. We will examine some of these techniques.

Changes in job structure

job rotation

the systematic movement of workers from one type of task to another to alleviate boredom and monotony (as well as training workers on different tasks; see Chapter 6)

Three techniques have been used to try to increase employee satisfaction by changing the structure of jobs. The first technique, job rotation, which was introduced in Chapter 7, involves moving workers from one specialized job to another. Although job rotation can be used to train workers in a variety of tasks, it can also be used to alleviate the monotony and boredom associated with performing the same work, day in and day out. For example, an employee in a retail store may move from maintenance and cleanup duties to stocking merchandise to bagging merchandise on a weekly basis. A receptionist in a large organization might rotate from greeting visitors and answering telephones to simple clerical duties such as filing and photocopying. Research shows that job rotation can be related to job satisfaction, as well as contributing to increases in salary and opportunities for promotion (Campion, Cheraskin, & Stevens, 1994).

job enlargement

the expansion of a job to include additional, more varied work tasks

Job enlargement is the practice of allowing workers to take on additional, varied tasks in an effort to make them feel that they are more valuable members of the organization. For example, a custodian who is responsible for the cleaning and upkeep of several rooms might progressively have the job enlarged until the job's duties involve the maintenance of an entire floor. Job enlargement is tricky to implement because it means that workers are required to do additional work, which some might perceive as negative. However, if used correctly, job enlargement can positively affect job satisfaction by giving an employee a greater sense of accomplishment and improving valuable work skills. One study of enlarged jobs found that they led to greater employee satisfaction, improved employee initiative, and better customer service than persons in nonenlarged jobs. However, enlarged jobs carried the "costs" of requiring more skilled, more highly trained, and more costly (higher paid) workers than those performing nonenlarged jobs (Campion & McClelland, 1991).

Job enrichment, which we studied in depth in Chapter 8, can also be used to increase employee engagement and job satisfaction. Recall that job enrichment involves raising the level of responsibility associated with a particular job by allowing workers a greater voice in the planning, execution, and evaluation of their own activities. For example, in one such program, assembly-line workers were divided into teams, each of which was given many of the responsibilities that were previously held by frontline supervisors, including ordering supplies, setting output rates, creating quality control inspection systems, and even appraising their own performance. This independence and increased responsibility can go a long way toward increasing motivation and job satisfaction for many workers. Although job enrichment and job enlargement seem somewhat similar because both require more work from employees, job enrichment raises the level of tasks, whereas job enlargement does not raise the level of responsibility associated with the work.

Changes in pay structure

According to research, the perception of fairness in pay is associated with greater job satisfaction (Witt & Nye, 1992). And although the relationship between pay and job satisfaction is not always a direct, positive one, there is some evidence that employees who are compensated well are less likely to search for jobs elsewhere (Cotton & Tuttle, 1986; Trevor et al., 1997). Although most innovative compensation programs are introduced primarily in an effort to improve job performance, many changes also increase levels of job satisfaction.

One innovative compensation program is skill-based pay (also known as *knowledge-based pay*), which involves paying employees an hourly rate based on their knowledge and skills rather than on the particular job to which they are assigned (Lawler, Mohrman, & Ledford, 1992). In other words, workers are paid for the level of the job that they are able to perform rather than for the level of the position that they hold. For skill-based pay programs to be cost effective, it is imperative that employees be assigned to jobs that match the levels of their skills and knowledge. Research indicates that workers are more satisfied in organizations that use this system than in those that use conventional pay plans, and there is also evidence that they are more productive, more concerned with quality, less prone to turnover, and more likely to be motivated to grow and develop on the job (Dierdorff & Surface, 2008; Guthrie, 2000; Murray & Gerhart, 1998). There is also some evidence that skill-based pay works better in manufacturing as opposed to service organizations (Shaw, Gupta, Mitra, & Ledford, 2005). Particularly satisfied are those who receive skill-based pay and who also have high levels of ability and motivation (Tosi & Tosi, 1987). One explanation for the effectiveness of skill-based pay systems is that employees may perceive these compensation plans as more fair (Lee, Law, & Bobko, 1999). With the current emphasis on the "knowledge worker," and with a dwindling supply of workers possessing the highest levels of technical knowledge and skills, skill-based pay systems may increase in the future.

The Porter–Lawler model (see Figure 9.3) suggested that job performance leads to job satisfaction by way of increased rewards, one of the most important of which is pay. If this is the case, then a system of compensation based directly on performance should be an effective strategy for increasing job satisfaction. One such pay-for-performance system is merit pay, a plan in which the amount of compensation is directly a function of an employee's performance. In merit pay plans, workers receive a financial bonus based on their individual output. Although sensible in theory, such systems do not work well in practice for a

skill-based pay
a system of compensation in which workers are paid based on their knowledge and skills rather than on their positions in the organization

merit pay
a compensation system in which employees receive a base rate and additional pay based on performance

number of reasons (Campbell, Campbell, & Chia, 1998). First, and perhaps most important, difficulties in the objective assessment of performance mean that it is often impossible to distinguish the truly good performers from the more average performers. This leads to feelings of unfairness in the distribution of merit pay and subsequent employee dissatisfaction (Salimaki & Jamsen, 2010; St-Onge, 2000). Second, most merit pay systems emphasize individual goals, which may hurt the organization's overall performance and disrupt group harmony, especially if jobs require groups to collaborate for the production of a product. Finally, in many such plans the amount of merit compensation is quite small in proportion to base salaries. In other words, the merit pay is simply not viewed as a strong incentive to work harder (Balkin & Gomez-Mejia, 1987; Pearce, Stevenson, & Perry, 1985). Research has suggested that a merit pay raise needs to be at least 7% to have a significant impact on employee attitudes and motivation (Mitra, Gupta, & Jenkins, 1997). Although they are extremely popular, merit pay systems can only be effective when great care is taken in how these programs are created (Campbell et al., 1998).

Another strategy for the implementation of pay-for-performance systems is to make pay contingent on effective group performance, a technique termed gainsharing (Lawler, 1987). The notion of group- or team-based rewards was introduced in Chapter 8. In gainsharing, if a work group or department reaches a certain performance goal, all members of the unit receive a bonus. Because the level of productivity among workers usually varies, the gainsharing program must be viewed as being fair to all involved (Welbourne, 1998; Welbourne & Ferrante, 2008). For example, in one program, workers decided that the most fair plan was to set a minimum amount that could be received by any worker, and then base additional pay on each worker's level of productivity. Thus, the low producers received some base compensation, but they found that greater pay would result only if they increased production. The high producers, on the other hand, were well rewarded for their efforts (Cooper, Dyck, & Frohlich, 1992). One longitudinal study of gainsharing found that it was related to more positive employee attitudes and greater commitment than employees not participating in gainsharing (Hanlon, Meyer, & Taylor, 1994). Another study found that gainsharing improved members' teamwork as well as their satisfaction with pay (O'Bannon & Pearce, 1999). Rather than focusing on productivity increases, some gainsharing programs reward workers who cut production costs through suggestions and innovations, then passing a portion of the savings on to the workers (Arthur & Huntley, 2005). Gainsharing may not be appropriate for all organizations or for all groups of workers. Therefore, implementation of a gainsharing program must be based on careful planning and a thorough knowledge of the groups of workers involved (Gomez-Mejia, Welbourne, & Wiseman, 2000; Graham-Moore & Ross, 1990). One important consideration is that a failed attempt at a major change in pay structure, such as a gainsharing plan, could lead to massive worker dissatisfaction (Collins, 1995).

A more common plan is profit sharing, in which all employees receive a small share of the organization's profits (Rosen, Klein, & Young, 1986). The notion underlying profit sharing is to instill a sense of ownership in employees, to increase both commitment to the organization and to improve motivation and productivity

gainsharing
a compensation system based on effective group performance

Stop & Review
Describe three techniques for changing job structure.

profit sharing
a plan where all employees receive a small share of an organization's profits

As part of a gainsharing system, this team of auto mechanics competes with other teams for monthly bonuses.

(Chiu & Tsai, 2007; Cox, 2001; Duncan, 2001). For profit-sharing programs to be effective, it is imperative that employees buy into the program (Orlitzky & Rynes, 2001). One drawback is that it is often difficult for employees to see how their individual performances have an impact on the company's total output. This may be one reason why profit sharing seems to work better in small companies than in large ones (Bayo-Moriones & Larraza-Kintana, 2009). In addition, there is typically quite a long delay between reaching performance goals and receiving individual shares of the company's profits (see box Applying I/O Psychology).

Employee ownership is a program where employees own all or part of an organization. Employee ownership can take one of two forms: direct ownership or employee stock ownership. In direct ownership, the employees are the sole owners of the organization. In employee stock ownership programs, which are the more common of the two, stock options are considered part of a benefit package whereby employees acquire shares of company stock over time. Each employee eventually becomes a company stockholder and has voting rights in certain company decisions. Proponents of these programs claim that although they are expensive, the costs are offset by savings created by increased employee organizational commitment, productivity, work quality, and job satisfaction, and decreases in rates of absenteeism and turnover (Buchko, 1992; Rosen, Case, & Staubus, 2005).

Of course tales of the quick success of employee-owned companies in the 1990s, such as Southwest Airlines, United Airlines, and Wheeling Steel quickly became legendary, but were offset by the ethical scandals of the early 2000s, and the financial meltdown, which meant that employees who had their retirement funds in stock in Enron, WorldComm, or a variety of Wall Street firms lost a bundle.

employee ownership
a program where employees own all or part of an organization

Research on the success of employee ownership programs is somewhat inconsistent, and results show that employee ownership does not necessarily lead to increased job satisfaction or organizational commitment (Oliver, 1990; Orlitzky & Rynes, 2001). Other research indicates that if employee ownership is going to increase organizational commitment, certain criteria must be met, the most obvious being that the program must be financially rewarding to employees (French & Rosenstein, 1984). Moreover, higher-level employees may have more positive reactions to employee ownership programs than do lower-level workers (Wichman, 1994). One investigation further qualified the conditions required for the success of employee ownership programs. Examining 37 employee stock ownership companies, the study found that rates of employee organizational commitment and satisfaction were highest when the companies made substantial financial contributions to the employee stock purchases, when management was highly committed to the program, and when there was a great deal of communication about the program (Klein, 1987). In addition, the Oliver (1990) study found that the rewards of employee ownership would only have a positive impact on the workers if they place a high value on those rewards. For example, if a worker values the work for its own merits, the worker would likely feel about the same level of satisfaction whether she was working for an employee-owned company or not.

Flexible work schedules

Another strategy for improving worker satisfaction and commitment is to provide alternative or flexible work schedules. Flexible work schedules give workers greater control over their workday, which can be important in large urban areas, where workers are able to commute at nonpeak times, or for workers with child-care responsibilities.

APPLYING I/O PSYCHOLOGY

Using Assessment to Enhance Employee Engagement

Throughout the years, I have used employee surveys, including standardized job satisfaction and organizational commitment measures, and instruments designed for specific organizations, as a means to gauge levels of employee job satisfaction. Often these are the starting point for programs designed to spot programs, policies, and procedures that are favorable or unfavorable among employees.

In one large banking institution, the employees became very involved in the surveys, and in the programs designed to enhance employee life and well-being that followed the assessments. The surveys looked specifically at the programs that employees viewed favorably (these were continued and sometimes expanded) and those practices that employees disliked, or problems that surfaced from the surveys. The president of the bank would then ask for volunteers to serve on task forces to address the problems and to try to make the workplace better. Employees were so engaged in this program that the number of volunteers exceeded by 4–5 times the number of available slots on the task forces. It was no wonder that over time, this organization was identified as one of the "great places to work" in annual rankings.

One type of flexible schedule is compressed workweeks, in which the number of workdays is decreased while the number of hours worked per day is increased. Most common are four 10-hour days, and certain groups, such as nurses, may work three 12-hour shifts per week. Workers may prefer a compressed schedule because the extra day off allows workers time to take care of tasks that need to be done Monday through Friday, such as going to the doctor, dentist, or tax accountant. Usually compressed workweeks include a three-day weekend, which allows workers more free time to take weekend vacations. Both of these benefits should cut down on absenteeism, because workers previously might have called in sick to take an extra day of "vacation" or to run errands. An extended shift might also allow a worker to miss peak traffic times. However, a drawback is that working parents might have difficulty finding child care for the extended workday. Also on the negative side, a 10-hour (or 12-hour) workday is more exhausting than the typical 8-hour day (Cunningham, 1989; Ronen & Primps, 1981; Rosa, Colligan, & Lewis, 1989). This fatigue may lead to decreases in work productivity and concern for work quality (although many people say that the extra couple of hours are not necessarily tiring). Meta-analyses suggest that although employees tend to be satisfied with compressed workweeks and exhibit higher overall job satisfaction, there is no reduction in absenteeism associated with compressed schedules (Baltes, Briggs, Huff, Wright, & Neuman, 1999; Di Milia, 1998). In addition, one study found that workers had more favorable attitudes toward compressed work schedules if they had participated in the decision to implement the schedule change (Latack & Foster, 1985).

compressed workweeks
schedules that decrease the number of days in the workweek while increasing the number of hours worked per day

Flextime is a scheduling system whereby a worker is committed to a specified number of hours per week (usually 40) but has some flexibility concerning the starting and ending times of any particular workday. Often flextime schedules operate around a certain core of hours during which all workers must be on the job (such as 10 A.M. to 2:30 P.M.). However, the workers can decide when to begin and end the workday as long as they are present during the core period and work an 8-hour day. Some flextime schedules even allow workers to borrow and carry hours from one workday to the next or, in some extremely flexible programs, from one week to another. The only stipulation is that an average of 40 hours per week is maintained. Obviously, only certain types of jobs can accommodate flextime

flextime
a schedule that commits an employee to working a specified number of hours per week, but offers flexibility in regard to the beginning and ending times for each day

What are the primary advantages of flextime? For the worker, it affords a sense of freedom and control over planning the working day (Hicks & Klimoski, 1981; Ralston, 1989). Workers can sleep in and begin work later in the morning, as long as they make up the time by staying late. Employees who want to leave work early to do some late-afternoon shopping can arrive early to work that day. One study of commuting workers showed that flextime commuters reported less driver stress than workers not on flextime (Lucas & Heady, 2002). A study of flextime programs found that flextime reduced stress levels for workers in three countries (Canada, Israel, Russia; Barney & Elias, 2010). Research indicates that flextime programs increase employee satisfaction and commitment and is sometimes positively related to worker productivity (Baltes et al.,

1999). Interestingly, flextime pays off for companies that can implement this type of schedule, achieving reduced rates of absenteeism and the virtual elimination of tardiness (Baltes et al., 1999; Ronen, 1981).

Benefit programs

Perhaps the most common way for employers to try to increase employees' job satisfaction and organizational commitment is through various benefit programs. Benefit programs can include flexible working hours, a variety of health-care options, different retirement plans, profit sharing, career development programs, health promotion programs, and employee-sponsored child care. This last program has the potential of becoming one of the most popular and sought-after benefits and may have the extra advantage of helping to decrease absenteeism caused by employees' occasional inability to find adequate child care (Milkovich & Gomez, 1976). Interestingly, however, studies of the effects of employee-sponsored, on-site child-care programs have found that although they increase worker job satisfaction, the expected reductions in absenteeism rates have been small (Goff, Mount, & Jamison, 1990; Kossek & Nichol, 1992).

Growing in popularity are flexible, or "cafeteria-style," benefit plans, where employees choose from a number of options (Barringer & Milkovich, 1998). Lawler (1971) long ago argued that allowing employees to choose their own benefits led to increases in job satisfaction and ensured that the benefits suited each employee's unique needs. One study demonstrated, however, that it is important that employees receive adequate information and guidance regarding the characteristics of the various benefit programs, to help them make an informed choice of benefits that best suit their needs, and to avoid dissatisfaction caused by making incorrect choices (Sturman, Hannon, & Milkovich, 1996). Research suggests that cafeteria-style benefits are perceived as a more fair system than traditional benefit plans (Cole & Flint, 2004).

It is important to bear in mind that the costs of employee benefits are rising rapidly—with benefits costing U.S. employers 30–40% of total compensation (U.S. Department of Labor, 2011). Benefit costs in some European countries are even higher. As a result, organizations often reduce benefit programs as a cost-saving strategy during times of economic downturn. Yet, organizations must be aware of the potential damaging effects of such cuts in benefits on employee job satisfaction and morale.

The effectiveness of programs designed to increase job satisfaction and organizational commitment depends on various factors. Although most of the techniques intended to increase job satisfaction do indeed appear to do so, there is less evidence that these programs then lead to changes in other important outcome variables such as productivity, work quality, absenteeism, and ultimately turnover. If a company implements a program aimed at increasing employee job satisfaction, and if management is perceived by employees to be taking positive steps toward the improvement of the workplace, job satisfaction will likely improve immediately after the introduction of the program. However, it may be unclear whether the program actually

Stop & Review

List and define four alternative pay structure techniques.

caused the increase or if it is really a sort of Hawthorne effect, in which employees' positive expectations about management's good intentions lead to increases in satisfaction, merely because something was done. Regardless of the reason for measured improvements following the implementation of some satisfaction-enhancing program, the increases may tend to disappear over time as some of the novelty wears off, which long-term follow-up evaluations would reveal.

Positive Employee Behaviors

Although employers want their employees to be satisfied and committed to the organization, job satisfaction and organizational commitment are attitudes. What employers really care about are how job satisfaction and organizational commitment translate into positive employee behaviors. We have already explored the connections between job satisfaction, organizational commitment, and the important work behaviors of job performance, absenteeism, and turnover. However, there are other forms that positive employee behaviors can take.

ORGANIZATIONAL CITIZENSHIP BEHAVIORS

Early research on positive employee behaviors focused on altruistic, or prosocial, behaviors. Bateman and Organ (1983) and Brief and Motowidlo (1986) first defined organizational prosocial behaviors as those that go beyond specific job requirements. They are behaviors performed to promote the welfare of the work group and the organization. Protecting an organization from unexpected dangers, suggesting methods of organizational improvement without expecting a payoff, undertaking deliberate self-development, preparing oneself for higher levels of organizational responsibility, and speaking favorably about the organization to outsiders are all forms of prosocial behavior. Subsequent research suggested that workers have deep-seated motives for performing prosocial behaviors (Rioux & Penner, 2001). Not only do prosocial behaviors have positive influences on the ability of individuals and teams to do their jobs, but there is also evidence of a positive relationship with job satisfaction (Organ, 1988; Smith, Organ, & Near, 1983).

Researchers have looked more broadly at worker behaviors that benefit the organization. This cluster of "pro-organizational" behaviors, which includes organizational prosocial behaviors, has been termed "organizational citizenship behavior" (Graham, 1991; Organ, 1988; Penner, Midili, & Kegelmeyer, 1997; Schnake, 1991). Organizational citizenship behavior **(OCB)** consists of efforts by organizational members who advance or promote the work organization, its image, and its goals. Job satisfaction, as well as motivating job characteristics, such as jobs that provide workers with autonomy and meaningful work (recall our discussion of motivating "job characteristics" in Chapter 8), combine to help produce organizational citizenship behaviors (Van Dyne, Graham, & Dienesch, 1994). In addition, certain personality types, particularly persons

organizational citizenship behavior
efforts by organizational members who advance or promote the work organization and its goals

TABLE 9.1

Types of Organizational Citizenship Behaviors (OCB)

Helping Behavior—voluntarily helping others with work-related problems; helping prevent others from encountering problems; keeping the peace/managing conflict

Sportsmanship—maintaining a positive attitude in the face of challenges or problems; tolerating inconveniences and impositions; not taking rejection personally; sacrificing personal interests for the sake of the group

Organizational Loyalty—promoting the organization to outsiders; defending the organization from external threats; remaining committed to the organization even under adverse conditions

Organizational Compliance—accepting and adhering to the organization's rules and procedures; being punctual; not wasting time

Individual Initiative—volunteering to take on additional duties; being particularly creative and innovative in one's work; encouraging others to do their best; going above and beyond the call of duty

Civic Virtue—participating in organizational governance; looking out for the organization (e.g., turning out lights to save energy, reporting possible threats, etc.); keeping particularly informed about what the organization is doing

Self-development—voluntarily working to upgrade one's knowledge and skills; learning new skills that will help the organization

Source: Podsakoff, P. M., MacKenzie, S. B., Paine, J. B., & Bachrach, D. G. (2000). Organizational citizenship behaviors: A critical review of the theoretical and empirical literature and suggestions for future research. *Journal of Management, 26,* 513–563.

who are "agreeable" and conscientious employees, are more likely to perform OCBs (Chiaburu, Oh, Berry, Li, & Gardner, 2011; Ilies, Scott, & Judge, 2006). Table 9.1 presents a list of categories of OCB.

OCBs are positively correlated with both job satisfaction and organizational commitment (Podsakoff, MacKenzie, Paine, & Bachrach, 2000). In addition,

Demonstrating positive feelings about your organization are examples of organizational citizenship behaviors.

employees who engage in more OCBs are less likely to turnover than those who do not engage in OCBs (Chen, Hui, & Sego, 1998) and less likely to be voluntarily absent (Lee, Mitchell, Sablynski, Burton, & Holtom, 2004). Moreover, there is evidence that supervisors notice OCBs, tending to give more positive performance appraisals to employees who engage in citizenship behaviors as opposed to those who simply do their jobs. In addition, managers and leaders have been found to play a critical role in the incidence of employees' OCBs if the leaders engage in OCBs themselves (Yaffe & Kark, 2011). There is even a study that suggests that employees who regularly engage in OCBs are more safety conscious (Gyekye & Salminen, 2005). An important question, however, is, "Do OCBs affect the bottom line?" Do employees' organizational citizenship behaviors affect organizational performance? Research suggests that employees who "go the extra mile" and exhibit OCBs do indeed have work groups and organizations that are more productive and produce higher-quality work than work groups exhibiting low levels of OCBs (Podsakoff & MacKenzie, 1997a). Organizational citizenship behaviors seem to affect work performance in groups as diverse as salespersons (Podsakoff & MacKenzie, 1994), manufacturing workers (Allen & Rush, 1998; Bommer, Dierdorff, & Rubin, 2007), machine crews in a paper mill (Podsakoff, Ahearne, & MacKenzie, 1997), and restaurant crews (Koys, 2001; Walz & Niehoff, 1996).

Podsakoff and MacKenzie (1997a) suggested a number of reasons why OCBs may be related to organizational effectiveness. They include the following:

- Workers who help new coworkers "learn the ropes" help them to speedup the orientation and socialization process and become more productive employees faster.
- Employees who help each other need less managerial supervision, freeing up the managers' time for other important duties.
- Employees who have positive attitudes toward one another are more cooperative and avoid destructive conflicts with other workers.
- Workers freely and voluntarily meet outside work times and regularly touch base with one another, improving the flow of organizational communication.
- OCBs lead to a positive work environment and help in the recruitment and retention of the best-qualified workers.
- Workers pick up the slack and "cover" for one another during absences or times of heavy individual workloads.
- Employees are more willing to take on new responsibilities or learn new technology or work systems.

As can be seen, organizational citizenship behaviors lead to work groups that engage in the best sorts of organizational and personnel processes and may help explain what separates the top-performing work groups and organizations from those who have substandard levels of performance. On the other hand, some workers might be so involved in work and going above and beyond their job descriptions, engaging in so many OCBs that it might interfere with their personal lives, similar to the "workaholic" syndrome we saw in Chapter 8 (Bolino & Turnley, 2005).

An interesting question concerns whether workers in various countries engage in the same organizational citizenship behaviors and at the same levels. Research suggests that although OCBs seem to be more or less universal, there are differences in how workers and organizations view these behaviors. For example, workers and supervisors in China and Japan are more likely to view OCBs as an everyday, expected part of one's jobs than do workers in the United States or Australia (Lam, Hui, & Law, 1999). Nevertheless, there is evidence that OCBs are positively correlated with measures of the productivity and service quality of Taiwanese bank employees (Yen & Niehoff, 2004), government employees in China (Liu & Cohen, 2010), Korean travel agents (Yoon & Suh, 2003), and U.S. insurance agents (Bell & Menguc, 2002).

As you can imagine, it is in the organization's best interest to encourage organizational citizenship behaviors. Research shows that OCBs are affected by whether or not employees perceive the organization as treating them fairly (Haworth & Levy, 2001; Tepper & Taylor, 2003). In addition, employees who feel that their values are aligned with the organization are more likely to engage in more OCBs (Deckop, Mangel, & Cirka, 1999).

POSITIVE AFFECT AND EMPLOYEE WELL-BEING

positive affect
positive emotions that affect mood in the workplace

In the past two decades there has been an explosion of research examining the role of positive emotions, or positive affect, in influencing employee attitudes, such as job satisfaction, and fostering positive employee behaviors (Ashkanasy, Härtel, & Zerbe, 2000; Brief, 2001). Simply stated, an individual's mood, positive or negative, can affect all aspects of work (we will look at negative emotions and their effects in Chapter 10). Not only is a person's emotional state important, but also there are clearly individual differences in dispositions toward positive or negative affect (Judge & Larsen, 2001). This is why, as we saw in the box On the Cutting Edge, some individuals just tend to be more satisfied in jobs than others.

Most researchers agree that positive affect influences work behavior through job satisfaction. That is, job satisfaction mediates the relationship between state and trait (dispositional) affect and important work outcomes, such as absenteeism, turnover, and performance. For example, one study of a group of hotel managers found that the affective dispositions of the managers influenced their job satisfaction, which, in turn, affected their job performance (Hochwater, Perrewé, Ferris, & Brymer, 1999). Emotionally positive managers showed more job satisfaction and had better job performance than emotionally negative managers who were dissatisfied and tended to be poorer performers. Similarly, dispositional positive affect is related to lower rates of stress (Janssen, Lam, & Huang, 2010) and absenteeism, whereas negative affect is related to both higher absenteeism and higher turnover (Pelled & Xin, 1999). There is evidence that affectively positive workers are more prone to engage in OCB and to have a broader view of what their job entails (e.g., being more willing to take on "extra" tasks) than emotionally negative workers (Bachrach & Jex, 2000; Podsakoff et al., 2000).

So, is a positive disposition or emotional state, and resulting job satisfaction, the "cure-all"? Not necessarily. There is some evidence that when workers become dissatisfied with some aspect of the work situation, they become motivated to change it. Job dissatisfaction has been linked to both creativity and voicing of concern (Zhou & George, 2001). Importantly, no matter how strong an individual's positive emotions or disposition, if she or he is not fairly treated, or is undercompensated, job satisfaction and positive work behaviors will decline.

It is important to also mention that satisfaction with one's job is not enough. Workers may have job satisfaction, but other aspects of their lives (family relationships, physical health, etc.) may not be as positive. I/O psychology has two important objectives in this regard: to improve the physical and social environment at work in an effort to enhance worker well-being, satisfaction, and life quality and to improve organizational outcomes, such as increased productivity, work quality, and reduced absenteeism and turnover through increasing employee participation in, and commitment to, organizational processes (Adams, King, & King, 1996; Beehr & McGrath, 1992; Danna & Griffin, 1999).

Stop & Review

List and define five categories of organizational citizenship behaviors.

Summary

Job satisfaction, which involves the positive feelings and attitudes one has about a job, can be conceptualized in overall, or global, terms or in terms of specific components or facets and can be measured through interviews or with self-report instruments. The most widely used self-report measures are the *Minnesota Satisfaction Questionnaire* (*MSQ*) and the *Job Descriptive Index* (*JDI*). Research indicates that there is a slight positive relationship between job satisfaction and job performance, although the link may be moderated by a third variable, such as the receipt of work rewards. Job satisfaction is positively correlated with *organizational commitment*, or employees' feelings and attitudes about the entire work organization.

Both job satisfaction and organizational commitment tend to be negatively correlated with voluntary employee absenteeism. However, the relationships are complex and difficult to decipher, partly due to the difficulty involved in distinguishing voluntary absenteeism from involuntary absenteeism. Job satisfaction and organizational commitment are also related to voluntary employee turnover.

Programs designed to increase job satisfaction include changes in job structure through techniques such as *job rotation, job enlargement,* and *job enrichment.* Other satisfaction-enhancing techniques suggest changing the pay structure by using methods such as *skill-based pay, pay-for-performance* programs like *merit pay, gainsharing,* or *profit sharing,* which are sometimes contingent on effective group performance. Flexible work schedules, such as *compressed workweeks* and *flextime,* improve satisfaction by giving workers greater control over their jobs. Still other methods of improving satisfaction involve increasing job-related benefits.

Positive employee behaviors beyond the normal job routine are termed *organizational citizenship behaviors*, and these are positively related to desirable work outcomes. Most recently, research has focused on the role of *positive affect* in employee behavior, with job satisfaction mediating the relationship between affect and work outcomes. This emphasis on positive employee attitudes, emotions, and behaviors reflects I/O psychology's concern with both organizational functioning and employee well-being.

Study Questions and Exercises

1. What are some of the difficulties in the measurement of employee job satisfaction? How might I/O psychologists try to deal with these problems?

2. How does job satisfaction relate to the important "bottom-line," outcome variables of performance, absenteeism, and turnover?

3. What would a good, comprehensive program to increase job satisfaction contain? What elements would you include in each?

4. Consider a job or occupation that you are familiar with. What are the "normal" job duties associated with this job, and what might be considered "organizational citizenship behaviors" for this job or occupation? Try to come up with examples of each type of OCB for this job.

5. In what ways have the working lives of U.S. workers changed over the past 60 years? What sorts of changes do you expect to see in the future?

Web Links

http://www.bgsu.edu/departments/psych/io/jdi/
Information on the Job Descriptive Index (JDI).

Suggested Readings

Macey, W. H., Schneider, B., Barbera, K. M., & Young, S. A. (2009). *Employee engagement: Tools for analysis, practice, and competitive advantage.* Chichester, UK: Wiley-Blackwell. *A book focusing on research and practice implications for employee engagement. Part of a series for practitioners called "Talent Management Essentials."*

Organ, D. W., Podsakoff, P. M., & MacKenzie, S. B. (2006). *Organizational citizenship behavior: Its nature, antecedents, and consequences.* Thousand Oaks, CA: Sage. *A detailed, high-level review of research on OCB.*

Spector, P. E. (1997). *Job satisfaction: Application, assessment, causes, and consequences.* Thousand Oaks, CA: Sage. *A very readable overview of the effects of job satisfaction on work behavior.*

Worker Stress, Negative Employee Attitudes and Behaviors

Inside Tips
THE NEGATIVE ASPECTS OF WORK

Life stress is a topic with which most of us will be familiar because it is discussed often in the popular press and media. This chapter deals primarily with worker stress: the stress that occurs at work and affects work behavior. So be careful not to confuse what you have heard from the media about life stress and what you read in this chapter. For instance, a common misconception is that all stress is bad. As you will find out, a little bit of stress can be motivating and challenging. Yet, it is the negative type of stress that gets most of the attention. Another misconception is that the strategies used in dealing with stress in everyday life will also work in dealing with worker stress. This is not always the case. For example, some stressors can be alleviated by organizational changes and are therefore under the control of management, whereas others must be addressed by the individual worker. In addition, some of the techniques for dealing with stress in the workplace are not so much stress-reduction techniques as they are simply good management and human resource practices. Social scientists have had a great deal of difficulty in precisely defining and measuring stress. Be aware of this. Some of the concepts in this chapter are quite abstract and are initially difficult to understand.

This chapter fits well with Chapter 9 that focused on worker satisfaction and positive worker behaviors and attitudes. In some ways, satisfaction and stress can be opposite sides of the coin. Jobs can create a great deal of satisfaction, contributing to a sense of well-being and "worth." At the same time, however, jobs can subject us to uncomfortable (and potentially harmful) stress and can lead to negative attitudes and work behaviors.

The first few weeks of your job were exciting, you were challenged to learn new things and accomplish important objectives. You felt good about the job and about yourself. But now work has become routine and there is a great sense of pressure. It is sometimes hard to drag yourself out of bed in the morning. Some of this is due to the increasing workload, but you are also having trouble getting along with a particularly difficult coworker. Sometimes, the pressure from work makes it hard to concentrate; other times you feel sick and unhappy.

As we saw in Chapter 9, most workers feel some sense of purpose and accomplishment about their jobs, which can be very rewarding and self-satisfying. However, work can also be a tremendous burden. Deadlines, work overload, and difficult bosses or coworkers can all place considerable pressure and strain on workers. Thus, jobs and the work environment commonly produce stress, with which workers must learn to deal. Moreover, the negative behaviors of people at work, ranging from bad attitudes to acts of sabotage and workplace violence, make the work world a difficult (and sometimes dangerous) place. In this section, we will define worker stress, see how it affects work behavior, look at how it is measured, examine ways that the individual worker can attempt to cope with it, and consider strategies that organizations can use to try to decrease stress. We will also look at negative attitudes and dysfunctional behaviors at work and what organizations and individuals can do to try to limit or eliminate these.

Defining Worker Stress

The construct of stress is quite complex. So much so, in fact, that researchers cannot agree on a single definition for stress (Kahn & Boysiere, 1992). Consequently, there are at least eight different definitions (models) for stress (Cooper, Dewe, & O'Driscoll, 2002; Ivancevich & Matteson, 1980).

According to the early stress researcher, Hans Selye (1976), stress is primarily a physiological reaction to certain threatening environmental events. From Selye's perspective, worker stress would simply refer to the stress caused by events in the work environment. Psychologist John French and his colleagues (French, Caplan, & Harrison, 1982; French, Rogers, & Cobb, 1974) say that worker stress results from a lack of "fit" between a person's skills and abilities and the demands of the job and the workplace. In other words, a worker who is totally unqualified for a particular job should feel a tremendous amount of stress. For example, imagine a worker with little previous experience with computer systems applying for and being hired as a communication specialist, only to find out that the job requires a thorough knowledge of various computer networking systems. Richard Lazarus (1991; Richard Lazarus & Folkman, 1984), in his "transactional" view of worker stress, saw stress as resulting from the worker's perception that a certain environmental event is a threat or a challenge, factoring in your perception of how capable you will be at managing the threat. From Richard Lazarus's perspective, you and I might interpret the same event very differently—I might find it stressful, you might view it as totally harmless (or perhaps even as pleasantly challenging!).

To arrive at a definition of worker stress for our purposes, we need to look at what these three different approaches to stress have in common. All three definitions view worker stress as an interaction between the person and some environmental event, or **stressor**. In addition, all the definitions emphasize that there are some important reactions to the stressful event. These reactions can be either physiological or psychological in nature, or both. Therefore, we will define **worker stress** as physiological and/or psychological reactions to an event that is perceived to be threatening or taxing.

Although we most often think of stress as an unpleasant state, it can have both negative and positive aspects. For example, imagine that you have been working for several years as an assistant manager for a large company and find out that you have just received a promotion to department manager, a position you have been trying to obtain for some time. With your new position come feelings of stress. Some of these are negative, such as the stress that will result from having to work many overtime hours without additional compensation; being required to make formal presentations regularly to your peers and superiors (and having your presentations critically evaluated by them); and taking on the responsibility to take the criticism for any problems occurring in your department. On the other hand, there are many positive reactions associated with the promotion, including feelings of accomplishment, anticipation, pride, and challenge. Like the negative aspects, these positive responses also induce physiological and psychological reactions in the body. Some stress researchers distinguish

stressor
an environmental event that is perceived by an individual to be threatening

worker stress
the physiological and/or psychological reactions to events that are perceived to be threatening or taxing

the negative stress, termed *distress*, from the positive kind of stress, called *eustress* (see, e.g., Golembiewski, Munzenrider, & Stevenson, 1986; Nelson & Simmons, 2011).

We are all likely familiar with the physiological reactions to stress. They include signs of arousal such as increased heart and respiratory rates, elevated blood pressure, and profuse sweating. The psychological reactions to stress include feeling anxiety, fear, frustration, and despair, as well as appraising or evaluating the stressful event and its impact, thinking about the stressful experience, and mentally preparing to take steps to try to deal with the stress.

In many ways, stress is a perceptual process. An event that one individual perceives to be stressful may not be labeled as such by someone else. For example, making a formal presentation in front of a large audience may be perceived as extremely stressful for the average college student, but may be perceived as energizing (and perhaps fun) by a person who is accustomed to public speaking. Because stress may cause a variety of reactions and feelings, and because perceptions of stress may vary from person to person, stress has not been particularly easy to define, and it is very difficult to measure. We will deal with methods of measuring stress shortly.

Companies and managers have become more and more concerned with the effects of stress on workers and on important "bottom-line" variables, such as productivity, absenteeism, and turnover. Why all of the interest in worker stress? The most obvious reason is that too much stress can cause illness. Stress-related illnesses include ulcers, hypertension and coronary heart disease, migraines, asthma attacks, and colitis. If worker stress leads to stress-related illnesses, rates of absenteeism can increase. At the psychological level, stress can cause mental strain, feelings of fatigue, anxiety, and depression that can reduce worker productivity and quality of work. If a job becomes too stressful, a worker may be compelled to quit and find a less-stressful position. Thus, worker stress may influence turnover as well.

Managers and workers may also be concerned about stress at a more personal level. Worker stress can be, in many ways, the flip side of job satisfaction. Whereas job satisfaction represents the "positives" associated with work, stress is a way of conceptualizing the "negatives" associated with jobs—the pressures, the strains, the conflicts. No doubt, much of the interest in worker stress results from the fact that managers, business owners, and all other sorts of workers experience stress on a day-to-day basis.

Sources of Worker Stress

Generally, stress can arise from either the environment (situational stress) or from an individual's personal characteristics (dispositional stress). Situational stress can come from all aspects of our lives. We are subjected to a wide range of stressors at home, at school, and in our interpersonal relationships, as well as the stressors we encounter at work. No doubt, all these various sources of stress accumulate and add to our overall stress levels. That is, stress at home can spill over to work situations and vice versa. Most stress researchers realize

situational stress
stress arising from certain conditions that exist in the work environment, or in the worker's personal life

this and emphasize that when studying stress, it is important to look at the broad picture of an individual's total stress, rather than focusing narrowly on stress derived from work (Erickson, Nichols, & Ritter, 2000; Frone, Russell, & Cooper, 1991).

For our purposes, however, we will focus primarily on the stress that comes from workplace sources. We will first examine stressful occupations and then focus on the elements of jobs and of work organizations that can cause worker stress. Finally, we will look at how worker stress can result from characteristics of the workers themselves, as we examine individual sources of worker stress, or what we might call dispositional stress.

STRESSFUL OCCUPATIONS

It is generally believed that certain occupations, such as air traffic controller, physician or other health-care provider, police officer, and firefighter, are particularly stressful. There has been increased attention to postal workers' stress, following highly publicized cases of postal workers attacking and killing coworkers. This has even led to the slang term "going postal." Is it true that certain occupations are particularly stress prone? There is some evidence to support this. For example, studies of air traffic controllers indicate that they do indeed experience high levels of work-related stress, as do medical doctors and nurses (Leonhardt & Vogt, 2011; Rutledge et al., 2009; Sparks & Cooper, 1999). Similarly, studies of dentists suggest that dentistry is a high-stress occupation (Cooper, Mallinger, & Kahn, 1978; DiMatteo, Shugars, & Hays, 1993). High-level managers and business executives are also believed to hold extremely stressful jobs.

Police officers' and firefighters' jobs are particularly stressful because of the physical dangers involved (Chamberlin & Green, 2010; Tehrani & Piper, 2011). We saw the dangers associated with these jobs during and after the September 11, 2001, tragedy. The day-to-day dangers facing police officers and firefighters are indeed stressful. However, some studies suggest that rather than causing stress, the excitement and challenge of dealing with physical danger may actually be motivating and "enriching" to many police officers and firefighters (Jermier, Gaines, & McIntosh, 1989; Riggio & Cole, 1995). Interestingly, studies of police officers suggest that they suffer from the same sources of stress, such as increased responsibilities and workloads and difficulties with coworkers, as persons in other occupations (Brown, Cooper, & Kircaldy, 1996). In sum, trying to determine levels of worker stress merely by looking at a person's occupation or job title may not be very accurate.

Research on these and other stereotypically stressful occupations has begun to discover exactly why these jobs are characterized as stressful. For instance, air traffic controllers' jobs are stressful because of the heavy workloads, the constant fear of causing accidents, equipment problems, and poor working environments (Shouksmith & Burrough, 1988). The primary sources of dentists' occupational stress come from difficult patients, heavy workloads, and the dentists' own concern that their patients hold negative views about them and about dentists in general (Coster, Carstens, & Harris, 1987; DiMatteo et al., 1993).

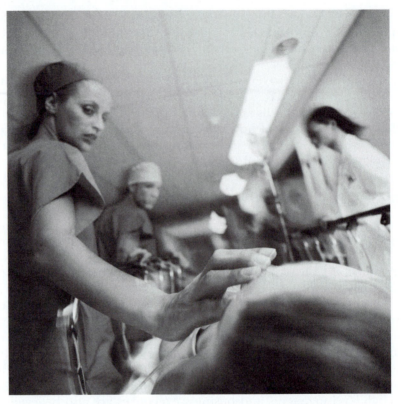

Although they are often seen as having fewer work responsibilities than physicians, nurses often experience very high levels of work stress.

Stop & Review

Discuss why worker stress is difficult to define.

Rather than focusing only on high-stress occupations, it makes sense to examine those sources of worker stress that are common to all kinds of jobs, even those that are not typically considered high-stress jobs. Such sources of stress can be divided into two general categories: organizational and individual. Organizational sources of stress come from the work environment and can be broken down into two subcategories: stress derived from work tasks and stress resulting from work roles. Individual sources of stress include a person's history of exposure to stress as well as certain stress-related personality characteristics and behavioral patterns. For example, there is evidence that certain personality traits make people more prone to stress (and stress-related illnesses), and some characteristics seem to make people more resistant to stress and its negative outcomes.

ORGANIZATIONAL SOURCES OF WORK STRESS: SITUATIONAL STRESSORS

A great deal of worker stress is caused by stressors in the environment of the work organization. Some of this organizational stress is caused by the work tasks themselves—the physical and psychological demands of performing a job. Organizational stress may also be caused by work roles because work organizations are complex social systems in which a worker must interact with many people. Therefore, the work relationships of various kinds that must be created and maintained for a worker to perform the job adequately can also lead to stress. These two types of situational stress—work task and work role stressors—can often be alleviated by management actions.

WORK TASK STRESSORS

Work overload

A common work task source of stress is work overload, also known as *role overload*, which results when the job requires excessive work speed, output, or concentration (Brown, Jones, & Leigh, 2005). More recently, attention has been given to technology-related work overload, such as the increased volume of information, leading to things such as "e-mail overload" (Bellotti, Ducheneaut, Howard, Smith, & Grinter, 2005; Soucek & Moser, 2010). Work overload is widely believed to be one of the greatest sources of work stress. Research on work overload indicates that it is related to physiological indicators of stress, such as elevated serum cholesterol and increased heart rate (Caplan & Jones, 1975; Cobb & Rose, 1973); to psychological measures of stress (Spector, 1987; Spector, Dwyer, & Jex, 1988); and to lower quality of work and job dissatisfaction (Kirmeyer & Dougherty, 1988). In fact, work overload has been reported as a common source of stress for jobs as diverse as clerical workers, soldiers, air traffic controllers, courtroom attorneys, and health-care workers (Bliese & Halverson, 1996; Carayon, 1994; Iverson, Olekalns, & Erwin, 1998; Shouksmith & Burrough, 1988).

| **work overload** a common source of stress resulting when a job requires excessive speed, output, or concentration |

Underutilization

Work overload can cause stress, but having too little to do—underutilization— can also be stressful (French & Caplan, 1972; Ganster, Fusilier, & Mayes, 1986). Underutilization may also occur when workers feel that the job does not use their work-related knowledge, skills, or abilities, or when jobs are boring and monotonous (Melamed, Ben-Avi, Luz, & Green, 1995). Some college graduates in low-level clerical or customer service positions may feel some stress due to underutilization of their knowledge and skills (French, Caplan, & Harrison, 1982). There is also evidence that some individuals may be more susceptible to stress relating to underutilization than others (Vodanovich, 2003).

| **underutilization** a source of stress resulting from workers feeling that their knowledge, skills, or energy are not being fully used |

WORK ROLE STRESSORS

Job ambiguity

A potential source of work role stress is job ambiguity, which occurs when aspects of a job, such as tasks and requirements, are not clearly outlined. When workers are unsure of their responsibilities and duties, stress can result (Breaugh & Colihan, 1994; Jackson & Schuler, 1985). Job ambiguity is also sometimes referred to as "job uncertainty." However, job uncertainty may better refer to the uncertainty caused by a lack of regular performance feedback concerning

| **job ambiguity** a source of stress resulting from a lack of clearly defined jobs and/or work tasks |

how well or how poorly workers are doing their jobs. Research suggests that supervisors can play an important part in reducing job uncertainty for subordinates by clarifying job roles and duties (Schaubroeck, Ganster, Sime, & Ditman, 1993). Findings that job uncertainty can have negative influences on job satisfaction highlight the importance of the supervisor's role in alleviating uncertainty and its accompanying stress (O'Driscoll & Beehr, 1994).

Conflict between roles can also occur and can become an additional source of stress (Greenhaus & Beutell, 1985). For instance, a worker's job may require excessive overtime that conflicts with the worker's family roles of spouse and parent. Or, having to play different roles at work simultaneously can cause stress. We will discuss roles and role conflict in more depth in Chapter 12.

Lack of control

lack of control

a feeling of having little input or effect on the job and/or work environment; typically results in stress

Another important source of work stress results from workers sensing that they have little control over the work environment and over their own work behavior. Stress resulting from this feeling of lack of control is particularly common in lower-level jobs or in highly structured organizations. Jobs that are so constrained and rule-driven that employees are unable to have any sort of input in work decisions and procedures are likely to be stress inducing, particularly for those workers who want to have some input (see Dwyer & Ganster, 1991; Karasek, 1979; Theorell, Westerlund, Alfredsson, & Oxenstierna, 2005). Research indicates that providing workers with a sense of control over their work environment, through techniques such as giving them a voice in decision-making processes or allowing them to plan their own work tasks, reduces work stress and fatigue and increases job satisfaction (Jackson, 1983; Jimmieson & Terry, 1998; Sonnentag & Zijlstra, 2006). On the other hand, some studies suggest that a sense of a lack of control over one's job may not be stressful for many workers (see Carayon, 1994). It may be the case that different types of workers are more or less concerned with having sense of control over their jobs (recall our discussion in Chapter 8 on the Job Characteristics Model and individual differences in workers' desire for autonomy). In fact, research has found that certain personality characteristics may determine whether or not an individual is stressed by a perceived lack of job control (Ivancevich, Matteson, & Preston, 1982).

Physical work conditions

Physical conditions in the work environment are another organizational source contributing to worker stress (Frese & Zapf, 1988). Jobs that must be performed under extreme temperatures, loud and distracting noise, or poor lighting or ventilation can be quite stressful. Dangerous jobs that place workers at risk of loss of health, life, or limb are an additional source of work stress (Booth, 1986). Cramped, crowded, and excessively noisy work environments can also cause stress. For example, one study showed that noise levels in open-space office environments (offices with partitioned cubicles and open ceilings) constituted a significant source of stress (Evans & Johnson, 2000). Similarly, working late night ("graveyard") shifts can disrupt natural sleep and waking cycles and may lead to problems such as high stress, fatigue, job dissatisfaction, and performance errors (Monk, Fokard, & Wedderburn, 1996; Smith & Folkard, 1993).

Interpersonal stress

One of the greatest sources of work stress results from difficulties in interpersonal relationships on the job. Interpersonal stress stems from difficulties in developing and maintaining relationships with other people in the work setting. Having a harsh, critical boss with a punitive management style would likely be stressful for just about anyone. With the rise of virtual work, some workers feel a lack of social connections and support and experience a stressful sense of social isolation (Avolio & Kahai, 2003; Wiesenfeld, Raghuram, & Garud, 2001).

Interpersonal stress can also result when coworkers are placed in some sort of conflict situation. Imagine, for example, that two employees are both being considered for an important promotion. A great deal of stress may be generated if the two individuals must work together while both are competing for the same honor. There is also evidence that organizational politics and struggles over power can be important sources of stress in the workplace (Ferris, Frink, Gilmore, & Kacmar, 1994). We will discuss power and politics in depth in Chapter 14. Whatever its causes, the inability to get along with other workers is one of the most common sources of stress in the workplace (Matteson & Ivancevich, 1987).

Another form of interpersonal stress occurs frequently in service organizations and involves the stress of providing good customer service. When one is dealing with impatient and difficult customers, the pressure to maintain one's

> **interpersonal stress**
> stress arising from difficulties with others in the workplace

Attentive supervisors may play an important part in reducing job uncertainty, thus reducing job stress.

emotional labor
the demands of regulating and controlling emotions in the workplace

cool and offer service with a smile can be quite taxing and stressful. Researchers have examined this emotional labor—the demands of regulating and controlling emotions and emotional displays as part of a job requirement (Diefendorff & Gosserand, 2003; Hochschild, 1983). The very common stress caused by emotional labor can cause workers to become dissatisfied and cynical about their jobs, reduce job satisfaction, performance, and lead to frequent absenteeism and turnover (Bono & Vey, 2005; Hulsheger, Lang, & Maier, 2010; Rubin, Tardino, Daus, & Munz, 2005).

Harassment

All forms of harassment, including sexual harassment, harassment due to group membership (e.g., gender, race, sexual orientation), and being singled out by an abusive supervisor or colleague, are all extremely stressful (Malamut & Offermann, 2001; Raver & Nishii, 2010; Tepper, Duffy, & Shaw, 2001). Research has suggested that victims of workplace sexual harassment, as well as victims of more general harassment at work, including bullying (see box *On the Cutting Edge: Workplace Bullying: An Invisible Epidemic?*), have increased odds of work-related illness, injury, or being assaulted (Rospenda, Richman, Ehmke, & Zlatoper, 2005). A study of over 6,000 telephone company employees across the United States showed that incidence of sexual harassment increased stress and decreased job satisfaction, but that the culture of the organization/unit in terms of whether the culture fostered and appeared to tolerate harassment or discouraged it played a part in levels of employee stress (Law, Dollard, Tuckey, & Dormann, 2011; Mueller, De Coster, & Estes, 2001). Moreover, there is evidence that sexual and other forms of harassment tended to co-occur in certain organizations, along with generally uncivil behavior (Lim & Cortina, 2005).

Organizational change

A common organizational source of stress is change (Rafferty & Griffin, 2006). (We will spend a great deal of time on organizational change in Chapter 15.) People tend to grow accustomed to certain work procedures and certain work structures, and they resist change. Most of us prefer things to remain stable and predictable. Such stability in our working environments seems comforting and reassuring. Therefore, it should not be surprising that major changes in a work organization tend to cause stress (Dahl, 2011; Leiter & Harvie, 1998). Some common change situations that lead to worker stress include company reorganizations, mergers of one company with another or acquisitions of one organization by another, changes in work systems and work technology, changes in company policy, and managerial or personnel changes (see Table 10.1; Judge, Thoresen, Pucik, & Welbourne, 1999; Wanberg & Banas, 2000). For example, research has shown that physiological stress responses are stronger in novel or unfamiliar circumstances that involve a threat or challenge (Rose, 1987). An event like a company-wide reorganization, or a merger or acquisition, would certainly be perceived as threatening and stressful by many employees (Marks & Mirvis, 2010).

TABLE 10.1
Characteristics of Jobs that Cause Worker Stress

Work overload (e.g., time pressures and too much work)	Interpersonal conflict
Underutilization of worker knowledge, skills, ability, or energy	Decision making
	Organizational change
Dangerous work conditions	Lack of support from supervisors or coworkers
Responsibility for the health and well-being of others	Lack of control over the work situation
Difficult or complex work tasks	Work–family conflict
Unpleasant or uncomfortable physical work conditions	Personal factors (e.g., Type A behavior or stress-prone personality)

Coping with the loss of a job, or potential job loss, is another major stressor (Moore, Grunbeg, & Greenberg, 2006; Prussia, Fugate, & Kinicki, 2001).

Work–family conflict

A very important source of stress, one that extends beyond the boundaries of the organization, is work–family conflict, which results from efforts to balance the often competing demands of work roles and requirements and those of family and nonworking life. A great deal of attention has been devoted to research on work–family conflict and efforts to achieve balance between the world of work and the world of family (Halpern & Murphy, 2005; Kossek & Lambert, 2005). Importantly, work–family conflict is a source of stress that is common internationally and is on the rise because of the increased demands of work (Poelmans, 2005; Rantanen, Mauno, Kinnunen, & Rantanen, 2011).

> **work–family conflict**
> cumulative stress that results from duties of work and family roles

ON THE *CUTTING* EDGE

Workplace Bullying: An "Invisible" Epidemic?

A 2007 survey of US workers found that more than one third of them reported that they had been bullied at work, including such behaviors as threats, aggression, ridiculing, sabotage of their work, and giving them the silent treatment. Targets of bullies report anxiety, fear, depression, and in extreme cases suffer a post-traumatic stress disorder (Namie & Namie, 2009). The cost of workplace bullying to organizations, in terms of reduced productivity and increased absenteeism and turnover, likely runs into the billions of dollars.

Because many of the targets of workplace bullies are not members of protected groups, there is often no legal recourse, and many witnesses of workplace bullying don't speak up for fear they will be targeted themselves. Some countries have begun to enact legislation to combat workplace bullying, including Australia, Canada, and several European nations. In the United States there is a movement to enact the Healthy Workplace bill, but anti-bullying legislation has not reached the federal level, but is being considered by several states.

INDIVIDUAL SOURCES OF WORK STRESS: DISPOSITIONAL STRESSORS

Although a great deal of worker stress is created by factors in the organization or by features of jobs and work tasks, some is caused by characteristics of the workers themselves. We will consider two such individual sources of work stress: the Type A behavior pattern and susceptibility to stress and to stress effects. It is the individual worker—not management—who must work to alleviate these sources of stress.

Type A behavior pattern

When many people think of individuals who are extremely stressed in the workplace, they immediately picture the stereotypical hard-driving, competitive executive who seeks a job with a heavy workload and many responsibilities—a person who takes on too much work and never seems to have enough time to do it. Is there any truth to this characterization? Research evidence indicates that there is. Researchers have uncovered the Type A behavior pattern, or Type A personality, which is characterized by excessive drive and competitiveness, a sense of urgency and impatience, and underlying hostility (Table 10.2; Friedman & Rosenman, 1974; Rosenman, 1978). This behavior pattern is particularly significant because there is evidence that persons who possess the Type A personality are slightly more prone to develop stress-related coronary heart disease, including fatal heart attacks, than persons who do not have the behavior pattern, termed Type Bs (Allan, 2011; Booth-Kewley & Friedman, 1987; Schaubroeck, Ganster, & Kemmerer, 1994).

> **Type A behavior pattern**
> a personality characterized by excessive drive, competitiveness, impatience, and hostility that has been linked to greater incidence of coronary heart disease

---

TABLE 10.2

Type A Behavior Pattern

Two popular self-report instruments designed to assess Type A behavior are the Jenkins Activity Survey (JAS; Jenkins, Zyzanski, & Rosenman, 1979) and the Framingham Type A Scale (FTAS; Haynes, Feinleib, Levine, Scotch, & Kannel, 1978). Examples of some of the types of questions asked by the FTAS and JAS are presented below:

FTAS

- Are you hard driving and competitive?
- Are you bossy or dominating?
- Do you have a strong need to excel?
- Are you pressed for time after work?

JAS

- Do you have trouble finding time to get your hair cut?
- Do you feel and act impatient when you have to wait in a line?
- Do you get irritated easily?
- When you were younger, was your temper fiery and hard to control?

Affirmative answers to these questions indicate possession of the Type A behavior pattern.

An important question is how does the Type A behavior pattern relate to stress and to stress-related heart disease? Early research on Type A behavior hypothesized that it was the Type A's hardworking, competitive drive that caused stress and subsequent heart problems (Rosenman et al., 1964). Later research, however, suggested that the Type A's underlying hostility, and the lack of appropriate expression of that hostility, is also partly responsible for increased stress reactions in Type A's (Dembroski & Costa, 1987; Friedman, Hall, & Harris, 1985; Smith & Pope, 1990). Other studies suggest that the more global construct of "negative affectivity," or the expression of negative emotions, such as anger, hostility, anxiety, impatience, and aggression, is what combines with a Type A personality to increase stress-related health risks (Chen & Spector, 1991; Ganster, Schaubroeck, Sime, & Mayes, 1991). (We will discuss negative affectivity in more depth later.)

Do Type A's experience more stress than others? Research into this question has produced mixed results. For example, some studies indicate that Type A's are more likely to experience or report high stress than are other personality types under the same workload (Kirmeyer & Dougherty, 1988; Payne, Jabri, & Pearson, 1988). Other studies show that Type A's do not report or experience greater stress, but simply have stronger physiological stress reactions to stressful situations (Ganster, 1986). Perhaps the subjective experience of stress has less negative influence on health than the physiological responses. In other words, Type A's may have stronger stress-induced physiological responses that they are not necessarily aware of, and it is these strong physiological responses over time that lead to increased health risks. If this is the case, Type A's may simply not realize that their long, intense work style is creating wear and tear on their bodies.

Although there are obvious stress-related costs to the Type A behavior pattern, there are also some gains. Studies consistently show that Type A's tend to work harder (Byrne & Reinhardt, 1989), work well in high-variety jobs (Lee, Earley, & Hanson, 1988), and have higher positions and salaries than Type B's (Boyd, 1984; Chesney & Rosenman, 1980; Payne et al., 1988). This aspect of Type A behavior is conceptually related to strong achievement orientation or "workaholism" discussed in the motivation chapter (see Chapter 8, Up Close).

An important question is whether the Type A behavior pattern is something related to Western or U.S. work culture, or whether Type A's occur in other countries and cultures. Although there is some evidence that other cultures have Type A and Type B workers (e.g., Jamal, 1999; Li & Shen, 2009), there are most certainly differences across cultures and countries in the prevalence and rates of the Type A behavior pattern (Al-Mashaan, 2003).

Susceptibility/resistance to stress

Another dispositional source of stress may stem from the fact that some persons are simply more susceptible to stress, whereas others have stress-resistant, hardy personalities. The concept of **hardiness** was outlined by psychologist Suzanne Kobasa (1982; Maddi & Kobasa, 1984), who argued that hardy personality types are resistant to the harmful effects of stress because

Stop & Review

List and define five organizational/ situational sources of worker stress.

hardiness
the notion that some people may be more resistant to the health-damaging effects of stress

of their style of dealing with stressful events. A meta-analysis shows that hardy individuals experience less stress and are better at coping with stress than non-hardy individuals (Eschleman, Bowling, & Alarcon, 2010). Rather than viewing a stressful situation as a threat, hardy types view it as a challenge and derive meaning from these challenging experiences (Britt, Adler, & Bartone, 2001). Moreover, they also believe that they can control and influence the course of their lives (recall that a sense of lack of control can contribute to stress) and are committed to their jobs. Conversely, a lack of hardiness is associated with higher levels of self-perceived stress, and there is evidence that such "unhardy" or "disease-prone" persons may be more susceptible to stress-related illnesses and depression (Friedman & Booth-Kewley, 1987; Kobasa & Puccetti, 1983). Thus, it appears that certain types of workers are more "stress prone." That is, they are more likely to suffer stress-related physical illness and psychological symptoms (depression, anxiety, etc.) than are more hardy workers.

There have been attempts to increase hardiness through what has been called HardiTraining. (Khoshaba & Maddi, 2001). In essence, training for hardiness actually involves the development of workers' coping skills, and a combination of relaxation training, a program of diet and exercise, and developing supportive networks to help reduce stress (Maddi & Khoshaba, 2003). More recently, hardiness training was found to be successful in helping college students deal with the stresses of college life (Maddi, Harvey, Khoshaba, Fazel, & Resurreccion, 2009). We will examine other programs to cope with stress later in this chapter.

Self-efficacy

self-efficacy
an individual's beliefs in his or her abilities to engage in courses of action that will lead to desired outcomes

Research has also identified another characteristic that seems to increase resistance to stress: self-efficacy. Self-efficacy is defined as an individual's beliefs in his or her abilities to engage in courses of action that will lead to desired outcomes (Bandura, 1997). In other words, self-efficacy is related to one's sense of competence and effectiveness. Self-efficacy is a very important concept that not only relates to one's ability to cope with stressful situations (i.e., the possession of *coping* self-efficacy), but it is also an important factor relating to a worker's ability to perform his or her job (*job-related* self-efficacy), to lead a work team (*leadership* self-efficacy), and to deal effectively with relationships at work (*relationship* self-efficacy). There is evidence that a sense of self-efficacy can have positive effects in reducing stress in the workplace (Jex & Bliese, 1999; Rennesund & Saksvik, 2010; Saks, 1994; Van Yperen, 1998). In one study, it was found that having a sense of control over a stressful work situation only decreased stress if the employees had a high sense of self-efficacy about their abilities to do their jobs under stress and strain (Jimmieson, 2000).

Measurement of Worker Stress

Because stress is such a complex phenomenon and because stress researchers cannot agree on a single definition of stress, you might suspect that the measurement of stress is extremely difficult. For the most part, measurement of stress in general, and of worker stress in particular, is problematic. There have been a number of approaches to measuring stress. We will consider several of these.

Physiological measures

As has been stated, the stress response involves physiological reactions as well as psychological and emotional responses. Therefore, one strategy for measuring stress has focused on measuring signs of physiological arousal and strain that accompany stress. This includes blood pressure monitoring, electrocardiogram (EKG) for monitoring heart rate, or blood tests for monitoring levels of certain hormones, such as the stress-linked hormone, cortisol, and cholesterol in the bloodstream. One problem with using such physiological indicators of stress is the amount of variation that can occur from hour to hour, day to day, or person to person (Herd, 1988). Another drawback to the use of such stress tests is the requirement for trained medical personnel, as well as the associated costs for equipment and analysis procedures.

Self-report assessments

Another approach to measuring stress, one that is favored by psychologists, is to ask people directly to report on their own perceived stress through various rating scales. Most self-report assessments fall into one of two major categories: reports about organizational conditions or reports about psychological and/or physical states.

Reports on organizational conditions typically contain items that ask about facets of the job such as autonomy, feedback, task identity, task significance, skill variety, complexity, dealing with others, ambiguity, and workload (Spector, 1992). For example, questions dealing with workload might include the following (Matteson & Ivancevich, 1987):

- Number of projects/assignments you have
- Amount of time spent in meetings
- Amount of time spent at work
- Number of phone calls and visitors you have during the day.

There are several standardized self-report measures of psychological and physiological stress and strain, such as the *Stress Diagnostic Survey* (*SDS*; Ivancevich & Matteson, 1980), the *Occupational Stress Indicator* (*OSI*; Cooper, Sloan, & Williams, 1988), and the *Job Stress Survey* (*JSS*; Spielberger & Reheiser, 1994). For example, the SDS measures workers' perceptions of stress in 15 work-related areas, including time pressure, workload, role ambiguity, and supervisory style. The JSS is a 30-item instrument that measures the severity and frequency with which workers experience certain stressful working conditions. These instruments have been used in research or by organizations to quickly gauge employees' stress levels.

Stop & Review

What is the Type A behavior pattern, and how does it relate to worker stress?

Measurement of stressful life events

As was mentioned earlier, situational stress in one area of an individual's life, such as the home or school, can affect stress levels at work (Levi, Frankenhaeuser, &

stressful life events
significant events in a
person's recent history
that can cause stress

Gardell, 1986; Martin & Schermerhorn, 1983). Particularly important is the worker's experience of traumatic or stressful life events, which include negative events such as the death of a spouse or loved one, divorce or separation, major illness, and financial or legal troubles, as well as positive events such as marriage, the birth of a child, and vacations. This approach to measuring stress assumes that such events can bring on stress-related illness and may impair job performance.

One measure is a checklist where individuals total the numerical "stress severity" scores associated with the significant life events that they have experienced in the past year (Holmes & Rahe, 1967; see Table 10.3). This provides a personal life events stress index. Half of the 10 most stressful life events are

TABLE 10.3

Sample Items from the Social Readjustment Rating Scale

Life Event	Stress Value
Death of spouse	100
Divorce	73
Marital separation	65
Jail term	63
Death of close family member	63
Personal injury or illness	53
Marriage	50
Fired at work	47
Change to different line of work	36
Change in number of arguments with spouse	35
Mortgage over $10,000	31
Foreclosure of mortgage or loan	30
Change in responsibilities at work	29
Outstanding personal achievement	28
Spouse begin or stop work	26
Trouble with boss	23
Change in work hours or conditions	20
Change in residence	20
Change in schools	20
Change in number of family get-togethers	15
Change in eating habits	15
Vacation	13
Christmas	12
Minor violations of the law	11

Source: Holmes, T. H., & Rahe, R. H. (1967). The social readjustment rating scale. *Journal of Psychosomatic Research, 11,* 213–218.

directly related to work (Hobson & Delunas, 2001). Research suggests that persons with high personal stress indexes tend to perform more poorly, have higher absenteeism, and change jobs more frequently than persons who experience fewer stressful life events (Bhagat, 1983; Weiss, Ilgen, & Sharbaugh, 1982). Moreover, there is some evidence that stressful life events have a greater stress impact on younger as opposed to older persons based on the notion that young people do not have as well-developed coping mechanisms (Jackson & Finney, 2002). Yet, there has been a great deal of criticism of the stressful life events approach to assessing stress (e.g., Hurrell, Murphy, Sauter, & Cooper, 1988). Much of the criticism is that this approach is too general. Certain life events may affect people very differently. For example, it has been suggested that a simple additive weighting of the Social Readjustment Rating Scale does not accurately assess the effect of an additional stressful event when an individual is already experiencing other stressful events (Birnbaum & Sotoodeh, 1991). In addition, assessment of stressful life events may not reveal the impact of day-to-day stressors influencing the individual.

Measurement of person–environment fit

Person–environment (P–E) fit refers to the match between a worker's abilities, needs, and values, and organizational demands, rewards, and values. P–E fit has been found to have a positive correlation with organizational commitment, well-being, and a negative correlation with turnover (Hult, 2005; Ostroff, 1993b; Verquer, Beehr, & Wagner, 2003; Yang, Che, & Spector, 2008). According to the P–E fit approach, a mismatch between the worker and the work organization/environment is believed to be a primary cause of worker stress. For example, imagine a worker who has a high need for job clarification, job structure, and feedback and who accepts a job with a small, fast-growing company where jobs are neither well defined nor structured, and where supervisors have little time for feedback due to constant production demands. In such a case, there would be a poor person–environment fit.

person–environment (P–E) fit
the match between a worker's abilities, needs, and values, and organizational demands, rewards, and values

Typically, measurement of person–environment fit involves measuring some characteristics of the worker, such as worker skills and/or abilities, and assessing the work environment and job demands. The discrepancy between these two sets of measures is then calculated as an index of fit (e.g., Edwards & Cooper, 1990). It can be argued, however, that the concept of person–environment fit is overly broad, and that measures that specifically look at "subcategories" of P–E fit—such as person–organization fit, person–job fit, and the extent to which a particular job fits an individual's motivational needs (see Chapter 8)—are needed (see Kristoff, 1996; Medcof & Hausdorf, 1995; Sutherland, Fogarty, & Pithers, 1995).

Effects of Worker Stress

Much of the growing interest in worker stress (it is one of the most studied areas of I/O psychology) is due to the very powerful impact that it can have on workers and work behavior, and, most dramatically, on employee health.

It is believed that more than one half of all physical illnesses are stress related. Some common stress-related illnesses are ulcers, colitis, high blood pressure, heart disease, respiratory illnesses, and migraine headaches. Moreover, stress can worsen common colds, flus, and infections, making recovery time longer. It is estimated that these illnesses, attributed in part to work stress, cost billions of dollars annually in health-care costs and in employee absenteeism and turnover (Beehr & Bhagat, 1985; Clark, 2005; Hart & Cooper, 2001). Importantly, polls of workers show that the majority believes that job stress causes them problems (Clark, 2005).

Worker stress can also have an adverse impact on employees' psychological states. High levels of stress are associated with depression, anxiety, and chronic fatigue. Stress may also contribute to alcoholism and drug abuse in workers and may influence accident rates on the job (Frone, 2008; Wolf, 1986; we will discuss these in more depth later). Emotional exhaustion, detachment from coworkers, negative self-evaluations, and lowered self-esteem are also associated with worker stress (Cordes & Dougherty, 1993).

As you might imagine, stress can have an effect on important work outcomes. Stress is believed to cause decreased work performance and increased absenteeism and turnover. However, the relationships between work stress and these key bottom-line variables are quite complex. For example, it has been suggested that the relationship between stress and performance may often take the form of an inverted U (see Figure 10.1), rather than being direct

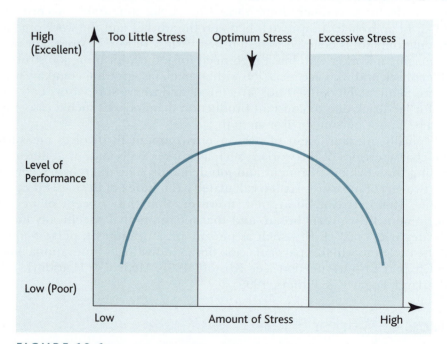

FIGURE 10.1

Relationship Between Performance and Stress

Source: Adapted from Cohen, S. V. (1980). After-effects of stress on human behavior and social behavior: A review of research theory. *Psychological Bulletin, 88,* 85.

and linear, with greater stress leading to poorer performance. In other words, very low levels of stress (or no stress) and very high levels of stress are associated with poor work performance, whereas low to moderate levels of stress seem to be related to better performance (Cohen, 1980; Muse, Harris, & Field, 2003). This makes sense, because very high levels of stress will interfere with job performance. For instance, there is evidence that severe, acute stress results in poor performance because stress interferes with workers' mental processing (Ellis, 2006). On the other end, having little or no stress likely means that workers are not being challenged or motivated (LePine, Podsakoff, & LePine, 2005). In short, a little bit of stress might not be a bad thing. Of course, both stress and job performance are extremely complex variables, and this inverted U relationship may not hold for all types of stressors or for all aspects of job performance (Beehr, 1985).

The effects of work stress on job performance might also be affected by other variables. For example, one study showed that the effect of stress on the job performance of nurses was mediated by feelings of depression. That is, work stress caused the nurses to be depressed, and the depression led to decreased quality of patient care and problems with relationships with coworkers (Motowidlo, Packard, & Manning, 1986). If stress is caused by an inability to get along with a certain coworker, an employee may try to cope with this situation by avoiding all interactions with the individual. This avoidance strategy may impair the employee's job performance if the coworker has some valuable information that the employee needs to perform his or her job. In this case, it is not the stress that is causing poor job performance, but the coping strategy!

A great deal of evidence suggests that work stress can lead to increased turnover and absenteeism (Boswell & Olson-Buchanan, 2004; Cavanaugh, Boswell, Roehling, & Boudreau, 2000; Mayes & Ganster, 1988). Gupta and Beehr (1979) found this to be true for a variety of occupations in five organizations. Another study concluded that it was a combination of high levels of work stress and low levels of organizational commitment that predicted voluntary turnover rates for workers in a food processing company (Parasuraman & Alutto, 1984). Further, if stress levels are to blame for certain illnesses, it is a given that stress must be responsible for some absenteeism and some turnover caused by disabling illness.

JOB BURNOUT

Employees exposed to such things as unresolved interpersonal conflicts, lack of clearly defined work tasks and responsibilities, extreme overwork, lack of appropriate rewards, or presence of inappropriate punishment may become victims of burnout, a process by which they become less committed to their jobs and begin to withdraw from work. The process of withdrawal may include such reactions as increased tardiness and absenteeism and decreased work performance and work quality (Gaines & Jermier, 1983; Sutherland & Cooper, 1988; Ybema, Smulders, & Bongers, 2010). Moreover, work-related burnout can spill over to an individual's family life, as we saw with stress earlier (Maslach, 2005; Maslach, Schaufeli, & Leiter, 2001).

burnout
a syndrome resulting from prolonged exposure to work stress that leads to withdrawal from the organization

TABLE 10.4

Sample Items from the Maslach Burnout Inventory (MBIHSS)

Directions: The purpose of this survey is to discover how various persons in the human services or helping professions view their jobs and the people with whom they work closely. Because persons in a wide variety of occupations will answer this survey, it uses the term "recipients" to refer to the people for whom you provide your service, care, treatment, or instruction. When you answer this survey please think of these people as recipients of the service you provide, even though you may use another term in your work.

Please read each statement carefully and decide if you ever feel this way about your job. If you have never had this feeling, write a "0" (zero) before the statement. If you have had this feeling, indicate how often you feel it by writing the number (from 1 to 6) that best describes how frequently you feel that way.

How Often:	0	1	2	3	4	5	6
	Never	A few times a year	Once a month or less	A few times a month	Once a week	A few times a week	Every day

I. Depersonalization
5. I feel I treat some recipients as if they were impersonal objects.

II. Personal Accomplishment
9. I feel I'm positively influencing other people's lives through my work.

III. Emotional Exhaustion
20. I feel like I'm at the end of my rope.

Source: From the *Maslach Burnout Inventory—Human Services Survey* by Christina Maslach and Susan E. Jackson. Copyright 1988 by CPP, Inc. All rights reserved. Further reproduction is prohibited without the Publisher's consent.

Modified and reproduced by special permission of the Publisher CPP, Inc., Mountain View, CA 94043 for Maslach Burnout Inventory-HSS by Christina Maslach and Susan E. Jackson. Copyright 1986 by CPP, Inc. All rights reserved. Further reproduction is prohibited without the Publisher's written consent.

Burnout usually occurs in three phases. The first phase is *emotional exhaustion* caused by excessive demands placed on the worker. The second phase is *depersonalization,* or the development of a cynical, insensitive attitude toward people (other workers or customers) in the work site. The third phase is marked by feelings of *low personal accomplishment.* Here the burned-out workers feel a sense of frustration and helplessness. They begin to believe that their work efforts fail to produce the desired results, and they may quit trying (Jackson, Schwab, & Schuler, 1986; Lee & Ashforth, 1990). Table 10.4 presents sample items from the Maslach Burnout Inventory Human Services Survey (MBI; Maslach & Jackson, 1986), an instrument that assesses the three hypothesized components of burnout.

Research has shown that burnout is especially high in human service professions that involve helping others, such as health-care providers (physicians, nurses, counselors), teachers, social workers, and policemen (Burke, 1997; Carlson & Thompson, 1995; Cherniss, 1980). A study of nurses found that burnout led to decreased organizational commitment and increased negative interactions with supervisors (Leiter & Maslach, 1988). Similarly, the effects of burnout on teachers include insensitivity toward students, lower tolerance for disruption in the

Research indicates that job burnout is particularly high in the human service professions, including teachers.

classroom, inadequate preparation for classes, and the feeling that they are no longer able to help students learn (Byrne, 1993). A longitudinal study of social welfare workers found that the emotional exhaustion component of Maslach's Burnout Inventory was related to both voluntary turnover and declines in job performance over a 1-year period (Wright & Cropanzano, 1998). Although much of the research on burnout focuses on the "helping professions," there is evidence that burnout can occur in many different occupations (Leiter & Schaufeli, 1996; Sonnentag, Brodbeck, Heinbokel, & Stolte, 1994). Clearly, however, the emotional labor of providing services to clients, customers, and patients, plays a big part in causing burnout (Brotherridge & Grandey, 2002; Zapf, Seifert, Schmutte, Mertini, & Holz, 2001).

It is important to note that there is some debate among researchers about the definition and the complexity of the burnout phenomenon. For instance, researchers have disagreed about the number of components that comprise the burnout syndrome (Demerouti, Bakker, Nachreiner, & Schaufeli, 2001; Evans & Fischer, 1993; Schaufeli & Van Dierendonck, 1993). Yet, burnout is a serious problem and illustrates some of the long-term psychological and behavioral effects of work-related stress.

Stop & Review

Discuss four ways of measuring worker stress.

Coping with Worker Stress

The tremendous variety of strategies and techniques designed to cope with work stress can all be categorized into two general approaches: individual strategies and organizational strategies. Individual strategies are those that can be used by individual employees to try to reduce or eliminate personal stress. Organizational strategies are techniques and programs that organizations can implement to try to reduce stress levels for groups of workers or for the organization as a whole.

Individual coping strategies

individual coping strategies
techniques such as exercise, meditation, or cognitive restructuring that can be used to deal with work stress

Individual coping strategies are behavioral or cognitive efforts made in an attempt to manage internal demands and conflicts that have exceeded an individual's usual coping resources (Lazarus & Launier, 1978; Sethi & Schuler, 1984). The most obvious of such techniques are programs developed to improve the individual's physical condition, such as exercise and diet plans. The primary rationale behind such health programs is to make the body more resistant to stress-related illnesses. Some claim that exercise itself may directly reduce the anxiety associated with stress, or that it may have a certain tranquilizing effect on stressed individuals (Jette, 1984). However, it is unclear whether it is the exercise that directly alleviates the physiological symptoms of stress or simply that an individual "feels good" after exercising because of positive psychological factors. For instance, because exercising and keeping physically fit are valued highly by our culture, it may be that physically active persons feel better about themselves and thus psychologically reduce perceived stress. More rigorous evaluation is needed to determine the precise physiological and psychological influences of exercise and diet programs in alleviating stress.

Another individual coping strategy is the inducement of states of relaxation to reduce the negative arousal and strain that accompany stress. A variety of techniques have been used to achieve this, including systematic relaxation training, meditation, and biofeedback (Stein, 2001). In systematic relaxation training, individuals are taught how to relax all the muscles of the body systematically, from the feet to the face. Meditation is a deep relaxed state that is usually brought on by intense concentration on a single word, idea, or object. Supposedly, meditative states are "free of anxiety, tension, or distress" (Sethi, 1984a, p. 145). Biofeedback uses some measure of physiological activity, typically brain waves or muscle tension, that is associated with relaxed states. When the person is in the state of relaxation, the measurement machinery provides some sort of feedback, such as a tone. The individual then learns through practice how to enter into the relaxed, stress-free state. Although relaxation, meditation, and biofeedback are intended principally to reduce the physiological arousal associated with stress, they may also induce positive psychological reactions to stress.

These various methods of coping with stress through relaxation processes are widely touted, but there has been very little systematic investigation of their effectiveness. In fact, some findings indicate that such programs are not very effective at all (Ganster, Mayes, Sime, & Tharp, 1982; Sallis, Johnson, Trevorrow, Hovell, & Kaplan, 1985).

One possible reason why systematic relaxation coping strategies may not be effective is that most of the relaxation techniques require quite a bit of dedication and practice to be used effectively. Not all persons find it easy to induce a deeply relaxed state; others may not be able to adhere to a regular program of systematic relaxation or meditation. Also, many of these programs last only a few hours, which may not be enough time to teach someone difficult relaxation techniques. The timing of the relaxation technique is another problem. Many people would find it difficult (and perhaps inappropriate) to meditate at work, and relaxing before or after work may or may not significantly reduce stress while at work. The same argument can be made for exercise programs—the benefits will only occur if people adhere to their exercise regimens (see Erfurt, Foote, & Heirich, 1992). In short, although any and all of these techniques may be good in theory, they may not function well in practice.

Other individual coping strategies include a variety of techniques to try to fend off work stress through better, more efficient work methods. Courses in time management are often advertised as methods of reducing stress caused by overwork and inefficiency (Schuler & Sethi, 1984; Wratcher & Jones, 1986). For example, learning to approach work tasks systematically by budgeting and assigning parcels of time to specific tasks and by planning ahead to avoid last-minute deadlines may be quite effective in helping reduce stress for some workers. Again, however, these strategies depend on the individual's commitment to the technique and willingness and ability to use it regularly (Shahani, Weiner, & Streit, 1993). (See Applying I/O Psychology for guidelines on how organizations should implement stress management programs.)

Individuals may also try to cope with stress by removing themselves, temporarily or permanently, from the stressful work situation. It is not uncommon for workers to exchange a stressful job for one that is less stressful (although many do seek more challenging and more stressful jobs). Although a vacation may temporarily eliminate work stress, certain trips, such as intense tours of eight European countries in seven days, may create a different kind of stress themselves (Lounsbury & Hoopes, 1986). Research indicates that although vacations do indeed reduce work stress and feelings of burnout, the effects are temporary. In fact, levels of stress and burnout are reduced immediately before, during, and immediately after the vacation, but may go back to original levels a few weeks after the vacation (Etzion, 2003; Westman & Eden, 1997).

It is interesting to note that workers might use absence from work—voluntarily taking a day off—as a coping strategy. If absence is used as an attempt to cope with a particularly stressful job, then the lost work time must be balanced against the possible gains in terms of the employee's long-term performance and well-being (Hackett & Bycio, 1996).

Finally, cognitive efforts to cope may include cognitive restructuring, which entails changing the way one thinks about stressors (Lazarus, 1991; Lowe & Bennett, 2003). For example, instead of thinking negative thoughts when faced with a stressor, the individual practices thinking neutral or positive thoughts (e.g., "this is not important," "this is really a challenge"). Studies of teachers and nurses who used cognitive restructuring found that it reduced their perceptions of stress and stress-related illnesses (Begley, 1998; Gardner, Rose, Mason, Tyler, & Cushway, 2005; Schonfeld, 1990). Cognitive restructuring is often used to treat post-traumatic stress disorder in workers and others who have experienced severe trauma (Mueser, Rosenberg, & Rosenberg, 2009).

Individual coping strategies may be effective in combating stress if they increase an individual's self-efficacy for coping with stress. Research shows that self-efficacy can help cope with work demands, such as work overload, but only if the person has the resources to help reduce the job demands (Jex, Bliese, Buzzell, & Primeau, 2001).

Organizational coping strategies

organizational coping strategies techniques that organizations can use to reduce stress for all or most employees

Individual coping strategies are steps that workers themselves can take to alleviate personal stress, and organizational coping strategies are steps that organizations can take to try to reduce stress levels in the organization for all, or most, employees (Burke, 1993). Because work stress can come from a variety of organizational sources, there are many things that organizations can do to reduce situational stressors in the workplace. These strategies include the following:

Improve the person–job fit—We have already seen that work stress commonly arises when workers are in jobs they dislike or jobs for which they are ill suited

---

APPLYING I/O PSYCHOLOGY

Designing Effective Work Stress Management Training Programs

A wide range of programs are used to help employees manage work stress. According to two leading researchers, such programs must follow certain guidelines to ensure their effectiveness: They must be systematic; they must teach knowledge, skills, or attitudes that are useful in coping with stress; and their success must be evaluated and documented (Matteson & Ivancevich, 1987; Munz & Kohler, 1997).

The first step in designing a stress management program is the same as in designing any sort of training program: an assessment of training needs. An organizational stress analysis is needed and might include answering such questions as: What are the major producers of stress in the organization? Do these stressors necessarily detract from the accomplishment of organizational goals? (In other words, are they "bad"?) What sort of resources will be committed to the training program?

According to Matteson and Ivancevich, most stress management programs take one of two forms: knowledge acquisition programs or skill training programs. Knowledge acquisition programs provide participants with some information about stress and a number of coping techniques. An outline of a sample four-part stress knowledge acquisition program is presented next:

1. *Overview of stress and its potential consequences (3 hours)*—This might include lecture and readings on facts and myths about stress, the impact of stress on physical and psychological health and on work performance, and potential sources of stress.

2. *Self-analysis: Learning about your personal stress (3 hours)*—This section can include assessments of personal stressors using instruments such as the stressful life events scale or workers' self-reports.

3. *Methods of coping with work stress (3 hours)*—Here various individual coping strategies are presented and perhaps demonstrated.

4. *Developing a personalized coping plan (3 hours)*—In this final part participants work on developing customized programs for managing stress, including setting personal stress management goals and finding means to assess their attainment.

The major advantages of knowledge acquisition programs are that they are relatively inexpensive, do not require a lot of time, and do not place heavy demands on participants. Unfortunately, these "one-shot" training programs may not be as effective as the more involved skill training programs in alleviating work stress (Hemingway & Smith, 1999).

Skill training programs are designed to improve specific coping skills in areas such as problem solving, time management, communication, social interaction, cognitive coping, or strategies for making changes in lifestyle.

APPLYING I/O PSYCHOLOGY

(Continued)

An example of a step-by-step problem-solving skill program developed by Wasik (1984) is illustrated next:

1. Identify problem (What is my problem?)
2. Select goals (What do I want to accomplish by solving the problem?)
3. Generate alternatives (What else can I do?)
4. Review the consequences (What might happen?)
5. Make a decision (What is my decision?)
6. Implement the decision (Did I do what I decided?)
7. Evaluate the decision (Does it work?)

This step-by-step program would be conducted in a series of 1- to 2-hour sessions over many weeks. Participants learn each of the steps, practice them using role-playing, and receive feedback concerning their skill development. They are also encouraged to use the skills to deal with actual work problems and then report back to discuss the success or failure of the strategy. The key to these programs is to practice using and applying the coping strategies to real and simulated stressful situations.

The final stage in any stress management program is to evaluate its effectiveness. Too often, stress management programs are not properly evaluated (Loo, 1994). It has been suggested that an assessment should consider trainees' reactions; how well the program accomplished its immediate objectives; actual behavioral changes; the impact of the program on organizational outcomes such as productivity, absenteeism, morale, and employee health; and the cost effectiveness of the program (Kirkpatrick, 1976).

(French & Caplan, 1972). A mismatch between a worker's interests or skills and job requirements can be very stressful. By maximizing the person–job fit through the careful screening, selection, and placement of employees, organizations can alleviate a great deal of this stress.

Improve employee training and orientation programs—Perhaps the most stressed groups of workers in any organization are new employees. Although they are usually highly motivated and want to make a good impression on their new bosses by showing that they are hardworking and competent, their lack of certain job-related skills and knowledge means that new employees are often unable to perform their jobs as well as they would like. This mismatch between expectations and outcomes can be very stressful for new workers. Moreover, they feel a great deal of stress simply because they are in a new and unfamiliar environment in which there is much important information to be learned. Companies can help eliminate some of this stress by ensuring that new workers receive proper job training and orientation to the organization. Not only does this lead to a more capable and productive new workforce, but it also helps to reduce the stress-induced turnover of new employees.

Increase employees' sense of control—We have seen that the lack of a sense of control over one's job can be very stressful. By giving workers a greater feeling of control through participation in work-related decisions, more responsibility, or increased autonomy and independence, organizations can alleviate some of this stress (Caplan, Cobb, French, Harrison, & Pinneau, 1980; Ganster, Fox, & Dwyer, 2001; Jimmieson & Terry, 1993; Schaubroeck, Jones, & Xie, 2001). Programs such as job enrichment, participative decision making, and systems of delegating authority all help increase employees' sense of control over their jobs and the work environment.

Eliminate punitive management—It is well known that humans react strongly when they are punished or harassed, particularly if the punishment or harassment is believed to be unfair and undeserved. The very act of being threatened or punished at work can be very stressful. If organizations take steps to eliminate company policies that are perceived to be threatening or punitive, a major source of work stress will also be eliminated. Training supervisors to minimize the use of punishment as a managerial technique will also help control this common source of stress.

Remove hazardous or dangerous work conditions—In some occupations stress results from exposure to hazardous work conditions, such as mechanical danger of loss of limb or life, health-harming chemicals, excessive fatigue, or extreme temperatures. The elimination or reduction of these situations is another way of coping with organizational stress.

Provide a supportive, team-oriented work environment—There is considerable research evidence that having supportive colleagues—people who can help deal with stressful work situations—can help reduce worker stress (Fenlason &

UP CLOSE   Stress Levels and Stress Sources of Executives Around the World

A common stereotype in the United States is the highly stressed, top-level business executive (Friedman, Hall, & Harris, 1985). Is this characterization accurate, and if so, are high-level managers in other nations similarly stressed? The first question—"Are executives highly stressed?"—does not have an easy answer. For example, many executives constantly work under such stressful conditions as work overload, high levels of responsibility, and interrole conflict (e.g., being required to travel extensively on business, which interferes with family and personal commitments). The finding that executives have a higher rate of certain types of ulcers than certain blue-collar workers attests to the existence of executive stress (Hurrell, Murphy, Sauter, & Cooper, 1988). On the other hand, executives have the benefit of some working conditions that are believed to moderate stress, such as control over the job.

The answer to the question of whether executives worldwide experience similar stressors is also not completely clear. There is some indication, however, that executives in different nations experience different types or sources of stress. For example, executives in less-developed countries such as Nigeria and Egypt seem to experience a great deal of stress due to lack of autonomy, whereas those from more developed countries, such as the United States, the United Kingdom, the Netherlands, and Japan, experience greater stress from work overload (Carayon & Zijlstra, 1999; Cooper & Hensman, 1985). Workers in India rated lack of job structure, not workload, as their greatest source of stress (Narayanan, Menon, & Spector, 1999). One study found that executives in New Zealand experience less job-related stress than executives in nine other countries (McCormick & Cooper, 1988). These researchers mention that this may be due to the more relaxed lifestyle in New Zealand and the fact that many of these executives worked for rather small organizations.

An interesting study by Kirkcaldy and Cooper (1993) found some evidence that work stress for executives may be modified by preference for leisure activities—and that preferred leisure activities may be related to culture. For example, managers from Germany, who tend to prefer nonaggressive leisure activities, experienced less job stress than British managers, who typically prefer aggressive leisure activities.

Overall, such studies seem to indicate that although executive job stress is universal, the amount of stress experienced, and the sources of the stress, may vary depending on country or culture.

Beehr, 1994; House, 1981; Lim, 1996). This is particularly true for workers involved in the emotional labor of service work (Korczynski, 2003). Meta-analyses suggest that social support in the workplace reduces perceptions of threat, lessens the perceived strength of the stressors, and helps in coping with work-related stress (Viswesvaran, Sanchez, & Fisher, 1999). The more organizations can foster good interpersonal relationships among coworkers and an integrated, highly functioning work team, the more likely that workers will be able to provide support for one another in times of stress (Heaney, Price, & Rafferty, 1995; Unden, 1996). We will look at work group processes and teamwork in more depth in Chapter 12.

Improve communication—Much of the stress at work derives from difficulties in interpersonal relations with supervisors and coworkers. The better the communication among workers, the lower the stress created because of misunderstandings. In addition, stress occurs when workers feel cut off from or uninformed about organizational processes and operations. In one study, merely providing more job-related information helped in reducing stress caused by task overload (Jimmieson & Terry, 1999). Proper organizational communication, which will be examined in Chapter 11, can prevent workers from experiencing stress from job uncertainty and feelings of isolation.

Negative Employee Attitudes and Behaviors

In Chapter 9 we saw how individual differences in positive affectivity had a favorable impact on job satisfaction and other work outcomes and that workers with negative affectivity tended to have low levels of satisfaction (Connolly & Viswevaran, 2000). What are the relationships between negative affectivity, worker stress, and undesirable work outcomes? There is mixed evidence about how negative affectivity influences perceived stress; however, it seems that individuals prone to negative emotions do indeed perceive that they have more stress on their jobs (Cassar & Tattersall, 1998; Spector, Chen, & O'Connell, 2000). However, the true relationship may be complex. For example, there is evidence that negative affectivity interacts with other variables, such as perceptions of being treated inequitably or unjustly—with persons prone toward negative emotionality reacting more strongly to being treated unfairly (Aquino, Lewis, & Bradfield, 1999). Workers with high negative affectivity were also more likely to leave work early, before the scheduled end of the workday (Iverson & Deery, 2001). In addition, there is some evidence that workers high in negative affectivity may not respond as well to feedback from supervisors about how to improve their work performance (Lam, Yik, & Schaubroeck, 2002).

Beyond the role of negative emotions, what are some negative employee behaviors that are of major concern to organizations? I/O psychologists have investigated counterproductive work behaviors (CWBs), which are deviant behaviors that are harmful to an employee's organization and its members (Bennett &

⏱ Stop & Review

List and describe five organizational coping strategies.

---

counterproductive work behaviors (CWBs)

deviant, negative behaviors that are harmful to an organization and its workers

Employee theft is one form of counterproductive work behavior.

Robinson, 2000; Spector & Fox, 2005). Counterproductive work behaviors include such things as stealing from employers, vandalism, sabotage, harassment of coworkers, deliberately missing work, and using drugs or alcohol on the job (see Table 10.5).

TABLE 10.5

Examples of Counterproductive Work Behaviors (CWBs)

Said something hurtful to, or made fun of, a coworker

Acted rudely or publicly embarrassed a coworker

Taken property from work without permission

Falsified a receipt to get reimbursed for more than you spent on a business expense

Taken an additional or longer work break than is acceptable

Come in late to work without permission

Neglected to follow your boss's instructions

Used an illegal drug or consumed alcohol on the job

Dragged out work in order to get paid overtime

Discussed confidential company information with an unauthorized person

Made a derogatory ethnic, religious, or racial remark at work

Littered your work environment

Intentionally worked slower than you could have worked

Source: Bennett, R. J., & Robinson, S. L. (2000). Development of a measure of workplace deviance. *Journal of Applied Psychology, 85,* 349–360.

Research has shown that CWBs can result from stress, frustration at work, or feelings of inequity, causing attempts to retaliate against the employer and seek revenge, or even from jealousy (Aquino, Tripp, & Bies, 2001; Fox & Spector, 1999; Jensen, Opland, & Ryan, 2010; Vecchio, 2000). Meta-analyses suggest that CWBs are more prevalent in younger employees and those with lower job satisfaction (Lau, Au, & Ho, 2003). Counterproductive work behaviors, and even workplace aggression and violence, are also linked to trait negative affectivity, anger, and other personality variables (Douglas & Martinko, 2001; Spector, 1997b). Interestingly, a meta-analysis showed that the incidence of CWBs is negatively related to ($r = -0.32$) the incidence of organizational citizenship behaviors (Dalal, 2005), but they are distinct constructs (Spector, Bauer, & Fox, 2010).

Researchers suggest that organizations should engage in programs to try to alleviate sources of stress and provide strategies to give workers greater control over their jobs, as a way to reduce CWBs. There is evidence that CWBs are not just individually motivated ("bad apples"), but can also be influenced by the norms and values of the group and organization ("bad barrels"; O'Boyle, Forsyth, & O'Boyle, 2011.) (We will discuss group level influences on behavior fully in Chapter 12). Also, making sure that employees are treated fairly, providing reasonable workloads, clearly defining jobs, and having supervisors trained to mediate interpersonal disputes among workers, are other strategies to prevent counterproductive behavior and workplace violence (Atwater & Elkins, 2009; Spector, 2001).

ALCOHOL AND DRUG USE IN THE WORKPLACE

A problem that is of great concern to businesses and to industrial/organizational psychologists is employee's use and abuse of alcohol and drugs (Frone, 2011). No doubt a great many industrial accidents occur because of worker intoxication. The combination of alcohol or drugs and heavy machinery or motor vehicles is deadly. Drug and alcohol abuse is also directly responsible for decreased productivity and increased absenteeism and turnover, not to mention all the problems that it can cause in the home lives of workers. The costs of all of this are staggering. A conservative estimate is that substance abuse costs U.S. employers more than $100 billion dollars a year, and substance abuse is a worldwide problem.

A study of young workers found that workers who reported problems with alcohol and drugs had greater job instability and reduced job satisfaction in comparison to their peers who did not abuse drugs (Galaif, Newcomb, & Carmona, 2001). Moreover, this is likely a cyclical process. Studies suggest that workers who are under severe stress, such as heavy job demands or the stress of job loss, may turn to alcohol or drugs (Begley, 1998; Frone, 2008; Murphy, Beaton, Pike, & Johnson, 1999). This, in turn, leads to problems on the job, and the cycle continues.

There is some evidence that organizational policies that ban substance abuse in the workplace and advocate against illicit drug use reduce employees' use of drugs both on and off the job (Carpenter, 2007). A number of programs have been used to try to deter drug use by employees (Ghodse, 2005).

In an effort to combat substance abuse, many companies have **employee assistance programs (EAPs)**, programs that offer counseling for a variety of

employee assistance programs (EAPs)
counseling provided for a variety of worker problems, particularly drug and alcohol abuse

employee problems. Of particular concern is counseling for drug and alcohol abuse, although EAPs also help employees to deal with work stress and personal problems that may adversely affect their performance and well-being (Cairo, 1983; Cooper, Dewe, & O'Driscoll, 2011). Although employee counseling has long been offered by companies, only in the past 20 years have comprehensive EAPs become commonplace in large organizations. This increase is likely due to the growing concern over the devastating consequences of substance abuse in terms of harming worker health and organizational productivity. The majority of large American companies today have some type of formalized employee assistance program.

Although industrial/organizational psychologists are greatly concerned about the adverse impact of substance abuse and work stress on employee productivity and well-being, clinical and counseling psychologists, social workers, and drug rehabilitation counselors, rather than I/O psychologists, typically staff EAPs. However, I/O psychologists may have a hand in the design, implementation, and evaluation of EAPs.

Employee assistance programs usually take one of two forms. External programs are those in which the company contracts with an outside agency to provide counseling services for its employees. Internal EAPs offer services at the work site. The advantage of an internal program is its convenience for the employees, although they are expensive to maintain. Usually only large organizations can afford internal EAPs. The main advantages of external programs are the lower costs and the increased employee confidentiality.

Despite the increasing popularity of employee assistance programs, there has been surprisingly little research on their effectiveness (Weiss, 1987; Kirk & Brown, 2003). The problem results partly from the difficulty of evaluating any counseling program, because it is not always clear which variables will best determine a program's "success" (Mio & Goishi, 1988). For example, some programs measure success by the number of workers treated, whereas others may use some standard of recovery or "cure." Furthermore, it is difficult to determine how EAP counseling affects bottom-line variables such as employee performance. It is also difficult to determine the effectiveness of EAPs because the large number of external agencies that offer counseling services for businesses usually conduct their own evaluations, and it is unclear how objective and accurate these self-assessments are. Although there are questions about the effectiveness of employee assistance programs in general, it is likely that even a few cases of employee recovery would lead an employer to label an EAP a success because of the severity of drug and alcohol addiction. Moreover, there is some evidence that EAPs do help reduce long-term health-care costs for employees (Cummings & Follette, 1976). One critic of substance abuse EAPs argues that they focus primarily on treating alcohol and drug problems after they have reached the problem stage, but give little attention to their prevention (Nathan, 1983). Despite the uncertainty of the effectiveness of employee assistance programs, it is likely that they will become a mainstay in most work organizations and another service that will be considered an essential part of any employee benefit package.

Stop & Review

Give five examples of counterproductive work behaviors

Summary

Although there is a great deal of disagreement over definitions of stress, *worker stress* can be defined as physiological or psychological reactions to an event that is perceived to be threatening or taxing. Stress is actually a perception, so there is tremendous individual variation in what one perceives to be stressful. Negative stress, or distress, can cause stress-related illness, and it can affect absenteeism, turnover, and work performance.

Certain occupations, such as air traffic controller and health-care provider, are stereotypically associated with high levels of stress. Worker stress can also come from either organizational sources or individual sources, which are commonly classified as *situational* or *dispositional sources,* respectively. Organizational sources may include having too much to do—*work overload*—or too little to do—*underutilization. Job ambiguity,* which occurs when job tasks and responsibilities are not clearly defined or from inadequate performance feedback or job insecurity, and *interpersonal stress,* which arises from relations with coworkers, are other organizational sources of stress, as are workers' sense of a *lack of control* over their jobs, *organizational change,* and *work–family conflict.* Individual sources of work stress include the worker's experience of traumatic *life events*; susceptibility to stress, such as the lack of *hardiness,* or resistance to stress-related illnesses; and certain personality characteristics such as the *Type A behavior pattern,* which is the coronary-prone personality.

Attempts to measure stress have included physiological measures, self-report assessments, the measurement of stressful life events, and the match between worker characteristics and the demands of the work situation, referred to as the *person–environment fit* approach. Stress has been shown to be related to certain physical illnesses such as ulcers, high blood pressure, and heart disease. These stress-related illnesses as well as stress itself are tied to rates of employee absenteeism and turnover and to job performance, although the relationship between stress and performance is complex. Long-term stress can lead to *job burnout,* a multidimensional construct that relates to one's tendency to withdraw from work.

Strategies for coping with work stress can be divided into *individual coping strategies* and *organizational coping strategies.* Individual strategies include programs of exercise, diet, systematic relaxation training, meditation, biofeedback, time management, work planning, and cognitive coping strategies. Organizational strategies include improving the person–job fit, offering better training and orientation programs, giving workers a sense of control over their jobs, eliminating punitive management styles, removing hazardous work conditions, and improving organizational communication.

Counterproductive work behaviors, which can result from stress, frustration, or feelings of inequity or can be due to personality differences, such as trait negative affectivity, are destructive behaviors designed to harm employers or fellow employees. An important concern of management is reducing counterproductive work behaviors and dealing with alcohol and drug use in the workplace. One strategy is to offer *Employee Assistance Programs* to help workers deal with alcohol and drug problems, as well as personal issues and workplace stress.

Study Questions and Exercises

1. List the sources of stress in your own life. Ask a friend to do the same. Are there important differences in your two lists, or are they quite similar? What are the implications for defining and understanding stress?

2. Consider how the work world will be changing in the next several years. What are the implications for worker stress? Will there be more of it, or less? What are some sources of technology-related stress (technostress) addressed in On the Cutting Edge that will increase in the future?

3. Consider the various means of assessing stress. Which seems most accurate, and why?

4. Based on the material in the chapter, design a stress management program for use in an organization.

5. What are the connections between worker stress and counterproductive work behaviors? How can counterproductive work behaviors be reduced?

Web Links

www.jobstresshelp.com
A site offering information on job stress.

www.eapweb.com
A site designed to help workers deal with stress and trauma.

Suggested Readings

Fox, S., & Spector, P. E. (2005). *Counterproductive work behavior: Investigations of actors and targets.* Washington, DC: American Psychological Association. *An edited book of research on counterproductive behavior in the workplace, including such topics as aggression and violence at work and bullying in the workplace.*

Leiter, M. P., & Maslach, C. (2005). *Banishing burnout: Six strategies for improving your relationship with work.* San Francisco: Jossey-Bass. *This applied book reviews what is known about stress and burnout and what individuals and organizations can do to deal with them.*

Sulsky, L., & Smith, C. (2005). *Work stress.* Belmont, CA: Thompson-Wadsworth. *A very detailed textbook on work stress.*

PART FOUR

CHAPTER

11

Communication
in the Workplace

CHAPTER OUTLINE

Inside Tips

COMMUNICATION: A COMPLEX PROCESS IN WORK ORGANIZATIONS

Communication is a constant, ongoing process involving all members of the organization. As a result, it is extremely complex and difficult to study. In contrast to the previous chapters, this chapter is more general. The theories and models tend to represent general aspects of communication, and relatively little new terminology is introduced. In this chapter, rather than concentrating on learning new terms or specific theories, think about the complexity of organizational communication and the difficulties encountered in trying to measure and understand this important, ongoing process. Consider the number and types of communication you send and receive each day, the various ways that messages are communicated, and the different settings in which this occurs.

Most of us do not work alone but rather with others in the context of small groups. In large organizations, these groups are in turn members of larger work groups or departments, which in combination make up the work organization. Depending on the size of the organization, our coworkers may number in the tens, hundreds, or even thousands. Much energy in organizations, particularly from the management perspective, involves coordinating the activities of the various members. In the next few chapters, we will examine work behavior in terms of this organizational interaction. We will investigate the dynamics of work groups—how they coordinate activities and make decisions—as well as the very factors that hold them together. We will see how workers differ in terms of their power and status within the organization, paying particular attention to the relationship between those persons designated as leaders and other workers. We will examine the politics within work organizations and the structure of work groups and larger work organizations. However, before we begin to explore these topics, we must understand one of the most basic processes that occurs among workers in organizational settings: communication.

Y ou return from vacation. On your desk is a foot-high stack of mail, your "in-basket" is overflowing, and your voice mail says you have 27 messages. Logging on, you find that you have 312 e-mail messages and wonder if the company's spam filter is working. A colleague stops by, reminds you that you have an important staff meeting in five minutes, and gives you an odd look—sort of a scowl—and you start to wonder what it means. You have always felt a sense of "communication overload" at work, but this is definitely too much.

The Communication Process: A Definition and a Model

communication

the passage of information between one person or group to another person or group

Communication can be defined as the transmission of information from one person or group to another person or group. In work settings, communication takes many forms, such as written or spoken orders, informal chatter, electronic messaging, printed reports or procedure manuals, discussion among executives in a corporate boardroom, announcements posted on bulletin boards, or Web-based communication. Communication is an ongoing process that serves as the lifeblood of the organization. Communication is also extremely complex and can occur in a variety of ways: through the written or spoken word; through nonverbal means such as gestures, nods, or tone of voice; or through a picture or diagram. We can also communicate in a number of contexts, including face-to-face conversation, telephone, text messaging, letters or memos, e-mail, charts and diagrams, a videoconference, or a public address. This complexity, coupled with its almost continuous nature (even our silence can communicate), makes communication very difficult to study.

sender

the originator of a communication, who encodes and transmits a message; also known as the encoder

Communication involves the process of the exchange of information among two or more parties, which is best represented by a simple model of communication between two persons: the sender and the receiver (see Figure 11.1). The **sender** (also known as the *encoder*) is the originator of the communication; the

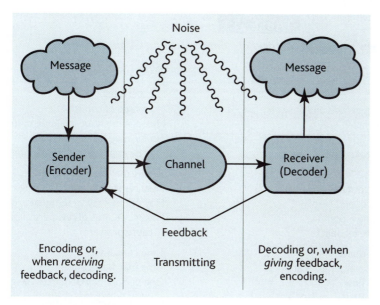

FIGURE 11.1
The Communication Process

receiver (also called the *decoder*) is the recipient. Communication begins with some information—a message—that the sender wishes to transmit to a receiver. The sender's task is to take the information and put it into some form in which it can be communicated to the receiver. This process of preparing a message for transmission is referred to as encoding, because the sender chooses some sort of shared code as a means of communication. In work settings, this code is usually the shared verbal language, but it might also consist of some common nonverbal code, or "body language."

The next step is for the sender to select a channel, the vehicle through which the message will flow from the sender to the receiver. The sender may choose the spoken word, confronting the receiver face-to-face or through the telephone, or the written word, using a memo, or a typed message sent through a text or e-mail. Different methods of communication have various advantages and disadvantages (see Table 11.1). For example, face-to-face, text messaging, or telephone communication is typically quick and convenient, whereas formal reports or detailed memos can be time consuming to prepare. However, the more formal, written channels of communication are less likely to be misunderstood or misinterpreted because of their length, detail, and careful preparation. Importantly, the sender must also choose the channel of communication that is appropriate for the situation. For example, personal information is usually conveyed verbally, face-to-face, while an important directive concerning a project deadline might be put in the form of a detailed, typed memo or e-mail that is distributed to all relevant parties, with follow-up reminders sent as the deadline nears.

receiver
the recipient of a communication who decodes the message; also known as the decoder

encoding
the process of preparing a message for transmission by putting it into some form or code

channel
the vehicle through which a message flows from sender to receiver

TABLE 11.1

Advantages and Disadvantages of Communication Channels

Channel	Advantages	Disadvantages
Telephone	Verbal Permits questions and answers Convenient Two-way flow Immediate feedback	Less personal No record of conversation Message might be misunderstood Timing may be inconvenient May be impossible to terminate
Face-to-Face	Visual Personal contact Can "show" and "explain" Can set the mood Immediate feedback	Timing may be inconvenient Requires spontaneous thinking May not be easy to terminate Power or status of one person may cause pressure
Meetings	Can use visuals Involves several minds at once Two-way flow	Time consuming Time may be inconvenient One person may dominate the group
Memorandum	Brief Provides a record Can prethink the message Can disseminate widely	No control over receiver Less personal One-way flow Delayed feedback
Formal Report	Complete; comprehensive Can organize material at writer's leisure Can disseminate widely	Less personal May require considerable time in reading Language may not be understandable Expensive One-way flow Delayed feedback
Teleconference	Saves time for travel Visual Lessens impact of power/ makes users be better prepared	Miss interpersonal contact Not good for initial brainstorming sessions Expensive

Electronic Mail &
Text Messaging
	Convenient
	
	Messages sent/received at all hours
	Extremely fast compared to other
	   written messages
	Can be sent to multiple parties
	   Simultaneously
		Ease can lead to message "overload"
		
		No nonverbal communication
		Others may be able to get access to
		   messages

Web-Based	Convenient
	Can interact in real time
	Can communicate with multiple parties
	   simultaneously
	Can present drawings/figures/
	   pictures/videos easily
		Ease can lead to message "overload"
		Difficult to control flow of messages
		   (e.g., turn-taking)

Source: Organizational Communication: The Essence of Effective Management by Lewis, Philip V. © reprinted by permission of Pearson Education, Inc., Upper Saddle River, NJ.

In the two-person communication model, the receiver picks up the message and is responsible for decoding it, or translating it in an effort to understand the meaning intended by the sender. Of course, in many communications some of the original message—that information drawn from the thought processes of the encoder—will be lost or distorted, either through the encoding process, through transmission, or in decoding. (That is why the second, received "Message" in the communication model is not identical to the original Message.)

Typically, when the receiver has decoded the message, feedback, or a response, is transmitted to the sender. The receiver acknowledges receipt of the message and either tells the sender that the message is understood or requests clarification. In the feedback stage of the process, the communication model actually reverses, with the receiver becoming the sender and vice versa. Feedback can be as simple as a nod of the head, a text saying "ok," or as formal as a letter of receipt or the initialing of a memo that is returned to the sender.

Although this model represents communication as a simple and relatively foolproof process, the effective flow of information from sender to receiver can break down at many points. The sender can have difficulty in encoding the message, making comprehension by the receiver difficult. For example, a supervisor might tell an employee, "I would really like you to try to make this deadline," when what she really means is that the deadline must be met, with no exceptions. On the other side, the receiver may inaccurately decode the message and interpret it in a way wholly different from what the sender had in mind. For example, the employee might interpret the "deadline" statement to mean that the supervisor has now turned entire responsibility for the project over to him and will no longer be available to help meet the deadline. A poor choice of channel may also result in a breakdown of effective communication. For example, giving a coworker lengthy and detailed instructions about a work task over the telephone rather than in writing may lead to inadequate performance of the job. Furthermore, the work environment may provide any number of distractions that can disrupt the communication process, such as competing conversations, loud machinery, or inconsistent or contradictory messages. Such distractions are collectively called noise. Noise may also refer to psychological factors such as biases, perceptual differences, or selective attention, all of which make it difficult for persons to communicate with and to understand one another. For example, psychological noise can occur when the receiver ignores the sender because of a belief that the sender "has nothing important to say."

decoding
the process of translating a message so that it can be understood

feedback
an acknowledgment that a message has been received and understood

noise
physical or psychological distractions that disrupt the effective flow of communication

RESEARCH ON THE COMMUNICATION PROCESS

Much of the research on the communication process in work settings has focused on factors that can increase or decrease its effectiveness. Among the factors that can affect the flow of communication from sender to receiver are source factors, channel factors, and audience factors.

A channel is any vehicle of communication, such as the spoken word via telephone or the written word via e-mail.

Source factors

source factors

characteristics of the sender that influence the effectiveness of a communication

Source factors are characteristics of the sender—the source of the message—that can facilitate or detract from the effective flow of communication. One such factor is the status of the source, which can affect whether potential receivers attend to a message. Generally, the higher the organizational status of the sender, the more likely the communication will be listened to and acted on. For example, messages from the president or owner of a company are usually given top priority. ("When the boss talks, people listen.")

Another source factor is the credibility, or believability, of the sender. If the source is trusted, particularly if someone is in a supervisory or leadership role, it is more likely that the message will receive proper attention (Mackenzie, 2010). Variables such as the expertise, knowledge, and reliability of the source (e.g., Has this person provided truthful information in the past?) contribute to the credibility of the sender (O'Reilly & Roberts, 1976). Employees learn which sources can be trusted and pay closest attention to their messages. Research suggests that a sender's communication style is also important. For instance, more expressive and more organized trainers tended to do a better job of imparting learning to trainees (Towler & Dipboye, 2001).

A final source factor is the encoding skills of the sender, or the source's ability to translate an abstract message into some sort of shared code, usually the written or spoken language, so that it can be clearly conveyed to the receiver. For example, the communication skills of a CEO may be critical when she or he is trying to articulate the company's vision or goals for the future. In short, these skills include the abilities to speak and write clearly and to select the appropriate channel for transmitting information. Generally, the better the encoding skills of the sender, the smoother and more effective is the flow of communication.

Channel factors

Channel factors, which are positive or negative characteristics related to the vehicle through which the message is communicated, can also influence the effectiveness of the communication process. Selection of the proper channel can have an important effect on the accurate flow of communication. For example, using a visual device such as a chart or graph to present complex information on sales and profit figures is likely to be a more effective channel than the spoken word. The channel selected can also affect the impact of the message. For example, a face-to-face reprimand from a supervisor might carry more weight than the same reprimand conveyed over the telephone. Whenever possible, using multiple channels to present complicated information will increase the likelihood that it will be attended to and retained. Research on organizational communication has focused on specific types, or "genres," of messages, such as business letters, memos, or group meetings (Yates & Orlikowski, 1992). In one study, it was found that persons higher in the organizational hierarchy had a preference for more formal modes of written communication (word-processed letters and memos) over more informal, handwritten messages (Reinsch & Beswick, 1995). Another study has found that managers are indicating a growing preference for using e-mail to communicate messages, even in situations such as responding to another's telephone message, or when the recipient is in an office just down the hall (Markus, 1994).

Semantic problems are common channel factors that can lead to a breakdown in communication. These difficulties occur because different people may interpret the meanings of certain words differently. For example, if your work supervisor tells you that you are doing a "good" job, you may infer that your performance is well above average. However, if the supervisor defines "good" as work that is barely passable (but really he expects "excellent," "superior," or "outstanding" performance), you may be missing the meaning of the message. Semantic problems may arise through the use of technical language, or jargon, the special language that develops within a specific work environment. Jargon is typically filled with abbreviated words, acronyms, special vocabularies, and slang. For example, industrial/organizational psychology could be abbreviated as "I/O Psych" and might be described as the field in which topics such as RJPs, BARS, and validity generalization are studied.

Although jargon serves the purpose of speeding up communication between those who speak the language, it can create problems when the receiver is not "fluent" in its use. The use of jargon can also create problems when a team of workers is composed of members from different professional disciplines, all of who may use different jargon (Cooley, 1994). For example, imagine the potential communication breakdowns that occurred during some of the NASA space projects, where decision-making teams were made up of aerospace engineers, military officers, and research scientists, each using their own technical jargon.

Stop & Review

Explain each of the steps in two-person communication.

channel factors
characteristics of the vehicle of transmission of a message that affect communication

jargon
special language developed in connection with certain jobs; also called technical language

The type of channel used to communicate can affect important work-related outcomes, such as job satisfaction. Research suggests that the frequency and quality of face-to-face communication between supervisors and subordinates is positively related to workers' job satisfaction (Callan, 1993; Lee, 1998; Muchinsky, 1977b). The type of channel may also have some influence on work performance and efficiency. For example, a company policy of keeping written documentation of all orders and directives rather than simply relying on spoken orders may decrease the likelihood that workers will forget what they are supposed to be doing, which in turn may have positive effects on the productivity and efficiency of the work unit.

A topic of great interest has been the use of computer-mediated meetings, where workers interconnect and hold meetings at their individual computer work stations, or teleconference via the Web (Sadowski-Rasters, Duysters, & Sadowski, 2006; Trevino & Webster, 1992; Weisband, 1992). Research indicates that computer-mediated meetings have the advantages of convenience, with members getting more equal participation in the interaction than occurs in face-to-face meetings (Weisband, Schneider, & Connolly, 1995). Low-status or shy members may be more willing to share information in computer-mediated meetings. However, the lack of "social dynamics," including the loss of nonverbal cues available in face-to-face interactions, tends to lead members of computer-mediated meetings to engage in more extreme or "risky" decisions. Members communicating via computer may also be more outspoken, and members may engage in "rude" behaviors, including "put-downs" of other participants, because the members do not have to face the disapproving looks of other participants (Kiesler & Sproull, 1992; Savicki & Kelley, 2000). There may also be some difficulties in coordinating the flow of communication and in taking turns—actually causing electronic meetings to be longer than face-to-face ones (Carey & Kacmar, 1997). However, as video–computer interfaces become more common, and the technology evolves, computer-mediated meetings may eventually become quite similar to face-to-face meetings (Fussell & Benimoff, 1995).

Audience factors

audience factors
characteristics of the receiver that influence the effectiveness of a communication

Audience factors are elements related to the receiver, such as the person's attention span and perceptual abilities, which can facilitate or impair the communication process. For example, it is important that training information be presented at a level that matches the audience's ability to perceive and process that information, or much of the communication may be lost. Moreover, it is critical to consider the attention span of the target audience. Although all-day classroom training sessions might be appropriate for management trainees who are used to such long sessions, the attention of assembly-line workers might be lost after an hour's lecture because of their unfamiliarity with this format.

The receiver's relationship to the sender can also affect the communication process. For example, if the receiver is subordinate to the sender, the message may be better attended to because the receiver is supposed to listen to superiors.

Videoconferencing offers instantaneous, face-to-face communication over long distances.

If, however, the situation is reversed, a message from a lower-ranking organizational member may not receive much attention from a higher-ranking employee.

Finally, the decoding skills of the receiver can influence the effectiveness of communication. Workers vary greatly in their ability to receive, decode, and understand organizational messages. Although managers are often considered the source rather than the audience of much organizational communication, research has shown that effective managers have good decoding skills in listening and responding to the needs and concerns of their subordinates (Baron, 1986). In fact, because much of the communication in work settings involves spoken communication, oral decoding skills, often referred to as listening skills, are considered to be the most important decoding skills of all (Hunt, 1980).

Research suggests that "active listening"—where the decoder asks clarifying questions, repeats the encoder's words, and provides feedback ("Yes, I see." "Uh-hum," etc.)—has positive effects on the effectiveness of the communication flow, in terms of greater comprehension and mutual understanding, and greater participant satisfaction (Kraut, Lewis, & Swezey, 1982; Rao, 1995). Bays (2007) argues that college students should be taught *both* speaking *and* listening skills in order to prepare them for the workplace.

NONVERBAL COMMUNICATION IN WORK SETTINGS

We commonly think of communication in work settings as taking one of two forms, either written or spoken. However, people can and do use a great deal of nonverbal communication, which is sent and received by means other than the written or spoken word. Broadly defined, nonverbal communication can occur through facial expressions, gesture, tone of voice, body movements, posture,

nonverbal communication
messages sent and received through means other than the spoken or written word

style of dress, touching, and physical distance between sender and receiver (Andersen, 2008). We use nonverbal communication to convey a wide range of feelings and attitudes.

To understand the role of nonverbal communication in work settings, we can examine its use from both the sender's and the receiver's perspective. For the sender, nonverbal communication can be used in three ways. First, nonverbal cues can be substituted for verbal communication. Nodding to show approval, shaking your head in disagreement, or gesturing for a person to come closer or to go away are all ways of sending clear, unspoken messages. In particular, noisy work environments or situations in which coworkers are positioned out of hearing range may necessitate the use of a set of nonverbal signals, which decreases the reliance on verbal communication. The hand signals used by ground crews to guide airline pilots or the gestures used by land surveyors are examples of the use of nonverbal communication.

Nonverbal cues can also be used to enhance verbal messages. We often use our tone of voice, facial expressions, and body movements to emphasize what we are saying. If you want to compliment a subordinate for doing an outstanding job, the words will have greater impact if they are accompanied by an enthusiastic tone of voice and an approving smile. A board member who pounds her fist on the table while voicing disagreement with a

Stop & Review

List several source and audience factors that affect communication flow.

ON THE *CUTTING* EDGE

Communicating in a Diverse, Multicultural Work Environment

The world of work is becoming more and more diverse. The workforce in most organizations is made up of people from various cultural backgrounds, many of who are nonnative speakers of the dominant language (Brislin, 2008; Orasnu, Fischer, & Davison, 1997). Moreover, many companies are engaged in international business and interact with workers from a variety of nations and cultures.

Such cultural diversity has many advantages. Diverse workforces tend to be more creative, more adaptable, and more tolerant of others (Adler, 1991). As you can imagine, however, cultural and language differences can present challenges to the effective flow of communication within organizations (Schachaf, 2008). Moreover, cultural differences can threaten a common, shared commitment to organizational goals (Fine, 1991; Granrose, 1997). Culturally based communication differences can also affect the ability of companies from different nations and cultures to work with one another. For example, the communication style of most North American managers tends to be direct and "confrontation-centered." The Japanese business communication style, however, tends to be indirect and "agreement-centered" (Kume, 1985). Such differences can lead to serious communication breakdowns.

Realizing the need to prevent cross-cultural communication breakdown, organizations have taken several steps to facilitate intercultural organizational communication. For example, many organizations have developed multicultural awareness and training programs (Clements & Jones, 2008; Kossek & Zonia, 1993). In addition, many international businesses have training programs specifically designed for preparing employees for assignments in other countries (see Chapter 7). One model of preparing managers for working with culturally diverse and multinational work groups suggests that general communication competence, proficiency in other languages, an awareness of cultural differences, and an ability to negotiate with people of diverse backgrounds are the keys to success (Tung, 1997). In short, the issues of multicultural and cross-cultural communication are going to be important ones in the world of work as we move into the future (Rost-Roth, 2010).

proposal is going to command greater attention by including this nonverbal emphasizer.

Given the increase in electronic communication, particularly e-mail, one problem is the absence of nonverbal cues in electronic text messages. It is very difficult to convey emotional meaning, sarcasm, and the like. As a result, savvy e-mail users (and programmers) have developed symbols, typically called "emoticons" (the little smiley faces—), to help compensate and put some "nonverbal" into these verbal interactions.

Nonverbal cues are also important for conveying certain impressions in organizations (Rosenfeld, Giacalone, & Riordan, 2002). For example, it is often important that persons in positions of leadership or authority convey their power and authority nonverbally if they want to get others' attention and be persuasive (Goethals, 2005; Riordan, 1989). Similarly, customer service representatives, such as salespersons or waitpersons, need to convey an image of helpfulness, positive emotions, and customer concern if they are to be successful (Grove & Fisk, 1989; Tsai, 2001).

Nonverbal cues can be used to convey underlying feelings. In situations in which a person is restricted in what can be said verbally to get the true message across, the verbal message may be accompanied by a nonverbal "disclaimer" (see Mehrabian, 1981). For example, at a new employee orientation, the trainer may verbally praise the company but with her tone of voice she may convey that things are not really going as well as they seem.

A sender's nonverbal communication can also subtly communicate his or her expectations to other workers and influence the workers' behaviors in line with those expectations, in what is called the Pygmalion effect (Rosenthal, 1994; Rosenthal & Jacobson, 1968). An example of the Pygmalion effect would be a supervisor who expects a team to perform very well (or very poorly), who nonverbally communicates those expectations to the team members, perhaps through an enthusiastic (or unenthusiastic) tone of voice, actually spurring the team to better (or worse) performance (Eden, 1990). A meta-analysis suggests that the Pygmalion effect does indeed occur in work organizations, but is stronger in initially low-performing groups and in the military, presumably because of the strong influence leaders have on followers in the armed forces (Kierein & Gold, 2000).

Pygmalion effect
when a sender nonverbally communicates expectations to a receiver influencing his/her behavior

From the perspective of a receiver, nonverbal cues serve two important functions. First, they provide additional information. When verbal communication is limited or when the receiver has reason to mistrust the verbal message, the receiver will look to nonverbal cues as a source of more data. This is particularly likely when the receiver feels that the verbal message may be deceptive, although research has shown that most people do not read the nonverbal cues of deception very accurately (DePaulo, Stone, & Lassiter, 1985; Kraut, 1980; O'Sullivan, 2005).

Nonverbal cues are also used by receivers in person perception, that is, in making judgments about a person's attitudes, personality, and competence. There is evidence that styles of nonverbal behavior play an important part in person perception (Schneider, Hastorf, & Ellsworth, 1979). This is particularly important in personnel decisions such as in performance feedback sessions or in hiring (Riggio, 2005). For example, it has been found that persons exhibiting more expressive nonverbal behaviors, such as more smiling and greater eye contact, are more favorably evaluated in hiring interviews than are nonexpressive individuals (DeGroot & Motowidlo, 1999; Forbes & Jackson, 1980; Gifford, Ng, & Wilkinson, 1985; Imada & Hakel, 1977). However, the relationship between nonverbal cues and interviewing success may be more complex than just simply "more is better" (see Rasmussen, 1984). In other words, rather than looking only at the amount of expressiveness, interviewers or other judges of applicants may look for particular styles of expressive nonverbal behavior, which indicate that the person is honest, ambitious, or easy to work with. Other nonverbal cues, such as style of dress, physical attractiveness, and indications of dominance, may likewise play an important role in how people are perceived in work settings (Henley, 1977; Riggio & Throckmorton, 1988). For example, it has been shown that attractively dressed and well-groomed individuals make better first impressions in certain work settings than persons who appear sloppy and unkempt (Arvey & Campion, 1982; Cann, Siegfried, & Pearce, 1981).

Ability to decode subtle nonverbal cues accurately is critically important for work supervisors, not only in helping to understand the subtle messages sent by supervisees, but also in building rapport and in helping the supervisor be responsive to the legitimate needs of workers (Riggio, 2001; Uhl-Bien, 2004).

Although nonverbal communication sometimes facilitates the flow of communication in work settings, misinterpreting such messages can also lead to considerable confusion and may disrupt work operations. Although there are well-known rules and techniques for learning to use appropriate written and spoken language, there are no firm guidelines governing nonverbal communication. Often the misunderstandings that occur in organizational communication, verbal and nonverbal, are related to the inadequate skills of the sender or receiver, or both. A great deal of attention is paid to trying to improve the verbal and writing skills of employees, and less concern is focused on nonverbal communication skills, even though they may represent a great deal of the critical communication that occurs in work settings.

The Flow of Communication in Work Organizations

Just as blood flows through the arteries, giving life to the body, messages flow through communication lines and networks, giving life to the work organization. If you look at the organizational chart of most organizations, you will see positions arranged in a pyramid-like hierarchy. Although this hierarchy is most commonly thought of as representing the lines of status and authority within the organization, it also depicts the lines of communication between superiors and subordinates. Formal messages travel back and forth along these routes between the top levels and the lower levels of the organization.

Downward, Upward, and Lateral Flow of Communication

The communication flow in work organizations is usually classified into three types: It can flow downward, through the organizational hierarchy; upward, through the same chain of command; or laterally, from colleague to colleague. Typically, each type of communication flow takes different forms and tends to contain different kinds of messages.

Downward communication consists of those messages sent from superiors to subordinates. Most commonly, they are one of several types: (a) instructions or directions concerning job performance, (b) information about organizational procedures and policies, (c) feedback to the supervisee concerning job performance, or (d) information to assist in the coordination of work tasks (Katz & Kahn, 1966). As you might guess, much of the formal communication that occurs in work organizations involves this downward flow, which makes sense, because the top levels are involved in making important decisions that must be communicated to the lower levels.

Although much formal communication in organizations is downward, research indicates that most organizations still do not have enough of this communication. A number of studies have found that workers would like more information from their superiors about work procedures and about what is happening elsewhere in the organization. One reason that downward communication is insufficient in some organizations is that superiors may overestimate the amount of information that their subordinates possess and may underestimate the amount they desire (Likert, 1961). Part of this problem is related to the fact that supervisors tend to overestimate how frequently and how clearly they communicate to supervisees (Callan, 1993).

It also appears that certain types of downward communication may be particularly limited, such as feedback concerning work performance (Baird, 1977). This is especially true in companies that fail to conduct regular performance appraisals. Also, organizations that neglect to provide workers with job descriptions and adequate orientation and training may experience a shortage of downward communication involving proper work procedures and company policies.

Research has shown that the frequency and quality of superior–subordinate communication influences important organizational outcomes (de Vries, Bakker-Pieper, & Oostenveld, 2010; Jablin, 1979). For example, downward communication from supervisors can affect new employees' adjustment to and satisfaction with the work group (Kramer, 1995). Research also suggests that supervisors need to be fair and consistent in their communication with subordinates, or workers can become concerned that supervisors are "playing favorites" (Sias & Jablin, 1995). Analysis of leader communication suggests that critical elements are that leaders should communicate that they are supportive of followers and that they are confident and assured in their leadership, and that leaders should be precise in their communications (de Vries, et al., 2010).

downward communication messages flowing downward in an organizational hierarchy, usually from superiors to subordinates

upward communication

messages flowing upward in an organizational hierarchy, usually taking the form of feedback

Upward communication is the flow of messages from the lower levels of the organization to the upper levels. It most typically consists of information managers need to perform their jobs, such as feedback concerning the status of lower-level operations, which could include reports of production output or information about any problems. The upward communication of feedback is critical for managers, who must use this information to make important work-related decisions. Upward communication can also involve complaints and suggestions for improvement from lower-level workers and is significant because it gives subordinates some input into the functioning of the organization. Research suggests that supervisors are more accepting of that feedback if they believe it is motivated by a desire for better performance/productivity (Lam, Huang, & Snape, 2007). Finally, an important form of upward feedback concerns subordinates' evaluations of the particular supervisor's effectiveness as a leader/supervisor (Smither, Wohlers, & London, 1995) (as we saw in Chapter 6 during our discussion of subordinate performance appraisals). Research indicates that the upward flow of suggestions for improvement can be increased when workers feel highly engaged in their jobs and they have a sense of self-efficacy (e.g., a sense that their suggestions will actually be considered and implemented) (Axtell, Holman, Unsworth, Wall, & Waterson, 2000; Frese, Teng, & Wijnen, 1999).

Unfortunately, in many organizations, there is simply not enough upward communication (see box Applying I/O Psychology). The upward communication of feedback about problems or difficulties in operations may be restricted because lower-level workers fear that the negative information might reflect poorly on their abilities, because managers neglect to ask for it, or because subordinates believe that management will not really listen to their suggestions and concerns.

lateral communication

messages between two parties at the same level in an organizational hierarchy

Lateral communication flows between people who are at the same level in the organizational hierarchy are particularly important when coworkers must coordinate their activities to accomplish a goal. Lateral communication can also occur between two or more departments within an organization. For example, effective lateral communication between the production and quality control departments in a television manufacturing plant can help the two departments to coordinate efforts to find and correct assembly errors. Lateral communication between departments also allows the sharing of news and information and helps in the development and maintenance of interpersonal relationships on the job (Hart, 2001; Koehler, Anatol, & Applbaum, 1981). Although it can help in coordinating worker activities within or between departments, thereby leading to increased productivity, "unauthorized" lateral communication, such as too much socializing on the job, can detract from effective job performance (Katz & Kahn, 1966).

BARRIERS TO THE EFFECTIVE FLOW OF COMMUNICATION

The upward, downward, and lateral flow of communication within an organization are subject to various types of information distortion that disrupt communication effectiveness by eliminating or changing key aspects of the message, so that the message that should be sent is not the one that the recipient receives. We will look closely at two types of distortion that affect communication flow in work organizations: filtering and exaggeration (Gaines, 1980).

Filtering is the selective presentation of the content of a communication; in other words, certain pieces of information are left out of the message. In downward communication, information is often filtered because it is considered to be unimportant to lower-level employees. Often, messages are sent telling workers what to do but not telling why it is being done. Information from upper levels of the organization may also be filtered because management fears the impact of the complete message on workers. For example, management may send a memo to workers about proposed cost-cutting measures, telling them that these actions are needed to increase efficiency and productivity. However, the fact that these cost-cutting measures are needed for the company to stay financially solvent is filtered out, because management is afraid that this information might cause workers to anticipate layoffs and thus begin to look for jobs elsewhere. Filtering of content in upward communication can occur if the information is unfavorable and the communicator fears incurring the wrath of the superior. In such cases, the negative information might be altered to make it appear less negative. Filtering in lateral communication can occur when two employees feel that they are in competition with one another for important organizational rewards, such as promotions and recognition from superiors. In such cases, workers continue to communicate, but may filter out any important information that is seen as giving the other person a competitive edge.

Sometimes, there is purposeful omission of a message to a receiver when a sender believes that the receiver does not need the information because it

filtering
the selective presentation of the content of a communication

APPLYING I/O PSYCHOLOGY

Increasing the Upward Flow of Organizational Communication

Most communication problems in work organizations relate to the insufficient flow of information, which results from a shortage in either downward communication or upward communication. However, because downward communication predominates in most work settings, and because it originates from those who have the most power and control over the organizational environment, attention must be given to increasing the flow of communication from those individuals at the bottom of the organization to those at the top, for a shortage of this communication has been associated with employee dissatisfaction and feelings that management is out of touch with employee needs and concerns. Several strategies that can increase upward communication follow.

Employee Suggestion Systems

There are a variety of procedures by which workers can submit ideas for improving some aspect of company operations. The suggestions are then reviewed by company decision makers, and beneficial ideas are implemented. Usually, suggestions are encouraged by some sort of incentive, such as recognition awards or cash prizes that are either fixed monetary amounts or amounts based on percentages of the savings that the suggestion produces. This form of upward communication can lead to innovations and improvement in company operations and can increase feelings of lower-level employees that they can indeed have some influence in the organization. One potential problem with suggestion systems

APPLYING I/O PSYCHOLOGY

(Continued)

is that employees may use it to voice complaints about conditions that management is unable to change.

Grievance Systems

A related concept is the establishment of formal complaint or grievance procedures. Whereas suggestion systems focus on positive changes, grievances are designed to change existing negative situations and thus must be handled more delicately to protect the employee from the retribution that can result when the complaint concerns mistreatment by someone higher in the organizational hierarchy. Also, to keep communication open and flowing, company officials must acknowledge the receipt of grievances and make it clear what action is to be taken (or why action will not or cannot be taken).

Subordinate Appraisals of Supervisory Performance

As we saw in our discussion of performance appraisals in Chapter 6, upward, subordinate appraisals of managerial performance can provide valuable feedback to improve supervisors' job performance, air the concerns of subordinates, and provide a starting point for the eventual improvement of supervisor–subordinate relationships.

Open-door Policies

The bottom-to-top flow of organizational communication can also be stimulated if upper-level managers establish an open-door policy, which involves setting aside times when employees can go directly to managers and discuss whatever is on their minds. This procedure bypasses the intermediate steps in the upward organizational chain, ensuring that important messages do indeed get to the top intact. The obvious drawback to the open-door policy is that a lot of the manager's time may be taken up by dealing with trivial or unimportant employee concerns.

Employee Surveys

Conducting an employee survey is an efficient and quick way to measure employees' attitudes about any aspect of organizational operations in an effort to target particular problem areas or solicit suggestions for improvement. (We discussed employee job satisfaction surveys in Chapter 9.) Because surveys offer the added benefit of anonymity, workers can respond honestly without fear of reprisal from management. As in all methods, feedback from management, in the form of either action taken or justification for not taking action, is critical for the program to operate effectively. Many times, companies will conduct an employee survey, look at the results, and do nothing. If feedback is not given, respondents will begin to see the survey as a waste of time, and future efforts will not be taken seriously.

Participative Decision Making

A number of strategies based on democratic or participative styles of management facilitate the upward flow of communication by involving employees in the process of making important decisions (Harrison, 1985). In participative decision making, employees can submit possible plans and discuss their benefits and drawbacks. They are then allowed to vote on the courses of action the company or work group will take. This strategy covers a wide range of programs and techniques that we will be studying in later chapters. However, any management technique that solicits employee input serves to increase the upward flow of communication.

is unimportant or would be disruptive to the receiver. Davis (1968) examined this sort of selective omission of information in the downward communications in a large manufacturing company. In this study, top management presented middle-level managers with two messages that were to be sent downward. The first message was important and concerned tentative plans for laying off workers. The second message was relatively unimportant, dealing with changes in the parking situation. The results of the study indicated that the middle managers altered the messages as a function of who was receiving the information. The important layoff information was passed on to 94% of the supervisors, who in turn presented it to only 70% of the assistant supervisors. The unimportant message about the parking changes was rarely communicated, with only 15% of the assistant supervisors eventually getting the message. In this case, the message was believed to be irrelevant to lower-level workers.

A potential sender may not forward a message when it involves bad news. This has been labeled the "MUM effect" (Tesser & Rosen, 1975). The MUM effect can be particularly detrimental to organizational functioning and effectiveness. For example, during the building of the U.S. Air Force's Stealth Bomber, the MUM effect was in operation as officers systematically suppressed bad news about the project's many problems from reaching higher-level officers. As a result, Pentagon officials continued to fund the project, because they were uninformed about the project's many technical problems and errors (Lee, 1993). In the space shuttle *Challenger* disaster, it was found that engineers believed that there was a reasonable probability that an engine might fail and explode, but they did not allow this to be conveyed to upper-level managers due to the MUM effect. Management may also be reluctant to communicate information downward concerning planned organizational downsizing (Guiniven, 2001).

Exaggeration is the distortion of information, which involves elaborating or overemphasizing certain aspects of the message. To draw attention to a problem, people may exaggerate its magnitude and impact. In downward communication, a supervisor might emphasize that if performance does not improve, subordinates may lose their jobs. In upward communication, workers might present a problem

exaggeration
the distortion of information by elaborating, overestimating, or minimizing parts of the message

"All those in favor say 'Aye.'"
"Aye."   "Aye."   "Aye."
"Aye."   "Aye."

Spoken messages are especially prone to distortion. © The New Yorker Collection 2002 Henry Martin from cartoonbank.com. All rights reserved.
Source: The Cartoon Bank.

as a crisis to get management to react and make some quick decisions. On the other hand, exaggeration may occur through the minimization of an issue, which involves making it seem like less of a problem than it actually is. This can happen, for example, when a worker wants to give the impression of competence and thus says that everything is under control when it is not (see box Up Close).

Certain factors increase or decrease the likelihood of distortion taking place in organizational communication. For example, spoken messages are more prone to distortion than are written messages. Regardless of form, a downward-flowing message from a high-status source is less likely to be intentionally altered than a communication originating from a low-status member. O'Reilly (1978) studied several factors related to communication distortion and specifically found a tendency for the greater distortion of upward messages that are unfavorable in content and less distortion of upward-flowing positive information. He also discovered that low trust in the receiver of a message resulted in a tendency toward distortion, particularly if the information reflected unfavorably on the sender.

CLOSE   Why Are Communication Breakdowns So Common in Organizations?

In many ways, the success of an organization depends on the efficient and effective flow of communication among its members. Even in very efficient and productive organizations, however, miscommunication seems to occur almost daily. Why are such breakdowns so common?

One answer is that many informal rules (or norms) in organizations appear to work against open and honest communication. Organizational members learn that it is important to engage in impression management, that is, to present oneself in a favorable light to get ahead in the company. It is not considered wise to admit to personal faults or limitations. Likewise, it is seen as important to project an air of self-confidence and competence. This may lead to a worker trying to tackle a very difficult task or problem alone, rather than asking for assistance. As we saw in studying hiring interviews, job applicants are particularly concerned with impression management. The resulting restricted communication may lead to a total mismatch between a worker's skills and abilities and the job requirements.

In competitive organizational settings, an air of mistrust of others may arise. As a result, verbal messages may not be entirely believed or may be seen as containing underlying alternative meanings ("What was he really saying to me?"). Mistrust is often present in organizations that have a history of not dealing honestly and openly with employees. This lack of trust may lead to limited communication, which is a serious problem for organizations whose lifeblood is the open flow of messages.

Another reason for communication breakdowns is employees' feelings of defensiveness, which often develop when their performance is criticized or questioned. Defensive postures by one participant are often followed by a defensive stance in another (Gibb, 1961). For example, when a work group has failed at some task, one group member might act defensively—"It wasn't my fault"—which then causes others to act in the same way. When employees become overly defensive, a communication breakdown can result. This defensiveness can also stifle employee creativity, as workers become afraid to take chances or to try new things for fear of being criticized.

Organizational communication breakdowns can also be caused by the tendency for people to undercommunicate. Workers generally assume that everyone in the work setting has access to the same information and possesses the same knowledge. Therefore, to avoid redundancy, a communicator may neglect to convey some important information to coworkers, assuming that they already know it. In reality, the other workers may not have the information or may have forgotten it and thus need to be reminded. Supervisors and managers are particularly prone to undercommunication, believing that subordinates do not need to be (or should not be) given certain information. This lack of communication flow can seriously disrupt productivity and may cause dissatisfaction among workers who feel as if they are left in the dark.

COMMUNICATION NETWORKS

In our discussion of the communication model and the downward, upward, and lateral flow of communication, we have been focusing on communication between two individuals, such as superior-to-subordinate or colleague-to-colleague. When we look beyond two-person communication to the linkages among work group, departmental, or organizational members, we are concerned with communication networks, which are systems of communication lines linking various senders and receivers.

The flow of organizational communication is regulated by several factors: the proximity of workers to one another, the rules governing who communicates with whom, the status hierarchy, and other elements of the work situation, such as job assignments and duties (Zahn, 1991). Thus, communication usually follows predictable patterns, or networks. Considerable research has been conducted on these networks and the properties associated with each. Five major types of communication networks have been studied in depth (Shaw, 1978; see Figure 11.2). The first three are termed centralized networks because the flow of information is centralized, or directed, through specific members. The next two are called decentralized networks, because the communication flow can originate at any point and does not have to be directed through certain central group members. Centralized networks are governed by members' status within the organization; decentralized networks typically are not. Often, decentralized networks are controlled by factors such as proximity of members to one another, or the personal preferences of the sender.

Centralized networks

The first centralized communication network, which is known as the *chain*, represents a five-member status hierarchy. A message typically originates at the top or at the bottom of the chain and works its way upward or downward

communication networks
systematic lines of communication among various senders and receivers

🕑 Stop & Review

List and describe four strategies for improving the upward flow of communication in organizations.

centralized networks
communication networks in which the flow of communication is directed through specific members

decentralized networks
communication networks in which messages can originate at any point and need not be directed through specific group members

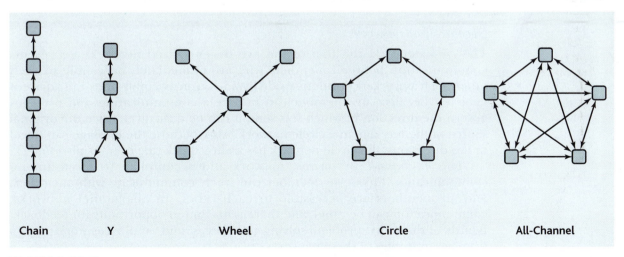

| Chain | Y | Wheel | Circle | All-Channel |

FIGURE 11.2
Communication Networks

through the different links. An example might be a message concerning some changes in the formula for payroll deductions. The director of human resources is the source of the message, which is then passed to the payroll manager, who in turn gives the instructions to the assistant payroll manager, who then tells the payroll supervisor. Finally, the payroll supervisor passes the message along to the clerk who will implement the changes. A message that is to go from the clerk to the human resources director must follow the same pattern. As you might guess, the chain is a relatively slow process, but it is direct, with all levels of the hierarchy being made aware of the message because it must pass through each link. A related communication network is the *Y* (which is actually an upside-down Y). The Y is also a hierarchical network, representing four levels of status within the organization, but its last link involves communication to more than one person. The inverted Y is a model of the communication network typically involved in a traditional, pyramid-shaped organization. The president issues an order to the chief of operations, who then tells the work supervisor. The work supervisor then gathers the bottom-line workers and gives them the order. In the other direction, the front-line supervisor is responsible for gathering information from bottom-line workers that must be sent upward. The chain and the Y networks are very similar in terms of speed of transmission and the formality of who communicates with whom.

The *wheel* network involves two status levels: a higher-status member (usually a work supervisor) and four lower-level members. The higher-status member is the hub, or center, through which all communication must pass. In the wheel network, there are no direct communication links between the lower-level members. An example might be a sales manager and four salespersons out in the field, each of who receives instructions directly from the manager and then sends information about sales activities back to the manager. However, the salespersons do not have any direct contact with one another, only indirect contact as information is relayed through the supervisor.

Decentralized networks

The *circle* network, the first of the two decentralized networks, represents communication between members who are immediately accessible to each other, such as workers positioned side by side on an assembly line or in adjacent cubicles. Because any member can initiate a communication and no rules govern the direction in which it is sent, it can be difficult to trace the original source of the message in a circle network. Also, because the message can travel in two directions, the circle network has a fairly quick rate of transmission.

The *all-channel*, or *comcon*, network allows complete freedom among communication links. Any member can freely communicate with any other, and all members are accessible to each other. In all-channel networks, communication can be rapid, and there is maximum opportunity for feedback. Boards of directors, problem-solving task forces, and employees working as a team are examples of these networks.

There has been extensive research on communication networks, most of which has been conducted in laboratory settings. The results of these studies indicate that each of the different networks has different strengths and weaknesses. For example, the centralized networks (the chain, Y, and wheel) are faster and make fewer errors in dealing with simple, repetitive tasks than do decentralized networks. This makes sense because the central person through whom all messages must pass can coordinate group activities because that individual has all the information needed to perform the simple tasks. Decentralized networks (circle and all-channel), on the other hand, are better at dealing with complex tasks, such as abstract problem solving (Leavitt, 1951; Shaw, 1964). In general, straightforward, repetitive tasks, such as assembly or manufacturing work, tend to operate well with a centralized communication network, whereas creative tasks, such as a group working on a product advertising campaign, are best accomplished using a decentralized network. One reason why centralized networks may have difficulty in solving complex problems is because the central people may be subject to information overload: They may have too much information to deal with efficiently. Because all the messages cannot be passed on intact to the various network members efficiently and quickly, group performance suffers.

The type of communication network used can also affect the satisfaction of network members. Generally, because of the restrictions on who can initiate communication and on who can communicate with whom, members in centralized networks have lower levels of satisfaction than those in decentralized networks (Shaw, 1964). More specifically, in the centralized networks, the persons holding the central positions tend to have high levels of satisfaction due to their role, whereas the noncentral members have extremely low satisfaction (Bavelas, 1950).

Some of the research on communication networks has been criticized for oversimplifying the communication process. Evidence suggests that the differences in speed and efficiency among the various networks may disappear over time, as the group involved learns to adjust to the required communication patterns (Burgess, 1968). For example, members of decentralized networks may learn to cut down on the amount of member discussion to speed up the decision-making process. Because most of the research on communication networks has been conducted in controlled laboratory settings, there is some concern about whether the results of these studies will generalize to communication networks in actual work settings, although the findings do indeed allow us to model (although simplistically) the communication patterns in work organizations.

Stop & Review

Define and give examples of the two barriers to effective communication.

FORMAL AND INFORMAL LINES OF COMMUNICATION: THE HIERARCHY VERSUS THE GRAPEVINE

So far we have been discussing the formal lines of communication, or how organizational members are supposed to communicate with one another. We have also seen that the official lines of communication in an organization are illustrated in the company's organizational chart, or organigram, which is a diagram of the hierarchy. When official messages must be sent up or down the hierarchy, they typically follow the lines shown in the organigram. The

organigram
a diagram of an orga-nization's hierarchy representing the formal lines of communication

formal lines of communication are usually governed by the organizational status or authority of the different members. However, although every organization possesses formal lines of communication, each also has informal communication lines, known as the grapevine. Just as a real grapevine twists and turns, branching out wherever it pleases, the organizational grapevine can follow any course through a network of organizational members. Throughout the workday, messages are passed from one worker to another along the grapevine. Because much of the daily communication that occurs in work organizations is informal, the organizational grapevine is an important element for I/O psychologists to study.

Whereas formal communication lines are represented by the organigram, the informal lines of communication among work group or organizational members are illustrated by the sociogram. In effect, the sociogram is a diagram of the organizational grapevine. Sociograms are used to study the informal contacts and communications occurring among organizational members (see Figure 11.3). In studying informal communication networks, workers are surveyed to determine which other organizational members they typically interact with (Monge & Eisenberg, 1987; Stork & Richards, 1992).

Baird (1977) suggested that three factors determine the pattern of communication links that form the grapevine: friendship, usage, and efficiency. In the informal communication network, people pass information on to their friends, which is only natural. We communicate with those people we like and avoid communicating informally with those people we do not like. Friendship is thus perhaps the most important factor that holds the grapevine together. In addition, persons who are used as communication links for other purposes will also be used as links in the grapevine. For example, workers who often come into contact with one another for job-related reasons are more likely to start sharing information informally. Finally, the grapevine sometimes develops because it is easier and more efficient for workers to follow their own informal networks rather than the formal lines of communication. An organizational member who needs to communicate something immediately may try to get the message through via the grapevine rather than by using the slow and cumbersome formal communication lines. For example, a low-ranking organizational member who wants to get a message to somebody high up in the organizational hierarchy may find it quicker and more efficient to rely on the grapevine to transmit the message, rather than going through the formal organizational channels that involve relaying the message through a successive chain of higher-status managers.

In addition to being a substitute network for formal lines of communication, the grapevine also serves a vital function in maintaining social relationships among workers. Because most formal communication tends to be task-oriented, focusing on jobs and job outcomes, the grapevine helps to meet the social communication needs of workers (which Mayo and his associates in the human relations movement long ago determined were so important to workers). Through informal communication contacts and the subsequent development of strong work friendships, the grapevine can help to bring workers together and encourage them to develop a sense of unity and commitment to the work group and the organization, which can play a big part in reducing absenteeism

grapevine
the informal communication network in an organization

sociogram
a diagram of the informal lines of communication among organizational members

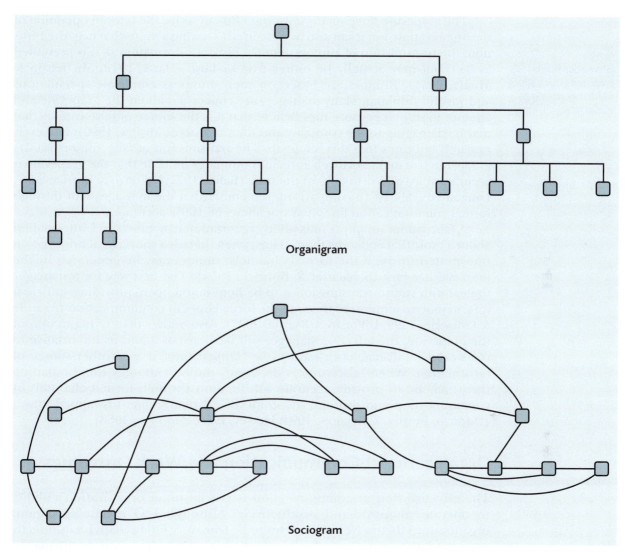

Organigram

Sociogram

FIGURE 11.3
The Organigram versus the Sociogram

and turnover rates (Baird, 1977). The grapevine can also help in reiterating important messages that have been sent through formal communication channels. For example, an employee might be reminded through the grapevine of important deadlines or company policies that were originally announced in memos or bulletins. In one interesting study, it was found that when innovations or changes were introduced to an organization, workers first learned about the innovation through formal communication channels. However, it was the amount of communication flowing through the organization's informal channels that influenced how quickly the innovation would actually be adopted by the work groups (Weenig, 1999).

The grapevine serves many important functions for the smooth operation of the organization, but it can also be perceived as having a somewhat negative function: the transmission of rumors. Rumors involve information that is presented as fact, but may actually be either true or false (Davis, 1972; Michelson & Mouly, 2004). Rumors are based on such things as employee speculations and wishful thinking. Many managers are concerned about the grapevine and attempt to stifle it because they believe that it is the source of false rumors that may be damaging to the company and the workforce (Mishra, 1990). However, research indicates that this is a myth. The transmission of false rumors via the grapevine is actually relatively rare, and estimates indicate that the grapevine is accurate at least 75% to 80% of the time (Baird, 1977; DiFonzo & Bordia, 2007; Langan-Fox, 2001). In comparison, remember that the messages sent through formal communication lines may not always be 100% accurate.

A false rumor usually results when organizational members lack information about a topic that concerns them. Thus, when there is a shortage of information transmitted through the formal channels, rumors may be generated by the informal network (Schachter & Burdick, 1955). The best way for a manager to deal with rumor transmission is to be honest and open, providing sufficient information to employees through the formal lines of communication (Akande & Odewale, 1994; DiFonzo & Bordia, 2007). Also, rather than trying to uproot the grapevine, the effective manager will be aware of it and its importance to the workers and may even want to be "tapped into" it as another source of information. When false rumors do occur, the best strategy for combatting them may be to provide accurate information through formal channels of communication and through the grapevine, if management is tapped into it (Difonzo, Bordia, & Rosnow, 1994; Hersey, 1966; Zaremba, 1988).

rumors
information that is presented as fact, but which may actually be true or false

Organizational Communication and Work Outcomes

The effective flow of communication is crucial to an organization's ability to operate smoothly and productively. Although I/O psychologists and organizations themselves believe this to be true, very little research has directly examined the impact of communication on organizational performance (Porter & Roberts, 1976). In 12 district offices of a state social services agency, one comprehensive study looked at the relationships among reported organizational communication effectiveness and five independent measures of organizational performance, including the number of clients served, the costs of operation, and the costs of operation per client served (Snyder & Morris, 1984). Questionnaires administered to more than 500 employees assessed perceptions of different types of organizational communication, which included two forms of downward communication—the adequacy of information provided concerning organizational policies and procedures, and the skills of supervisors as communicators. One form of lateral communication—the information exchange within the work group, and one type of downward communication—the feedback given about individual performance, were also measured. The results indicated that the amount of communication, particularly the lateral communication within work groups, and the communication skills of supervisors were related to more cost-effective organizational performance. In another study, it was found that employees' satisfaction with the amount and quality of organizational communication was positively correlated with measures of worker productivity—those who reported receiving more and better communication were the most productive workers (Clampitt & Downs, 1993). A laboratory study found that group performance on a manual task—assembling a complex toy—was related to the quality of communication. Specifically, if the groups engaged in high-quality "cycles" of communication, including interactions that involved orienting the group to the task, planning how the work would be done, and evaluating the outcomes, then the groups outperformed those who did not have systematic cycles of communication (Tschan, 1995). Finally, it is clear that communication technology, such as e-mail, cellular phones, and Web-based communications, have had an important impact on increasing worker productivity, although workers can waste their valuable work time on personal e-mail communications and non-work-related Web surfing (Langan-Fox, 2001).

Although effective communication can lead to bottom-line payoffs in terms of increased productivity, it can also create increased levels of employee satisfaction. Research suggests positive relationships between the amount of upward communication in an organization and feelings of satisfaction in lower-level workers (Koehler, Anatol, & Applbaum, 1981). It has also been demonstrated that employees who receive a great deal of information about the organization in the form of downward communication tend to be more satisfied and have higher organizational commitment than those who do not (Ng, Butts, Vandenberg, DeJoy, & Wilson, 2006). In fact, even employees who were overloaded with so much downward communication that their job performance was hampered tended to be satisfied with more downward communication (O'Reilly, 1980). Moreover, serving as a communication source is also linked to increased levels of satisfaction (Muchinsky, 1977b).

In addition to job performance and job satisfaction, effective communication may also have an impact on absenteeism and turnover rates. Although research has not directly addressed this relationship, one study found that open and supportive downward communication helped one organization retain its "surviving" workers after a companywide downsizing. Moreover, communication seemed to be very important in reducing worker stress and maintaining job satisfaction during the downsizing (Johnson, Bernhagen, Miller, & Allen, 1996). Keeping downward and upward communication flowing is considered to be a crucial best practice when effectively managing a major organizational change such as downsizing or organizational restructuring (Marks, 2007; Marks & Mirvis, 2010).

Although it makes sense that organizations with free and open lines of communication would tend to have more satisfied workers, leading to lowered rates of absenteeism and turnover, open communication among workers can also have some drawbacks. For example, researchers who examined the patterns of turnover among workers in three fast-food restaurants found that workers tended to quit their jobs in clusters. Most importantly, the clusters tended to be among workers who communicated freely with one another, a phenomenon that has been termed the "snowball effect" (Krackhardt & Porter, 1986).

Stop & Review

List the five communication network types and give examples of each.

All in all, when dealing with organizational communication, more is usually better, although there may be a few exceptions, as when workers engage in so much non-work-related communication or are so deluged with messages and other information that job performance is impaired. Although much evidence indicates that it is usually better to keep communication flowing, open, and honest, some researchers claim that, because of organizational politics, at times organizational members might want to close some communication lines and keep certain types of information to themselves (see, e.g., Eisenberg & Witten, 1987).

In summary, it appears that many organizations can benefit from greater amounts of communication and that companies can work to make organizational communication more accurate and effective. Top-level managers need to be aware of employees' needs for information and must open the flow of downward communication to provide for these needs. On the other hand, there needs to be a greater upward flow of communication to make management aware of what is going on at the lower levels of the company and to increase employee participation in and commitment to the organization. It also appears that increased lateral communication plays an important role in the ability of work groups to get the job done and in the development and maintenance of inter-personal relationships on the job. All of this can lead to more positive outcomes for the individuals, work groups, and organizations involved.

Summary

Communication is crucial for effective organizational performance. The basic communication model begins with the *sender*, who is responsible for *encoding* the message, which involves choosing some mutually understood code for transmitting the message to another person. The sender also selects a vehicle for communication, or the *channel*. The task of the *receiver* is to *decode* the message in an effort to understand its original meaning. The receiver also sends *feedback* to indicate that the message was received and understood. Any factors that disrupt the effective flow of communication from sender to receiver are referred to as *noise*.

Research on the communication process has examined the factors that can influence communication effectiveness. *Source factors* are variables related to the sender, such as status, credibility, and communication skills, which can influence the effectiveness of communication. *Channel factors* are variables related to the actual communication vehicle that can enhance or detract from the flow of communication from sender to receiver. In verbal communication, semantic problems, or the use of technical language termed *jargon*, can sometimes disrupt the communication flow. *Audience factors*, such as the decoding skills and attention span of the receiver, can also play a role in the communication process.

Nonverbal communication has a subtle but important effect on communication in work settings. It can be used as a substitute for verbal communication, to enhance verbal messages or to send true feelings. Receivers may also use nonverbal cues as an additional information source or as a means of forming impressions about people. A *Pygmalion effect* can occur if a sender holds positive expectations about a worker's performance and subtly influences that worker's performance via nonverbal communication.

Communication can flow in three directions through the organizational hierarchy: upward, downward, or laterally. *Downward communication* typically involves messages sent from superiors to subordinates; *upward communication* flows from the lower levels of the organization; and *lateral communication* occurs between persons at the same status level. *Filtering* and *exaggeration* are two types of distortion that often disrupt the effective flow of organizational communication.

Much of our knowledge of organizational communication patterns comes from research conducted on *communication networks*, which can be grouped into two types: *centralized*, in which messages move through central members, and *decentralized*, in which communication paths are not directed through specific network members. The formal communication patterns in organizations are represented in the organizational chart, or *organigram*. The informal lines of communication, or *grapevine*, are illustrated in a *sociogram*. The formal lines of communication carry messages that are sanctioned by the organization, whereas the grapevine is an informal network through which messages are passed from worker to worker. Managers are sometimes wary of the grapevine because they see it as a source of *rumors*, although research indicates that the grapevine can be a highly accurate and important information network.

Research suggests that greater and more effective organizational communication is linked to improved levels of performance and job satisfaction. Moreover, there may be links between open, flowing organizational communication and rates of employee absenteeism and turnover.

Study Questions and Exercises

1. List the steps in the basic communication model. Which factors influence the effective flow of communication at each of the steps?

2. In what ways can nonverbal communication affect the interaction between a supervisor and a subordinate? Between two same-status coworkers?

3. Think of an organization with which you have had some contact, such as a work organization, a club or social group, or your college or university. What forms of downward, upward, and lateral communication take place in this organization? How could the flow of each direction of communication be improved?

4. Consider the five types of communication networks. What are the characteristics of each? Can you think of any special work groups that illustrate each network?

5. In what ways will the sources, channels, and audiences of the formal lines of communication and the informal lines of communication (grapevine) in an organization differ?

Web Links

www.aom.pace.edu/ocis
Site for the Academy of Management's Division of Organizational Communication and Information Systems.

Suggested Readings

Matsumoto, D. (Ed.). (2010). *APA handbook of inter-cultural communication training.* Washington, DC: American Psychological Association. *This edited book covers all areas of intercultural communication— edited by a recognized research expert in intercultural issues.*

Putnam, L., & Krone, K. J. (Eds.). (2006). *Organizational communication.* Thousand Oaks, CA: Sage. *This 5-volume set covers all areas of organizational communication—a good starting point for an in-depth research paper.*

Manusov, V. L., & Patterson, M. L. (Eds.). (2006). *The SAGE handbook of nonverbal communication.* Thousand Oaks, CA: Sage. *A detailed guidebook to all aspects of nonverbal communication, including nonverbal communication in the workplace.*

Management Communication Quarterly and *Journal of Business and Technical Communication*, both published by Sage Publications, and *The Journal of Business Communication*, published by the Association for Business Communication. *These journals contain articles on the theory and practice of management and business communication. Recent topics include intercultural communication, computer-mediated communication, and state-of-the-art communication technology.*

CHAPTER

12

Group Processes
in Work Organizations

CHAPTER OUTLINE

Inside Tips

GROUP PROCESSES: THE CORE OF ORGANIZATIONS

A knowledge of group dynamics, or the processes by which groups function, is central to understanding how work organizations operate, because they are made up of smaller work groups. This chapter builds on Chapter 11's discussion of workplace communication, for it is communication that holds people together in work groups. This chapter also sets the stage for the next three chapters on organizational processes. In particular, Chapter 13, on leadership, studies a very important ongoing process in work groups: the relationship between the leader and the other members of the group. Chapter 14, which examines influence, power, and politics, continues the discussion of group processes presented in this chapter by considering how these three social processes operate in work groups and larger work organizations. Chapter 15 moves to the next level—the design and structure of work organizations—to explore how work groups link to form larger organizations.

You may already be familiar with some of the concepts presented in this chapter. For example, conformity, roles, norms, and conflict are central not only in industrial/organizational psychology but also in other specialty areas of psychology and in other behavioral sciences. Here, however, we will be applying these concepts specifically to the study of behavior in work settings. Other topics, such as organizational socialization and interorganizational conflict, are more particular to I/O psychology. This chapter represents a blending of some older, traditional concepts with some newer ones.

Many of the issues involved in describing group processes are particularly complex. Specifically, the concept of groupthink, with its many interrelated symptoms, merits attention. The different levels of conflict described in this chapter also have similar-sounding names that can be confusing. An inside tip is to remember that the prefix "intra-" means "within," whereas the prefix "inter-" means "between" or "among." Therefore, "intragroup" means within a group, whereas "intergroup" means between groups.

You have been working for some time with the same group of coworkers. At first, you felt like an outsider, but you soon learned your way around and began to feel like an accepted team member. You have noticed, however, that although group members often cooperate with one another, they don't always. Moreover, when the pressure is on, group members can engage in some very interesting (and seemingly bizarre) behavior. There is an important and much anticipated meeting of the entire department where crucial issues will be discussed and important decisions made. As you enter the room, with a mixture of anticipation and trepidation, you wonder how it will all go…

Work organizations are made up of individuals, but typically these individuals are tied together by their membership in particular work groups. A work group might be a department, a job classification, a work team, or an informal group of coworkers who socialize during lunch and after work to discuss work-related problems and issues. Groups are very important to the functioning of work organizations, for the members of a group can pool their talents, energy, and knowledge to perform complex tasks. Work groups also help provide professional identities for members and satisfy human needs for social interaction and the development of interpersonal relationships on the job. Finally, groups help establish rules for proper behavior in the work setting and play a part in determining the courses of action that the work group and the organization will follow. The study of work groups is an important topic in I/O psychology (Sanna & Parks, 1997).

In this chapter, we will examine work groups and their processes. We will begin by defining groups, looking at the different roles within groups, and considering what holds groups together. Next, we will study the processes of cooperation, competition, and conflict, which are regular parts of work group functioning. We will then look at how work groups affect organizational decision making and how group decision making affects organizational outcomes. Finally, we will focus on those special groups or interconnected workers that we refer to as teams.

Defining Work Groups and Teams

A group can be defined as two or more individuals, engaged in social interaction, for the purposes of achieving some goal. In work settings this goal is usually work related, such as producing a product or service. However, groups at work may form merely to develop and maintain social relationships. Work groups can be either formal—put together by the organization to perform certain tasks and handle specific responsibilities—or informal, developing naturally. Informal work groups might include groups of workers who regularly get together after work to discuss their jobs.

Whereas groups are individuals working toward a goal, a team consists of interdependent workers with complementary skills working toward a shared goal or outcome. We will be discussing historical and recent research on group processes, and the term "group" is typically used, but some of these groups are clearly "teams" with interdependency and shared goals. At the end of the chapter we will focus more specifically on research that involves clearly defined teams.

ROLES

Within work groups (and teams), members can play various roles, or patterns of behavior, that are adopted on the basis of expectations about the functions of a particular position. Group roles are important because they help provide some specific plan for behavior. When a worker is playing a particular role within a group, that person usually knows something about the responsibilities and requirements of the role, or the role expectations. In most work groups, members are quite aware of the various expectations associated with each of the different positions within the group.

As a work group develops, the various members learn to become responsible for different aspects of its functioning. In other words, members begin to play different roles within the work group. This process whereby group members learn about and take on various defined roles is called role differentiation. For example, a new worker who enters a work group may immediately fall into the role of novice worker. However, that person may later develop a reputation for having a good sense of humor and thus begin to play the role of jokester, providing levity when situations get too tense or when boredom sets in.

One important role that is clearly differentiated in most work groups is that of leader. The leader in a formal work group or department plays an important part in directing group activities, being spokesperson for the group, and deciding which courses of action the group will follow. Because of its significance, we will consider the topic of leadership in great depth in Chapter 13.

group
two or more individuals engaged in social interaction to achieve some goal

team
interdependent workers with complementary skills working toward a shared goal

roles
patterns of behavior that are adapted based on expectations about the functions of a position

role expectations
beliefs concerning the responsibilities and requirements of a particular role

role differentiation
the process by which group members learn to perform various roles

As a civilian analyst, this woman plays a clearly defined role in this military group, identifying tactical problems and possible solutions.

The various roles in work groups are often created based on factors such as position or formal job title, status within the group, the tasks to which a member is assigned, or the possession of some particular work skill or ability. For example, employees who are designated as assistant supervisor, senior mechanic, or communications specialist perform specific roles and engage in certain behaviors consistent with these job titles. Although workers can be designated as playing certain usual roles within the work group, they can perform different functional roles at different times. Two early researchers outlined a wide range of work roles, which they grouped into three categories (Benne & Sheats, 1948; see Table 12.1). The first category, *group task roles*, is related to getting the job done. Group task roles are given such titles as information giver, procedural technician, and evaluator–critic. For example, a machinist in a cardboard container factory who outlines the steps necessary for the work group to construct and assemble a new type of box is playing the procedural technician role. The second category of functional roles is *group building and maintenance* roles. These deal with the maintenance of interpersonal relations among group members and include such roles as encourager, harmonizer, and compromiser. A worker who plays an active part in settling an argument between two coworkers may be taking on the harmonizer role. The third category, called *self-centered roles*, involves satisfying personal rather than group goals. Titles of these roles include recognition seeker, aggressor, and help seeker. Employees who look to others for assistance in completing their own work assignments are playing the help-seeker role. It has been suggested that workers may or may not define prosocial behaviors—the organizational citizenship behaviors that we discussed in Chapter 9—as part of their defined work role, rather than viewing OCBs (Organizational Citizenship Behaviors) as "extrarole" behaviors (Tepper,

---

TABLE 12.1

The Various Roles Individuals Play in Work Groups

Group Task Roles

Initiator–contributor: Recommends new ideas about, or novel solutions to, a problem
Information seeker: Emphasizes getting facts and other information from others
Opinion seeker: Solicits inputs concerning the attitudes or feelings about ideas under
    consideration
Information giver: Contributes relevant information to help in decision making
Opinion giver: Provides own opinions and feelings
Elaborator: Clarifies and expands on the points made by others
Coordinator: Integrates information from the group
Orientor: Guides the discussion and keeps it on the topic when the group digresses
Evaluator–critic: Uses some set of standards to evaluate the group's accomplishments
Energizer: Stimulates the group to take action
Procedural technician: Handles routine tasks such as providing materials or supplies
Recorder: Keeps track of the group's activities and takes minutes

Group Building and Maintenance Roles

Encourager: Encourages others' contributions
Harmonizer: Tries to resolve conflicts between group members
Compromiser: Tries to provide conflicting members with a mutually agreeable solution
Gatekeeper: Regulates the flow of communication so that all members can have a say
Standard setter: Sets standards or deadlines for group actions
Group observer: Makes objective observations about the tone of the group interaction
Follower: Accepts the ideas of others and goes along with group majority

Self-centered Roles

Aggressor: Tries to promote own status within group by attacking others
Blocker: Tries to block all group actions and refuses to go along with group
Recognition seeker: Tries to play up own achievements to get group's attention
Self-confessor: Uses group discussion to deal with personal issues
Playboy: Engages in humor and irrelevant acts to draw attention away from the tasks
Dominator: Attempts to monopolize the group
Help seeker: Attempts to gain sympathy by expressing insecurity or inadequacy
Special interest pleader: Argues incessantly to further own desires

Source: Benne K. D., & Sheats, P. (1948). Functional roles of group members. *Journal of Social Issues, 4,* 41–49.

Lockhart, & Hoobler, 2001). The fact that there are so many different roles that members can play in work group functioning illustrates the complexity of the processes that occur daily in work groups.

It is important to mention that sometimes workers are unclear about the requirements of the various roles they are expected to play in the workplace. This can lead to role ambiguity, or a sense of uncertainty over the requirements of a particular role an individual is expected to play. Role ambiguity, like job ambiguity (see Chapter 10), is an important source of workplace stress.

role ambiguity
a sense of uncertainty over the requirements of a particular role

In organizations, persons often are expected to play more than one role at a time. In some cases, the behaviors expected of an individual due to one role may not be consistent with the expectations concerning another role. Instances such as these give rise to role conflict. Role conflict is quite common, particularly in positions that require workers to be members of different groups simultaneously. For example, imagine that you are the supervisor of a work group. One of your roles involves holding the group together and protecting the interests of its members. However, you are also a member of the organization's management team, and in this role you are ordered to transfer a very talented and very popular work group member, against her wishes, to another department. Because you cannot satisfy the two incompatible goals of holding the team together while carrying out the organization's plan to transfer the worker, you experience role conflict, another form of stress that can have negative effects on job satisfaction, performance, and mental and physical well-being.

role conflict
conflict that results when the expectations associated with one role interfere with the expectations concerning another role

Norms

Work groups contain various members, each playing different roles, but all members, regardless of their role, must adhere to certain group rules. Norms are the rules that groups adopt to indicate appropriate and inappropriate behavior for members. Group norms can be formalized as written work rules, but are most commonly informal and unrecorded. Norms can govern any work activity, including the speed with which a person should perform a job, proper modes of dress, acceptable topics for group conversation, and even who sits where in the employee lunchroom. According to Feldman (1984), norms develop in a number of ways. They can come from explicit statements made by supervisors or coworkers. For example, a supervisor might tell group members, "No one goes home until the work area is spotlessly clean." This leads to a norm that all workers stop working 15 minutes before quitting time to clean up the work area. Group leaders or powerful group members often play an important role in such norm formation. Norms can also evolve from the group's history. For example, if a certain work procedure leads to a disastrous outcome, the group may place a ban on its use. In other instances, norms may be carried over from past situations. When a member changes groups, norms from the old group may be imported to the new one. For example, a sales supervisor was transferred from the corporate office to a regional sales office. On her first day in the new office, she commented on the casual dress of employees by saying, "At the corporate office, men always wear suits and ties and women always wear skirts or dresses." From the next day on, a new dress code of more formal attire developed.

norms
rules that groups adopt governing appropriate and inappropriate behavior for members

Norms serve many important purposes for groups. First and foremost, they are established to help the group survive. A group must be able to produce enough to ensure the economic success of the group and the organization. Therefore, some norms will develop to facilitate group production. On the other hand, if members feel that production rates are too high and will possibly lead to layoffs, norms to restrict group output (called "rate setting") may arise. Norms can also develop that help commit work group members to producing higher-quality products or services, and norms can even develop in organizations and groups that compel workers to be innovative and "entrepreneurial" (Anderson & West, 1998; Russell & Russell, 1992). Work groups can develop norms that result in high levels of positive work behaviors, such as organizational citizenship behavior (Erhart & Naumann, 2004), but norms encouraging counterproductive work behaviors can also occur (Fox & Spector, 2005).

Norms also help increase the predictability of members' behavior. For example, norms regarding speaking turns and the length of time that one may hold the floor in group meetings, as well as norms regarding the structure and content of meetings, may ease the flow of the meetings and avoid embarrassment (Niederman & Volkema, 1999). Researchers have even studied the norms that evolve in online communication and chat networks (Dietz-Uhler, Bishop-Clark, & Howard, 2005). Finally, norms provide a sense of identity for the group by giving members a chance to express their shared values and beliefs. For example, if an advertising agency believes that they are responsible for setting advertising trends, a norm for producing advertisements that are unique or novel may develop.

In summary, both roles and norms help provide a structure and plan for group members' behavior. They play an important part in regulating group activities and in helping group members to achieve shared goals. In addition, norms and, to some extent, roles provide some of the foundation of a company's organizational culture (a topic we will consider in Chapter 15).

ORGANIZATIONAL SOCIALIZATION: LEARNING GROUP ROLES AND NORMS

A critical area of research that has received a great deal of attention from I/O psychologists is organizational socialization, or the process by which new employees become integrated into work groups. Companies today often refer to organizational socialization as the "onboarding process" (Bauer & Erdogan, 2011). Organizational socialization includes three important processes: (a) the development of specific work skills and abilities, (b) the acquisition of a set of appropriate role behaviors, and (c) adjustment to the work group's norms and values (Anakwe & Greenhaus, 1999; Feldman, 1981; Schein, 1968). The first process—learning specific work skills and abilities—is the main goal of personnel training, which was discussed in depth in Chapter 7. The other two processes—the acquisition of roles and role behaviors and the learning of group norms—are of particular interest here. New employees learn about group roles and norms in the same way that they learn new job skills, specifically by observing and imitating the behaviors of others. Newcomers may look to established workers as role models and try to copy their successful work behaviors (Louis, Posner, & Powell, 1983). For example, a novice trial attorney may watch the way that a seasoned senior partner handles herself in court and at firm meetings to learn about the expected role behaviors for the firm's successful attorneys. New employees may also learn about group norms by being reinforced for performing appropriate behaviors and being punished for inappropriate actions. A new salesperson in a busy clothing store may learn about norms for

> **Stop & Review**
>
> Describe and define three categories of work roles.

> **organizational socialization**
> the process by which new employees learn group roles and norms and develop specific work skills and abilities

appropriate employee dress and the usual procedures for handling impatient customers through receiving a reinforcing smile and nod, or a disapproving frown, from the sales manager.

Typically, organizational socialization occurs in stages, as one moves from being a newcomer to a fully functioning and contributing member of the work group (Wanous, Reichers, & Malik, 1984). One model outlines three stages in the socialization of new employees (Feldman, 1976a, 1976b). The first is *anticipatory socialization.* Here newcomers develop a set of realistic expectations concerning the job and the organization and determine if the organization will provide the right match with their abilities, needs, and values. The second stage in the process is *accommodation.* In this stage, new employees learn about the various roles that work group members play and about their own specific roles in the group. They also begin to "learn the ropes" as they discover important work group norms and standards. In this second stage, the newcomers begin to develop interpersonal relationships with other group members. In the third stage, *role management,* newcomers make the transition to regular members or insiders, mastering the tasks and roles they must perform. As they move through this stage, they eventually have a thorough knowledge of all facets of work group norms and operations.

Although all new employees are likely to pass through the same stages in the organizational socialization process, research indicates that employees may be socialized at different rates, depending on the characteristics of the workers and of the work environment (Reichers, 1987; Taormina, 2009). For example, workers who are forced to move from an old, established work group or organization to a new setting because of layoffs or geographical moves may have a more difficult time becoming socialized than workers who voluntarily make the move. Research has clearly shown that supervisors and coworkers play an important part in the successful socialization of new employees by establishing positive relationships and mentoring newcomers (Major, Kozlowski, Chao, & Gardner, 1995; Ostroff & Kozlowski, 1993). Research suggests that structured and regular socialization that focuses on employees' job learning and career progression is better than less-systematic socialization processes (Cable & Parsons, 2001). The lesson is that new employee socialization should be planned and systematic—part of an integrated employee orientation and training program.

Workers can also play an active part in their own socialization (Ashford & Black, 1996; Saks & Ashforth, 1997). For example, newcomer attitudes and willingness to become a part of the new work group can play an important role in how quickly and smoothly socialization occurs. It may also be the case that prior work experience and personality characteristics of workers may affect socialization rates (Adkins, 1995; Ostroff & Kozlowski, 1992).

Organizations can also greatly facilitate the socialization of new employees (Ashforth & Saks, 1996). Good employee orientation and training programs are essential to the process, as are the work group's openness and willingness to welcome new members. One technique for encouraging employee socialization is to link newcomers with established, knowledgeable workers, an approach similar to the mentoring concept discussed in Chapter 7. The more quickly new employees are socialized into the work group and organization, the faster they will become productive and valuable workers. Research also indicates that effective socialization is related to reduced work stress, reductions in employee turnover rates, increased organizational commitment, and employee career success (Allen, 2006; Ashforth, Saks, & Lee, 1998; Cable & Parsons, 2001; Feldman, 1989; Nelson, 1987).

Basic Group Processes

Several basic social processes that occur in all work groups help to hold the groups together, regulate group behavior, coordinate group activities, and stimulate action by group members. In the following section we will consider five of these processes: conformity, group efficacy, cohesiveness, cooperation, and competition. A final group process, conflict, will be considered under a separate heading because of its importance.

CONFORMITY

Conformity is the process of adhering to group norms. Because these norms are so important to a group's identity and activities, groups exert considerable pressure on members to follow them. Violation can result in subtle or overt pressure to comply with the rules, which can take the form of a look of disapproval, verbal criticism, or isolation of the offending individual (giving the person the "silent treatment"). Once the violator conforms to the norm, the pressure is removed, and the person is again included in normal group activities. Generally, conformity to norms is very strong and helps maintain order and uniformity in the group's behavior.

> **conformity**
> the process of adhering to group norms

Because pressure to conform to group norms is so strong, we need to consider the circumstances in which an individual might choose to violate a norm. Usually, someone will not conform to a group norm if the individual's goals are different from those of the group. For example, imagine that a manufacturing group has a norm of steady but less-than-optimal production. If a worker within the group wants to be noticed by management as an exceptionally hard worker who would be a good candidate for a promotion to a supervisory position, that person might break the group's production rate norm. Of course, the group will exert pressure in an effort to get the "rate buster" to conform. Extreme and repeated cases of norm violation may eventually lead to ostracism from the group (Scott, Mitchell, & Birnbaum, 1981). An individual might also resist the pressure to conform to demonstrate that the member believes that the norm is incorrect and should not be followed (Hackman, 1992). Generally, members who have more power and influence in the group, such as the leader, will have a better chance of resisting the group's conformity pressure and persuading the group to change or eliminate the norm. Also, if the violator has a past history of being a "good," conforming member, the nonconformity will be tolerated more and have a better chance of being accepted by the group than if it is done by a member known for repeated norm violations (Feldman, 1984).

⏱ Stop & Review
Describe the three stages of organizational socialization.

Although conforming to group norms is typically functional in a work setting, in some instances conformity pressure may attempt to get members to engage in undesirable, counterproductive, or even unethical behavior. In addition there is evidence that conformity among work group members can sometimes stifle individual innovation and creativity (Pech, 2001).

GROUP COHESIVENESS

cohesiveness
the degree of attraction among group members

Another basic group process, cohesiveness, is like the social "glue" that holds people together in groups. Cohesiveness refers simply to the amount or degree of attraction among group members. It is cohesiveness that explains the team spirit that many work groups possess. It is generally assumed that cohesive groups are more satisfied and more productive than noncohesive groups because their members tend to interact more, participate more fully in group activities, and accept and work toward the groups' goals (Cartwright, 1968; Hare, 1976). In fact, however, although cohesive groups are usually more satisfied than non-cohesive groups, the relationship between cohesiveness and productivity is rather weak (Gully, Devine, & Whitney, 1995). That is because typically, for a cohesive group to be productive, the reason for the cohesiveness must be work related (Evans & Dion, 1991; Klein & Mulvey, 1995). For example, groups with strong, work-related norms, such as the willingness to work overtime and a norm of workers taking personal responsibility for doing a good job, had higher group performance than work teams without such strong work-related norms (Langfred, 1998). However, a group may be cohesive yet have as a goal to do as little work as possible. In this case, cohesiveness is high and group satisfaction may be high, but productivity is likely to be very low (Tziner, 1982).

In a very interesting study of U.S. and Hong Kong bank employees, it was found that increases in job complexity and autonomy—two critical, motivating elements of the job characteristics model (see Chapter 8)—led to greater cohesiveness among work group members. This cohesiveness, in turn, caused the groups to be more productive (Man & Lam, 2003). A simple explanation is that the challenges of the more complex tasks and the group's increased responsibility/autonomy caused the group to come together in a way that motivated higher levels of performance.

Because group cohesiveness is theoretically linked to member satisfaction and, under certain circumstances, productivity, there has been considerable research on the factors that increase group cohesiveness. The most important of these factors are the size of the group, the equality of status of members, member stability, member similarity, and the existence of a common threat or enemy.

Generally, the smaller the group, the more cohesive and the more satisfied its members. This makes sense, because small groups offer many more chances to interact with members and to form closer ties than do large groups (Forsyth, 2006). As smaller businesses become larger, gaining more and more employees, cohesiveness often declines. Older workers often lament the strong cohesiveness of the earlier, smaller work group ("In the old days it used to be like a family around here"). Therefore, one way to regain some of the cohesiveness would be to break the large group into smaller work teams.

The more equivalent the status of group members, generally the greater the cohesiveness (Cartwright, 1968). When a status hierarchy exists, the lower-status members may feel resentful of those of higher status, which leads to disharmony. Conversely, the higher-status members may try to use their authority to direct or control the activities of the lower-status members, which can also erode group cohesiveness. Many team approaches, such as job enrichment, attempt to eliminate status differences in groups to increase cohesiveness. For example, in many job enrichment programs team members are all given the same work classification and job title.

The stability of group membership can also have positive effects on cohesiveness (Forsyth, 2006). Generally, the more stable the membership, the more time members have to develop strong ties with one another. New members may often disrupt group harmony because they are unaware of group norms and may unwittingly violate them as they try to learn the ropes. Thus, high rates of member turnover and the presence of many new members can be detrimental to group cohesiveness.

Another factor that affects group cohesiveness is the similarity of group members. The more similar the characteristics of the group members, the more cohesive the group is likely to be. If members have similar backgrounds, education, and attitudes, it is reasonable to assume that they will develop closer ties to one another. Years of research on group processes indicate that member similarity is a very powerful force in determining social ties; we tend to be attracted to, and establish close relationships with, persons who are similar to us (Forsyth, 2006; Jackson et al., 1991). It is important to emphasize, however, that similarity of group members can limit a group's potential to be creative and to innovate, as similar members may tend to "think alike." Research has emphasized that group member diversity can lead to more creative, innovative, and perhaps more productive work groups (Rogelberg & Rumery, 1996; Watson, Kumar, & Michaelsen, 1993).

The presence of an external threat or enemy can likewise increase the cohesiveness of a work group (Shaw, 1981). When a group perceives itself as under attack, the members tend to pull together. Cohesiveness of this type is often referred to as the **we–they feeling** ("We're the good guys, they're the bad guys"). Often, small, up-and-coming companies will characterize large competitor companies as "threatening" or even "evil," in an effort to increase cohesiveness of workers as they try to overcome the ominous giant company that threatens the smaller company's, and its workers', very existence. The smaller company is hoping that the increased cohesiveness will result in greater productivity as the workers pull together in an effort to beat the competition. Unfortunately, within organizations, this we–they feeling often develops between the workers and management. This can lead to increased cohesiveness within the work group but can be disruptive in coordinated efforts to achieve organizational goals if the workers perceive management as the enemy.

In sum, all these factors tend to increase group cohesiveness, which can in turn be related to improved work outcomes, particularly increased levels of member satisfaction, organizational commitment, and reduced rates of absenteeism and turnover (Wech, Mossholder, Steel, & Bennett, 1998). Moreover,

we–they feeling
intragroup cohesiveness created by the existence of a common threat, which is typically another group

regardless of the actual relationship between group cohesiveness and group productivity, many managers believe that cohesiveness is critical for work group success. And, if part of the reason for the work group's cohesiveness is task related, then cohesive groups are usually high-performing groups (Carless & DePaola, 2000; Mullen & Copper, 1994).

GROUP EFFICACY

group efficacy
a group's shared belief that they can attain organizational outcomes

In the same way that individual workers can possess a sense of self-efficacy, as we saw in our discussion of coping with stress (Chapter 10), groups can have a collective sense of efficacy. Group efficacy is the group's shared beliefs in their ability to engage in courses of action that will lead to desired outcomes (Bandura, 1997). Research has demonstrated that group members' levels of individual self-efficacy help contribute to group efficacy, which in turn can have a positive impact on the group's cohesiveness and on their productivity (Baker, 2001; Pescosolido, 2003). A meta-analysis showed a moderately strong relationship between group/team efficacy and performance (Gully, Incalcaterra, Joshi, & Beaubein 2002). Importantly, group efficacy levels seem to be a better predictor of group performance than the sum of individual members' self-efficacy (Lent, Schmidt, & Schmidt, 2006). There is also some evidence that group efficacy predicts levels of job satisfaction and organizational commitment, and that leaders can have an important impact on developing group members' sense of collective efficacy (Walumbwa, Wang, Lawler, & Shi, 2004).

COOPERATION AND COMPETITION IN WORK GROUPS

We have mentioned that the main purpose of work groups and teams is to facilitate the attainment of personal and organizational work goals. This often requires that people work together, coordinating their activities, cooperating with one another, and sometimes helping each other. Yet work groups are also rife with competition as workers try to outperform one another to attain scarce bonuses, raises, and promotions. Competition may also be encouraged when one employee's performance is compared to that of others. Incentive programs are specifically designed to increase motivation by inducing competition—pitting one worker against another. These two seemingly incompatible processes, cooperation and competition, exist simultaneously in all work groups (Lu, Tjosvold, & Shi, 2010; Tjosvold, Morishima, & Belsheim, 1999). Because they are such important group processes, we will consider each in depth.

Cooperation

Cooperation is critical to the effective functioning of work groups/teams and organizations. Consider three employees in a bookstore as an example. The employees take turns performing the tasks that their jobs require. At any time, two are at the front desk, serving customers. The third worker is opening boxes of books, pricing them, and putting them on the appropriate shelves. The workers are coordinating their efforts in an attempt to meet the organizational goals of selling books and providing good customer service. If one of the workers at the front desk goes on a lunch break, the person stocking shelves moves to the front to help customers. If an employee does not know the answer to a customer's question, he may turn to a more knowledgeable and experienced coworker for assistance. The store employees also coordinate their time off, developing a mutually agreeable vacation schedule.

For the most part, such cooperation among work group members is the rule rather than the exception, chiefly because it is often difficult to achieve work goals alone. As long as workers hold to the same goals, they will usually cooperate with one another. Employees might also go out of their way to help each other because of the **reciprocity rule** (Gouldner, 1960), which is illustrated by the sayings, "One good turn deserves another," and "Do unto others as you would have them do unto you." Thus workers help each other because they believe that when they need assistance, they will be paid back in kind. The reciprocity rule is very strong, and people do indeed tend to reciprocate helping behaviors (Eisenberger, Armeli, Rexwinkel, Lynch, & Rhoades, 2001).

One element that helps increase cooperation among work group members is the degree of **task interdependence**, or the degree to which an individual worker's task performance depends on the efforts or skills of others (Campion, Medsker, & Higgs, 1993; Somech, Desivilya, & Lidogoster, 2009). In large part, it is task interdependence that differentiates work "groups" from work "teams." Research has shown that task interdependence fosters positive feelings about coworkers and increases cooperative behavior in work groups and teams (van der Vegt, Emans, & van de Vliert, 1998, 2000; Wageman & Baker, 1997).

Group members also cooperate because achieving organizational goals can lead to payoffs for the individual workers in terms of raises, bonuses, and promotions. This, in turn, can increase group member satisfaction and subsequent performance (consistent with the Porter–Lawler model introduced in Chapter 9) (Alper, Tjosvold, & Law, 2000; Tjosvold, 1998b). Moreover, when work-related rewards are based on effective group performance, such as in the gainsharing programs discussed in Chapter 9, it helps foster cooperation among work group members.

Although the presence of cooperative group members often helps facilitate work performance, there are instances where work group members refuse to cooperate and "pull their load." **Social loafing** is the name given to the phenomenon whereby individuals working in a group put forth less effort than when working alone (Latane, Williams, & Harkins, 1979). Research has shown that social loafing occurs most frequently when workers believe that their individual performance or contribution will not be measured and when working on simple, additive tasks, rather than complex, interdependent tasks (Comer, 1995; Karau & Williams, 1993). Social loafing has also occurred in virtual teams (Suleiman & Watson, 2008). In addition, social loafing is more likely to occur in groups that are low in cohesiveness (Liden, Wayne, Jaworski, & Bennett, 2004).

Research suggests what some of us have believed all along—that some individuals may be more prone to social loafing than others (Smith, Kerr, Markus, & Stasson, 2001; Tan & Tan, 2008). Another study (Robbins, 1995) found that if group members perceived others as engaging in social loafing,

reciprocity rule
the tendency for persons to pay back those to whom they are indebted for assistance

task interdependence
the degree to which an individual's task performance depends on the efforts or skills of others

social loafing
the phenomenon whereby individuals working in groups exert less effort than when working alone

Stop & Review
Name five factors that increase group cohesiveness.

it increased their tendency to loaf—good evidence for the equity theory of motivation (see Chapter 8) ("If they're going to slack off, I'll slack off, too").

Competition

competition

the process whereby group members are pitted against one another to achieve individual goals

Like cooperation, **competition** is also a natural behavior that commonly arises in group dynamics (Tjosvold, 1988; Tjosvold, XueHuang, Johnson, & Johnson, 2008). Whereas cooperation involves group members working together toward shared common goals, competition within groups involves members working against one another to achieve individual goals, often at the expense of other members. For example, in a sales competition, all members of a sales group compete with one another, but only one can be named top salesperson. Most work groups are rife with competition as members struggle to get ahead. One study by Campbell and Furrer (1995) found evidence that the introduction of competition in a work situation where goals were already set actually led to a decrease in performance, so managers should be cautious in their use of competition as a motivational strategy, as we will see shortly in our discussion of conflict.

Because both cooperation and competition are very natural human processes, they often both exist side by side in work groups, and work organizations

ON THE *CUTTING* EDGE

Work Group Diversity and Performance

As work groups become increasingly diverse, how might this diversity—in cultural and ethnic background, gender, and perspectives—influence group and team processes? Let's look at group performance. Research on group processes suggests that diversity might enhance some aspects of performance, but detract from other types of work performance (van Knippenberg & van Ginkel, 2010). For example, diversity is particularly important when the task is complex and involves creativity, due to the differing opinions and points of view of the diverse members. However, along with these differing viewpoints is an increase in potentially disruptive intragroup conflict. One study of teams in a wide range of U.S. organizations found that this was indeed the case. Work groups that were more diverse in terms of gender, age, status, and work background/experience were evaluated as more effective groups, but were also more prone to conflict (Devine et al., 1999).

As we might also expect from research on group dynamics and personnel psychology, gender and ethnic diversity can lead to the development of factions, such as when same-sex or same-race subgroups develop and impede the overall functioning of the group and discriminate against members of the other factions (Williams & O'Reilly, 1998). So, the answer is unclear. There are instances where diversity should be, and is, advantageous to work group performance and instances where it inhibits successful group functioning.

The critical element is not diversity per se, but the ability of the group and the organization to effectively manage diversity, by creating a culture that accepts, supports, and values diverse individuals and diverse perspectives, by ensuring equitable treatment of all group members, and from creating an environment where team members learn from one another (Benschop, 2001; Ely & Thomas, 2001; Ivancevich & Gilbert, 2000; Jackson & Ruderman, 1995). Although the relationship between work group diversity and performance is complex, there is one clear benefit of diversity. Organizations that have diverse workforces, and organizations that value and successfully manage diversity, have more loyal, committed employees, are more attractive to potential workers, and tend to have lower rates of absenteeism and turnover than less-diverse, less-accepting organizations (Cox & Tung, 1997; Gilbert & Ivancevich, 2001).

and work culture actually encourage both. The very fact that work organizations exist indicates that there must be some advantage in having workers cooperate by pooling their efforts to perform some complex tasks. At the same time, the compensation systems adopted by U.S. organizations, and companies in most Western countries, emphasize the rewarding of individual efforts, which breeds competition. Much of this competition is viewed as healthy because it often motivates people to improve their work performance. Indeed, in the United States and many other industrialized Western nations, being competitive is a highly valued characteristic that is considered imperative for individual and organizational success.

CONFLICT IN WORK GROUPS AND ORGANIZATIONS

Whereas competition refers to a motivating state, conflict is used to describe competitiveness of individual workers or work groups that become exposed. Conflict is behavior by a person or group that is purposely designed to inhibit the attainment of goals by another person or group (Gray & Starke, 1984). There are many typical instances of conflict between members of an organization, such as two delivery persons arguing over who gets to drive the new company truck, union and management representatives in heated negotiations over a new contract, or two applicants competing for a single job. Conflict in work organizations and in other areas of everyday life is indeed a common state of affairs.

> **conflict**
> behavior by a person or group intended to inhibit the attainment of goals by another person or group

The key element in the definition of conflict is that the conflicting parties have incompatible goals (Tjosvold, 1998a). Thus, both delivery persons cannot drive the same truck, the union cannot attain its goals unless management is willing to give up some of its goals, and two people cannot hold the same job. Because in extreme cases conflict can lead to a variety of negative behaviors, such as shouting, name-calling, and acts of aggression, and perhaps because there is often a "loser" in conflict outcomes, it is commonly believed that conflict is bad. However, this is not necessarily true. Conflict is a natural process that occurs in all work groups and organizations. It can have negative, destructive consequences, but it can also be constructive and lead to positive outcomes for work groups and organizations, but only under very specific and controlled circumstances (De Dreu, 2008). Generally, the only way to be certain when conflict is bad or good is to examine whether it has positive or negative consequences for the conflicting parties and for the work group or organization as a whole. Although the consequences of conflict are very important, we must first examine the different levels of conflict that occur in organizations and the potential sources of conflict.

Levels of conflict

Conflict can occur at different levels within a work organization. We typically think of conflict as occurring between two people or two groups. However, workers can have internal conflict (what we discussed in Chapter 10 as role conflict) when one person is faced with two sets of incompatible goals. For example, the business owner who hires her son is going to be faced with serious internal conflict when dealing with him as a work employee. Her roles as mother and as work superior may come into conflict.

Conflict between two people, or interindividual conflict, is quite common in work groups and organizations, and a major source of interpersonal stress. Two persons vying for the same promotion could create interindividual conflict, because the person who gets the promotion would block the other from attaining the goal.

The next level of conflict, intragroup conflict, occurs between one person or faction within a group and the other group members. An individual who violates a group norm is creating intragroup conflict, as are members of a work group who disagree over the course of action for the group. Assume, for example, that a legal firm is trying to decide how to conduct their billing operations. Some of the attorneys favor hiring someone in-house who will handle billing, whereas others believe that billing should be contracted with an outside agency. Until the group settles on one of the plans, the firm will experience high levels of intragroup conflict.

When two groups are in conflict with each other, intergroup conflict exists. Such conflict occurs annually in many organizations when departments are asked to submit their budget requests for the upcoming year. Usually, the sum of the requests greatly exceeds the total amount of money available, which creates a great deal of intergroup conflict as each department tries to achieve its budgetary goals at the expense of the others (Greenberg, 1987).

Each of these four levels of conflict takes place *within* a particular organization, but interorganizational conflict occurs *between* organizations. Businesses that are fighting over the same consumer market are likely to engage in interorganizational conflict as each organization tries to achieve its sales goals at the expense of those of the other. This can cause organizations to compete to provide better goods and services for consumers. Interorganizational conflict can also have negative outcomes, such as when a managed care organization and a group of health-care providers conflict causing problems in health-care delivery to patients (Callister & Wall, 2001).

Sources of conflict

Conflict in work groups and organizations comes from many sources. Sometimes it is caused by the organizational structure. For example, status differences are a common source of conflict. Sometimes conflict results because of simple disagreements between two parties over the appropriate work behavior or course of action. Although it would be difficult to list all potential sources of conflict, we will examine some of the more common causes.

A scarcity of important resources—money, materials, tools, and supplies—is perhaps the most common source of conflict in work organizations (Greenberg & Baron, 1997). It is a rare organization that has enough resources to satisfy the needs of all of its members. When members are forced to compete with one another for these resources, conflict usually follows.

Individuals and work groups usually must rely on the activities of other persons and groups to get their own jobs done. Therefore, individual and group interdependence is an important source of conflict (Victor & Blackburn, 1987). Generally, the greater the interdependence of work activities, the greater the potential for conflict (Walton & Dutton, 1969). For example, in the airline industry, flight crews must depend on the maintenance crews, luggage handlers, and passenger boarding personnel to do their jobs in servicing and loading the aircraft before they can do their job. Intergroup conflict can result if one group does not feel that another is doing its job. If the flight crew feels that the luggage handlers are too slow, causing delays in takeoff, the fact that the flight crew may be blamed for the delays creates a potential conflict situation.

We have seen that the we–they feeling plays a large role in fostering group cohesiveness; nothing can draw a group together better than having a common enemy to fight. However, a problem occurs when the "enemy" is within your own organization. This is what often causes the conflict in wage negotiations between workers and managers. The workers ask for a wage increase, whereas management, in an effort to keep costs down, rejects the request. What commonly results is that each group views the other as an enemy blocking its goal attainment. Although the common enemy helps draw the members together within their respective groups, it also tends to draw the two groups further away from each other.

One of the most common sources of conflict results from the fact that certain individuals simply do not get along with each other (Labianca, Brass, & Gray, 1998). This important source of conflict thus comes from interpersonal sources. Two organizational members who dislike each other may refuse to cooperate. This sort of interpersonal conflict can be very disruptive to the larger work group and the organization in general, especially if the problem is between two powerful people, such as two department heads who may turn their supervisees against members of the other department. What was once a conflict between two persons can thus escalate into conflict between two groups.

Most organizational conflict occurs behind the scenes, but in extreme instances the dispute becomes public.

Research evidence also suggests that some people are more conflict prone than others. Differences in personality and temperament mean that certain persons may be likely to engage in conflict. Indeed, studies have shown that some people try to stir up interindividual conflict because of their desire to gain at others' expense (McClintock, Messick, Kuhlman, & Campos, 1973; see also Knight & Dubro, 1984). Inability to deal effectively with negative emotions may also make certain people more conflict prone (Yang & Mossholder, 2004).

A final characteristic that can be a potential source of conflict is age. A good deal of evidence indicates that younger workers are more conflict prone than older workers, presumably because they have less to lose and more to gain from the outcomes of conflict situations (Robbins, 1974). Some research also suggests that young workers, particularly those who are trying to balance work and school, are more negatively influenced by interpersonal conflict, experiencing greater job dissatisfaction and stress than older workers (Frone, 2000; Harvey, Blouin, & Stout, 2006).

Conflict outcomes

It has been stated that conflict in work settings can produce both positive and negative outcomes for the organization. Attention is usually given to how conflict affects the important organizational outcomes of job performance or productivity, job satisfaction, and employee attendance. First, we will examine the positive outcomes of conflict.

A primary question is how conflict within a work group or organization relates to performance. One way that conflict can indirectly affect performance is by increasing the motivation and energy level of group members. A little bit of conflict seems to energize members, which in turn may increase their motivation to perform their jobs. The complete absence of conflict in work groups can cause workers to become complacent and unmotivated. (It can also be very dull.)

Another positive outcome of conflict is that it can stimulate creativity and innovation (James, Chen, & Goldberg, 1992). When people challenge the existing system, a form of conflict results. But out of this type of conflict come new, and often better, ideas. For example, in many groups, workers continue to use the same old "tried and true" work procedures. When a worker suggests a new, improved method, there may be some initial conflict as members resist having to learn a new technique. However, if the new procedure is effective, group productivity may increase. Thus, although people tend to resist changes, when change is for the better, the organization and its members benefit.

Another performance-related positive outcome of conflict occurs when conflict improves the quality of decisions (Cosier & Dalton, 1990). Giving all members of a group some input into the decision-making process leads to conflict because the group must consider a wide range of opposing views and opinions. Conflict occurs as each member tries to be heard and pushes for what he or she thinks is right. The positive result of all of this, however, is that decisions made are usually of high quality, being the result of a very critical process. (We will return to a discussion of group decision-making processes later in this chapter.)

In Chapters 9 and 11, we saw that employees who feel that they have an active role in affecting group or organizational processes tend to be more satisfied than those who have no influence. Being able to communicate freely with coworkers, having a voice in decision making, and being allowed to make suggestions or criticize group or organizational operations are all ways in which workers can have some impact on group processes. Although some conflict is likely to arise every time workers are allowed to introduce their own opinions, the fact that they can take part in this positive, productive type of conflict is associated with greater group member satisfaction. Therefore, some forms of conflict can be directly associated with member satisfaction and commitment to the work group.

Among the various negative outcomes of conflict, one of the most obvious is the reduction of group cohesiveness. Although a little bit of conflict can energize group members, too much can erode cohesiveness and, in extremes, diminish the members' abilities to work with each other. This may contribute to increased voluntary absenteeism and eventually employee turnover.

Conflict can also hamper effective group performance when it retards communication. People who are in conflict may avoid communicating with each other, making it difficult to work together. Conflict can also be destructive to group member satisfaction when conflicting parties begin to send misleading or deceptive messages to one another or when false and disparaging rumors are started. Evidence also suggests that when a great deal of interpersonal conflict occurs among work group members, supervisors may begin to avoid allowing subordinates to participate in decision-making processes, thus shutting down this type of communication, presumably in an effort to avoid further conflict (Fodor, 1976). Conflict is especially damaging to performance when it allows group goals to become secondary to the infighting. Sometimes members direct so much energy to the conflict situation that they neglect to perform their jobs (Robbins, 1979). A meta-analysis suggests that conflict can have negative impacts on both team productivity and on job satisfaction (De Dreu & Weingart, 2003).

In summary, neither too much nor too little conflict is beneficial for the work group members and the organization. This means that there must be some optimal level of conflict. Because conflict is so pervasive in work groups and organizations, it would be very difficult to assess whether all forms of conflict were at their optimal levels at any given time. Because some excess or shortage of conflict is inevitably going to exist, the smart thing to do at all times in all work groups is to learn to manage conflict.

Managing conflict

To manage conflict—to keep it at an optimal level—one of two things must be done. If the conflict becomes too great, leading to severe negative outcomes, it must be resolved. If, on the other hand, the level of conflict is too low, conflict stimulation is needed.

There is little doubt that too much conflict can have devastating consequences on both the work group and the organization. Therefore, a great deal of attention has been given to the development and application of various conflict resolution strategies, which can be of two types. Individual conflict resolution strategies are those that the conflicting parties can use themselves to try to resolve the conflict; managerial conflict resolution strategies are steps that managers or other third parties can take to encourage conflict resolution. Thomas (1976, 1992) has identified five individual conflict resolution strategies:

dominating (forcing)
a conflict resolution strategy of persisting in a conflict until one party attains personal goals at the expense of the other's

1. **Dominating (Forcing)**—Persisting in the conflict until one party's goals are achieved at the expense of those of the other. This can be labeled a win–lose strategy: One party wins, the other loses.

accommodation
a conflict resolution strategy of making a sacrifice to resolve a conflict

2. **Accommodation**—Giving in or acting in a self-sacrificing manner to resolve the conflict. This is a lose–win strategy. Often, this strategy of appeasement is done to cut losses or in an effort to save the relationship between the conflicting parties.

compromise
a conflict resolution strategy in which both parties give up some part of their goals

3. **Compromise**—Each party must give up something. This is a lose–lose strategy. Compromise is typical in bargaining situations. For example, in union–management negotiations, management may offer a $1.50-an-hour raise, whereas the union wants a $3.00 raise. They compromise at $2.00, but neither group has achieved its complete goal. They have each lost something from their original position—a lose–lose outcome. Compromise is not an appropriate strategy if both parties cannot afford to yield part of their goals (Harris, 1993).

collaboration
a conflict resolution strategy in which the parties cooperate to reach a solution that satisfies both

4. **Collaboration**—The parties try to cooperate and reach a mutually beneficial solution. This is a win–win situation. Unfortunately, this is not always possible, particularly when the conflict is over scarce resources, and there is not enough to satisfy both parties' needs. It has been suggested that if both parties work at it, many conflicts can be resolved collaboratively (Ury, Brett, & Goldberg, 1988).

avoidance
withdrawing from or avoiding a conflict situation

5. **Avoidance**—Suppressing the conflict, not allowing it to come into the open, or simply withdrawing from the situation. Although this strategy avoids open conflict, the differences between the two parties still exist and will likely continue to affect their ability to work with one another. Avoidance can be appropriate if the timing for open conflict is not right or if the conflicting parties need a "cooling-off" period.

Although the two conflicting parties can take such steps to try to resolve their differences, managers, because of their status and power in the organization, can play a major role in resolving conflict between subordinates (Blake, Shepard, & Mouton, 1964; Pinkley, Brittain, Neale, & Northcraft, 1995; Sheppard, 1974). Managers may try to force an end to the conflict by deciding in favor of one or the other parties. Although this may end the conflict, resentment may be built up in the losing person that may surface later in actions against the manager or the coworker (van de Vliert, Euwema, & Huismans, 1995). Managers can also act as arbitrators or mediators to resolve conflict in a way that may satisfy both parties. For example, two graphic artists were constantly fighting over use of a computer scanner needed to perform their jobs. When one worker needed the scanner, it always seemed that the other person was using it, which led to constant arguments. When the manager became aware of the problem, he instantly resolved it by simply purchasing another scanner.

In other circumstances, outside consultants or arbitrators may be called in specifically to resolve internal conflicts in organizations (Thomas, 1992).

One managerial conflict resolution strategy, outlined in a series of studies by Sherif and his colleagues (Sherif, Harvey, White, Hood, & Sherif, 1961), deals with resolving intragroup conflict by stimulating intragroup cohesiveness through the introduction of a common, superordinate goal that is attractive to both parties. When a group is split over some minor issue, introducing a more important superordinate goal may draw the two sides together as they strive to attain the common end. For example, commissioned salespersons in the men's clothing section of a large chain department store were constantly fighting over who would be the first to grab a customer who walked into the area. The manager helped to resolve much of this conflict by introducing a bonus program that pitted the department's overall sales against those of men's departments in other stores. By focusing on pooled sales figures, the employees became oriented toward beating the other stores rather than beating each other.

> **superordinate goal**
> a goal that two conflicting parties are willing to work to attain

Managers can also help resolve conflict in group decision making (Conlon & Ross, 1993). For example, they may use their authority to call an issue to a vote, which means that the majority of workers will win the conflict situation. However, there may be a disgruntled minority of losers, who may then carry on the conflict by refusing to follow the elected plan or by some other means. The manager will need to deal with this residual conflict if it is deemed serious enough to require resolution.

The key to successful conflict resolution from the managerial perspective is to maintain a broad perspective, trying to find a workable solution and considering the potential side effects, such as disgruntled losers, that may result from the resolution process (see box Applying I/O Psychology).

In certain situations, such as when group members appear to have become complacent and disinterested in work activities, managers may feel that some specific types of conflict are needed. A number of strategies can be used to stimulate conflict. One tactic is simply to ask for it. Asking employees for their suggestions or for complaints about the organization and its policies may lead to some conflict as employees critically evaluate the organization and management. However, it is hoped that this type of conflict will lead to constructive change and improvement. When top management feels that work groups have become too cohesive, to the detriment of the groups' energy and motivational levels, they may decide to break up that cohesiveness and inject a little stimulating conflict by making personnel changes such as bringing in new employees or rotating workers to different departments or work sites. Restaurant and retail chains use this strategy when they rotate managers among stores.

Sales or performance competition programs are another way of stimulating some positive group conflict. The key to a successful competition program, however, is to ensure that members do not engage in dysfunctional behaviors, such as sabotaging others' work activities, in an effort to win the competition. Ideally, a good program should allow all participants to achieve a goal. For example, a bonus should be given to each employee who reaches a certain performance level, instead of only to the top performer.

APPLYING I/O PSYCHOLOGY

Reducing Management–Union Conflict

A common type of intergroup conflict in large work organizations exists between management and unions. The behavioral scientists Blake, Mouton, and Sloma (1964) outlined a case in which such conflict was reduced through a two-day workshop designed to refocus the two groups' efforts on common work-related goals. The company was a large electronics manufacturing plant with more than 4,000 employees. Because there was a history of disagreement between management and the labor union, one of the most difficult tasks for the behavioral scientists was to get both sides to agree to the "experiment." Finally, however, they agreed that the hostility between the two groups was so high that something needed to be done.

The scientists believed that the key to reducing conflict was to get the two groups to increase their understanding of each other and to see that in many ways, they had compatible rather than competing goals. The workshop designed to achieve this mutual awareness was broken down into eight phases, as follows:

In the first few phases, the management and union representatives wrote down their images of themselves, particularly in their relationship with the other group, and their images of the other side. These images were exchanged, and heated discussion ensued. In these early discussions, the two groups continued their intense conflict. For example, one manager said, "I can't even talk with these union officials. I just 'see red' and clam up every time I see one of them coming." Eventually, however, as the groups moved through the middle phases of the workshop, they began to gain insight into each other's positions and some of the misunderstandings began to disappear. This was helped along by the fifth phase in which both groups' task was to try to discover why the conflict had become what it was. In the discussion that followed, the two sides began to find that they had some common goals:

The employee relations manager, who had been listening intently all this time, stood up with a look of disbelief on his face. He didn't seem to realize he was on his feet. "Do you mean to say you people are really interested in production?" He had listened to the union say this for two days, but he had just "heard" it for the first time. His next question was a simple one, but it triggered an hour-long discussion. He asked, "What could management do to use people more effectively?" (Blake, Mouton, & Sloma, 1964, p. 189)

By finding that they shared common goals, the two groups set an agenda to work together not only to reduce the management–union conflict further but also to develop some cooperative strategies for dealing with work-related problems. From this workshop arose a plan of action for creating better lines of communication between the two groups and for implementing strategies that would increase plant efficiency and productivity for the benefit of all.

Phase	Activity	Time (hours)
1	Orientation; purposes of workshop explained	½
2	Intragroup development of own images and images of other group	5
3	Exchange of images across groups	1
4	Clarification of images	2
5	Intragroup diagnosis of present relationship	4
6	Exchange of diagnoses across groups	3
7	Consolidation of key issues and sources of friction	2
8	Planning of next steps to be taken	1

A widely used conflict stimulation strategy that can often lead to positive outcomes is to move from centralized decision-making procedures to a group decision-making process, in which all group members have a say in certain work-related issues. Although this automatically increases conflict by allowing each worker to state his or her opinion and argue for a particular course of action, it is presumed that this type of conflict will yield positive results because it allows for consideration of a wider range of plans and greater critiquing of the various possible decisions.

Group Decision-Making Processes

One of the most important processes in work groups is group decision making, which includes establishing group goals, choosing among various courses of action, selecting new members, and determining standards of appropriate behavior. The processes by which groups make these decisions have been of interest to I/O psychologists for many years.

Groups can make work-related decisions in a number of ways. The simplest and most straightforward strategy, known as autocratic decision making, is when the group leader makes decisions alone, using only the information that the leader possesses. The major advantage of autocratic decision making is that it is fast. Decisions are made quickly by the leader and are then expected to be carried out by group members. However, because the decision is made based only on what the leader knows the quality of the decision may suffer. For example, suppose a leader of a group of accountants has to decide which accounting software to order. If the leader actually knows which program is the best for the group, there will be no drawback to the autocratic approach. If, however, the leader cannot make an informed choice, the decision may be faulty. In this case, input from the group members would be helpful. A variation on the strict autocratic decision-making approach occurs when the leader solicits information from group members to assist in reaching a decision, but still holds the final say. This is sometimes referred to as *consultative decision making*. In the software decision, soliciting input from group members about which systems they favor might lead to a higher quality decision.

A very different strategy is democratic decision making, in which all group members are allowed to discuss the decision and then vote on a particular course of action. Typically, democratic decision making is based on majority rule. One advantage of this approach is that decisions are made using the pooled knowledge and experience of all the group members. Moreover, because all members have a chance to voice an opinion or suggest a different course of action, a greater number of alternatives are considered. Also, because group members have a role in the decision making, they are more likely to follow the chosen course.

The most obvious drawback to democratic decision making is that it is time consuming. Because it encourages conflict, it can also be inefficient. Although the democratic, majority-rule approach results in a satisfied majority who will back the decision, there may be a disgruntled minority who resist its implementation.

⏱ *Stop & Review*

Compare and contrast competition and conflict.

---

autocratic decision making
a process by which group decisions are made by the leader alone, based on information the leader possesses

---

democratic decision making
a strategy by which decisions are made by the group members based on majority-rule voting

consensus

decision making based on 100% member agreement

A strategy that overcomes some of the weaknesses of democratic decision making is to make decisions based on consensus, which means that all group members have agreed on the chosen course of action. Because consensus decision making is especially time consuming, it is usually used only for very important decisions. For example, juries use this strategy because the decision affects the freedom and future of the accused. Some company executive boards may strive for a consensus when making major decisions about changes in the direction of the organization or in organizational structure or company policy. As you might imagine, the outcome of consensus decision making is usually a high-quality, highly critiqued decision, backed by all members of the group. The obvious drawback is the tremendous amount of time it may take for the group to reach a consensus. In fact, in many situations, arriving at a consensus may be impossible, particularly if one or more group members is strongly resistant to the majority's decision (the courtroom analogy would be a "hung" jury).

Stop & Review

Define the five individual conflict resolution strategies.

EFFECTIVENESS OF GROUP DECISION MAKING

Organizations often rely on group strategies for making important work-related decisions. Part of this is fueled by beliefs in the inherent advantages of group over individual decision making. However, although group decision making has many positive aspects, it also has some drawbacks (see Table 12.2). The key is to know not only how group-made decisions can be more effective than those made by individuals, but also when group decision making is superior.

As mentioned, the major advantage of group decision making is that it offers increased knowledge and experience on which to base the decision. But do groups actually make better decisions than individuals? Research does give the edge to group decision making, on the average. The average group will make a higher-quality decision than the average individual. However, some research indicates that the best decision-making individual—one who possesses all the information needed to make a high-quality decision—will be able to perform as well as or better than a group (Hill, 1982; Miner, 1984). In other circumstances, groups may arrive at decisions that are superior to even those made by the group's best decision maker (Michaelson, Watson, & Black, 1989). Moreover, certain members, such as a group leader or respected individual, may have more influence in affecting the outcome and may be able to sway a

TABLE 12.2

Advantages and Disadvantages of Group Decision Making

Advantages	Disadvantages
Works from a broad knowledge base	Slow (can be a problem in crisis situations)
Decision is accepted by members	Creates intragroup conflict
Decision is highly critiqued	Potential for groupthink and group polarization
Aspects of the problem can be divided among group members	Certain members, such as leaders, may dominate the decision-making process

group toward accepting a particular course of action. If the influential member is not knowledgeable or well informed about the alternatives, however, the group may be led to make a poor decision.

We have also seen that group decision making tends to be slower than individual decision making, which can be a problem in situations such as an emergency or crisis. At these times, it may be better for an individual to take charge and make decisions for the group (Tjosvold, 1984a). However, if a problem is complex and multifaceted, with many steps required to arrive at a decision, a group may make the decision faster than an individual, because the various aspects of the problem can be divided among group members.

Perhaps the strongest argument in support of group decision making is that it tends to lead to increased member satisfaction and greater member commitment to the course of action than does individual decision making. But what happens if the group-made decision is a bad one? Research indicates that when this occurs, members may increase their commitment to the poor decision (Bazerman, Giuliano, & Appleman, 1984). If the poor decision was made by an individual, group members will not be as committed and may be more likely to see its faults and try another course of action.

Group members may also be widely distributed geographically. As a result, there has been an increase in electronic decision-making meetings. A meta-analysis that compared decision making in face-to-face versus computer-mediated groups suggested that face-to-face groups were perceived as more effective, more efficient, with group members feeling more satisfied than the computer-mediated decision-making groups (Baltes, Dickson, Sherman, Bauer, & LaGanke, 2002).

In summary, although group decision making has certain limitations, it offers many advantages over individual decision making, particularly in improving the quality of decisions and in increasing the commitment to decisions once they are made. Trends toward greater use of teams and encouraging greater involvement of workers in organizational processes mean that group decision making is likely to increase in the future (De Dreu & West, 2001).

GROUP DECISION MAKING GONE AWRY: GROUPTHINK AND GROUP POLARIZATION

When making important work decisions, particularly those that have a major impact on the work procedures or working lives of group members, group decision making may be preferred over decision making by high-ranking members of the organization. This is done in an effort to increase the amount of relevant information available and to encourage member commitment to the eventually chosen course. However, psychologists have discovered two situations in which the usual advantages of group decision making may not be forthcoming: One is known as groupthink, and the other is termed group polarization.

Groupthink

Groups generally arrive at high-quality decisions because the alternative courses of action have been subjected to critical evaluation. This is particularly

UP CLOSE   What Is Brainstorming, and Does It Work?

In the 1950s an advertising executive developed a technique to encourage groups to come up with creative ideas (Osborn, 1957). The technique, termed brainstorming, involved 6–10 group members throwing out ideas in a noncritical and nonjudgmental atmosphere as a means of trying to generate as many creative ideas or solutions to a problem as possible. Since its invention, brainstorming has become very popular, and tremendous claims have been made regarding its success.

The basic rules in brainstorming sessions are: (a) no idea is too far out; (b) criticism of any idea is not allowed; (c) the more ideas the better; and (d) members should try to build on each other's ideas. The technique has been widely used in a variety of businesses, but does it work? Evidence from nearly 40 years of research indicates that, despite its popularity, brainstorming is not as effective as its proponents might lead one to believe (see, for example, Furnham, 2000; Litchfield, 2009; Taylor, Block, & Berry, 1958; Yetton & Bottger, 1982). The problem is that despite the rules, group dynamics are too powerful; the creativity of people in the brainstorming groups is often inhibited (Brown & Paulus, 1996; Diehl & Stroebe, 1987).

Research indicates that individuals are equal to or better than the brainstorming groups in generating creative ideas. At one point, researchers suggested that "electronic brainstorming"—having groups brainstorm virtually—might remove some of the groups processes that hinder the group's ability to generate good ideas present in face-to-face groups (e.g., fear that others are negatively evaluating one's ideas; "free-riding" members who allow other members to do the work) are absent in the electronic brainstorming groups (Gallupe, Bastianutti, & Cooper, 1991; Paulus, Larey, & Dzindolet, 2001). Yet, research has not found that electronic brainstorming groups perform better than either face-to-face brainstorming groups or individuals (Barki & Pinsonneault, 2001; Dornburg, Stevens, Hendrickson, & Davidson, 2009).

What is extremely interesting, however, is that members of brainstorming groups firmly believe that the group brainstorming was more productive than individual brainstorming, in terms of both the number and the quality of the ideas generated (Paulus & Dzindolet, 1993). The moral is that just because a technique sounds logical or is popular, this does not necessarily mean that it will work.

---

brainstorming
a group process generating creative ideas or solutions through a noncritical and nonjudgmental process

groupthink
a syndrome characterized by a concurrence-seeking tendency that overrides the ability of a cohesive group to make critical decisions

true in consensus decision making, because even one dissenting member can argue against a plan favored by all the rest. There is, however, an exception to this rule. A complex set of circumstances can sometimes occur in consensus decision making that retards the critical evaluation process. What results is a complete backfiring of the normal, critical decision making that results in a premature, hasty, and often catastrophic decision. This situation is termed groupthink. Groupthink is a syndrome that occurs in highly cohesive decision-making groups, where a norm develops to arrive at an early consensus, thereby reducing the effectiveness of the group's ability to make high-quality, critical decisions.

The concept of groupthink was researched by psychologist Irving Janis (1972, 1982; Janis & Mann, 1977). According to Janis, groupthink usually occurs only in highly cohesive groups in which the members' desire to maintain cohesiveness overrides the sometimes uncomfortable and disruptive process of critical decision making. A course of action is laid out on the table, and without it being adequately critiqued, the members rapidly move toward a consensus to adopt the plan. Despite Janis's assertion that groupthink usually only occurs in highly cohesive groups, research suggests that it is groups whose cohesiveness is "relationship based" that are more prone to groupthink than groups whose cohesiveness is "task based," or related to the decision-making and performance goals of the group (Bernthal & Insko, 1993).

In developing his theory of groupthink, Janis studied a number of poor decisions made by high-level decision-making groups, such as U.S. presidential administrations and boards of directors of large companies, the consequences of which were so bad that Janis labeled the outcomes "fiascoes." Janis investigated a number of historical fiascoes, such as the Kennedy administration's failed Bay of Pigs invasion, the Truman administration's decision to cross the thirty-eighth parallel in the Korean War, and the Johnson administration's decision to escalate the Vietnam War. He also studied catastrophic business decisions, such as the decision to market the drug Thalidomide, which led to thousands of birth deformities; the Buffalo Mining Company's decision about dam construction, which caused the deaths of 125 people; and the Ford Motor Company's decision to market the Edsel, one of the greatest failures in U.S. automotive history (Wheeler & Janis, 1980). In more recent history, researchers have studied NASA's catastrophic decision to launch the *Challenger* space shuttle (Esser, 1998), and the torture of Iraqi prisoners by the U.S. military in Abu Ghraib (Post, 2011). By studying the decision-making processes in each early case of groupthink, Janis noticed certain similarities that he has termed the "symptoms of groupthink"—specific group factors that work toward preventing the critical evaluation usually present in decision-making groups (see Table 12.3).

To understand how the symptoms of groupthink interfere with critical decision-making processes, consider the following example. A board of directors of an international air freight service must decide whether the company should

---

TABLE 12.3

The Eight Symptoms of Groupthink

1. *Illusion of invulnerability*—The highly cohesive decision-making group members see themselves as powerful and invincible. Their attraction to and faith in the group leads them to ignore the potential disastrous outcomes of their decision.

2. *Illusion of morality*—Members believe in the moral correctness of the group and its decision; related to the first symptom. Derived from the we–they feeling, members view themselves as the "good guys" and the opposition as bad or evil.

3. *Shared negative stereotypes*—Members have common beliefs that minimize the risks involved in a decision or belittle any opposing viewpoints.

4. *Collective rationalizations*—The members explain away any negative information that runs counter to the group decision.

5. *Self-censorship*—Members suppress their own doubts or criticisms concerning the decision.

6. *Illusion of unanimity*—Members mistakenly believe that the decision is a consensus. Because dissenting viewpoints are not being voiced, it is assumed that silence indicates support.

7. *Direct conformity pressure*—When an opposing view or a doubt is expressed, pressure is applied to get the dissenter to concur with the decision.

8. *Mindguards*—Some members play the role of protecting or insulating the group from any opposing opinions or negative information.

enter a cost-cutting war with their competitors. The board begins its decision-making meeting with the chairperson's loaded question, "Should we enter into this foolish price war, or just keep rates the way they are?" By labeling the price war as "foolish," the chairperson has already indicated her preferred course of action: Keep the rates as they are. Normally, the critical decision-making process would involve a great deal of discussion about the relative strengths and weaknesses of the various alternatives, and the decision that would result should be of high quality. However, in groupthink situations this does not occur. The symptoms of groupthink, themselves manifestations of such basic group processes as cohesiveness, stereotyped and rationalized views, and conformity, can counteract the critical evaluations that should be made. If groupthink does indeed occur, the consequences may be devastating, particularly because the group believes that the chosen action is the result of a critical and well-conducted decision-making process, when it is not.

If groupthink takes place at the air freight company, the board of directors would likely manifest three symptoms—the *illusion of invulnerability*, the *illusion of morality*, and the presence of *shared negative stereotypes*—that result from the we–they feeling that is typically present in highly cohesive groups. The members believe that they and their organization are powerful and good. Negative stereotypes about nonmembers or other groups (the enemy) also stem from the we–they feeling. Examples of these three symptoms might be seen in the board members' statements that they believe the group and the company are invulnerable ("We're the number one company in this business") and morally good ("We always provide the best possible service to our customers"). Other comments suggest that they hold shared negative stereotypes about the competition ("With their inept management and poor equipment, they will never be able to offer the kind of service that we do"). These three groupthink symptoms thus begin a tendency toward seeking concurrence, as the members strive to stick together and agree with one another (Janis, 1972).

Additional groupthink symptoms—*collective rationalizations* of opposing viewpoints, a tendency for members to engage in *self-censorship*, and the *illusion of unanimity*—lead the group to arrive at a premature consensus. Suppose that one of the board members suggests an alternative to the plan to keep rates as they are that the board is moving toward adopting. The dissenter wants to keep rates the same while starting an advertising campaign that tells customers, "You get what you pay for," thus emphasizing the company's higher quality of service. Collective rationalizations of members immediately put down the alternative plan ("People never listen to advertisements anyway" and "That will cost us more than lowering our rates!"). Other board members may see the merit in the alternative plan, but because it appears that most of the others, because of their silence, do not like it, they engage in self-censorship and keep their opinions to themselves. The fact that no one speaks up leads to the illusion of unanimity, the misconception that everybody is for the original plan.

If dissenters do speak up, two additional groupthink symptoms operate to stifle the critical decision-making process even further. *Direct conformity pressure* might be applied to force dissenters to keep their opinions to themselves and not break up the group's agreement. Some members may even play the role of *mindguards* by taking it on themselves to keep dissenting opinions from reaching the ears of the group leader and other members. The member advocating the advertisement plan, for example, might be told by a self-appointed mindguard to not bring the plan up again, "for the good of the group."

Janis believes that groupthink can be combated by breaking up some of the cohesiveness of the group through the interjection of productive conflict. This might involve using strategies such as bringing in outsiders to offer different viewpoints or having some members play the role of critical evaluators—"devil's advocates"—who are highly critical of any plan of action that is brought before the group (Schweiger, Sandberg, & Ragan, 1986). Similarly, a group norm that encourages critical evaluation will help prevent groupthink (Postmes, Spears, & Cihangir, 2001). Also, because groupthink is partly brought on by a sense of time urgency, if the group begins with the idea that they need to come up with the best possible decision, regardless of how long it takes, groupthink may be avoided (Chapman, 2006). tHart (1998) suggested that holding individual group members accountable and reducing pressures to conform will help combat groupthink. Baron (2005) suggested that groupthink may occur quite frequently in all sorts of decision-making groups.

Group polarization

The quality of group decisions may also be adversely affected by group polarization, or the tendency for groups to make decisions that are more extreme than those made by individuals (Myers & Lamm, 1976). Early research found evidence of the effects of group polarization when decisions carried a high degree of risk. In these studies, individuals were asked to make a decision between an attractive but risky course of action and one that was less attractive but also less risky. After making the decision, the respondents were put into groups and asked to come up with a group decision. It was found that the groups tended to make riskier decisions than the average individual (Wallach, Kogan, & Bem, 1962). This effect became known as the "risky shift" and was the topic of much research and theorizing. It had major implications for the making of important decisions in business and government because it suggested that group decisions might be more dangerous than decisions made by individuals. However, subsequent research began to challenge these early findings, failing to find a risky shift in some decision-making groups and occasionally finding evidence of a cautious shift. What we now know is that group discussion often leads individuals to become more extreme in their opinions. The attitudes and opinions of individuals who favor an idea tend to become even more positive after group discussion, whereas those who do not favor an idea tend to develop opinions that are even more negative (Isenberg, 1986; Lamm, 1988).

How does group polarization relate to decisions made in work situations, and why does it occur? Imagine that a company must choose which of several new products it should introduce. Some of the products are costly to develop and market, but if successful they could bring large profits. Other products are less costly but will lead to smaller financial gains. An individual who makes the decision might choose to introduce a product of medium-level risk and payoff.

group polarization
the tendency for groups to make decisions that are more extreme than those made by individuals

However, if the person is put into a group that is leaning toward marketing a risky product, the group's decision would be more extreme than the individual's. If, on the other hand, the group is leaning toward the side of caution, the group might shift to a more cautious choice than the typical individual would choose. Research suggests that virtual groups may be even more prone to group polarization than face-to-face groups (Sia, Tan, & Wei, 2002).

Two explanations for group polarization have been offered. The first is that in the group, the individual is presented with persuasive arguments by other members that bolster the individual's original positive or negative stance on an issue. After hearing others in the group argue for a decision that coincides with the individual's opinion, he or she becomes more certain that his or her opinion is correct, and there is a tendency for the group as a whole to become more extreme in its final decision. The other explanation is that individuals adopt the values of the group. If the group presents a positive opinion on an issue, the individuals go along with the group, becoming even more positive (or negative) about an idea than they would be alone. Individuals may support the viewpoint of the group to demonstrate that they endorse the group's values.

Regardless of why it occurs, the fact that some group decisions may be more extreme than those of individuals is a reason for some concern, particularly when a decision involves risks that may compromise the goals of the group, or when extremely cautious decisions inhibit the attainment of group goals.

Despite the persistence of group polarization, there are potential safeguards that may minimize its effect on decision making. Evidence has indicated that groups composed of individuals who all initially agree on an issue, before any group discussion has taken place, tend to make decisions that are the most extreme. That is, these decisions tend to be even more extreme than decisions made by groups composed of members who do not initially agree with one another (Williams & Taormina, 1992). Thus, when groups include members who have varying original opinions on an issue, the decisions made by those groups may be more resistant to the effects of group polarization, and thus less extreme. The presence of even a single dissenting member in a group may help to combat group polarization, just as a "devil's advocate" can help combat groupthink.

Teams and Teamwork

Early on, we differentiated between work groups and work teams, although in many instances the two terms are synonymous. We have already seen that the use of work teams is on the rise, with well more than half of U.S. workers reporting working in some sort of team, as opposed to only 5% of workers in the early 1980s. Although some scholars have touted the use of teams as the solution for improving productivity, we can draw on research in group processes and research on work teams to determine under what conditions teams and teamwork are most appropriate (Hackman, 1998; Stewart & Barrick, 2000).

Teams are most appropriate when the task is complex, requiring individuals with varied skills and competencies to work together. In today's world, that is likely the majority of tasks from construction, to surgery, to software engineering

Stop & Review

Describe the advantages and disadvantages of group decision making.

and design. That is why some researchers emphasize the importance of selecting the right individuals, based on members' knowledge, skills, abilities, and other characteristics (KSAOs), for a particular team and team task (LePine, Hanson, Borman, & Motowidlo, 2000; Stevens & Campion, 1994, 1999). It has been suggested that a common mistake is assigning a task to a team that is better done by individuals working alone. A simple example might be using a team to write a complex report that might be done easier and more effectively by an individual author (Hackman, 1998). Teams are also appropriate for complex decision-making tasks, or for tasks requiring innovation or creativity. However, it is important to emphasize the limitations of groups in creative tasks such as brainstorming (see Up Close). Teams are also appropriate when the situation is variable, requiring the team to adapt to changing external conditions (Dunphy & Bryant, 1996; Kozlowski & Ilgen, 2006).

In addition to team members possessing the required KSAOs to complement one another, effective team members should possess the kinds of characteristics that will make them highly functioning team members, such as good communication skills, skills in problem solving, and conflict management skills, and they should be self-motivated and committed to the team (Stevens & Campion, 1999). Because team members may not possess some of these characteristics, and because team members may come and go, I/O psychologists have advocated training for team members, as well as cross-training so that members have overlapping competencies in the event that a member leaves the team (Marks, Sabella, Burke, & Zaccaro, 2002; Moreland, Argote, & Krishnan, 1998).

In the group dynamics of the team, it is important that the team develop a sense of trust among members (Costa, 2003), a sense of task-related cohesiveness, and group efficacy if they are to perform effectively. Good leadership is also important for successful teams, whether the leadership involves a designated team leader/manager or leadership is shared among team members (Pearce & Conger, 2003). Leaders facilitate team performance by providing direction, constructive feedback, evaluating, coaching, and rewarding (Stagl, Salas, & Burke, 2007).

Another area that has received increasing research attention is the emotional climate and process in work groups and teams (Barsade, 2002; Hartel et al., 2005; Kozlowski & Ilgen, 2006). As we saw in Chapters 9 and 10, positive and negative emotions in the workplace can have huge effects on individual and team performance, job engagement, and commitment to the team and organization.

External to the team, effective teams must be supported by the organization, and they need to receive feedback and coaching about the team's performance and ways to improve it. Often, organizations evaluate team performance at both the team level and the individual level. Table 12.4 offers suggestions for the effective functioning of work teams.

A great deal of attention has been given to what are termed **self-managing work teams**, which are teams that have complete responsibility for whole tasks, products, or service lines (Cohen, Ledford, & Spreitzer, 1996; Kuipers & Stoker, 2009). Self-managing work teams often operate without a formal supervisor, or leader. We will discuss such "self-leading groups" in Chapter 13 on leadership.

self-managing work teams

teams that have complete responsibility for whole tasks

Stop & Review

List and define six symptoms of groupthink.

TABLE 12.4
Guidelines for Effective Functioning of Work Teams

1. The task is one that is appropriate for a work team.
2. The team is recognized as such by its own members and others in the organization.
3. The team has clear authority over the task (e.g., team must not be "second-guessed" by management).
4. The structure of the team, including the task, the team members, and the team norms, needs to promote teamwork.
5. The organization must support the team through policies and systems specifically designed to support the work teams' needs.
6. Expert coaching and feedback are provided to the teams when it is needed and when team members are ready to receive it.

Source: Hackman, J. R. (1998). Why teams don't work. In R. Scott Tindale et al. (Eds.). *Theory and research on small groups*. New York: Plenum Press.

Summary

A *group* is two or more individuals, engaged in social interaction to achieve some goal. *Teams* consist of interdependent workers with complementary skills working toward a shared goal or outcome. Within work groups, members play various *roles*, which are patterns of behavior adopted based on expectations held about the function of a position. Work groups also develop *norms*, or rules to help govern member behavior. The process of *organizational socialization* refers to the integration of individuals into work groups and organizations through learning work procedures, work roles, and organizational and group norms.

Certain basic processes occur in all work groups. One is *conformity*, the process of adhering to and following group norms. Another basic process, *cohesiveness*, is the degree of attraction among group members. A number of factors, such as group size, member status, member stability, and member similarity, can influence group cohesiveness.

Two common yet opposing forces that are evident in all groups are cooperation and competition. *Cooperation* is critical to coordinating the activities of work group members. However, *social loafing* can occur when workers in groups put in less effort than they would when working alone. *Competition* can lead to *conflict*, which is behavior by one party that is designed to inhibit the goal attainment of another party. Conflict can occur at a number of levels within work organizations, taking the form of *intraindividual*, interindividual, intragroup, intergroup, or interorganizational conflict. It can arise from various sources, most notably from a scarcity of desired resources and from individual and group interdependence. The effect of conflict can be both positive and negative; it is positive when it motivates workers or stimulates them to be creative or innovative and negative when it disrupts group work activities and social relationships. Managing conflict involves regulating the level of conflict, resolving it when it is negative, and stimulating it when it is positive or productive. A number of conflict resolution and conflict stimulation strategies are used in organizations.

An important function in work groups is group decision making, which has several advantages and disadvantages over individual decision making. Although group decision making is slow and conflict ridden, it can lead to high-quality decisions and greater member satisfaction with and commitment to the decision.

A type of breakdown in the effectiveness of decision-making groups is termed *groupthink*, which is a concurrence-seeking tendency that overrides the ability of a cohesive group to make critical decisions. *Group polarization* is the tendency for groups to make more extreme decisions, either more risky or more cautious, than individuals.

For teams to be effective, careful attention must be given to the appropriateness of the task, the characteristics of the team members, and organizational support for the team. The use of *self-managing work teams*, where members work on a complete task, product, or service, are on the rise.

Study Questions and Exercises

1. Consider a work or social group of which you are a member. What are the various roles that members play? What roles have you played? What are some of the norms that are particular to this group?

2. In what ways can group cohesiveness facilitate goal attainment in work groups? How might cohesiveness hinder goal attainment?

3. List the levels of conflict that occur in work groups. Give specific examples from your own life to illustrate each.

4. Discuss the ways in which cohesiveness and conflict can be seen as opposite forces in work groups.

5. What are some of the potential positive and negative outcomes of conflict? Using a work or social group with which you have had contact, think of examples of conflict that led to negative outcomes. How might these situations have been managed to reduce their negative impact?

6. Consider the eight symptoms of groupthink. What steps can decision-making groups take to try to avoid each of them?

Web Links

www.has.vcu.edu/group/gdynamic.htm
A group dynamics site designed to accompany Forsyth's text on Group Dynamics.

Suggested Readings

Forsyth, D. R. (2009). *Group dynamics* (5th ed.). Belmont, CA: Wadsworth. *This excellent textbook is a very good overview of group processes in general, but there are many applications to the workplace.*

Group Dynamics: Theory Research and Practice. Begun in 1997, this journal focuses on research in group processes, much of which has to deal with work groups.

Kozlowski, S. W. J., & Ilgen, D. R. (2006). Enhancing the effectiveness of work groups and teams. *Psychological Science in the Public Interest,* 7(3), 77–124. *A very readable overview of the use of groups and teams in organizations by leading I/O psychologists.*

Salas, E., Goodwin, G. F., & Burke, C. S. (Eds.). (2009). *Team effectiveness in complex organizations: Cross-disciplinary perspectives and approaches.* New York: Taylor & Francis. *An edited, academic book covering research on groups and teams. Part of SIOP's Organizational Frontiers series.*

Inside Tips
UNDERSTANDING LEADERSHIP THEORIES

This chapter presents some of the many theories of leadership in work organizations in more or less chronological order, beginning with the earliest (and simplest) theories and progressing to the more current (and usually more complex) models. Although each of these theories takes a somewhat different perspective in examining work group leadership, you will find common threads. Later theories tend to build on earlier theories, and so contain some of the same elements, but they are enhanced or looked at in different ways. You might also notice that different theoretical approaches sometimes lead to very different interventions to develop leadership.

The theories of leadership introduced in this chapter are directly related to topics discussed previously and also provide a background for upcoming chapters. Specifically, the topic of leadership follows the discussion of group processes in Chapter 12, as the relationship between leaders and other members of the work group is itself an important group process. Leadership and the leadership role are also linked to organizational communication (Chapter 11), particularly the downward flow of communication in organizations. Finally, this chapter will link with the discussion of influence, power, and politics in Chapter 14, for it is clear that the most influential and powerful members of work groups are usually the leaders.

What Is Leadership?

Following your recent promotion, you reflect and realize that for the first time you feel like you are truly a leader in your organization. Your elation is tempered by the fact that with your leadership position comes many new responsibilities. Your supervisees and others will look to you for guidance, to make decisions, and to settle disputes. As you ponder all of this, you wonder, "How can I be the best possible leader for my work group and for my company?"

In Chapter 12 we saw that individuals play various roles in work groups and organizations. One of these roles is that of leader, which in many groups is viewed as the key position. Rightly or wrongly, many people believe that the success or failure of a particular group is largely dependent on the leader and the type of leadership demonstrated. The importance placed on leadership has made it a major topic in politics, the military, and work organizations. Organizations spend millions of dollars annually trying to select managerial personnel who possess the qualities necessary to be effective leaders of work groups. Many millions more are spent on training employees to be more effective leaders and to develop important leadership characteristics. Before we can study the qualities of leaders, however, we must first define and understand leadership.

Defining Leadership

There are a great number of definitions of leadership, but most of these definitions involve the leader using his or her influence to assist groups in attaining goals (Yukl & Van Fleet, 1992). Therefore, for our purposes, we will define leadership as the ability to direct a group toward the attainment of goals. Often, the leader of a work group is the person who holds a particular position or title, such as supervisor, manager, vice president, or leadperson. But there are such things as informal leaders. Thus, a work group leader can be a person with no official title or status. These informal leaders emerge because they have some characteristics that the group members value.

leadership
ability to guide a group toward the achievement of goals

Regardless of whether a leader holds a formal leadership role or emerges informally, a true leader should move followers toward the attainment of goals. Consequently, the fact that a manager or supervisor holds a position of responsibility does not necessarily make that person a true leader. Of course, in work organizations, a powerful position or title can provide a strong starting point for a person to become an effective leader, but a position or title alone will not make an effective leader. Therefore, our definition deals with effective leadership. We may all know (or have worked under) managers who were not effective leaders. They may actually have done nothing to help the group achieve work goals, or they may have even hindered the group's work. Such leaders are "leaders" in name only. This chapter will concentrate on theories of effective leadership.

There has been a long history of research on and theorizing about leadership, and today leadership is one of the most widely studied areas of I/O psychology and management. Leadership theories tend to build on one another, with later theories using components of earlier models and expanding on or using them in new ways. The discussion will begin with the earliest theories, which are known as universalist theories because they were attempts to uncover the universal characteristics of effective leaders. The second category consists of the behavioral theories, which focus on the behaviors of effective leaders. The largest category contains the more complex contingency theories, which examine the interaction between leader characteristics and elements of the work situation. Finally, we will examine theories that focus on leaders as charismatic and transformational individuals who affect followers and organizations in profound ways. Throughout the discussion, relevant research and applications of the theories will also be presented. In particular, we will compare and contrast the various theories. At the end of the chapter, we will discuss how leadership theories can be used to improve the effectiveness of leadership in work organizations.

Universalist Theories of Leadership

universalist theories
theories that look for the major characteristics common to all effective leaders

Universalist theories of leadership search for the one key characteristic or a cluster of key characteristics held by effective leaders, arguing that leaders with these traits will be successful regardless of the situation. Universalist theories represent the earliest and simplest approaches to the study of leadership. We will briefly discuss two of these theories, the great man/woman theory, and the trait theory.

GREAT MAN/WOMAN THEORY

great man/woman theory
a universalist theory of leadership that maintains that great leaders are born, not made

The great man/woman theory, which is much older than any of the formal social science disciplines, reflects the adage that "great leaders are born, not made." Rather than being a formal theory, this theory is a belief that personal qualities and abilities make certain great persons natural leaders. Proponents of the great man/woman theory would state that if important historical leaders

Does the fact that generations of Kennedys have held leadership positions suggest a belief in the great man/woman theory?

such as Julius Caesar, Alexander the Great, or Joan of Arc were alive today, they would again rise to positions of leadership because of their natural abilities. Of course this is mere speculation, and there is little evidence to support the theory, but this does not mean that people do not still believe in it. The fact that in certain countries the relatives of great leaders are also put into positions of power may indicate that there is some general faith in this notion of inborn leadership ability.

TRAIT THEORY

In the early part of this century, psychologists made many attempts to isolate the specific traits, or consistent and enduring physical and personality attributes, that are associated with leader success. The trait theory of leadership refers to several of these investigations. Much of this research involved identifying certain physical characteristics, including height, appearance, and energy level; other characteristics, such as intelligence; and personality traits, like extroversion, dominance, or achievement that were associated with effective leaders (Hollander, 1985; Yukl, 1981). It was presumed, for example, that those who were more intelligent, extroverted, or dominant would be more likely to do well as leaders. Unfortunately, the results of these early studies were inconclusive and showed no solid evidence of any single trait common to all effective leaders (Hollander, 1985; Stogdill, 1948).

Since the 1980s, however, there has been a resurgence of interest in leadership traits (Kenny & Zaccaro, 1983; Lord, DeVader, & Alliger, 1986;

traits
enduring attributes associated with an individual's makeup or personality

trait theory
attempts to discover the traits shared by all effective leaders

Zaccaro, Foti, & Kenny, 1991). This newer work suggests that leadership traits are indeed important. For instance, meta-analytic studies with what is called the *Big5* core personality traits (the Big 5 are extraversion, conscientiousness, openness to experience, agreeableness, and emotional stability) show that in combination, these five traits correlate fairly strongly with measures of leadership emergence and effectiveness (Bono & Judge, 2004; Judge, Bono, Ilies, & Gerhardt, 2002). Furthermore, research on more complex "constellations" of leader characteristics, such as flexibility, charisma, or social intelligence, also suggests that possession of these complex traits are important for leadership. For example, Kenny and Zaccaro (1983, p. 678) described flexibility as "the ability to perceive the needs and goals of a constituency and to adjust one's personal approach to group action accordingly." As such, leader flexibility may not be a single trait but instead a very complex set of abilities to perceive and understand social situations, to communicate effectively, and to act wisely in a variety of social settings (Hall, Workman, & Marchioro, 1998; Marlowe, 1986; Riggio, 1986) that might be better termed "social intelligence" or "social competence" (Hollander, 1978). Certain characteristics, such as a leader's flexibility or social intelligence, may be significant in predicting leader success, although these key leader qualities are probably more complex and multifaceted than those investigated in early leadership research (Riggio, Murphy, & Pirozzolo, 2002).

The major problem with the original trait approach to leadership was that it was too general. It is unlikely that any one trait will be associated with effective leadership in all situations, with all kinds of tasks, and among all groups of followers. The world of work, with the variety of workers and work settings, is much too complex and diverse for any one type of leader to be universally successful. On the other hand, complex constellations of leader characteristics, such as "flexibility" or "charisma," may be related to leader effectiveness, but these complex leader characteristics involve the leader adapting his or her behavior to the leadership situation. We will examine this approach of looking at the interaction of leader characteristics and the leadership situation in later theories of leadership.

Behavioral Theories of Leadership

The general failure of the universalist theories to isolate the characteristics associated with leader effectiveness led to a change in focus. Rather than trying to measure characteristics in the leader's orientation or personality, researchers began to examine the actual behavior of effective leaders to determine what kinds of behavior led to success. In the late 1940s and throughout the 1950s, two research projects, one conducted at Ohio State University and the other at the University of Michigan, investigated the behaviors exhibited by effective leaders. Both projects arrived at some very similar conclusions concerning leaders, their behavior, and effective leadership. Theories based on these studies and focusing on the particular behaviors that related to effective leadership are called behavioral theories of leadership.

behavioral theories of leadership theories derived from studies at Ohio State and University of Michigan that focus on the behaviors common to effective leaders

OHIO STATE LEADERSHIP STUDIES

Using self-reports and detailed observations of leader behavior from both the leaders themselves and their subordinates, researchers at Ohio State University accumulated a list of hundreds of leader behaviors. Using a statistical process called factor analysis, they found that these hundreds of behaviors could all be narrowed into two general categories: initiating structure and consideration (Halpin & Winer, 1957). (Recall from the Statistical Appendix that factor analysis examines how variables are related to each other and clusters them together to form meaningful categories, or factors.) Initiating structure includes leader activities that define and organize, or structure, the work situation, such as assigning specific tasks, defining work group roles, meeting deadlines, making task-related decisions, and maintaining standards of work performance. Consideration describes behaviors that show a genuine concern for the feelings, attitudes, and needs of subordinates by developing rapport with them and showing them mutual respect and trust. Such activities include asking subordinates for their opinions and input, showing concern for the feelings of workers, encouraging communication from and between subordinates, bolstering workers' self-confidence and job satisfaction, and implementing their suggestions.

> **initiating structure**
> leader behaviors that define, organize, and structure the work situation

> **consideration**
> leader behaviors that show a concern for the feeling, attitudes, and needs of followers

Stop & Review
Discuss the limitations of universalist theories of leadership.

The Ohio State researchers concluded that these two dimensions, initiating structure and consideration, were independent of each other. That is, a leader's score on one did not relate to the score on the other. This means that both categories of leader behavior are associated with effective leadership but that they do not necessarily coexist. In other words, some effective leaders are high on initiating structure alone, others display only consideration behaviors, and still others exhibit both.

A great deal of research has been conducted to test the soundness of the initiating structure and consideration dimensions. Generally, the results show that most leader behavior can indeed be grouped into one of the two categories (Bass & Bass, 2008; Fleishman & Harris, 1962; Stogdill & Coons, 1957). Additional studies have looked at how the two categories are related to the important outcome variables of work performance and job satisfaction (Judge, Piccolo, & Ilies, 2004; Kerr & Schriesheim, 1974; Yukl, 1971). Initiating structure has been found to be correlated not only with effective work performance but also with lower group member job satisfaction and corresponding increases in turnover. On the other hand, consideration leader behaviors tend to be positively related to job satisfaction but may be unrelated to or even negatively correlated with work productivity (Bass, 1981; Locke & Schweiger, 1979). However, a meta-analysis of many studies over a long period of time suggested that both initiating structure and consideration are related to both performance and group member satisfaction in the expected relationships. That is, consideration was more strongly related to satisfaction, and initiating structure was more strongly related to performance (Judge et al., 2004).

Although the Ohio State behavioral approach stimulated a great deal of research on effective leader behaviors, it, like the universalist theories, is too simplistic. The Ohio State investigations leave us with two categories of leader behavior, both of which may or may not be related to certain indicators of leader effectiveness. Although the results had the positive effect of stimulating research on leader behaviors, it is clear that the Ohio State studies fall short when it comes to making firm predictions about the relationships between leader behaviors and specific work outcomes in all types of working situations.

UNIVERSITY OF MICHIGAN LEADERSHIP STUDIES

At about the same time as the Ohio State studies were being conducted, researchers at the University of Michigan were also focusing on the behaviors characteristic of effective leaders and came up with quite similar results. Studying leaders in a number of large industrial organizations, the Michigan researchers found that successful leaders tended to exhibit patterns of behavior that were labeled task-oriented, sometimes also called production-oriented, and relationship-oriented, also referred to as employee-oriented (Kahn & Katz, 1960). **Task-oriented behaviors** are concentrated on performing the job that the work group faces and are thus similar to those of the initiating structure factor. The leader is concerned with setting work standards, supervising the job, and meeting production goals. **Relationship-oriented behaviors** include showing concern for employees' well-being and involving them in decision-making processes. The primary difference between the Ohio State and University of Michigan studies was that the Michigan results tended to consider relationship-oriented leader behaviors to be more effective than task-oriented behaviors (Likert, 1967). One of the most famous Michigan studies examined the behavior of leaders in a large insurance company. The findings indicated that both task-oriented and relationship-oriented leadership behavior patterns were positively related to work group performance. However, subordinates of relationship-oriented leaders tended to be more satisfied and had lower turnover rates than employees who were managed by task-oriented leaders (Morse & Reimer, 1956; see also Up Close: How to Be an Effective Leader).

task-oriented behaviors
leader behaviors focused on the work task

relationship-oriented behaviors
leader behaviors focused on maintaining interpersonal relationships on the job

UP CLOSE   How to Be an Effective Leader

It is very likely that sometime in the near future you will find yourself in a leadership role. You may serve as a formal manager of a work group, you may be elected to serve as a leader of a club or civic organization, or you may be appointed head of some work task force. In any case, the research on leadership as well as other findings that we have studied in the areas of communication and group dynamics can help you to do a better job. Of course, as you should know by now, there is no one best way to lead. There are, however, some general principles that you can follow to increase your chances of success:

Become a More Effective Communicator

It has been estimated that as much as 80% of a manager's job involves communication (Mintzberg, 1973). As we saw in Chapter 11, communication is essential for the effective functioning of work groups, teams, and organizations. The better the channels of communication between the leader and followers, the more likely it is that the two will be able to cooperate to get the task done. It is particularly important to listen to supervisees and be sensitive to their needs and concerns. In fact, effective listening may be a leader's most important skill (Harris, 1993; Johnson & Bechler,

1998). The leader who steals away behind closed doors will be unable to meet these needs, which may lead to breakdowns in productivity and in work group satisfaction.

Be Both Task-Oriented and Relationship-Oriented

As the research indicates, both task-oriented and relationship-oriented behaviors are related to leader effectiveness (Bass, 1990). Therefore, leaders who are able to display concern for both the task and the people are more likely to be successful. In general, having a larger "repertoire" of leadership behaviors is a good thing (Hooijberg, 1996). Gaining insight into your own leader behavior patterns will help you to realize if you have a deficit in either area.

Give Careful Attention to Decision Making

One of the leader's most important tasks is decision making. As we have seen, in addition to reaching a good and workable solution, the process itself is also important. For example, involving employees in the decision can increase their levels of satisfaction but usually also leads to slower decision making. The decision-making leadership model emphasizes flexibility—adapting the leader's decision-making style to the situation. Certain decisions may call for more autocratic decision making; others demand a participative approach. Being able to determine what process to use in what situation is the key. However, because evidence indicates that supervisees are generally satisfied with participative decision making, when in doubt it may be wise to use this style.

Remember that Leadership Is a Two-Way Street

Although leaders influence their followers, followers also influence their leaders. A leader can be truly effective only if that person has the support of followers (Meindl, 1990; Palich & Hom, 1992; Riggio, Chaleff, & Lipman-Blumen, 2008). An effective leader knows what his or her own needs are and works to satisfy those needs, but the effective leader is also in tune with, and responsive to, the needs of followers.

Learn to Delegate

Effective leaders learn to delegate certain challenging and responsible tasks to followers, which often not only develops their work skills and abilities, thus making them more valuable to the leader and to the organization, but also gives the leader more time to work on other duties, leading to higher levels of productivity. Hughes, Ginnett, and Curphy (1996) provided guidelines for effective delegation. These include choosing what to delegate, and to whom; making the assignment clear and specific; allowing follower autonomy, but monitoring performance (after all, the leader is ultimately responsible that the task is completed); and "giving credit, not blame."

Have Leadership Self-Efficacy

Leadership self-efficacy is belief in one's ability to play a leadership role. Self-efficacy is important because leaders with higher levels of self-efficacy (e.g., who seem confident in their leadership abilities) are seen as more effective leaders. In addition, they are more persistent under stressful working conditions, and they enhance their followers' self-efficacy (Chemers, Watson, & May, 2000; Murphy, 2002).

Monitor Followers' Performance, Set Challenging Goals, and Give Constructive Feedback

Field studies of work groups from a variety of settings indicates that effective leaders keep tabs on what work group members are doing and provide constructive feedback to help them improve performance and correct errors (Chen, Lam, & Zhong, 2007; Komaki, 1986; Komaki, Desselles, & Bowman, 1989). In addition, effective leaders use effective goal setting to motivate followers (see Chapter 8), to help monitor performance, and to provide a forum for providing constructive feedback.

Be Flexible

Effective leadership means doing the right thing in the right situation. Effective leaders are thus flexible or adaptable (Zaccaro & Banks, 2004). One way to be more flexible is to step back and objectively analyze a situation before you act. Leaders should also be objective about their own feelings, behaviors, attitudes, and biases, and how they may negatively affect leadership ability. Sometimes, leaders fall into comfortable patterns of behavior, using the same leadership style in all situations simply because it is easier than adapting behavior to fit the situation. However, it is the objective, adaptable leaders who are successful.

Evaluation of the Behavioral Theories of Leadership

Although initiating structure (task-orientation) and consideration (relationship-orientation) seem to be reliable dimensions describing leader behavior, the behavioral approach has one major shortcoming: The two dimensions represent very different types of leader behavior, yet both have been linked to effective management (Bass, 1981; Morse & Reimer, 1956). If we believe the universalist contention that there is one set of effective leader characteristics or one best leadership style, such divergent leader behaviors simply cannot represent a single, effective leader. The most likely explanation is that other variables, particularly those related to the type of tasks or the characteristics of the work group, determine whether certain leadership behaviors will be effective. In other words, a task-oriented leader might be effective in certain situations under specific circumstances, whereas a relationship-oriented leader might be effective in another situation.

Leadership Grid
an application of the findings from the behavioral theories of leadership that stresses that effective leaders should be both task-oriented and relationship-oriented

---

APPLYING I/O PSYCHOLOGY

The Leadership Grid: The Marketing of Leadership Theory

One of the more successful and widespread applications of leadership theory to the business world is known as the Leadership Grid (formerly known as the Managerial Grid; Blake & McCanse, 1991; Blake & Mouton, 1985). This leadership intervention program encompasses two core dimensions—people emphasis and production emphasis. These are attitudinal in character and are to be distinguished from the behavioral dimensions identified in the research originating with the Ohio State and University of Michigan studies. The Leadership Grid is based on what has been called Situational Leadership Theory. The basic premise of the theory and the Leadership Grid is that the best leaders are those who show both high concern for the task and production and high concern for people. Each leader is rated on two 9-point scales, the first assessing the leader's production orientation, the second measuring the leader's people orientation. The best leader receives a score of 9, 9, meaning someone high in both production and people orientation (labeled a "team manager"); the worst leader receives a 1, 1 rating, meaning someone low in both production and people orientation (labeled an "impoverished manager"; see the accompanying diagram). By stating that there is one best leadership style (the 9, 9 leader), the Leadership Grid takes a universalist approach, which is a departure from the results of the Ohio State studies indicating that either task/production orientation or relationship/people orientation could be related to leader effectiveness (see Figure 13.1).

The Leadership Grid has been criticized primarily because of its universalist approach. Most researchers advocate that there is no one best leadership style and that effective leadership depends on how the leader's style fits with the particular work situation. Despite some criticisms, the Leadership Grid has had significant impact. According to the authors, the program has "boosted productivity and profits for thousands of corporations worldwide"; they claim that Leadership Grid training has been provided to nearly half a million leaders and managers. In fact, the program has been so well packaged that its name is a registered trademark. Most of these praises, however, are based on the testimonials of client organizations that have used (and paid for) the Leadership Grid. There has been little systematic research on the theory behind the grid by persons other than its authors (Vecchio, 2007), although Tjosvold (1984b) found that leaders who were task-oriented and who demonstrated a relationship orientation by expressing leader warmth led groups that were more productive than those led by leaders who lacked both of these orientations—but this is a far cry from conclusive support for the Leadership Grid.

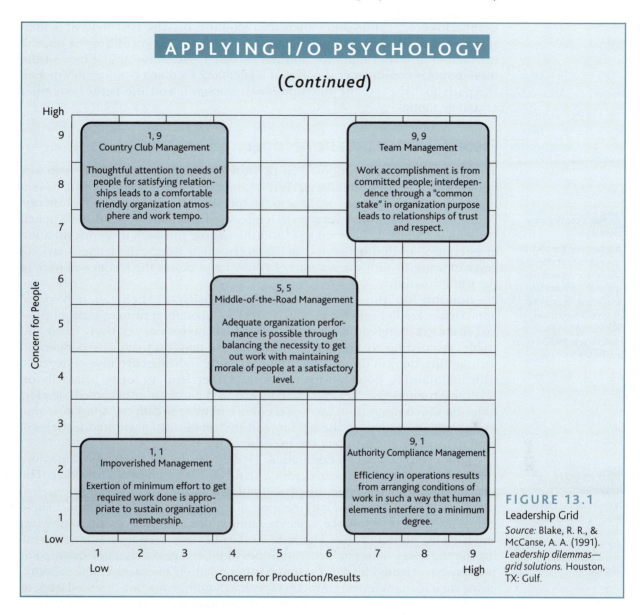

APPLYING I/O PSYCHOLOGY

(Continued)

1, 9
Country Club Management

Thoughtful attention to needs of people for satisfying relationships leads to a comfortable friendly organization atmosphere and work tempo.

9, 9
Team Management

Work accomplishment is from committed people; interdependence through a "common stake" in organization purpose leads to relationships of trust and respect.

5, 5
Middle-of-the-Road Management

Adequate organization performance is possible through balancing the necessity to get out work with maintaining morale of people at a satisfactory level.

1, 1
Impoverished Management

Exertion of minimum effort to get required work done is appropriate to sustain organization membership.

9, 1
Authority Compliance Management

Efficiency in operations results from arranging conditions of work in such a way that human elements interfere to a minimum degree.

Concern for People (vertical axis: Low to High, 1–9)

Concern for Production/Results (horizontal axis: Low to High, 1–9)

FIGURE 13.1
Leadership Grid
Source: Blake, R. R., & McCanse, A. A. (1991). *Leadership dilemmas—grid solutions.* Houston, TX: Gulf.

Contingency Theories of Leadership

The next stage in the evolution of leadership theories produced contingency theories, which examine the interaction of characteristics of the leader and the situation, stating that effective leadership depends on the proper match between the two. Many of the contingency theories do, however, build on the behavioral theories, using the leader behavior dichotomies—task-oriented/initiating structure and relationship-oriented/consideration—as a starting

contingency theories
theories that look at the interaction of characteristics of both the leader and the situation

point. However, contingency theories recognize no one best style of leadership behavior. Rather, leader effectiveness depends, or is contingent on, the interaction of leader behavior and the situation. We will examine four of the more popular contingency theories of leadership: Fiedler's contingency model, the path-goal theory, the decision-making model, and the leader–member exchange model.

FIEDLER'S CONTINGENCY MODEL

The leadership theory proposed by psychologist Fred Fiedler (1967) is so well known that it is often simply referred to as *the* contingency model. But, as outlined, the term *contingency model* actually specifies a certain category of theory. Fiedler's contingency model argues that effective leadership depends on a match between a leader's behavioral style and the degree to which the work situation gives control and influence to the leader. In other words, the leader's style of behavior must fit with the amount of control and power the leader will have in the work situation.

Building on the Ohio State and University of Michigan behavioral approaches, Fiedler's theory divides leaders based on their primary motivation—task-oriented or relationship-oriented—which he sees as relatively fixed and stable. According to Fiedler, certain leaders may be primarily concerned with getting the job done (task-oriented), although they are also concerned with maintaining good group relations. Other leaders focus primarily on relationships and give "secondary" concern to the task. In other words, leaders differ on which motivation takes precedence in most situations. A task-oriented leader will attend less to the group, and the relationship-oriented leader will tend to focus on the group at the expense of the task.

To measure a leader's orientation, Fiedler developed a self-report measure referred to as the LPC measure, which stands for least preferred coworker. The LPC requires leaders to rate the person with whom they had worked least well—"the person with whom you had the most difficulty in getting a job done." These ratings are done using bipolar adjective rating scales, such as pleasant/unpleasant and friendly/unfriendly (see Figure 13.2). The LPC is scored by summing the ratings on the scales. This total score indicates whether a person is a task-oriented or relationship-oriented leader. Persons scoring relatively low on the LPC measure, giving their least preferred coworkers very harsh ratings, are task-oriented leaders. Individuals who rate their least preferred coworker somewhat leniently, leading to relatively high LPC scores, are considered to be relationship-oriented. Scores from normative populations help determine what are low and high LPC scores. The rationale behind this scoring system is that task-oriented leaders will be very critical of a poor worker because they value task success. A relationship-oriented leader, on the other hand, values interpersonal relationships and is likely to rate the least preferred coworker more leniently (Rice, 1978). According to Fiedler, task-oriented leaders with low LPC scores link a worker's poor performance with undesirable personality characteristics, whereas relationship-oriented leaders with high LPC scores can separate the least preferred coworker's personality from the individual's work performance (Fiedler, 1967).

Fiedler's contingency model

a leadership theory that maintains that effective leadership depends on a match between the leader's style and the degree to which the work situation gives control and influence to the leader

least preferred coworker (LPC)

a measure that assesses leaders' task or relationship orientation by having them rate their most difficult fellow worker

Stop & Review

Compare and contrast the findings of the Ohio State and University of Michigan behavioral studies of leadership.

NAME _____

People differ in the ways they think about those with whom they work. This may be important in working with others. Please give your immediate, first reaction to the items on the following two pages.

Below are pairs of words which are opposite in meaning, such as "Very neat" and "Not neat." You are asked to describe someone with whom you have worked by placing an "X" in one of the eight spaces on the line between the two words.

Each space represents how well the adjective fits the person you are describing, as if it were written.

Very neat | 8 | 7 | 6 | 5 | 4 | 3 | 2 | 1 | Not neat
Very neat / Quite neat / Some-what neat / Slightly neat / Slightly untidy / Some-what untidy / Quite untidy / Very untidy

FOR EXAMPLE If you were to describe the person with whom you are able to work least well, and you ordinarily think of him or her as being quite neat, you would put an "X" in the second space from the words Very neat, like this

Very neat | 8 | X(7) | 6 | 5 | 4 | 3 | 2 | 1 | Not neat

If you ordinarily think of the person with whom you can work least well as being only slightly neat, you would put your "X" as follows

Very neat | 8 | 7 | 6 | X(5) | 4 | 3 | 2 | 1 | Not neat

If you think of the person as being very untidy, you would use the space nearest the words Not Neat

Very neat | 8 | 7 | 6 | 5 | 4 | 3 | X(2) | 1 | Not neat

Look at the words at both ends of the line before you put in your "X." Please remember that there are *no right or wrong answers.* Work rapidly, your first answer is likely to be the best. Please do not omit any items, and mark each item only once.

LPC

Think of the person *with whom you can work least well.* He or she may be someone you work with now or someone you knew in the past.

He or she does not have to be the person you like least well, but should be the person with whom you had the most difficulty in getting a job done. Describe this person as he or she appears to you.

Pleasant	8	7	6	5	4	3	2	1	Unpleasant
Friendly	8	7	6	5	4	3	2	1	Unfriendly
Rejecting	8	7	6	5	4	3	2	1	Accepting
Helpful	8	7	6	5	4	3	2	1	Frustrating
Unenthusiastic	8	7	6	5	4	3	2	1	Enthusiastic
Tense	8	7	6	5	4	3	2	1	Relaxed
Distant	8	7	6	5	4	3	2	1	Close
Cold	8	7	6	5	4	3	2	1	Warm
Cooperative	8	7	6	5	4	3	2	1	Uncooperative
Supportive	8	7	6	5	4	3	2	1	Hostile
Boring	8	7	6	5	4	3	2	1	Interesting
Quarrelsome	8	7	6	5	4	3	2	1	Harmonious
Self-assured	8	7	6	5	4	3	2	1	Hesitant
Efficient	8	7	6	5	4	3	2	1	Inefficient
Gloomy	8	7	6	5	4	3	2	1	Cheerful
Open	8	7	6	5	4	3	2	1	Guarded

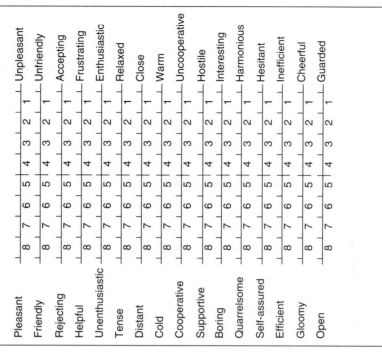

FIGURE 13.2
Least Preferred Coworker (LPC) Measure

Source: Fiedler, F. E. (1967). *A theory of leadership effectiveness* (pp. 40–41). New York: McGraw-Hill.

Determining a leader's task or relationship orientation with the LPC is only the first part of Fiedler's contingency model. The next step is defining characteristics of the work situation to find the proper match between leadership style and the situation. The characteristics of a work situation are defined using three variables—leader–member relations, task structure, and position power—that combine to create circumstances that are either very favorable, very unfavorable, or neither favorable nor unfavorable for the leader.

leader–member relations

the quality of the relationship between leader and followers

Leader–member relations is the relationship between the leader and followers—in other words, how well liked, respected, and trusted the leader is by subordinates. According to Fiedler, this dimension can be measured on a scale involving good and poor ratings by having group members indicate their loyalty for and acceptance of the leader.

task structure

an assessment of how well elements of the work task are structured

The second dimension, task structure, assesses how well a job is structured by considering such factors as whether the group's output can be easily evaluated, whether the group has well-defined goals, and whether clear procedures for reaching those goals exist. Tasks can be defined as "structured" or "unstructured."

position power

a leader's authority to punish or reward followers

The third dimension that Fiedler uses to define the situation is position power, or the leader's authority over subordinates, which is usually defined as the leader's ability to hire, fire, discipline, and reward. Position power is assessed as either strong or weak. It is usually easy to determine position power, because it is clearly outlined in company policies.

Recall that according to Fiedler's contingency model, the key to effective leadership is the leader's control and influence in a specific situation. Obviously, the situation that is going to be most favorable for the leader is one

According to Fiedler, leader–member relations reflect the respect workers have for their leader.

in which the leader–member relations are good, the task is structured, and the leader has strong position power. The least favorable situation for the leader is one where leader–member relations are poor, the task is unstructured, and the leader has weak position power. Research indicates that task-oriented leaders with low LPC scores are most effective in situations that are either highly favorable or highly unfavorable for the leader—the two extremes of the continuum. Relationship-oriented leaders are more effective in "middle situations" in which the leader's control and influence are neither low nor high.

According to Fiedler, task-oriented leaders with low LPC scores are successful in very unfavorable situations because their take-charge style puts some structure into the circumstances and may encourage the group to perform the job. In other words, in an extremely unfavorable situation, the task-oriented leader has nothing to lose. Taking a firm hand and focusing on task performance and task-related goals may produce results, which is what is needed in such a crisis. At these times followers might walk all over a relationship-oriented leader. In very favorable situations, groups are already likely to be productive because the task is straightforward and structured, relations between leader and members are good, and the leader has the power to reward for good performance.

Relationship-oriented leaders are more successful when their situational control and influence are neither very high nor low. In these "middle" circumstances, it is important that leaders be well equipped to deal with the interpersonal conflicts that inevitably arise. This is the specialty of the high-LPC, relationship-oriented leaders. Because such situations may lack one of the three situational variables, a leader who shows increased concern for workers and allows them to voice opinions may increase group member satisfaction levels and even job performance. By contrast, being task-oriented in these situations may be counterproductive, alienating members and decreasing levels of satisfaction, because the leader appears to care only about the task. Fiedler also argued that high-LPC leaders may be more cognitively complex, or better able to deal with complex situations. Situations that are neither clearly favorable nor clearly unfavorable for the leader are complex and are best handled by such a person.

Figure 13.3 is a graphic representation of the predictions made by the Fiedler model. The graph shows that task-oriented leaders (solid line) have higher group performance when in very favorable or very unfavorable situations. Relationship-oriented leaders (dotted line) lead higher-performing groups in situations of moderate favorability.

Although some studies have failed to find the predictions made by Fiedler's theory (Vecchio, 1977), others have generally supported the model (Peters, Hartke, & Pohlmann, 1985; Strube & Garcia, 1981). However, the predictions hold up better in laboratory studies than in studies conducted in actual work settings (Peters, Hartke, & Pohlmann, 1985). Critics have focused primarily on the use of the LPC measure, arguing that it is not clear exactly what it measures because it only infers a leader's orientation from feelings about a coworker rather than directly assessing task and relationship orientation (Ashour, 1973; Schriesheim, Bannister, & Money, 1979). Another criticism concerns individuals who score near the middle of the LPC scale. In fact, one researcher divided the

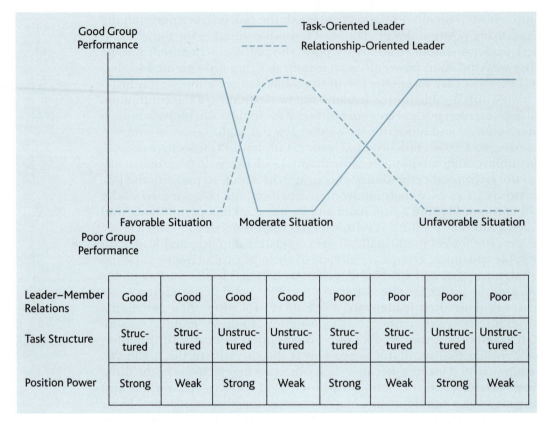

FIGURE 13.3
Fiedler's Contingency Model Predictions

ratings into high, low, and middle scores and found that the middle-LPC leaders seemed to be effective in a range of situations (Kennedy, 1982). Another weakness in Fiedler's predictions concerns the assessment of situations, for it is not clear how actual work situations would break down in terms of their favorableness for the leader. In other words, we do not know how many real-world situations would be favorable or very unfavorable for the leader and thus demand a task-oriented leader. Nor do we know how many situations are moderately favorable for the leader or what distinctions there are between moderately favorable situations (e.g., are there "low moderate" and "high moderate" favorable situations?).

Despite these criticisms, the Fiedler contingency model is important for many reasons. First, it was the first highly visible leadership theory to present the contingency approach. Second, its detailed attention to the situation emphasized the importance of both situation and leader characteristics in determining leader effectiveness. Third, Fiedler's model stimulated a great deal of research, including tests of its predictions and attempts to improve on the model, and inspired the formulation of alternative contingency theories. Finally, it also led to the development of a program by Fiedler and his colleagues (Fiedler & Chemers, 1984) to apply his theory to actual leadership situations. Known as Leader Match, their program consists of a workbook containing an LPC measure, leadership problems that the leader must analyze and solve, directions on how to assess elements of the leader's situation, guidelines for changing elements of the situation, and suggestions for helping subordinates improve performance. Basically, Leader Match teaches managers to recognize their own leadership orientation using the LPC and then trains them to recognize those situations in which they are most likely to succeed. If a mismatch is discovered between the leader's orientation and the work situation, suggestions are made for changing one or more of the three situational variables to provide a more appropriate fit. For example, if a low-LPC, task-oriented leader is in a situation of moderate favorability in which leader–member relations are fair, the task is unstructured, but position power is strong, an attempt might be made either to improve leader–member relations or to make the group work task more structured to increase the favorability of the situation and thus make it more compatible with the leader. The Leader Match program holds that it is more effective to change the situation, or to fit certain types of leaders to appropriate situations, than it is to try to change the leader's style of behavior.

Leader Match has been widely used. Fiedler claims that it has been used by more than 40,000 managers. Although the program has been shown to be quite successful in increasing managers' leadership effectiveness (Leister, Borden, & Fiedler, 1977), it is not without its critics, who argue that at times Leader Match does not follow the predictions made by the theory (Jago & Ragan, 1986; Kabanoff, 1981).

In sum, Fiedler's contingency model was one of the first detailed theories of leadership. It makes certain predictions about the situations in which certain types of leaders will be effective and has been a straightforward and widely used intervention for improving leader effectiveness (Ayman, Chemers, & Fiedler, 1995).

THE PATH-GOAL THEORY

Expanding on the definition of leadership presented at the start of this chapter, the path-goal theory states that a leader's job is to help the work group attain the goals that they desire (House, 1971; House & Mitchell, 1974). The leader is accordingly seen as a facilitator, or guide, who helps the group overcome the various barriers and roadblocks they may encounter on the way to achieving their goals. Usually these goals involve increasing worker motivation to perform the job and attempting to gain increases in worker satisfaction. As is reflected in its emphasis on worker motivation, the expectancy theory of motivation (see Chapter 8) was used as the foundation for the path-goal theory (Yukl, 1998).

To help the group reach its goals, the leader may adopt one of four categories of behavior—directive, achievement-oriented, supportive, and participative—the selection of which depends on the characteristics of the situation. Directive behavior provides instructions and suggestions for getting the job done. Examples include giving workers specific guidelines and procedures, setting up schedules and work rules, and coordinating work group activities.

path-goal theory
states that a leader's job is to help the work group achieve their desired goals

directive behavior
leader behavior that provides instructions and suggestions for performing a job

achievement-oriented behavior
leader behavior concentrated on particular work outcomes

supportive behavior
leader behavior focusing on interpersonal relationships and showing concern for workers' well-being

participative behavior
leader behavior that encourages members to assume an active role in group planning and decision making

Achievement-oriented behavior focuses on specific work outcomes and may involve setting challenging goals for the group and measuring and encouraging improvements in performance. Supportive behavior concentrates on the interpersonal relations among group members by showing concern for workers' well-being and providing a friendly work environment. Finally, participative behavior encourages members to take an active role in work group planning and decision making through actions such as soliciting information from workers about how to do the job and asking for opinions and suggestions. These four types of leader behaviors outlined in the path-goal theory offer a more detailed breakdown of the initiating structure (task-oriented) and consideration (relationship-oriented) behaviors: Directive and achievement-oriented behaviors are two kinds of initiating structure behavior, while the supportive and participative behaviors are two kinds of consideration behaviors.

The choice of leader behavior is contingent on the type of work task and the characteristics of the followers. For example, if a task is routine and easy to understand and if the work group is made up of experienced, self-motivated individuals, the directive style of leadership would probably not be needed because followers can perform the job without much supervision. Instead, supportive behavior might be called for to maintain a harmonious work setting, or participative behavior may be necessary to encourage employees to suggest ways to improve work procedures and the work environment. On the other hand, if the task is fairly complex and the workers are somewhat inexperienced, a directive style might be appropriate.

The results of research on the path-goal theory have been mixed (House, 1996). Although there has been some support for the model (Dixon & Hart, 2010; House & Dessler, 1974; Wofford & Liska, 1993), its general approach and its inability to make specific and precise predictions in actual work settings have been criticized (Schriesheim & Kerr, 1977; Yukl, 1989). The theory does offer some idea of how leaders must change their behavior to fit the situation, but the biggest disappointment is that it has not led to a specific type of intervention for use on the job (Miner, 1983). On the positive side, like Fiedler's contingency model, the path-goal theory offers a rather detailed assessment of the situation in an effort to relate the leader's behavior to the characteristics of a specific situation. It also goes a step beyond the simple dichotomy of task orientation and relationship orientation in defining leader behavior.

THE DECISION-MAKING MODEL

decision-making model
a theory that matches characteristics of the situation with leader decision-making strategies

As seen in Chapter 12, one of the major tasks of a work group leader is to preside over important work-related decisions. Vroom and his colleagues (Vroom & Jago, 1988; Vroom & Yetton, 1973) have developed a contingency theory of leadership called the decision-making model that is based on the premise that leaders are basically decision makers. This theory is somewhat unique in that it not only makes predictions about proper leader behavior in making decisions but also actually gives "prescriptions" for the decision maker to follow. The decision-making theory holds that a leader can make work decisions using a number of strategies, ranging from acting alone (purely autocratic decision

TABLE 13.1

Five Decision-Making Strategies: The Model

Decision-Making Strategy Process

1. Autocratic decision I The leader makes the decision alone, using information available only to the leader.
2. Autocratic decision II The leader obtains information from subordinates and then makes the decision alone.
3. Consultative decision I The leader shares the problem with relevant subordinates and gets their ideas and input individually, but makes the decision alone.
4. Consultative decision II The leader shares the problem with subordinates as a group, gets their collective input, but makes the decision alone.
5. Group decision The leader shares the problem with subordinates as a group and together they make a consensus decision.

Source: Vroom, V. H., & Yetton, P. W. (1973). *Leadership and decision-making* (p. 13). Pittsburgh: University of Pittsburgh Press.

making) to arriving at a decision on the basis of group consensus (completely participative decision making). In the latter type of decision making the leader is just another group member. The five decision-making styles used in the decision-making model are presented in Table 13.1.

To define the decision-making situation, the theory provides a series of yes–no, work-related questions that a leader must ask before adopting a particular strategy. For example, the first question is whether or not a high-quality decision is needed. If the leader answers "yes," it is likely that a more participative style is needed; if the answer is "no," it is likely that a more autocratic style is appropriate. Of course, the decision-making style chosen is a composite of all questions. The decision-making model presents a decision tree framework for the leader to follow, with each of the seven questions representing a choice point that eventually leads to the correct behavior for the decision that needs to be made (see Figure 13.4). Consider, for example, the manager of the parts department of an automobile dealer who must purchase a computer software inventory system for the department. A number of systems are available, each with its own advantages and drawbacks. The leader answers each of the questions on the decision tree as follows:

a. Yes, there is a need for quality—a system that will work best in our department.
b. No, the leader doesn't have enough information to make a quality decision alone.
c. No, the problem is not structured, because there is no clear-cut way to decide among the various systems.
d. Yes, subordinates will be using the system and need to accept it.
e. No, if subordinates did not like the system they might avoid using it.
f. Yes, workers do share organizational goals (they want a system that will do the job).
g. Not applicable.

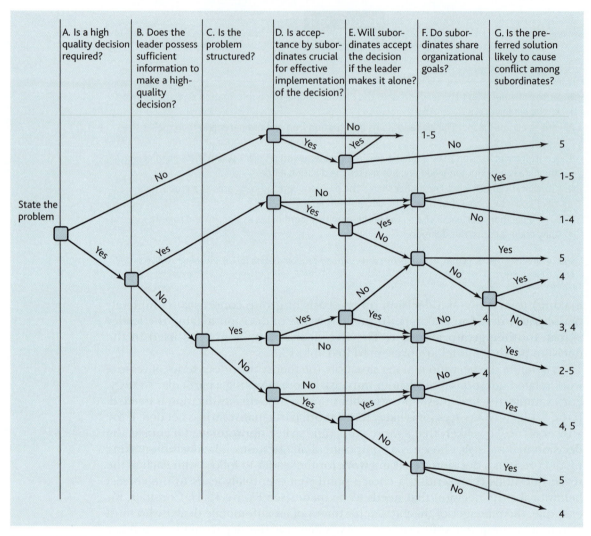

FIGURE 13.4
Decision Tree Flow Chart (see Table 12.1 for decision-making strategies)

This framework suggests that the leader should use a group strategy to arrive at a consensus. Because the department is small and the workers are involved in their jobs, they can contribute a great deal to the decision-making process, and it is critical that they accept the decision.

Research has largely supported this decision-making model (Field, 1982; Field & Andrews, 1998; Margerison & Glube, 1979; Paul & Ebadi, 1989). For example, a study found that the effective strategies used by actual managers to solve important work-related decisions were consistent with the theory's prescriptions (Vroom & Jago, 1978). Because of the normative nature of the model, it is also a unique combination of theory and application. As a contingency model, it is effective because it considers how a leader's individual behavior fits with the dynamics of a specific situation. Moreover, it provides a very detailed definition of the situation, as outlined by the decision-related questions. The major problem with the model is its complexity, which may make it difficult for managers to understand and to learn to use. (In fact, revisions to the decision-making theory have further refined it, and made it even more complex and precise than what is presented in Figure 13.4 (Vroom & Jago, 1995).) This occurs to theories in general: As they get closer to modeling real-world complexity, they may also become harder to apply. There is a general tendency for people to look for relatively simple solutions to problems. Thus, although complex contingency models, such as the decision-making model, might be sound and accurate, they may not be widely used or accepted in actual work settings due to their complex nature.

Stop & Review

Define the three situational characteristics in Fiedler's contingency model.

THE LEADER–MEMBER EXCHANGE MODEL

The previous contingency models of leadership, including Fiedler's model and the path-goal theory, fit the leader's behavior to various characteristics of the work situation. Fiedler's model also considers the amount of power a leader has in a given situation, whereas the decision-making theory weighs a variety of characteristics related to a situation. The leader–member exchange model (LMX) takes a different approach and considers that effective leadership is determined by the quality of the interaction between the leader and a particular work group member (Dansereau, Graen, & Haga, 1975; Graen & Uhl-Bien, 1995). According to this theory, the worker is the situation. Basically, the model (which was formerly called the vertical dyad linkage model) states that the types of one-on-one, or dyadic, relationships that develop between the leader and each follower will be somewhat different. In any work group, the leader tends to develop better relationships with a few subordinates (the in-group), whereas the rest receive less attention or concern from the leader (the out-group). The character of the leader–member exchange can range from low quality, in which the leader has a negative image of the subordinate, and the subordinate does not respect or trust the leader, to high quality, in which the leader has a positive view of the worker, and the worker feels that the leader is supportive and provides encouragement. Of course, such differences affect important outcomes such as work performance, employee loyalty and attendance, and job satisfaction (Gerstner & Day, 1997; Graen, Novak, & Sommerkamp, 1982; Howell & Hall-Merenda, 1999; Kim, Lee, & Carlson, 2010; Wayne & Ferris, 1990). As one might expect, in high-quality leader–member relations, there is frequent communication between the leader and subordinate, and these interactions are generally positive. In low-quality LMX relationships, communication is infrequent and/or less positive in tone (Kacmar, Witt, Zivnuska, & Gully, 2003).

leader–member exchange model (LMX) a theory that effective leadership is determined by the quality of the interaction between the leader and particular group members

The notion that leaders develop different types and quality of relationships with subordinates makes sense. For example, the president of a large company may have to interact with a number of department managers. Some of them

Stop & Review

What are the four leader behaviors central to the path-goal theory?

may be the trusted advisers with whom the president interacts quite frequently and to whom he gives an important role in establishing company policy. The president's relationships with other managers may not be close at all, and they may in fact have very little actual contact with the president. Naturally, and as the LMX model predicts, the motivation to perform and the levels of satisfaction of the in-group managers are likely to be high, whereas the out-group managers may not be very motivated or satisfied.

The authors of the LMX theory claim that their approach is an improvement over other leadership theories because previous models assume that leaders act in a relatively uniform way toward all subordinates. Because these traditional approaches look only at typical, or average, leader behavior and ignore the nontypical behavior displayed in very good or very poor leader–member exchanges, a focus on specific leader–member relations will lead to better predictions of the effects of that leader behavior on work outcomes (Dansereau et al., 1975; Graen, 1976; see also Vecchio, 1982). In other words, rather than looking at how the leader's behavior influences a particular outcome in subordinates, the LMX approach generally emphasizes how a leader's particular behavior with particular subordinates—both in-group and out-group members—affects their specific job outcomes.

The leader–member exchange model is quite popular and has generated a considerable amount of research. A number of improvements have been made to the theory, including improvements in measuring in-group/out-group membership and the quality of leader–member exchanges (Duchon, Green, & Taber, 1986; Graen & Scandura, 1985; Liden & Maslyn, 1998; Phillips & Bedeian, 1994). Evidence suggests that LMX is a two-way street, with the quality of relationships being influenced by the effort and energy put into the relationships by both the leader and the follower (Maslyn & Uhl-Bien, 2001).

The strategy for applying LMX to improving leader effectiveness seems relatively straightforward: Improve the quality of leader–member relationships. Tests of leadership training programs aimed at this goal have been encouraging. For example, in one study of 83 computer-processing employees of a large service organization, a program that trained leaders to listen and communicate their expectations to subordinates led to a 19% increase in work group productivity and significant increases in subordinates' job satisfaction (Scandura & Graen, 1984). In another study, the quality of leader–member exchanges between supervisors and newly hired employees in the newcomers' first five days on the job predicted the quality of leader–member exchanges at six months, indicating the importance of developing good-quality supervisor–subordinate interactions early on (Liden, Wayne, & Stilwell, 1993).

Charismatic and Transformational Leadership Theories

Whereas contingency theories of leadership focus on the interaction between a leader's behavior or style and elements of the situation, other leadership theorists have focused on the truly "exceptional" leaders. For example, when we think of exceptional leaders throughout history and the truly great leaders of

Former U.S. President William Clinton is considered by many to be a charismatic leader.

today, they seem to do more than simply adapt their behavior to the situation. These leaders seem to have the ability to inspire or "energize" followers toward organizational goals. They often are able to "transform" groups of workers into highly effective teams. Great leaders, in effect, inspire followers to become leaders themselves. We will briefly examine two additional theories of leadership that deal with these exceptional types of leaders: charismatic leadership theory and transformational leadership.

CHARISMATIC LEADERSHIP THEORY

We can all think of great political and social leaders who possessed charisma—Winston Churchill, Martin Luther King Jr., Eleanor Roosevelt, John F. Kennedy, Mahatma Gandhi. There are also charismatic business leaders who seem to inspire and captivate their employees—GE's former CEO Jack Welch, Richard Branson of Virgin Atlantic, Apple's Steve Jobs. Charismatic leadership theory focuses on such exceptional leaders and tries to identify and define the characteristics that

charismatic leadership theory
states that leaders possess some exceptional characteristics that cause followers to be loyal and inspired

these leaders possess that inspire followers to identify with and to be devoted to them and also outlines the nature of the relationship charismatic leaders have with followers (Klein & House, 1995; Trice & Beyer, 1986; Weierter, 1997). According to House (1977), charismatic leaders have the ability to communicate shared group goals, and they convey confidence in their own abilities as well as those of their followers. Elements of the situation also come into play, however, because charismatic leaders are often most effective in situations where goals are unclear and environmental conditions are uncertain or unstable, presumably because charismatic leaders are able to provide some vision of where the group should be headed (House & Singh, 1987).

⏱ Stop & Review

Describe the strengths and weaknesses of the decision-making theory of leadership.

There is some speculation that the "exceptional" characteristics or qualities of charismatic leaders are related to the possession of exceptionally high social skills and an ability to relate to (and inspire) followers at a deep, emotional level (Hogan, Raskin, & Fazzini, 1990; Riggio, 1987). Conger and Kanungo (1987, 1988) propose that the key characteristics of charismatic leaders include sensitivity to followers and the situation/environment, ability to inspire, and a desire to change the status quo. It has also been suggested that follower characteristics, such as identification with the leader, susceptibility to the leader's emotional messages, and a willingness to follow, are components of charismatic leadership. Thus, charismatic leadership is indeed an interaction of leader, follower, and situation, as shown in Figure 13.5.

An interesting study applied charismatic leadership theory to the effectiveness of U.S. presidents (House, Spangler, & Woycke, 1991). In this study, the charisma of all U.S. presidents from Washington to Reagan were rated using historical documents. It was found that the more charismatic the president, the more effective he was in dealing with the economy and with domestic affairs—those factors that most directly affect the followers. Another approach

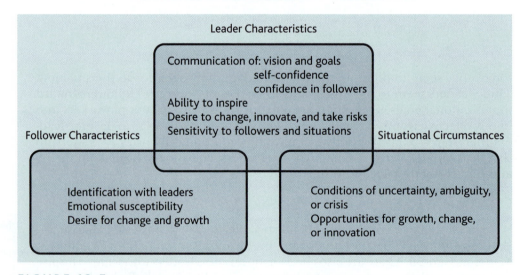

FIGURE 13.5
Charismatic Leadership Theory Is an Interaction among Leader Characteristics, Follower Characteristics, and Elements of the Situation

emphasizes the role of third-party individuals, called "surrogates," who promote and defend the top-level leader, which enhances follower perceptions of the top-level leader's charisma (Galvin, Balkundi, & Waldman, 2010).

TRANSFORMATIONAL LEADERSHIP THEORY

Another prominent leadership theory distinguishes between transactional and transformational leadership (Burns, 1978). Transactional leadership occurs when the relationship between leader and followers is based on some sort of exchange or "transaction," such as exchanging money or praise for work, or exchanging leader consideration behaviors for employee loyalty and commitment. Transformational leadership involves the leader changing the values, beliefs, and attitudes of followers. In other words, in transactional approaches the leader and followers can be seen as involved in an implicit or explicit agreement whereby followers devote time and energy to pursuing organizational goals, and the leader, in exchange, provides rewards and job security. The transformational leader, however, inspires followers by providing a vision of where the group is headed and developing a work culture that stimulates high-performance activities (Bass, 1985; Bass & Riggio, 2006). Transformational leaders are viewed as responsible for performance beyond ordinary expectations as they transmit a sense of mission, stimulate workers' learning experiences, and inspire new and creative ways of thinking (Hater & Bass, 1988). Both charismatic and transformational leadership may be particularly important for leading organizations through significant change processes (Eisenbach, Watson, & Pillai, 1999).

Four components make up transformational leadership and can be referred to as the four "Is." These are

> *Idealized Influence*—refers to the transformational leader being a positive role model for followers. Transformational leaders "walk the talk" and would not behave in a manner inconsistent with their beliefs or values. As a result, transformational leaders are respected and admired by followers.
>
> *Inspirational Motivation*—Like charismatic leaders, transformational leaders are able to arouse and inspire followers by providing a compelling vision of a positive future and important and meaningful outcomes.
>
> *Intellectual Stimulation*—Transformational leaders stimulate followers' curiosity and their innovation and creativity. This is done in an intellectually challenging way, allowing followers to have input into brainstorming sessions and in decision making.
>
> *Individualized Consideration*—involves the leader's personalized attention to each follower's feelings, needs, and concerns. Through this individualized attention, each follower is developed to his or her full potential.

The results of a great deal of research suggest that both transactional and transformational leadership are associated with leader effectiveness (Judge & Piccolo, 2004; Wang, Oh, Courtright, & Colbert, 2011), but transformational leaders have extraordinarily successful work groups (Bass & Riggio, 2006). For example, meta-analyses demonstrate that groups led by transformational

transactional leadership
leadership based on some transaction, such as exchanging money for work

transformational leadership
focuses on the leader's ability to provide shared values and a vision for the future for the work group

leaders have moderately higher performance than groups led by nontransformational leaders (Lowe, Kroeck, & Sivasubramaniam, 1996). Moreover, followers of transformational leaders are much more satisfied than those led by other types of leaders (Dumdum, Lowe, & Avolio, 2002).

Research on transformational leadership has grown because of the development of an instrument that measures both elements of transactional and transformational leadership, the Multifactor Leadership Questionnaire (MLQ; Bass & Avolio, 1997). The MLQ surveys the followers of a particular leader who evaluate the leader on the four components of transformational leadership. In addition to the MLQ, alternative measures of transformational leadership have also been developed (Alimo-Metcalfe & Alban-Metcalfe, 2001). Importantly, transformational leaders play an important part in empowering followers and developing them into budding leaders (Avolio, 1999).

Recent years have seen an explosion of research interest in both charismatic and transformational leadership. As mentioned, a meta-analysis of more than 20 studies found that transformational leadership was superior to transactional leadership in fostering work group effectiveness (Lowe et al., 1996). Moreover, the positive effects of transformational leadership on group performance hold for groups as varied as student leaders in laboratory experiments (Kirkpatrick & Locke, 1996; Sosik, Avolio, & Kahai, 1997), the military (Bass, 1998), nursing and healthcare supervisors (Bycio, Hackett, & Allen, 1995; Mullen & Kelloway, 2009), Turkish hotel managers (Erkutlu, 2008), and German and Indian bank managers (Geyer & Steyrer, 1998; Majumdar & Ray, 2011).

Led by research on transformational leadership, scholars have begun to pay careful attention to the ethics of leaders. For example, charismatic leaders have been separated into those who are more oriented toward the common good, such as Gandhi and Martin Luther King Jr., and self-serving and corrupt charismatics, such as Hitler and Saddam Hussein. As a result, leaders are being distinguished as "socialized" or "authentic" leaders, versus the "personalized" or "inauthentic" types (Bass & Steidlmeier, 1999; Howell & Avolio, 1993).

Comparing and Contrasting Theories of Leadership

Table 13.2 presents a summary of the various leadership theories we have reviewed. The early universalist theories of leadership were limited because they were too simplistic—leadership is too complex a phenomenon to be captured in terms of a single characteristic, or group of leader characteristics. The behavioral theories of leadership suggested that two very different sets of leader behaviors—task-oriented and person-oriented—were associated with effective leadership. But this perspective too was limited because different leader behaviors will be more or less successful depending on characteristics of the leadership situation. This brought us to the contingency models.

Each of the contingency theories of leadership presents a different way of examining leader effectiveness by focusing on the leader–situation interaction. To understand better the perspectives that these theories take in predicting leader effectiveness, we need to compare the various models.

TABLE 13.2
Summary of Leadership Theories

Theory	Elements/Components	Applications
Universalist Theories		
Great Man/Woman Theory	Effective leaders are born, not made	(no direct intervention programs)
Trait Theory	Searching for traits common to all effective leaders	(no direct intervention programs)
Behavioral Theories		
Ohio State Studies	Two leader behaviors: Initiating Structure and Consideration	(no direct intervention)
University of Michigan Studies	Two leader behaviors: Task-oriented and Relationship-oriented	Leadership Grid
Contingency Theories		
Fiedler's Contingency Theory	Leader style must be matched to situational characteristics	Leader Match
Path-Goal Theory	Leader must play roles to help groups attain goals	(no specific interventions)
Decision-Making Model	Leader asks situation-related questions before choosing decision-making style	Model contains its own application
Leader–Member Exchange	Focuses on quality of leader–member relationship	Leadership training
Charismatic & Transformational Theories		
Charismatic Leadership	Followers are drawn to "exceptional" characteristics possessed by leader	Leadership training
Transformational Leadership	Leader inspires, provides a "vision" and develops followers	Leadership training

One obvious difference among the contingency theories is how they view the leader's primary task. For example, Fiedler's model sees the leader as determining the course the work group should take; the path-goal theory considers the leader as merely a facilitator who helps the group achieve its goals; the decision-making model sees the leader's main job as work-related decision making; and the leader–member exchange theory focuses on the leader's role with subordinates. The models also differ in how they define effective leadership. In Fiedler's contingency model, in contrast to the other models, the leader's style is seen as relatively fixed and unchangeable. Thus, the leader must seek out or create situations that are compatible with the leader's behavioral orientation. All the other contingency models assume that leaders are more flexible and require leaders to change their behavior in accordance with the situation. For example, according to the decision-making model, a leader should be participative and democratic in dealing with decision making in one situation and be more autocratic and directive in another. Likewise, according to the path-goal theory, a leader may change roles from time to time to meet the varying goals of the work group. As we shall see, this notion of the flexibility or stability of leader behavior is very important to the application of leadership theory.

Finally, charismatic and transformational leadership theories seem at the same time, to combine and to move beyond both the trait approaches and the contingency approaches to leadership. That is, these newer approaches to leadership focus on characteristics of the leader and how these extraordinary leader characteristics interact with situational elements, including the attitudes, beliefs, and loyalty of the followers. The charismatic and transformational leadership theories, however, go a step beyond contingency models because in these newer models, the leader's behavior is more than just a simple adjusting or adapting to situational constraints.

Applications of Leadership Theories

The various leadership theories suggest several possible interventions for improving leaders' effectiveness. For example, Fiedler's Leader Match program offers suggestions for changing a work situation to fit with the leader's behavioral orientation; the decision-making theory prescribes the appropriate decision-making strategy for any situation; and the leader–member exchange model advocates teaching leaders to be more attentive and responsive to group members. The most common suggestion by far is trying to change the leader's behavior. Spurred by this, tremendous energy and resources have gone into programs to train leaders. From the other perspective, some effort has also gone into ways of redesigning jobs to fit particular leaders' styles.

LEADERSHIP TRAINING & DEVELOPMENT

Leadership training programs take a number of forms, although most follow two general approaches. The first approach teaches leaders diagnostic skills, that is, how to assess a situation to determine the type of leader behavior that will work best. The assumption is that a leader who knows the particular behavior that a situation requires will be able to adjust behavior accordingly. The path-goal and decision-making theories emphasize such a diagnosis. The path-goal theory requires leaders to determine the goal expectations of the work group, whereas the decision-making model asks the leader to perform a detailed assessment of a situation before adopting a decision-making strategy.

The second approach teaches leaders specific skills or behaviors that they lack. For example, such programs might train task-oriented leaders to be more relationship-oriented or train transactional leaders to become more transformational (Barling, Weber, & Kelloway, 1996). Probably a combination of both approaches—teaching diagnostic skills plus increasing the leader's behavioral repertoire—is likely to be most effective.

Organizations invest a great deal of time and money in programs designed to train their leaders to be more effective. Although research indicates that many of these programs are successful (Burke & Day, 1986; Collins & Holton, 2004; Latham, 1988), a number of factors must be considered to maximize the chances of such effectiveness.

First, as in all types of training programs, training needs must be determined (see Chapter 7). In leadership training it is important to identify the specific behaviors or diagnostic skills that the trainee lacks. A second, related concern is the leader trainee's openness and acceptance of the training program. This has been termed *leader developmental readiness*—which relates to whether a leader is prepared and motivated to develop and advance his or her leadership skills. If leaders are to be successful in a program that involves a substantial change in behavior, they must see the merit in learning new leadership behaviors and perhaps abandoning past leadership behaviors. This is a problem in many training programs in which managers are "forced" to attend, and the program may fail because of resistance from the participants.

Third, the more time and energy invested in the program, the more successful it is likely to be. Changing the behavior of practicing managers is neither quick nor easy, for old leadership patterns have likely become deeply ingrained. A two-hour program is not likely to have much impact.

Another important consideration is whether the particular leadership behaviors taught in the training program will be accepted in the work group and organization. In many cases, when the leaders try to use their newly acquired leadership behaviors in the work environment, they meet with resistance from both supervisees and colleagues. The new behaviors may be incompatible with the usual operating procedures within the organization or the work group, and the new leadership style may not fit the expectations of group members. For example, a training program that taught police sergeants to replace task-oriented, authoritarian styles with participative behaviors was a spectacular failure. Although the sergeants accepted the change, it was met with considerable resistance by their subordinates, who felt that the program had made their leaders "soft," a condition that they perceived as dangerous in the life-and-death situations that police officers often face. Thus for leadership training to be effective, the organization must accept and support the new leader behavior.

Finally, sound evaluations of leadership training programs must be conducted routinely to determine whether the programs are indeed successful (Hannum, Martineau, & Reinelt, 2007). Such evaluations include measuring the effects of leadership training programs on organizational outcomes such as work group productivity, work quality, and member satisfaction. One measure that has been suggested is to estimate the return on investment in leadership development, but looking at the costs of the leader development program and the resulting increases in work group performance (Avolio, Avey, & Quisenberry, 2010). Training programs that deal with these various concerns can improve the quality of leadership in work groups and organizations.

ON THE *CUTTING* EDGE

Transcultural Leadership: Training Leaders in the 21st Century

The increasing internationalization of business, with multinational organizations routinely doing business worldwide, coupled with the increasing diversity of the workforce, means that leaders today and in the future must be specially trained for a more complex work world (Adler, 1991; Bass & Bass, 2008; Javidan & House, 2001; Rost-Roth, 2010). The majority of large U.S. organizations now routinely do business with companies in other countries. Women and members of ethnic minority groups will be the majority of workers of the future.

One model of leadership training (Conger, 1993) suggests that future leaders will need, among other things, the following areas of training:

• *Global awareness*—Leaders will need to be knowledgeable of worldwide issues that may affect the organization and the organizations and organizational members it must interact with.
• *Capability of managing highly decentralized organizations*—As more and more work is done in independently functioning work teams, leaders will need to play more of a "coaching" or "consultant" role, than the traditional authority role of "boss."

• *Sensitivity to diversity issues*—Leaders will be looked to as "diversity experts," so they must be able to deal effectively with groups that have different values and worldviews.
• *Interpersonal skills*—The changing and expanding role of work group leaders (e.g., from "bosses" to "coaches") will require them to become more interpersonally skilled.
• *Community-building skills*—Effective leaders of the future will have to build work groups into cooperating, interdependent "communities" of workers. The leader will need to build group cohesiveness and commitment to goals. More and more, group members will turn to leaders for the "vision" of where the work group and the organization is going.

It appears that once again, leader flexibility is called for. Leaders of the future will be required to be "culturally" flexible and adaptable if they are going to be effective in leading diverse work groups in an increasingly complex world of work.

JOB REDESIGN AND SUBSTITUTES FOR LEADERSHIP

Certain critics, such as Fiedler, have suggested that leadership training may be ineffective and a waste of organizational resources. Because Fiedler believes that a leader's orientation is inflexible, he argued that organizations should concentrate on changing the job to fit the leader rather than vice versa (Fiedler, 1965). The most obvious example of this approach is his Leader Match program, which offers suggestions for altering the work situation to fit the leader's predominantly task-oriented or relationship-oriented pattern, usually by increasing or decreasing task structure or position power. The main problem with this approach is that many work situations may be unchangeable. In such cases, Fiedler (1973) suggested that it might be easier to transfer the leader to a situation that is more compatible with the leader's orientation than to try to alter the leader's behavioral orientation. However, changing the situation to fit the leader's style may prove to be quite successful.

Research in redesigning jobs indicates that in certain instances leaders may be unnecessary, leading to a search for "substitutes for leadership" (Hackman, 1990; Kerr & Jermier, 1978; Podsakoff & MacKenzie, 1997b). For example, a group that is cohesive and has very structured norms for operation may have no need for a leader. Examples of such leaderless groups include some of the job enrichment teams mentioned in Chapter 8, in which all members have equal status and authority, as well as groups of professionals such as physicians or real estate agents, who all have high levels of ability, experience, training, and knowledge. In addition, a leader would be redundant in a situation in which the task is well structured and routine and the work is intrinsically satisfying to workers, because there would be no need for direction or for encouragement. Finally, it has been suggested that a form of self-leadership, or self-management, might substitute for the traditional supervision provided by a formal leader (Manz, 1986; Manz & Sims, 1980; Spreitzer, Cohen, & Ledford, 1999; Stewart & Manz, 1995; Vanderslice, 1988).

Finally, many of today's work groups and teams in areas that require creative output (e.g., software development teams, research and development groups) or high levels of interdependency require that group members share the load of leadership. Pearce and Conger (2003) defined **shared leadership** "as a dynamic, interactive influence process among individuals in groups for which the objective is to lead one another to the achievement of group or organizational goals" (p. 1). This definition is quite consistent with our earlier definition of leadership. There is little doubt that in many work groups and teams leadership is indeed shared. However, although some work groups may be able to operate well without formal leaders, such groups probably represent a relatively small percentage of work groups (Pearce, Manz, & Sims, 2009). It is likely that leaders will remain an important part of most work groups.

> **Stop & Review**
>
> What are the five needs for transcultural leaders outlined by Conger (1993)?

> **shared leadership**
> where leadership is shared among the group members rather than being centralized in one person

> **Stop & Review**
>
> Describe three applications of leadership theories.

Summary

Leadership is the ability to direct a group toward the attainment of goals. Leadership theories can be divided into three categories: *universalist theories, behavioral theories,* and *contingency theories.* The *great man/woman theory,* a universalist theory, holds that some people are natural, born leaders. The *trait theory* specifies certain personality traits, or characteristics, that are common to all effective leaders. These universalist theories suffer from the facts that they are simplistic and that they focus on individual leader characteristics.

The behavioral theories of leadership are typified by studies conducted at Ohio State and the University of Michigan that looked directly at leader behavior, rather than at inferred leader characteristics. Two dimensions of leader behavior emerged: *initiating structure* (also called *task-oriented behaviors*), which focuses on work task production, and *consideration* (also known as *relationship-oriented behaviors*), which emphasizes interpersonal relationships among workers. The *Leadership Grid* is an application of the findings from the behavioral theories—a program that stresses both task-oriented and relationship-oriented behaviors as the keys to leader success.

Next to emerge were the contingency theories of leadership. *Fiedler's contingency model* states that effective leadership depends on a match between the leader's style and the favorableness of the work situation. Leader style is assessed through the *least preferred coworker (LPC)* measure. Task-oriented leaders are most effective in either very favorable or very unfavorable situations, whereas relationship-oriented leaders do better in moderately favorable situations. The favorability of situations in Fiedler's model is determined by three variables: *leader–member relations, task structure,* and the leader's *position power.*

The *path-goal theory* asserts that the leader is a facilitator who chooses the type of behavior that will most help the work group to achieve their goals. According to the path-goal theory, the leader can adopt four types of leader behavior: *directive, achievement-oriented, supportive,* or *participative.*

The *decision-making model* sees the leader's main role as making work-related decisions. This prescriptive model contains a decision tree framework for the leader to follow to decide the appropriate decision-making strategy (ranging from autocratic to democratic) to use in a particular situation. The *leader–member exchange* (*LMX*) model examines the quality of the relationship between the leader and each subordinate, which leads to a more precise determination of work outcomes. Finally, *transformational* and *charismatic leadership theories* focus on exceptional characteristics or qualities that leaders possess that inspire loyalty in followers and motivate them to achieve extraordinary goals.

The application of leadership theories involves one of two strategies: instituting leadership training programs or redesigning the job to fit the leader. The majority of the theories advocate leadership training, either by teaching specific leader behaviors (e.g., task-oriented or relationship-oriented) or by training leaders to diagnose situations that call for either task-oriented or relationship-oriented behaviors. Job redesign usually involves changing characteristics of the situation to fit the leader's typical style or orientation. However, work situations that are amenable to such job redesigns may be limited. In other situations, particularly where roles and procedures are well defined, substitutes for leadership, such as self-managing work teams, or *shared leadership*, may be appropriate.

Study Questions and Exercises

1. Discuss the limitations of the universalist leadership theories. Why do you suppose they had, and continue to have, such popular appeal?

2. Consider the distinction between task-oriented (initiating structure) and relationship-oriented (consideration) leader behaviors. List the role that they play in each of the various contingency theories.

3. Think of a leader of a work or social group whom you have known. How would you characterize this person's leadership style or orientation? What theory of leadership best describes and explains this person's leadership situation?

4. All contingency theories of leadership measure some characteristics of both the leader and the work situation. How do the different theories—Fiedler's, path-goal, decision-making, leader–member exchange—define characteristics of the work situation?

5. Design a leadership training program for leaders of student organizations. Keep in mind the program characteristics that will maximize the effectiveness of the training program.

6. What sorts of groups might operate efficiently without a leader? How would leadership be shared in these groups?

Web Links

http://research.mckenna.edu/kli/
Our Kravis Leadership Institute site containing some resources about leadership.

http://www.ila-net.org/
Website for the International Leadership Association, a professional organization for scholars and practitioners from many disciplines who are interested in the study and practice of leadership.

Suggested Readings

Avolio, B. J. (2005). *Leadership development in balance: Made/born.* Mahwah, NJ: Erlbaum. *This book is a personal guide to leadership development from one of the top leadership scholars.*

Bass, B. M. & Bass, R. (2008). *Bass & Stogdill's handbook of leadership: Theory, research, and managerial applications* (4th ed.). New York: Free Press. *A classic, comprehensive review of theory and research on leadership from the earliest days through the late 1980s. An excellent resource with well over 5,000 references to research articles relating to leadership.*

Bass, B. M., & Riggio, R. E. (2006). *Transformational leadership* (2nd ed.). Mahwah, NJ: Erlbaum. *A comprehensive review of leadership on transformational and charismatic leadership.*

Pearce, C. L., & Conger, J. A. (Eds.). (2003). *Shared leadership: Reframing the hows and whys of leadership.* Thousand Oaks, CA: Sage. *A collection of work on the relatively new concept of shared leadership.*

CHAPTER

14

Influence, Power, and Politics

Inside Tips

DEFINING AND DIFFERENTIATING INFLUENCE, POWER, AND POLITICS

This chapter presents and discusses three topics: influence, power, and organizational politics. Although each is a distinct concept, they are also three facets of the same general process, for all involve one party trying to affect the behavior of another. However, it is important to be able to distinguish among the three. The differences are subtle.

Influence, power, and politics are extremely significant and pervasive processes in all work groups and organizations. Power and influence in particular are important aspects of leadership (see Chapter 13), because leaders use their power and influence to help work groups attain their goals. Influence, power, and politics are also important factors in group processes, which we discussed in Chapter 12. For example, conformity to group norms will occur only if the group can influence members to follow the rules. Also, managers can use their power and authority to help resolve conflicts among group members. Furthermore, group decision making, by its very nature, is a political process. Finally, because certain forms of power are linked to the very structure of the organizational hierarchy, our discussion in this chapter will provide some groundwork for examining organizational structure in Chapter 15.

As you reflect on your work organization, you marvel at how people use their power and influence in their efforts to perform their jobs and to get ahead. You have noticed that some high-level executives seem to enjoy the power and control that they have over others, and some are very low key in using their power and authority. You notice that two managers, at the same level in a company, still may not be equal in terms of their power and influence. One is more powerful because she is well liked and respected by subordinates and superiors and because she understands the politics of the company and knows how to "play the game." And you don't even want to get started thinking about organizational politics—that's a whole game unto itself...

Although influence, power, and politics are ongoing processes in the day-to-day life of any work organization, with important implications for organizational performance and employee satisfaction, social scientists only began to study them in the past three decades (Ferris & Hochwater, 2011; Pfeffer, 1981, 1992). The concepts of influence, power, and politics are also closely intertwined with the topics of group processes and leadership that were discussed earlier. For example, individuals in work groups use influence and power to affect and alter the behavior of other members. Leaders also use their power and influence to achieve group goals. Moreover, they must often act politically to gain and hold their powerful leadership positions, and individuals may also engage in politics to improve their positions in organizations. Influence, power, and politics likewise play major roles in group decision-making processes. For example, a powerful, influential member can have an important impact in deciding the courses of action a group will take. Democratic decision making, by its very nature, involves political behaviors, such as lobbying for and voting on particular plans. Moreover, because influence, power, and politics affect the behavior of others, they can help determine the amount of conflict and coordination within work groups.

Defining Influence, Power, and Politics

In one sense, influence, power, and politics are similar, because all three involve getting others to do something. There are, however, some important differences among them.

influence
the ability to use social forces to affect the behavior of others

Influence can be viewed as a form of social control or social power. It is an individual's ability to get another person to perform a certain action. Usually, influence is exerted by using informal strategies such as persuasion, peer pressure, or compliance techniques. For example, an individual might use persuasive influence in trying to obtain a loan from a friend or when attempting to persuade a coworker to help complete a work task. Peer pressure influence might take the form of a worker's plea to a colleague to break a company rule because "everybody does it." Influence might also involve the use of compliance techniques. For example, an executive might use flattery or the offer of a favor to get a clerical assistant to work overtime to finish producing a report. In this definition, the term might be called "social influence," which is a more restricted usage than the more general notion of influence, which is defined as any process of affecting behavioral change in others (Allen & Porter, 1983).

power
the use of some aspect of a work relationship to compel another to perform a certain action despite resistance

Power in the workplace is a more formal process that can be defined as the use of some aspect of a work relationship to force or compel another person to perform a certain action despite resistance. For example, a company president can give an order to a vice president and expect it to be carried out because of the power associated with the status relationship. A safety inspector may be able to demand that operators shut down a piece of machinery that has a potentially dangerous malfunction by virtue of the person's position as an acknowledged safety expert. Although influence resides primarily in the individual, power usually derives from the relationship between two parties. For example, a coworker might use persuasion skills—a form of influence—to try to get an unmotivated worker to increase work output by appealing to the worker to "pull his own weight." However, a supervisor, by virtue of the status relationship that gives the person authority over the worker, can use power to order the worker to improve productivity or face the consequences. Thus, power resides in the relationship between parties or in their positions, rather than in the individuals themselves.

organizational politics
self-serving actions designed to affect the behavior of others to achieve personal goals

Organizational politics is a very different process that involves any actions taken to influence the behavior of others to reach personal goals. The one thing that distinguishes political behaviors from power and influence is the fact that organizational politics are always self-serving, whereas power and influence are not necessarily self-serving.

The following example shows how a person might use influence, power, and politics to achieve a certain outcome: Marilyn James has a problem. The vacation schedules at her company, Mackenzie Electronics, have been set up for several months. However, she has just found out that her husband's vacation will come two weeks earlier than they had anticipated. She now needs to exchange her vacation time with Dan Gibbons, who will be taking his vacation during the two weeks she needs. Marilyn could use influence by trying to persuade Dan to change his plans; she might promise to do him a favor, or she might simply make an appeal to Dan's generous nature and willingness to help. Marilyn would be using power if she ordered a change in the vacation schedule, which she could do because she is assistant manager of the marketing department and Dan is a newcomer, far down in the departmental hierarchy. Finally, she might use politics to get what she wants. Marilyn could encourage the marketing director to assign an important project to Dan, saying, "He's a real hard worker, and he deserves to handle this assignment." The project would require that Dan make a formal presentation on August 24, right in the middle of his vacation. Later, when Dan mentions that he needs to trade vacation times to work on the assignment, Marilyn would be ready to jump right in and offer to switch. In short, Marilyn could use any one of these methods—influence, power, or politics—to affect Dan's behavior.

Influence, power, and politics are pervasive processes in all work organizations that involve efforts by some organizational members to control the actions of others. However, the means exerted in using each process are quite different and thus will be examined separately.

Influence: The Use of Social Control

People often attempt to persuade, cajole, convince, or induce others to provide assistance, change an opinion, offer support, or engage in a certain behavior in both work organizations and in everyday social life. A study by Kipnis, Schmidt, and Wilkinson (1980) attempted to classify the various influence tactics used in the workplace by having 165 lower-level managers write essays describing incidents in which they influenced either their superiors, coworkers, or subordinates. The 370 tactics were put into eight categories: assertiveness, ingratiation, rationality, sanctions, exchanges, upward appeals, blocking, and coalitions (see Table 14.1; it is important to note that this classification includes behaviors that, by our definitions, would include both influence and power tactics). Subsequent research has supported the existence of these categories of influence/power tactics (Schriesheim & Hinkin, 1990; Yukl, 2007; Yukl & Falbe, 1990).

In addition to trying to influence others by being assertive or by using logical arguments, one might also employ **ingratiation** by increasing one's personal appeal through such tactics as doing favors, praising, or flattering another (Kumar & Beyerlein, 1991). There is some evidence that interviewees' use of ingratiation tactics work well in hiring interviews (Higgins & Judge, 2004). Other categories of influence include offering exchanges of favors or

ingratiation
influencing others by increasing one's personal appeal to them

TABLE 14.1

Categories of Influence Tactics

Assertiveness	*Exchanges*
Making orders or demands	Offering an exchange of favors
Setting deadlines and making sure they are met	Reminding another of past favors
Emphasizing rules that require compliance	Offering to make some personal sacrifice in exchange for a favor
Ingratiation	*Upward Appeals*
Using praise or making the other person feel important	Obtaining the support of superiors
Showing a need for the other person's help	Sending the target person to see superiors
Being polite and/or friendly	Filing a report about the target person to superiors
Rationality	*Blocking*
Using logic to convince someone else	Threatening to stop working with the other person
Writing a detailed justification of a plan	Ignoring the other person or withdrawing friendship
Presenting information to support a request along with the request	Engaging in a work slowdown
Sanctions	*Coalitions*
Withholding salary increases	Obtaining coworkers' support of a request
Threatening to fire someone or to give a poor performance evaluation	Making a request at a formal conference
Promising or giving a salary increase	Obtaining subordinates' support of a request

Source: Kipnis, D., Schmidt, S. M., & Wilkinson, I. (1980). Intraorganizational influence tactics: Explorations in getting one's way. *Journal of Applied Psychology, 65,* 445–448.

threatening the other person with negative sanctions, such as a demotion or firing. The final three categories of influence are making appeals to persons higher in the status hierarchy; engaging in behaviors that block, interfere with, or prohibit the others' work activities; or building coalitions by getting the support of coworkers or subordinates.

The Kipnis et al.'s study found that the choice of influence tactic was determined by the situation, the status of the individuals involved, and other characteristics of the organization such as size and whether or not the organization was unionized. For example, higher-status persons were more likely to use assertiveness or sanctions, whereas lower-status individuals used rational appeals to influence superiors. Coworkers commonly employed ingratiation and exchange when attempting to influence one another and to obtain personal favors, whereas rational and coalition tactics were often used to institute changes in the work task or in the work context. Interestingly, there were no sex differences in the use of the various influence tactics. Men and women seem to use the same tactics in the same ways, and with similar results (see also Aguinis & Adams, 1998; Driskell, Olmstead, & Salas, 1993). A meta-analysis suggests that ingratiation and rationality are effective influence tactics for workers, but self-promotion tactics were not (Higgins, Judge, & Ferris, 2003).

Other studies have found that subordinates use different upward influence tactics with superiors, depending on whether they are seeking personal goals, such as a pay raise or promotion, or organizational goals, such as gaining the supervisor's approval of a new, more efficient work procedure. When seeking personal goals, subordinates tended to use tactics such as ingratiation. When seeking organizational goals, they favored strategies such as upward appeals and rational persuasion to try to influence superiors (Ansari & Kapoor, 1987; Schmidt & Kipnis, 1984). Moreover, subordinates' influence tactics varied depending on whether the superior was autocratic and task oriented or participative and relationship oriented. Subordinates tended to use ingratiation, blocking, and upward appeal techniques with autocratic managers but rational persuasion strategies with participative superiors (Ansari & Kapoor, 1987). Studies of supervisors' influence tactics found that rational persuasion was a very effective managerial influence strategy, whereas pressure tactics, such as threats, were least effective. Additionally, the influence tactics of ingratiation and exchange were moderately effective in influencing both subordinates and other managers (Yukl & Tracey, 1992).

Research has suggested some cross-cultural differences in the use of influence tactics. For example, U.S. managers rated rational persuasion and exchange as more effective influence tactics, whereas Chinese managers believed that coalition tactics, upward appeals, and gifts would be more effective (Fu & Yukl, 2000). However, few differences in preferences for influence tactics were found between Asian-American and Caucasian-American managers (Xin & Tsui, 1996).

Like individuals, groups will also use a wide variety of tactics to exert influence. For example, groups tend to use influence to get members to conform to group norms. As we saw in Chapter 12, if a member is in violation of a group norm, pressure will be exerted in the form of criticism, isolation (the "silent treatment"), or in extreme cases, expulsion. Such pressure to conform is a very common and very important influence process in work groups and organizations (Feldman, 1984; Moscovici, 1985; see Up Close).

Power: A Major Force in Work Organizations

Power, in contrast to influence, is a more formal force in work organizations that derives from an individual's role or position or from some specific characteristics of the individual, such as work-related expertise or admirable leadership qualities. Whereas influence depends on the skill of the influencer in affecting another person at a particular place or time, power is a consistent force that is likely to work across situations and time. In organizations, power is a fairly stable capacity or potential that can consistently affect the behavior of others, as long as the power remains with the individual (Hocker & Wilmot, 1985). In other words, the use of influence strategies to affect the behavior of others is sometimes successful, but the use of power is almost always successful.

organizational power

power derived from a person's position in an organization and from control over important resources afforded by that position

individual power

power derived from personal characteristics that are of value to the organization, such as particular expertise or leadership ability

POWER SOURCES

Power can take many forms and is derived from a variety of sources that are of two main types (Yukl & Falbe, 1991). Most often, power comes from the organization. Organizational power comes from an individual's position in the organization and from the control over important organizational resources conveyed by that position. These organizational resources can be tangible, such as money, work assignments, or office space, or more intangible, such as information or communication access to other people. Individual power is derived from personal characteristics, such as particular expertise or leadership ability, that are of value to the organization and its members.

Astley and Sachdeva (1984) outlined three important sources of organizational power. One is the hierarchical structure of the organization. Power derived from the status hierarchy is inherent in one's position in the

UP CLOSE How to Resist Social Influence Tactics

Social psychologist Robert Cialdini (2000) has discussed the various uses of social influence tactics by "compliance professionals," such as salespersons, advertisers, and con artists, who are those people whose job it is to get others to do something. Using the technique of participant observation, he infiltrated such groups by posing as a door-to-door vacuum cleaner salesman, a car dealer, and a telephone fund-raiser. Through his research, Cialdini was able to identify the most frequently used influence tactics. Three of the more common strategies are the reciprocity rule, the rule of commitment and consistency, and the scarcity principle. With the reciprocity rule, a "favor" is done to get something in return. The rule of commitment and consistency is used in getting people to commit to a small initial request and then hitting them with a larger request. The most infamous example of this is the "foot-in-the-door" tactic used by salespersons or people seeking donations. The compliance professional might begin with the question, "You are concerned about the plight of the whales, aren't you?" Answering affirmatively commits you to agreeing with the next question: "Then you would like to make a donation to the Save the Whales Fund, wouldn't you?" The scarcity principle is used to create the illusion of a limited supply, as is done by advertisements that read, "Act now, supply is limited."

A fourth influence tactic identified by Cialdini seems to involve the use of guilt in getting individuals to comply with requests. This additional tactic, called the "door-in-the-face" technique, is a two-step compliance technique that is like using the foot-in-the-door tactic in reverse. In using the door-in-the-face, the influencer prefaces the real request with a first request that is so large that it is certain to be rejected. For example, an influencer who wants to borrow 10 dollars from a friend will start out asking for a loan of a hundred dollars. When the exorbitant request is denied, the second request for 10 dollars is made, and it seems reasonable by contrast, making the friend more likely to grant the 10-dollar loan than he or she would have if the smaller request had been made alone.

Finally, Cialdini also emphasized the importance of liking in influence attempts—we are more easily influenced by people we like—and what better way for influence "peddlers" to get you to like them but by ingratiation. Research has demonstrated that ingratiation is not only used by salespersons, but is often used in the workplace by supervisors to influence supervisees (Aguinis, Nesler, Hosoda, & Tedeschi, 1994), and by subordinates to try to influence the promotion process (Thacker & Wayne, 1995).

As you can see, all the tactics of influence mentioned by Cialdini can be used by coworkers or bosses to influence people to do what they might not otherwise do. For example, reciprocity is often invoked by management after workers are given a cost-of-living raise. Workers, feeling as if management has just done them a favor, may be more compliant than usual, even though the raise was tied to some factor other than management's generosity.

UP CLOSE *(continued)*

A company may try to use the commitment and consistency rule to increase company loyalty and cut down on voluntary turnover. For example, each month the company might hold a contest in which employees submit essays about why the company is a great place to work. Winning essays could be published in the company newsletter. This may make it tougher for employees to consider leaving for work elsewhere, as they have made such a public act of loyalty. An organization might employ the scarcity principle in performance incentive programs by encouraging employees to work hard to obtain one of a very few scarce rewards.

Cialdini maintains that the best way to combat unethical use of influence tactics is to be able to recognize them. By understanding that people are trying to use these strategies to take unfair advantage of you, you may be able to resist them simply by seeing such obvious exploitation attempts for what they really are.

---

organization. Workers lower in the hierarchy often obey their superiors simply because they believe that their superiors' higher position gives them the right to exercise power (Astley & Zajac, 1991). Organizational power can also result from control of important resources such as money, fringe benefits, knowledge, and work-related expertise. Finally, organizational power can come from being in a position of network centrality that is crucial to the flow of information (recall Chapter 11's discussion of communication networks). Persons in such positions may have access to information that others do not possess and may develop social relationships with important individuals or groups within the organization. For example, an executive's secretary may have low levels of power due to ranking in the organizational hierarchy and little control over resources, but may still be powerful because of a position of network centrality that involves contact with important people and information.

French and Raven (1959) looked at different types of power that they called **power bases**, which are the sources of a person's power over others in the organization. They specified five important power bases: coercive power, reward power, legitimate power, expert power, and referent power.

Coercive power is the ability to punish or to threaten to punish others. For example, threatening to fine, demote, or fire someone are all means of exercising coercive power, as is assigning a person to an aversive work task. An individual may possess coercive power by holding a position in the organization that allows the person to punish others. However, any individual, regardless of position, can use coercive power by threatening to harm someone either physically or psychologically with tactics such as damaging a reputation by spreading false rumors.

We have seen that the use of coercive power, with its punishment and threats of punishment, carries certain risks, because it may create anger and resentment in the subject. Coercive power must be exercised carefully, with awareness of the potential strengths and weaknesses of punitive strategies. For example, although coercive threats may get quick action, the threatened person may try to retaliate later. Raven (1992) said that if a leader is to use coercive

> **Stop & Review**
>
> Describe the eight categories of influence tactics and give examples of each.

> **power bases**
> sources of power possessed by individuals in organizations

> **coercive power**
> the use of punishment or the threat of punishment to affect the behavior of others

power effectively, the leader must be ready and willing to follow through on threats, regardless of the costs involved. Moreover, the leader who uses coercive power must be ready to maintain surveillance over the target, to ensure that the target is behaving appropriately. Thus, to be used effectively, coercive power can put a drain on the manager who uses it, because the manager must constantly watch subordinates to apply sanctions quickly when undesirable work behaviors occur.

reward power
power that results from having the ability to offer something positive, such as money or praise

In many ways, reward power is the opposite of coercive power, for although coercive power is the ability to do harm, reward power is the ability to give something positive, such as money, praise, promotions, and interesting or challenging work assignments. The ability to reward others is a very common source of power in work organizations, where it often derives from having control over the resources that others value. Having the ability to administer pay raises, bonuses, promotions, or coveted work tasks can be an extremely strong power base.

legitimate power
the formal rights or authority accompanying a position in an organization

Legitimate power involves the formal rights or authority that an individual possesses by virtue of a position in an organization. Titles such as manager, shift supervisor, director, or vice president are all bases for legitimate power. When employees carry out a request simply because "the boss" asked them to do it, they are responding to such power. In work organizations, legitimate power is typically combined with the reward and coercive power bases. That is, most persons with legitimate authority also have the power to reward or punish subordinates. These three power bases are usually, although not always, tied together. There can be some rare instances in which persons are given some formal position that is not accompanied by reward and coercive power—a position of power in name only. Such is the case of the vice president for public affairs in a relatively small insurance company. The organizational chart for this company reveals that this vice president probably lacks much reward or coercive power to back up his legitimate title because he is the sole employee in the department, with no subordinates! Yet, there is good evidence that workers respond well to persons who possess legitimate power (Hinkin & Schriesheim, 1994; Yukl & Falbe, 1991), perhaps because most individuals are taught from an early age to respect those in authority.

expert power
power derived from having certain work-related knowledge or skill

Expert power is one of the strongest power bases an individual can possess because it results from the possession of some special, work-related knowledge, skill, or expertise. In high-tech organizations, or companies that are based on knowledge and ideas, such as software development, the development of complex drugs and medical devices, and the like, knowledge and expertise are valuable commodities. Research has shown that the possession of work-related expertise was found to be strongly related to supervisors awarding subordinates pay raises (Bartol & Martin, 1990). Expert power is also the source of power behind many health-care professionals. For example, you are willing to take the advice of a physician because you believe that this individual has some special knowledge concerning your health.

referent power
power resulting from the fact that an individual is respected, admired, and liked by others

A very different type of power base is referent power, which develops because an individual is respected, admired, and liked by others. Because the person is liked or admired, workers respond to the person's wishes in an effort to please

To be effective, members of a racecar pit crew must be high in expert power.

the person and to gain favor. The most dramatic illustration of referent power is the charismatic political leader who can spur an entire population to action merely because of their admiration and respect for that person (see Chapter 13). Certain leaders in work settings may also have a strong referent power base and thus be very influential in controlling the activities of others.

Because of the renewed interest in studying organizational power, researchers have developed a number of scales to measure the different French and Raven power bases (Hinkin & Schriesheim, 1989; Nesler, Aguinis, Quigley, Lee, & Tedeschi, 1999; Raven, Schwarzwald, & Koslowsky, 1998; Schriescheim, Hinkin, & Podsakoff, 1991). One such instrument is presented in Table 14.2 and is designed to be administered to workers to assess which power bases are used by their supervisors and helps further illustrate these power bases.

In sum, the different power bases indicate that power can indeed take many forms and arise from many sources. For example, expert power and referent power reside within the individual and thus are forms of individual power. More often than not, legitimate, reward, and coercive power are derived from organizational rather than personal sources and thus are types of organizational power. As you might expect, the various power bases can combine to further increase an individual's power in an organization. At the same time, possession of certain power bases, coupled with the effective use of influence tactics (e.g., assertiveness, ingratiation, upward appeals) can even further increase the power an individual wields in a group or organization (Brass & Burkhardt, 1993). A great deal of research has been conducted on power dynamics, or on how the different power bases operate in work settings and how they affect work outcomes. Let's explore power dynamics in work organizations.

Stop & Review

Name and describe three influence tactics identified by Cialdini.

TABLE 14.2
A Measure of Power Bases

Instructions: Following is a list of statements that may be used in describing behaviors that supervisors in work organizations can direct toward their subordinates. First, carefully read each descriptive statement, thinking in terms of your supervisor. Then decide to what extent you agree that your supervisor could do this to you. Mark the number that most closely represents how you feel. Use the following numbers for your answers:

(5) = strongly agree
(4) = agree
(3) = neither agree nor disagree
(2) = disagree
(1) = strongly disagree

My supervisor can …

(Reward Power)
  increase my pay level.
  influence my getting a pay raise.
  provide me with special benefits.
  influence my getting a promotion.

(Coercive Power)
  give me undesirable job assignments.
  make my work difficult for me.
  make things unpleasant here.
  make being at work distasteful.

(Legitimate Power)
  make me feel that I have commitments to meet.
  make me feel like I should satisfy my job requirements.
  give me the feeling I have responsibilities to fulfill.
  make me recognize that I have tasks to accomplish.

(Expert Power)
  give me good technical suggestions.
  share with me his/her considerable experience and/or training.
  provide me with sound, job-related advice.
  provide me with needed technical knowledge.

(Referent Power)
  make me feel valued.
  make me feel like he/she approves of me.
  make me feel personally accepted.
  make me feel important.

Source: Hinkin, T. R., & Schriesheim, C. A. (1989). Development and application of new scales to measure French and Raven (1959) bases of social power. *Journal of Applied Psychology, 74,* 561–567. (American Psychological Association.)

POWER DYNAMICS IN WORK ORGANIZATIONS

The topic of power in work settings is an important one, and research on the topic has increased particularly on the dynamics of power in work organizations (Bacharach & Lawler, 1980; Gandz & Murray, 1980). For example, researchers have investigated such issues as the distribution of power in organizations, the attempts of organizational members to increase power, power and dependency relationships, and the effects of power on important organizational outcomes—specifically job performance and satisfaction.

Differences in power distribution

We know that power, because of its many forms, is unevenly distributed in work settings. Usually, organizations are arranged in a power hierarchy, with people at the upper levels possessing great power and those at the bottom having relatively little power. However, individual differences in the expert and referent power bases ensure that no two people, even those at the same status level, have exactly equal power. Therefore, although persons high in the hierarchy tend to possess more power than those at lower levels, even a low-ranking member can wield considerable power because of personal sources of power, such as expert power and referent power.

McClelland (1975) and others (Winter, 1973) have shown that people place different values on the gain and use of power, with some people being high in the need for power and others having a low need for power (see Chapter 8). Thus, organizations may have some individuals who are "power hungry" and others who have little interest in gaining much power. However, although people may differ in their needs for power, once individuals have obtained power, they are usually reluctant to give it up (Kipnis, 1976). Perhaps this is what underlies the common notion that power can be "intoxicating" or "addicting." This makes sense, because it is power that enables organizational members to satisfy their various work-related goals. Does possession of power "corrupt"? Evidence suggests that when people are given more power, they may tend to behave in self-serving ways (Mitchell, Hopper, Daniels, Falvy, & Ferris, 1998).

Ways to increase power

One way for an organizational member to increase power is to gain work-related expertise or knowledge (Mechanic, 1962). Learning to solve complex problems, being able to operate or repair sophisticated machinery, and knowing complicated procedures are all linked to an expert power base. Low-power individuals may also increase their organizational power by developing a relationship with a higher-ranking member (Bartol & Martin, 1988). Protégés often benefit from their association with a mentor, leading to greater organizational status and power (see Chapter 6). In fact, it has been shown that networking within the organization, and even simply possessing the knowledge of important social networks in the organization, are related to an individual's possession of power (Krackhardt, 1990).

Low-ranking members may also gain power by forming a coalition, which involves a group of workers banding together to achieve common goals (Bacharach & Lawler, 1998). A coalition can be a very powerful force because of its ability to slow or shut down organizational operations. A group of low-level workers acting together as a unit can become very powerful by sheer virtue of their numbers. In other words, a few workers may be easily replaced, but an entire line of workers cannot. A strong coalition can be created when employees join a union, which can exercise its power by threatening to strike or by actually striking. Generally, the larger the coalition, the greater its power. There can indeed be "power in numbers."

coalition
a group of individuals who band together to combine their power

Stop & Review
Name and describe the five French and Raven power bases.

Power and dependency relationships

When a nonreciprocal dependency relationship exists such that party A is dependent on party B, but B is not dependent on A, B will have power over A (Blalock, 1989). In work settings, it is very common for certain individuals or groups to depend on others for certain resources needed to do a job. If the dependency does not go both ways, the individuals or groups who control the scarce resources will have power over the have-nots (Hickson, Hinnings, Less, Schneck, & Pennings, 1971). Workers who have a great deal of expertise often have such power because those without the expert knowledge must rely on them to perform their jobs correctly. Because expert power is based in the individual, the dependent party sometimes has higher status than the expert. For example, in the military, commissioned officers attain their positions by attending officer training school. Although they have more formal education than noncommissioned officers, they have virtually no on-the-job experience. Thus, when junior lieutenants receive their first assignments, they quickly find out who holds the expert power—the noncommissioned officers, especially the master sergeants, who have many years of experience. A dependency relationship develops. A lieutenant who does not learn to get along with the master sergeants is in trouble and will be unable to command effectively because of a shortage of expert knowledge. Similar situations exist in business when a new manager may have to rely on the expertise of a longtime employee to get the job done.

Businesses strive to avoid dependency relationships on the organizational level. For example, a company will try hard not to have to rely on a single supplier for needed materials because such sole dependency gives the supplier power over the company. One famous fast-food chain has eliminated most dependency relationships by controlling the supply within the company. This restaurant chain owns their own cattle ranches to supply meat, farms to supply grain products, and even paper mills to make bags and containers. The resulting independence allows the company to increase its power over competitors who may be hurt if, for example, their meat suppliers go on strike.

Power and work outcomes

The possession and use of power bases can be directly related to important organizational outcomes such as performance and job satisfaction. For example, expert power is generally related to effective job performance (Bachman, Bowers, & Marcus, 1968) because expert power is based on knowing how to do the job. Referent power, on the other hand, is consistently linked to member satisfaction with the person wielding the power (Carson, Carson, & Roe, 1993). This should not be surprising, because referent power results from the subjects' willingness to submit to the power of someone they admire and respect. In contrast, coercive power tends to decrease the attractiveness of the power wielder and may lead to decreased job satisfaction in work group members. Moreover, the use of coercive power may erode the individual's referent power base. In other words, we lose respect for people who consistently punish or threaten us. In practice, the exercise of coercive power more often involves threats of punishment rather than actual punishment. Although drastic threats can be effective means for gaining compliance, the person who makes such threats runs the risk of having someone "call their bluff" and refuse to comply. The exerciser is now faced with a dilemma: If the person does not follow through with the punishment, some coercive power will be lost because the subject learns that it is an empty threat.

On the other hand, the exerciser who administers the punishment risks infuriating, or in the case of threats of dismissal, losing the employee. In many instances, the use of coercive power is a no-win situation. Although it may be used to threaten workers into higher levels of performance, satisfaction is likely to decrease, and the organization may lose in the long run through increases in voluntary absenteeism and turnover in the dissatisfied workforce. It is probably for these reasons that studies of practicing managers indicate that coercive power is the least used of the five power bases (e.g., Stahelski, Frost, & Patch, 1989).

The power corollary

One aspect of power dynamics is known as the **power corollary** (Robbins, 1979), which states that for every use of power, there is a tendency for a corollary use of power—a return power play by the subject ("for every action there is a reaction"). In other words, when people are the subject of an obvious power play, they tend to try to assert their own power. According to French and Raven (1959), this is why it is important to possess a legitimate power base when exercising other power bases, particularly coercive power, for the combination will limit the form a corollary use of power can take. For example, if a coworker tries to use coercive tactics on you, you might respond in kind, with threats of your own. However, if the person using coercive power is your supervisor, your response options are limited. In other words, it is unlikely that you will directly threaten someone who has legitimate authority.

power corollary
the concept that for every exercise of power, there is a tendency for the subject to react with a return power play

Power and leadership

The concepts of power and leadership are closely intertwined. Leaders use their power to help followers attain desired goals. Ideally, to be effective, a leader should possess a number of power bases. Having high levels of all five would be ideal (although it may often be rare), because the various power bases often complement one another (Raven, Schwarzwald, & Koslowsky, 1998). As we have seen, legitimate power tends to validate the use of reward and coercive power. Expert power should also exist in legitimate power positions, because the most qualified persons are usually the supervisors. If the work group is committed to doing a good job, and if they have a leader who is high in legitimate and reward power and who has the expert power to lead a group to high levels of productivity, the leader is likely to develop a strong referent power base as well. Conversely, because of their strong admiration for a leader with referent power, followers may also assume the leader has expertise (Podsakoff & Schriesheim, 1985).

Looking back to some of the concepts of leadership presented in Chapter 13, we can see the importance of power in leader effectiveness. Power is either explicitly or implicitly a crucial part of some of the contingency theories of leadership. For example, the decision-making model views leaders as possessing the power to make major work-related decisions alone or to delegate some of the decision-making power to subordinates. Decision-making power can be a form of legitimate power. The leader–member exchange (LMX) model focuses on the quality of leader–member relations as a key to effective leadership. Referent power is important here because the quality of leader–member relations may depend on the leader's referent power. Perhaps the leadership theory that is most strongly linked to notions of power and specific power bases is Fiedler's (1967) contingency model. According to Fiedler, a leader is effective when the leader's style—task-oriented or relationship-oriented—matches the leader's power and control in a given situation. Recall that Fiedler outlined

APPLYING I/O PSYCHOLOGY

The Empowerment Process: A Key to Organizational Success

A major focus of research in the past two decades has centered on the notion of empowerment, which is the process by which organizational members are able to increase their sense of power and personal control in the work environment. Workers can be empowered by managers or other persons in authority positions or by increasing important work-related skills or responsibilities. A manager can empower subordinates by giving them some decision-making power or assigning some legitimate power, but workers can also be empowered when conditions in the work environment that make them feel powerless are removed. Individual workers can also become empowered by developing a sense of self-efficacy, which is, as we saw in Chapter 10, a belief in one's abilities to engage in courses of action that will lead to desired outcomes (Bandura, 1997; Conger & Kanungo, 1988). Other ways in which leaders can empower workers include the following:

Express confidence in subordinates' abilities and hold high expectations concerning their performance—Considerable evidence suggests that supervisors who have high expectations about their work group's performance may subtly communicate these feelings to the workers and thus positively influence their behavior (Eden & Shani, 1982). We saw this in Chapter 11 in the discussion of the Pygmalion effect, and there is good evidence that leaders can significantly impact followers' performance through holding and communicating positive expectations about their performance (Avolio et al., 2009).

Allow workers to participate in decision-making processes—Workers who share in decision making are more committed to the chosen courses of action (see Chapter 12).

Allow workers some freedom and autonomy in how they perform their jobs—For example, let workers be creative or innovative in work methods. The job enrichment programs discussed in Chapter 8 can empower workers by giving them increased responsibility over how their jobs are performed and evaluated.

Set inspirational and/or meaningful goals—Again, there is considerable evidence that goal setting is an important motivational strategy (see Chapter 8). Also, according to the path-goal theory of leadership (see Chapter 13), setting meaningful goals is one of the important moves that leaders can make to help work groups become more effective.

Use managerial power in a wise and positive manner, such as limiting the use of coercive tactics—Our discussion of the use of different power bases emphasized that coercive power can lead to dissatisfaction in the targets of the power and a reduction in the power user's referent power base. By contrast, reward, expert, and referent power bases allow workers greater choice and flexibility in following the power user. They can decide to strive for the reward or can choose to follow someone who is knowledgeable or admired. These are generally more effective strategies for achieving positive work group outcomes.

The empowerment process can have very positive effects on organizational outcomes. For example, empowering workers can help lessen the impact of demoralizing organizational changes. If workers feel that they have some sort of personal control over aspects of the work environment, and if they have had a say in some of the organizational changes, they can more easily adapt to and accept the changes (Greenberger & Strasser, 1986). Empowered workers may be more satisfied, less prone to leave the organization (Dewettinck & van Ameijde, 2011), and also be better able to deal with certain types of organizational stress (Spreitzer, 1996), particularly stress that results from a sense of lack of control or from job uncertainty (see Chapter 10). There is considerable evidence that empowerment and feelings of self-efficacy play an important role in motivating workers to achieve challenging work-related goals (Gist, 1987), especially if they have a hand in setting the goals and feel that the goals are within reach. In addition, empowered workers are more likely to persist at a task despite difficult organizational or environmental obstacles (Block, 1987; Conger & Kanungo, 1988). Finally, empowerment may be related to future career development and career success of workers (London, 1993).

three dimensions for defining the leadership situation: position power, leader-member relations, and task structure. Two of these are strongly linked to certain power bases. Position power deals with the leader's power to reward and punish subordinates. It actually refers to a combination of the three types of organizational power: legitimate, reward, and coercive power. Leader–member relations refer to the quality of the relationship between leader and followers, which represents the leader's referent power. In short, power is a key element in theories of leadership because the role of leader, by its very nature, must be accompanied by some form of power over followers (see box Applying I/O Psychology).

> **empowerment**
> the process by which organizational members can increase their sense of power and personal control in the work setting

Organizational Politics

The use of politics occurs daily at all levels of all organizations (Schein, 1977). For example, a qualified individual is passed over for a promotion that goes to a coworker who is clearly less qualified; organizational members say that it was a political decision. Two office workers who have a history of never getting along suddenly file a joint formal complaint about a mutually disliked supervisor; observers explain that their collaboration is due to office politics. A junior-level manager gives up a planned weekend trip to stay at home and take care of the boss's dog while the executive is out of town. The manager's motivation? Obviously political. Anyone who has had the chance to observe the operations of an organization has seen organizational politics in action.

Although the study of organizational politics is relatively new in industrial/organizational psychology, research interest in the topic is growing rapidly (Ferris & Hochwater, 2011). This makes sense because politics in organizations is quite common (Ferris & Kacmar, 1992), occurs at all levels, and can have serious effects on job performance, satisfaction, and turnover (Ferris & King, 1991; Madison, Allen, Porter, Renwick, & Mayes, 1980). However, before we begin to explore the effects of organizational politics, we must start by clearly defining the term.

Stop & Review
Outline three strategies for increasing power in organizations.

DEFINING ORGANIZATIONAL POLITICS

Earlier definitions stated that organizational politics involved the self-serving, or selfish, use of power or influence to achieve desired outcomes. This covers a very wide range of behaviors; in fact, just about any behavior can be interpreted as being political. Typically, the types of political behaviors in which we are interested involve the use of power or influence that is not part of one's position or role within the organization (Mayes & Allen, 1977). Because political behaviors are not "sanctioned" by the organization, it is assumed that organizational politics are bad or harmful to the organization's functioning, but this is not always true. Although a worker may act politically to satisfy selfish goals, using means that are not considered to be acceptable organizational procedures, the outcome might actually be favorable to the organization (Cropanzano & Grandey, 1998). In other words, political behaviors sometime lead to successful organizational

functional politics

political behaviors that help the organization to attain its goals

dysfunctional politics

political behaviors that detract from the organization's ability to attain its goals

outcomes. Such behavior might be called functional politics—behaviors that assist the organization in attaining its goals. On the other hand, political behavior that inhibits the attainment of organizational goals is dysfunctional politics. The same political behavior may be either functional or dysfunctional, depending on how it affects the goals of the organization. For example, a salesperson may use high-pressure tactics to make a sale, despite an organizational policy that frowns on such techniques. However, if the sale is made and the customer is satisfied, the tactics are functional, because the goals of both the salesperson and the organization have been met. On the other hand, if the salesperson uses the unapproved techniques and makes the sale, but the customer is unhappy with being subjected to high-pressure tactics and vows never to buy another of the company's products, the political behavior can be termed dysfunctional. The salesperson's goals have been met, but the organization's goal of keeping customers happy and loyal has been thwarted. It is not always easy to distinguish between functional and dysfunctional political behavior because the difference between the two often depends on looking at the broad picture of how the behavior affects the organization and its goals (Cavanagh, Moberg, & Velasquez, 1981). Yet, employees seem to be able to distinguish the "positive" political behavior from the "negative" (Fedor, Maslyn, Farmer, & Bettenhausen, 2008)—at least in terms of their perceptions. We will see that employee perceptions of political behavior are very important.

Ideally, if political behavior is going to occur in organizations (and it is), it should be functional. However, in any organization some of the political behavior will be functional and some will be dysfunctional. Figure 14.1 shows how political behavior that operates in the individual's self-interest can sometimes overlap with the organization's goals. The political behavior that satisfies the goals of both is functional; the behavior that satisfies the goals of the individual but not those of the organization is dysfunctional.

Although some of the political behavior that takes place in government and work organizations is dysfunctional, oriented toward achieving personal goals

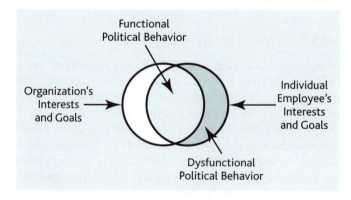

FIGURE 14.1

Political Behavior

Source: Robbins, S. P. (1979). *Organizational behavior: Concepts and controversies* (p. 404). Englewood Cliffs, NJ: Prentice Hall.

to the detriment of organizational goals, much political behavior is actually functional, helping both the individual and the organization achieve respective goals. However, it is the dysfunctional politics that often gain the most attention, because they sometimes violate the organization's codes of ethical and moral behavior. For example, in one organization, reporting negative information about another worker to management might be considered a breach of ethics, whereas in another organization such political behavior might be more accepted. In one company, management might view workers' unionization as an acceptable political practice, whereas the management of a rival organization might see it as mutiny.

EMPLOYEE PERCEPTIONS OF ORGANIZATIONAL POLITICS

Research has examined how organizational politics and the political "climate" at work are perceived by workers and work teams. First, it is important to emphasize that employees tend to view organizational politics negatively—often as a sort of necessary "evil," likely because of its self-serving nature. As a result, perceptions of high levels of organizational political behavior, or a climate that seems to tolerate politicking, are associated with negative employee outcomes. For example, a meta-analysis found that perceptions of politics led to decreased levels of job satisfaction, commitment, task performance, and organizational citizenship behaviors. There were also increased employee perceptions of "strain" and intention to turnover (Chang, Rosen, & Levy, 2009). Figure 14.2 shows a model of how employee perceptions of negative politics impact stress/strain and morale, which in turn lead to negative work outcomes.

As the meta-analysis suggests, for many workers organizational politics is seen as a significant source of stress, and highly political organizations can

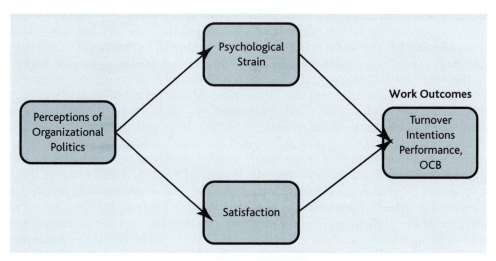

FIGURE 14.2
Model of Effects of Perceptions of Politics on Employee Outcomes

experience high levels of turnover and job dissatisfaction (Ferris, Russ, & Fandt, 1989; Poon, 2003; Vigoda, 2000). Other workers seem to truly enjoy engaging in organizational politics. Although lower-level employees may view politics as an additional burden, managers tend to view organizational politics as "part of the job" (Ferris et al., 1996). Employees at different levels of the organization also seem to perceive politics differently. One study found that top-level managers and lower-level employees believed that there was less politicking going on in their organizations than did managers at the middle levels (Parker, Dipboye, & Jackson, 1995). In addition, there may be cultural variations in reactions to organizational politics. For example, Israeli workers appear to be more tolerant of high levels of organizational politicking than British workers (Vigoda, 2001).

TYPES OF POLITICAL BEHAVIORS

Political behavior was defined as any self-serving behavior. This means that politics includes many different types of behaviors. To better understand organizational politics, it is important to have some scheme for classifying political behaviors. Farrell and Petersen (1982) have suggested that political behaviors can be grouped along three dimensions: *internal–external, lateral–vertical*, and *legitimate–illegitimate*.

The internal–external dimension refers to whether political behavior involves only members of the organization, or if it extends beyond the boundaries of the organization to include outside people and resources. Examples of external political behaviors would be bringing a lawsuit against an organization or an organizational member, consulting with members of competitor organizations, or leaking secret company information to the press. The lateral–vertical dimension concerns whether the political behavior occurs between members of the same status within the organization, or if it crosses vertical status levels. Political behaviors involving superiors and subordinates would be an example of vertical politics, whereas two coworkers campaigning for the same promotion are engaging in lateral politics. If a subordinate bypasses the typical chain of command and goes to someone higher in the organization to complain about an immediate supervisor, this is vertical politics. Several coworkers of the same status who form a coalition are engaging in lateral politics. The third dimension is whether a particular political behavior is legitimate or illegitimate. This legitimate–illegitimate dimension concerns whether the behavior is "normal everyday" politics, or some extreme form of political behavior that violates the generally accepted "rules of the game." As mentioned earlier, organizations and work groups establish their own codes of what is appropriate, or legitimate, and what is unacceptable, or illegitimate. Illegitimate political behavior is most likely to be used by alienated members of the organization who feel that they have no other alternatives and nothing to lose, such as a worker who is about to be fired. For example, slowing down work output—rate setting—may be a legitimate form of political behavior in many organizations, whereas sabotage, such as purposely breaking an important piece of work equipment, will always be considered illegitimate.

Interestingly, the distinction between whether a particular political behavior is legitimate or illegitimate, acceptable or unacceptable, or good or bad is in large part a value judgment. The same type of behavior may be considered unacceptable in one situation, but acceptable when performed in another.

It is also true that political behaviors performed by certain organizational members might be approved, whereas the same behavior from other workers may be disapproved. For example, political behaviors are usually considered a way of life at the top levels of an organization, but such behaviors among the lower-level members are often labeled subversive and potentially dangerous to the organization. The perspective of the person making the judgment also affects whether a political behavior is considered acceptable or unacceptable. What one person considers to be a perfectly reasonable action, another may consider to be dirty politics. Moreover, actions that many might agree are reasonable political behaviors can, if taken to extremes, lead to very negative and very dysfunctional ends. For example, forming coalitions can be seen as a good way for low-ranking members to gain some collective power and influence within the organization. However, management may perceive such coalitions as precursors to negative outcomes such as work stoppages and striking. At extremes, striking workers may engage in activities to disrupt organizational operations by forming picket lines to keep "scab" workers out, destroying company property, and rioting. The same basic process can thus be perceived as either good or bad, depending on the timing, the circumstances, and the people involved (see Table 14.3 and box On the Cutting Edge).

TABLE 14.3
Organizational Political Behaviors: The Good, The Bad, and The Ugly

Good	Bad	Ugly
Forming coalitions	Striking	Rioting
Blame placing (pointing out who is legitimately at fault)	Passing the buck (avoiding personal blame)	Scapegoating (blaming an individual who is likely not at fault)
Image building (making yourself look good by emphasizing your positive attributes)	Discrediting others (pointing out others' faults so that you look good in comparison)	Mudslinging (bringing up negative and possibly false information about another person)
Making demands and bargaining	Blackmailing	Sabotaging
Limiting communication	Withholding information	Lying
Refusing to comply	Stalling	"Stonewalling"
Forming alliances	Displaying favoritism	"Brownnosing"

The same basic political behavior, which may initially be seen as "good" or acceptable, can be misused or can be seen as being misused, and can thus be labeled "bad." Certain political behaviors can be taken to extremes that can be very disruptive to the organization and its functioning.

ON THE *CUTTING* EDGE

Are Some Workers More Politically Skilled Than Others?

There is little doubt that there are individual differences in workers' tendencies to engage in organizational politicking, as well as their tolerance for it (Ferris & Hochwater, 2011; Hochwater, Witt, & Kacmar, 2000; Kacmar & Baron, 1999). It has been suggested that given the fact that political behavior is so common in organizations, wise employees need to develop their "political skill" (Ferris, Perrewé, Anthony, & Gilmore, 2000). In fact, with increased use of teams, the overlapping and interdependent nature of jobs, as well as increasing job ambiguity and the great mobility of workers today, it is likely that political skill is even more important today than it was when jobs and organizations were more stable and predictable.

What are the elements of political skill? It has been suggested that social intelligence, emotional intelligence, and self-efficacy—all constructs that we looked at earlier—are important elements of political skill. Another important component of political skill is called "tacit knowledge" and refers to what one needs to know to succeed in a given environment (Sternberg, 2002). Tacit knowledge is related to political "savvy" and is often unspoken and needs to be acquired on-the-job. Scholars have developed a measure of political skill, and their research suggests that political skill helps people cope with some aspects of work stress and is advantageous for leaders to possess (Ferris et al., 2005; Perrewé et al., 2005).

---

whistle-blowing
political behavior whereby an employee criticizes company policies and practices to persons outside the organization

One particular political behavior that has received a great deal of attention is termed "whistle-blowing." Whistle-blowing is when employees convey criticisms about their organization's policies and practices to persons or authorities outside the organization (Perry, 1998). (Note that in Farrell and Petersen's scheme, whistle-blowing is external political behavior.) Typically, whistle-blowers believe that the organization's practices are illegal, immoral, or illegitimate, regardless of whether the criticisms are indeed valid (Johnson, 2003; Near & Miceli, 1985, 1995). Well-known instances of whistle-blowing include employees of chemical companies, who have reported instances of dumping of hazardous waste; Enron employees, who exposed the company's financial scandals; a staffer, who exposed the FBI's slow actions in dealing with terrorists prior to the 9/11 attacks; and exposures of the criminal activities of politicians by members of their office staffs.

Whistle-blowing is a particularly complicated form of organizational politics. The whistle-blower may face an ethical dilemma between doing what he or she believes to be right and hurting a company toward which the worker may feel a sense of loyalty and commitment by exposing the company to possible fines, sanctions, and costs (Jubb, 1999). Moreover, there is the possibility that the organization will retaliate against the whistle-blower. For this reason, in the United States, the United Kingdom, Canada, and India there are laws that partially protect whistle-blowers. Of course, disgruntled employees may file false complaints as a way of getting back at the company that they feel has wronged them.

Not surprisingly, it has been found that employees in organizations that have policies encouraging whistle-blowing, and workers whose supervisors support their whistle-blowing, have greater instances of reporting inappropriate company practices to external agencies (Kaptien, 2011; King, 1999). In addition,

⏱ *Stop & Review*

Distinguish between functional and dysfunctional political behavior and give examples of each.

workers who have strong values are more likely to whistle-blow (Sims & Keenan, 1998). One author has advised the HR departments to have whistle-blowing policies and procedures in place for the benefit of all concerned (Lewis, 2002).

Whistle-blowing is only one type of organizational politics, but it is one that receives a great deal of attention because it involves parties outside the organization (often the press or consumer protection agencies) and because of the ethical and loyalty implications of whistle-blowing. Interestingly, many organizational political behaviors, like whistle-blowing, are labeled using slang terminology (see Table 14.3).

CAUSES OF ORGANIZATIONAL POLITICS

Organizational politics are attempts by organizational members to use their influence and power to achieve personal goals, such as increased pay and career advancement. Often, in order to achieve these goals, workers must engage in certain types of political behaviors. To understand organizational politics, which is an inevitable, ongoing process with important implications for the operations of work organizations, we need to explore the factors that contribute to increasing the incidence of political behaviors in work organizations. These include such things as competition for power and scarce resources, difficulties in measuring important work outcomes, compensation for worker inadequacies, and increased group decision making.

Competition for power and resources

When resources such as money, promotions, and status are scarce, people may try to exercise their power to obtain what they need to satisfy their goals (Parker, Dipboye, & Jackson, 1995). The scarcer the resources and the more difficult they are to obtain, due to "red tape" or arbitrary allocation procedures, the greater the potential that organizational members will act politically to get what they want. For example, an individual who forms a strong relationship with someone in the organization who has control over distributing important resources may be able to get a larger share of the resources (and to get them more quickly). In a publishing company, a manager noticed that new computers were often distributed first to persons who were friendly with the departmental manager, rather than to those who needed them most. In a city government, an employee saw that the incidence of political behaviors increased whenever the city obtained a large state or federal grant, as each department lobbied for a greater share of the money. Generally, competition for power resources increases the incidence of organizational politics.

Subjective performance appraisals

When job performance is not measured objectively, it means that performance may be unrelated to career success. When personnel decisions, such as pay raises and promotions, are based on poorly defined or poorly measured subjective criteria, workers may resort to political tactics such as forming alliances, discrediting others, and lobbying to gain favor with the appraisers and get ahead. This can be extremely dysfunctional for the organization, because the best workers may not be recognized and encouraged for their efforts. Even worse, poor performers who are good politicians will occasionally be placed in positions of responsibility.

When criteria other than performance, such as dressing a certain way or espousing company philosophy, are overemphasized in personnel decisions, workers may make efforts to look good rather than to perform well. When managers make comments like, "He looks like a real company man," they are likely giving weight to factors that are unrelated to good work performance. This is another reason that sound and objective performance appraisals are a necessity (see Chapter 6).

Delay in measurement of work outcomes

In many jobs, particularly white-collar positions, workers are faced with a variety of tasks. Some tasks see immediate results, whereas with others, the results may not be observed for a long time. A problem occurs when management wants periodic appraisals of workers' performance. Workers who are involved in long-term activities may be at a disadvantage over those engaged in "quick-and-dirty" tasks, particularly if existing performance appraisal methods do not take into account performance on long-term tasks. This means that workers faced with long-term jobs may be faced with two choices: focus their energy into short-term tasks or engage in political behaviors to convince management that they are indeed good workers. Either case can be dysfunctional for the organization, because it directs effort away from the long-term tasks, which are often very important to the organization.

University professors are subject to this delay in measurement with their research activities. Although both longitudinal and field research projects are valuable, they often require a great deal of time, often even several years, to complete. Meanwhile, professors are under pressure to "publish or perish." This leads many to abandon valuable long-term projects for simpler laboratory studies in which the results, and the subsequent publications, appear more quickly.

Compensation for inadequacies

When jobs are ambiguous and workers do not know how to perform them correctly, there is the potential for dysfunctional political behavior as the workers try to look as if they know what they are doing. Defining jobs and work procedures clearly and effectively orienting new employees eliminate much of this problem and reduce the likelihood that workers will engage in political behaviors to compensate for being confused or inadequately trained.

According to one management theory, there is a tendency for members in an organizational hierarchy to be continually promoted upward, until they reach a level at which they have exceeded their abilities to perform the job well. This has been labeled the "Peter principle" (Peter & Hull, 1969), which basically states that employees will eventually rise to their level of incompetency. If this is true—and it probably is more true for some employees than for others—then these workers who have "peaked out" must engage in organizational politics to maintain their positions and to make further upward progress. This practice is obviously very dysfunctional for the organization.

In certain instances, workers may engage in politics to cover up another's inadequacies. This might occur if a worker, out of pity, helps and covers up for someone who does not have the skills to perform a job. In other instances, subordinates may protect a leader who is incompetent because of strong positive feelings for that person. However, covering up for a leader who is under legitimate attack is a form of dysfunctional politics. Although subordinates may feel that they are being loyal to their boss, having a poor leader can be very harmful for the organization.

Lack of cooperation and interdependence

Work groups that are not highly interdependent, that do not have a strong norm for cooperation, or that do not support one another tend to engage in greater levels of political behavior than groups that are cooperative, interdependent, and supportive. In fact, the results of one study suggested that work groups could be defined along a continuum, with highly politicized groups at one end and supportive, cooperative groups at the other end (Randall, Cropanzano, Bormann, & Birjulin, 1999).

Increased group decision making

The more that group decision-making procedures are used in organizations, the greater is the potential for politics. Group decision making is basically a political process, with members lobbying for certain courses of action and engaging in a variety of exchanges of favors and support to obtain certain outcomes. For the most part, group decision making, when properly regulated, leads to functional outcomes. However, if the process begins to break down, so that high-quality decisions are not being accepted because of opponents' political savvy and power, the results can be dysfunctional. In extremes, group members may begin to focus more and more energy into the political process, ignoring the implementation of decisions, which is also dysfunctional.

CONSEQUENCES OF ORGANIZATIONAL POLITICS

Because organizational politics can be functional or dysfunctional—either helping or hindering the organization from achieving its performance-related goals—connections between politics and productivity are not straightforward. Clearly, if too much dysfunctional politicking is occurring in an organization, it will have a negative effect on work group productivity. In extreme cases, employees may spend so much time politicking that they spend little time doing their work. However, at least one study suggests that organizational politics are positively related to work performance if workers and supervisors share similar goals (Witt, 1998).

The relationship between organizational politics and job satisfaction is a bit clearer. Research has shown a fairly consistent negative relationship between political behaviors and job satisfaction (Cropanzano, Howes, Grandey, & Toth,

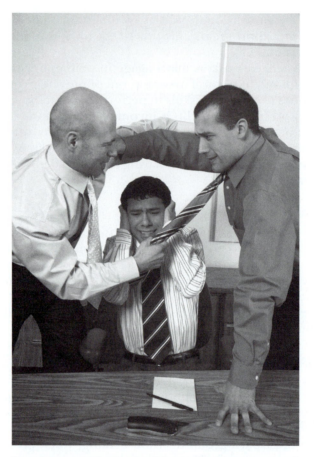

Sometimes organizational politics can lead to extreme and aggressive behaviors.

1997; Ferris et al., 1996; Gandz & Murray, 1980; Larwood, Wright, Desrochers, & Dahir, 1998; Parker, Dipboye, & Jackson, 1995; Vigoda, 2000). In addition, organizational politics is negatively related to organizational commitment and to the incidence of organizational citizenship behaviors (Ferris & Kacmar, 1992; Randall et al., 1999; Shore & Wayne, 1993; Witt, 1998). Low levels of organizational politics are also associated with better organizational communication (Rosen, Levy, & Hall, 2006). Finally, organizational politics may be positively related to both absenteeism and turnover, as workers in highly political work environments get tired of the "political games" and call in sick or begin to look for work elsewhere (Cropanzano et al., 1997; Ferris et al., 1993; Gilmore, Ferris, Dulebohn, & Harrell-Cook, 1996).

MANAGING ORGANIZATIONAL POLITICS

It is clear that politics can be stimulated by a number of factors in work organizations and that political behaviors take many forms. An important concern is how to manage organizational politics. In many ways, the management of organizational politics is much like the management of conflict that was discussed in Chapter 12: The first step is simply to know when it occurs. Learning the causes of political behavior—particularly factors that are likely to lead to dysfunctional political behavior, such as inappropriate performance measures, inadequate job descriptions and procedures, or poor training for new employees—can help to ensure that conditions do not encourage too much political behavior. On the other hand, a certain amount of politics is natural and may even lead to functional outcomes for the organization. Group decision-making processes, workers' critiques of established work procedures and suggestions for alternatives and improvements, and competition among workers may all result in functional political behaviors and improved organizational outcomes.

One model suggests five strategies for managing organizational politics (Mayes, 1995):

1. *Remove ambiguity and uncertainty*—Written job descriptions and procedures manuals can help clarify jobs and organizational procedures and help eliminate some dysfunctional politicking.

2. *Provide "slack" resources*—Giving managers slightly more than minimal resources (e.g., discretionary funds, extra positions) means that they will not have to trade political favors to meet goals.

3. *Create a positive and ethical organizational climate*—From the top levels of the organization down, executives and managers should encourage a climate that discourages negative political behavior. If top-level management is engaging in dysfunctional political behavior, lower-level workers will follow their example, and vice versa.

4. *Clarify personnel selection and appraisal processes*—All personnel decisions should be made devoid of politics.

5. *Reward performance, not politics*—Workers should not be able to succeed in the organization through politics alone.

A Contingency Approach to Organizational Power and Politics

The use and effectiveness of organizational power and politics depends on a number of factors. We have seen that individuals vary in their tendencies, abilities, and willingness to use power and politics. Research continues to explore individual differences in the desire and ability to use organizational power and politics (e.g., Kirchmeyer, 1990). We also know that the ability to use power effectively is related to the characteristics of those who are the subject(s) of the power play (Yukl, Guinan, & Sottolano, 1995). Moreover, organizations and work groups differ in the extent to which they will allow certain types of power and political maneuvering by members (e.g., Near, Dworkin, & Miceli, 1993). All of this indicates that power and politics in work organizations are extremely complex phenomena that are best explained and understood through a contingency approach, which looks at the interaction of characteristics of the individual or group and factors related to the situation in which the individual or group is behaving.

Researchers have attempted to put power and politics into contingency frameworks. Gray and Ariss (1985) proposed that politics vary across the stages of an organization's "life cycle." That is, the political behaviors observed in a very new organization (termed the "birth and early growth stage") are very different than those occurring in a more "mature," established organization. According to this model, appropriate political behaviors are critical for success in managing an organization effectively. The manager must be able to adapt political strategies to those appropriate to the organization and its particular life cycle stage (see also Mintzberg, 1984; Salancik & Pfeffer, 1977). For example, in the earliest stages of an organization, the manager is actually the entrepreneur who founded the organization. At this point, the manager should wield absolute power, controlling and distributing resources as the manager sees fit. The entrepreneur–manager also controls decision-making power and aligns the organization's goals with the manager's self-interest. In other words, the organization is created in the image and likeness of the manager. As the organization moves toward maturity, the manager will switch to more of a "bargaining" political strategy of exchanging resources for favors.

In another contingency approach, Cobb (1984), building on the work of Porter, Allen, and Angle (1981), proposed an "episodic model of power" that examines power episodes, or the use of power in actual work settings (see Figure 14.3). The episodic model includes consideration of aspects of the

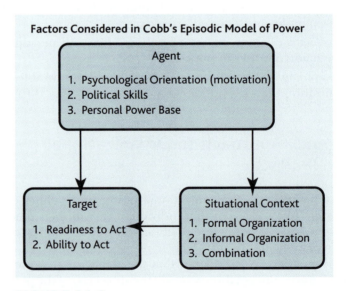

FIGURE 14.3

Factors Considered in Cobb's Episodic Model of Power

Factors Considered in Cobb's "An Episodic Model of Power: Toward an Integration of Theory and Research." Cobb, A. T. (1984). *Academy of Management Review* (Vol. 9, pp. 482–493). Reprinted by permission of the Academy of Management.

exerciser, or agent, of power and the subject, or target, as well as elements of the power situation. For example, in trying to understand the use of power, this model looks at three factors related to the agent of power. The first, psychological orientation, is the motivation to use power. The second, political skills, is the agent's understanding of organizational politics and her or his ability to act politically. Finally, personal power base is the amount and type(s) of power a person possesses. The model also considers two factors related to the target of power: the readiness to act and the ability to act. Readiness is defined as the extent to which the target is inclined to act in a manner consistent with the agent's desires. Ability is whether the target can indeed perform the act the agent desires. Finally, this model looks at the power situation, examining whether the "power episode" occurs in the context of the formal organization, the informal organization, or in both. If the power episode is a formal situation, the agent's legitimate power and authority will likely play a greater role in influencing the target than will the agent's political skills. However, if the situation is informal, the agent's influence skills may be more important than legitimate power bases. This model thus attempts to integrate the scattered research on power in organizations to offer a broad and complex approach to understanding power dynamics.

In sum, the topics of power and politics in organizations are still relatively new, although they have been the focus of a growing amount of research in the past several years. The contingency models briefly presented here represent future directions in the study of organizational power processes.

⏱ **Stop & Review**

Name and define the three power agent factors that affect the use of power in the episodic model of power (Cobb).

Summary

Influence, power, and politics are important processes in work groups and organizations. *Influence* is the use of informal social strategies to get another to perform specific actions. *Power* is the use of some aspect of a social relationship to compel another to perform an action despite resistance. *Organizational politics* is the use of power to achieve selfish, or self-serving, goals. A wide variety of influence tactics are commonly employed in work organizations. One such strategy, *ingratiation*, occurs when an individual tries to influence others by increasing personal appeal through doing favors or through flattery.

There are five major power bases, or sources of power: *coercive power*, which involves the use or threat of punishment; *reward power*, which is the ability to give organizational rewards to others; *legitimate power*, which involves the formal rights and authorities that accompany a position; *expert power*, which derives from an individual's work-related knowledge, skill, or expertise; and *referent power*, which comes from the fact that an individual is respected and admired by others. Research indicates that the various power bases have different effects on important organizational outcomes, such as work performance and job satisfaction.

Organizational political behaviors can be divided into two categories. The first, *functional politics*, is political behavior on the part of an organizational member that helps the organization to attain its goals. The second, *dysfunctional politics*, inhibits the organization's goal attainment. Organizational politics arise from a variety of sources, including competition for power and resources, subjective performance appraisals, delay in measurement of work outcomes, compensation for inadequacies, and increased group decision making. Research has attempted to categorize political behaviors and recognize conditions under which they are likely to occur. One goal of management is to try to eliminate dysfunctional political behavior by eliminating conditions that give rise to it. The most recent approaches to studying organizational power and politics take a contingency approach, examining the interaction of individual power characteristics, the target of the power play, and the situational context.

Study Questions and Exercises

1. In what ways are influence, power, and organizational politics different? In what ways are they similar?
2. Consider the five power bases described by French and Raven (1959). Give examples of how a manager might use each to increase work group productivity.
3. Recall some instances in which you observed power used in a work or social group. Which power bases were used in each case? How effective were they in influencing others' behavior?
4. What is the distinction between functional and dysfunctional political behavior? Give examples of each.
5. List some of the potential causes of political behaviors.

Web Links

www.influenceatwork.com
   A site based on Cialdini's research on social influence.

Suggested Readings

Cialdini, R. B. (2008). *Influence: Science and practice* (5th ed.). Boston, MA: Pearson. *An enjoyable explanation of how social influence is used by compliance professionals to affect the behavior of others.*

Clegg, S., Courpasson, D., & Phillips, N. (2006). *Power and organizations.* Thousand Oaks, CA: Sage. *A very scholarly review of research and theory on organizational power.*

Vigoda-Gadot, E., & Drory, A. (Eds.). (2006). *Handbook of organizational politics.* Cheltenham, UK: Edward Elgar. *A scholarly, edited review of research and theory on organizational politics.*

CHAPTER OUTLINE

Inside Tips

ORGANIZATIONAL STRUCTURE, CULTURE, AND DEVELOPMENT:
UNIFYING CONCEPTS IN INDUSTRIAL/ORGANIZATIONAL
PSYCHOLOGY

In this chapter, we view organizations at their most general level: looking at how the organization, as a whole, can affect the behavior of the typical worker. Take organizational structure, for example. In rigid, rule-driven, traditional organizations, it is likely that employees will be expected to adhere closely to strict company regulations and policies. By contrast, in nontraditional organizations, there is a lack of rigid structure and rules, which means that workers will have quite a bit of freedom and are expected to take on responsibility and to demonstrate initiative. Knowing about the structure and culture of an organization can help us to understand and analyze the work behavior that occurs within the organization.

Although this chapter focuses on the organization as a whole, the concepts of organizational structure and culture have been touched on previously. For example, in Chapter 11, we saw that the organizational chart, or organigram, illustrates the lines of formal communication within an organization, or the organization's communication structure. In this chapter we will focus more on the organization's authority structure, because the organizational chart also represents the formal lines of status and authority. The general concept of authority was also discussed in Chapter 14, when the topic of legitimate power was introduced. There are strong ties between the concept of power and the structure of organizations because organizations can be viewed as power structures. The concept of organizational culture has been hinted at in several previous chapters. Organizational culture is connected to workers' feelings about their jobs and their organization—recall Chapter 9 and the discussions of job engagement and organizational commitment. In addition, the group processes chapter (Chapter 12) explored the elements that contribute to an organization's total "culture."

The field of organizational development (OD), which is introduced in this chapter, emphasizes that organizations must take steps to keep up with the changing world around them. Organizational development is an eclectic area of I/O psychology, for it draws on many theories and applications from a variety of topics within the broader field and uses them to help organizations change. In our discussion of OD, you will see many of the concepts and topics from earlier chapters, but here they will be applied in an effort to help organizations change and innovate.

Y ou have begun working for a new organization. You have had experience with several other organizations and noticed that each was hierarchical and somewhat bureaucratic. Your last company had many layers of management. Even your university was structured, with many levels of administration between the students and the president. But this organization is quite different. The employees act more like a team. Everyone is on a first-name basis, and the head of the company is indistinguishable from some of the other, older employees. Most importantly, the climate of the organization is completely different. People seem more "loose," but they are highly motivated, work long hours, and seem to take real pride in their work and the company. You begin to wonder how organizations can vary so greatly.

So far, we have studied work behavior at a number of levels. We looked at work behavior at the individual level, examining the processes by which individual workers are selected and assigned to jobs, trained, and evaluated, and the internal processes that affect the behavior of individual workers, including the factors that influence worker motivation, job satisfaction, and stress. We have also explored work behavior at the group level. It is now time to look at work behavior from a larger perspective: the organizational level. This larger perspective will allow an exploration of how the structure, dynamics, and culture of the organization itself can affect the behavior of its work groups and individuals (Williams & Rain, 2007).

We will begin by studying the structure of organizations, or how they are designed and operate. We will consider how factors both inside and outside the organization affect its structure, focusing on how different structures affect behavior within the organization. We will then look at how organizations develop their own individual cultures, which can influence nearly all aspects of behavior at work. Finally, we will look at how organizations can change and develop to meet the demands placed on them from both within and without. In particular, we will study some of the various techniques used to help organizations change to become more effective and to become better places to work.

Organizational Structure

Organizational structure refers to the arrangement of positions in an organization and the authority and responsibility relationships among them. This means that every organization is made up of persons holding particular positions or playing certain roles in an organization. The organization's structure is then determined by the interrelationships among the responsibilities of these various positions or roles. Consider, for example, a simple Internet retail business that has three positions.

The first is the director of operations, who has authority over the other two positions. The director's responsibilities include selecting and acquiring the products that will be offered through the business and handling the organization's finances. The second position is the marketing specialist, whose responsibilities consist of designing the Web-based advertisements for the organization's products and placing the ads in various outlets. In terms of authority, the marketing specialist is subordinate to the director but superior to the third position: the shipping clerk. The clerk's responsibilities

organizational structure
refers to the arrangement of positions in an organization and the authority and responsibility relationships among them

are solely to package and mail orders. In this very small organization, positions and responsibilities are clearly defined, and the responsibilities are linked in such a way that all functions of the company are handled smoothly and efficiently.

Of course, most work organizations are extremely complex, made up of dozens, hundreds, or thousands of workers. Each has an arrangement of positions and responsibilities that is in some way unique. There are a number of different dimensions of organizational structure. For example, organizations can be classified under a general continuum of structure that ranges from the very formal and traditional to the completely informal and nontraditional. Organizations can also be classified by their size or the "shape" of their organizational hierarchy. We will begin our discussion by examining some of the dimensions on which organizations can be structured.

Dimensions of Organizational Structure

Traditional versus Nontraditional Organizational Structures

Traditional organizations have formally defined roles for their members, are very rule driven, and are stable and resistant to change. Jobs and lines of status and authority tend to be clearly defined in traditional structures, which means that much of the work behavior tends to be regulated and kept within organizational guidelines and standards. Sometimes, traditional organizational structures are called "mechanistic" or "bureaucratic" structures (we will discuss bureaucracies shortly).

Nontraditional organizational structures are characterized by less-formalized work roles and procedures. As a result, they tend to be rather flexible and adaptable, without the rigid status hierarchy characteristic of more traditional structures. Nontraditional organizational structures are sometimes referred to as "organic." Generally, nontraditional organizations have fewer employees than the traditional structures, and nontraditional structures may also occur as a small organization that is a subunit of a larger, more traditionally structured organization. For example, an organization that manufactures state-of-the-art jet airliners may be made up of a nontraditional organizational unit that is responsible for designing new aircraft and a traditional organizational unit that is charged with producing dozens of the new jets.

Traditional organizational structures arose around the turn of the 20th century, when advancements in technology had led to the growth of manufacturing organizations and the increase in their output. As these manufacturing organizations became larger and larger, there was greater need for establishing rules to coordinate the various activities of the growing numbers of workers in each organization. These traditional structures began to replace the small, family-type manufacturing organizations, and today many work organizations, such as major manufacturers and service organizations—including banks, the Internal Revenue Service, the department of motor vehicles, and your college or university administration—are traditional organizational structures.

Nontraditional structures are often organized around a particular project or product line and are responsible for all aspects of the job. Motion picture production crews are an example of a nontraditional structure. Film crews contain a number of types of experts and professionals—camerapersons, actors/actresses, lighting specialists, editors—who work together, pooling their knowledge and talents to produce a creative, quality product. Nontraditional structures have also been set up in hospitals and health-care agencies, financial institutions, and government (Burns, 1989; Burns & Wholey, 1993; Kolodny, 1979). Nontraditional organizations typically have four important characteristics: (a) high flexibility and adaptability, (b) collaboration among workers, (c) less emphasis on organizational status, and (d) group decision making. We will look at examples of both traditional and nontraditional organizational structures a bit later.

CHAIN OF COMMAND AND SPAN OF CONTROL

Traditional organizational structures are characterized by an authority hierarchy that is represented in the organizational chart, or organigram. The organigram depicts graphically the various levels of status or authority in a traditional organization and the number of workers that report to each position of authority. The chain of command is the number of authority levels in a particular organization. The chain of command follows the lines of authority and status vertically through the organization. The span of control is the number of workers who must report to a single supervisor. An organization with a wide span of control has many workers reporting to each supervisor; an organization with a narrow span has few subordinates reporting to each superior. Based on these dimensions of chain of command and span of control, traditional organizations are often described as being either "tall" or "flat" in structure (see Figure 15.1). A tall organizational structure has a long chain of command—many authority levels—and a narrow span of control. A flat organizational structure has a short chain of command but a wide span of control. It is important to note that both dimensions are more descriptive of traditional rather than nontraditional structures. Very nontraditional organizations may have a very small chain of command or none at all, because they de-emphasize authority levels.

An organization's shape, either tall or flat, can have important implications for work life in the organization. For example, in tall organizational structures, workers at the bottom levels may feel cut off from those above, because they are separated by many levels of middle-ranking superiors. On the positive side, tall organizations may offer lower-level employees many different promotional opportunities throughout their careers. Another advantage of such structures is that there is usually adequate supervision because the span of control is narrow; each supervisor is only responsible for a few employees. However, tall organizational structures can become "top heavy" with administrators and managers, because the ratio of line workers to supervisors is very low. Conversely,

chain of command
the number of authority levels in an organization

span of control
the number of workers who must report to a single supervisor

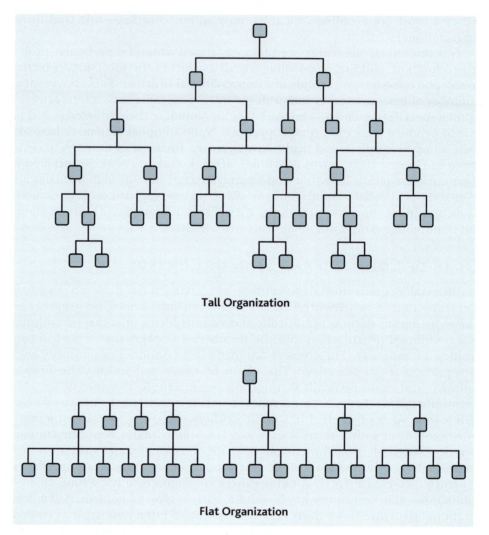

Tall Organization

Flat Organization

FIGURE 15.1
Tall and Flat Organizational Structures

in a flat structure few levels separate top-level managers from bottom-level workers, possibly leading to greater interaction between the top and bottom of the organization. However, flat structures offer few promotional opportunities to workers, and supervision may not always be adequate, because many workers report to the same supervisor.

The type of structure, tall or flat, follows from its functions and goals. For example, flat organizational structures may be more common when the task is routine or repetitive, thus requiring a large number of workers who need minimal supervision. Organizations with complex and multifaceted goals or products may have taller structures, with different levels handling the various aspects of the company's goals.

FUNCTIONAL VERSUS DIVISIONAL STRUCTURE

Organizations can also be structured by either functions or divisions. Functional structure divides the organization into departments based on the functions or tasks performed. For example, a manufacturing firm may be made up of a production department, sales department, and finance department. An amusement park might be divided into operations, publicity, and maintenance.

Divisional structure is based on types of products or customers. Each division may perform the same range of functions, but those functions only serve the goals of the particular division. In other words, each division operates almost as if it were a separate organization. For example, a major motion picture company might have multiple products—one that focuses on films for theatres, another producing movies for television, and one that focuses on DVD products—each of which is represented by a separate division. Within each division are people who handle manufacturing, marketing, and financing, but only for their particular product. Figure 15.2 provides examples of organizations structured by function and division.

A primary advantage of functional structure is that it creates job specialists, such as experts in marketing or finance, and eliminates duplication of functions. One disadvantage of functional structure is that workers may become overly focused on their own department and area of specialization, and this may breed interdepartmental rivalry and conflict. Another disadvantage is that work must move from one large department to another to be completed, which may decrease productivity, particularly when work is lost in the shuffle or when one department is particularly slow in accomplishing its functions, thereby creating a bottleneck.

Divisional structure has positive and negative aspects as well. One advantage is that the company can easily expand products or services merely by adding a new division. Also, because each division operates as a separate entity, with its own production goals and profit picture, there is greater accountability. It is easy to determine which units are performing at either exceptional or substandard levels. One of the major drawbacks to divisional structure concerns the duplication of areas of expertise, because each division contains its own departments for production, sales, research, and other functions. Another potential weakness is that workers with similar skills and expertise may not be able to benefit from professional interaction with each other because they are housed in different divisions.

CENTRALIZED VERSUS DECENTRALIZED STRUCTURE

Another dimension of organizational structure deals with how important work-related decisions are made, which can be either centralized or decentralized. Centralization is the degree to which decision-making authority is concentrated at the top of the organizational hierarchy (Fry & Slocum, 1984). In highly centralized organizations, the decision-making power is firmly held by the top levels of the organization. Decentralization is the process of taking the decision-making power out of the hands of the top level and distributing some of it to lower levels.

functional structure
an organizational structure that divides the organization into departments based on the functions or tasks they perform

divisional structure
an organizational structure that divides the organization according to types of products or customers

centralization
the degree to which decision-making power rests at the upper levels of the organizational hierarchy

decentralization
the process of taking the decision-making authority away from the top levels of the organization and distributing it to lower levels

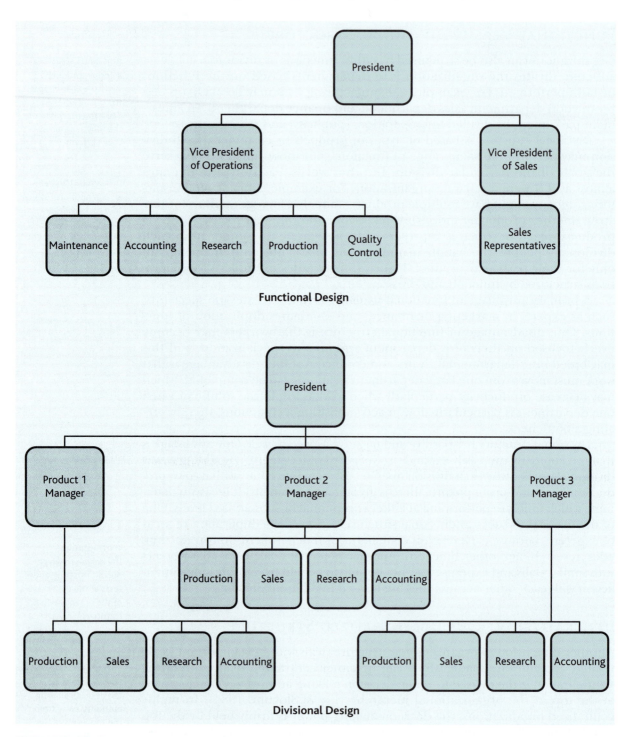

FIGURE 15.2
Functional and Divisional Organizational Design

For example, a chain of ice cream stores could have either a very centralized or a very decentralized structure. In the centralized structure, top-level executives in the corporate office would control all the decision making. They would decide what flavors of ice cream should appear in the stores each month, the number of personnel each store can hire, and how the advertising budget for each store will be spent. In contrast, if the same chain had a decentralized structure, each of the store managers would be allowed to make decisions concerning the selection of ice cream flavors, advertising, and personnel. The centralized organization has the advantage of uniformity, which means that each store should operate with some average level of quality and efficiency. However, this structure may limit the ability of individual stores to adjust to special circumstances. For example, one store manager in the centralized chain may complain that his store has special personnel and advertising needs that the corporate decision makers do not consider. In the decentralized company, each store can make its own decisions, but this could backfire if the store managers make poor or uninformed decisions. One study found that employees felt that they were treated more fairly by organizations with decentralized, as opposed to centralized, structures (Schminke, Ambrose, & Cropanzano, 2000).

Examples of Traditional and Nontraditional Organizational Structures

TRADITIONAL ORGANIZATIONAL STRUCTURES

The bureaucracy

The prototypical traditional organizational structure is the bureaucracy, which is characterized by a well-defined authority hierarchy with strict rules for governing work behavior. The bureaucratic organization is often represented as a pyramid, with the few members with highest status on the top, leading directly down to the many bottom-level workers who carry out the organization's goal of producing goods or services. The bureaucratic model was developed in the early 20th century by the German sociologist Max Weber, who formulated a theory of organizational structure that was based on formality and authority (Weber, 1947). Weber believed the bureaucracy established order in the work setting and increased productivity by reducing inefficiencies in organizational operations. According to him, a true bureaucratic organization should possess six characteristics outlined in Table 15.1: the division or specialization of labor, a well-defined authority hierarchy, formal rules and procedures, impersonality, merit-based employment decisions, and an emphasis on written records.

Manufacturing organizations and those providing simple customer service are the most likely candidates for bureaucratic structure, which, with its emphasis on job specialization, tends to lead to greater productivity when the manufacturing of goods or the delivery of services is routine. Many of the organizations you deal with on a daily basis, such as the post office, supermarkets, department stores, and fast-food restaurants, are built on the bureaucratic model. And, contrary to popular notions, these bureaucracies are usually efficient organizations.

bureaucracy
a traditional organizational structure typified by a well-defined authority hierarchy and strict rules governing work behavior

TABLE 15.1

Six Characteristics of a Bureaucratic Organization

Specialization of labor—The complex goals or outputs of the organization are broken down into separate jobs with simple, routine, and well-defined tasks. In this way, each person becomes a specialized expert at performing a certain task.

A well-defined authority hierarchy—Bureaucracies are characterized by a pyramid-type arrangement in which each lower position is controlled and supervised by the next higher level. Every position is under the direct supervision of someone higher up, so that there is no confusion about who reports to whom (see Figure 15.3).

Formal rules and procedures—In a bureaucracy there are strict rules and regulations to ensure uniformity and to regulate work behavior. Because of these extensive rules and procedures, there should never be any doubt about what a particular worker is supposed to be doing. Everyone's job is well defined, and procedures for coordinating activities with other workers should be clearly established.

Impersonality—In bureaucracies, behavior is based on logical rather than emotional thinking. This means that personal preferences and emotional factors do not have a place in any work-related decisions. For example, a true bureaucratic service organization would never give preferential treatment to one customer over another.

Employment decisions based on merit—Hiring and promotion decisions are based on who is best qualified for the job rather than on the personal preferences of those making the personnel decisions. In a true bureaucracy, people who are effective workers should be the only ones advancing to higher-level positions.

Emphasis on written records—To ensure uniformity of action and fair and equitable treatment of employees, bureaucracies keep meticulous records of past decisions and actions. All behaviors occurring in the organization are recorded, which contributes to the image of bureaucrats as compulsive "paper-shufflers."

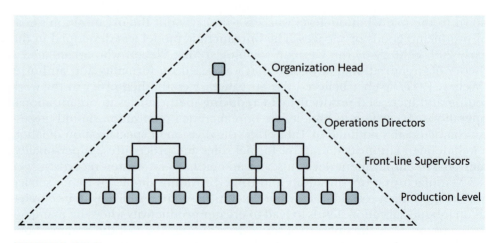

FIGURE 15.3
A Bureaucratic Organization is Arranged Like a Pyramid with Decreasing Authority Levels Leading Down to the Production Line.

However, the formal nature of the bureaucratic organization, with inflexible rules that stifle individual creativity and initiative, may lead to dissatisfied employees (Adler & Borys, 1996). The bureaucratic model may restrict an organization's ability to grow and innovate.

The line–staff organizational structure

As organizations grew in complexity, a variation of the traditional bureaucratic model began to emerge. This structure was designated the line–staff organizational structure (see Figure 15.4). This traditional structure is made up of two groups of employees, each with different goals. The first group is the line, or those workers who are directly engaged in the tasks that accomplish the primary goals of the organization. For example, in manufacturing organizations, line employees are the ones making products on the assembly lines or shop floors. In service organizations, line workers are involved in the distribution of services to customers. The second group of employees is designated as the staff, which consists of specialized positions designed to support the line. In today's complex organizations, many organizational members hold staff positions that have very little to do directly with the primary goals of the organization. For example, in a computer assembly plant, many employees' jobs involve functions that have nothing to do with assembling computers, such as bookkeeping, plant maintenance, public relations, marketing research, and maintaining employee records (Nossiter, 1979). Recent research suggests that staff managers are, as a group, better at managing relationships and are more open to change and innovation than are line managers. Line managers are more service oriented than staff managers, but they are less open to change (Church & Waclawski, 2001).

line–staff organizational structure
a traditional organizational structure composed of one group of employees who achieve the goals of the organization (the line), and another group who support the line (staff)

line
employees in an organization who are engaged directly in tasks that accomplish its goals

staff
specialized employee positions designed to support the line

⏱ Stop & Review

Define three dimensions used to classify organizational structure.

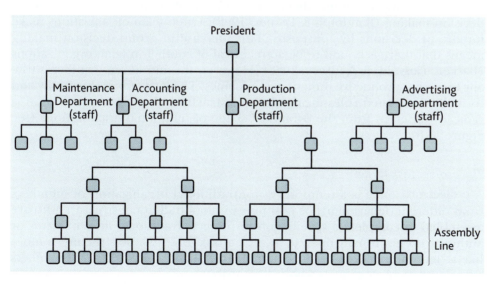

FIGURE 15.4

Line–staff Organizational Structure. In a manufacturing organization, the line is represented by production line workers. The staff consists of specialized positions or departments designed to support the line.

NONTRADITIONAL ORGANIZATIONAL STRUCTURES

The team organization

team organization

a nontraditional orga-
nizational structure
consisting of a team
of members organized
around a particular
project or product

The **team organization** typifies the nontraditional organization structure. In team organizations, workers have broadly defined jobs, not the narrowly specialized positions common to traditionally structured organizations. Workers in a team structure thus know a great deal about the product or goals of the organization and tend to possess a variety of work-related skills. This enables both the workers and the organization to adopt new technology readily, to take on new projects, and to develop innovative work strategies. A second characteristic of team organizations is the collaboration among workers. Rather than each worker independently contributing a "piece" to the final product, as in a traditional organization, employees in team organizations share skills and resources, working collaboratively to get the job done. Because of this tendency to work together, a great deal of communication in the form of meetings, problem-solving groups, and conferences goes on in team organizations (Ford & Randolph, 1992).

Team organizations also place much less emphasis on organizational status than do traditional structures. Although team organizations may have a formal project leader and supervisors or managers, these workers do not typically possess the "ultimate" authority that leaders or managers have in traditional organizations. Each worker is viewed as a knowledgeable and skilled professional who is expected to be self-motivated and committed to the goals of the organization.

A final characteristic of team organizations is the tendency toward group decision making. Team members have considerable input into organizational decision making (Randolph & Posner, 1992). Often team organizations make important decisions by consensus. This increase in group decision making means that there is bound to be a great deal of conflict in team organizations (Barker, Tjosvold, & Andrews, 1988). However, this intragroup conflict is usually turned to productive, functional outcomes. The lack of both hierarchy and formally designated roles means that the structure of a team organization is radically different from the pyramidal shape of traditional organizations (see Figure 15.5).

The project task force

project task force

a nontraditional organi-
zation of workers who
are assembled tempo-
rarily to complete
a specific job or project

A **project task force** is a temporary, nontraditional organization of members from different departments or positions within a traditional structure who are assembled to complete a specific job or project. Traditional lines of status or authority do not usually operate in such a task force, whose structure is more like a "temporary" team organization (Ford & Randolph, 1992). All members are viewed as professionals who will contribute collaboratively to the group's output.

A project task force might be created in an organization that is suddenly faced with hosting the annual two-day conference of executives from all the divisions and affiliates. A task force is put together to handle all facets of the

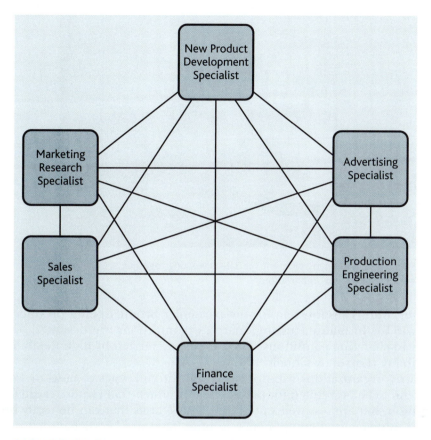

FIGURE 15.5
A Simple Team Organizational Structure

meeting, including obtaining space, arranging accommodations for out-of-town participants, assembling the program, mailing information, and conducting the sessions. In creating the task force, persons with varied skills and expertise are selected, including budgeting specialists to handle finances, graphic artists to produce designs for printed programs, and clerical workers to deal with correspondence. All members work together until the task is completed and then return to their original positions. Some companies may even have standing task forces that, like volunteer fire departments, assemble ready for action whenever special projects arise.

The matrix organization: A hybrid of traditional and nontraditional organizational designs

The **matrix organization** is an organizational design that is structured both by product and function simultaneously. This offers the best of both traditional and nontraditional designs. In matrix organizations, workers have two reporting lines: one to a functional manager, a person responsible for the worker's area of expertise (e.g., engineering, marketing), and one to a product

matrix organization
an organizational design that blends functional and product structures

Film crews, with many different specialists working together, are an example of a team organization.

manager, who is responsible for the particular product being produced (see Figure 15.6). In manufacturing, matrix organizations are designed to adapt rapidly to changing conditions. They are characterized by high flexibility and adaptability (Larson & Gobeli, 1987).

Matrix organizations will not work well with all types of tasks or workers. They tend to be best suited for projects and products that require creativity and innovation, but are less well suited for routine tasks that can be easily broken down into specialized components. Routine tasks are better handled in more traditional organizational structures. Matrix organizations tend to have high levels of performance in dealing with complex, creative work products (Ford & Randolph, 1992). Also, because of the amount of interaction among members in matrix structures, and the high levels of responsibility they possess, matrix organizations usually have greater worker communication and job satisfaction. The drawbacks to matrix organizations are obvious: reporting to two bosses simultaneously can cause confusion and potentially disruptive conflict.

CONTINGENCY MODELS OF ORGANIZATIONAL STRUCTURE

It is clear that no one type of structure is appropriate for all work organizations. Organizations differ in many ways, including the number and type of goods or services they produce, their size, their customers, their employees, and the environment in which they reside. All these factors can help determine which structure is "best" for an organization. Many theorists argue that organizational structure should be addressed with contingency models. Recall that these models look at the interaction of characteristics of the individual—in this case, the organization—and characteristics of the situation—in this case, the setting in which the organization operates.

One of the earliest contingency models of organizational structure was proposed by sociologist Joan Woodward (1965). Focusing solely on manufacturing

Stop & Review

Compare and contrast traditional and non-traditional organizational structures and give examples of each.

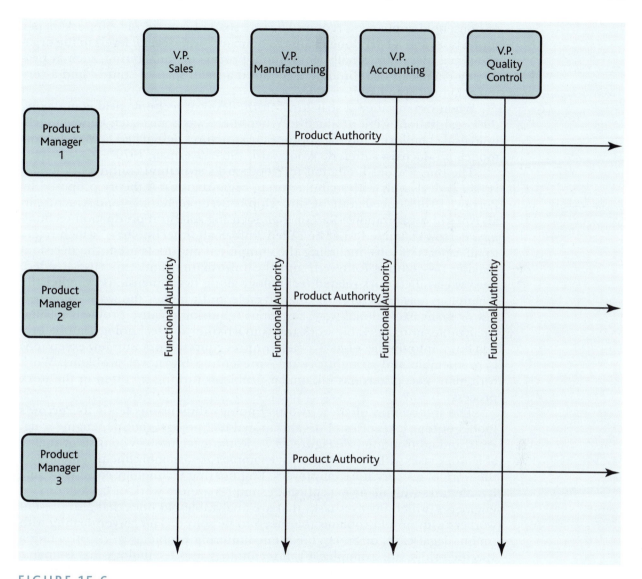

FIGURE 15.6
A Matrix Organization Is a Hybrid of Functional and Product Designs

organizations, Woodward stated that for maximal performance, organizational structure needed to match the type of production technology. Woodward classified manufacturers into three types: small-batch production, mass production, and continuous-process production. According to Woodward's model, producers of small batches of specialty products, such as specialized electronic components or construction equipment, required a span of control that was moderate in size, with about 20 to 30 workers reporting to a supervisor, and a short chain of command. Mass-production organizations, referred to as "large-batch" companies, such as automobile assemblers and manufacturers of household appliances, required a large span of control (40–50 workers per supervisor) and a fairly long chain of command, with several levels in the organizational hierarchy. Finally, continuous-process manufacturing, such as producing chemicals or refining oil, required a small span of control and a very long chain of command.

When organizational structures fit the level of technological complexity, the organizations were productive. When there was a mismatch between technological complexity and the appropriate structures designated by Woodward's model, productivity suffered (Woodward, 1965; Zwerman, 1970).

The one obvious limitation to Woodward's structural contingency model is that it deals only with manufacturing organizations. A theory proposed by Perrow (1970) looked at the relationship between technology and structure in all types of organizations. Rather than focusing solely on production technology, Perrow examined what he called "information technology," which refers to all aspects of jobs, including the equipment and tools used, the decision-making procedures followed, and the information and expertise needed. Perrow classified work-related technology along two dimensions: whether the technology was analyzable or unanalyzable and whether the work contained few or many exceptional work situations requiring creative problem solving. Analyzable/nonanalyzable work refers to whether the technology can be broken down into simple, objective steps or procedures. Work with few exceptions is predictable and straightforward—presenting few novel problems. Work with many exceptions has unfamiliar problems turning up often in the work process.

The interaction of these two technology dimensions leads to Perrow's model of four categories of organizational technology: routine, engineering, craft, and nonroutine (see Figure 15.7). Routine technology consists of analyzable work tasks with few exceptions; examples are assembly-line production or the work of grocery store employees. Engineering technology consists of analyzable tasks with many exceptions; examples are the work of lawyers or civil engineers, which involves tasks that are analyzable but ones that also present workers with novel problems that need to be solved. The lawyer dealing with unique legal cases or an engineer encountering problems in constructing a specific bridge are examples. Craft technology uses technology that is unanalyzable, with no discrete steps, and has few exceptions; examples include the jobs of a skilled woodcarver and a social worker. Both of these jobs involve specialized experience and knowledge, but both present workers with similar types of problems. Finally, nonroutine technology is represented by the work of scientific researchers or professional artists and musicians in which there are no clearly defined steps to follow, yet, there are many unique problems to be solved.

According to Perrow's model, the structure of the organization adjusts to the technology. For example, organizations with routine technology tend to be formal, highly rule driven, and centralized in structure. Nonroutine technology leads to a less formal, more flexible structure, such as a team or matrix organization. The craft and engineering technologies tend to result in structures that are neither completely traditional nor completely nontraditional

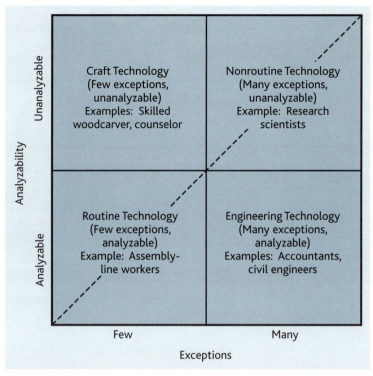

FIGURE 15.7
Perrow's Contingency Model of Organizational Structure

but rather a combination of both (Lynch, 1974; Van de Ven & Delbecq, 1974; Withey, Daft, & Cooper, 1983).

Both Woodward's and Perrow's contingency models emphasize that organizational structure must adjust to fit the technology used by the organization. Woodward's theory focused on the different forms of technology used in manufacturing organizations, whereas Perrow's model expanded the definition of technology to look at all forms of organizations.

Although it is clear that the structure of an organization can be greatly affected by the technology used (David, Pearce, & Randolph, 1989), the organization is also affected by external factors: elements in the outside world that exert some influence on the work organization, affecting its operations and its structure (Bluedorn, 1993). Some common environmental factors that have an impact on work organizations include economic forces, competitors, consumer demand, the supply of raw materials, the supply of human resources, and government regulations. Lawrence and Lorsch (1967) have developed a contingency model of organizational structure that looks at how structure must adapt to fit changing environmental conditions. They assert that two processes determine a company's ability to keep up with external changes: differentiation and integration. Differentiation is the complexity of the organizational structure: the number of units, the various orientations and philosophies of the managers, and the goals and interests of the organization's members. Integration is the

Stop & Review
List and define the six characteristics of a bureaucracy.

differentiation
the complexity of an organization's structure that is based on the number of units, the orientations of managers, and the goals and interests of members

integration
the amount and quality of collaboration among the divisions of an organization

Because performing artists face many unique problems with no clearly defined steps to follow, they require a nonroutine technology.

amount and quality of collaboration among the various units of the organization. As the external environment becomes more complex and turbulent, the organization must increase its differentiation and integration to match its internal complexity to the external complexity.

APPLYING I/O PSYCHOLOGY

The Role of Organizational Structure in Computer-aided Manufacturing

Since the 1980s, there have been profound advances made in manufacturing technology. The greatest impact has been in the area of computer-aided manufacturing (CAM). More and more, product manufacturing is being controlled and monitored by sophisticated computer systems (Cecil, 2001). The changeover to CAM has led to significant organizational restructuring for the purposes of adapting and better integrating state-of-the-art production techniques (Shaiken, 1984).

In a study of nearly 200 U.S. metal-working factories, the impact of CAM technology on organizational structure was explored (Dean, Yoon, & Susman, 1992). Of particular concern was how CAM affected the decentralization of decision making and the formalization of rules in the organizations. It was found that the use of CAM technology

led to increased decentralization, as production workers took on greater responsibility for making important work-related decisions. A great deal of the increased decision making being done by lower-level workers was related to the increased flexibility offered by CAM technology. Specifically, it was found that the computers could be more quickly and easily reprogrammed by lower-level personnel, rather than going through the time-consuming process of going up the chain of command to make reprogramming decisions. Yet, with this increase in decentralization came an increase in the development of rules governing production-related decisions in the factories. The greater decision making of production workers seemed to increase the adoption of specific rules to govern the computer-related decisions they were now shouldered with.

For example, in today's marketplace, a manufacturer of photocopiers must be highly differentiated, with a number of departments designed to meet certain organizational goals. The engineering and research and development departments must keep up with the latest technology in developing improved office and home copier machines, the advertising department must be able to develop eye-catching and convincing ads to rival those of the competition, the sales department must maintain high sales rates, and the service department must provide courteous and efficient service to customers. As environmental conditions change, with consumers demanding better-quality photocopiers and the competition continuing to present new product lines and new advertising and sales campaigns, the organization with its various departments must innovate to survive. The organizational complexity must increase to meet more complex environmental demands. This means that there must be good integration among the various departments, so that they are able to work together to achieve shared goals. Therefore, the organization must use a great deal of its resources to make sure that the various departments are well integrated, for it would do no good to have the best copiers on the market if the servicing of the machines is so poor that it drives away customers.

The Lawrence and Lorsch model makes us aware of the effect of the external environment on the organization, its structure, and its ability to meet its goals. Organizations today exist in a constantly changing world. The work organization that fails to keep up with evolving consumer trends, technology, and industrial developments may have a tough time surviving. This notion that organizations can be structured to adapt to environmental changes is a central tenet of the area of behavioral science known as organizational development. We will discuss organizational development later. However, now that we have some understanding of the formal structure of organizations, and how that formal structure affects work behavior, we need to look at the impact of the informal organization on workers. We represent these informal "forces" of the organization as aspects of organizational culture.

Organizational Culture

Although organizations have a formal structure, there are also "informal" forces that operate to shape the organization and behavior within the organization. A popular approach to viewing these informal aspects of the organization is to refer to them collectively as the "organizational culture." Organizational culture can be defined as the shared values, beliefs, assumptions, and patterns of behavior within an organization (Ott, 1989). In many ways, organizational culture is somewhat akin to the organization's "personality" (Kilman, Saxton, & Serpa, 1985). It is differences in organizational culture that cause two companies—similar in most important ways, such as company size, goods produced, and regional location—to "feel" completely different to workers and visitors (Schein, 1992). Organizational culture is different than "organizational climate," with culture being more deeply embedded in the organization (Denison, 1996).

organizational culture
the shared values, beliefs, assumptions, and patterns of behavior within an organization

Organizational culture develops from many sources. For example, organizations develop certain assumptions and norms governing behavior through a history of experience concerning what seems to "work" and what doesn't work for the organization. Shared norms, values, and goals contribute greatly to an organization's culture (O'Reilly & Chatman, 1996). An organization's culture is also reflected in the stories and "myths" that are told within the organization, and the culture can become communicated and further shaped by those stories (Schneider, Erhart, & Macey, 2011). The technology used in the organization, the markets it sells its products and/or services to, and the organization's competition all influence organizational culture. Organizational culture can also be affected by the societal culture in which the organization is located and the makeup of its workers. Finally, the organizational culture can be shaped by the personalities of the companies' founders and their most dominant early leaders, as with companies like Hewlett-Packard, Kellogg's, Wal-Mart, and J. C. Penney (Schneider, Brief, & Guzzo, 1996).

It has been suggested that organizations vary in terms of the strength and influence of their organizational cultures, with some organizations having strong, dominant cultures, and other companies having weaker cultures (O'Reilly, 1989). It has also been suggested that having a strong organizational culture can be beneficial to companies that provide services because it is crucial that representatives of service organizations provide a strong sense of company identity to customers (Chatman & Jehn, 1994). In other words, it is important that customers of service organizations understand what the company "stands for."

In one study, it was found that companies that have a strong commitment to good human resources practices foster a climate that involves mutual trust, cooperation, and a greater sharing of information among organizational

Shared values, beliefs, and behavioral norms make up each company's unique organizational culture.

members. This very positive organizational culture led to greater company performance (Collins & Smith, 2006). Organizations that gain a reputation for having an exceptional organizational culture are better able to recruit job applicants (Catanzaro, Moore, & Marshall, 2010).

In many of the earlier chapters we have touched on elements of organizational culture. For example, in employee selection, particularly in hiring interviews, there are often efforts made to see if a potential employee "fits" with the company's organizational culture (i.e., "Does he or she hold values consistent with our organization?"). For example, Southwest Airlines prefers hiring employees who have a good sense of humor and know how to have fun, consistent with their fun-loving company culture. Initial training and socialization of new employees often includes efforts to convey elements of the organization's culture to newcomers. For example, Starbucks makes efforts to impress on new employees the importance of its emphasis on corporate social responsibility. In addition, companies may develop specific norms that help convey corporate culture. For example, at Google, employees are encouraged to eat in the Google café, and there are on-site exercise rooms, washers and dryers, game rooms, and locker rooms to make it easier for employees to work together (and work late).

Organizational culture can, by its very nature, serve as a force that guides behavior within the organization. However, organizational culture can oftentimes make an organization resistant to change and innovation (Hilton & Hertzbach, 1997; Schein, 1996). By understanding and assessing an organization's culture, it becomes easier to predict organizational behavior under different circumstances (Hofstede, Neuijen, Ohayv, & Sanders, 1990; Ott, 1989). For example, studies have found that organizations with strong cultural values that involved flexibility, openness, and responsiveness were more likely to grow, expand, and innovate, whereas organizations whose culture valued consistency and adherence to the company's mission were more productive and profitable (Denison & Mishra, 1995; Naranjo-Valencia, Jimenez-Jimenez, & Sanz-Valle, 2011).

SOCIETAL INFLUENCES ON ORGANIZATIONAL CULTURE

The larger culture of a nation, society, or ethnic group can have important influences on the development of the organizational culture of a work organization. The most influential work on societal culture is by Hofstede (1980, 1997). According to Hofstede, there are five key dimensions on which societal cultures differ, such as whether the culture has an *individualistic* base, where values are centered on the individual and individual achievements, or a *collectivistic* base, where values are focused on the group or collective. The United States, for example, is very individualistic in its societal/national orientation, whereas Mexico and Japan are more collectivistic (see Table 15.2 for a description of these five cultural dimensions).

One large study by House and his colleagues (1999; House, Hanges, Javidan, Dorfman, & Gupta, 2004), called the Global Leadership and Organizational Behavior Effectiveness project (GLOBE), is looking at

TABLE 15.2
Five Dimensions of Societal/National Culture

Individualism versus collectivism—Concerned with the extent to which individual interests and goals are emphasized versus a focus on the larger group, or collective.

Power distance—Deals with the extent to which members of the culture accept and expect that there are differences in the way that power is distributed unequally among members.

Masculinity versus femininity—Represents the extent to which members of the culture value traits and practices that are stereotypically "masculine" such as assertiveness and competitiveness, or stereotypically "feminine" traits such as caring for others and being modest in presentation of accomplishments.

Uncertainty avoidance—Concerns the extent to which members of the culture avoid or tolerate uncertainty and ambiguity.

Long-term versus short-term orientation—This dimension concerns whether members of the culture emphasize long-term orientations such as perseverance and working hard today for future payoffs, versus short-term fulfillment of immediate needs.

Source: Based on Hofstede, 1980, 1997.

⏱ Stop & Review

Give two examples of contingency models of organizational structure.

cross-national differences in work organizations, in their cultures, and in their leadership. Although societal culture can have a direct influence on a work organization's culture, these cultural influences are also important in organizations whose workers are made up of members from diverse cultural backgrounds. By understanding systematic differences in the society in which a work organization is embedded, and cultural differences in workers from different nations and societies, it will help to improve our general understanding of work behavior.

MEASURING ORGANIZATIONAL CULTURE

There are a variety of ways of measuring organizational culture. One qualitative strategy is to focus on the "artifacts" of the organization's culture (Ashkanasy & Jackson, 2001; Rafaeli & Pratt, 2006). These might include important symbols that carry meaning for organizational members, such as employees wearing pins with the word *quality*, suggesting that this is an important focus of the organization. Commonly shared stories about a company, its founders, or heroes, might be another type of cultural artifact, as would be certain rituals, such as a company that has a monthly "service day," where employees get together to engage in a joint community service project. One Southern California company has a ritual of employees helping to construct the company's float for the annual Pasadena Tournament of Roses parade.

Another strategy is to rely on a survey instrument, such as the instrument developed by O'Reilly, Chatman, and Caldwell (1991), called the *Organizational Culture Profile* (*OCP*). In measuring organizational culture using the OCP, organizational representatives sort 54 "value statements" describing such things as organizational attitudes toward quality, risk taking, and the respect the organization gives to workers into meaningful categories to provide a descriptive profile of the organization. Research using the OCP in a number of different companies indicated that important dimensions of organizational culture include the company's concern with innovation, stability, orientation toward people, orientation toward producing results, and team orientation (Chatman & Jehn, 1994).

Another measure is Hofstede et al.'s (1990) *Organizational Practices Scale.* This instrument, designed specifically to measure organizational culture (as opposed to societal culture) assesses the company's culture in terms of dimensions such as whether the organization is "process versus results oriented," "employee versus job oriented," or has "loose" or "tight" control over employees' behavior, as well as other dimensions. A revised version includes scales of whether an organization is "self-interested versus socially responsible" and "market" versus "internally" oriented (Verbeke, 2000). Other measures of organizational culture are more specific, such as one measure that assesses an organization's culture for quality (Johnson, 2000).

The study of organizational culture is an increasingly popular approach for I/O psychologists studying organizations at a global level. Organizational culture is intertwined with the topics of job satisfaction (Chapter 9) and group processes (Chapter 12) covered earlier.

Organizational Development

It is very common for organizations to cease operating because they were unable to change to keep up with the times (Mone, McKinley, & Barker, 1998). Companies that do not use the latest marketing or production techniques can lose out to competitors who take advantage of state-of-the-art technology. Retail stores and Internet businesses that are unable to keep pace with changing consumer tastes have gone out of business. Furthermore, organizations have to adapt not only to external conditions but also to internal factors (Burke & Litwin, 1992). For example, as new generations of workers enter the workforce with different types of skills and different ideas about what they want from their jobs, the organization must adjust to utilize their skills and to meet their demands. Otherwise, the better workers will leave the organization, or disgruntled employees may be able to slow down productivity through costly work stoppages and strikes. In addition, the trend toward downsizing means that many organizations must produce more with fewer organizational members. In short, the ability to change is critical to an organization's survival (Greenwood & Hinings, 1996; Martins, 2011; Nutt & Backoff, 1997).

Why is change such a problem for organizations? Research in I/O psychology has demonstrated time and time again that individuals, groups, and organizations strongly resist any sort of change (McMurry, 1947; Watson, 1971; Zander, 1950). People and organizations get comfortable with the familiar and the "tried and true." Moreover, characteristics of bureaucracies, as we saw earlier, are designed for stability and consistency, so bureaucratic organizations are particularly resistant to change. It has been argued that the biggest task of today's business leaders is to recognize the need for organizations to change and to manage that change process (Martins, 2011). In fact, an analysis of the reasons given for boards of directors firing chief executive officers (CEOs) found that the most common reason was the failure of the CEO to appropriately manage change (Hempel, 2005).

The study of organizational change is an important topic. In addition to studying organizational change processes, social scientists have made use of certain interventions to help organizations prepare for and manage organizational change (Gallos, 2006; Porras & Robertson, 1992). The specific specialty area concerned with helping organizations develop, adapt, and innovate is known as organizational development (OD). Organizational development often involves altering the organization's work structure or influencing workers' attitudes or behavior to help the organization to adapt to fluctuating external and internal conditions.

organizational development (OD)
the process of assisting organizations in preparing for and managing change

OD typically takes place in a series of phases. The first phase is usually a diagnosis of the organization to identify significant problems. In the next phase, appropriate interventions are chosen to try to deal with the problems. The third phase is the implementation of the interventions, or OD techniques. Finally, the results of the interventions are evaluated (Burke, 1987). Organizational development does not involve one single theory or approach, but rather a variety of orientations and methods for helping organizations manage change. Although OD is its own subdiscipline, with its own dedicated journals and associations, much of organizational development rests on a foundation created by research in I/O psychology.

Organizational development is both a general philosophy about the nature of modern organizations as well as a discipline that studies ways to help organizations be more effective. Most OD programs are oriented toward long-term organizational improvement rather than focused on solving immediate problems. In fact, most OD practitioners believe that their role is not to solve the organization's problems but to help improve the organization's ability to solve its own problems. Typically, employees of all levels collaborate in the development and implementation of the OD program. Moreover, many OD programs use team approaches to deal with problems at the group or organizational level, rather than focusing on problems associated with individual workers (see Up Close). One goal of such programs is to help the organization become aware of its own operations and problems (Friedlander, 1980). Often, this is done by opening up organizational communication channels and increasing members' involvement in the planning and execution of work activities (Monge, Cozzens, & Contractor, 1992). The rationale is that workers who are more involved in and who have a better understanding of important organizational processes will be more committed to helping the organization achieve its goals (French, 1969).

change agent
name for an OD practitioner, referring to the person's role as a catalyst who helps organizations through the process of change

Organizational development is an applied, practice-oriented area of the behavioral sciences. The OD practitioner is oriented toward helping the organization design and implement a program for dealing with change-related problems. The OD practitioner is often referred to as a change agent, one who

UP CLOSE   How to Develop Effective Work Teams

Many innovative strategies for improving work performance involve the development and use of work teams. If work teams or committees are to be effective in solving organizational problems, certain criteria must be met. Care must be taken to select appropriate participants for problem-solving teams and to ensure that certain procedures are followed. Galbraith (1973, 1977) has developed a set of rules for making high-level, decision-making work teams effective:

1. *Team members should perceive their participation as important and personally rewarding*—To build commitment to the team, members must view their work as beneficial. One way to do this is to offer some sort of formal rewards for contributions to the team.

2. *The work team should include some persons of organizational power who will be responsible for helping to implement any decisions made by the group*—If a team is to develop innovative strategies, it is important that these efforts are implemented. It is important to have some managers with organizational power as part of the work team to make sure that team suggestions are listened to and implemented.

3. *Team members should have knowledge and information relevant to the decision*—In any problem-solving work team, it is critical that members have job-related knowledge relevant to the decisions that are being made. This involves including lower-level workers who have firsthand experience with the job.

4. *Team members should have the authority to commit their respective departments to the decision*—The work team participants must be able to commit valuable resources (human and otherwise) to help in the successful implementation of the strategies developed by the team.

5. *Team members should represent and inform nonteam workers*—If the problem-solving work team or committee is a select group of a larger body of workers, it is crucial that the team members inform nonteam members about the committee tasks and decisions.

6. *The influence of team members on decisions should be based on expertise*—This is especially important when members come from various levels in the organization. Work-related decisions should be based on relevant knowledge, not on organizational politics.

7. *Work team conflict should be managed to maximize the problem-solving process*—The conflict that arises in problem-solving committees should be functional and help to develop a high-level and highly critiqued course of action. It is important that such conflict be controlled to avoid dysfunctional outcomes.

8. *Team members should have good interpersonal skills and adequate leadership*—The success of a work team is going to be directly related to the smooth flow of communication among members. The better their interpersonal skills, the better the group's ability to reach high-quality decisions. It is also important for the team leader to take an appropriate but not too dominant role to facilitate team interaction and to help resolve nonproductive conflicts.

coaches or guides the organization in developing problem-solving strategies. The change agent, however, is not a problem solver. The change agent works with the various levels of the organization, developing or deciding on problem-solving techniques. The change agent is a behavioral scientist, often an industrial/organizational psychologist, who is expert at assisting organizations in diagnosing problems and skilled in helping organizational members deal with sensitive situations. The change agent will have some special knowledge of particular OD interventions that may be used to help solve the organization's problems. The change agent also acts as an educator who trains the organization to

🕐 Stop & Review

What are three
sources of organiza-
tional culture?

action research

an OD methodologi-
cal model that applies
social science research
methods to collecting
relevant organizational
data that are used for
solving organizational
problems

implement strategies for coping with future problems (Burke, 1987; Gottlieb, 1998). Waclawski and Church (2002) argued that OD is a very data-driven process so the effective OD practitioner should be well steeped in social science research methods and how to apply them.

Organizational development programs usually follow one of several procedural models, all of which typically use an OD consultant, or change agent, and go through the four phases outlined earlier. One popular OD model is **action research**, which is the process of applying social science research methods to collect relevant data within the organization to study an organization and to help it understand and solve its problems (Aguinis, 1993; Frohman, Sashkin, & Kavanagh, 1976). The application-oriented goal of action research means that it is somewhat different than the traditional hypothesis-testing research discussed in Chapter 2. Whereas hypothesis-testing research attempts to find new knowledge that is applicable to a wide range of organizations, action research tries to solve problems specific to a particular organization. Action research involves some of the same tools used by hypothesis-testing research, namely objective observation and the collection and analysis of research data. However, their goals and scope are quite different, for action research is oriented toward producing some specific result.

The first step in the action research process is data gathering and problem diagnosis. Here, the OD consultant collects data to diagnose the problem situation. In the next step, feedback is given as the data, and the OD consultant's interpretation of the data, are presented to the organization's members. The next step is joint action planning. Here the OD consultant and the organizational members design a problem-solving program, which might be one of a variety of OD interventions that we will discuss later. Once the program is implemented, the action research process repeats itself. Now, however, the data gathering is an attempt to determine the effectiveness of the OD program. If it is successful, the organization and the OD consultant might discuss ways to make it a regular part of the organization's operations. If unsuccessful, the program might need some alterations, or a different program might be tried. Figure 15.8 graphically depicts the steps in the action research model.

ORGANIZATIONAL DEVELOPMENT TECHNIQUES

In solving organizational problems, OD programs use a wide variety of established techniques (Fagenson & Burke, 1990), some of which we have already discussed. For example, recall from Chapter 8 that job enrichment is a process of increasing the levels of responsibility associated with jobs to improve worker satisfaction and commitment to the work effort. Although job enrichment was presented in Chapter 8 as a motivational technique, it could also be used in OD efforts because it involves the collaboration of workers in work teams that play an important part in solving change-related problems that may affect the groups' work performance. Organizational behavior modification programs (also presented in Chapter 8), which reinforce desirable work behaviors, can likewise be used as

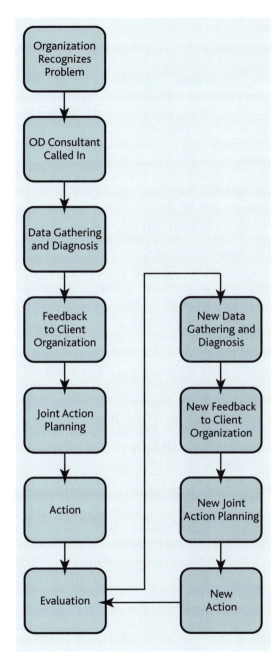

FIGURE 15.8
Steps in the Action Research Process

an OD technique. Of the other procedures that have been used by OD practitioners, we will discuss six of the more popular: survey feedback, t-groups, team building, process consultation, management by objectives, and quality circles.

Survey feedback

The use of employee surveys is a common OD strategy. **Survey feedback** is the process by which the OD consultant works with the organization to develop a survey instrument to collect data that is then used to solve specific problems or to institute a program for managing change. The survey is usually designed to assess employee attitudes about important work-related issues such as the organization in general, company policies and practices, quality of leadership, and coordination among work units. Once constructed, the survey is distributed either to all workers or to a representative sample. The OD consultant then tabulates the survey data and puts them into a form that will be easily understood by organizational members. Next the results are presented to organizational members. This feedback can be done in a number of ways: via the Internet, in written form, in small- or large-group discussions, or in a general meeting. As we saw in 360-degree feedback, survey data from multiple sources, such as from management and line employees, as well as other constituents, can be very useful. This is also the case in OD-oriented surveys (Church, Walker, & Brockner, 2002). Because the survey is merely an assessment tool to indicate which areas of the organization need attention or improvement, the final, crucial step in a survey feedback program involves developing strategies to deal with any problems or concerns that arise from the results. The survey is a starting point for solving organizational problems or for instituting future programs for planned organizational change (Born & Mathieu, 1996; Faletta & Combs, 2002).

One of the direct benefits of the survey is that it can increase the upward flow of communication from lower-level workers to management (see Chapter 11). The survey may also have a positive effect on workers' attitudes, as they perceive that management is interested in hearing their views and concerns (Gavin, 1984). This will only occur, however, if steps are taken to address problems. If not, workers may develop negative attitudes about management and the survey process. Finally, the survey results can show workers that they are not alone and that others share their attitudes and concerns.

Research indicates that survey feedback is an effective OD technique, if followed by some positive actions (Bowers, 1973; Bowers & Hauser, 1977; Guzzo, Jette, & Katzell, 1985). Surveys have additional advantages as well. They are an efficient way of collecting a large amount of information from a large number of workers. Also, because surveys can be conducted anonymously, lower-level workers feel that they can safely voice their opinions, which can lead to very honest appraisals of work situations. Because it requires considerable training to create valid and reliable employee surveys and to analyze and interpret the results, I/O psychologists or other social science professionals are most often involved in survey feedback programs.

⏱ Stop & Review

Outline the methods and terms used in organizational development.

T-groups

The OD strategy known as **t-groups** (also called **sensitivity training**) actually refers to the use of unstructured group interaction to help workers gain insight into their motivations and their behavior patterns in dealing with others. T-groups, which stands for "training groups," consists of small groups of workers who meet in a nonwork setting for an unstructured discussion of their attitudes and beliefs concerning their work, the work environment, and their interactions with supervisors and coworkers. The eventual goals of t-groups are for participants to gain insight concerning their own behavior, to develop greater openness, and to improve skills in understanding and dealing with others. Typically, a professional serves as group leader, although the leader usually plays a nondirective role in merely keeping the goals of the session in everyone's minds and keeping the discussion from getting out of hand. An effective leader will usually prevent problems such as "psychological casualties," which occur when the group targets one or more persons for intense criticism or when participants suffer from airing sensitive personal information in a public forum.

T-groups were very popular in the 1960s and early 1970s, when interest in self-exploration and group encounters was at its height. Although it is not as popular today, this method is still used by some OD practitioners who report very positive results, particularly in improving the communication skills of managers. However, research on the effectiveness of t-groups has been inconclusive. T-groups and related techniques have been shown to be related to improved employee attitudes and increased job satisfaction (Neuman, Edwards, & Raju, 1989; Sundstrom, de Meuse, & Futrell, 1990). Although there is some evidence that managers can achieve insight into their behavior and develop interpersonal skills through the process, there is some concern over whether the insights and skills gained from sensitivity training generalize to actual work settings (Campbell & Dunnette, 1968; Mirvis & Berg, 1977). In other words, it is not clear that gaining insight about one's own behavior, and developing communication skills in the "safe" setting of the t-group, will then translate into changes in a worker's behavior in the actual work setting.

Team building

Team building is an OD intervention in which groups of workers meet to discuss ways to improve their performance by identifying strengths and weaknesses in their interaction with one another (Liebowitz & de Meuse, 1982). In some ways, team building is similar to t-groups, although the focus is no longer on individual growth and skill development but on improving team functioning and goal attainment. Because of its emphasis on the group, rather than the individual, team building does not have the threat of psychological casualties that may exist in t-groups. Although some emphasis is put on improving members' abilities to communicate with one another, greater stress is placed on helping the team to achieve performance-related goals. Because of the increase in work teams, and because of its focus on improving team dynamics and performance, team building is becoming one of the most popular OD techniques today.

Team building can use existing groups of workers or construct new work teams. The first session is a diagnostic meeting. The OD consultant serves as moderator, while the team discusses its current level of functioning in an unstructured setting similar to that used in t-groups. Each team member is allowed to present personal views and suggestions for improving the team's performance. Through this process, the group should eventually agree on strategies

team building
an OD technique in which teams of workers discuss how to improve team performance by analyzing group interaction

In team building, groups of employees discuss methods of improving their work.

for implementing positive changes. Subsequent sessions involve evaluating and "fine-tuning" new procedures or suggesting alternate approaches. One evaluation of various OD techniques found that team building was the technique that had the largest and most consistent positive effects on increasing employee job satisfaction and morale (Neuman et al., 1989). Two meta-analytic evaluations of the effects of team building found positive relationships between team building and team performance; however, team building worked best when the focus of team building was on the skills and roles of team members than when it was focused on goal setting or on improving interpersonal relationships within the team (Salas, Rozell, Mullen, & Driskell, 1999; Svyantek, Goodman, Benz, & Gard, 1999). With the increase in virtual teams—interdependent work groups that rarely meet face-to-face—team building might be a good strategy for bringing team members closer together, although evaluation of the team-building program should be done to ensure that it is having a positive impact.

Process consultation

process consultation
an OD technique in which a consultant helps a client-organization study its problems objectively and learn to solve them

Process consultation is an OD technique in which a consultant helps a client organization to "perceive, understand, and act upon process events which occur in the client's environment" (Schein, 1969, p. 9). In process consultation, the OD consultant helps the organization to learn how to solve its own problems. In many ways, process consultation epitomizes many of the central themes of organizational development. It uses a change agent, the process consultant, who works as a teacher to assist the client-organization in learning how to use objective methods, such as survey instruments, structured interviews, or the collection of relevant performance data, to diagnose and solve its own problems.

The consultant also instructs organizational members in how to implement specific OD problem-solving techniques. The goal is for the organization to become self-reliant by knowing how to deal with change-related problems once the process consultant is gone.

To understand the specific steps in process consultation outlined by Schein (1969), we will use the example of a consultant who is working with CDE company, which produces and sells cosmetics. The first step is the *initial contact* with the client-organization, which is usually initiated by someone in the organization who realizes that problems exist and is willing to try to solve them. In the case of CDE, the vice president of sales called in the process consultant, Dr. Io, because of what he considers to be high turnover of sales personnel and managers.

The second step is *developing the contract.* In initial, exploratory meetings, the vice president of sales meets with top decision makers—the other vice presidents and the company president—to determine the problems, explain the consultant's role, and formulate actions to be taken. A formal contract is drawn up to determine matters such as client time and compensation. A "psychological" contract, which includes the expectations and goals of the organization as well as Dr. Io's goals, is also formulated: The company wants to reduce costly turnover, and Dr. Io wants the organization to take steps not only to reduce turnover, but also to ensure that the company can deal with future turnover problems. In addition, she also wants the organization to explore any related problems that the consultation uncovers.

The third step is the *selection of a setting and a method of work.* A site for study is selected collaboratively with the client and is usually a unit near the top of the organization. Those workers who are being observed by the consultant must be made aware of her presence and purpose. Together, Dr. Io and the CDE decision makers choose the largest regional headquarters as the site for study. Because this office is adjacent to corporate headquarters, Dr. Io will have easy contact with the company's top-level executives.

The fourth step is *data gathering and diagnosis.* By using interviews (particularly exit interviews), direct observation, and surveys of employees, Dr. Io tries to obtain an in-depth picture of the organization and its internal processes. She works with certain CDE personnel, instructing them in data collection methods. Through analysis of these data and consultation with relevant CDE personnel and executives, specific problem areas are targeted. The data reveal that turnover is linked to three factors: (a) Salespersons perceive their sales commissions rates to be lower than those in other sales positions; (b) salespersons feel they do not receive enough attention from sales managers; and (c) some salespersons are hired without much experience, and CDE provides little specific training of new personnel.

The next step is the *intervention.* A variety of intervention strategies are used in process consultation. Some are as simple as providing feedback of the consultant's observations to workers. Others may involve counseling work groups or individuals or setting agendas to increase a group's awareness of its own internal processes. In the case of CDE, Dr. Io and company executives jointly decide to develop a "sales force improvement task force," composed of both management personnel and salespersons, who will formulate a proposal to improve the hiring and training procedures for new salespersons. Other goals of the task force will be to conduct a survey of sales commission rates in other companies and to develop a program for improving sales managers' supervision.

The final step in process consultation is the *evaluation of results and disengagement.* According to Schein (1969, p. 123), successful process consultation improves organizational performance by "changing some of the values of the organization and by increasing the interpersonal skills of key managers." If these goals are met, CDE should see some changes in the organization's perception of the value of the sales force and in the selection, training, and treatment of sales personnel. There will also likely be some improvement in the interpersonal skills of sales managers. The relationship between consultant and client is terminated by mutual agreement. In the case of CDE, Dr. Io may or may not work with the organization in implementing and evaluating the various new programs. Sometimes, a slow disengagement process is used whereby the consultant gradually lessens involvement with the client-organization. This is likely in the case of Dr. Io, because the programs for organizational improvement will probably take a long time to design and implement, and their evaluation will likely initially require her assistance.

Process consultation is a detailed OD program, involving an extensive and long-term relationship between the consultant and the client-organization. Some authors have likened this technique to the psychotherapeutic process in which a therapist works with a client over a long period of time to diagnose and work toward solving the client's problems (Landy, 1989). Unfortunately, there has not been a great deal of research evaluating the effectiveness of process consultation (Kahnweiler, 2002).

Management by objectives (MBO)

management by objectives (MBO)
a goal-setting OD technique in which supervisors and subordinates jointly set performance goals; at the end of the goal period, their attainment is evaluated and new goals are set

Management by objectives, or MBO, is a goal-setting technique that is often used as an OD intervention. In MBO, subordinates work with superiors in jointly setting performance goals. The basic rationales behind the procedure are that work-related goals must be clearly specified and measurable, and that employees should participate in setting them to become committed to their fulfillment. MBO is closely related to the goal-setting techniques of motivation discussed in Chapter 8. Management by objectives can also be used as an alternative to traditional rating methods of performance appraisal, because successful MBO programs must accurately and objectively measure the attainment of performance goals (see Chapter 6). At the end of the goal period—usually 3 to 6 months and occasionally 12 months—employees again meet with supervisors and receive feedback concerning the goal attainment. If the goals have not been met, suggestions for improvement are made. If they have been attained, new and perhaps even more challenging goals are set.

The MBO technique actually predates the organizational development movement. Popularized in the 1950s by Drucker and his associates (Drucker, 1954), it has been an often-used method for improving worker performance. Unfortunately, MBO has also been widely misused. Often any type of goal setting is labeled MBO, even though it does not follow the MBO model (McConkie, 1979). For MBO to be implemented correctly, the following criteria must be met:

- *Employees must participate in setting personal performance goals*   A potential weakness of MBO goal setting, however, is that workers may take advantage of the freedom they are afforded and set goals that are much too easy and do not represent a motivating challenge. Alternatively, if the supervisor too strongly influences the setting of goals, MBO may not be effective because employees may feel that they have no real voice in the goal-setting process.

- *Feedback concerning goal attainment must be provided*   As in any performance appraisal system, the strength of the appraisal depends on the ability to assess performance objectively. Objective measurement of goal attainment must take place, and this information must be presented to the employees.

- *Guidelines for improvement must be provided*   In the case of the failure to reach goals, supervisors should provide suggestions for improving work performance. Otherwise, employees may become frustrated and unmotivated by their inability to achieve set goals.

- *Goals must be realistic*   They must neither be too high nor too low. If goals are unrealistically high, the workers will be frustrated. If they are too low, the employees are not challenged.

- *The upper levels of the organization must support the program*   Because MBO is a time-consuming process for supervisors, their efforts must be recognized. The best way to do this is to include effective participation in the MBO program as part of the supervisors' own performance goals.

- *Individual, work group, and organizational goals must be equally emphasized*   If jobs involve cooperation with other employees (and most jobs do), overemphasis on individual goals may inhibit the group's ability to work together. Thus, workers must be oriented toward achieving not only their own goals but also those of the group and the organization as a whole.

Management by objectives is one of the most widely used OD techniques, partly because it can be implemented in just about any work organization and with almost any type of job. MBO is also one of the most successful OD programs. A meta-analysis of 70 studies of MBO programs found that there were productivity gains caused by MBO in 68 of the 70 cases (Rodgers & Hunter, 1991).

Quality circles

One OD intervention that is typically associated with Japanese management techniques popularized in the 1980s is the concept of quality circles, which are small groups of volunteer employees from the same work areas who meet regularly to identify, analyze, and solve product quality problems and other work-related problems (Adam, 1991; Munchus, 1983). In initial quality circle meetings, members are trained in quality control, work on developing

quality circles
small groups of volunteer employees from the same work area who meet regularly to solve work-related problems

communication skills, and learn problem-solving techniques. They then select a particular problem to study and use a variety of methods to gather information pertinent to the issue. Finally, a recommendation is made to management about how to solve the problem. The goal of quality circles is to get employees more involved in their jobs and to increase their feelings of having some control over their work. This increased employee involvement should lead to greater worker satisfaction, work quality (and perhaps productivity), and worker commitment to the organization.

Research indicates that quality circles can indeed lead to increased quality and productivity in both Japanese and American manufacturing organizations and may also enhance participants' job satisfaction (Barrick & Alexander, 1987; Buch & Spangler, 1990; Marks, Mirvis, Hackett, & Grady, 1986). However, in certain instances U.S. applications of quality circle programs have failed, although analysis suggests that the failures have more to do with poor implementation than with any inherent flaws in the theory underlying quality circles. The failure of quality circle programs, and indeed of other OD programs, can often be traced to a lack of support from management and/ or workers or to poor training and preparation of participants (Marks, 1986; Tang, Tollison, & Whiteside, 1987, 1991, 1996). Moreover, there is evidence that unless quality circles are maintained and fully integrated into the organizational system, their effectiveness will diminish in a year or two (Ledford, Lawler, & Mohrman, 1988).

Other "quality-oriented" programs include total quality management (TQM), the implementation of continuous improvement work processes (Coyle-Shapiro, 1999 ; Omachonu & Ross, 1994; Teboul, 1991; Waldman, 1994), and Six Sigma, a quality improvement process popularized by former GE CEO Jack Welch (Pande, Neuman, & Cavanagh, 2000). The success of all quality enhancement programs involves some fundamental changes in organizational climate and culture to get workers committed to improving quality of output. Yet, this is very important because many organizations have found that unless they produce high-quality products or services, they cannot compete in the increasingly competitive global market.

THE EFFECTIVENESS OF ORGANIZATIONAL DEVELOPMENT

A variety of techniques have been used as interventions in organizational development programs. However, the important question is, "Does OD work?" There is no firm answer to this question. A number of factors make it difficult to ascertain the effectiveness of OD programs (Martineau & Preskill, 2002). One difficulty concerns the variety of OD techniques that can be used as part of OD programs. Some of these techniques may simply be better than others. For example, evidence suggests that goal-setting based programs and survey feedback are moderately successful (Kondrasuk, 1981; Miner, 1983), whereas there has been some question about the effectiveness of t-groups (Odiorne, 1963; Miner, 1983). A second reason lies in the nature of the organization that conducts the OD program. What works in one organization may not be effective in another because of differences in the attitudes of organizational members or in the workers' and management's commitment to OD efforts. Another concern is the abilities of the OD consultants overseeing the intervention—some OD consultants may simply do a better job than others (O'Driscoll & Eubanks, 1993). Furthermore, determining the effectiveness of organizational development is hard because of difficulties in conducting good evaluation research. Because OD interventions usually take place on a large scale, often involving an entire organization, much of the evidence for their effectiveness is based on case studies. The unit of measurement—the "participant" in the evaluation of an OD program—is the organization. It is very difficult to combine the results of a specific OD strategy with those of the same method used in other companies because the circumstances may be very different. This often leaves us with only a series of case studies as evidence for the effectiveness of OD programs.

Overall, the results of evaluations of organizational development programs are mixed. There have been some reports of glowing successes and other reports of failures (French & Bell, 1990; Woodman & Pasmore, 1987). Bass (1983) proposed that the positive effects may be greater in job satisfaction and organizational commitment than in increased organizational productivity. Moreover, he suggested that many of the successes of OD programs may be long-term changes that do not show up for months or years, long after the evaluation of the OD program is completed. Until more rigorous evaluation research of OD programs is routinely conducted, it will be very difficult to draw

Stop & Review

List and describe five organizational development techniques.

ON THE *CUTTING* EDGE

Organizational Change: The Case of Downsizing

A very common and profound organizational change occurs when organizations choose to downsize and eliminate permanent employees. There are many reasons for downsizing—the introduction of labor-saving technology, the need to cut personnel costs, and mergers and acquisitions that lead to duplicated positions (Budros, 1999; De Meuse, Marks, & Dai, 2011). OD researchers tend to approach downsizing as just another of many planned organizational changes (Legatski, 1998).

Research suggests that downsizing has important negative effects on the survivors of layoffs. For example, downsizing can lead to decreased commitment and loyalty on the part of survivors, particularly if the layoffs are seen as unfair (Allen et al., 2001; Grunberg, Anderson-Connolly, & Greenberg, 2000). These effects may be even stronger for managers than for line employees (Wiesenfeld, Brockner, & Thibault, 2000).

In addition, the loss of knowledgeable and experienced workers may lead to a "brain drain" to the organization, adversely affecting the company's ability to learn and innovate (Fisher & White, 2000). Downsizing also leads to a great deal of stress among employees (Zeitlin, 1995).

There is evidence, however, that utilizing a systematic OD approach can help reduce the negatives associated with downsizing (Freeman, 1999). Deal and Kennedy (1999), as well as Marks and Mirvis (1998, 2010), have looked at downsizing and mergers and acquisitions from an OD model and suggest that planning, providing clear and straightforward information to employees about the process, taking steps to manage the inevitable stress felt by survivors, and building a shared organizational culture—and getting employees committed to the new culture—are the keys to success.

firm conclusions about their effectiveness. It has been suggested however, that OD is moving in a positive direction, with greater attention given to interventions that are driven by theory, and greater attention to research rigor (Martins, 2011). However, organizational development remains quite popular, largely because its underlying theory—that organizations must adapt to keep up with the rapid changes in the world at large—makes sense.

Summary

Organizational structure is the arrangement of positions in an organization and the relationships among them. Organizational structures can be generally classified into traditional and nontraditional forms. Traditional organizational structures tend to be stable and rule driven, whereas nontraditional structures are characterized by their flexibility, adaptability, and lack of formal authority lines. Important dimensions of organizational structure are the number of authority levels in an organization, or *chain of command*, and the number of workers reporting to a single work supervisor, or the *span of control*. Organizations can also be divided by the kinds of tasks performed—a *functional structure*—or by the types of products produced or customers served—a *divisional structure*. Decision-making power can either be concentrated at the top levels of the organization (*centralization*), or dispersed throughout the organization (*decentralization*).

The *bureaucracy* and the *line–staff organization* typify the traditional structure. The bureaucracy is a structure based on authority relationships among organizational members that operate through a system of formal rules and procedures. The line–staff organization is a formal structure in which the line executes organizational objectives, whereas the staff is designed to support the line. Nontraditional organizational structures are exemplified by the *team organization*, a permanent team of competent workers designed for maximizing organizational adaptability, and by the *project task force*, a more temporary structure. A *matrix organization* is a combination of both product and functional organizational designs.

The most recent approaches to organizational structure are contingency models, whereby the most effective type of structure depends on the fit between structure and the external or internal environment of the work organization.

Organizational culture refers to the shared values, beliefs, assumptions, and patterns of behavior in organizations. Organizational culture derives from many sources, can be stronger in some organizations than in others, and has important influences on organizational behavior. Societal/national influences on organizational culture can be very strong. Recently, a great deal of attention has been given to developing methods for assessing organizational culture.

Organizational development (OD) is the process of preparing for and managing change in organizations. OD programs use a consultant who is commonly called a change agent. OD programs usually occur in phases. One model for such a program is *action research*, which involves collecting data, diagnosing organizational problems, and developing strategies to take action to solve them. A variety of interventions are used in OD programs, including *survey feedback*, a technique of using data about organizational members' feelings and concerns as the basis for planned change; *t-groups*, a process of increasing workers' awareness of their own and other members' behavior; *team building*, the development of teams of workers to focus on ways to improve group performance; *process consultation*, a long-term method of helping an organization to develop problem-solving strategies; *management by objectives (MBO)*, a goal-setting technique designed to increase worker commitment to the attainment of personal and organizational goals; and *quality circles*, which are groups of employees who meet regularly to discuss quality-related work problems. Evaluation of OD programs indicates that they can be effective for improving certain aspects of organizational effectiveness, although neither their implementation nor their evaluation is easy.

Study Questions and Exercises

1. Consider an organization with which you have had some contact. Describe the structure of this organization using the dimensions of traditional–nontraditional, functional–divisional, and centralized–decentralized. If you have access to the organization's chart, describe its chain of command and span of control.

2. Based on what you know about traditional and nontraditional organizational structures, contrast the work life of the typical worker in a traditional organization with that of a worker in a nontraditional organization.

3. Compare and contrast the contingency models of organizational structure.

4. Describe the organizational culture of a company or firm you are familiar with. What are some of the sources of this company's organizational culture?

5. Consider a common problem in classrooms, such as a difficulty in communication between professor and students or an unclear grading policy. How might an OD consultant solve this problem? What OD techniques might be used?

6. Drawing on your knowledge of research methods, what are the difficulties in evaluating the success of OD programs?

Web Links

www.odnetwork.org
The OD Network site. A professional network of OD practitioners.

Suggested Readings

Anderson, D. L. (2011). *Organization development: The process of leading organizational change.* Thousand Oaks, CA: Sage. *A comprehensive textbook covering all facets of OD.*

Marks, M. L. & Mirvis, P. H. (2010). *Joining forces: Making one plus one equal three in mergers, acquisitions, and alliances.* San Francisco: Jossey-Bass. A very good book that discusses how organizations ought to change and adapt after large-scale changes brought about by mergers or downsizings.

Schein, E. H. (2003). *Organizational culture and leadership.* San Francisco: Jossey-Bass. *The top authority on organizational culture and change discusses the implications of both for leaders.*

A number of journals are specifically devoted to organizational development and related topics. These include *Organization Development Journal, Journal of Organizational Change Management, Leadership & Organization Development Journal, OD Practitioner,* and *Action Research.*

GLOSSARY

A

accommodation a conflict resolution strategy of making a sacrifice to resolve a conflict.

achievement motivation theory McClelland's model of motivation that emphasizes the importance of three needs—achievement, power, and affiliation—in determining worker motivation.

achievement-oriented behavior leader behavior concentrated on particular work outcomes.

action learning teams assembled to work on a company-related problem or issue to learn by doing.

action research an OD methodological model that applies social science research methods to collecting relevant organizational data that are used for solving organizational problems.

actor–observer bias the tendency for observers to overattribute cause to characteristics of the actor and the tendency for the actor to over-attribute cause to situational characteristics.

adverse impact when members of a protected group are treated unfairly by an employer's personnel action.

affirmative action the voluntary development of policies that try to ensure that jobs are made available to qualified individuals regardless of sex, age, or ethnic background.

apprenticeship a training technique, usually lasting several years, that combines on-the-job experience with classroom instruction.

assessment center a detailed, structured evaluation of job applicants using a variety of instruments and techniques.

audience factors characteristics of the receiver that influence the effectiveness of a communication.

audiovisual instruction the use of films, videotapes, and other electronic media to convey training material.

autocratic decision making a process by which group decisions are made by the leader alone, based on information the leader possesses.

avoidance withdrawing from or avoiding a conflict situation.

B

behavior modeling training a training method that exposes trainees to role models performing appropriate and inappropriate work behaviors and their outcomes and then allows trainees to practice modeling the appropriate behaviors.

behavioral observation scales (BOS) performance appraisal methods that require appraisers to recall how often a worker has been observed performing key work behaviors.

behavioral theories of leadership theories derived from studies at Ohio State and University of Michigan that focus on the behaviors common to effective leaders.

behaviorally anchored rating scales (BARS) performance appraisal technique using rating scales with labels reflecting examples of poor, average, and good behavioral incidents.

biodata background information and personal characteristics that can be used in employee selection.

bona fide occupational qualifications the term used for actual qualifications needed in order to perform a particular job.

brainstorming a group process generating creative ideas or solutions through a noncritical and nonjudgmental process.

bureaucracy a traditional organizational structure typified by a well-defined authority hierarchy and strict rules governing work behavior.

burnout a syndrome resulting from prolonged exposure to work stress that leads to withdrawal from the organization.

C

case study a research investigation involving a one-time assessment of behavior.

causal attribution the process by which people assign cause to events or behaviors.

central tendency error the tendency to give all workers the midpoint rating in performance appraisals.

centralization the degree to which decision-making power rests at the upper levels of the organizational hierarchy.

centralized networks communication networks in which the flow of communication is directed through specific members.

chain of command the number of authority levels in an organization.

change agent name for an OD practitioner, referring to the person's role as a catalyst who helps organizations through the process of change.

channel the vehicle through which a message flows from sender to receiver.

channel factors characteristics of the vehicle of transmission of a message that affect communication.

charismatic leadership theory states that leaders possess some exceptional characteristics that cause followers to be loyal and inspired.

checklists performance appraisal methods using a series of statements about job performance.

coaching a one-on-one relationship where a consultant helps an executive improve his or her performance.

coalition a group of individuals who band together to combine their power.

coercive power the use of punishment or the threat of punishment to affect the behavior of others.

cognitive theories of learning learning theories that emphasize that humans are information processors.

cohesiveness the degree of attraction among group members.

collaboration a conflict resolution strategy in which the parties cooperate to reach a solution that satisfies both.

communication the passage of information between one person or group to another person or group.

communication networks systematic lines of communication among various senders and receivers.

comparable worth the notion that jobs that require equivalent KSAOs should be compensated equally.

comparative methods performance appraisal methods involving comparisons of one worker's performance against that of other worker's.

comparison others persons used as a basis for comparison in making judgments of equity/inequity.

compensable factors the job elements that are used to determine appropriate compensation for a job.

competition the process whereby group members are pitted against one another to achieve individual goals.

compressed workweeks schedules that decrease the number of days in the workweek while increasing the number of hours worked per day.

compromise a conflict resolution strategy in which both parties give up some part of their goals.

computer-assisted instruction programmed instruction delivered by computer that adapts to the trainee's learning rate.

conference an unstructured management training technique in which participants share ideas, information, and problems; also called a group discussion.

conflict behavior by a person or group intended to inhibit the attainment of goals by another person or group.

conformity the process of adhering to group norms.

consensus decision making based on 100% member agreement.

consideration leader behaviors that show a concern for the feeling, attitudes, and needs of followers.

construct validity refers to whether an employment test measures what it is supposed to measure.

content validity the ability of the items in a measurement instrument to measure adequately the various characteristics needed to perform a job.

contingency theories theories that look at the interaction of characteristics of both the leader and the situation.

control group a comparison group in an experimental investigation that receives no treatment.

correlation coefficient a statistical technique used to determine the strength of a relationship between two variables.

correlational method a research design that examines the relationship among or between variables as they naturally occur.

counterproductive work behaviors (CWBs) deviant, negative behaviors that are harmful to an organization and its workers.

criteria measures of job success typically related to performance.

criterion contamination the extent to which performance appraisals contain elements that detract from the accurate assessment of job effectiveness.

criterion deficiency the degree to which a criterion falls short of measuring job performance.

criterion relevance the extent to which the means of appraising performance is pertinent to job success.

criterion usefulness the extent to which a performance criterion is usable in appraising a particular job.

criterion-related validity the accuracy of a measurement instrument in determining the relationship between scores on the instrument and some criterion of job success.

critical incidents technique (CIT) a job analysis technique that relies on instances of especially successful or unsuccessful job performance.

D

decentralization the process of taking the decision-making authority away from the top levels of the organization and distributing it to lower levels.

decentralized networks communication networks in which messages can originate at any point and need not be directed through specific group members.

decision-making model a theory that matches characteristics of the situation with leader decision-making strategies.

decoding the process of translating a message so that is can be understood.

democratic decision making a strategy by which decisions are made by the group members based on majority-rule voting.

dependent variable in the experimental method, the variable that is acted on by the independent variable; the outcome variable.

descriptive statistics arithmetical formulas for summarizing and describing research data.

Dictionary of Occupational Titles (DOT) a reference guide that classifies and describes over 40,000 jobs.

differentiation the complexity of an organization's structure that is based on the number of units, the orientations of managers, and the goals and interests of members.

directive behavior leader behavior that provides instructions and suggestions for performing a job.

divisional structure an organizational structure that divides the organization according to types of products or customers.

dominating (forcing) a conflict resolution strategy of persisting in a conflict until one party attains personal goals at the expense of the other's.

downward communication messages flowing downward in an organizational hierarchy, usually from superiors to subordinates.

dysfunctional politics political behaviors that detract from the organization's ability to attain its goals.

E

effect size an estimate of the magnitude of a relationship or effect found in a research investigation.

emotional intelligence ability to understand, regulate, and communicate emotions and to use them to inform thinking.

emotional labor the demands caused from the need to regulate and control emotions and emotional displays in the workplace.

employee assistance programs (EAPs) counseling provided for a variety of worker problems, particularly drug and alcohol abuse.

employee ownership ownership of all or part of an organization by its workers, typically through stock purchases.

Employee engagement a psychological state characterized by vigor, dedication, and absorption in one's work/organization.

employee placement the process of assigning workers to appropriate jobs.

employee recruitment the process by which companies attract qualified applicants.

employee screening the process of reviewing information about job applicants used to select workers.

employee selection the process of choosing applicants for employment.

employee training planned organizational efforts to help employees learn job-related knowledge, skills, and other characteristics.

empowerment the process by which organizational members can increase their sense of power and personal control in the work setting.

encoding the process of preparing a message for transmission by putting it into some form or code.

Equal Employment Opportunity Commission (EEOC) the federal agency created to protect against discrimination in employment.

equity theory a theory that workers are motivated to reduce perceived inequities between work inputs and outcomes.

ERG theory Alderfer's motivation model that categorizes needs into existence, relatedness, and growth needs.

exaggeration the distortion of information by elaborating, overestimating, or minimizing parts of the message.

exceptioning the practice of ignoring pay discrepancies between particular jobs possessing equivalent duties and responsibilities.

expectancy (in expectancy theory) the perceived relationship between the individual's effort and performance of a behavior.

expectancy theory a cognitive theory of motivation that states that workers weigh expected costs and benefits of particular courses before they are motivated to take action.

experimental method a research design characterized by a high degree of control over the research setting to allow for the determination of cause-and-effect relationships among variables.

expert power power derived from having certain work-related knowledge or skill.

external validity whether research results obtained in one setting will apply to another setting.

extraneous variables variables other than the independent variable that may influence the dependent variable.

F

facet approach (to job satisfaction) views job satisfaction as made up of several components, or "facets."

faking purposely distorting one's responses to a test to try to "beat" the test.

false-negative errors erroneously rejecting applicants who would have been successful in a particular job or occupation.

false-positive errors erroneously accepting applicants for a job who are later proven to be unsuccessful at performing the job.

feedback an acknowledgment that a message has been received and understood.

Fiedler's contingency model a leadership theory that maintains that effective leadership depends on a match between the leader's style and the degree to which the work situation gives control and influence to the leader.

filtering the selective presentation of the content of a communication.

fixed-interval schedule reinforcement that follows the passage of a specified amount of time.

fixed-ratio schedule reinforcement that is contingent on the performance of a fixed number of behaviors.

flextime a schedule that commits an employee to working a specified number of hours per week, but offers flexibility in regard to the beginning and ending times for each day.

forced distributions assigning workers to established categories of poor to good performance with fixed limitations on how many employees can be assigned to each category.

frequency distribution a descriptive statistical technique that arranges scores by categories.

functional job analysis (FJA) a structured job analysis technique that examines the sequence of tasks in a job and the processes by which they are completed.

functional politics political behaviors that help the organization to attain its goals.

functional structure an organizational structure that divides the organization into departments based on the functions or tasks they perform.

G

gainsharing a compensation system based on effective group performance.

glass ceiling limitations placed on women and minorities preventing them from advancing into top-level positions in organizations.

global approach (to job satisfaction) views job satisfaction as a general, unitary construct.

goal-setting theory the motivational theory that emphasizes the setting of specific and challenging performance goals.

grapevine the informal communication network in an organization.

graphic rating scales performance appraisal methods using a predetermined scale to rate the worker on important job dimensions.

great man/woman theory a universalist theory of leadership that maintains that great leaders are born, not made.

group two or more individuals engaged in social interaction to achieve some goal.

group efficacy a group's shared belief that they can attain organizational outcomes.

group polarization the tendency for groups to make decisions that are more extreme than those made by individuals.

groupthink a syndrome characterized by a concurrence-seeking tendency that overrides the ability of a cohesive group to make critical decisions.

growth need strength the need and desire for personal growth on the job.

H

halo effect an overall positive evaluation of a worker based on one known positive characteristic or action.

hardiness the notion that some people may be more resistant to the health-damaging effects of stress.

Hawthorne effect changes in behavior occurring as a function of participants' knowledge that they are being observed and their expectations concerning their role as research participants.

human relations movement a movement based on the studies of Elton Mayo that emphasizes the importance of social factors in influencing work performance.

hygienes elements related to job context that, when absent, cause job dissatisfaction.

hypotheses statements about the supposed relationships between or among variables.

I

independent variable in the experimental method, the variable that is manipulated by the researcher.

individual coping strategies techniques such as exercise, meditation, or cognitive restructuring, that can be used to deal with work stress.

individual methods performance appraisal methods that evaluate an employee by himself or herself, without explicit reference to other workers.

individual power power derived from personal characteristics that are of value to the organization, such as particular expertise or leadership ability.

industrial/organizational (I/O) psychology the branch of psychology that is concerned with the study of behavior in work settings and the application of psychology principles to change work behavior.

inferential statistics statistical techniques used for analyzing data to test hypotheses.

influence the ability to use social forces to affect the behavior of others.

informed consent fully informing a research participant of the nature of a study or experiment and informing the individual about the right to refuse participation.

ingratiation influencing others by increasing one's personal appeal to them.

initiating structure leader behaviors that define, organize, and structure the work situation.

inputs elements that a worker invests in a job, such as experience and effort.

instrumentality the perceived relationship between the performance of a particular behavior and the likelihood of receiving a particular outcome.

integration the amount and quality of collaboration among the divisions of an organization.

integrity tests measures of honest or dishonest attitudes and/or behaviors.

interindividual conflict conflict that occurs when two people are striving to attain their own goals, thus blocking the other's achievement.

internal consistency a common method of establishing a measurement instrument's reliability by examining how the various items of the instrument intercorrelate.

internal validity the extent to which extraneous or confounding variables are removed from a study.

interorganizational conflict conflict between organizations with incompatible goals.

interpersonal stress stress arising from difficulties with others in the workplace.

intragroup conflict conflict that arises when a person or faction within a group attempts to achieve a goal that interferes with the group's goal attainment.

intraindividual conflict conflict that occurs when an individual is faced with two sets of incompatible goals.

intrinsic motivation the notion that people are motivated by internal rewards.

J

jargon special language developed in connection with certain jobs; also called technical language.

job ambiguity a source of stress resulting from a lack of clearly defined jobs and/or work tasks.

job analysis the systematic study of the tasks, duties, and responsibilities of a job and the qualities needed to perform it.

job characteristics model a theory that emphasizes the role that certain aspects of jobs play in influencing work motivation.

job description a detailed description of job tasks, procedures, and responsibilities; the tools and equipment used; and the end product or service.

Job Descriptive Index (JDI) a self-report job satisfaction rating scale measuring five job facets.

Job Diagnostic Survey (JDS) a questionnaire that measures core job characteristics.

job element method a job analysis method that analyzes jobs in terms of the knowledge, skills, abilities, and other characteristics (KSAOs) required to perform the jobs.

job enlargement the expansion of a job to include additional, more varied work tasks.

job enrichment a motivational program that involves redesigning jobs to give workers a greater role in the planning, execution, and evaluation of their work.

job evaluation an assessment of the relative value of a job to determine appropriate compensation.

job rotation a method of rotating workers among a variety of jobs to increase their breadth of knowledge.

job rotation the systematic movement of workers from one type of task to another to alleviate boredom and monotony (as well as training workers on different tasks; see Chapter 6).

job satisfaction the positive and negative feelings and attitudes about one's job.

job specification a statement of the human characteristics required to perform a job.

L

lack of control a feeling of having little input or effect on the job and/or work environment; typically results in stress.

lateral communication messages between two parties at the same level in an organizational hierarchy.

leader–member exchange model (LMX) a theory that effective leadership is determined by the quality of the interaction between the leader and particular group members.

leader–member relations the quality of the relationship between leader and followers.

leadership ability to guide a group toward the achievement of goals.

Leadership Grid an application of the findings from the behavioral theories of leadership that stresses that effective leaders should be both task oriented and relationship oriented.

least preferred coworker (LPC) a measure that assesses leaders' task or relationship orientation by having them rate their most difficult fellow worker.

legitimate power the formal rights or authority accompanying a position in an organization.

leniency error the tendency to give all workers very positive performance appraisals.

line employees in an organization who are engaged directly in tasks that accomplish its goals.

line–staff organizational structure a traditional organizational structure composed of one group of employees who achieve the goals of the organization (the line), and another group who support the line (staff).

M

management by objectives (MBO) a goal-setting OD technique in which supervisors and subordinates jointly set performance goals; at the end of the goal period, their attainment is evaluated and new goals are set.

management games a management training technique using scaled-down enactments of the operations and managements of organizations.

matrix organization an organizational design that blends functional and product structures.

mean a measure of central tendency; also known as the average.

measures of central tendency present the center point in a distribution of scores.

median a measure of central tendency; the midpoint of a distribution of scores.

mentoring a program in which an inexperienced worker develops a relationship with an experienced worker who serves as an advisor.

merit pay a compensation system in which employees receive a base rate and additional pay based on performance.

meta-analysis a technique that allows results from several different research studies to be combined and summarized.

Minnesota Satisfaction Questionnaire (MSQ) a self-report measure of job satisfaction that breaks satisfaction down into 20 job facets.

modeling learning that occurs through the observation and imitation of the behavior of others.

motivation the force that energizes, directs, and sustains behavior.

motivators elements related to job content that, when present, lead to job satisfaction.

multiple cutoff model an employee selection method using a minimum cutoff score on each of the various predictors of job performance.

multiple hurdle model an employee selection strategy that requires that an acceptance or rejection decision be made at each of several stages in a screening process.

multiple regression model an employee selection method that combines separate predictors of job success in a statistical procedure.

N

narratives open-ended written accounts of a worker's performance used in performance appraisals.

need hierarchy theory a motivation theory, proposed by Maslow, that arranges needs in a hierarchy from lower, more basic needs to higher-order needs.

Needs physiological or psychological deficiencies that an organism is compelled to fulfill.

negative reinforcers events that strengthen a behavior through the avoidance of an existing negative state.

noise physical or psychological distractions that disrupt the effective flow of communication.

nonverbal communication messages sent and received through means other than the spoken or written word.

normal distribution (bell-shaped curve) a distribution of scores along a continuum with known properties.

norms rules that groups adopt governing appropriate and inappropriate behavior for members.

O

O*NET the U.S. Department of Labor's Web site that provides comprehensive information about jobs and careers.

objective performance criteria measures of job performance that are easily quantified.

objectivity the unbiased approach to observation and interpretations of behavior.

obtrusive observation research observation in which the presence of the observer is known to the participants.

on-the-job training an employee training method of placing a worker in the workplace to learn firsthand about a job.

operationalized clearly defining a research variable so that it can be measured.

organigram a diagram of an organization's hierarchy representing the formal lines of communication.

organizational behavior modification the application of conditioning principles to obtain certain work outcomes.

organizational citizenship behavior (OCB) efforts by organizational members that advance or promote the work organization and its goals.

organizational commitment a worker's feelings and attitudes about the entire work organization.

organizational coping strategies techniques that organizations can use to reduce stress for all or most employees.

organizational culture the shared values, beliefs, assumptions, and patterns of behavior within an organization.

organizational development (OD) the process of assisting organizations in preparing for and managing change.

organizational downsizing a strategy of reducing an organization's workforce to improve organizational efficiency and/or competitiveness.

organizational politics self-serving actions designed to affect the behavior of others to achieve personal goals.

organizational power power derived from a person's position in an organization and from control over important resources afforded by that position.

organizational socialization the process by which new employees learn group roles and norms and develop specific work skills and abilities.

organizational structure refers to the arrangement of positions in an organization and the authority and responsibility relationships among them.

outcomes those things that a worker expects to receive from a job, such as pay and recognition.

outsourcing contracting with an external organization in order to accomplish some work or organizational tasks.

overpayment inequity worker's perception that outcomes are greater than inputs.

P

paired comparison performance appraisal method in which the rater compares each worker with each other worker in the group.

parallel forms a method of establishing the reliability of a measurement instrument by correlating scores on two different but equivalent versions of the same instrument.

participative behavior leader behavior that encourages members to assume on active role in group planning and decision making.

path-goal theory states that a leader's job is to help the work group achieve their desired goals.

performance appraisals the formalized means of assessing worker performance in comparison to certain established organizational standards.

performance criteria measures used to determine successful and unsuccessful job performance.

performance feedback the process of giving information to a worker about performance level with suggestions for future improvement.

personality tests instruments that measure psychological characteristics of individuals.

person–environment (P–E) fit the match between a worker's abilities, needs, and values, and organizational demands, rewards, and values.

personnel psychology the specialty area of I/O psychology focusing on an organization's human resources.

polygraphs instruments that measure physiological reactions presumed to accompany deception; also known as lie detectors.

Porter-Lawler model a theory where the relationship between job satisfaction and performance is mediated by work-related rewards.

Position Analysis Questionnaire (PAQ) a job analysis technique that uses a structured questionnaire to analyze jobs according to 187 job statements, grouped into six categories.

position power a leader's authority to punish or reward followers.

positive affect positive emotions that affect workers' moods in the workplace.

positive reinforcers desirable events that strengthen the tendency to respond.

posttest-only design a program evaluation that simply measures training success criterion following completion of the training program.

power the use of some aspect of a work relationship to compel another to perform a certain action despite resistance.

power bases sources of power possessed by individuals in organizations.

power corollary the concept that for every exercise of power, there is a tendency for the subject to react with a return power play.

predictors variables about applicants that are related to (predictive of) the criteria.

pretest–posttest design a design for evaluating a training program that makes comparisons of criterion measures collected before and after the introduction of the program.

problem-solving case study a management training technique that presents a real or hypothetical organizational problem that trainees attempt to solve.

process consultation an OD technique in which a consultant helps a client-organization study its problems objectively and learn to solve them.

profit sharing a plan where all employees receive a small share of an organization's profits.

programmed instruction self-paced individualized training in which trainees are provided with training materials and can test how much they have learned.

project task force a nontraditional organization of workers who are assembled temporarily to complete a specific job or project.

protected groups groups including women and certain ethnic and racial minorities that have been identified as previous targets of employment discrimination.

psychology the study of behavior and mental processes.

punishment unpleasant consequences that reduce the tendency to respond.

Pygmalion effect when a sender nonverbally communicates expectations to a receiver influencing his/her behavior.

Q

qualitative (categorical or frequency) data data that measure some category or measurement quality.

quality circles small groups of volunteer employees from the same work area who meet regularly to solve work-related problems.

quantitative (measurement) data data that measure some numerical quantity.

quasi-experiment a study that follows the experimental design but lacks random assignment of participants and/or manipulation of the independent variable.

R

random assignment a method of assigning subjects to groups by chance to control for the effects of extraneous variables.

random sampling the selection of research participants from a population so that each individual has an equal probability of being chosen.

rankings performance appraisal methods involving the ranking of supervisees from best to worst.

realistic job preview (RJP) an accurate presentation of the prospective job and organization made to applicants.

receiver the recipient of a communication who decodes the message; also known as the decoder.

recency effect the tendency to give greater weight to recent performance and lesser weight to earlier performance.

reciprocity rule the tendency for persons to pay back those to whom they are indebted for assistance.

referent power power resulting from the fact that an individual is respected, admired, and liked by others.

reinforcement theory the theory that behavior is motivated by its consequences.

relationship-oriented behaviors leader behaviors focused on maintaining interpersonal relationships on the job.

reliability the consistency of a measurement instrument or its stability over time.

reward power power that results from having the ability to offer something positive, such as money or praise.

role ambiguity a sense of uncertainty over the requirements of a particular role.

role conflict conflict that results when the expectations associated with one role interfere with the expectations concerning another role.

role differentiation the process by which group members learn to perform various roles.

role expectations beliefs concerning the responsibilities and requirements of a particular role.

role-playing a management training exercise that requires trainees to act out problem situations that often occur at work.

roles patterns of behavior that are adapted based on expectations about the functions of a position.

rumors information that is presented as fact, but which may actually be true or false.

S

sampling the selection of a representative group from a larger population for study.

scientific management begun by Frederick Taylor, a method of using scientific principles to improve the efficiency and productivity of jobs.

self-efficacy an individual's beliefs in his or her abilities to engage in courses of action that will lead to desired outcomes.

self-managing work teams teams that have complete responsibility for whole tasks.

self-report techniques measurement methods relying on research participants' reports of their own behavior or attitudes.

seminar a common training method in which an expert provides job-related information in a classroomlike setting.

sender the originator of a communication, who encodes and transmits a message; also known as the encoder.

severity error the tendency to give all workers very negative performance appraisals.

shared leadership where leadership is shared among the group members rather than being centralized in one person.

simulation training that replicates job conditions without placing the trainee in the actual work setting.

situational exercise assessment tools that require the performance of tasks that approximate actual work tasks.

situational stress stress arising from certain conditions that exist in the work environment or in the worker's personal life.

skill-based pay a system of compensation in which workers are paid based on their knowledge and skills rather than on their positions in the organization.

snap judgment arriving at a premature, early overall evaluation of an applicant in a hiring interview.

social learning theory learning theory that emphasizes the observational learning of behavior.

social loafing the phenomenon whereby individuals working in groups exert less effort than when working alone.

sociogram a diagram of the informal lines of communication among organizational members.

Solomon four-group design a method of program evaluation using two treatment groups and two control groups.

source factors characteristics of the sender that influence the effectiveness of a communication.

span of control the number of workers who must report to a single supervisor.

staff specialized employee positions designed to support the line.

standard deviation a measure of variability of scores in a frequency distribution.

statistical significance the probability of a particular result occurring by chance, used to determine the meaning of research outcomes.

stratified sampling the selection of research participants based on categories that represent important distinguishing characteristics of a population.

stressful life events significant events in a person's recent history that can cause stress.

stressor an environmental event that is perceived by an individual to be threatening.

subject matter expert (SME) an individual who has detailed knowledge about a particular job.

subjective performance criteria measures of job performance that typically consist of ratings or judgments of performance.

superordinate goal a goal that two conflicting parties are willing to work to attain.

supportive behavior leader behavior focusing on interpersonal relationships and showing concern for workers' well-being.

survey feedback an OD technique whereby the consultant works with the organization to develop and administer a survey instrument to collect data that are fed back to organizational members and used as the starting point for change.

surveys a common self-report measure in which participants are asked to report on their attitudes, beliefs, and/or behaviors.

T

task interdependence the degree to which an individual's task performance depends on the efforts or skills of others.

task structure an assessment of how well elements of the work task are structured.

task-oriented behaviors leader behaviors focused on the work task.

team an interdependent group of workers with complementary skills working toward shared goals.

team building an OD technique in which teams of workers discuss how to improve team performance by analyzing group interaction.

team organization a nontraditional organizational structure consisting of a team of members organized around a particular project or product.

test battery a combination of employment tests used to increase the ability to predict future job performance.

test utility the value of a screening test in determining important outcomes, such as dollars gained by the company through its use.

test–retest reliability a method of determining the stability of a measurement instrument by administering the same measure to the same people at two different times and then correlating the scores.

t-groups (sensitivity training) an OD technique that uses unstructured group interaction to assist workers in achieving insight into their own motivations and behavior patterns in dealing with other organizational members.

Thematic Apperception Test (TAT) a projective test that uses ambiguous pictures to assess psychological motivation.

theory/model the organization of beliefs into a representation of the factors that affect behavior.

360-degree feedback a method of gathering performance appraisals from a worker's supervisors, subordinates, peers, customers, and other relevant parties.

time-and-motion studies procedures in which work tasks are broken down into simple component movements and the movements timed to develop a more efficient method for performing the tasks.

trainee readiness the individual's potential for successful training.

trait theory attempts to discover the traits shared by all effective leaders.

traits enduring attributes associated with an individual's makeup or personality.

transactional leadership leadership based on some transaction, such as exchanging money for work.

transfer of training concept dealing with whether training is actually applied in the work setting.

transformational leadership focuses on the leader's ability to provide shared values and a vision for the future for the work group.

treatment group the group in an experimental investigation that is subjected to the change in the independent variable.

t-test a statistical test for examining the difference between the means of two groups.

turnover intentions workers' self-reported intentions to leave their jobs, often used as a substitute for actual turnover measures.

two-factor theory Herzberg's motivational theory that proposes that two factors—motivators and hygienes—are important in determining worker satisfaction and motivation.

Type A behavior pattern a personality characterized by excessive drive, competitiveness, impatience, and hostility that has been linked to greater incidence of coronary heart disease.

U

underpayment inequity worker's perception that inputs are greater than outcomes.

underutilization a source of stress resulting from workers feeling that their knowledge, skills, or energy are not being fully used.

universalist theories theories that look for the major characteristics common to all effective leaders.

unobtrusive observation research observation in which the presence of the observer is not known to the participants.

upward communication messages flowing upward in an organizational hierarchy, usually taking the form of feedback.

V

valence the desirability of an outcome to an individual.

validity a concept referring to the accuracy of a measurement instrument and its ability to make accurate inferences about a criterion.

validity generalization the ability of a screening instrument to predict performance in a job or setting different from the one in which the test was validated.

variable-interval schedule of reinforcement that follows the passage of a specified amount of time, with exact time of reinforcement varying.

variable-ratio schedule reinforcement that depends on the performance of a specified but varying number of behaviors.

variables the elements measured in research investigations.

variability estimates the distribution of scores around the middle or average score.

vestibule training training that uses a separate area adjacent to the work area to simulate the actual work setting.

W

weighted application forms forms that assign different weights to the various pieces of information provided on a job application.

we–they feeling intragroup cohesiveness created by the existence of a common threat, which is typically another group.

whistle-blowing political behavior whereby an employee criticizes company policies and practices to persons outside the organization.

work–family conflict the cumulative stress that can result from the duties of trying to fulfill both work role and family role requirements.

work overload a common source of stress resulting when a job requires excessive speed, output, or concentration.

work sample tests used in job skill tests to measure applicants' abilities to perform brief examples of important job tasks.

worker stress the physiological and/or psychological reactions to events that are perceived to be threatening or taxing.

REFERENCES

Ackerman, P. L., & Kanfer, R. (1993). Integrating laboratory and field study for improving selection: Development of a battery for predicting air traffic controller success. *Journal of Applied Psychology, 78*, 413–432.

Adam, E. E. (1991). Quality circle performance. *Journal of Management, 17*, 25–39.

Adams, G. A., King, L. A., & King, D. W. (1996). Relationships of job and family involvement, family social support, and work-family conflict with job and life satisfaction. *Journal of Applied Psychology, 81*, 411–420.

Adams, J. A. (1987). Historical review and appraisal of research on the learning, retention, and transfer of human motor skills. *Psychological Bulletin, 101*, 41–74.

Adams, J. S. (1965). Inequity in social exchange. In L. Berkowitz (Ed.), *Advances in experimental social psychology* (Vol. 2, pp. 267–299). New York: Academic Press.

Adkins, C. E. (1995). Previous work experience and organizational socialization: A longitudinal examination. *Academy of Management Journal, 38*, 839–862.

Adler, N. J. (1991). *International dimensions of organizational behavior* (2nd ed.). Boston, MA: PWS-Kent.

Adler, N. J. (1993). An international perspective on the barriers to the advancement of women managers. *Applied Psychology: An International Review, 42*, 289–300.

Adler, P. S., & Borys, B. (1996). Two types of bureaucracy: Enabling and coercive. *Administrative Science Quarterly, 41*, 61–89.

AFSCME v. State of Washington, 578 F. supp. 846 (W.D. Wash. 1983).

Aguinis, H. (1993). Action research and scientific method: Presumed discrepancies and actual similarities. *Journal of Applied Behavioral Science, 29*, 416–431.

Aguinis, H., & Adams, S. K. R. (1998). Social-role versus structural models of gender and influence use in organizations: A strong inference approach. *Group & Organization Management, 23*, 414–446.

Aguinis, H., Nesler, M. S., Hosoda, M., & Tedeschi, J. T. (1994). The use of influence tactics in persuasion. *The Journal of Social Psychology, 134*, 429–438.

Aiello, J. R., & Kolb, K. J. (1995). Electronic performance monitoring and social context: Impact on productivity and stress. *Journal of Applied Psychology, 80*, 339–353.

Akande, A., & Odewale, F. (1994). One more time: How to stop company rumours. *Leadership & Organization Development Journal, 15(4)*, 27–30.

Albermarle Paper v. Moody, 74–389 (1975).

Alderfer, C. P. (1972). *Existence, relatedness, and growth: Human needs in organizational settings.* New York: Free Press.

Alge, B. J. (2001). Effects of computer surveillance on perceptions of privacy and procedural justice. *Journal of Applied Psychology, 86*, 797–804.

Alimo-Metcalfe, B., & Alban-Metcalfe, R. J. (2001). The development of a new transformational leadership questionnaire. *Journal of Occupational and Organizational Psychology, 74*, 1–27.

Allan, R. (2011). Type A behavior pattern. In R. Allan & J. Fisher (Eds.), *Heart and mind: The practice of cardiac psychology* (2nd ed., pp. 287–290). Washington, DC: American Psychological Association.

Allen, D. G. (2006). Do organizational socialization tactics influence newcomer embeddedness and turnover? *Journal of Management, 32*, 237–256.

Allen, D. G., Weeks, K. P., & Moffitt, K. R. (2005). Turnover intentions and voluntary turnover: The moderating roles of self-monitoring, locus of control, proactive personality, and risk aversion. *Journal of Applied Psychology, 90*, 980–990.

Allen, R. W., & Porter, L. W. (Eds.). (1983). *Organizational influence processes.* Glenview, IL: Scott, Foresman.

Allen, T. D., & Eby, L. T. (Eds.). (2007). *The Blackwell handbook of mentoring: A multiple perspectives approach.* New York: Wiley-Blackwell.

Allen, T. D., Freeman, D. M., Russell, J. E. A., Reizenstein, R. C., & Rentz, J. O. (2001). Survivor reactions to organizational downsizing: Does time ease the pain? *Journal of Occupational and Organizational Psychology, 74*, 145–164.

Allen, T. D., & Rush, M. C. (1998). The effects of organizational citizenship behavior on performance judgments: A field study and a laboratory experiment. *Journal of Applied Psychology, 83*, 247–260.

Allen, W. R., Bacdayan, P., Kowalski, K. B., & Roy, M. H. (2005). Examining the impact of ethics training on business student values. *Education & Training, 47*, 170–182.

Al-Mashaan, O. S. (2003). Comparison between Kuwaiti and Egyptian teachers in Type A behavior and job satisfaction: A cross-cultural study. *Social Behavior and Personality, 31*, 523–534.

Alper, S., Tjosvold, D., & Law, K. S. (2000). Conflict management, efficacy, and performance in organizational teams. *Personnel Psychology, 53*, 625–642.

Ambrose, M. L., & Alder, G. S. (2000). Designing, implementing, and utilizing computerized performance monitoring: Enhancing organizational justice. *Research in Personnel and Human Resources Management, 18*, 187–219.

Ambrose, M. L., Alder, G. S., & Noel, T. W. (1998). Electronic performance monitoring: A consideration of rights. In M. Schminke (Ed.), *Managerial ethics: Moral management of people and processes* (pp. 61–80). Mahwah, NJ: Erlbaum.

American Psychological Association. (2002). *Ethical principles of psychologists and code of conduct.* Retrieved from http://www.apa.org/ethics/code2002.html

Anakwe, U. P., & Greenhaus, J. H. (1999). Effective socialization of employees: Socialization content perspective. *Journal of Managerial Issues, 11(3),* 315–329.

Andersen, P. A. (2008). *Nonverbal communication: Forms and functions* (2nd ed.). Long Grove, IL: Waveland.

Anderson, L., & Wilson, S. (1997). Critical incident technique. In D. L. Whetzel & G. R. Wheaton (Eds.), *Applied measurement methods in industrial psychology* (pp. 89–112). Palo Alto, CA: Davies-Black.

Anderson, N., Herriot, P., & Hodgkinson, G. P. (2001). The practitioner-researcher divide in Industrial, Work and Organizational (IWO) psychology: Where are we now, and where do we go from here? *Journal of Occupational and Organizational Psychology, 74,* 391–411.

Anderson, N. R., & West, M. A. (1998). Measuring climate for work group innovation: Development and validation of the team climate inventory. *Journal of Organizational Behavior, 19,* 235–258.

Ansari, M. A., & Kapoor, A. (1987). Organizational context and upward influence tactics. *Organizational Behavior and Human Decision Processes, 40,* 39–49.

Antecol, H., & Cobb-Clark, D. (2003). Does sexual harassment training change attitudes? A view from the federal level. *Social Science Quarterly, 84,* 826–842.

Aquino, K., Lewis, M. U., & Bradfield, M. (1999). Justice constructs, negative affectivity, and employee deviance: A proposed model and empirical test. *Journal of Organizational Behavior, 20,* 1073–1091.

Aquino, K., Tripp, T. M., & Bies, R. J. (2001). How employees respond to personal offense: The effects of blame attribution, victim status, and offender status on revenge and reconciliation in the workplace. *Journal of Applied Psychology, 86,* 52–59.

Argyris, C. (1964). *Integrating the individual and the organization.* New York: Wiley.

Argyris, C. (1980). Some limitations of the case method: Experiences in a management development program. *Academy of Management Review, 5,* 251–298.

Arnold, D. W., & Thiemann, A. J. (1992). To test or not to test: The status of psychological testing with the ADA. *The Industrial-Organizational Psychologist, 29,* 25–27.

Arnold, H. J., & Feldman, D. C. (1982). A multivariate analysis of the determinants of job turnover. *Journal of Applied Psychology, 67,* 350–360.

Arthur, J. B., & Huntley, C. L. (2005). Ramping up the organizational learning curve: Assessing the impact of deliberate learning on organizational performance under gainsharing. *Academy of Management Journal, 48,* 1159–1170.

Arthur, W. J., Bell, S. T., Villado, A. J., & Doverspike, D. (2006). The use of person-organization fit in employment decision making: An assessment of its criterion-related validity. *Journal of Applied Psychology, 91,* 786–801.

Arvey, R. D., & Begalla, M. E. (1975). Analyzing the homemaker job using the Position Analysis Questionnaire (PAQ). *Journal of Applied Psychology, 60,* 513–518.

Arvey, R. D., Bouchard, T. J., Segal, N. L., & Abraham, L. M. (1989). Job satisfaction: Environmental and genetic components. *Journal of Applied Psychology, 74,* 187–192.

Arvey, R. D., & Campion, J. E. (1982). The employment interview: A summary and review of recent research. *Personnel Psychology, 35,* 281–322.

Arvey, R. D., Maxwell, S. E., & Salas, E. (1992). The relative power of training evaluation designs under difficult cost configurations. *Journal of Applied Psychology, 77,* 155–160.

Arvey, R. D., Miller, H. E., Gould, R., & Burch, P. (1987). Interview validity for selecting sales clerks. *Personnel Psychology, 40,* 1–12.

Arvey, R. D., & Murphy, K. R. (1998). Performance evaluation in work settings. *Annual Review of Psychology, 49,* 141–168.

Ashford, S. J., & Black, J. S. (1996). Proactivity during organizational entry: The role of desire for control. *Journal of Applied Psychology, 81,* 199–214.

Ashforth, B. E., & Saks, A. M. (1996). Socialization tactics: Longitudinal effects on newcomer adjustment. *Academy of Management Journal, 39,* 149–178.

Ashforth, B. E., Saks, A. M., & Lee, R. T. (1998). Socialization and newcomer adjustment: The role of organizational context. *Human Relations, 51,* 897–926.

Ashkanasy, N. M., & Cooper, C. L. (Eds.). (2008). *Research companion to emotion in organizations.* Cheltenham, UK: Edward Elgar.

Ashkanasy, N. M., & Jackson, C. R. A. (2001). Organizational culture and climate. In N. Anderson, D. S. Ones, H. K. Sinangil, & C. Viswesvaran (Eds.), *Handbook of Industrial, work and organizational psychology* (Vol. 2, pp. 398–415). London, UK: Sage.

Ashkanasy, N. M., Hartel, C. E. J., & Zerbe, W. J. (Eds.). (2000). *Emotions in the workplace: Research, theory, and practice.* Westport, CT: Quorum/Greenwood.

Ashour, A. S. (1973). The contingency model of leadership effectiveness: An evaluation. *Organizational Behavior and Human Performance, 9,* 339–355.

Astley, W. G., & Sachdeva, P. S. (1984). Structural sources of intraorganizational power: A theoretical synthesis. *Academy of Management Review, 9,* 104–113.

Astley, W. G., & Zajac, E. J. (1991). Intraorganizational power and organizational design: Reconciling rational and coalitional models of organization. *Organization Science, 4,* 399–411.

Atkin, R. S., & Goodman, P. S. (1984). Methods of defining and measuring absenteeism. In P. S. Goodman & R. S. Atkin (Eds.), *Absenteeism: New approaches to understanding, measuring, and managing employee absence* (pp. 47–109). San Francisco, CA: Jossey-Bass.

Atwater, L. E., Brett, J. F., & Waldman, D. (2003). Understanding the benefits and risks of multi-source feedback. In S. E. Murphy & R. E. Riggio (Eds.), *The future of leadership development* (pp. 89–106). Mahwah, NJ: Erlbaum.

Atwater, L. E., Carey, J. A., & Waldman, D. A. (2001). Gender and discipline in the workplace: Wait until your father gets home. *Journal of Management, 27,* 537–561.

Atwater, L., & Elkins, T. (2009). Diagnosing, understanding, and dealing with counterproductive work behavior. In J. W. Smither & M. London (Eds.), *Performance management: Putting research into action* (pp. 359–410). San Francisco, CA: Jossey-Bass.

Atwater, L. E., Waldman, D. A., Atwater, D., & Cartier, P. (2000). An upward feedback field experiment: Supervisors' cynicism, reactions, and commitment to subordinates. *Personnel Psychology, 53,* 275–297.

Austin, J., Kessler, M. L., Riccobono, J. E., & Bailey, J. S. (1996). Using feedback and reinforcement to improve the performance and safety of a roofing crew. *Journal of Organizational Behavior Management, 16,* 49–75.

Austin, J. T., & Villanova, P. (1992). The criterion problem: 1917–1992. *Journal of Applied Psychology, 77,* 836–874.

Avery, D. R., & McKay, P. F. (2006). Target practice: An organizational impression management approach to attracting minority and female job applicants. *Personnel Psychology, 59,* 157–187.

Avolio, B. J. (1999). *Full leadership development: Building the vital forces in organizations.* Thousand Oaks, CA: Sage.

Avolio, B. J., Avey, J. B., & Quisenberry, D. (2010). Estimating return on leadership development investment. *The Leadership Quarterly, 21(4),* 633–644.

Avolio, B. J., & Kahai, S. (2003). Placing the "E" in E-leadership: Minor tweak or fundamental change. In S. E. Murphy & R. E. Riggio (Eds.), *The future of leadership development* (pp. 49–70). Mahwah, NJ: Erlbaum.

Avolio, B. J., Reichard R. J., Hannah, S. T., Walumbwa, F. O., & Chan, A. (2009). A meta-analytic review of leadership impact research: Experimental and quasi-experimental studies. *The Leadership Quarterly, 20(5),* 764–784.

Axtell, C. M., Holman, D. J., Unsworth, K. L., Wall, T. D., & Waterson, P. E. (2000). Shopfloor innovation: Facilitating the suggestion and implementation of ideas. *Journal of Occupational and Organizational Psychology, 73,* 265–285.

Ayman, R., Chemers, M. M., & Fiedler, F. (1995). The contingency model of leadership effectiveness: Its levels of analysis. *Leadership Quarterly, 6,* 147–167.

Baba, V. V., & Jamal, M. (1991). Routinization of job context and job content as related to employees' quality of working life: A study of Canadian nurses. *Journal of Organizational Behavior, 12,* 379–386.

Bacharach, S. B., & Lawler, E. J. (1980). *Power and politics in organizations: The social psychology of conflict, coalitions, and bargaining.* San Francisco, CA: Jossey-Bass.

Bacharach, S. B., & Lawler, E. J. (1998). Political alignments in organizations: Contextualization, mobilization, and coordination. In R. M. Kramer & M. A. Neale (Eds.), *Power and influence in organizations* (pp. 67–88). Thousand Oaks, CA: Sage.

Bachman, J. G., Bowers, D. G., & Marcus, P. M. (1968). Bases of supervisory power: A comparative study in five organizational settings. In A. S. Tannenbaum (Ed.), *Control in organizations* (pp. 229–238). New York: McGraw-Hill.

Bachrach, D. G., & Jex, S. M. (2000). Organizational citizenship and mood: An experimental test of perceived job breadth. *Journal of Applied Social Psychology, 30,* 641–663.

Back, M. D., Stopfer, S. V., Gaddis, S., Schmukle, S. C., Egloff, B., & Gosling, S. D. (2010). Facebook profiles reflect actual personality, not self-idealization. *Psychological Science.* doi:10.1177/0956797609360756.

Bailey, C., & Fletcher, C. (2002). The impact of multiple source feedback on management development: Findings from a longitudinal study. *Journal of Organizational Behavior, 23,* 853–867.

Baird, J. E. (1977). *The dynamics of organizational communication.* New York: Harper & Row.

Baker, D. F. (2001). The development of collective efficacy in small task groups. *Small Group Research, 32,* 451–474.

Baldwin, T. T., & Ford, J. K. (1988). Transfer of training: A review and directions for future research. *Personnel Psychology, 41,* 63–105.

Baldwin, T. T., & Magjuka, R. (1997). Training as an organizational episode: Pre-training influences on trainee motivation. In J. K. Ford (Ed.), *Improving training effectiveness in work organizations* (pp. 99–127). Mahwah, NJ: Erlbaum.

Baldwin, T. T., Magjuka, R. J., & Loher, B. T. (1991). The perils of participation: Effects of choice of training on trainee motivation and learning. *Personnel Psychology, 44,* 51–65.

Balkin, D. B., & Gomez-Mejia, L. R. (Eds.). (1987). *New perspectives on compensation.* Englewood Cliffs, NJ: Prentice Hall.

Baltes, B. B., Briggs, T. E., Huff, J. W., Wright, J. A., & Neuman, G. A. (1999). Flexible and compressed workweek schedules: A meta-analysis of their effects on work-related criteria. *Journal of Applied Psychology, 84,* 496–513.

Baltes, B. B., Dickson, M. W., Sherman, M. P., Bauer, C. C, & LaGanke, J. S. (2002). Computer-mediated communication and group decision making: A meta-analysis. *Organizational Behavior and Human Decision Processes, 87,* 156–179.

Bamberger, P. A., & Levi, R. (2009). Team-based reward allocation structures and the helping behaviors of interdependent team members. *Journal of Managerial Psychology, 24(4),* 300–327.

Bandura, A. (1977). *Social learning theory.* Englewood Cliffs, NJ: Prentice Hall.

Bandura, A. (1997). *Self-efficacy: The exercise of control.* San Francisco, CA: W. H. Freeman.

Barber, A. E., Wesson, M. J., Roberson, Q. M., & Taylor, M. S. (1999). A tale of two job markets: Organizational size and its effects on hiring practices and job search behavior. *Personnel Psychology, 52,* 841–867.

Bar-Hillel, M., & Ben-Shakhar, G. (2000). The a priori case against graphology: Methodological and conceptual bases. In T. Connelly, H. R. Arkes, & K. R. Hammond (Eds.), *Judgment and decision making: An interdisciplinary reader* (Vol. 2, pp. 556–569). New York: Cambridge University Press.

Barker, J., Tjosvold, D., & Andrews, R. I. (1988). Conflict approaches of effective and ineffective project managers: A field study in a matrix organization. *Journal of Management Studies, 25,* 167–178.

Barki, H., & Pinsonneault, A. (2001). Small group brainstorming and idea quality: Is electronic brainstorming the most effective approach? *Small Group Research, 32(2),* 158–205.

Barling, J., Weber, T., & Kelloway, E. K. (1996). Effects of transformational leadership training on attitudinal and financial outcomes: A field experiment. *Journal of Applied Psychology, 81,* 827–832.

Barnett, R. B., & Bradley, L. (2007). The impact of organizational support for career development on career satisfaction. *Career Development International, 12(7),* 617–636.

Barney, C. E., & Elias, S. M. (2010). Flex-time as a moderator of the job stress-work motivation relationship: A three nation investigation. *Personnel Review, 39(4),* 487–502.

Baron, R. A. (1986). *Behavior in organizations: Understanding and managing the human side of work* (2nd ed.). Boston, MA: Allyn & Bacon.

Baron, R. S. (2005). So right it's wrong: Groupthink and the ubiquitous nature of polarized group decision making. In M. P. Zanna (Ed.), *Advances in Experimental Social Psychology, 37,* 219–253.

Barrett, G. V., & Depinet, R. L. (1991). A reconsideration of testing for competence rather than intelligence. *American Psychologist, 46,* 1012–1024.

Barrett, G. V., & Kernan, M. C. (1987). Performance appraisal and terminations: A review of court decisions since *Brito v. Zia* with implications for personnel practices. *Personnel Psychology, 40,* 489–503.

Barrett, G. V., Phillips, J. S., & Alexander, R. A. (1981). Concurrent and predictive validity designs: A critical reanalysis. *Journal of Applied Psychology, 66,* 1–6.

Barrick, M. R., & Alexander, R. A. (1987). A review of quality circle efficacy and the existence of positive-finding bias. *Personnel Psychology, 40,* 579–592.

Barrick, M. R., & Mount, M. K. (1991). The Big Five personality dimensions and job performance: A meta-analysis. *Personnel Psychology, 44,* 1–26.

Barrick, M. R., & Mount, M. K. (1993). Autonomy as a moderator of the relationship between the Big Five personality dimensions and job performance. *Journal of Applied Psychology, 78,* 111–118.

Barrick, M. R., Mount, M. K., & Strauss, J. P. (1994). Antecedents of involuntary turnover due to reduction in force. *Personnel Psychology, 47,* 515–535.

Barringer, M. W., & Milkovich, G. T. (1998). A theoretical exploration of the adoption and design of flexible benefit plans: A case of human resource innovation. *Academy of Management Review, 23,* 305–324.

Barron, L. G., & Sackett, P. R. (2008). Asian variability in performance rating modesty and leniency bias. *Human Performance, 21(3),* 277–290.

Barsade, S. G. (2002). The ripple effect: Emotional contagion and its influence on group behavior. *Administrative Science Quarterly, 47,* 644–675.

Bartol, K. M., & Martin, D. C. (1988). Influences on managerial pay allocations: A dependency perspective. *Personnel Psychology, 41,* 361–378.

Bartol, K. M., & Martin, D. C. (1990). When politics pays: Factors influencing managerial compensation decisions. *Personnel Psychology, 43,* 599–614.

Bartram, D. (2000). Internet recruitment and selection: Kissing frogs to find princes. *International Journal of Selection and Assessment, 8,* 261–274.

Bass, B. M. (1954). The leaderless group discussion. *Psychological Bulletin, 51,* 465–492.

Bass, B. M. (1981). *Stogdill's handbook of leadership* (rev. and enl. ed.). New York: Free Press.

Bass, B. M. (1983). Issues involved in relations between methodological rigor and reported outcomes in evaluations of organizational development. *Journal of Applied Psychology, 68,* 197–199.

Bass, B. M. (1985). *Leadership and performance beyond expectations.* New York: Free Press.

Bass, B. M. (1990). *Bass & Stogdill's handbook of leadership: Theory, research, and managerial applications* (3rd ed.). New York: Free Press.

Bass, B. M. (1998). *Transformational leadership: Industry, military, and educational impact.* Mahwah, NJ: Erlbaum.

Bass, B. M., & Avolio, B. J. (1997). *Manual for the multifactor leadership questionnaire.* Palo Alto, CA: Mindgarden.

Bass, B. M., & Bass, R. (2008). *The Bass handbook of leadership.* New York: Free Press.

Bass, B. M., & Riggio, R. E. (2006). *Transformational leadership* (2nd ed.). Mahwah, NJ: Erlbaum.

Bass, B. M., & Steidlmeier, P. (1999). Ethics, character, and authentic transformational leadership. *The Leadership Quarterly, 10,* 181–217.

Bateman, T. S., & Organ, D. W. (1983). Job satisfaction and the good soldier: The relationship between affect and employee "citizenship." *Academy of Management Journal, 26,* 587–595.

Bateman, T. S., & Strasser, S. (1984). A longitudinal analysis of the antecedents of organizational commitment. *Academy of Management Journal, 27,* 95–112.

Bauer, T. N., & Erdogan, B. (2011). Organizational socialization: The effective onboarding of new employees. In S. Zedeck (Ed.), *APA handbook of industrial and organizational psychology, Vol. 3: Maintaining, expanding, and contracting the organization* (pp. 51–64). Washington, DC: American Psychological Association.

Bavelas, A. (1950). Communication patterns in task-oriented groups. *Journal of Acoustical Society of America, 22,* 725–730.

Bayo-Moriones, A., & Larraza-Kintana, M. (2009). Profit-sharing plans and affective commitment: Does the context matter? *Human Resource Management, 48(2),* 207–226.

Bays, G. (2007). Let's talk: Preparing students for speaking and listening in the workplace. In C. L. Selfe (Ed.), *Resources in technical communication: Outcomes and approaches* (pp. 281–291). Amityville, NY: Baywood.

Bazerman, M. H., Giuliano, T., & Appleman, A. (1984). Escalation of commitment in individual and group decision making. *Organizational Behavior and Human Performance, 33,* 141–152.

Becker, T. E., & Billings, R. S. (1993). Profiles of commitment: An empirical test. *Journal of Organizational Behavior, 14,* 177–190.

Beehr, T. A. (1985). Organizational stress and employee effectiveness: A job characteristics approach. In T. A. Beehr & R. S. Bhagat (Eds.), *Human stress and cognition in organizations: An integrated perspective* (pp. 57–81). New York: Wiley.

Beehr, T. A., & Bhagat, R. S. (Eds.). (1985). *Human stress and cognition in organizations: An integrated perspective.* New York: Wiley.

Beehr, T. A., & McGrath, J. E. (1992). Social support, occupational stress and anxiety. *Anxiety, Stress, and Coping, 5,* 7–19.

Begley, T. M. (1998). Coping strategies as predictors of employee distress and turnover after an organizational consolidation: A longitudinal analysis. *Journal of Occupational and Organizational Psychology, 71,* 305–329.

Bell, S. J., & Menguc, B. (2002). The employee-organization relationship, organizational citizenship behaviors, and superior service quality. *Journal of Retailing, 78,* 131–146.

Bellotti, V., Ducheneaut, N., Howard, M., Smith, I., & Grinter, R. E. (2005). Quality versus quantity: E-mail centric task management and its relation with overload. *Human-Computer Interaction, 20,* 89–138.

Bemis, S. E., Belenky, A. H., & Soder, D. A. (1983). *Job analysis: An effective management tool.* Washington, DC: The Bureau of National Affairs.

Benne, K. D., & Sheats, P. (1948). Functional roles of group members. *Journal of Social Issues, 4,* 41–49.

Bennett, G. K. (1980). *Bennett mechanical comprehension test.* San Antonio, TX: The Psychological Corporation.

Bennett, G. K. (1981). *Hand-tool dexterity test.* San Antonio, TX: The Psychological Corporation.

Bennett, R. J., & Robinson, S. L. (2000). Development of a measure of workplace deviance. *Journal of Applied Psychology, 85,* 349–360.

Benschop, Y. (2001). Pride, prejudice, and performance: Relations between HRM, diversity, and performance. *The International Journal of Human Resource Management, 12*, 1166–1181.

Ben-Shakhar, G., Bar-Hillel, M., Bilu, Y., Ben-Abba, E., & Flug, A. (1986). Can graphology predict occupational success? Two empirical studies and some methodological ruminations. *Journal of Applied Psychology, 71*, 645–653.

Berger, M. A. (1983). In defense of the case method: A reply to Argyris. *Academy of Management Review, 8*, 329–333.

Bernardin, H. J., & Beatty, R. W. (1984). *Performance appraisal: Assessing human behavior at work.* Boston, MA: Kent.

Bernardin, H. J., & Bulkley, M. R. (1981). Strategies in rater training. *Academy of Management Review, 6*, 205–242.

Bernardin, H. J., Dahmus, S. A., & Redmon, G. (1993). Attitudes of first-line supervisors toward subordinate appraisals. *Human Resource Management, 32*, 315–324.

Bernardin, H. J., Hagan, C. M., Kane, J. S., & Villanova, P. (1998). Effective performance management: A focus on precision, customers, and situational constraints. In J. W. Smither (Ed.), *Performance appraisal: State of the art in practice* (pp. 3–48). San Francisco, CA: Jossey-Bass.

Bernthal, P. R., & Insko, C. A. (1993). Cohesiveness without groupthink: The interactive effects of social and task cohesion. *Group and Organization Management, 18*, 66–87.

Bertrand, M. (2000). *The gender gap in top corporate jobs.* Cambridge, MA: National Bureau of Economic Research.

Bertua, C., Anderson, N., & Salgado, J. F. (2005). The predictive validity of cognitive ability tests: A UK meta-analysis. *Journal of Occupational and Organizational Psychology, 78*, 387–409.

Bhagat, R. S. (1983). Effects of stressful life events on individual performance effectiveness and work adjustment processes within organizational settings: A research model. *Academy of Management Review, 8*, 660–671.

Binning, J. F., & Barrett, G. V. (1989). Validity of personnel decisions: A conceptual analysis of the inferential and evidential bases. *Journal of Applied Psychology, 74*, 478–494.

Birati, A., & Tziner, A. (1999). Economic utility of training programs. *Journal of Business and Psychology, 14*, 155–164.

Birdi, K. (2007). A lighthouse in the desert? Evaluating the effects of creativity training on employee innovation. *Journal of Creative Behavior, 41(4)*, 249–270.

Birnbaum, M. H., & Sotoodeh, Y. (1991). Measurement of stress: Scaling the magnitudes of life changes. *Psychological Science, 2*, 236–243.

Blake, R. R., & McCanse, A. A. (1991). *Leadership dilemmas—Grid solutions.* Houston, TX: Gulf.

Blake, R. R., & Mouton, J. S. (1985). *The managerial grid III.* Houston, TX: Gulf.

Blake, R. R., Mouton, J. S., & Sloma, R. L. (1964). An actual case history of resolving intergroup conflict in union-management relations. In R. R. Blake, H. A. Shepard, & J. S. Mouton (Eds.), *Managing intergroup conflict in industry* (pp. 155–195). Houston, TX: Gulf.

Blake, R. R., Shepard, H. A., & Mouton, J. S. (1964). *Managing intergroup conflict in industry.* Houston, TX: Gulf.

Blakely, G. L., Blakely, E. H., & Moorman, R. H. (1998). The effects of training on perceptions of sexual harassment allegations. *Journal of Applied Social Psychology, 28*, 71–83.

Blalock, H. M. (1989). *Power and conflict: Toward a general theory.* Newbury Park, CA: Sage.

Blanchard, C., Poon, P., Rodgers, W., & Pinel, B. (2000). Group environment questionnaire and its applicability in an exercise setting. *Small Group Research, 31*, 210–224.

Blau, F. D., & Kahn, L. M. (2007). The gender pay gap: Have women gone as far as they can? *Academy of Management Perspective, 21*, 7–23.

Bliese, P. D., & Halverson, R. R. (1996). Individual and nomothetic models of job stress: An examination of work hours, cohesion, and well-being. *Journal of Applied Social Psychology, 26*, 1171–1189.

Block, P. (1987). *The empowered manager.* San Francisco, CA: Jossey-Bass.

Bluedorn, A. C. (1993). Pilgrim's progress: Trends and convergence in research on organizational size and environment. *Journal of Management, 19*, 163–191.

Blumstein, A., & Nakamura, K. (2009). Redemption in the presence of widespread criminal background checks. *Criminology, 47(2)*, 327–359.

Bobrow, W., & Leonards, J. S. (1997). Development and validation of an assessment center during organizational change. *Journal of Social Behavior & Personality, 12*, 217–236.

Bolino, M. C., & Turnley, W. H. (2005). The personal costs of citizenship behavior: The relationship between individual initiative and role overload, job stress, and work-family conflict. *Journal of Applied Psychology, 90*, 740–748.

Bolino, M. C., & Turnley, W. H. (2008). Old faces, new places: Equity theory in cross-cultural contexts. *Journal of Organizational Behavior, 29(1)*, 29–50.

Bommer, W. H., Dierdorff, E. C., & Rubin, R. S. (2007). Does prevalence mitigate relevance? The moderating effect of group-level OCB on employee performance. *Academy of Management Journal, 50(6)*, 1481–1494.

Bono, J. E., & Judge, T. A. (2004). Personality and transformational and transactional leadership: A meta-analysis. *Journal of Applied Psychology, 89*, 901–910.

Bono, J. E., & Vey, M. A. (2005). Toward understanding emotional management at work: A quantitative review of emotional labor research. In C. E. J. Härtel, W. J. Zerbe, & N. M. Ashkanasy (Eds.), *Emotions in organizational behavior* (pp. 213–233). Mahwah, NJ: Erlbaum.

Booth, R. T. (1986). Machinery hazards. In J. Ridley (Ed.), *Safety at work* (2nd ed; pp. 549–571). London: Butterworth.

Booth-Kewley, S., & Friedman, H. S. (1987). Psychological predictors of heart disease: A quantitative review. *Psychological Bulletin, 101*, 343–362.

Borman, W. C. (1998). 360-ratings: An analysis of assumptions and a research agenda for evaluating their validity. *Human Resources Management Review, 7*, 299–315.

Born, D. H., & Mathieu, J. E. (1996). Differential effects of survey-guided feedback: The rich get richer and the poor get poorer. *Group & Organization Management, 21*, 388–403.

Boswell, W. R., & Boudreau, J. W. (2002). Separating the developmental and evaluative performance appraisal uses. *Journal of Business and Psychology, 16*, 391–412.

Boswell, W. R., & Olson-Buchanan, J. B. (2004). Experiencing mistreatment at work: The role of grievance filing, nature of mistreatment, and employee withdrawal. *Academy of Management Journal, 47*, 129–139.

Bowen, C., Swim, J. K., & Jacobs, R. R. (2000). Evaluating gender biases on actual job performance of real people: A meta-analysis. *Journal of Applied Social Psychology, 30*, 2194–2215.

Bowers, D. G. (1973). OD techniques and their results in 23 organizations: The Michigan ICL study. *Journal of Applied Behavioral Science, 9*, 21–43.

Bowers, D. G., & Hauser, D. L. (1977). Work group types and intervention effects in organizational development. *Administrative Science Quarterly, 22*, 76–94.

Boyd, D. P. (1984). Type A behavior, financial performance, and organizational growth in small business firms. *Journal of Occupational Psychology, 57*, 137–140.

Brannick, M. T., Levine, E. L., & Morgeson, F. P. (2007). *Job and work analysis: Methods, research, and applications for human resource management* (2nd ed.). Thousand Oaks, CA: Sage.

Brannon, D., Streit, A., & Smyer, M. A. (1992). The psychosocial quality of nursing home work. *Journal of Aging and Health, 4*, 369–389.

Brass, D. J., & Burkhardt, M. E. (1993). Potential power and power use: An investigation of structure and behavior. *Academy of Management Journal, 36*, 441–470.

Braver, M. C. W., & Braver, S. L. (1988). Statistical treatment of the Solomon four-group design: A meta-analytic approach. *Psychological Bulletin, 104*, 150–154.

Bray, D. W., Campbell, R. J., & Grant, D. L. (1974). *Formative years in business: A long-term AT&T study of managerial lives.* New York: Wiley.

Breaugh, J. A. (1981). Relationships between recruiting sources and employee performance, absenteeism, and work attitudes. *Academy of Management Journal, 24*, 142–147.

Breaugh, J. A. (2008). Employee recruitment: Current knowledge and important areas for future research. *Human Resource Management Review, 18*, 103–118.

Breaugh, J. A. (2009). The use of biodata for employee selection: Past research and future directions. *Human Resource Management Review, 19*, 219–231.

Breaugh, J. A., & Colihan, J. P. (1994). Measuring facets of job ambiguity: Construct validity evidence. *Journal of Applied Psychology, 79(2)*, 191–202.

Breaugh, J. A., Greising, L. A., Taggart, J. W., & Chen, H. (2003). The relationship of recruiting sources and pre-hire outcomes: Examination of yield ratios and applicant quality. *Journal of Applied Social Psychology, 33*, 2267–2287.

Bretz, R. D., Milkovich, G. T., & Read, W. (1992). The current state of performance appraisal research and practice: Concerns, directions, and implications. *Journal of Management, 18*, 321–352.

Bretz, R. D., & Thomas, S. L. (1992). Perceived equity, motivation, and final-offer arbitration in major league baseball. *Journal of Applied Psychology, 77*, 280–287.

Brewer, N., & Ridgway, T. (1998). Effects of supervisory monitoring on productivity and quality of performance. *Journal of Experimental Psychology: Applied, 4*, 211–227.

Brief, A. P. (2001). Organizational behavior and the study of affect: Keep your eyes on the organization. *Organizational Behavior and Human Decision Processes, 86*, 131–139.

Brief, A. P., & Motowidlo, S. J. (1986). Prosocial organizational behaviors. *Academy of Management Review, 11*, 710–725.

Brislin, R. (2008). *Working with cultural differences: Dealing effectively with diversity in the workplace.* Westport, CT: Praeger/Greenwood.

Britt, T. W., Adler, A. B., & Bartone, P. T. (2001). Deriving benefits from stressful events: The role of engagement in meaningful work and hardiness. *Journal of Occupational Health Psychology, 6*, 53–63.

Brockner, J., Spreitzer, G., Mishra, A., Hochwarter, W., Pepper, L., & Weinberg, J. (2004). Perceived control as an antidote to the negative effects of layoffs on survivors' organizational commitment and job performance. *Administrative Science Quarterly, 49*, 76–100.

Brodbeck, F. C., Zapf, D., Prumper, J., & Frese, M. (1993). Error handling in office work with computers: A field study. *Journal of Occupational and Organizational Psychology, 66*, 303–317.

Brotherridge, C. M., & Grandey, A. A. (2002). Emotional labor and burnout: Comparing two perspectives of "people work." *Journal of Vocational Behavior, 60*, 17–39.

Brown, B. B. (1991). Staff changes at EEOC, DOL; Focuses on ADA, "Glass-ceiling initiative." *Employment Relations Today*, 107–111.

Brown, J., Cooper, C., & Kirkcaldy, B. (1996). Occupational stress among senior police officers. *British Journal of Psychology, 87*, 31–41.

Brown, K. G. (2001). Using computers to deliver training: Which employees learn and why? *Personnel Psychology, 54*, 271–296.

Brown, S. P., Jones, E., & Leigh, T. W. (2005). The attenuating effect of role overload on relationships linking self-efficacy and goal level to work performance. *Journal of Applied Psychology, 90*, 972–979.

Brown, V., & Paulus, P. B. (1996). A simple dynamic model of social factors in group brainstorming. *Small Group Research, 27*, 91–114.

Brown, V. R., & Vaughn, E. D. (2011). The writing on the (Facebook) wall: The use of social networking sites in hiring decisions. *Journal of Business Psychology, 26*, 219–225. doi: 10.1007/s10869-011-9221-x

Buch, K., & Spangler, R. (1990). The effects of quality circles on performance and promotions. *Human Relations, 43*, 573–582.

Buchko, A. A. (1992). Employee ownership, attitudes, and turnover: An empirical assessment. *Human Relations, 45*, 711–733.

Buckly, R. (1993). *Job analysis and examination specifications study.* Sacramento, CA: Department of Real Estate.

Budros, A. (1999). A conceptual framework for analyzing why organizations downsize. *Organization Science, 10*, 69–82.

Burgess, R. (1968). Communication networks: An experimental reevaluation. *Journal of Experimental Social Psychology, 4*, 324–337.

Burke, M. J. (1992). Computerized psychological testing. In N. Schmitt & W. C. Borman (Eds.), *Personnel selection* (pp. 203–239). San Francisco, CA: Jossey-Bass.

Burke, M. J., & Day, R. R. (1986). A cumulative study of the effectiveness of managerial training. *Journal of Applied Psychology, 71*, 232–245.

Burke, R. J. (1993). Organizational-level interventions to reduce occupational stressors. *Work & Stress, 7*, 77–87.

Burke, R. J. (1997). Toward an understanding of psychological burnout among police officers. *International Journal of Stress Management, 4*, 13–27.

Burke, R. J. (2000a). Workaholism in organizations: Psychological and physical well-being consequences. *Stress Medicine, 16,* 11–16.

Burke, R. J. (Ed.). (2006). *Research companion to working time and work addiction.* Northampton, MA: Edward Elgar.

Burke, R. J., McKeen, C. A., & McKenna, C. (1993). Correlates of mentoring in organizations: The mentor's perspective. *Psychological Reports, 72,* 883–896.

Burke, W. W. (1987). *Organization development: A normative view.* Reading, MA: Addison-Wesley.

Burke, W. W., & Litwin, G. H. (1992). A causal model of organizational performance and change. *Journal of Management, 18,* 523–545.

Burns, J. M. (1978). *Leadership.* New York: Harper & Row.

Burns, L. R. (1989). Matrix management in hospitals: Testing theories of matrix structure and development. *Administrative Science Quarterly, 34,* 349–368.

Burns, L. R., & Wholey, D. R. (1993). Adoption and abandonment of matrix management programs: Effects of organizational characteristics and interorganizational networks. *Academy of Management Journal, 36,* 106–138.

Bushnell, I. W. R. (1996). A comparison of the validity of handwriting analysis with that of the Cattell 16PF. *International Journal of Selection and Assessment, 4,* 12–17.

Butterfield, L. D., Borgen, W. A., Amundson, N. E., & Asa-Sophia, T. M. (2005). Fifty years of the critical incident technique: 1954–2004 and beyond. *Qualitative Research, 5,* 475–497.

Bycio, P., Hackett, R. D., & Allen, J. S. (1995). Further assessments of Bass's (1985) conceptualization of transactional and transformational leadership. *Journal of Applied Psychology, 80,* 468–478.

Byrne, B. M. (1993). The Maslach Burnout Inventory: Testing for factorial validity and invariance across elementary, intermediate, and secondary teachers. *Journal of Occupational and Organizational Psychology, 66,* 197–212.

Byrne, D. G., & Reinhardt, M. I. (1989). Work characteristics, occupational achievement, and the Type A behaviour pattern. *Journal of Occupational Psychology, 62,* 123–134.

Cable, D. M., & Graham, M. E. (2000). The determinants of job seekers' reputation perceptions. *Journal of Organizational Behaviour, 21,* 929–947.

Cable, D. M., & Parsons, C. K. (2001). Socialization tactics and person-organization fit. *Personnel Psychology, 54,* 1–23.

Cable, D. M., & Turban, D. B. (2001). Establishing the dimensions, sources and value of job seekers' employer knowledge during recruitment. *Research in Personnel and Human Resources Management, 20,* 115–163.

Cable, D. M., & Turban, D. B. (2003). The value of organizational reputation in the recruitment context: A brand-equity perspective. *Journal of Applied Social Psychology, 33,* 2244–2266.

Cairo, P. C. (1983). Counseling in industry: A selected review of the literature. *Personnel Psychology, 36,* 1–18.

Caligiuri, P., Tarique, I., & Jacobs, R. (2009). Selection for international assignments. *Human Resource Management Review, 19,* 251–262.

Callan, V. J. (1993). Subordinate-manager communication in different sex dyads: Consequences for job satisfaction. *Journal of Occupational and Organizational Psychology, 66,* 13–27.

Callinan, M., & Robertson, I. T. (2000). Work sample testing. *International Journal of Selection and Assessment, 8,* 248–260.

Callister, R. R., & Wall, J. A. (2001). Conflict across organizational boundaries: Managed care organizations versus health care providers. *Journal of Applied Psychology, 86,* 754–763.

Camara, W. J. (1988). Senate approves bill to ban polygraph testing in the workplace. *The Industrial-Organizational Psychologist, 25(4),* 57–58.

Campbell, D. J., Campbell, K. M., & Chia, H. (1998). Merit pay, performance appraisal, and individual motivation: An analysis and alternative. *Human Resource Management, 37,* 131–146.

Campbell, D. J., & Furrer, D. M. (1995). Goal setting and competition as determinants of task performance. *Journal of Organizational Behavior, 16,* 377–389.

Campbell, D. J., & Lee, C. (1988). Self-appraisal in performance evaluation: Development versus evaluation. *Academy of Management Review, 13,* 302–314.

Campbell, D. T., & Stanley, J. C. (1963). *Experimental and quasi-experimental designs for research.* Chicago, IL: Rand McNally.

Campbell, J. P., & Dunnette, M. D. (1968). Effectiveness of t-group experiences in management training and development. *Psychological Bulletin, 70,* 73–104.

Campbell, J. P., Dunnette, M. D., Lawler, E. E., & Weick, K. E. (1970). *Managerial behavior, performance, and effectiveness.* New York: McGraw-Hill.

Campbell, J. P., & Kuncel, N. R. (2001). Individual and team training. In N. Anderson, D. S. Ones, H. K. Sinangil, & C. Viswesvaran (Eds.), *Handbook of industrial, work & organizational psychology* (pp. 278–312). London, UK: Sage.

Campbell, J. P., & Pritchard, R. (1976). Motivation theory in industrial and organizational psychology. In M. D. Dunnette (Ed.), *Handbook of industrial and organizational psychology* (pp. 63–130). Skokie, IL: Rand McNally.

Campion, M. A. (1991). Meaning and measurement of turnover: Comparison of alternative measures and recommendations for research. *Journal of Applied Psychology, 76,* 199–212.

Campion, M. A., Cheraskin, L., & Stevens, M. J. (1994). Career-related antecedents and outcomes of job rotation. *Academy of Management Journal, 37,* 1518–1542.

Campion, M. A., Medsker, G. J., & Higgs, A. C. (1993). Relations between work group characteristics and effectiveness: Implications for designing effective work group. *Personnel Psychology, 46,* 823–850.

Campion, M. A., & McClelland, C. L. (1991). Interdisciplinary examination of the costs and benefits of enlarged jobs: A job design quasi-experiment. *Journal of Applied Psychology, 76,* 186–198.

Campion, M. A., Palmer, D. K., & Campion, J. E. (1998). Structuring employment interviews to improve reliability, validity, and users' reactions. *American Psychological Society, 7,* 77–82.

Campion, M. A., Pursell, E. D., & Brown, B. K. (1988). Structured interviewing: Raising the psychometric properties of the employment interview. *Personnel Psychology, 41,* 25–42.

Cann, E., Siegfried, W. D., & Pearce, L. (1981). Forced attention to specific applicant qualifications: Impact of physical attractiveness and sex on applicant biases. *Personnel Psychology, 34,* 65–76.

Cannon-Bowers, J. A., Rhodenizer, L. Salas, E., & Bowers, C. A. (1998). A framework for understanding pre-practice conditions and their impact on learning. *Personnel Psychology, 51,* 291–320.

Cannon-Bowers, J. A., & Salas, E. (1997). A framework for developing team performance measures in training. In M. T. Brannick, E. Salas, & C. Prince (Eds.), *Team performance assessment and measurement: Theory, methods, and applications* (pp. 45–62). Hillsdale, NJ: Erlbaum.

Caplan, R. D., Cobb, S., French, J. R. P., Harrison, P. V., & Pinneau, S. R. (1980*). Job demands and worker health*. Ann Arbor, MI: University of Michigan Institute for Social Research.

Caplan, R. D., & Jones, K. W. (1975). Effects of workload, role ambiguity, and Type A personality on anxiety, depression, and heart rate. *Journal of Applied Psychology, 60*, 713–719.

Carayon, P. (1994). Stressful jobs and non-stressful jobs: A cluster analysis of office jobs. *Ergonomics, 37*, 311–323.

Carayon, P., & Zijlstraw, F. (1999). Relationship between job control, work pressure and strain: Studies in the USA and The Netherlands. *Work & Stress, 13*, 32–48.

Carey, J. M., & Kacmar, C. J. (1997). The impact of communication mode and task complexity on small group performance and member satisfaction. *Computers in Human Behavior, 13*, 23–49.

Carless, S. A., & De Paolo, C. (2000). The measurement of cohesion in work teams. *Small Group Research, 31*, 71–88.

Carlson, B. C., & Thompson, J. A. (1995). Job burnout and job leaving in public school teachers: Implications for stress management. *International Journal of Stress Management, 2*, 15–29.

Carnevale, A. P., Gainer, L. J., & Villet, J. (1990). *Training in America: The organization and strategic role of training*. San Francisco, CA: Jossey-Bass.

Carpenter, C. S. (2007). Workplace drug testing and worker drug use. *Health Services Research, 42(2)*, 795–810.

Carrell, M. R. (1978). A longitudinal field assessment of employee perceptions of equitable treatment. *Organizational Behavior and Human Performance, 21*, 108–118.

Carretta, T. R., & Ree, M. J. (2000). General and specific cognitive and psychomotor abilities in personnel selection: The prediction of training and job performance. *International Journal of Selection and Assessment, 8*, 227–236.

Carroll, S. J., Paine, F. T., & Ivancevich, J. J. (1972). The relative effectiveness of training methods: Expert opinion and research. *Personnel Psychology, 25*, 495–510.

Carson, P. P., Carson, K. D., & Roe, C. W. (1993). Social power bases: A meta-analytic examination of interrelationships and outcomes. *Journal of Applied Social Psychology, 23*, 1150–1169.

Cartwright, D. (1968). The nature of group cohesiveness. In D. Cartwright & A. Zander (Eds.), *Group dynamics: Research and theory* (3rd ed., pp. 91–109). New York: Harper & Row.

Cascio, W. F. (1987). *Applied psychology in personnel management* (3rd ed.). Englewood Cliffs, NJ: Prentice Hall.

Cascio, W. F. (2003). *Managing human resources: Productivity, quality of work life, profits* (6th ed.). Burr Ridge, IL: Irwin/McGraw-Hill.

Cascio, W. F. (2009). *Managing human resources: Productivity, quality of work life, profits* (8th ed.). Burr Ridge, IL: Irwin/McGraw-Hill.

Cascio, W. F., & Aguinis, H. (2008). Research in industrial and organizational psychology from 1963 to 2007: Changes, choices, and trends. *Journal of Applied Psychology, 93(5)*, 1062–1081.

Cascio, W. F., Alexander, R. A., & Barrett, G. V. (1988). Setting cutoff scores: Legal, psychometric, and professional issues and guidelines. *Personnel Psychology, 41*, 1–24.

Cascio, W. F., & Phillips, N. F. (1979). Performance testing: A rose among thorns? *Personnel Psychology, 32*, 751–766.

Cascio, W. F., & Wynn, P. (2004). Managing a downsizing process. *Human Resource Management, 43*, 425–436.

Cassar, V., & Tattersall, A. (1998). Occupational stress and negative affectivity in Maltese nurses: Testing moderating influences. *Work & Stress, 12*, 85–94.

Catanzaro, D., Moore, H., & Marshall, T. R. (2010). The impact of organizational culture on attraction and recruitment of job applicants. *Journal of Business and Psychology, 25(4)*, 649–662.

Cattell, R. B. (1986). *Sixteen oersonality factors questionnaire*. Champaign, IL: Institute for Personality and Ability Testing.

Cavanagh, G. F., Moberg, D. J., & Velasquez, M. (1981). The ethics of organizational politics. *Academy of Management Review, 6*, 363–374.

Cavanaugh, M. A., Boswell, W. R., Roehling, M. V., & Boudreau, J. W. (2000). An empirical examination of self-reported work stress among U.S. managers. *Journal of Applied Psychology, 85*, 65–74.

Cecil, J. (2001). Computer-aided fixture design: A review and future trends. *International Journal of Advanced Manufacturing Technology, 18*, 790–793.

Cederblom, D. (1982). The performance appraisal interview: A review, implications, and suggestions. *Academy of Management Review, 7*, 219–227.

Chalykoff, J., & Kochan, T. A. (1989). Computer-aided monitoring: Its influence on employee job satisfaction and turnover. *Personnel Psychology, 42*, 807–829.

Chamberlin, M. J. A., & Green, H. J. (2010). Stress and coping strategies among firefighters and recruits. *Journal of Loss and Trauma, 15(6)*, 548–560.

Chan, D., Schmitt, N., DeShon, R. P., Clause, C. S., & Delbridge, K. (1997). Reactions to cognitive ability tests: The relationships between race, test performance, face validity perceptions, and test-taking motivation. *Journal of Applied Psychology, 82*, 300–310.

Chang, C., Rosen, C. C., & Levy, P. E. (2009). The relationship between perceptions of organizational politics and employee attitudes, strain, and behavior: A meta-analytic examination. *Academy of Management Journal, 52(4)*, 779–801.

Chao, G. T., Walz, P. M., & Gardner, P. D. (1992). Formal and informal mentorships: A comparison on mentoring functions and contrast with nonmentored counterparts. *Personnel Psychology, 45*, 619–636.

Chapman, D., Uggerslev, K. L., Carroll, S. A., Piasentin, K. A., & Jones, D. A. (2005). Applicant attraction to organizations and job choice: A meta-analytic review of the correlates of recruiting outcomes. *Journal of Applied Psychology, 90(5)*, 928–944.

Chapman, D. S., & Rowe, P. M. (2001). The impact of videoconference technology, interview structure, and interviewer gender on interviewer evaluations in the employment interview: A field experiment. *Journal of Occupational and Organizational Psychology, 74*, 279–298.

Chapman, J. (2006). Anxiety and defective decision making: An elaboration of the groupthink model. *Management Decision, 44(10)*, 1391–1404.

Chatman, J. A., & Jehn, K. A. (1994). Assessing the relationship between industry characteristics and organizational culture: How different can you be? *Academy of Management Journal, 37*, 522–553.

Chemers, M. M., Watson, C. B., & May, S. T. (2000). Dispositional affect and leadership effectiveness: A comparison of self-esteem, optimism, and efficacy. *Personality and Social Psychology Bulletin, 26*, 267–277.

Chen, P. Y., & Spector, P. E. (1991). Negative affectivity as the underlying cause of correlations between stressors and strains. *Journal of Applied Psychology, 76*, 398–407.

Chen, X., Hui, C., & Sego, D. J. (1998). The role of organizational citizenship behavior in turnover: Conceptualization and preliminary tests of key hypotheses. *Journal of Applied Psychology, 83*, 922–931.

Chen, Z., Lam, W., & Zhong, J. A. (2007). Leader-member exchange and member performance: A new look at individual-level negative feedback-seeking behavior and team level empowerment climate. *Journal of Applied Psychology, 92(1)*, 202–212.

Cherniss, C. (1980). *Staff burnout: Job stress in human services*. Beverly Hills, CA: Sage.

Chesney, M. A., & Rosenman, R. H. (1980). Type A behaviour in the work setting. In C. L. Cooper & R. Payne (Eds.), *Current concerns in occupational stress* (pp. 187–212). Chichester, England: Wiley.

Chiaburu, D. S., Oh, I., Berry, C. M., Li, N., & Gardner, R. G. (2011). The five-factor model of personality traits and organizational citizenship behaviors: A meta-analysis. *Journal of Applied Psychology, 96*, 1140–1166.

Chiu, S., & Tsai, W. (2007). The linkage between profit sharing and organizational citizenship behavior. *International Journal of Human Resource Management, 18(6)*, 1098–1115.

Christiansen, N. D., Janovics, J. E., & Siers, B. P. (2010). Emotional intelligence in selection contexts: Measurement method, criterion-related validity, and vulnerability to response distortion. *International Journal of Selection and Assessment, 18(1)*, 87–101.

Church, A. H., & Waclawski, J. (2001). Hold the line: An examination of line vs. staff differences. *Human Resource Management, 40*, 21–34.

Church, A. H., Walker, A. G., & Brockner, J. (2002). Multisource feedback for organization development and change. In J. Waclawski & A. H. Church (Eds.), *Organization development: A data-driven approach to organizational change* (pp. 27–54). San Francisco, CA: Jossey-Bass.

Clampitt, P. G., & Downs, C. W. (1993). Employee perceptions of the relationship between communication and productivity: A field study. *The Journal of Business Communication, 30*, 5–28.

Clark, M. C. (2005, July). *The cost of job stress*. Retrieved from http://www.mediate.com/articles/clarkM1.cfm.

Clay-Warner, J., Reynolds, J., & Roman, P. (2005). Organizational justice and job satisfaction: A test of three competing models. *Social Justice Research, 18*, 391–409.

Clements, P., & Jones, J. (2008). *The diversity training handbook* (3rd ed.). London, UK: Kogan Page.

Cleveland, J. N., Murphy, K. R., & Williams, R. E. (1989). Multiple uses of performance appraisal: Prevalence and correlates. *Journal of Applied Psychology, 74*, 130–135.

Cobb, A. T. (1984). An episodic model of power: Toward an integration of theory and research. *Academy of Management Review, 9*, 482–493.

Cobb, S., & Rose, R. M. (1973). Hypertension, peptic ulcer, and diabetes in air traffic controllers. *Journal of the American Medical Association, 224*, 489–492.

Cober, R. T., Brown, D. J., Levy, P. E., Cober, A. B., & Keeping, L. M. (2003). Organizational web sites: Web site content and style as determinants of organizational attraction. *International Journal of Selection and Assessment, 11*, 158–169.

Cohen, S. (1980). Aftereffects of stress on human behavior and social behavior: A review of research and theory. *Psychological Bulletin, 88*, 82–108.

Cohen, S. G., Ledford, G. E., Jr., & Spreitzer, G. M. (1996). A predictive model of self-managing work team effectiveness. *Human Relations, 49*, 643–676.

Cole, N. D., & Flint, D. H. (2004). Perceptions of distributive and procedural justice in employee benefits: Flexible versus traditional benefit plans. *Journal of Managerial Psychology, 19*, 19–40.

Collins, C. J., Hanges, P. J., & Locke, E. A. (2004). The relationship of achievement motivation to entrepreneurial behavior: A meta-analysis. *Human Performance, 17*, 95–117.

Collins, C. J., & Smith, K. G. (2006). Knowledge exchange and combination: The role of human resource practices in the performance of high-technology firms. *Academy of Management Journal, 49*, 544–560.

Collins, D. (1995). Death of a gainsharing plan: Power politics and participatory management. *Organizational Dynamics, 24*, 23–38.

Collins, D. B., & Holton, E. F. (2004). The effectiveness of managerial leadership development programs: A meta-analysis of studies from 1982 to 2001. *Human Resource Development Quarterly, 15(2)*, 217–248.

Combs, G. M., & Luthans, F. (2007). Diversity training: The impact of self-efficacy. *Human Resource Development Quarterly, 18(1)*, 91–120.

Comer, D. R. (1995). A model of social loafing in real work groups. *Human Relations, 48*, 647–667.

Conger, J. A. (1993). The brave new world of leadership training. *Organizational Dynamics, 21*, 46–58.

Conger, J. A., & Kanungo, R. N. (1987). Toward a behavioral theory of charismatic leadership in organizational settings. *Academy of Management Review, 12*, 637–647.

Conger, J. A., & Kanungo, R. N. (1988). The empowerment process: Integrating theory and practice. *Academy of Management Review, 13*, 471–482.

Conger, J. A., & Toegel, G. (2003). Action learning and multi-rater feedback: Pathways to leadership development? In S. E. Murphy & R. E. Riggio (Eds.), *The future of leadership development* (pp. 107–125). Mahwah, NJ: Erlbaum.

Conger, J. A., & Xin, K. (2000). Voices from the field: Executive education among global corporations. *Journal of Management Education, 24*, 73–101.

Conlon, D. E., & Ross, W. H. (1993). The effects of partisan third parties on negotiator behavior and outcome perception. *Journal of Applied Psychology, 78*, 280–290.

Connolly, J. J., & Viswesvaran, C. (2000). The role of affectivity in job satisfaction: A meta-analysis. *Personality and Individual Differences, 29*, 265–281.

Conway, J. M., & Huffcutt, A. I. (1996, April). *Testing assumptions of 360-degree feedback: A meta-analysis of supervisor, peer, subordinate and self-ratings*. Paper presented at the 11th annual conference of the Society for Industrial and Organizational Psychology, San Diego, CA.

Conway, J. M., Jako, R. A., & Goodman, D. F. (1995). A meta-analysis of interrater and internal consistency reliability of selection interviews. *Journal of Applied Psychology, 80*, 565–579.

Conway, J. M., Lombardo, K., & Sanders, K. C. (2001). A meta-analysis of incremental validity and nomological networks for subordinate and peer rating. *Human Performance, 14,* 267–303.

Cook, T. D., Campbell, D. T., & Peracchio, L. (1991). Quasi-experiments. In M. D. Dunnette & L. M. Hough (Eds.), *Handbook of industrial/organizational psychology* (2nd ed., Vol. 2, pp. 4991–5076). Palo Alto, CA: Consulting Psychologists Press.

Cooley, E. (1994). Training an interdisciplinary team in communication and decision-making skills. *Small Group Research, 25,* 5–25.

Cooper, C. L., Dewe, P. J., & O'Driscoll, M. P. (2002). *Organizational stress: A review and critique of theory, research, and applications.* Thousand Oaks, CA: Sage.

Cooper, C. L., Dewe, P. J., & O'Driscoll, M. P. (2011). Employee assistance programs: Strengths, challenges, and future roles. In J. C. Quick & L. E. Tetrick (Eds.), *Handbook of occupational health psychology* (2nd ed., pp. 337–356). Washington, DC: American Psychological Association.

Cooper, C. L., Dyck, B., & Frohlich, N. (1992). Improving the effectiveness of gainsharing: The role of fairness and participation. *Administrative Science Quarterly, 37,* 471–490.

Cooper, C. L., & Hensman, R. (1985). A comparative investigation of executive stress: A ten-nation study. *Stress Medicine, 1,* 295–301.

Cooper, C. L., Mallinger, M., & Kahn, R. (1978). Identifying sources of occupational stress among dentists. *Journal of Occupational Psychology, 51,* 227–234.

Cooper, C. L., Sloan, S. G., & Williams, S. (1988). *The occupational stress indicator: Management guide.* Oxford: NFER-Nelson.

Cordes, C. L., & Dougherty, T. W. (1993). A review and an integration of research on job burnout. *Academy of Management Review, 18,* 621–656.

Cortina, J. M., Goldstein, N. B., Payne, S. C., Davison, H. K., & Gilliland, S. W. (2000). The incremental validity of interview scores over and above cognitive ability and conscientiousness scores. *Personnel Psychology, 53,* 325–351.

Cosier, R. A., & Dalton, D. R. (1990). Positive effects of conflict: A field assessment. *The International Journal of Conflict Management, 1,* 81–92.

Costa, A. C. (2003). Work team trust and effectiveness. *Personnel Review, 32,* 605–622.

Costa, P. T., & McCrae, R. R. (1992). *The revised NEO personality inventory (NEO-PI-R) and NEO five-factor inventory (NEO-FFI) professional manual.* Odessa, FL: Psychological Assessment Resources.

Coster, E. A., Carstens, I. L., & Harris, A. M. P. (1987). Patterns of stress among dentists. *Journal of the Dental Association of South Africa, 42,* 389–394.

Cotton, J. L., & Tuttle, J. M. (1986). Employee turnover: A meta-analysis and review with implications for research. *Academy of Management Review, 11,* 55–70.

Cox, A. (2001). Achieving a sense of ownership among employees: A critical look at the role of reward systems. *Trends in Organizational Behavior, 8,* 81–95.

Cox, T. H., & Tung, R. (1997). The multicultural organization revisited. In C. C. Cooper & S. E. Jackson (Eds.), *Creating tomorrow's organization: A handbook for future research in organizational behavior* (pp. 7–28). New York: Wiley.

Coyle-Shapiro, J. A.-M. (1999). TQM and organizational change: A longitudinal study of the impact of a TQM intervention on work attitudes. *Research in Organizational Change and Development, 12,* 129–169.

Craiger, J. P. (1997). Technology, organizations, and work in the 20th century. *The Industrial-Organizational Psychologist, 34,* 89–96.

Crampton, S. M., Hodge, J. W., & Mishra, J. M. (1997). The Equal Pay Act: The first 30 years. *Public Personnel Management, 26,* 335–344.

Crawford, J. (1981). *Crawford small parts dexterity test.* San Antonio, TX: The Psychological Corporation.

Cromwell, S. E., & Kolb, J. A. (2004). An examination of work-environment support factors affecting transfer of supervisory skills training to the workplace. *Human Resource Development Quarterly, 15(4),* 449–471.

Cropanzano, R., & Grandey, A. A. (1998). If politics is a game, then what are the rules?: Three suggestions for ethical management. In M. Schminke (Ed.), *Managerial ethics: Moral management of people and processes* (pp. 133–152). Mahwah, NJ: Erlbaum.

Cropanzano, R., Howes, J. C., Grandey, A. A., & Toth, P. (1997). The relationship of organizational politics and support to work behaviors, attitudes, and stress. *Journal of Organizational Behavior, 18,* 159–180.

Crown, D. F., & Rosse, J. G. (1995). Yours, mine, and ours: Facilitating group productivity through the integration of individual and group goals. *Organizational Behavior and Human Decision Processes, 64,* 138–150.

Cummings, L. L., & Schwab, D. P. (1978). Designing appraisal systems for information yield. *California Management Review, 20,* 18–25.

Cummings, N. A., & Follette, W. T. (1976). Brief psychotherapy and medical utilization: An eight-year follow-up. In H. Dorken (Ed.), *The professional psychologist today: New developments in law, health, insurance, and health practice.* San Francisco, CA: Jossey-Bass.

Cunningham, J. B. (1989). A compressed shift schedule: Dealing with some of the problems of shift-work. *Journal of Organizational Behavior, 10,* 231–245.

Dahl, M. S. (2011). Organizational change and employee stress. *Management Science, 57(2),* 240–256.

Dalal, R. S. (2005). A meta-analysis of the relationship between organizational citizenship behavior and counterproductive work behavior. *Journal of Applied Psychology, 90,* 1241–1255.

Dalton, D. R., & Mesch, D. J. (1991). On the extent and reduction of avoidable absenteeism: An assessment of absence policy provisions. *Journal of Applied Psychology, 76,* 810–817.

Dalton, D. R., Krackhardt, D. M., & Porter, L. W. (1981). Functional turnover: An empirical assessment. *Journal of Applied Psychology, 66,* 716–721.

Danna, K., & Griffin, R. W. (1999). Health and well-being in the workplace: A review and synthesis of the literature. *Journal of Management, 25,* 357–384.

Dansereau, F., Graen, G., & Haga, B. (1975). A vertical dyad linkage approach to leadership within formal organizations: A longitudinal investigation of the role making process. *Organizational Behavior and Human Performance, 13,* 46–78.

David, F. R., Pearce, J. A., & Randolph, W. A. (1989). Linking technology and structure to enhance group performance. *Journal of Applied Psychology, 74,* 233–241.

Davis, K. (1968). Success of chain-of-command oral communication in a manufacturing management group. *Academy of Management Journal, 11*, 379–387.

Davis, K. (1972). *Human behavior at work.* New York: McGraw-Hill.

Davis-Blake, A., & Broschak, J. P. (2009). Outsourcing and the changing nature of work. *Annual Review of Sociology, 35*, 321–340.

De Dreu, C. K. W. (2008). The virtue and vice of workplace conflict: Food for (pessimistic) thought. *Journal of Organizational Behavior, 29*, 5–18.

De Dreu, C. K. W., & Weingart, L. R. (2003). Task versus relationship conflict, team performance, and team member satisfaction: A meta-analysis. *Journal of Applied Psychology, 88(4)*, 741–749.

De Dreu, C. K. W., & West, M. A. (2001). Minority dissent and team innovation: The importance of participation in decision making. *Journal of Applied Psychology, 86*, 1191–1201.

de Jonge, J., Dormann, C., Janssen, P. P. M., Dollard, M. F., Landeweerd, J. A., & Nijhuis, F. J. N. (2001). Testing reciprocal relationships between job characteristics and psychological well-being: A cross-lagged structural equation model. *Journal of Occupational and Organizational Psychology, 74*, 29–46.

de Lara, P. Z. M. (2006). Research note: Fear in organizations: Does intimidation by formal punishment mediate the relationship between interactional justice and workplace Internet deviance? *Journal of Managerial Psychology, 21(6)*, 580–592.

De Meuse, K. P., Marks, M. L., & Dai, G. (2011). Organizational downsizing, mergers and acquisitions, and using strategic alliances using theory and research to enhance practice. In S. Zedeck (Ed.), *APA handbook of industrial and organizational psychology* (Vol. 3, pp. 729–768). Washington, DC: American Psychological Association.

De Varo, J., Li, R., & Brookshire, D. (2007). Analysing the job characteristics model: New support from a cross-section of establishments. *The International Journal of Human Resource Management, 18(6)*, 986–1003.

de Vries, R. E., Bakker-Pieper, A., & Oostenveld, W. (2010). Leadership = communication? The relations of leaders' communication styles with leadership styles, knowledge sharing and leadership outcomes. *Journal of Business and Psychology, 25(3)*, 367–380.

Deal, T. E., & Kennedy, A. A. (1999). *The new corporate cultures: Revitalizing the workplace after downsizing, mergers, and reengineering.* Reading, MA: Perseus.

Dean, J. W., Yoon, S. J., & Susman, G. I. (1992). Advanced manufacturing technology and organization structure: Empowerment or subordination. *Organization Science, 3*, 203–229.

Dean, M. A. (2004). An assessment of biodata predictive ability across multiple performance criteria. *Applied Human Resource Management Research, 9*, 1–12.

DeAngelis, T. (1994). New tests allow takers to tackle real-life problems. *APA Monitor, 25*, 14–15.

Deci, E. L. (1972). The effects of contingent and noncontingent rewards and controls on intrinsic motivation. *Organizational Behavior and Human Performance, 8*, 212–229.

Deci, E. L. (1992). On the nature and functions of motivation theories. *Psychological Science, 3*, 167–171.

Deci, E. L., Koestner, R., & Ryan, R. M. (1999). A meta-analytic review of experiments examining the effects of extrinsic rewards on intrinsic motivation. *Psychological Bulletin, 125*, 627–688.

Deci, E. L., & Ryan, R. M. (1985). *Intrinsic motivation and self-determination in human behavior.* New York: Plenum Press.

Decker, P. J., & Nathan, B. R. (1985). *Behavior modeling training: Principles and applications.* New York: Praeger.

Deckop, J. R., Mangel, R., & Cirka, C. C. (1999). Getting more than you pay for: Organizational citizenship behavior and pay-for-performance plans. *Academy of Management Journal, 42*, 420–428.

DeGroot, T., & Motowidlo, S. J. (1999). Why visual and vocal interview cues can affect interviewers' judgments and predict performance. *Journal of Applied Psychology, 84*, 986–993.

Delery, J. E., Gupta, N., Jenkins, G. D., Jr., & Walker, B. C. (1998). Interdimensional correlations in individual and dyadic performance ratings. *Journal of Organizational Behavior, 19*, 577–587.

DeMatteo, J. S., Eby, L. T., & Sundstrom, E. (1998). Team-based rewards: Current empirical evidence and directions for future research. In B. M. Staw & L. L. Cummings (Eds.), *Research in organizational behavior* (Vol. 20, pp. 141–148). Greenwich, CT: Jai Press.

Dembroski, T. M., & Costa, P. T. (1987). Coronary-prone behavior: Components of the Type A pattern and hostility. *Journal of Personality, 55*, 211–236.

Demerouti, E., Bakker, A. B., Nachreiner, F., & Schaufeli, W. B. (2001). The job demands-resources model of burnout. *Journal of Applied Psychology, 86*, 499–512.

DeNisi, A. S., & Peters, L. H. (1996). Organization of information in memory and the performance appraisal process: Evidence from the field. *Journal of Applied Psychology, 81*, 717–737.

DeNisi, A. S., Randolph, W. A., & Blencoe, A. G. (1983). Potential problems with peer ratings. *Academy of Management Journal, 26*, 457–464.

DeNisi, A. S., Robbins, T., & Cafferty, T. P. (1989). Organization of information used for performance appraisals: Role of diary-keeping. *Journal of Applied Psychology, 74*, 124–129.

Denison, D. R. (1996). What is the difference between organizational culture and organizational climate? A native's point of view on a decade of paradigm wars. *Academy of Management Review, 21*, 619–654.

Denison, D. R., & Mishra, A. K. (1995). Toward a theory of organizational culture and effectiveness. *Organization Science, 6*, 204–223.

DePaulo, B. M., Stone, J. I., & Lassiter, G. D. (1985). Deceiving and detecting deceit. In B. R. Schlenker (Ed.), *The self and social life* (pp. 323–370). New York: McGraw-Hill.

Devine, D. J., Clayton, L. D., Philips, J. L., Dunford, B. B., & Melner, S. B. (1999). Teams in organizations: Prevalence, characteristics, and effectiveness. *Small Group Research, 30*, 678–711.

Devine, D. J., Habig, J. K., Martin, K. E., Bott, J. P., & Grayson, A. L. (2004). TINSEL TOWN: A top management simulation involving distributed expertise. *Simulation & Gaming, 35*, 94–134.

Dewettinck, K., & van Ameijde, M. (2011). Linking leadership empowerment behaviour to employee attitudes and behavioural intentions: Testing the mediating role of psychological empowerment. *Personnel Review, 40(3)*, 284–305.

DeWitt, R. (1993). The structural consequences of downsizing. *Organization Science, 4*, 30–40.

Di Milia, L. (1998). A longitudinal study of the compressed workweek: Comparing sleep on a weekly rotating 8-hour system to a faster rotating 12-hour system. *International Journal of Industrial Ergonomics, 21*, 199–207.

Diefendorff, J. M., & Chandler, M. M. (2011). Motivating employees. In S. Zedeck (Ed.), *APA handbook of industrial and organizational psychology, Vol. 3: Maintaining, expanding, and contracting the organization* (pp. 65–135). Washington, DC: American Psychological Association.

Diefendorff, J. M., & Gosserand, R. H. (2003). Understanding the emotional labor process: A control theory perspective. *Journal of Organizational Behavior, 24*, 945–959.

Diehl, M., & Stroebe, W. (1987). Productivity loss in brainstorming groups: Toward the solution of a riddle. *Journal of Personality and Social Psychology, 53*, 497–509.

Dierdorff, E. C., & Surface, E. A. (2007). Placing peer ratings in context: Systematic influences beyond rate performance. *Personnel Psychology, 60(1)*, 93–126.

Dierdorff, E. C., & Surface, E. A. (2008). If you pay for skills, will they learn? Skill change and maintenance under a skill-based pay system. *Journal of Management, 34(4)*, 721–743.

Dietz-Uhler, B., Bishop-Clark, C., & Howard, E. (2005). Formation of and adherence to a self-disclosure norm in an on-line chat. *CyberPsychology & Behavior, 8(2)*, 114–120.

DiFonzo, N., & Bordia, P. (2007). *Rumor psychology: Social and organizational approaches.* Washington, DC: American Psychological Association.

Difonzo, N., Bordia, P., & Rosnow, R. L. (1994). Reining in rumors. *Organizational Dynamics, 23*, 47–62.

DiMatteo, M. R., Shugars, D. A., & Hays, R. D. (1993). Occupational stress, life stress, and mental health among dentists. *Journal of Occupational and Organizational Psychology, 66*, 153–162.

Dipboye, R. L. (1982). Self-fulfilling prophecies in the selection-recruitment interview. *Academy of Management Review, 7*, 579–587.

Dipboye, R. L. (1989). Threats to the incremental validity of interviewer judgments. In R. W. Eder & G. R. Ferris (Eds.), *The employment interview: Theory, research, and practice* (pp. 45–60). Newbury Park, CA: Sage.

Dipboye, R. L. (1994). Structured and unstructured selection interviews: Beyond the job-fit model. *Research in Personnel and Human Resources Management, 12*, 79–123.

Dipboye, R. L. (1997). Organizational barriers to implementing a rational model of training. In M. A. Quiñones & A. Ehrenstein (Eds.), *Training for a rapidly changing workplace: Applications of psychological research* (pp. 31–60). Washington, DC: American Psychological Association.

Dipboye, R. L., Fontenelle, G. A., & Garner, K. (1984). Effects of previewing the application on interview process and outcomes. *Journal of Applied Psychology, 69*, 118–128.

Dipboye, R. L., Wooten, K., & Halverson, S. K. (2004). Behavioral and situational interviews. In J. C. Thomas (Ed.), *Comprehensive handbook of psychological assessment, Vol. 4: Industrial and organizational assessment* (pp. 297–316). New York: Wiley.

Dixon, M. L., & Hart, L. K. (2010). The impact of path-goal leadership styles on work group effectiveness and turnover intention. *Journal of Managerial Issues, 22(1)*, 52–69.

Donaldson, T., Earl, J. K., & Muratore, A. M. (2010). Extending the integrated model of retirement adjustment: Incorporating mastery and retirement planning. *Journal of Vocational Behavior, 77*, 279–289.

Dormann, C., Fay, D., Zapf, D., & Frese, M. (2006). A state-trait analysis of job satisfaction: On the effect of core self-evaluations. *Applied Psychology: An International Review, 55*, 27–51.

Dormann, C., & Zapf, D. (2001). Job satisfaction: A meta-analysis of stabilities. *Journal of Organizational Behavior, 22*, 483–504.

Dornburg, C. C., Stevens, S. M., Hendrickson, S. M. L., & Davidson, G. S. (2009). Improving extreme-scale problem solving: Assessing electronic brainstorming effectiveness in an industrial setting. *Human Factors, 51(4)*, 519–527.

Dose, J. J. (2003). Information exchange in personnel selection decisions. *Applied Psychology: An International Review, 52*, 237–252.

Dotlich, D. L., & Noel, J. L. (1998). *Action learning.* San Francisco, CA: Jossey-Bass.

Douglas, S. C., & Martinko, M. J. (2001). Exploring the role of individual differences in the prediction of workplace aggression. *Journal of Applied Psychology, 86*, 547–559.

Driskell, J. E., Olmstead, B., & Salas, E. (1993). Task cues, dominance cues, and influence in task groups. *Journal of Applied Psychology, 78*, 51–60.

Driskell, J. E., Willis, R. P., & Copper, C. (1992). Effect of overlearning on retention. *Journal of Applied Psychology, 77*, 615–622.

Driver, R. W., Buckley, M. R., & Frink, D. D. (1996). Should we write off graphology? *International Journal of Selection and Assessment, 4*, 78–86.

Drucker, P. F. (1954). *The practice of management.* New York: Harper & Row.

Duchon, D., Green, S. G., & Taber, T. D. (1986). Vertical dyad linkage: A longitudinal assessment of antecedents, measures, and consequences. *Journal of Applied Psychology, 71*, 56–60.

Dumdum, U. R., Lowe, K. B., & Avolio, B. J. (2002). A meta-analysis of transformational and transactional leadership correlates of effectiveness and satisfaction: An update and extension. In B. J. Avolio & F. J. Yammarino (Eds.), *Transformational and charismatic leadership: The road ahead.* Oxford, England: JAI/Elsevier.

Duncan, W. J. (2001). Stock ownership and work motivation. *Organizational Dynamics, 30*, 1–11.

Dunnette, M. D. (1990). Blending the science and practice of industrial and organizational psychology: Where are we and where are we going. In M. D. Dunnette & L. M. Hough (Eds.), *Handbook of industrial and organizational psychology* (Vol. 1, 2nd ed., pp. 1–27). Palo Alto, CA: Consulting Psychologists Press.

Dunnette, M. D. (1993). My hammer or your hammer? *Human Resource Management, 32*, 373–384.

Dunnette, M. D., Campbell, J. P., & Hakel, M. D. (1967). Factors contributing to job satisfaction and dissatisfaction in six occupational groups. *Organizational Behavior and Human Performance, 2*, 143–174.

Dunphy, D., & Bryant, B. (1996). Teams: Panaceas or prescriptions for improved performance? *Human Relations, 49*, 677–699.

Dwyer, D. J., & Ganster, D. C. (1991). The effects of job demands and control on employee attendance and satisfaction. *Journal of Organizational Behavior, 12*, 595–608.

Eagly, A. H. (2007). Female leadership advantage and disadvantage: Resolving the contradictions. *Psychology of Women Quarterly, 31*, 1–12.

Eagly, A. H., & Carli, L. L. (2007). Women and the labyrinth of leadership. *Harvard Business Review, 85*, 62–71.

Eckert, R., Ekelund, B. Z., Gentry, W. A., & Dawson, J. F. (2010). I don't see me like you see me, but is that a problem? Cultural influences on rating discrepancy in 360-degree feedback instruments. *European Journal of Work and Organizational Psychology, 19(3)*, 259–278.

Eden, D. (1990). *Pygmalion in management.* Lexington, MA: Lexington Books.

Eden, D., & Shani, A. B. (1982). Pygmalion goes to boot camp: Expectancy, leadership, and trainee performance. *Journal of Applied Psychology, 67,* 194–199.

Edwards, J. R., & Cooper, C. L. (1990). The person-environment fit approach to stress: Recurring problems and some suggested solutions. *Journal of Organizational Behavior, 11,* 293–307.

Efraty, D., & Sirgy, M. J. (1990). The effects of quality of working life (QWL) on employee behavioral responses. *Social Indicators Research, 22,* 31–47.

Eisenbach, R., Watson, K., & Pillai, R. (1999). Transformational leadership in the contextor organizational change. *Journal of Organizational Change Management, 12,* 80–88.

Eisenberg, E. M., & Witten, M. G. (1987). Reconsidering openness in organizational communication. *Academy of Management Review, 12,* 418–426.

Eisenberger, R., Armeli, S., Rexwinkel, B., Lynch, P. D., & Rhoades, L. (2001). Reciprocation of perceived organizational support. *Journal of Applied Psychology, 86,* 42–51.

Elenkov, S. E. (1998). Can American management concepts work in Russia? A cross-cultural comparative study. *California Management Review, 40,* 133–156.

Ellis, A. P. J. (2006). System breakdown: The role of mental models and transactive memory in the relationship between acute stress and team performance. *Academy of Management Journal, 49,* 576–589.

Ely, R. J., & Thomas, D. A. (2001). Cultural diversity at work: The effects of diversity perspectives on work group processes and outcomes. *Administrative Science Quarterly, 46,* 229–273.

Englebrecht, A. S., & Fischer, A. H. (1995). The managerial performance implications of a developmental assessment center process. *Human Relations, 48,* 387–404.

Ensher, E. A., & Murphy, S. E. (2005). *Power mentoring: How successful mentors and proteges get the most out of their relationships.* San Francisco, CA: Jossey-Bass.

Ensher, E. A., Thomas, C., & Murphy, S. E. (2001). Comparison of traditional, step-ahead, and peer mentoring on protégés' support, satisfaction, and perceptions of career success: A social exchange perspective. *Journal of Business and Psychology, 15,* 419–438.

Erez, M. (1994). Toward a model of cross-cultural industrial and organizational psychology. In H. C. Triandis, M. D. Dunnette, & L. M. Hough (Eds.), *Handbook of industrial and organizational psychology* (2nd ed., Vol. 4, pp. 557–607). Palo Alto, CA: Consulting Psychologists Press.

Erez, M. (2011). Cross-cultural and global issues in organizational psychology. In S. Zedeck (Ed.), *APA handbook of industrial and organizational psychology* (Vol. 3, pp. 807–854). Washington, DC: American Psychological Association.

Erez, M., & Arad, R. (1986). Participative goal-setting: Social, motivational, and cognitive factors. *Journal of Applied Psychology, 71,* 591–597.

Erez, M., & Gati, E. (2004). A dynamic, multi-level model of culture: From the micro level of the individual to the macro level of a global culture. *Applied Psychology: An International Journal, 53,* 583–598.

Erez, M., & Zidon, I. (1984). Effect of goal acceptance on the relationship of goal difficulty to performance. *Journal of Applied Psychology, 69,* 69–78.

Erfurt, J. C., Foote, A., & Heirich, M. A. (1992). The cost-effectiveness of worksite wellness programs for hypertension, weight loss, smoking cessation, and exercise. *Personnel Psychology, 45,* 5–27.

Erhart, M. G., & Naumann, S. E. (2004). Organizational citizenship behavior in work groups: A group norms approach. *Journal of Applied Psychology, 89,* 960–974.

Erickson, R. J., Nichols, L., & Ritter, C. (2000). Family influences on absenteeism: Testing an expanded process model. *Journal of Vocational Behavior, 57,* 246–272.

Erkutlu, H. (2008). The impact of transformational leadership on organizational and leadership effectiveness: The Turkish case. *Journal of Management Development, 27(7),* 708–726.

Eschleman, K. J., Bowling, N. A., & Alarcon, G. M. (2010). A meta-analytic examination of hardiness. *International Journal of Stress Management, 17(4),* 277–307.

Esposito, M. D. (1992). There's more to writing job descriptions than complying with the ADA. *Employment Relations Today, 19,* 273–281.

Esser, J. K. (1998). Alive and well after 25 years: A review of groupthink research. *Organizational Behavior and Human Decision Processes, 73,* 116–141.

Etzion, D. (2003). Annual vacation: Duration of relief from job stressors and burnout. *Anxiety, Stress, and Coping, 16,* 213–226.

Evans, B. K., & Fischer, D. G. (1993). The nature of burnout: A study of the three-factor model of burnout in human service and non-human service samples. *Journal of Occupational and Organizational Psychology, 66,* 29–38.

Evans, C. R., & Dion, K. L. (1991). Group cohesion and performance: A meta-analysis. *Small Group Research, 22,* 175–186.

Evans, G. W., & Johnson, D. (2000). Stress and open-office noise. *Journal of Applied Psychology, 85,* 779–783.

Evers, W. J., Brouwers, A., & Tomic, W. (2006). A quasi-experimental study on management coaching effectiveness. *Consulting Psychology Journal: Practice and Research, 58,* 174–182.

Fagenson, E. A. (1989). The mentor advantage: Perceived career/job experiences of protégés vs. non-protégés. *Journal of Organizational Behavior, 10,* 309–320.

Fagenson, E. A., & Burke, W. W. (1990). The activities of organization development practitioners at the turn of the decade of the 1990s: A study of their predictions. *Group and Organization Studies, 15,* 366–380.

Fagenson, E. A., & Jackson, J. J. (1993). The status of women managers in the United States. *International Studies of Management and Organizations, 23,* 93–112.

Faletta, S. V., & Combs, W. (2002). Surveys as a tool for organization development and change. In J. Waclawski & A. H. Church (Eds.), *Organization development: A data-driven approach to organizational change* (pp. 78–102). San Francisco, CA: Jossey-Bass.

Fantuzzo, J. W., Riggio, R. E., Connelly, S., & Dimeff, L. A. (1989). Effects of reciprocal peer tutoring on academic achievement and psychological adjustment: A component analysis. *Journal of Educational Psychology, 81,* 173–177.

Farh, J., & Dobbins, G. H. (1989). Effects of comparative performance information on the accuracy of self-ratings and agreement between self- and supervisor ratings. *Journal of Applied Psychology, 74*, 606–610.

Farh, J., Dobbins, G. H., & Cheng, B. (1991). Cultural relativity in action: A comparison of self-ratings made by Chinese and U.S. workers. *Personnel Psychology, 44*, 129–147.

Farr, J. L. (1993). Informal performance feedback: Seeking and giving. In H. Schuler, J. L. Farr, & M. Smith (Eds.), *Personnel selection and assessment: Individual and organizational perspectives* (pp. 163–180). Hillsdale, NJ: Erlbaum.

Farrell, D., & Petersen, J. C. (1982). Patterns of political behavior in organizations. *Academy of Management Review, 7*, 403–412.

Fedor, D., Maslyn, J., Farmer, S., & Bettenhausen, K. (2008). The contributions of positive politics to prediction of employee reactions. *Journal of Applied Social Psychology, 38*, 76–96.

Feild, H. S., & Holley, W. H. (1982). The relationship of performance appraisal system characteristics to verdicts in selected employment discrimination cases. *Academy of Management Journal, 25*, 392–406.

Feldman, D. C. (1976a). A contingency theory of socialization. *Administrative Science Quarterly, 21*, 433–454.

Feldman, D. C. (1976b). A practical program for employee socialization. *Organizational Dynamics, 57*, 64–80.

Feldman, D. C. (1981). The multiple socialization of organization members. *Academy of Management Review, 6*, 309–318.

Feldman, D. C. (1984). The development and enforcement of group norms. *Academy of Management Review, 9*, 47–54.

Feldman, D. C. (1989). Socialization, resocialization, and training: Reframing the research agenda. In I. L. Goldstein (Ed.), *Training and development in organizations* (pp. 376–416). San Francisco, CA: Jossey-Bass.

Feldman, D. C., & Klich, N. R. (1991). Impression management and career strategies. In R. A. Giacalone & P. Rosenfeld (Eds.), *Applied impression management: How image-making affects managerial decisions* (pp. 67–80). Newbury Park, CA: Sage.

Feldman, J. M. (1981). Beyond attribution theory: Cognitive processes in performance appraisal. *Journal of Applied Psychology, 66*, 127–148.

Fenlason, K. J., & Beehr, T. A. (1994). Social support and occupational stress: Effects of talking to others. *Journal of Organizational Behavior, 15*, 157–175.

Ferris, G. R., Brand, J. F., Brand, S., Rowland, K. M., Gilmore, D. C., King, T. R., Kacmar, K. M., & Burton, C. A. (1993). Politics and control in organizations. In E. J. Lawler, B.Markovsky, J. O'Brien, & K. Heimer (Eds.), *Advances in group processes* (Vol. 10, pp. 83–111). Greenwich, CT: JAI Press.

Ferris, G. R., Frink, D. D., Galang, M. C., Zhou, J., Kacmar, K. M., & Howard, J. L. (1996). Perceptions of organizational politics: Prediction, stress-related implications, and outcomes. *Human Relations, 49*, 233–266.

Ferris, G. R., Frink, D. D., Gilmore, D. C., & Kacmar, K. M. (1994). Understanding as an antidote for the dysfunctional consequences of organizational politics as a stressor. *Journal of Applied Social Psychology, 24*, 1204–1220.

Ferris, G. R., & Hochwater, W. A. (2011). Organizational politics. In S. Zedeck (Ed.), *APA handbook of industrial and organizational psychology* (Vol. 3, pp. 435–459). Washington, DC: American Psychological Association.

Ferris, G. R., & Kacmar, K. M. (1992). Perceptions of organizational politics. *Journal of Management, 18*, 93–116.

Ferris, G. R., & King, T. R. (1991). Politics in human resources decisions: A walk on the dark side. *Organizational Dynamics, 20*, 59–71.

Ferris, G. R., Perrewé, P. L., Anthony, W. P., & Gilmore, D. C. (2000). Political skill at work. *Organizational Dynamics, 28*, 25–37.

Ferris, G. R., Russ, G. S., & Fandt, P. M. (1989). Politics in organizations. In R. A. Giacalone & P. Rosenfeld (Eds.), *Impression management in the organization* (pp. 143–170). Hillsdale, NJ: Erlbaum.

Ferris, G. R., Treadway, D. C., Kolodinsky, R. W., Hochwater, W. A., Kacmar, C. J., Douglas, C., & Frink, D. D. (2005). Development and validation of the Political Skill Inventory. *Journal of Management, 31*, 126–152.

Festinger, L. (1957). *A theory of cognitive dissonance.* Evanston, IL: Row, Peterson.

Fiedler, F. E. (1965). Engineer the job to fit the manager. *Harvard Business Review, 43*, 115.

Fiedler, F. E. (1967). *A theory of leadership effectiveness.* New York: McGraw-Hill.

Fiedler, F. E. (1973). How do you make leaders more effective? New answers to an old puzzle. *Organizational Dynamics, 54*, 3–18.

Fiedler, F. E., & Chemers, M. M. (1984). *Improving leadership effectiveness: The Leader Match concept* (rev. ed.). New York: Wiley.

Field, R. H. (1982). A test of the Vroom-Yetton normative model of leadership. *Journal of Applied Psychology, 67*, 523–532.

Field, R. H. G., & Andrews, J. P. (1998). Testing the incremental validity of the Vroom-Jago versus Vrooom-Yetton models of participation in decision making. *Journal of Behavioral Decision Making, 11*, 251–261.

Fine, M. G. (1991). New voices in the workplace: Research directions in multicultural communication. *The Journal of Business Communication, 23*, 259–275.

Fine, S. A., & Cronshaw, S. F. (1999). *Functional job analysis: A foundation for human resources management.* Mahwah, NJ: Erlbaum.

Fine, S. A., & Getkate, M. (1995). *Benchmark tasks for job analysis: A guide for Functional Job Analysis (FJA) scales.* Hillsdale, NJ: Erlbaum.

Fine, S. A., & Wiley, W. W. (1971). *An introduction to functional job analysis.* Kalamazoo, MI: W. E. Upjohn Institute.

Finegan, J. E. (2000). The impact of person and organizational values on organizational commitment. *Journal of Occupational and Organizational Psychology, 73*, 149–169.

Fisher, C. B. (2009). *Decoding the ethics code: A practical guide for psychologists* (2nd ed.). Thousand Oaks, CA: Sage.

Fisher, S. R., & White, M. A. (2000). Downsizing in a learning organization: Are there hidden costs? *Academy of Management Review, 25*, 244–251.

Fitzgerald, L. F., Drasgow, F., Hulin, C. L., Gelfand, M. J., & Magley, V. J. (1997). Antecedents and consequences of sexual harassment in organizations: A test of an integrated model. *Journal of Applied Psychology, 82*, 578–589.

Flanagan, J. C. (1954). The critical incidents technique. *Psychological Bulletin, 51*, 327–358.

Fleishman, E. A., & Harris, E. F. (1962). Patterns of leadership behavior related to employee grievances and turnover. *Personnel Psychology, 15*, 43–56.

Fletcher, C., & Perry, E. L. (2001). Performance appraisal and feedback: A consideration of national culture and a review of contemporary research and future trends. In N. Anderson, D. S. Ones, H. K. Sinangil, & C. Viswesvaran (Eds.), *Handbook of industrial, work, & organizational psychology* (pp. 127–144). London, UK: Sage.

Flint, D. H. (1999). The role of organizational justice in multi-source performance appraisal: Theory-based applications and directions for research. *Human Resource Management Review, 9,* 1–20.

Fodor, E. M. (1976). Group stress, authoritarian style of control, and use of power. *Journal of Applied Psychology, 61,* 313–318.

Forbes, R. J., & Jackson, P. R. (1980). Nonverbal behaviour and the outcome of selection interviews. *Journal of Occupational Psychology, 53,* 65–72.

Ford, J. K., & Noe, R. A. (1987). Self-assessed training needs: The effects of attitudes toward training, managerial level, and function. *Personnel Psychology, 40,* 39–53.

Ford, R. C., & Randolph, W. A. (1992). Cross-functional structures: A review and integration of matrix organizations and project management. *Journal of Management, 18,* 267–294.

Forsyth, D. R. (2006). *Group dynamics* (4th ed.). Pacific Grove, CA: Brooks/Cole.

Forsythe, S., Drake, M. F., & Cox, C. E. (1985). Influence of applicant's dress on interviewer's selection decisions. *Journal of Applied Psychology, 70,* 374–378.

Fox, S., & Spector, P. E. (1999). A model of work frustration-aggression. *Journal of Organizational Behavior, 20,* 915–931.

Fox, S., & Spector, P. E. (Eds.). (2005). *Counterproductive work behavior: Investigations of actors and targets.* Washington, DC: American Psychological Association.

Franke, R. H., & Kaul, J. D. (1978). The Hawthorne experiments: First statistical interpretation. *American Sociological Review, 43,* 623–643.

Fredericksen, N. (1962). Factors in in-basket performance. *Psychological Monographs, 76* (Entire issue no. 541).

Freeman, S. J. (1999). The gestalt of organizational downsizing: Downsizing strategies as packages of change. *Human Relations, 52,* 1505–1541.

French, J. L., & Rosenstein, J. (1984). Employee ownership, work attitudes, and power relationships. *Academy of Management Journal, 27,* 861–869.

French, J. R. P., & Caplan, R. D. (1972). Organizational stress and individual strain. In A. J. Marrow (Ed.), *The failure of success* (pp. 30–66). New York: AMACOM.

French, J. R. P., Caplan, R. D., & Harrison, R. V. (1982). *The mechanisms of job stress and strain.* Chichester, England: Wiley.

French, J. R. P., & Raven, B. H. (1959). The bases of social power. In D. Cartwright (Ed.), *Studies in social power* (pp. 150–167). Ann Arbor, MI: University of Michigan Press.

French, J. R. P., Rogers, W., & Cobb, S. (1974). A model of person-environment fit. In G. V. Coelho, D. A. Hamburgh, & J. E. Adams (Eds.), *Coping and adaptation.* New York: Basic Books.

French, W. L. (1969). Organization development objectives, assumptions, and strategies. *California Management Review, 12,* 23–46.

French, W. L., & Bell, C. H. (1990). *Organization development: Behavioral science interventions for organization improvement* (4th ed.). Englewood Cliffs, NJ: Prentice Hall.

Frese, M., Teng, E., & Wijnen, C. J. D. (1999). Helping to improve suggestion systems: Predictors of making suggestions in companies. *Journal of Organizational Behavior, 20,* 1139–1155.

Frese, M., & Zapf, D. (1988). Methodological issues in the study of work stress: Objective vs. subjective measurement of work stress and the question of longitudinal studies. In C. L. Cooper & R. Payne (Eds.), *Courses, coping and consequences of stress at work* (pp. 375–411). New York: Wiley.

Fried, Y. (1991). Meta-analytic comparison of the Job Diagnostic Survey and Job Characteristics Inventory as correlates of work satisfaction and performance. *Journal of Applied Psychology, 76,* 690–697.

Fried, Y., & Ferris, G. R. (1987). The validity of the job characteristics model: A review and meta-analysis. *Personnel Psychology, 40,* 287–322.

Friedlander, F. (1980). The facilitation of change in organizations. *Professional Psychology, 11,* 520–530.

Friedman, H. S., & Booth-Kewley, S. (1987). The "disease-prone personality": A meta-analytic view of the construct. *American Psychologist, 42,* 539–555.

Friedman, H. S., Hall, J. A., & Harris, M. J. (1985). Type A behavior, nonverbal expressive style, and health. *Journal of Personality and Social Psychology, 48,* 1299–1315.

Friedman, M., & Rosenman, R. H. (1974). *Type A behavior and your heart.* New York: Knopf.

Fritz, J. M. H., Arnett, R. C., & Conkel, M. (1999). Organizational ethical standards and organizational commitment. *Journal of Business Ethics, 20,* 289–299.

Frohman, M. A., Sashkin, M., & Kavanagh, M. J. (1976). Action research as applied to organization development. *Organization and Administrative Sciences, 7,* 129–142.

Frone, M. R. (2000). Interpersonal conflict at work and psychological outcomes: Testing a model among young workers. *Journal of Occupational Health Psychology, 5,* 246–255.

Frone, M. R. (2008). Are work stressors related to employee substance use? The importance of temporal context assessments of alcohol and illicit drug use. *Journal of Applied Psychology, 93(1),* 199–206.

Frone, M. R. (2011). Alcohol and illicit drug use in the workforce and workplace. In J. C. Quick & L. E. Tetrick (Eds.), *Handbook of occupational health psychology* (2nd ed., pp. 277–296). Washington, DC: American Psychological Association.

Frone, M. R., Russell, M., & Cooper, M. L. (1991). Relationship of work and family stressors to psychological distress: The independent moderating influence of social support, mastery, active coping, and self-focused attention. *Journal of Social Behavior and Personality, 6,* 227–250.

Fry, W., & Slocum, J. W. (1984). Technology, structure, and work-group effectiveness: A test of a contingency model. *Academy of Management Journal, 27,* 221–246.

Fu, P. P., & Yukl, G. (2000). Perceived effectiveness of influence tactics in the United States and China. *Leadership Quarterly, 11,* 251–266.

Furnham, A. (1997). Knowing and faking one's five-factor personality score. *Journal of Personality Assessment, 69,* 229–243.

Furnham, A. (2000). The brainstorming myth. *Business Strategy Review, 11,* 21–28.

Furnham, A., & Stringfield, P. (1994). Congruence of self and subordinate ratings of managerial practices as a correlate of supervisor evaluation. *Journal of Occupational and Organizational Psychology, 67,* 57–67.

Fussell, S. R., & Benimoff, N. I. (1995). Social and cognitive processes in interpersonal communication: Implications for advanced telecommunications technologies. *Human Factors, 37,* 228–250.

Gaertner, S. (2000). Structural determinants of job satisfaction and organizational commitment in turnover models. *Human Resource Management Review, 9,* 479–493.

Gaffney, S. (2005). Career development as a retention and succession planning tool. *Journal for Quality and Participation, 28(3),* 7–10.

Gagne, M., & Deci, E. L. (2005). Self-determination theory and work motivation. *Journal of Organizational Behavior, 26,* 331–362.

Gaines, J. H. (1980). Upward communication in industry: An experiment. *Human Relations, 33,* 929–942.

Gaines, J. H., & Jermier, J. M. (1983). Emotional exhaustion in a high stress organization. *Academy of Management Journal, 26,* 567–586.

Galaif, E. R., Newcomb, M. D., & Carmona, J. V. (2001). Prospective relationships between drug problems and work adjustment in a community sample of adults. *Journal of Applied Psychology, 86,* 337–350.

Galbraith, J. (1973). *Designing complex organizations.* Reading, MA: Addison-Wesley.

Galbraith, J. (1977). *Organization design.* Reading, MA: Addison-Wesley.

Gallois, C., Callan, V., & Palmer, J. M. (1992). The influence of applicant communication style and interviewer characteristics on hiring decisions. *Journal of Applied Social Psychology, 22,* 1041–1060.

Gallos, J. V. (Ed.). (2006). *Organization development.* San Francisco, CA: Jossey-Bass.

Gallupe, R. B., Bastianutti, L., & Cooper, W. H. (1991). Unblocking brainstorms. *Journal of Applied Psychology, 76,* 137–142.

Galvin, B. M., Balkundi, P., & Waldman, D. A. (2010). Spreading the word: The role of surrogates in charismatic leadership processes. *Academy of Management Review, 35(3),* 477–494.

Gamst, G., & Otten, C. M. (1992). Job satisfaction in high technology and traditional industry: Is there a difference? *The Psychological Record, 42,* 413–425.

Gandz, J., & Murray, U. V. (1980). The experience of workplace politics. *Academy of Management Journal, 23,* 237–251.

Ganster, D. C. (1986). Type A behavior and occupational stress. *Journal of Organizational Behavior Management, 8,* 61–84.

Ganster, D. C., Fox, M. L., & Dwyer, D. J. (2001). Explaining employees' health care costs: A prospective examination of stressful job demands, personal control, and physiological reactivity. *Journal of Applied Psychology, 86,* 954–964.

Ganster, D. C., Fusilier, M. R., & Mayes, B. T. (1986). Role of social support in the experience of stress at work. *Journal of Applied Psychology, 71,* 102–110.

Ganster, D. C., Mayes, B. T., Sime, W. E., & Tharp, G. D. (1982). Managing organizational stress: A field experiment. *Journal of Applied Psychology, 67,* 533–542.

Ganster, D. C., Schaubroeck, J., Sime, W. E., & Mayes, B. T. (1991). The nomological validity of the Type A personality among employed adults. *Journal of Applied Psychology, 76,* 143–168.

Gardner, B., Rose, J., Mason, O., Tyler, P., & Cushway, D. (2005). Cognitive therapy and behavioural coping in the management of work-related stress: An intervention study. *Work & Stress, 19,* 137–152.

Gardner, D. G., & Pierce, J. L. (1998). Self-esteem and self-efficacy within the organizational context: An empirical examination. *Group & Organization Management, 23,* 48–70.

Gatewood, R. D., Field, H. S., & Barrick, M. (2008). *Human resource selection* (6th ed.). Mason, OH: Thomson South-Western.

Gattiker, U. E., & Howg, L. (1990). Information technology and quality of work life: Comparing users with non-users. *Journal of Business and Psychology, 5,* 237–260.

Gaugler, B. B., Rosenthal, D. B., Thornton, G. C., & Bentson, C. (1987). Meta-analyses of assessment center validity. *Journal of Applied Psychology, 72,* 493–511.

Gavin, J. F. (1984). Survey feedback: The perspectives of science and practice. *Group and Organization Studies, 9,* 29–70.

Gellatly, I. R. (1995). Individual and group determinants of employee absenteeism: Test of a causal model. *Journal of Organizational Behavior, 16,* 469–485.

Georgesen, J. C., & Harris, M. J. (1998). Why's my boss always holding me down? A meta-analysis of power effects on performance evaluations. *Personality and Social Psychology Review, 2,* 183–195.

Gerstner, C. R., & Day, D. V. (1997). Meta-analytic review of leader-members exchange theory: Correlates and construct issues. *Journal of Applied Psychology, 82,* 827–844.

Geyer, A. L. J., & Steyrer, J. M. (1998). Transformational leadership and objective performance in banks. *Applied Psychology: An International Review, 47,* 397–420.

Ghiselli, E. E. (1973). The validity of aptitude tests in personnel selection. *Personnel Psychology, 26,* 461–477.

Ghorpade, J. V. (1988). *Job analysis: A handbook for the human resource director.* Englewood Cliffs, NJ: Prentice Hall.

Gibb, J. R. (1961). Defensive communication. *Journal of Communication, 11,* 81–84.

Gibby, R., & McCloy, R. A. (2011). Computerized adaptive testing. In N. Tippins & S. Adler (Eds.), *Technology enhanced assessments of talent.* San Francisco, CA: Wiley.

Gifford, R., Ng, C. F., & Wilkinson, M. (1985). Nonverbal cues in the employment interview: Links between applicant qualities and interviewer judgments. *Journal of Applied Psychology, 70,* 729–736.

Gilbert, J. A., & Ivancevich, J. M. (2000). A re-examination of organizational commitment. *Journal of Social Behavior and Personality, 14,* 385–396.

Gilbert, J. A., & Ivancevich, J. M. (2001). Effects of diversity management on attachment. *Journal of Applied Social Psychology, 31,* 1331–1349.

Gilbreth, F. B. (1916). Motion study in surgery. *Canadian Journal of Medicine and Surgery, 1,* 1–10.

Gillet, B., & Schwab, D. P. (1975). Convergent and discriminant validities of corresponding Job Descriptive Index and Minnesota Satisfaction Questionnaire scales. *Journal of Applied Psychology, 60,* 313–317.

Gilliland, S. W., & Langdon, J. C. (1998). Creating performance management systems that promote perceptions of fairness. In J. W. Smither (Ed.), *Performance appraisal: State of the art in practice* (pp. 209–243). San Francisco, CA: Jossey-Bass.

Gilmore, D. C., Ferris, G. R., Dulebohn, J. H., & Harrell-Cook, G. (1996). Organizational politics and employee attendance. *Group & Organization Management, 21,* 481–494.

Gist, M. E. (1987). Self-efficacy: Implications for organizational behavior and human resource management. *Academy of Management Review, 12,* 472–485.

Gist, M. E., Schwoerer, C., & Rosen, B. (1989). Effects of alternative training methods on self-efficacy and performance in computer software training. *Journal of Applied Psychology, 74,* 884–891.

Goethals, G. R. (2005). Nonverbal behavior and political leadership. In R. E. Riggio & R. S. Feldman (Eds.), *Applications of nonverbal communication* (pp. 95–115). Mahwah, NJ: Lawrence Erlbaum.

Goff, S. J., Mount, M. K., & Jamison, R. L. (1990). Employer supported child care, work/family conflict, and absenteeism: A field study. *Personnel Psychology, 43*, 793–809.

Goffin, R. D., & Gellatly, I. R. (2001). A multi-rater assessment of organizational commitment: Are self-report measures biased? *Journal of Organizational Behavior, 22*, 437–451.

Goldberg, C. B., & Waldman, D. A. (2000). Modeling employee absenteeism: Testing alternative measures and mediated effects based on job satisfaction. *Journal of Organizational Behavior, 21*, 665–676.

Goldman, R. B. (1976). *A work experiment: Six Americans in a Swedish plant.* New York: Ford Foundation.

Goldsmith, M., & Carter, L. (Eds.). (2010). *Best practices in talent management.* San Francisco, CA: Wiley.

Goldstein, I. L., & Ford, J. K. (2002). *Training in organizations: Needs assessment, development, and evaluation* (4th ed.). Belmont, CA: Wadsworth/Thomsen.

Goldstein, I. L., & Sorcher, M. A. (1974). *Changing supervisory behavior.* New York: Pergamon.

Golembiewski, R. T., Munzenrider, R. F., & Stevenson, J. G. (1986). *Stress in organizations: Toward a phase model of burnout.* New York: Praeger.

Gomez-Mejia, L. R., Welbourne, T. M., & Wiseman, R. M. (2000). The role of risk sharing and risk taking under gainsharing. *Academy of Management Review, 25*, 492–507.

Goodale, J. G. (1989). Effective employment interviewing. In R. W. Eder & G. R. Ferris (Eds.), *The employment interview: Theory, research, and practice* (pp. 307–323). Newbury Park, CA: Sage.

Gottfredson, L. S. (1986). Societal consequences of the g factor in employment. *Journal of Vocational Behavior, 29*, 293–450.

Gottlieb, J. Z. (1998). Understanding the role of organization development practitioners. *Research in Organizational Change and Development, 11*, 117–158.

Gough, H. G. (1984). A managerial potential scale for the California Psychological Inventory. *Journal of Applied Psychology, 69*, 233–240.

Gough, H. G. (1985). A work orientation scale for the California Psychological Inventory. *Journal of Applied Psychology, 70*, 505–513.

Gough, H. G. (1987). *California psychological inventory.* Palo Alto, CA: Consulting Psychologists Press.

Gouldner, A. W. (1960). The norm of reciprocity: A preliminary statement. *American Sociological Review, 25*, 161–178.

Graen, G. B. (1969). Instrumentality theory of work motivation: Some experimental results and suggested modifications. *Journal of Applied Psychology Monograph, 53* (Vol. 2, Pt. 2).

Graen, G. B. (1976). Role-making processes within complex organizations. In M. D. Dunnette (Ed.), *Handbook of industrial and organizational psychology* (pp. 1201–1245). Chicago, IL: Rand McNally.

Graen, G. B., Novak, M., & Sommerkamp, P. (1982). The effects of leader-member exchange and job design on productivity and satisfaction: Testing a dual attachment mode. *Organizational Behavior and Human Performance, 30*, 109–131.

Graen, G. B., & Scandura, T. A. (1985). *Leader-member exchange scale–17.* Cincinnati, OH: University of Cincinnati.

Graen, G. B., Scandura, T. A., & Graen, M. R. (1986). A field experimental test of the moderating effects of growth need strength on productivity. *Journal of Applied Psychology, 71*, 484–491.

Graen, G. B., & Uhl-Bien, M. (1995). Relationship-based approach to leadership: Development of leader-member exchange (LMX) theory of leadership over 25 years: Applying a multi-level multi-domain perspective. *Leadership Quarterly, 6*, 219–247.

Graham, J. W. (1991). An essay on organizational citizenship behavior. *Employee Responsibilities and Rights Journal, 4*, 249–270.

Graham-Moore, B., & Ross, T. L. (1990). *Gainsharing: Plans for improving performance.* Washington, DC: Bureau of National Affairs.

Grandey, A. A. (2001). Family friendly policies: Organizational justice perceptions of need-based allocations. In R. Cropanzano (Ed.), *Justice in the workplace: From theory to practice* (pp. 145–173). Mahwah, NJ: Erlbaum.

Granrose, C. S. (1997). Cross-cultural socialization of Asian employees in U.S. organizations. In C. S. Granrose & S. Oskamp (Eds.), *Cross-cultural work groups* (pp. 186–211). Thousand Oaks, CA: Sage.

Graves, L. M., & Karren, R. J. (1996). The employee selection interview: A fresh look at an old problem. *Human Resource Management, 35*, 163–180.

Gray, B., & Ariss, S. S. (1985). Politics and strategic change across organizational life cycles. *Academy of Management Review, 10*, 707–723.

Gray, J. L., & Starke, F. A. (1984). *Organizational behavior: Concepts and applications* (3rd ed.). Columbus, OH: Charles E. Merrill.

Greenberg, J. (1982). Approaching equity and avoiding inequity in groups and organizations. In J. Greenberg & R. L. Cohen (Eds.), *Equity and justice in social behavior.* New York: Academic Press.

Greenberg, J. (1986). Determinants of perceived fairness of performance evaluations. *Journal of Applied Psychology, 71*, 340–342.

Greenberg, J. (1987). A taxonomy of organizational justice theories. *Academy of Management Review, 12*, 9–22.

Greenberg, J. (1990). Employee theft as a reaction to underpayment inequity: The hidden cost of pay cuts. *Journal of Applied Psychology, 75*, 561–568.

Greenberg, J., & Baron, R. A. (1997). *Behavior in organizations* (6th ed.). Upper Saddle River, NJ: Prentice Hall.

Greenberg, J., & Ornstein, S. (1983). High status job title as compensation for underpayment: A test of equity theory. *Journal of Applied Psychology, 68*, 285–297.

Greenberger, D. B., & Strasser, S. (1986). Development and application of a model of personal control in organizations. *Academy of Management Review, 11*, 164–177.

Greenhaus, J. H., & Beutell, N. J. (1985). Sources of conflict between work and family roles. *Academy of Management Review, 10*, 76–88.

Greenlaw, P. S., & Kohl, J. P. (1993). Now is the time to update salaries and job descriptions. *Journal of Compensation and Benefits, 9*, 61–64.

Greenwood, R., & Hinings, C. R. (1996). Understanding radical organizational change: Bringing together the old and the new institutionalism. *Academy of Management Review, 21*, 1022–1054.

Greguras, G. J., & Robie, C. (1997, April). *Reliability of 360-degree feedback ratings.* Paper presented at the 12th annual conference of the Society for Industrial and Organizational Psychology, St. Louis, MO.

Griffeth, R. W., & Gaertner, S. (2001). A role for equity theory in the turnover process: An empirical test. *Journal of Applied Social Psychology, 31,* 1017–1037.

Griffeth, R. W., Hom, P. W., & Gaertner, S. (2000). A meta-analysis of antecedents and correlates of employee turnover: Update, moderator tests, and research implications for the new millennium. *Journal of Management, 26,* 463–488.

Griggs v. Duke Power Co. (1971). 401 U.S. 424, 3EPD p8137, 3 FEP Cases 175.

Grove, S. J., & Fisk, R. P. (1989). Impression management in services marketing: A dramaturgical perspective. In C. S. Granrose & S. Oskamp (Eds.), *Cross-cultural work groups* (pp. 427–438). Thousand Oaks, CA: Sage.

Grunberg, L., Anderson-Connolly, R., & Greenberg, E. S. (2000). Surviving layoffs: The effects on organizational commitment and job performance. *Work and Occupations, 27,* 7–31.

Guiniven, J. E. (2001). The lessons of survivor literature in communicating decisions to downsize. *Journal of Business and Technical Communication, 15,* 53–71.

Guion, R. M. (1965). *Personnel testing.* New York: McGraw-Hill.

Guion, R. M., & Gibson, W. M. (1988). Personnel selection and placement. *Annual Review of Psychology, 39,* 349–374.

Guion, R. M., & Gottier, R. J. (1965). Validity of personality measures in personnel selection. *Personnel Psychology, 18,* 135–164.

Gully, S. M., Devine, D. J., & Whitney, D. J. (1995). A meta-analysis of cohesion and performance: Effects of level of analysis and task interdependence. *Small Group Research, 26,* 497–520.

Gully, S. M., Incalcaterra, K. A., Joshi, A., & Beaubien, J. M. (2002). A meta-analysis of team-efficacy, potency, and performance: Interdependence and levels of analysis as moderators of observed relationships. *Journal of Applied Psychology, 87,* 819–832.

Gunn, E. (1995). Mentoring: The democratic version. *Training, 32,* 64–67.

Gupta, N., & Beehr, T. A. (1979). Job stress and employee behaviors. *Organizational Behavior and Human Performance, 23,* 373–387.

Guthrie, J. P. (2000). Alternative pay practices and employee turnover: An organization economics perspective. *Group & Organizational Management, 25,* 419–439.

Guthrie, J. P., & Hollensbe, E. C. (2004). Group incentives and performance: A study of spontaneous goal setting, goal choice, and commitment. *Journal of Management, 30,* 263–284.

Guzzo, R. A., Jette, R. D., & Katzell, R. A. (1985). The effects of psychologically based intervention programs on worker productivity: A meta-analysis. *Personnel Psychology, 38,* 275–292.

Gyekye, S. A., & Salminen, S. (2005). Are "good soldiers" safety conscious? An examination of the relationship between organizational citizenship behaviors and perception of workplace safety. *Social Behavior and Personality, 33,* 805–820.

Gyllenhammer, P. (1977). *People at work.* Reading, MA: Addison-Wesley.

Haccoun, R. R., & Jeanrie, C. (1995). Self reports of work absence as a function of personal attitudes towards absence, and perceptions of the organisation. *Applied Psychology: An International Review, 44,* 155–170.

Hacker, C. A. (2004). New employee orientation: Make it pay dividends for years to come. *Information Systems Management, 21(1),* 89–93.

Hackett, R. D. (1990). Age, tenure, and employee absenteeism. *Human Relations, 43,* 601–619.

Hackett, R. D., & Bycio, P. (1996). An evaluation of employee absenteeism as a coping mechanism among hospital nurses. *Journal of Occupational and Organizational Psychology, 69,* 327–328.

Hackett, R. D., & Guion, R. M. (1985). A reevaluation of the absenteeism-job satisfaction relationship. *Organizational Behavior and Human Decision Processes, 35,* 340–381.

Hackman, J. R. (1990). *Groups that work (and those that don't).* San Francisco, CA: Jossey-Bass.

Hackman, J. R. (1992). Group influences on individuals in organizations. In M. D. Dunnette & L. M. Hough (Eds.), *Handbook of industrial and organizational psychology* (Vol. 3, 2nd ed., pp. 194–267). Palo Alto, CA: Consulting Psychologists Press.

Hackman, J. R. (1998). Why teams don't work. In R. S. Tindale (Ed.), *Theory and research on small groups* (pp. 245–267). New York: Plenum Press.

Hackman, J. R., & Oldham, G. R. (1975). Development of the job diagnostic survey. *Journal of Applied Psychology, 60,* 159–170.

Hackman, J. R., & Oldham, G. R. (1976). Motivation through the design of work: Test of a theory. *Organizational Behavior and Human Performance, 16,* 250–279.

Hackman, J. R., & Oldham, G. R. (1980). *Work redesign.* Reading, MA: Addison-Wesley.

Hakstian, A. R., & Cattell, R. B. (1975–1982). *Comprehensive ability battery.* Champaign, IL: Institute for Personality and Ability Testing.

Hall, R. J., Workman, J. W., & Marchioro, C. A. (1998). Sex, task, and behavioral flexibility effects on leadership perceptions. *Organizational Behavior and Human Decision Processes, 74,* 1–32.

Halpern, D. F., & Murphy, S. E. (Eds.). (2005). *From work-family balance to work-family interaction: Changing the metaphor.* Mahwah, NJ: Lawrence Erlbaum Associates.

Halpert, J. A., Wilson, M. L., & Hickman, J. L. (1993). Pregnancy as a source of bias in performance appraisals. *Journal of Organizational Behavior, 14,* 649–663.

Halpin, A. W., & Winer, B. J. (1957). A factorial study of the leader behavior descriptions. In R. M. Stogdill & A. E. Coons (Eds.), *Leader behavior: Its description and measurement.* Columbus, OH: Ohio State University Bureau of Business Research.

Hammer, T. H., & Landau, J. C. (1981). Methodological issues in the use of absence data. *Journal of Applied Psychology, 66,* 574–581.

Hamner, W. C., & Hamner, E. P. (1976). Behavior modification on the bottom line. *Organizational Dynamics, 4,* 8–21.

Hanlon, S. C., Meyer, D. G., & Taylor, R. R. (1994). Consequences of gainsharing: A field experiment revisited. *Group & Organization Management, 19,* 87–111.

Hannum, K. M., Martineau, J. W., & Reinelt, C. (Eds.). (2007). *The handbook of leadership development evaluation.* Hoboken, NJ: John Wiley & Sons.

Hanson, T. J., & Balestreri-Spero, J. C. (1985). An alternative to interviews. *Personnel Journal, 64,* 114–123.

Harder, J. W. (1991). Equity theory versus expectancy theory: The case of major league baseball free agents. *Journal of Applied Psychology, 76,* 458–464.

Hare, A. P. (1976). *Handbook of small group research* (2nd ed.). New York: Free Press.

Harris, M. M. (1989). Reconsidering the employment interview: A review of recent literature and suggestions for future research. *Personnel Psychology, 42,* 691–726.

Harris, M. M., & Schaubroeck, J. (1988). A meta-analysis of self-supervisor, self-peer, and peer-supervisor ratings. *Personnel Psychology, 41,* 43–62.

Harris, R., Simons, M., Willis, P., & Carden, P. (2003). Exploring complementarity in on- and off-job training for apprenticeships. *International Journal of Training and Development, 7,* 82–92.

Harris, T. E. (1993). *Applied organizational communication: Perspectives, principles, and pragmatics.* Hillsdale, NJ: Erlbaum.

Harrison, D. A., & Martocchio, J. J. (1998). Time for absenteeism: A 20-year review of origins, offshoots, and outcomes. *Journal of Management, 24,* 305–350.

Harrison, D. A., & McLaughlin, M. E. (1993). Cognitive processes in self-report responses: Tests of item context effects in work attitude measures. *Journal of Applied Psychology, 78,* 129–140.

Harrison, J. K. (1992). Individual and combined effects of behavior modeling and the cultural assimilator in cross-cultural management training. *Journal of Applied Psychology, 77,* 952–962.

Harrison, T. M. (1985). Communication and participative decision making: An exploratory study. *Personnel Psychology, 38,* 93–116.

Hart, P. M., & Cooper, C. L. (2001). Occupational stress: Toward a more integrated framework. In N. Anderson, D. S. Ones, H. K. Sinangil, & C. Viswesvaran (Eds.), *Handbook of industrial, work and organizational psychology* (Vol.2, pp. 93–114). London, UK: Sage.

Hart, R. K. (2001). Constituting relationships in communication: An interdisciplinary approach to understanding peer relationships in geographically dispersed teams. In M. M. Beyerlein, D. A. Johnson, & S. T. Beyerlein (Eds.), *Virtual teams* (pp. 85–106). New York: Elsevier/JAI Press.

Härtel, C. E. J. (1998). Vantage 2000: Recent advances in diversity research—When diversity has positive outcomes for organizations and when it does not. *The Industrial-Organizational Psychologist, 36,* 57–60.

Härtel, C. E. J., Ashkanasy, N. M., & Zerbe, W. (Eds.). (2005). *Emotions in organizational behavior.* Mahwah, NJ: Lawrence Erlbaum Associates.

Härtel, C. E. J., Zerbe, W., & Ashkanasy, N. M. (Eds.). (2005). *Emotions in organizational behavior.* Mahwah, NJ: Erlbaum.

Harvey, R. J. (1991). Job analysis. In M. D. Dunnette & L. M. Hough (Eds.), *Handbook of industrial and organizational psychology* (2nd ed., Vol. 2, pp. 71–163). Palo Alto, CA: Consulting Psychologists Press.

Harvey, S., Blouin, C., & Stout, D. (2006). Proactive personality as a moderator of outcomes for young workers experiencing conflict at work. *Personality and Individual Differences, 40,* 1063–1074.

Hater, J. J., & Bass, B. M. (1988). Supervisors' evaluations and subordinates' perceptions of transformational and transactional leadership. *Journal of Applied Psychology, 73,* 695–702.

Hathaway, S. R., & McKinley, J. C. (1970). *MMPI: Minnesota multiphasic personality inventory.* Minneapolis, MN: University of Minnesota Press.

Hauenstein, N. M. A. (1992). An information-processing approach to leniency in performance judgments. *Journal of Applied Psychology, 77,* 485–493.

Hauenstein, N. M. A. (1998). Training raters to increase the accuracy of appraisals and the usefulness of feedback. In J. W. Smither (Ed.), *Performance appraisal: State of the art in practice* (pp. 404–442). San Francisco, CA: Jossey-Bass.

Haworth, C. L., & Levy, P. E. (2001). The importance of instrumentality beliefs in the prediction of organizational citizenship behaviors. *Journal of Vocational Behavior, 59,* 64–75.

Haynes, S. G., Feinleib, M., Levine, S., Scotch, N. A., & Kannel, W. B. (1978). The relationship of psychosocial factors to coronary heart disease in the Framingham study. II. Prevalence of coronary heart disease. *American Journal of Epidemiology, 107,* 384–402.

Heaney, C. A., Price, R. H., & Rafferty, J. (1995). Increasing coping resources at work: A field experiment to increase social support, improve work team functioning, and enhance employee mental health. *Journal of Organizational Behavior, 16,* 335–353.

Heath, C. (1999). On the social psychology of agency relationships: Lay theories of motivation overemphasize extrinsic incentives. *Organizational Behavior and Human Decision Processes, 78,* 25–62.

Hedge, J. W., Borman, W. C., & Lammlein, S. E. (2006). *The aging workforce: Realities, myths, and implications for organizations.* Washington, DC: American Psychological Association.

Hedge, J. W., & Kavanagh, M. J. (1988). Improving the accuracy of performance evaluations: Comparison of three methods of performance appraiser training. *Journal of Applied Psychology, 73,* 68–73.

Heidemeier, H., and Moser, K. (2009). Self–other agreement in job performance ratings: A meta-analytic test of a process model. *Journal of Applied Psychology, 94*(2), 353–370.

Heilman, M. E., & Saruwatari, L. R. (1979). When beauty is beastly: The effects of appearance and sex on evaluations of job applicants for managerial and nonmanagerial jobs. *Organizational Behavior and Human Performance, 23,* 360–372.

Helmreich, R. L., Merritt, A. C., & Wilhelm, J. A. (1999). The evolution of crew resource management training in commercial aviation. *International Journal of Aviation Psychology, 9,* 19–32.

Hemingway, M. A., & Smith, C. S. (1999). Organizational climate and occupational stressors as predictors of withdrawal behaviours and injuries in nurses. *Journal of Occupational and Organizational Psychology, 72,* 285–299.

Hempel, J. (2005). Why the boss really had to say goodbye. *Business Week* (July 4, 2005), 10.

Heneman, R. L., & Wexley, K. N. (1983). The effects of time delay in rating and amount of information observed in performance rating accuracy. *Academy of Management Journal, 26,* 677–686.

Henley, N. M. (1977). *Body politics: Power, sex, and nonverbal communication.* Englewood Cliffs, NJ: Prentice Hall.

Herd, J. A. (1988). Physiological indices of job stress. In J. J. Hurrell, L. R. Murphy, S. L., Sauter, & C. L. Cooper (Eds.), *Occupational stress issues and developments in research* (pp. 124–154). Philadelphia, PA: Taylor & Francis.

Hermelin, E. Lievens, F., & Robertson, I. T. (2007). The validity of assessment centres for the prediction of supervisory performance ratings: A meta-analysis. *International Journal of Selection and Assessment, 15(4),* 405–411.

Hersey, R. (1966). Grapevine—Here to stay but not beyond control. *Personnel, 43,* 62–66.

Hertel, G., Konradt, U., & Orlikowski, B. (2004). Managing distance by interdependence: Goal setting, task interdependence, and team-based rewards in virtual teams. *European Journal of Work and Organizational Psychology, 13*, 1–28.

Herzberg, F. (1966). *Work and the nature of man.* Cleveland, OH: World.

Herzberg, F., Mausner, B., & Snyderman, B. B. (1959*). The motivation to work.* New York: Wiley.

Hicks, W. D., & Klimoski, R. J. (1981). The impact of flextime on employee attitudes. *Academy of Management Journal, 24*, 333–341.

Hickson, D. J., Hinings, C. R., Less, C. A., Schneck, R. E., & Pennings, J. M. (1971). A strategic contingencies theory of intraorganizational power. *Administrative Science Quarterly, 16*, 216–229.

Higgins, C. A., & Judge, T. A. (2004). The effect of applicant influence tactics on recruiter perceptions of fit and hiring recommendations: A field study. *Journal of Applied Psychology, 89*, 622–632.

Higgins, C. A., Judge, T. A., & Ferris, G. R. (2003). Influence tactics and work outcomes: A meta-analysis. *Journal of Organizational Behavior, 24*, 89–106.

Highhouse, S., & Becker, A. S. (1993). Facet measures and global job satisfaction. *Journal of Business and Psychology, 8*, 117–127.

Hill, G. W. (1982). Group versus individual performance: Are N+1 heads better than one? *Psychological Bulletin, 89*, 517–539.

Hilton, T. F., & Hertzbach, A. (1997). *Organizational culture reactions to upward feedback.* Washington, DC: Federal Aviation Administration.

Hinds, P. J., Patterson, M., & Pfeffer, J. (2001). Bothered by abstraction: The effect of expertise on knowledge transfer and subsequent novice performance. *Journal of Applied Psychology, 86*, 1232–1243.

Hinkin, T. R., & Schriesheim, C. A. (1989). Development and application of new scales to measure French and Raven (1959) bases of social power. *Journal of Applied Psychology, 74*, 561–567.

Hinkin, T. R., & Schriesheim, C. A. (1994). An examination of subordinate-perceived relationships between leader reward and punishment behavior and leader bases of power. *Human Relations, 47*, 779–800.

Hobson, C. J., & Delunas, L. (2001). National norms and life-even frequencies for the revised Social Readjustment Rating Scale. *International Journal of Stress Management, 8*, 299–314.

Hochschild, A. R. (1983). *The managed heart: Commercialization of human feeling.* Berkeley, CA: University of California Press.

Hochwater, W. A., Perrewé, P. L., Ferris, G. R., & Brymer, R. A. (1999). Job satisfaction and performance: The moderating effects of value attainment and affective disposition. *Journal of Vocational Behavior, 54*, 296–313.

Hochwater, W. A., Witt, L. A., & Kacmar, K. M. (2000). Perceptions of organizational politics as a moderator of the relationship between conscientiousness and job performance. *Journal of Applied Psychology, 85*, 472–478.

Hocker, J. L., & Wilmot, W. W. (1985*). Interpersonal conflict* (2nd ed.). Dubuque, IA: Brown.

Hoffman, C. C., Nathan, B. R., & Holden, L. M. (1991). A comparison of validation criteria: Objective versus subjective performance measures and self- versus supervisor ratings. *Personnel Psychology, 44*, 601–619.

Hofstede, G. (1980). *Culture's consequences: International differences in work-related values.* Beverly Hills, CA: Sage.

Hofstede, G. (1997). *Cultures and organizations: Software of the mind.* New York: McGraw-Hill.

Hofstede, G., Neuijen, B., Ohayv, D., & Sanders, G. (1990). Measuring organizational cultures: A qualitative and quantitative study across twenty cases. *Administrative Science Quarterly, 35*, 286–316.

Hogan, R., & Hogan, J. (1985). *Hogan Personnel Selection Series.* Minneapolis, MN: National Computer Systems.

Hogan, R., Raskin, R., & Fazzini, D. (1990). The dark side of charisma. In K. E. Clark & M. B. Clark (Eds.), *Measures of leadership* (pp. 171–184). West Orange, NJ: Leadership Library of America.

Hollander, E. P. (1978). *Leadership dynamics: A practical guide to effective relationships.* New York: Free Press.

Hollander, E. P. (1985). Leadership and power. In G. Lindzey & E. Aronson (Eds.), *The handbook of social psychology* (3rd ed., pp. 485–538). New York: Random House.

Hollenbeck, J. R. (1990). The past, present, and future of assessment centers. *The Industrial-Organizational Psychologist, 28*, 13–17.

Hollenbeck, J. R., DeRue, D. S., & Guzzo, R. (2004). Bridging the gap between I/O research and HR practice: Improving team composition, team training, and team task design. *Human Resource Management, 43*, 353–366.

Hollenbeck, J. R., & Williams, C. R. (1986). Turnover functionality versus turnover frequency: A note on work attitudes and organizational effectiveness. *Journal of Applied Psychology, 71*, 606–611.

Holmes, T. H., & Rahe, R. H. (1967). The Social Readjustment Rating Scale. *Journal of Psychosomatic Research, 11*, 213–218.

Hom, P. W., Griffeth, R. W., Palich, L. E., & Bracker, J. S. (1998). An exploratory investigation into theoretical mechanisms underlying realistic job previews. *Personnel Psychology, 61*, 421–451.

Honeywell-Johnson, J. A., & Dickinson, A. M. (1999). Small group incentives: A review of the literature. *Journal of Organizational Behavior Management, 19*, 89–120.

Hooijberg, R. (1996). A multidirectional approach toward leadership: An extension of the concept of behavioral complexity. *Human Relations, 49*, 917–946.

Hopkins, A. (1990). Stress, the quality of work, and repetition strain injury in Australia. *Work & Stress, 4*, 129–138.

Hough, L. (1998). Personality at work: Issues and evidence. In M. D. Hakel (Ed.), *Beyond multiple choice: Evaluating alternatives to traditional testing for selection* (pp. 131–166). Mahwah, NJ: Erlbaum.

Houkes, I., Janssen, P. P. M., de Jonge, J., & Bakker, A. B. (2004). Specific determinants of intrinsic work motivation, emotional exhaustion and turnover intention: A multisample longitudinal study. *Journal of Occupational and Organizational Psychology, 76*, 427–450.

House, J. S. (1981). *Work stress and social support.* Reading, MA: Addison-Wesley.

House, R. J. (1971). A path-goal theory of leader effectiveness. *Administrative Science Quarterly, 1*, 321–338.

House, R. J. (1977). A 1976 theory of charismatic leadership. In J. G. Hunt & L. L. Larsen (Eds.), *Leadership: The cutting edge* (pp. 189–207). Carbondale, IL: Southern Illinois University Press.

House, R. J. (1996). Path-goal theory of leadership: Lessons, legacy, and a reformulated theory. *Leadership Quarterly, 7*, 323–352.

House, R. J., & Dessler, G. (1974). The path-goal theory of leadership: Some post hoc and a priori tests. In J. G. Hunt & L. L. Larsen (Eds.), *Contingency approaches to leadership* (pp. 29–55). Carbondale, IL: Southern Illinois University Press.

House, R. J., Hanges, P. J., Javidan, M., Dorfman, P. W., & Gupta, V. (Eds.). (2004). *Culture, leadership, and organizations: The GLOBE study of 62 societies.* Thousand Oaks, CA: Sage.

House, R. J., & Mitchell, T. (1974). Path-goal theory of leadership. *Journal of Contemporary Business, 3,* 81–98.

House, R. J., & Singh, J. V. (1987). Organizational behavior: Some new directions for I/O psychology. *Annual Review of Psychology, 38,* 669–718.

House, R. J., Spangler, W. D., & Woycke, J. (1991). Personality and charisma in the U.S. presidency: A psychological theory of leader effectiveness. *Administrative Science Quarterly, 36,* 364–396.

Houston, W. M., Raymond, M. R., & Svec, J. C. (1991). Adjustments for rater effects in performance assessment. *Applied Psychological Measurement, 15,* 409–421.

Howard, A. (1997). A reassessment of assessment centers: Challenges for the 21st century. In R. E. Riggio & B. T. Mayes (Eds.), *Assessment centers: Research and applications* (pp. 13–52). Corte Madera, CA: Select Press.

Howard, G. S., & Dailey, P. R. (1979). Response-shift bias: A source of contamination of self-report measures. *Journal of Applied Psychology, 64,* 144–150.

Howell, J. M., & Avolio, B. J. (1993). Transformational leadership, transactional leadership, locus of control, and support for innovation: Key predictors of consolidated business unit performance. *Journal of Applied Psychology, 78,* 891–902.

Howell, J. M., & Hall-Merenda, K. E. (1999). The ties that bind: The impact of leader-member exchange, transformational and transactional leadership, and distance on predicting follower performance. *Journal of Applied Psychology, 84,* 680–694.

Howell, W. C., & Cooke, N. J. (1989). Training the human information processor: A look at cognitive models. In I. Goldstein (Ed.), *Training and development in work organizations* (pp. 121–183). New York: Jossey-Bass.

Hu, C., Su, H., & Chen, C. (2007). The effect of person-organization fit feedback via recruitment web sites on applicant attraction. *Computers in Human Behavior, 23,* 2509–2523.

Huber, G. P. (2011). Organizations: Theory, design, future. In S. Zedeck (Ed.), *APA handbook of industrial and organizational psychology, Vol. 1: Building and developing the organization* (pp. 117–160). Washington, DC: American Psychological Association.

Huffcutt, A. I., & Arthur, W. (1994). Hunter and Hunter (1984) revisited: Interview validity for entry-level jobs. *Journal of Applied Psychology, 79,* 184–190.

Huffcutt, A. I., Conway, J. M., Roth, P. L., & Stone, N. J. (2001). Identification and meta-analytic assessment of psychological constructs measured in employment interviews. *Journal of Applied Psychology, 86,* 897–913.

Huffcutt, A. I., Roth, P. L., & McDaniel, M. A. (1996). A meta-analytic investigation of cognitive ability in employment interview evaluations: Moderating characteristics and implications for incremental validity. *Journal of Applied Psychology, 81,* 459–473.

Huffcutt, A. I., & Woehr, D. J. (1999). Further analysis of employment interview validity: A quantitative evaluation of interviewer-related structuring methods. *Journal of Organizational Behavior, 20,* 549–560.

Hughes, G. L., & Prien, E. P. (1989). Evaluation of task and job skill linkage judgements used to develop test specifications. *Personnel Psychology, 42,* 283–292.

Hughes, R. L., Ginnett, R. C., & Curphy, G. J. (1996). *Leadership: Enhancing the lessons of experience* (2nd ed.). Chicago, IL: Irwin.

Hulsheger, U. R., Lang, J. W. B., & Maier, G. W. (2010). Emotional labor, strain, and performance: Testing reciprocal relationships in a longitudinal panel study. *Journal of Occupational Health Psychology, 15(4),* 505–521.

Hult, C. (2005). Organizational commitment and person-environment fit in six Western countries. *Organization Studies, 26,* 249–270.

Hunt, G. T. (1980). *Communication skills in the organization.* Englewood Cliffs, NJ: Prentice Hall.

Hunter, J. E., & Hunter, R. F. (1984). Validity and utility of alternative predictors of job performance. *Psychological Bulletin, 96,* 72–98.

Hunter, J. E., & Schmidt, F. L. (1982). Fitting people to jobs: The impact of personnel selection on national productivity. In M. D. Dunnette & E. A. Fleishman (Eds.), *Human performance and productivity: Human capability assessment* (pp. 233–284). Hillsdale, NJ: Erlbaum.

Hurrell, J. J., Murphy, L. R., Sauater, S. L., & Cooper, C. L. (Eds.). (1988). *Occupational stress issues and developments in research.* Philadelphia, PA: Taylor & Francis.

Huseman, R. C., Hatfield, J. D., & Miles, E. W. (1987). A new perspective on equity theory: The equity sensitivity construct. *Academy of Management Review, 12,* 222–234.

Hyland, A. M., & Muchinsky, P. M. (1991). Assessment of the structural validity of Holland's model with job analysis (PAQ) information. *Journal of Applied Psychology, 76,* 75–80.

Ilgen, D. R., Barnes-Farrell, J. L., & McKellin, D. B. (1993). Performance appraisal process research in the 1980s: What has it contributed to appraisals in use? *Organizational Behavior and Human Decision Processes, 54,* 321–368.

Ilgen, D. R., Fisher, C. D., & Taylor, M. S. (1979). Consequences of individual feedback on behavior in organizations. *Journal of Applied Psychology, 64,* 349–371.

Ilgen, D. R., & Hollenback, J. H. (1977). The role of job satisfaction in absence behavior. *Organizational Behavior and Human Performance, 19,* 148–161.

Ilies, R., Hauserman, N., Schwochau, S., & Stibal, J. (2003). Reported incidence rates of work-related sexual harassment in the United States: Using meta-analysis to explain reported rate disparities. *Personnel Psychology, 56,* 607–631.

Ilies, R., Scott, B. A., & Judge, T. A. (2006). The interactive effects of personal traits and experienced states on intraindividual patterns of citizenship behavior. *Academy of Management Journal, 49,* 561–575.

Imada, A. S., & Hakel, M. D. (1977). Influence of nonverbal communication and rater proximity on impressions and decisions in simulated employment interviews. *Journal of Applied Psychology, 62,* 295–300.

Ingate, M. (1992). ADA: We assume we will still be testing. *The Industrial-Organizational Psychologist, 30,* 35–38.

Ironson, G. H., Smith, P. C., Brannick, M. T., Gibson, W. M., & Paul, K. B. (1989). Construction of a job in general scale: A comparison of global, composite, and specific measures. *Journal of Applied Psychology, 74,* 193–200.

Isaac, R. G., Zerbe, W. J., & Pitt, D. C. (2001). Leadership and motivation: The effective application of expectancy theory. *Journal of Managerial Issues, 13(2),* 212–226.

Isenberg, D. J. (1986). Group polarization: A critical review. *Journal of Personality and Social Psychology, 50,* 1141–1151.

Ivancevich, J. M. (1979). Longitudinal study of the effects of rater training on psychometric error in ratings. *Journal of Applied Psychology, 64,* 502–508.

Ivancevich, J. M. (1982). Subordinates' reactions to performance appraisal interviews: A test of feedback and goal-setting techniques. *Journal of Applied Psychology, 67,* 581–587.

Ivancevich, J. M., & Gilbert, J. A. (2000). Diversity management: Time for a new approach. *Public Personnel Management, 29,* 75–92.

Ivancevich, J. M., & Matteson, M. T. (1980). *A managerial perspective: Stress and work.* Glenview, IL: Scott Foresman.

Ivancevich, J. M., Matteson, M. T., & Preston, C. (1982). Occupational stress, Type A behavior, and physical well-being. *Academy of Management Journal, 25,* 373–391.

Iverson, R. D., & Deery, S. J. (2001). Understanding the "personological" basis of employee withdrawal: The influence of affective disposition on employee tardiness, early departure, and absenteeism. *Journal of Applied Psychology, 86,* 856–866.

Iverson, R. D., Olekalns, M., & Erwin, P. J. (1998). Affectivity, organizational stressors, and absenteeism: A causal model of burnout and its consequences. *Journal of Vocational Behavior, 52,* 1–23.

Jablin, F. M. (1979). Superior–subordinate communication: The state of the art. *Psychological Bulletin, 86,* 1201–1222.

Jackson, D. N., Harris, W. G., Ashton, M. C., McCarthy, J. M., & Tremblay, P. F. (2000). How useful are work samples in validational studies? *International Journal of Selection and Assessment, 8,* 29–33.

Jackson, P. B., & Finney, M. (2002). Negative life events and psychological distress among young adults. *Social Psychology Quarterly, 65,* 186–201.

Jackson, S. E. (1983). Participation in decision making as a strategy for reducing job-related strain. *Journal of Applied Psychology, 68,* 3–19.

Jackson, S. E. (Ed.). (1994). *Diversity in the workplace: Human resources initiatives.* New York: Guilford.

Jackson, S. E., Brett, J. F., Sessa, V. I., Cooper, D. M., Julin, J. A., & Peyronnin, K. (1991). Some differences make a difference: Individual dissimilarity and group heterogeneity as correlates of recruitment, promotions, and tenure. *Journal of Applied Psychology, 76,* 675–689.

Jackson, S. E., & Joshi, A. (2011). Work team diversity. In S. Zedeck (Ed.), *APA handbook of industrial and organizational psychology* (Vol. 1, pp. 651–686). Washington, DC: American Psychological Association.

Jackson, S. E., & Ruderman, M. N. (Eds.). (1995). *Diversity in work teams: Research paradigms for a changing workplace.* Washington, DC: American Psychological Association.

Jackson, S. E., & Schuler, R. S. (1985). A meta-analysis and conceptual critique of research on role ambiguity and role conflict in work settings. *Organizational Behavior and Human Decision Processes, 36,* 16–78.

Jackson, S. E., Schwab, R. L., & Schuler, R. S. (1986). Toward an understanding of the burnout phenomenon. *Journal of Applied Psychology, 71,* 630–640.

Jacobs, R. R. (1986). Numerical rating scales. In R. A. Berk (Ed.), *Performance assessment: Methods and applications* (pp. 82–99). Baltimore, MD: The Johns Hopkins University Press.

Jago, A. G., & Ragan, J. W. (1986). The trouble with Leader Match is that it doesn't match Fiedler's contingency model. *Journal of Applied Psychology, 71,* 555–559.

Jamal, M. (1999). Job stress, Type-A behavior, and well-being: A cross-cultural examination. *International Journal of Stress Management, 6,* 57–67.

James, K., Chen, J., & Goldberg, C. (1992). Organizational conflict and individual creativity. *Journal of Applied Social Psychology, 22,* 545–566.

Janis, I. L. (1972). *Victims of groupthink: A psychological study of foreign-policy decisions and fiascoes.* Boston, MA: Houghton Mifflin.

Janis, I. L. (1982). *Groupthink: Psychological studies of policy decisions and fiascoes.* Boston, MA: Houghton-Mifflin.

Janis, I. L., & Mann, L. (1977). *Decision making: A psychological analysis of conflict, choice, and commitment.* New York: Free Press.

Janssen, O., Lam, C. K., & Huang, X. (2010). Emotional exhaustion and job performance: The moderating roles of distributive justice and positive affect. *Journal of Organizational Behavior, 31(6),* 787–809.

Janz, T. (1982). Initial comparisons of patterned behavior description interviews versus unstructured interviews. *Journal of Applied Psychology, 67,* 577–580.

Javidan, M., & House, R. J. (2001). Cultural acumen for the global manager: Lessons from Project GLOBE. *Organizational Dynamics, 29,* 289–305.

Jenkins, C. D., Zyzanski, S. J., & Rosenman, R. H. (1979). *Manual for the jenkins activity survey.* New York: Psychological Corporation.

Jensen, J. M., Opland, R. A., & Ryan, A. M. (2010). Psychological contracts and counterproductive work behaviors: Employee responses to transactional and relational breach. *Journal of Business and Psychology, 25(4),* 555–568.

Jermier, J. M., Gaines, J., & McIntosh, N. J. (1989). Reactions to physically dangerous work: A conceptual and empirical analysis. *Journal of Organizational Behavior, 10,* 15–33.

Jette, M. (1984). Stress coping through physical activity. In A. S. Sethi & R. S. Schuler (Eds.), *Handbook of organizational stress coping strategies* (pp. 215–231). Cambridge, MA: Ballinger.

Jex, S. M., & Bliese, P. D. (1999). Efficacy beliefs as a moderator of the impact of work-related stressors: A multilevel study. *Journal of Applied Psychology, 84,* 349–361.

Jex, S. M., Bliese, P. D., Buzzell, S., & Primeau, J. (2001). The impact of self-efficacy on stressor-strain relations: Coping style as an explanatory mechanism. *Journal of Applied Psychology, 86,* 401–409.

Jimmieson, N. L. (2000). Employee reactions to behavioural control under conditions of stress: The moderating role of self-efficacy. *Work & Stress, 14,* 262–280.

Jimmieson, N. L., & Terry, D. J. (1993). The effects of prediction, understanding, and control: A test of the stress antidote model. *Anxiety, Stress, and Coping, 6,* 179–199.

Jimmieson, N. L., & Terry, D. J. (1998). An experimental study of the effects of work stress, work control, and task information on adjustment. *Applied Psychology: An International Review, 47,* 345–369.

Jimmieson, N. L., & Terry, D. J. (1999). The moderating role of task characteristics in determining responses to a stressful work simulation. *Journal of Organizational Behavior, 20,* 709–736.

Johns, G. (1994a). Absenteeism estimates by employees and managers: Divergent perspectives and self-serving perceptions. *Journal of Applied Psychology, 79,* 229–239.

Johns, G. (1994b). How often were you absent? A review of the use of self-reported absence data. *Journal of Applied Psychology, 79*, 574–591.

Johnson, J. J. (2000). Differences in supervisor and non-supervisor perceptions of quality culture and organizational climate. *Public Personnel Management, 29*, 119–128.

Johnson, J. R., Bernhagen, M. J., Miller, V., & Allen, M. (1996). The role of communication in managing reductions in work force. *Journal of Applied Communication Research, 24*, 139–164.

Johnson, J. W. (1996). Linking employee perceptions of service climate to customer satisfaction. *Personnel Psychology, 49*, 831–851.

Johnson, R. A. (2003). *Whistleblowing: When it works—and why.* Boulder, CO: Lynne Rienner.

Johnson, S. D., & Bechler, C. (1998). Examining the relationship between listening effectiveness and leadership emergence: Perceptions, behaviors, and recall. *Small Group Research, 29*, 452–471.

Johnston, J. H., Driskell, J. E., & Salas, E. (1997). Vigilant and hypervigilant decision making. *Journal of Applied Psychology, 82*, 614–622.

Jones, E. E., & Nisbett, R. E. (1972). The actor and the observer: Divergent perceptions of the causes of behavior. In E. E. Jones, D. E. Kanouse, H. H. Kelley, R. E. Nisbett, S. Valins, & B. Weiner (Eds.), *Attribution: Perceiving the causes of behavior* (pp. 79–94). Morristown, NJ: General Learning Press.

Jubb, P. B. (1999). Whistleblowing: A restrictive definition and interpretation. *Journal of Business Ethics, 21*, 77–94.

Judd, K., & Gomez-Mejia, L. R. (1987). Comparable worth: A sensible way to end pay discrimination or the "looniest idea since looney tunes." In D. B. Balkin & L. R. Gomez-Mejia (Eds.), *New perspectives on compensation* (pp. 61–79). Englewood Cliffs, NJ: Prentice Hall.

Judge, T. A., Bono, J. E., Ilies, R., & Gerhardt, M. W. (2002). Personality and leadership: A qualitative and quantitative review. *Journal of Applied Psychology, 87*, 765–780.

Judge, T. A., & Ferris, G. R. (1993). Social context of performance evaluation decisions. *Academy of Management Journal, 36*, 80–105.

Judge, T. A., & Higgins, C. A. (1998). Affective disposition and the letter of reference. *Organizational Behavior and Human Decision Processes, 75*, 207–221.

Judge, T. A., & Larsen, R. J. (2001). Dispositional affect and job satisfaction: A review and theoretical extension. *Organizational Behavior and Human Decision Processes, 86*, 67–98.

Judge, T. A., Parker, S., Colbert, A. E., Heller, D., & Ilies, R. (2001). Job satisfaction: A cross-cultural review. In N. Anderson, D. S. Ones, H. K. Sinangil, & C. Viswesvaran (Eds.), *Handbook of industrial, work and organizational psychology* (Vol. 2, pp. 25–52). London, UK: Sage.

Judge, T. A., & Piccolo, R. F. (2004). Transformational and transactional leadership: A meta-analytic test of their relative validity. *Journal of Applied Psychology, 89*, 755–768.

Judge, T. A., Piccolo, R. F., & Ilies, R. (2004). The forgotten ones? The validity of consideration and initiating structure in leadership research. *Journal of Applied Psychology, 89*, 36–51.

Judge, T. A., Piccolo, R. F., Podsakoff, N. P., Shaw, J. C., & Rich, B. L. (2010). The relationship between pay and job satisfaction: A meta-analysis of the literature. *Journal of Vocational Behavior, 77*, 157–167.

Judge, T. A., Piccolo, R. F., & Remus, I. (2004). The forgotten ones? The validity of consideration and initiating structure in leadership research. *Journal of Applied Psychology, 89(1)*, 36–51.

Judge, T. A., Thoresen, C. J., Bono, J. E., & Patton, G. K. (2001). The job satisfaction—job performance relationship: A qualitative and quantitative review. *Psychological Bulletin, 127*, 376–407.

Judge, T. A., Thoresen, C. J., Pucik, V., & Welbourne, T. M. (1999). Managerial coping with organizational change: A dispositional perspective. *Journal of Applied Psychology, 84*, 107–122.

Kabanoff, B. (1981). A critique of Leader Match and its implications for leadership research. *Personnel Psychology, 34*, 749–764.

Kacmar, K. M., & Baron, R. A. (1999). Organizational politics: The state of the field, links to related processes, and an agenda for future research. *Research in Personnel and Human Resources Management, 7*, 1–39.

Kacmar, K. M., Delery, J. E., & Ferris, G. R. (1992). Differential effectiveness of applicant impression management tactics on employment interview decisions. *Journal of Applied Social Psychology, 22*, 1250–1272.

Kacmar, K. M., Witt, L. A., Zivnuska, S., & Gully, S. M. (2003). The interactive effect of leader-member exchange and communication frequency on performance ratings. *Journal of Applied Psychology, 88*, 764–772.

Kahn, R. L., & Boysiere, P. (1992). Stress in organizations. In M. D. Dunnette & L. M. Hough (Eds.), *Handbook of industrial/organizational psychology* (2nd ed., pp. 571–650). Palo Alto, CA: Consulting Psychologists Press.

Kahn, R. L., & Katz, D. (1960). Leadership practices in relation to productivity and morale. In D. Cartwright & A. Zander (Eds.), *Group dynamics: Research and theory* (2nd ed., pp. 554–571). Elmsford, NY: Row, Peterson.

Kahnweiler, W. M. (2002). Process consultation: A cornerstone of organization development practice. In J. Waclawski & A. H. Church (Eds.), *Organization development: A data-driven approach to organizational change* (pp. 149–163). San Francisco, CA: Jossey-Bass.

Kampa-Kokesch, S., & Anderson, M. Z. (2001). Executive coaching: A comprehensive review of the literature. *Consulting Psychology Journal: Practice and Research, 53*, 205–228.

Kanfer, R., & Ackerman, P. L. (1989). Motivation and cognitive abilities: An integrative/aptitude-treatment approach to skill acquisition. *Journal of Applied Psychology, 74*, 657–690.

Kantrowitz, T. M., Dawson, C. R., & Fetzer, M. S. (2011). Computer adaptive testing (CAT): A faster, smarter, and more secure approach to pre-employment testing. *Journal of Business Psychology, 26*, 227–232.

Kaplan, A. (1964). *The conduct of inquiry.* New York: Harper & Row.

Kaptein, M. (2011). From inaction to external whistleblowing: The influence of the ethical culture of organizations on employee responses to observed wrongdoing. *Journal of Business Ethics, 98(3)*, 513–530.

Kaptien, M. (2011). Understanding unethical behavior by unraveling ethical culture. *Human Relations, 64(6)*, 843–869.

Karasek, R. (1979). Job demands, job decision latitude, and marital strain: Implications for job redesign. *Administrative Science Quarterly, 24*, 285–306.

Karau, S. J., & Williams, K. D. (1993). Social loafing: A meta-analytic review and theoretical integration. *Journal of Personality and Social Psychology, 65*, 681–706.

Kass, S. J., Vodanovich, S. J., & Callender, A. (2001). State-trait bore-dom: Relationship to absenteeism, tenure, and job satisfaction. *Journal of Business and Psychology, 16*, 317–327.

Katz, D., & Kahn, R. L. (1966). *The social psychology of organizations.* New York: Wiley.

Katzell, R. A., & Austin, J. T. (1992). From then to now: The devel-opment of industrial-organizational psychology in the United States. *Journal of Applied Psychology, 77*, 803–835.

Keller, L. M., Bouchard, T. J., Arvey, R. D., Segal, N. L., & Dawis, R. V. (1992). Work values: Genetic and environmental issues. *Journal of Applied Psychology, 77*, 79–88.

Kennedy, J. K. (1982). Middle LPC leaders and the contingency model of leadership effectiveness. *Organizational Behavior and Human Performance, 30*, 1–14.

Kenny, D. A., & Zaccaro, S. J. (1983). An estimate of variance due to traits in leadership. *Journal of Applied Psychology, 68*, 678–685.

Kernan, M. C., & Lord, R. G. (1990). Effects of valence, expectancies, and goal-performance discrepancies in single and multiple goal environments. *Journal of Applied Psychology, 75*, 194–203.

Kerr, S., & Jermier, J. M. (1978). Substitutes for leadership: Their meaning and measurement. *Organizational Behavior and Human Performance, 22*, 375–403.

Kerr, S., & Schriesheim, S. (1974). Consideration, initiating struc-ture, and organizational criteria: An update of Korman's 1966 review. *Personnel Psychology, 27*, 555–568.

Keys, B., & Wolfe, J. (1990). The role of management games and simulations in education and research. *Journal of Management, 16*, 307–336.

Khanna, C., & Medsker, G. J. (2010). 2009 income and employment survey results for the Society for Industrial and Organizational Psychology. *The Industrial Organizational Psychologist, 48(1)*, 23–38.

Khoshaba, D. M., & Maddi, S. R. (2001). *HardiTraining* (3rd ed.). Newport Beach, CA: Hardiness Institute.

Kierein, N. M., & Gold, M. A. (2000). Pygmalion in work organi-zations: A meta-analysis. *Journal of Organizational Behavior, 21*, 913–928.

Kiesler, S., & Sproull, L. (1992). Group decision making and com-munication technology. *Organizational Behavior and Human Decision Processes, 52*, 96–123.

Kilburg, R. R. (2000). *Executive coaching: Developing managerial wisdom in a world of chaos.* Washington, DC: American Psycho-logical Association.

Kilman, R. H., Saxton, M. J., & Serpa, R. (Eds.). (1985). *Gaining con-trol of the corporate culture.* San Francisco, CA: Jossey-Bass.

Kim, B., Lee, G., & Carlson, K. D. (2010). An examination of the nature of the relationship between Leader-Member-Exchange (LMX) and turnover intent at different organizational levels. *International Journal of Hospitality Management, 29(4)*, 591–597.

Kim, H. (2004). Transfer of training as a sociopolitical process. *Human Resource Development Quarterly, 15*, 497–501.

Kim, H., & Gong, Y. (2009). The roles of tacit knowledge and OCB in the relationship between group-based pay and firm perfor-mance. *Human Resource Management Journal, 19(2)*, 120–139.

Kim, J. E., & Moen, P. (2001). Moving into retirement: Preparation and transitions in late midlife. In M. E. Lachman (Ed.), *Hand-book of midlife development* (pp. 487–527). Hoboken, NJ: Wiley.

King, G., III. (1999). The implications of an organization's struc-ture on whistleblowing. *Journal of Business Ethics, 20*, 315–326.

Kinicki, A. J., McKee-Ryan, F. M., Schriesheim, C. A., & Carson, K. P. (2002). Assessing the construct validity of the Job Descriptive Index: A review and meta-analysis. *Journal of Applied Psychology, 87*, 14–32.

Kinicki, A. J., Prussia, G. E., Wu, B., & McKee-Ryan, F. M. (2004). A covariance structure analysis of employees' response to perfor-mance feedback. *Journal of Applied Psychology, 89*, 1057–1069.

Kipnis, D. (1976). *The powerholders.* Chicago, IL: The University of Chicago Press.

Kipnis, D., Schmidt, S. M., & Wilkinson, I. (1980). Intraorganiza-tional influence tactics: Explorations in getting one's way. *Journal of Applied Psychology, 65*, 440–452.

Kirby, E. G., Kirby, S. L., & Lewis, M. A. (2002). A study of the effec-tiveness of training proactive thinking. *Journal of Applied Social Psychology, 32*, 1538–1549.

Kirchmeyer, C. (1990). A profile of managers active in office poli-tics. *Basic and Applied Social Psychology, 11*, 339–356.

Kirk, A. K., & Brown, D. F. (2003). Employee assistance programs: A review of the management of stress and well-being through workplace counseling and consulting. *Australian Psychologist, 38(2)*, 138–143.

Kirkcaldy, B. D., & Cooper, C. L. (1993). The relationship between work stress and leisure style: British and German managers. *Human Relations, 46*, 669–675.

Kirkpatrick, D. L. (1959–1960). Techniques for evaluating training programs. *Journal of the American Society of Training Directors, 13*, 3–9, 21–26; 14, 13–18, 28–32.

Kirkpatrick, D. L. (1976). Evaluating in-house training programs. *Training and Development Journal, 32*, 6–9.

Kirkpatrick, S. A., & Locke, E. A. (1996). Direct and indirect effects of three core charismatic leadership components on perfor-mance and attitudes. *Journal of Applied Psychology, 81*, 36–51.

Kirmeyer, S. L., & Dougherty, T. W. (1988). Work load, tension, and coping: Moderating effects of supervisor support. *Personnel Psychology, 41*, 125–139.

Klein, H. J., & Mulvey, P. W. (1995). Two investigations of the rela-tionships among group goals, goal commitment, cohesion, and performance. *Organizational Behavior and Human Decision Processes, 61*, 44–53.

Klein, K. J. (1987). Employee stock ownership and employee atti-tudes: A test of three models. *Journal of Applied Psychology, 72*, 319–332.

Klein, K. J., & House, R. J. (1995). On fire: Charismatic leadership and levels of analysis. *Leadership Quarterly, 6*, 183–198.

Kleinmann, M. (1993). Are rating dimensions in assessment centers transparent for participants? Consequences for criterion and construct validity. *Journal of Applied Psychology, 78*, 988–993.

Kleinmann, M., & Strauss, B. (1998). Validity and application of computer-simulated scenarios in personnel assessment. *International Journal of Selection and Assessment, 6*, 97–106.

Klimoski, R. J., & Brickner, M. (1987). Why do assessment centers work? The puzzle of assessment center validity. *Personnel Psy-chology, 40*, 243–260.

Kluger, A. N., & DeNisi, A. (1996). The effects of feedback inter-ventions on performance: A historical review, a meta-analysis, and a preliminary feedback intervention theory. *Psychological Bulletin, 119*, 254–284.

Knight, G. P., & Dubro, A. F. (1984). Cooperative, competitive, and individualistic social values: An individualized regression and clustering approach. *Journal of Personality and Social Psychology, 46*, 98–105.

Knouse, S. B. (1994). Impressions of the resumé: The effects of applicant education, experience, and impression management. *Journal of Business and Psychology, 9*, 33–45.

Knowlton, W. A., & Mitchell, T. R. (1980). Effects of causal attributions on a supervisor's evaluation of subordinate performance. *Journal of Applied Psychology, 65*, 459–466.

Kobasa, S. C. (1982). The hardy personality: Toward a social psychology of stress and health. In J. Suls & G. Sanders (Eds.), *The social psychology of health and illness* (pp. 3–32). Hillsdale, NJ: Erlbaum.

Kobasa, S. C., & Puccetti, M. C. (1983). Personality and social resources in stress resistance. *Journal of Personality & Social Psychology, 45*, 839–850.

Koehler, J. W., Anatol, K. W. E., & Applbaum, R. L. (1981). *Organizational communication: Behavioral perspectives* (2nd ed.). New York: Holt, Rinehart and Winston.

Kolodny, H. F. (1979). Evolution to a matrix organization. *Academy of Management Review, 4*, 543–553.

Komaki, J. L. (1986). Toward effective supervision: An operant analysis and comparison of managers at work. *Journal of Applied Psychology, 71*, 270–279.

Komaki, J. L., Coombs, T., & Schepman, S. (1991). Motivational implications of reinforcement theory. In R. M. Steers & L. W. Porter (Eds.), *Motivation and work behavior* (5th ed., pp. 87–107). New York: McGraw-Hill.

Komaki, J. L., Desselles, M. L., & Bowman, E. D. (1989). Definitely not a breeze: Extending an operant model of effective supervision to teams. *Journal of Applied Psychology, 74*, 522–529.

Kondrasuk, J. N. (1981). Studies in MBO effectiveness. *Academy of Management Review, 6*, 419–430.

Konradt, U., Hertel, G., & Joder, K. (2003). Web-based assessment of call center agents: Development and validation of a computerized instrument. *International Journal of Selection and Assessment, 11*, 184–193.

Kooij, D., De Lange, A. H., Jansen, P. G. W., Kanfer, R., & Dikkers, J. S. E. (2011). Age and work-related motives: Results of a meta-analysis. *Journal of Organizational Behavior, 32*, 197–225.

Korczynski, M. (2003). Communities of coping: Collective emotional labour in service work. *Organization, 10*, 55–79.

Korsgaard, M. A., Meglino, B. M., & Lester, S. W. (2004). The effect of other orientation on self-supervisor rating agreement. *Journal of Organizational Behavior, 25*, 873–891.

Kossek, E. E., & Lambert, S. J. (Eds.). (2005). *Work and life integration: Organizational, cultural, and individual perspectives.* Mahwah, NJ: Erlbaum.

Kossek, E. E., & Nichol, V. (1992). The effects of on-site child care on employee attitudes and performance. *Personnel Psychology, 45*, 485–509.

Kossek, E. E., Roberts, K., Fisher, S., & DeMarr, B. (1998). Career self-management: A quasi-experimental assessment of the effects of a training intervention. *Personnel Psychology, 51*, 935–962.

Kossek, E. E., & Zonia, S. C. (1993). Assessing diversity climate: A field study of reactions to employer efforts to promote diversity. *Journal of Organizational Behavior, 14*, 61–81.

Kottke, J. L., & Shultz, K. S. (1997). Using an assessment center as a developmental tool for graduate students: A demonstration.

In R. E. Riggio & B. T. Mayes (Eds.), *Assessment centers: Research and applications* (pp. 289–302). Corte Madera, CA: Select Press.

Koys, D. J. (2001). The effects of employee satisfaction, organizational citizenship behavior, and turnover on organizational effectiveness: A unit-level, longitudinal study. *Personnel Psychology, 54*, 101–114.

Kozlowski, S. W. J., & Ilgen, D. R. (2006). Enhancing the effectiveness of work groups and teams. *Psychological Science in the Public Interest, 7(3)*, 77–124.

Kozlowski, S. W. J., & Salas, E. (1997). An organizational systems approach for the implementation and transfer of training. In J. K. Ford (Ed.), *Improving training effectiveness in work organizations* (pp. 247–287). Hillsdale, NJ: Erlbaum.

Krackhardt, D. (1990). Assessing the political landscape: Structure, cognition, and power in organizations. *Administrative Science Quarterly, 35*, 342–369.

Krackhardt, D., & Porter, L. W. (1986). The snowball effect: Turnover embedded in communication networks. *Journal of Applied Psychology, 71*, 50–55.

Kraiger, K., & Ford, J. K. (1985). A meta-analysis of rat race effects in performance ratings. *Journal of Applied Psychology, 70*, 56–65.

Kraiger, K., Ford, J. K., & Salas, E. (1993). Application of cognitive, skill-based and affective theories of learning outcomes to new methods of training evaluation. *Journal of Applied Psychology, 78*, 311–328.

Kraiger, K., & Jung, K. M. (1997). Linking training objectives to evaluation criteria. In M. A. Quinones & A. Ehrenstein (Eds.), *Training for a rapidly changing workplace: Applications of psychological research* (pp. 151–175). Washington, DC: American Psychological Association.

Kram, K., & Hall, D. (1989). Mentoring as an antidote to stress during trauma, *Human Resource Management, 28*, 493–510

Kramer, M. W. (1995). A longitudinal study of superior-subordinate communication during job transfers. *Human Communication Research, 22*, 39–64.

Kraut, R. E. (1980). Humans as lie detectors: Some second thoughts. *Journal of Communication, 30*, 209–216.

Kraut, R. E., Lewis, H. L., & Swezey, L. W. (1982). Listener responsiveness and the coordination of conversation. *Journal of Personality and Social Psychology, 43*, 781–831.

Kravitz, D. A., & Balzer, W. K. (1992). Context effects in performance appraisal: A methodological critique and empirical study. *Journal of Applied Psychology, 77*, 24–31.

Kravitz, R. L., Linn, L. S., & Shapiro, M. F. (1990). Physician satisfaction under the Ontario health insurance plan. *Medical Care, 28*, 502–512.

Kristoff, A. L. (1996). Person-organization fit: An integrative review of its conceptualizations, measurement, and implications. *Personnel Psychology, 49*, 1–49.

Krueger, J., Ham, J. J., & Linford, K. M. (1996). Perceptions of behavioral consistency: Are people aware of the actor-observer effect? *Psychological Science, 7*, 259–264.

Kuipers, B. S., & Stoker, J. I. (2009). Development and performance of self-managing work teams: A theoretical and empirical examination. *The International Journal of Human Resource Management, 20(2)*, 399–419.

Kumar, K., & Beyerlein, M. (1991). Construction and validation of an instrument for measuring ingratiatory behaviors in organizational settings. *Journal of Applied Psychology, 76*, 619–627.

Kumara, U. A., & Koichi, F. (1989). Employee satisfaction and job climate: An empirical study of Japanese manufacturing employees. *Journal of Business and Psychology, 3,* 315–329.

Kume, T. (1985). Managerial attitudes toward decision-making: North American and Japan. In W. B. Gudykunst, L. P. Stewart, & S. Ting-Toomey (Eds.), *Communication, culture, and organizational processes* (pp. 231–251). Beverly Hills, CA: Sage.

Kuvaas, B. (2011). The interactive role of performance appraisal reactions and regular feedback. *Journal of Managerial Psychology, 26(2),* 123–137.

Labianca, G., Brass, D. J., & Gray, B. (1998). Social networks and perceptions of intergroup conflict: The role of negative relationships and third parties. *Academy of Management Journal, 41,* 55–67.

Lam, S. S. K., Hui, C., & Law, K. S. (1999). Organizational citizenship behavior: Comparing perspectives of supervisors and subordinates across four international samples. *Journal of Applied Psychology, 84,* 594–601.

Lam, S. S. K., Yik, M. S. M., & Schaubroeck, J. (2002). Responses to formal performance appraisal feedback: The role of negative affectivity. *Journal of Applied Psychology, 87,* 192–201.

Lam, W., Huang, X., & Snape, E. (2007). Feedback-seeking behavior and leader-member exchange: Do supervisor attributed motives matter. *Academy of Management Journal, 50(2),* 348–363.

Lambert, L. S. (2011). Promised and delivered inducements and contributions: An integrated view of psychological contract appraisal. *Journal of Applied Psychoogy, 96(4),* 695–712.

Lamm, H. (1988). Review of our research on group polarization: Eleven experiments on the effects of group discussion on risk acceptance, probability estimation, and negotiations positions. *Psychological Reports, 62,* 807–813.

Lance, C. E., Johnson, C. D., Douthitt, S. S., Bennett, W., Jr., & Harville, D. L. (2000). Good news: Work sample administrators' global performance judgments are (about) as valid as we've suspected. *Human Performance, 13,* 253–277.

Lance, C. E., LaPointe, J. A., & Fisicaro, S. A. (1994). Tests of three causal models of halo rater error. *Organizational Behavior and Human Decision Processes, 57,* 83–96.

Landy, F. J. (1989). *Psychology of work behavior* (4th ed.). Pacific Grove, CA: Brooks/Cole.

Landy, F. J. (1993). Job analysis and job evaluation: The respondent's perspective. In H. Schuler, J. L. Farr, & M. Smith (Eds.), *Personnel selection and assessment: Individual and organizational perspectives.* Hillsdale, NJ: Erlbaum.

Landy, F. J., & Sigall, H. (1974). Beauty is talent: Task evaluation as a function of the performer's physical attractiveness. *Journal of Personality and Social Psychology, 29,* 299–304.

Langan-Fox, J. (2001). Communication in organizations: Speed, diversity, networks and influence on organizational effectiveness, human health, and relationships. In N. Anderson, D. S. Ones, H. K. Sinangil, & C. Viswesvaran (Eds.), *Handbook of industrial, work, & organizational psychology* (pp. 188–205). London, UK: Sage.

Lange, T. (2009). Attitudes, attributes, and institutions determining job satisfaction in central and eastern Europe. *Human Relations, 31(1),* 81–97.

Langfred, C. W. (1998). Is group cohesiveness a double-edged sword? An investigation of the effects of cohesiveness on performance. *Small Group Research, 29,* 124–143.

Larson, E. W., & Gobeli, D. H. (1987). Matrix management: Contradictions and insights. *California Management Review, 29,* 126–138.

Larwood, L., Wright, T. A., Desrochers, S., & Dahir, V. (1998). Extending latent role and psychological contract theories to predict intent to turnover and politics in business organizations. *Group & Organization Management, 23,* 100–123.

Latack, J. C., & Foster, L. W. (1985). Implementation of compressed work schedules: Participation and job redesign as critical factors for employee acceptance. *Personnel Psychology, 38,* 75–92.

Latane, B., Williams, K., & Harkins, S. (1979). Many hands make light the work: The causes and consequences of social loafing. *Journal of Personality and Social Psychology, 37,* 822–832.

Latham, G. P. (1988). Human resource training and development. *Annual Review of Psychology, 39,* 545–582.

Latham, G. P. (1989). The reliability, validity, and practicality of the situational interview. In R. W. Eder & G. R. Ferris (Eds.), *The employment interview: Theory, research, and practice* (pp. 169–182). Newbury Park, CA: Sage.

Latham, G. P. (2001). The reciprocal transfer of learning from journals to practice. *Applied Psychology: An International Review, 50,* 201–211.

Latham, G. P., & Locke, E. A. (2007). New developments and directions for goal-setting research. *European Psychologist, 12(4),* 290–300.

Latham, G. P., & Saari, L. M. (1979). Application of social-learning theory to training supervisors through behavioral modeling. *Journal of Applied Psychology, 64,* 239–246.

Latham, G. P., & Saari, L. M. (1982). The importance of union acceptance for productivity improvement through goal setting. *Personnel Psychology, 35,* 781–787.

Latham, G. P., & Saari, L. M. (1984). Do people do what they say? Further studies on the situational interview. *Journal of Applied Psychology, 69,* 569–573.

Latham, G. P., Saari, L. M., Pursell, E. D., & Campion, M. A. (1980). The situational interview. *Journal of Applied Psychology, 65,* 422–427.

Latham, G. P., & Wexley, K. N. (1977). Behavioral observation scales for performance appraisal purposes. *Personnel Psychology, 30,* 225–268.

Lau, V. C. S., Au, W. T., & Ho, J. M. C. (2003). A qualitative and quantitative review of antecedents of counterproductive behavior in organizations. *Journal of Business and Psychology, 18,* 73–99.

Law, R., Dollard, M. F., Tuckey, M. R., & Dormann, C. (2011). Psychosocial safety climate as a lead indicator of workplace bullying and harassment, job resources, psychological health and employee engagement. *Accident Analysis and Prevention, 43(5),* 1782–1793.

Lawler, E. E. (1971). *Pay and organizational effectiveness.* New York: McGraw-Hill.

Lawler, E. E. (1987). Paying for performance: Future directions. In D. B. Balkin & L. R. Gomez-Mejia (Eds.), *New perspectives on compensation* (pp. 162–168). Englewood Cliffs, NJ: Prentice Hall.

Lawler, E. E., Mohrman, S. A., & Ledford, G. E. (1992). *Employee involvement and total quality management.* San Francisco, CA: Jossey-Bass.

Lawrence, P. R., & Lorsch, J. (1967). *Organization and environment.* Cambridge, MA: Harvard University Press.

Lazarus R. S. (1991). Psychological stress in the workplace. *Journal of Social Behavior and Personality, 6,* 1–13.

Lazarus, R. S., & Folkman, S. (1984). *Stress, appraisal and coping.* New York: Springer.

Lazarus, R. S., & Launier, R. (1978). Stress-related transactions between person and environment. In L. A. Pervin & M. Lewis (Eds.), *Perspectives in interactional psychology* (pp. 287–327). New York: Plenum Press.

Leavitt, H. J. (1951). Some effects of certain communication patterns on group performance. *Journal of Abnormal and Social Psychology, 46,* 38–50.

Ledford, G. E., Lawler, E. E., & Mohrman, S. A. (1988). The quality circle and its variations. In J. P. Campbell & R. J. Campbell (Eds.), *Productivity in organizations* (pp. 255–294). San Francisco, CA: Jossey-Bass.

Lee, C., Earley, P. C., & Hanson, L. A. (1988). Are type As better performers? *Journal of Organizational Behavior, 9,* 263–269.

Lee, C., Law, K. S., & Bobko, P. (1999). The importance of justice perceptions of pay effectiveness: A two-year study of a skill-based pay plan. *Journal of Management, 25,* 851–873.

Lee, F. (1993). Being polite and keeping MUM: How bad news is communicated in organizational hierarchies. *Journal of Applied Social Psychology, 23,* 1124–1149.

Lee, J. (1998). Effective maintenance communication in superior-subordinate relationships. *Western Journal of Communication, 62,* 181–208.

Lee, R. T., & Ashforth, B. E. (1990). On the meaning of Maslach's three dimensions of burnout. *Journal of Applied Psychology, 75,* 743–747.

Lee, T. W. (1989). The antecedents and prediction of employee attendance. *Journal of Business Issues, 17,* 17–22.

Lee, T. W., Ashford, S. J., Walsh, J. P., & Mowday, R. T. (1992). Commitment propensity, organizational commitment, and voluntary turnover: A longitudinal study of organizational entry processes. *Journal of Management, 18,* 15–32.

Lee, T. W., & Maurer, S. D. (1997). The retention of knowledge workers with the unfolding model of voluntary turnover. *Human Resource Management Review, 7,* 247–275.

Lee, T. W., & Mitchell, T. R. (1994). An alternative approach: The unfolding model of voluntary employee turnover. *Academy of Management Review, 19,* 51–89.

Lee, T. W., Mitchell, T. R., Sablynski, C. J., Burton, J. P., & Holtom, B. C. (2004). The effects of job embeddedness on organizational citizenship, job performance, volitional absences, and voluntary turnover. *Academy of Management Journal, 47,* 711–722.

Lefkowitz, J. (2000). The role of interpersonal affective regard in supervisory performance ratings: A literature review and proposed causal model. *Journal of Occupational and Organizational Psychology, 73,* 67–85.

Legatski, T. W. (1998). Downsizing, downscoping, and restructuring: Classifying organizational change. *Research in Organizational Change and Development, 11,* 253–270.

Leibowitz, Z. B., Farren, C., & Kaye, B. L. (1986). *Designing career development systems.* San Francisco, CA: Jossey-Bass.

Leister, A., Borden, D., & Fiedler, F. E. (1977). Validation of contingency model leadership training: Leader Match. *Academy of Management Journal, 20,* 464–470.

Leiter, M. P., & Harvie, P. (1998). Conditions for staff acceptance of organizational change: Burnout as a mediating construct. *Anxiety, Stress, and Coping, 11,* 1–25.

Leiter, M. P., & Maslach, C. (1988). The impact of interpersonal environment on burnout and organizational commitment. *Journal of Organizational Behavior, 9,* 297–308.

Leiter, M. P., & Schaufeli, W. B. (1996). Consistency of the burnout construct across occupations. *Anxiety, Stress, and Coping, 9,* 229–243.

Lent, R. W., Schmidt, J., & Schmidt, L. (2006). Collective efficacy beliefs in student work teams: Relation to self-efficacy, cohesion, and performance. *Journal of Vocational Behavior, 68,* 73–84.

Leonhardt, J., & Vogt, J. (2011). Critical incident stress and the prevention of psychological trauma in air traffic controllers. In N. Tehrani (Ed.), *Managing trauma in the workplace: Supporting workers and organizations* (pp. 63–80). New York: Routledge.

LePine, J. A., Hanson, M. A., Borman, W. C., & Motowidlo, S. J. (2000). Contextual performance and teamwork: Implications for staffing. *Research in Personnel and Human Resources Management, 19,* 53–90.

LePine, J. A., Podsakoff, N. A., & LePine, M. A. (2005). A meta-analytic test of the challenge stressor-hindrance stressor framework: An explanation for inconsistent relationships among stressors and performance. *Academy of Management Journal, 48,* 764–775.

Lester, T. (1993). A woman's place. *Management Today, 25,* 46–50.

Levi, L., Frankenhaeuser, M., & Gardell, B. (1986). The characteristics of the workplace and the nature of its social demands. In S. G. Wolf & A. J. Finestone (Eds.), *Occupational stress: Health and performance at work* (pp. 54–67). Littleton, MA: PSG Publishing.

Levine, E. L., Ash, R. A., & Bennett, N. (1980). Exploratory comparative study of four job analysis methods. *Journal of Applied Psychology, 65,* 524–535.

Levine, E. L., Ash, R. A., Hall, H., & Sistrunk, F. (1983). Evaluation of job analysis methods by experienced job analysts. *Academy of Management Journal, 26,* 339–347.

Levy, P. E., & Williams, J. R. (2004). The social context of performance appraisals: A review and framework for the future. *Journal of Management, 30,* 881–905.

Lewin, K. (1935). *Dynamic theory of personality.* New York: McGraw-Hill.

Lewis, D. (2002). Whistleblowing procedures at work: What are the implications for human resource practitioners? *Business Ethics: A European Review, 11,* 202–209.

Li, L., & Shen, Q. (2009). Relationships among nurse occupational stress, type-A behavior pattern, and subjective well being. *Chinese Mental Health Journal, 23(4),* 255–258.

Liden, R. C., & Maslyn, J. M. (1998). Multidimensionality of leader-member exchange: An empirical assessment through scale development. *Journal of Management, 24,* 43–72.

Liden, R. C., Wayne, S. J., Jaworski, R. A., & Bennett, N. (2004). Social loafing: A field investigation. *Journal of Management, 30,* 285–304.

Liden, R. C., Wayne, S. J., & Stilwell, D. (1993). A longitudinal study on the early development of leader-member exchanges. *Journal of Applied Psychology, 78,* 662–674.

Liebowitz, S. J., & de Meuse, K. P. (1982). The application of team building. *Human Relations, 16,* 1–18.

Lievens, F. (1998). Factors which improve the construct validity of assessment centers: A review. *International Journal of Selection and Assessment, 6,* 141–152.

Lievens, F. (2001). Assessors and use of assessment centre dimensions: A fresh look at a troubling issue. *Journal of Organizational Behavior, 22,* 203–221.

Lievens, F., Decaesteker, C., Coetsier, P., & Geirnaert, J. (2001). Organizational attractiveness for prospective applicants: A person-organisation fit perspective. *Applied Psychology: An International Review, 50,* 30–51.

Lievens, F., & DePaepe, A. (2004). An empirical investigation of interviewer-related factors that discourage the use of high structure interviews. *Journal of Organizational Behavior, 25,* 29–46.

Lievens, F., Klimoski, R. J. (2001). Understanding the assessment centre process: Where are we now? *International Review of Industrial and Organizational Psychology, 16,* 246–286.

Lievens, F., & Sackett, P. R. (2006). Video-based versus written situational judgment tests: A comparison in terms of predictive validity. *Journal of Applied Psychology, 91,* 1181–1188.

Likert, R. (1961). *New patterns of management.* New York: McGraw-Hill.

Likert, R. (1967). *The human organization.* New York: McGraw-Hill.

Lim, S., & Cortina, L. M. (2005). Interpersonal mistreatment in the workplace: The interface and impact of general incivility and sexual harassment. *Journal of Applied Psychology, 90,* 483–496.

Lim, V. K. G. (1996). Job insecurity and its outcomes: Moderating effects of work-based and nonwork-based social support. *Human Relations, 49,* 171–194.

Litchfield, R. C. (2009). Brainstorming rules as assigned goals: Does brainstorming really improve idea quality? *Motivation and Emotion, 33(1),* 25–31.

Liu, Y., & Cohen, A. (2010). Values, commitment, and OCB among Chinese employees. *International Journal of Intercultural Relations, 34(5),* 493–506.

Locke, E. A. (1968). Toward a theory of task motivation and incentives. *Organizational Behavior and Human Performance, 3,* 157–189.

Locke, E. A. (1976). The nature and causes of job satisfaction. In M. D. Dunnette (Ed.), *Handbook of industrial and organizational psychology* (pp. 1297–1350). Chicago, IL: Rand McNally.

Locke, E. A., & Latham, G. P. (1984). *Goal setting: A motivational technique that works.* Englewood Cliffs, NJ: Prentice Hall.

Locke, E. A., & Latham, G. P. (1990a). *A theory of goal setting and task performance.* Englewood Cliffs, NJ: Prentice Hall.

Locke, E. A., & Latham, G. P. (1990b). Work motivation and satisfaction: Light at the end of the tunnel. *Psychological Science, 1,* 240–246.

Locke, E. A., & Latham, G. P. (2004). What should we do about motivation theory? Six recommendations for the twenty-first century. *Academy of Management Review, 29,* 388–403.

Locke, E. A., & Latham, G. P. (2006). New directions in goal-setting theory. *Current Directions in Psychological Science, 15,* 265–268.

Locke, E. A., Latham, G. P., & Erez, M. (1988). The determinants of goal commitment. *Academy of Management Review, 13,* 23–39.

Locke, E. A., & Schweiger, D. M. (1979). Participation in decision making: One more look. In B. M. Staw (Ed.), *Research in organizational behavior* (pp. 265–340). Greenwich, CT: JAI Press.

Locke, E. A., Shaw, K. N., Saari, L. M., & Latham, G. P. (1981). Goal setting and task performance: 1969–1980. *Psychological Bulletin, 90,* 125–152.

Loden, M., & Rosener, J. B. (1991). *Workforce America! Managing employee diversity as a vital resource.* Homewood, IL: Business One Irwin.

London, M. (1993). Relationships between career motivation, empowerment, and support for career development. *Journal of Occupational and Organizational Psychology, 66,* 55–69.

London, M., & Bassman, E. (1989). Retraining midcareer workers for the future workplace. In I. L. Goldstein (Ed.), *Training and development in organizations.* San Francisco, CA: Jossey-Bass.

London, M., & Beatty, R. W. (1993). 360-degree feedback as a competitive advantage. *Human Resource Management, 32,* 353–372.

London, M., & Smither, J. W. (1995). Can multi-source feedback change perceptions of goal accomplishment, self-evaluations, and performance-related outcomes? Theory-based applications and directions for research. *Personnel Psychology, 48,* 803–839.

Loo, R. (1994). The evaluation of stress management services by Canadian organizations. *Journal of Business and Psychology, 9,* 129–136.

Lord, R. G., DeVader, C. L., & Alliger, G. M. (1986). A meta-analysis of the relation between personality traits and leadership perceptions: An application of validity generalization procedures. *Journal of Applied Psychology, 71,* 402–410.

Losey, M., Ulrich, D., & Meisinger, S. (Eds.). (2005). *The future of human resource management: 64 thought leaders explore the critical HR issues of today and tomorrow.* New York: Wiley.

Louis, M. R., Posner, B. Z., & Powell, G. N. (1983). The availability and helpfulness of socialization practices. *Personnel Psychology, 36,* 857–866.

Lounsbury, J. W., & Hoopes, L. L. (1986). A vacation from work: Changes in work and nonwork outcomes. *Journal of Applied Psychology, 71,* 392–401.

Lowe, K. B., Kroeck, K. G., & Sivasubramaniam, N. (1996). Effectiveness correlates of transformational and transactional leadership: A meta-analytic review of the MLQ literature. *Leadership Quarterly, 7,* 385–425.

Lowe, R., & Bennett, P. (2003). Exploring coping reactions to work-stress: Application of an appraisal theory. *Journal of Occupational and Organizational Psychology, 76,* 393–400.

Lowe, R. H., & Wittig, M. A. (Eds.). (1989). Approaching pay equity through comparable worth. *Journal of Social Issues, 45* (Whole issue number 4).

Lowman, R. L. (Ed.). (2006). *The ethical practice of psychology in organizations* (2nd ed.). Washington, DC: American Psychological Association.

Lowry, S. M., Maynard, H. B., & Stegemerten, G. J. (Eds.). (1940). *Time and motion study and formulas for wage incentives* (3rd ed.). New York: McGraw-Hill.

Lu, J., Tjosvold, D., & Shi, K. (2010). Team training in China: Testing and applying the theory of cooperation and competition. *Journal of Applied Social Psychology, 40(1),* 101–134.

Lucas, J. L., & Heady, R. B. (2002). Flextime commuters and their driver stress, feelings of time urgency, and commute satisfaction. *Journal of Business and Psychology, 16,* 565–572.

Ludwig, T. D., & Geller, E. S. (1997). Assigned versus participative goal setting and response generalization: Managing injury control among professional pizza deliverers. *Journal of Applied Psychology, 82,* 253–261.

Lundberg, C., Gudmundson, A., & Andersson, T. D. (2009). Herzberg's Two-Factor Theory of work motivation tested empirically on seasonal workers in hospitality and tourism. *Tourism Management, 30(6)*, 890–899.

Luthans, F., Rhee, S., Luthans, B. C., & Avey, J. B. (2008). Impact of behavioral performance management in a Korean application. *Leadership & Organization Development Journal, 29(5)*, 427–443.

Lynch, B. P. (1974). An empirical assessment of Perrow's technology construct. *Administrative Science Quarterly, 19*, 338–356.

Macan, T. H., & Dipboye, R. L. (1994). The effects of the application on processing of information from the employment interview. *Journal of Applied Social Psychology, 24*, 1291–1314.

Macey, W. H., & Scheider, B. (2008). The meaning of employee engagement. *Industrial and Organizational Psychology, 1(1)*, 3–30.

Machlowitz, M. M. (1976, October 3). Working the 100-hour week—and loving it. *The New York Times.*

Mackenzie, M. L. (2010). Manager communication and workplace trust: Understanding manager and employee perceptions in the e-world. *International Journal of Information Management, 30(6)*, 529–541.

Maddi, S. R., & Khoshaba, D. M. (2003). Hardiness training for resiliency and leadership. In D. Paton, J. M. Violanti, & L. M. Smith (Eds.), *Promoting capabilities to manage posttraumatic stress: Perspectives on resilience* (pp. 43–57). Springfield, IL: Charles C Thomas.

Maddi, S. R., & Kobasa, S. C. (1984). *The hardy executive: Health under stress.* Homewood, IL: Dow Jones-Irwin.

Maddi, S. R., Harvey, R. H., Khoshaba, D. M., Mostafa, F., & Resurreccion, N. (2009). Hardiness training facilitates performance in college. *The Journal of Positive Psychology, 4(6)*, 566–577.

Madison, D. L., Allen, R. W., Porter, L. W., Renwick, P. A., & Mayes, B. T. (1980). Organizational politics: An exploration of managers' perceptions. *Human Relations, 33*, 79–100.

Mael, F. A. (1991). A conceptual rationale for the domain and attributes of biodata items. *Personnel Psychology, 44*, 763–792.

Mael, F. A., Connerly, M., & Morath, R. A. (1996). None of your business: Parameters of biodata invasiveness. *Personnel Psychology, 49*, 613–650.

Major, D. A., Kozlowski, S. W. J., Chao, G. T., & Gardner, P. D. (1995). A longitudinal investigation of newcomer expectations, early socialization outcomes, and the moderating effects of role development factors. *Journal of Applied Psychology, 80*, 418–431.

Majumdar, B., & Ray, A. (2011). Transformational leadership and innovative work behaviour. *Journal of the Indian Academy of Applied Psychology, 37(1)*, 140–148.

Makiney, J. D., & Levy, P. E. (1997, April). *Supervisor's use of self- and peer ratings for appraisal decisions.* Paper presented at the 12th annual conference of the Society for Industrial and Organizational Psychology, St. Louis, MO.

Malamut, A. B., & Offermann, L. R. (2001). Coping with sexual harassment: Personal, environmental, and cognitive demands. *Journal of Applied Psychology, 86*, 1152–1166.

Malos, S. B. (1998). Current legal issues in performance appraisal. In J. W. Smither (Ed.), *Performance appraisal: State of the art in practice* (pp. 49–94). San Francisco, CA: Jossey-Bass.

Man, D. C., & Lam, S. S. K. (2003). The effects of job complexity and autonomy on cohesiveness in collectivistic and individualistic work groups: A cross-cultural analysis. *Journal of Organizational Behavior, 24*, 979–1001.

Mann, R. B., & Decker, P. J. (1984). The effect of key behavior distinctiveness on generalization and recall in behavior modeling training. *Academy of Management Journal, 27*, 900–909.

Manz, C. C. (1986). Self-leadership: Toward an expanded theory of self-influence processes in organizations. *Academy of Management Review, 11*, 585–600.

Manz, C. C., & Sims, H. P. (1980). Self-management as a substitute for leadership: A social learning perspective. *Academy of Management Review, 5*, 361–367.

Marcoulides, G. A., Mills, R. B., & Unterbrink, H. (1993). Improving preemployment screening: Drug testing in the workplace. *Journal of Management Issues, 5*, 290–300.

Margerison, C., & Glube, R. (1979). Leadership decision-making: An empirical test of the Vroom and Yetton model. *Journal of Management Studies, 16*, 45–55.

Markham, S. E., & McKee, G. H. (1995). Group absence behavior and standards: A multilevel analysis. *Academy of Management Journal, 38*, 1174–1190.

Markham, S. E., Scott, K. D., & McKee, G. H. (2002). Recognizing good attendance: A longitudinal, quasi-experimental field study. *Personnel Psychology, 55*, 639–660.

Marks, M. A., Sabella, M. J., Burke, C. S., & Zaccaro, S. J. (2002). The impact of cross-training on team effectiveness. *Journal of Applied Psychology, 87*, 3–13.

Marks, M. L. (1986). The question of quality circles. *Psychology Today, 20*, 36–46.

Marks, M. L. (2007). Best practices in leading organizational change: Workplace recovery following major organizational transitions. In J. A. Conger & R. E. Riggio (Eds.), *The practice of leadership: Preparing the next generation of leaders* (pp. 201–222). San Francisco, CA: Jossey-Bass.

Marks, M. L., & Mirvis, P. H. (1998). *Joining forces: Making one plus one equal three in mergers, acquisitions, and alliances.* San Francisco, CA: Jossey-Bass.

Marks, M. L., & Mirvis, P. H. (2010). *Joining forces.* San Francisco, CA: Jossey-Bass.

Marks, M. L., Mirvis, P. H., Hackett, E. J., & Grady, J. F. (1986). Employee participation in a quality circle program: Impact on quality of work life, productivity, and absenteeism. *Journal of Applied Psychology, 71*, 61–69.

Markus, M. L. (1994). Electronic mail as the medium of managerial choice. *Organization Science, 5*, 502–527.

Marlowe, H. A. (1986). Social intelligence: Evidence for multidimensionality and construct independence. *Journal of Educational Psychology, 78*, 52–58.

Martin, D. C., Bartol, K. M., & Kehoe, P. E. (2000). The legal ramifications of performance appraisal: The growing significance. *Public Personnel Management, 29*, 379–406.

Martin, J. E., & Peterson, M. M. (1987). Two-tier wage structures: Implications for equity theory. *Academy of Management Journal, 30*, 297–315.

Martin, T. N., & Schermerhorn, J. R. (1983). Work and nonwork influences on health: A research agenda using inability to leave as a critical variable. *Academy of Management Review, 8*, 650–659.

Martineau, J. W., & Preskill, H. (2002). Evaluating the impact of organization development interventions. In J. Waclawski & A. H. Church (Eds.), *Organization development: A data-driven approach to organizational change* (pp. 286–301). San Francisco, CA: Jossey-Bass.

Martins, L. L. (2011). Organizational change and development. In S. Zedeck (Ed.), *APA handbook of industrial and organizational psychology* (Vol. 3, pp. 691–728). Washington, DC: American Psychological Association.

Martocchio, J. J. (1993). Employee decisions to enroll in microcomputer training. *Human Resource Development Quarterly, 4*, 51–70.

Martocchio, J. J., & Webster, J. (1992). Effects of feedback and cognitive playfulness on performance in microcomputer software training. *Personnel Psychology, 45*, 553–578.

Marx, R. D. (1982). Relapse prevention for managerial training: A model for maintenance of behavior change. *Academy of Management Review, 7*, 433–441.

Maslach, C. (2005). Understanding burnout: Work and family issues. In D. F. Halpern & S. E. Murphy (Eds.), *From work-family balance to work-family interaction: Changing the metaphor* (pp. 99–114). Mahwah, NJ: Erlbaum.

Maslach, C., & Jackson, S. E. (1986). *MBI: Maslach burnout inventory.* Palo Alto, CA: Consulting Psychologists Press.

Maslach, C., Schaufeli, W. B., & Leiter, M. P. (2001). Job burnout. *Annual Review Psychology, 52*, 397–422.

Maslow, A. H. (1965). *Eupsychian management.* Homewood, IL: Irwin.

Maslow, A. H. (1970). *Motivation and personality* (2nd ed.). New York: Harper & Row.

Maslyn, J. M., & Uhl-Bien, M. (2001). Leader-member exchange and its dimensions: Effects of self-effort and other's effort on relationship quality. *Journal of Applied Psychology, 86*, 697–708.

Mathieu, J. E., Hofmann, D. A., & Farr, J. L. (1993). Job perception-job satisfaction relations: An empirical comparison of three competing theories. *Organizational Behavior and Human Decision Processes, 56*, 370–387.

Mathieu, J. E., Martineau, J. W., & Tannenbaum, S. I. (1993). Individual and situational influences on the development of self-efficacy: Implications for training effectiveness. *Personnel Psychology, 46*, 125–147.

Mathis, R. L., & Jackson, J. H. (1985). Personnel: Contemporary perspectives and applications. St. Paul, MN: West.

Matsui, T., Kagawa, M., Nagamatsu, J., & Ohtsuka, Y. (1977). Validity of expectancy theory as a within-person behavioral choice model for sales activity. *Journal of Applied Psychology, 62*, 764–767.

Matteson, M. T., & Ivancevich, J. M. (1987). *Controlling work stress: Effective human resource and management strategies.* San Francisco, CA: Jossey-Bass.

Maurer, S. D., & Faye, C. (1988). Effect of situational interviews, conventional structured interviews, and training on interview rating agreement: An experimental analysis. *Personnel Psychology, 41*, 329–344.

Maurer, S. D., Howe, V., & Lee, T. W. (1992). Organizational recruiting as marketing management: An interdisciplinary study of engineering graduates. *Personnel Psychology, 45*, 807–833.

Maurer, T. J. (2001). Career-relevant learning and development, worker age, and beliefs about self-efficacy for development. *Journal of Management , 27*, 123–140.

Mawhinney, T. C. (1992). Total quality management and organizational behavior management: An integration for continual improvement. *Journal of Applied Behavior Analysis, 25*, 525–543.

May, G. L., & Kahnweiler, W. M. (2000). The effect of a mastery practice design on learning and transfer in behavior modeling training. *Personnel Psychology, 53*, 353–373.

Mayer, J. D., Caruso, D. R., & Salovey, P. (1999). *The multifactor emotional intelligence scale.* Simsbury, CT: www.EmotionalIQ.com.

Mayer, J. D., & Salovey, P. (1997). What is emotional intelligence? In P. Salovey & D. Sluyter (Eds.), *Emotional development and emotional intelligence: Implications for educators* (pp. 3–31). New York: Basic Books.

Mayes, B. T. (1995). Power and organizational politics. In *McGraw-Hill's Virtual organizational behavior.* New York: McGraw-Hill.

Mayes, B. T., & Allen, R. W. (1977). Toward a definition of organizational politics. *Academy of Management Review, 2*, 672–678.

Mayes, B. T., & Ganster, D. C. (1988). Exit and voice: A test of hypotheses based on fight/flight responses to job stress. *Journal of Organizational Behavior, 9*, 199–216.

Mayo, E. (1933). *The human problems of an industrial civilization.* Cambridge: Harvard University Press.

McClelland, D. C. (1961). *The achieving society.* New York: Van Nostrand.

McClelland, D. C. (1970). The two faces of power. *Journal of International Affairs, 24*, 29–47.

McClelland, D. C. (1975). *Power: The inner experience.* New York: Irvington Press.

McClelland, D. C. (1980). Motive dispositions: The merits of operant and respondent measures. In L. Wheeler (Ed.), *Review of personality and social psychology* (Vol. 1, pp. 10–41). Beverly Hills, CA: Sage.

McClelland, D. C., Atkinson, J. W., Clark, R. A., & Lowell, E. L. (1953). *The achievement motive.* New York: Appleton-Century-Crofts.

McClelland, D. C., & Boyatzis, R. E. (1982). Leadership motive pattern and long-term success in management. *Journal of Applied Psychology, 67*, 737–743.

McClelland, D. C., & Burnham, D. H. (1976). Power is the great motivator. *Harvard Business Review, 54*, 100–111.

McClelland, D. C., & Franz, C. E. (1993). Motivational and other sources of work accomplishments at mid-life: A longitudinal study. *Journal of Personality, 60*, 679–707.

McClintock, C. G., Messick, D. M., Kuhlman, D. M., & Campos, F. T. (1973). Motivational bases of choice in three-choice decomposed games. *Journal of Experimental Social Psychology, 9*, 572–590.

McClurg, L. N. (2001). Team rewards: How far have we come? *Human Resource Management, 40*, 73–86.

McConkie, M. L. (1979). A clarification of the goal setting and appraisal processes in MBO. *Academy of Management Review, 4*, 29–40.

McCormick, E. J. (1979). *Job analysis: Methods and applications.* New York: AMACOM.

McCormick, E. J., & Cooper, C. L. (1988). Executive stress: Extending the international comparison. *Human Relations, 41*, 65–72.

McCormick, E. J., Jeanneret, P. R., & Mecham, R. C. (1969). *Position analysis questionnaire.* West Lafayette, IN: Occupational Research Center, Purdue University.

McElroy, J. C., Morrow, P. C., & Rude, S. N. (2001). Turnover and organizational performance: A comparative analysis of the effects of voluntary, involuntary, and reduction-in-force turnover. *Journal of Applied Psychology, 86*, 1294–1299.

McEvoy, G. M., & Buller, P. F. (1987). User acceptance of peer appraisals in an industrial setting. *Personnel Psychology, 40,* 785–797.

McEvoy, G. M., & Cascio, W. F. (1985). Strategies for reducing employee turnover: A meta-analysis. *Journal of Applied Psychology, 70,* 342–353.

McGaghie, W. C., Issenberg, S. B., Petrusa, E. R., & Scalese, R. J. (2010). A critical review of simulation-based medical education research: 2003–2009. *Medical Education, 44(1),* 50–63.

McGeehee, W., & Thayer, P. W. (1961). *Training in business and industry.* New York: Wiley.

McIntyre, R. M., Smith, D. E., & Hassett, C. E. (1984). Accuracy of performance ratings as affected by rater training and perceived purpose of rating. *Journal of Applied Psychology, 69,* 147–156.

McKay, P. F., & Avery, D. R. (2006). What has race got to do with it? Unraveling the role of racioethnicity in job seekers' reactions to site visits. *Personnel Psychology, 59,* 395–429.

McKenna, D. D., & Davis, S. L. (2009). Hidden in plain sight: The active ingredients of executive coaching. *Industrial and Organizational Psychology, 2(3),* 244–260.

McMurry, R. N. (1947). The problem of resistance to change in industry. *Journal of Applied Psychology, 31,* 589–593.

McNall. L. A., & Roch, S. G. (2009). A social exchange model of employee reaction to electronic performance monitoring. *Human Performance, 22,* 204–224.

Mead, A. D., & Drasgow, F. (1993). Equivalence of computerized and paper-and-pencil cognitive ability tests: A meta-analysis. *Psychological Bulletin, 114,* 449–458.

Mechanic, D. (1962). Sources of power of lower participants in complex organizations. *Administrative Science Quarterly, 7,* 349–364.

Medcof, J. W., & Hausdorf, P. A. (1995). Instruments to measure opportunities to satisfy needs, and degree of satisfaction with needs, in the workplace. *Journal of Occupational and Organizational Psychology, 68,* 193–208.

Medsker, G. J., Katkowski, D. A., & Furr, D. (2005). *2003 income and employment survey results for the Society for Industrial and Organizational Psychology.* Bowling Green, OH: SIOP.

Meehl, P. (1954). *Clinical vs. statistical prediction.* Minneapolis, MN: University of Minnesota Press.

Megargee, E. I., & Carbonell, J. L. (1988). Evaluating leadership with the CPI. In C. Spielberger & J. N. Butcher (Eds.), *Advances in personality assessment* (Vol. 7, pp. 121–139). Hillsdale, NJ: Erlbaum.

Mehrabian, A. (1981). *Silent messages* (2nd ed.). Belmont, CA: Wadsworth.

Meindl, J. R. (1990). On leadership: An alternative to the conventional wisdom. *Research in Organizational Behavior, 12,* 159–203.

Melamed, S., Ben-Avi, I., Luz, J., & Green, M. S. (1995). Objective and subjective work monotony: Effects on job satisfaction, psychological distress, and absenteeism in blue-collar workers. *Journal of Applied Psychology, 80,* 29–42.

Mento, A. J., Locke, E. A., & Klein, H. J. (1992). Relationship of goal level to valence and instrumentality. *Journal of Applied Psychology, 77,* 395–405.

Mento, A. J., Steele, R. P., & Karren, R. J. (1987). A meta-analytic study of the effects of goal-setting on task performance: 1966–1984. *Organizational Behavior and Human Decision Processes, 39,* 52–83.

Mentzer, M. S. (2005). Towards a psychological and cultural model of downsizing. *Journal of Organizational Behavior, 26,* 993–997.

Merwin, G. A., Thomason, J. A., & Sanford, E. E. (1989). Methodology and content review of organizational behavior management in the private sector: 1978–1986. *Journal of Organizational Behavior Management, 10,* 39–57.

Mesmer-Magnus, J. R., & Viswesvaran, C. (2007). Expatriate management: A review and directions for research in expatriate selection, training, and repatriation. In M. M. Harris (Ed.), *Handbook of research in international human resource management* (pp. 183–206). Mahwah, NJ: Lawrence Erlbaum.

Meyer, H. H., & Raich, M. S. (1983). An objective evaluation of a behavior modeling training program. *Personnel Psychology, 36,* 755–761.

Meyer, J. P., & Allen, N. J. (1997). *Commitment in the workplace: Theory, research, and application.* Thousand Oaks, CA: Sage.

Meyer, J. P., Allen, N. J., & Smith, C. A. (1993). Commitment to organizations and occupations: Extension and test of a three-component conceptualization. *Journal of Applied Psychology, 78,* 538–551.

Miceli, M. P. (1993). Justice and pay system satisfaction. In R. Cropanzano (Ed.), *Justice in the workplace: Approaching fairness in HRM* (pp. 257–283). Hillsdale, NJ: Erlbaum.

Michaelson, L. K., Watson, W. E., & Black, R. H. (1989). A realistic test of individual versus group consensus decision making. *Journal of Applied Psychology, 74,* 834–839.

Michelson, G., & Mouly, V. S. (2004). Do loose lips sink ships? The meaning, antecedents and consequences of rumour and gossip in organizations. *Corporate Communications, 9(3),* 189–201.

Milkovich, G. T., & Gomez, L. R. (1976). Child care and selected work behaviors. *Academy of Management Journal, 19,* 111–115.

Mills, P. R., Kessler, R. C., Cooper, J., & Sullivan, S. (2007). Impact of a health promotion program on employee health risks and work productivity. *American Journal of Health Promotion, 22(1),* 45–53.

Millsap, R. E., & Kwok, O. (2004). Evaluating the impact of partial factorial invariance on selection in two populations. *Psychological Methods, 9(1),* 93–115.

Milne, P. (2007). Motivation, incentives and organizational culture. *Journal of Knowledge Management, 11(6),* 28–38.

Miner, F. C. (1984). Group versus individual decision making: An investigation of performance measures, decision strategies, and process losses/gains. *Organizational Behavior and Human Performance, 31,* 112–124.

Miner, J. B. (1983). The unpaved road from theory: Over the mountains to application. In R. H. Kilmann, K. W. Thomas, D. P. Slevin, R. Nath, & S. L. Jerrel (Eds.), *Producing useful knowledge for organizations* (pp. 37–68). New York: Praeger.

Miner, J. B. (1984). The unpaved road over the mountains: From theory to applications. *The Industrial-Organizational Psychologist, 21,* 9–20.

Mintzberg, H. (1973). *The nature of managerial work.* New York: Harper & Row.

Mintzberg, H. (1984). Power and organization life cycles. *Academy of Management Review, 9,* 207–224.

Mio, J. S., & Goishi, C. K. (1988). The employee assistance program: Raising productivity by lifting constraints. In P. Whitney & R. B. Ochman (Eds.), *Psychology and productivity.* New York: Plenum Press.

Miron, D., & McClelland, D. C. (1979). The impact of achievement motivation training on small businesses. *California Management Review, 21,* 13–28.

Mirvis, P. H., & Berg, D. N. (1977). *Failures in organization development and change: Cases and essays for learning.* New York: Wiley.

Mishra, J. (1990). Managing the grapevine. *Public Personnel Management, 19,* 213–228.

Mitchell, K. E., Alliger, G. M., & Morfopoulos, R. (1997). Toward an ADA-appropriate job analysis. *Human Resource Management Review, 7,* 5–26.

Mitchell, T. R., & Kalb, L. S. (1982). Effects of job experience on supervisor attributions for a subordinate's poor performance. *Journal of Applied Psychology, 67,* 181–188.

Mitchell, T. R., Hopper, H., Daniels, D., Falvy, J. G., & Ferris, G. R. (1998). Power, accountability, and inappropriate actions. *Applied Psychology: An International Review, 47,* 497–517.

Mitra, A., Gupta, N., & Jenkins, G. D. (1997). A drop in the bucket: When is a pay raise a pay raise? *Journal of Organizational Behavior, 18,* 117–137.

Mitra, A., Jenkins, G. D., & Gupta, N. (1992). A meta-analytic review of the relationships between absenteeism and turnover. *Journal of Applied Psychology, 77,* 879–889.

Mobley, W. H. (1982). Some unanswered questions in turnover and withdrawal research. *Academy of Management Review, 7,* 111–116.

Molinsky, A., & Margolis, J. (2006). The emotional tightrope of downsizing: Hidden challenges for leaders and their organizations. *Organizational Dynamics, 35,* 145–159.

Mone, M. A., McKinley, W., & Barker, V. L. (1998). Organizational decline and innovation: A contingency framework. *Academy of Management Review, 23,* 115–132.

Monge, P. R., Cozzens, M. D., & Contractor, N. S. (1992). Communication and motivational predictors of the dynamics of organizational innovation. *Organization Science, 3,* 250–274.

Monge, P. R., & Eisenberg, E. M. (1987). Emergent communication networks. In F. Jablin, L. Putnam, K. Roberts, & L. Porter (Eds.), *Handbook of organizational communication: An interdisciplinary approach.* Beverly Hills, CA: Sage.

Monk, T. H., Folkard, S., & Wedderburn, A. I. (1996). Maintaining safety and high performance on shiftwork. *Applied Ergonomics, 27,* 17–23.

Moore, S., Grunberg, L., & Greenberg, E. (2006). Surviving repeated waves of organizational downsizing: The recency, duration, and order effects associated with different forms of layoff contact. *Anxiety, Stress & Coping: An International Journal, 19(3),* 309–329.

Moreland, R. L., Argote, I., & Krishnan, R. (1998). Training people to work in groups. In R. S. Tindale (Ed.), *Theory and research on small groups* (pp. 37–60). New York: Plenum Press.

Morgeson, F. P., & Campion, M. A. (1997). Social and cognitive sources of potential inaccuracy in job analysis. *Journal of Applied Psychology, 82,* 627–655.

Morrisby, J. R. (1955). *Mechanical ability test.* London, UK: Educational and Industrial Test Services.

Morrison, E. W. (1993). Longitudinal study of the effects of information seeking on newcomer socialization. *Journal of Applied Psychology, 78,* 173–183.

Morse, B. J., & Popovich, P. M. (2009). Realistic recruitment practices in organizations: The potential benefits of generalized expectancy calibration. *Human Resource Management Review, 19,* 1–8.

Morse, N. C., & Reimer, E. (1956). The experimental change of a major organizational variable. *Journal of Abnormal and Social Psychology, 52,* 120–129.

Moscoso, S. (2000). Selection interview: A review of validity evidence, adverse impact and applicant reactions. *International Journal of Selection and Assessment, 8,* 237–247.

Moscovici, S. (1985). Social influence and conformity. In G. Lindzey & E. Aronson (Eds.), *Handbook of social psychology* (3rd ed., pp. 347–412). New York: Random House.

Motowidlo, S. J., Carter, G. W., Dunnette, M. D., Tippins, N., Werner, S., Burnett, J. R., & Vaughan, M. J. (1992). Studies of the structured behavioral interview. *Journal of Applied Psychology, 77,* 571–587.

Motowidlo, S. J., Dunnette, M. D., & Carter, G. W. (1990). An alternative selection procedure: The low-fidelity simulation. *Journal of Applied Psychology, 75,* 640–647.

Motowidlo, S. J., Packard, J. S., & Manning, M. R. (1986). Occupational stress: Its causes and consequences for job performance. *Journal of Applied Psychology, 71,* 618–629.

Mount, M. K. (1984). Supervisor, self-and subordinate ratings of performance and satisfaction with supervision. *Journal of Management, 10,* 305–320.

Mount, M. K., Barrick, M. R., & Strauss, J. P. (1999). The joint relationship of conscientiousness and ability with performance: Test of the interaction hypothesis. *Journal of Management, 25,* 702–721.

Mount, M. K., Witt, L. A., & Barrick, M. R. (2000). Incremental validity of empirically keyed biodata scales over GMA and the five factor personality concerns. *Personnel Psychology, 53,* 299–323.

Mowday, R. T. (1979). Equity theory predictions of behavior in organizations. In R. M. Steers & L. W. Porter (Eds.), *Motivation and work behavior* (2nd ed.). New York: McGraw-Hill.

Mowday, R. T., Steers, R., & Porter, L. W. (1979). The measurement of organizational commitment. *Journal of Vocational Behavior, 14,* 224–247.

Muchinsky, P. M. (1977a). A comparison of within-and across-subjects analyses of the expectancy-valence model for predicting effort. *Academy of Management Journal, 20,* 154–158.

Muchinsky, P. M. (1977b). Organizational communication: Relationships to organizational climate and job satisfaction. *Academy of Management Journal, 20,* 592–607.

Muchinsky, P. M. (1979). The use of reference reports in personnel selection: A review and evaluation. *Journal of Occupational Psychology, 52,* 287–297.

Muchinsky, P. M. (1987). *Psychology applied to work* (2nd ed.). Chicago, IL: Dorsey.

Muchinsky, P. M. (1993). Validation of intelligence and mechanical aptitude tests in selecting employees for manufacturing jobs. *Journal of Business and Psychology, 7,* 373–382.

Mueller, C. W., De Coster, S., & Estes, S. B. (2001). Sexual harassment in the workplace: Unanticipated consequences of modern social control in organizations. *Work and Occupations, 28,* 411–446.

Mueser, K. T., Rosenberg, S. D., & Rosenberg, H. J. (2009). *Treatment of posttraumatic stress disorder in special populations: A cognitive restructuring program.* Washington, DC: American Psychological Association.

Mulcahy, A. (2010, October). How I did it: Xerox's former CEO on why succession shouldn't be a horse race. *Harvard Business*

Review. Retrieved from http://hbr.org/2010/10/how-i-did-it-xeroxs-former-ceo-on-why-succession-shouldnt-be-a-horse-race/ar/1

Mullen, B., & Copper, C. (1994). The relations between group cohesiveness and performance: An integration. *Psychological Bulletin, 115,* 210–227.

Mullen, J. E., & Kelloway, E. K. (2009). Safety leadership: A longitudinal study of the effects of transformational leadership on safety outcomes. *Journal of Occupational and Organizational Psychology, 82(2),* 253–272.

Mullins, W. C., & Kimbrough, W. W. (1988). Group composition as a determinant of job analysis outcomes. *Journal of Applied Psychology, 73,* 657–664.

Mumford, M. D., & Licuanan, B. (2004). Leading for innovation: Conclusions, issues, and directions. *Leadership Quarterly, 15,* 163–171.

Munchus, G. (1983). Employer-employee based quality circles in Japan: Human resource policy implications for American firms. *Academy of Management Review, 8,* 255–261.

Munnoch, K., & Bridger, R. (2008). The relationship between a mechanical comprehension test and weapons-training task. *Military Psychology, 20(2),* 95–101.

Munsterberg, H. (1913). *Psychology and industrial efficiency.* Boston, MA: Houghton Mifflin.

Munz, D. C., & Kohler, J. M. (1997). Do worksite stress management programs attract the employees who need them and are they effective? *International Journal of Stress Management, 4,* 1–11.

Murphy, K. R. (1993). *Honesty in the workplace.* Pacific Grove, CA: Brooks/Cole.

Murphy, K. R. (1998). Trends facing work, work organizations, and I-O psychologists. *The Industrial-Organizational Psychologist, 35,* 95–97.

Murphy, K. R., & Balzar, W. K. (1986). Systematic distortions in memory-based behavior ratings and performance evaluations: Consequences for rating accuracy. *Journal of Applied Psychology, 71,* 39–44.

Murphy, K. R., & Dzieweczynski, J. L. (2005). Why don't measures of broad dimensions of personality perform better as predictors of job performance. *Human Performance, 18,* 343–357.

Murphy, K. R., Philbin, T. A., & Adams, S. R. (1989). Effect of purpose of observation on accuracy of immediate and delayed performance ratings. *Organizational Behavior and Human Decision Processes, 43,* 336–354.

Murphy, S. A., Beaton, R. D., Pike, K. C., & Johnson, L. C. (1999). Occupational stressors, stress responses, and alcohol consumption among professional firefighters: A prospective, longitudinal analysis. *International Journal of Stress Management, 6,* 179–196.

Murphy, S. E. (2002). Leader self-regulation: The role of self-efficacy and multiple intelligences. In R. E. Riggio, S. E. Murphy, & P. J. Pirozzolo (Eds.), *Multiple intelligences and leadership* (pp. 165–186). Mahwah, NJ: Erlbaum.

Murray, B., & Gerhart, B. (1998). An empirical analysis of a skill-based pay program and plant performance outcomes. *Academy of Management Journal, 41,* 68–78.

Muse, L. A., Harris, S. G., & Field, H. S. (2003). Has the inverted-U theory of stress and job performance had a fair test? *Human Performance, 16,* 349–364.

Myers, D. G., & Lamm, H. (1976). The group polarization phenomenon. *Psychological Bulletin, 83,* 602–627.

Nahrgang, J. D., Morgeson, F. P., & Hofmann, D. A. (2011). Safety at work: A meta-analytic investigation of the link between job demands, job resources, burnout, engagement, and safety outcomes. *Journal of Applied Psychology, 96,* 71–94. doi: 10.1037/a0021484.

Namie, G., & Namie, R. (2009). *The bully at work: What you can do to stop the hurt and reclaim your dignity on the job* (2nd ed.). Napierville, IL: Sourcebooks.

Naranjo-Valencia, J. C., Jimenez-Jimenez, D., & Sanz-Valle, R. (2011). Innovation or imitation? The role of organizational culture. *Mangement Decision, 49(1),* 55–72.

Narayanan, L, Menon, S., & Spector, P. (1999). A cross-cultural comparison of job stressors and reactions among employees holding comparable jobs in two countries. *International Journal of Stress Management, 6,* 197–212.

Nathan, P. E. (1983). Failures in prevention: Why we can't prevent the devastating effect of alcoholism and drug abuse. *American Psychologist, 38,* 459–467.

Near, J. P., Dworkin, T. M., & Miceli, M. P. (1993). Explaining the whistle-blowing process: Suggestions from power theory and justice theory. *Organization Science, 4,* 393–411.

Near, J. P., & Miceli, M. P. (1985). Organizational dissidence: The case of whistle-blowing. *Journal of Business Ethics, 4,* 1–16.

Near, J. P., & Miceli, M. P. (1995). Effective whistle-blowing. *Academy of Management Review, 20,* 679–708.

Nebeker, D. M., & Tatum, C. (1993). The effects of computer monitoring, standards, and rewards on work performance, job satisfaction, and stress. *Journal of Applied Social Psychology, 23,* 508–536.

Nelson, D. L. (1987). Organizational socialization: A stress perspective. *Journal of Occupational Behavior, 8,* 311–324.

Nelson, D. L., & Simmons, B. L. (2011). Savoring eustress while coping with distress: The holistic model of stress. In J. C. Quick & L. E. Tetrick (Eds.), *Handbook of occupational health psychology* (2nd ed.) (pp. 55–74). Washington, DC: American Psychological Association.

Nesler, M. S., Aguinis, H., Quigley, B. M., Lee, S., & Tedeschi, J. T. (1999). The development and validation of a scale measuring global social power based on French and Raven's power taxonomy. *Journal of Applied Social Psychology, 29,* 750–771.

Neuman, G. A., Edwards, J. E., & Raju, N. S. (1989). Organizational development interventions: A meta-analysis of their effects on satisfaction and other attitudes. *Personnel Psychology, 42,* 461–489.

Ng, T. W. H., Butts, M. M., Vandenberg, R. J., DeJoy, D. M., & Wilson, M. G. (2006). Effects of management communication, opportunity for learning, and work schedule flexibility on organizational commitment. *Journal of Vocational Behavior, 68,* 474–489.

Nicklin, J. M., & Roch, S. G. (2009). Letters of recommendation: Controversy and consensus from expert perspectives. *International Journal of Selection and Assessmesnt, 17(1),* 76–91.

Niederman, F., & Volkema, R. J. (1999). The effects of facilitator characteristics on meeting preparation, set up, and implementation. *Small Group Research, 30,* 330–360.

Niehoff, B. P., Moorman, R. H., Blakely, G., & Fuller, J. (2001). The influence of empowerment and job enrichment on employee loyalty in a downsizing environment. *Group & Organization Management, 26,* 93–113.

Nisbett, R. D., & Wilson, T. D. (1977). The halo effect: Evidence for unconscious alteration of judgments. *Journal of Personality and Social Psychology, 35,* 250–256.

Noe, R. A. (1986). Trainees' attributes and attitudes: Neglected influences on training effectiveness. *Academy of Management Review, 11,* 736–749.

Noe, R. A. (1996). Is career management related to employee development and performance? *Journal of Organizational Behavior, 17,* 119–133.

Normand, J., Salyards, S. D., & Mahoney, J. J. (1990). An evaluation of preemployment drug testing. *Journal of Applied Psychology, 75,* 629–639.

Nossiter, V. (1979). A new approach toward resolving the line and staff dilemma. *Academy of Management Review, 4,* 103–106.

Nurse, L. (2005). Performance appraisal, employee development and organizational justice: Exploring the linkages. *International Journal of Human Resource Management, 16,* 1176–1194.

Nutt, P. C., & Backoff, R. W. (1997). Transforming organizations with second-order change. *Research in Organizational Change and Development, 10,* 229–274.

O'Bannon, D. P., & Pearce, C. L. (1999). An exploratory examination of gainsharing in service organizations: Implications for organizational citizenship behavior and pay satisfaction. *Journal of Managerial Issues, 11,* 363–378.

O'Boyle, E. H., Forsyth, D. R., & O'Boyle, A. S. (2011). Bad apples or bad barrels: An examination of group- and organizational-level effects in the study of counterproductive work behavior. *Group and Organization Management, 36(1),* 39–69.

O'Connor, F. (1977). *O'Connor finger dexterity test.* Lafayette, IN: Lafayette Instruments.

O'Driscoll, M. P., & Beehr, T. A. (1994). Supervisor behaviors, role stressors and uncertainty as predictors of personal outcomes for subordinates. *Journal of Organizational Behavior, 15,* 141–155.

O'Driscoll, M. P., & Eubanks, J. L. (1993). Behavioral competencies, goal-setting, and OD practitioner effectiveness. *Group & Organization Management, 18,* 308–327.

O'Driscoll, M. P., Ilgen, D. R., & Hildreth, K. (1992). Time devoted to job and off-job activities, interrole conflict and affective experiences. *Journal of Applied Psychology, 77,* 272–279.

O'Reilly, C. A. (1978). The intentional distortion of information in organizational communication: A laboratory and field approach. *Human Relations, 31,* 173–193.

O'Reilly, C. A. (1980). Individuals and information overload in organizations: Is more necessarily better? *Academy of Management Journal, 23,* 684–696.

O'Reilly, C. A. (1989). Corporations, culture, and commitment: Motivation and social control in organizations. *California Management Review, 31,* 9–25.

O'Reilly, C. A., & Chatman, J. A. (1996). Culture as social control: Corporations, cults, and commitment. *Research in Organizational Behavior, 18,* 157–200.

O'Reilly, C. A., Chatman, J. A., & Caldwell, D. (1991). People and organizational culture: A Q-sort approach to assessing person-organization fit. *Academy of Management Journal, 34,* 487–516.

O'Reilly, C. A., & Roberts, K. H. (1976). Relationships among components of credibility and communication behaviors in work units. *Journal of Applied Psychology, 61,* 99–102.

O'Sullivan, M. (2005). Emotional intelligence and deception detection: Why most people can't "read" others, but a few can. In R. E. Riggio & R. S. Feldman (Eds.), *Applications of nonverbal communication* (pp. 215–253). Mahwah, NJ: Erlbaum.

Odiorne, G. (1963). The trouble with sensitivity training. *Training Directors Journal, 17,* 12–19.

Offermann, L. R., & Phan, L. U. (2002). Culturally intelligent leadership for a diverse world. In R. E. Riggio, S. E. Murphy, & F. J. Pirozzolo (Eds.), *Multiple intelligences and leadership* (pp. 187–214). Mahwah, NJ: Lawrence Erlbaum.

Olian, J. D., Carroll, S. J., & Giannantonio, C. M. (1993). Mentor reactions to protégés: An experiment with managers. *Journal of Vocational Behavior, 43,* 266–278.

Oliver, N. (1990). Work rewards, work values, and organizational commitment in an employee-owned firm: Evidence from the U.K. *Human Relations, 43,* 513–526.

Omachonu, V. K., & Ross, J. E. (1994). *Principles of total quality.* Delray Beach, FL: St. Lucie Press.

Ones, D. S., & Viswesvaran, C. (1998a). Looking ahead in I-O psychology (If we had a crystal ball...). *The Industrial-Organizational Psychologist, 35,* 92–95.

Ones, D. S., & Viswesvaran, C. (1998b). Integrity testing in organizations. In R. W. Griffen (Ed.), *Dysfunctional behavior in organizations: Violent and deviant behavior* (pp. 243–276). Stamford, CT: JAI Press.

Ones, D. S., & Viswesvaran, C. (1998c). The effects of social desirability and faking on personality and integrity assessment for personnel selection. *Human Performance, 11,* 245–269.

Ones, D. S., & Viswesvaran, C. (2007). A research note on the incremental validity of job knowledge and integrity tests for predicting maximal performance. *Human Performance, 20(3),* 293–303.

Orasnu, J., Fischer, U., & Davison, J. (1997). Cross-cultural barriers to effective communication in aviation. In C. S. Granrose & S. Oskamp (Eds.), *Cross-cultural work groups* (pp. 134–162). Thousand Oaks, CA: Sage.

Organ, D. W. (1988). *Organizational citizenship behavior: The good soldier syndrome.* Lexington, MA: Lexington.

Organ, D. W. (1990). The motivational basis of organizational citizenship behavior. In B. M. Staw & L. L. Cummings (Eds.), *Research in organizational behavior* (Vol. 14, pp. 43–72). Greenwich, CT: JAI Press.

Organ, D. W., & Ryan, K. (1995). A meta-analytic review of attitudinal and dispositional predictors of organizational citizenship behavior. *Personnel Psychology, 48,* 775–802.

Orlitzky, M., & Rynes, S. L. (2001). When employees become owners: Can employee loyalty be bought? *Trends in Organizational Behavior, 8,* 57–79.

Ortega, J. (2001). Job rotation as a learning mechanism. *Management Science, 47,* 1361–1370.

Osborn, A. F. (1957). *Applied imagination.* New York: Charles Scribner's Sons.

Ostroff, C. (1993a). The effects of climate and personal influences on individual behavior and attitudes in organizations. *Organizational Behavior and Human Decision Processes, 56,* 56–90.

Ostroff, C. (1993b). Relationships between person-environment congruence and organizational effectiveness. *Group and Organization Management, 18,* 103–122.

Ostroff, C., & Ford, J. K. (1989). Assessing training needs: Critical levels of analysis. In I. L. Goldstein (Ed.), *Training and development in organizations* (pp. 25–62). San Francisco, CA: Jossey-Bass.

Ostroff, C., & Kozlowski, S. W. (1992). Organizational socialization as a learning process: The role of information acquisition. *Personnel Psychology, 45,* 849–874.

Ostroff, C., & Kozlowski, S. W. J. (1993). The role of mentoring in the information gathering processes of newcomers during early organizational socialization. *Journal of Vocational Behavior, 42,* 170–183.

Otis, A. S. (1929). *Self-administering test of mental ability.* Tarrytown-on-Hudson, NY: World.

Ott, J. S. (1989). *The organizational culture perspective.* Pacific Grove, CA: Brooks/Cole.

Owens, W. A. (1976). Background data. In M. D. Dunnette (Ed.), *Handbook of industrial and organizational psychology* (pp. 609–644). Chicago, IL: Rand McNally.

Palich, L. E., & Hom, P. W. (1992). The impact of leader power and behavior on leadership perceptions. *Group and Organization Management, 17,* 279–296.

Pande, P. S., Neuman, R. P., & Cavanagh, R. R. (2000). *The Six Sigma way: How GE, Motorola, and other top companies are honing their performance.* New York: McGraw-Hill.

Parasuraman, S., & Alutto, J. A. (1984). Sources and outcomes of stress in organizational settings: Toward the development of a structural model. *Academy of Management Journal, 27,* 330–350.

Parker, C. P., Dipboye, R. L., & Jackson, S. L. (1995). Perceptions of organizational politics: An investigation of antecedents and consequences. *Journal of Management, 21,* 891–912.

Parsons, H. M. (1974). What happened at Hawthorne? *Science, 183,* 922–932.

Paul, R. J., & Ebadi, Y. M. (1989). Leadership decision making in a service organization: A field test of the Vroom-Yetton model. *Journal of Occupational and Organizational Psychology, 62,* 201–211.

Paulus, P. B., & Dzindolet, M. T. (1993). Social influence processes in group brainstorming. *Journal of Personality and Social Psychology, 64,* 575–586.

Paulus, P. B., Larey, T. S., & Dzindolet, M. T. (2001). Creativity in groups and teams. In M. E. Turner (Ed.), *Groups at work: Theory and research* (pp. 319–339). Mahwah, NJ: Erlbaum.

Payne, R. L., Jabri, M. M., & Pearson, A. W. (1988). On the importance of knowing the affective meaning of job demands. *Journal of Organizational Behavior, 9,* 149–158.

Pearce, C. L., & Conger, J. A. (Eds.). (2003). *Shared leadership: Reframing the hows and whys of leadership.* Thousand Oaks, CA: Sage.

Pearce, C. L., Manz, C. C., & Sims, H. P. (2009). Where do we go from here?: Is shared leadership the key to team success. *Organizational Dynamics, 38(3),* 234–238.

Pearce, J. L., Stevenson, W. B., & Perry, J. L. (1985). Managerial compensation based on organizational performance: A time series analysis of the effects of merit pay. *Academy of Management Journal, 28,* 261–278.

Pech, R. J. (2001). Reflections: Termites, group behaviour, and the loss of innovation: Conformity rules! *Journal of Managerial Psychology, 16,* 559–574.

Pelled, L. H., & Xin, K. R. (1999). Down and out: An investigation of the relationship between mood and employee withdrawal behavior. *Journal of Management, 25,* 875–895.

Penner, L. A., Midili, A. R., & Kegelmeyer, J. (1997). Beyond job attitudes: A personality and social psychology perspective on the causes of organizational citizenship behavior. *Human Performance, 10,* 111–131.

Perlman, R., & Pike, M. (1994). *Sex discrimination in the labour market: The case for comparable worth.* Manchester, England: Manchester University Press.

Perrewé, P. L., Zellars, K. L., Rossi, A. M., Ferris, G. R., Kacmar, C. J., Liu, Y., Zinko, R., & Hochwater, W. A. (2005). Political skill: An antidote in the role overload-strain relationship. *Journal of Occupational Health Psychology, 10,* 239–250.

Perrow, C. (1970). *Organizational analysis: A sociological perspective.* Belmont, CA: Wadsworth.

Perry, N. (1998). Indecent exposures: Theorizing whistleblowing. *Organization Studies, 19,* 235–257.

Pescosolido A. T. (2003). Group efficacy and group effectiveness: The effects of group efficacy over time on group performance and development. *Small Group Research, 34,* 20–42.

Peter, L. J., & Hull, R. (1969). *The Peter principle.* New York: William Morrow.

Peters, L. H., Hartke, D. D., & Pohlmann, J. T. (1985). Fiedler's contingency theory of leadership: An application of the meta-analysis procedures of Schmidt and Hunter. *Psychological Bulletin, 97,* 274–285.

Peterson, D. B. (2011). Executive coaching: A critical review and recommendations for advancing the practice. In S. Zedeck (Ed.), *APA handbook of industrial and organizational psychology, Vol 2: Selecting and developing members for the organization* (pp. 527–566). Washington, DC: American Psychological Association.

Peterson, N. G., & Jeanneret, P. R. (1997). Job analysis: Overview and description of deductive methods. In D. L. Whetzel & G. R. Wheaton (Eds.), *Applied measurement methods in industrial psychology* (pp. 13–50). Palo Alto, CA: Davies-Black.

Pfeffer, J. (1981). *Power in organizations.* Boston, MA: Pitman.

Pfeffer, J. (1992). Understanding power in organizations. *California Management Review, 34,* 29–50.

Phillips, A. S., & Bedeian, A. G. (1994). Leader-follower exchange quality: The role of personal and interpersonal attributes. *Academy of Management Journal, 37,* 990–1001.

Pierce, J. L., Gardner, D. G., Dunham, R. B., & Cummings, L. L. (1993). Moderation by organization-based self-esteem of role condition-employee response relationships. *Academy of Management Journal, 36,* 271–286.

Pinder, C. (1984). *Work motivation.* Glenview, IL: Scott-Foresman.

Pinkley, R. L., Brittain, J., Neale, M. A., & Northcraft, G. B. (1995). Managerial third-party dispute intervention: An inductive analysis of intervenor strategy selection. *Journal of Applied Psychology, 80,* 386–402.

Pinzler, I. K., & Ellis, D. (1989). Wage discrimination and comparable worth: A legal perspective. *Journal of Social Issues, 45,* 51–65.

Pitt-Catsouphes, M., Kossek, E. E., & Sweet, S. (Eds.). (2006). *The work and family handbook: Multi-disciplinary perspectives and approaches.* Mahwah, NJ: Erlbaum.

Plachy, R. J., & Plachy, S. J. (1998). *More results-oriented job descriptions.* New York: AMACOM.

Ployhart, R. E. (2006). Staffing in the 21st century: New challenges and strategic opportunities. *Journal of Management, 32,* 868–897.

Ployhart, R. E., Schneider, B., & Schmitt, N. (2006). *Staffing organizations: Contemporary practice and theory.* (3rd ed.). Mahwah, NJ: Erlbaum.

Ployhart, R. E., Ziegert, J. C., & McFarland, L. A. (2003). Understanding racial differences on cognitive ability tests in selection contexts: An integration of stereotype threat and applicant reactions research. *Human Performance, 16,* 231–259.

Podsakoff, P. M., Ahearne, M., & MacKenzie, S. B. (1997). Organizational citizenship behavior and the quantity and quality of work group performance. *Journal of Applied Psychology, 82,* 262–270.

Podsakoff, P. M., & MacKenzie, S. B. (1994). Organizational citizenship behaviors and sales unit effectiveness. *Journal of Marketing Research, 31,* 351–363.

Podsakoff, P. M., & MacKenzie, S. B. (1997a). Impact of organizational citizenship behavior on organizational performance: A review and suggestions for future research. *Human Performance, 10,* 133–151.

Podsakoff, P. M., & MacKenzie, S. B. (1997b). Kerr and Jermier's substitutes for leadership model: Background empirical assessment and suggestions for future research. *Leadership Quarterly, 8,* 117–125.

Podsakoff, P. M., MacKenzie, S. B., Paine, J. B., & Bachrach, D. G. (2000). Organizational citizenship behaviors: A critical review of the theoretical and empirical literature and suggestions for future research. *Journal of Management, 26,* 513–563.

Podsakoff, P. M., & Schriesheim, C. A. (1985). Field studies of French and Raven's bases of power: Critique, reanalysis, and suggestions for future research. *Psychological Bulletin, 97,* 387–411.

Poelmans, S. A. Y. (Ed.). (2005). *Work and family: An international research perspective.* Mahwah, NJ: Erlbaum.

Poon, J. M. L. (2003). Situational antecedents and outcomes of organizational politics perceptions. *Journal of Managerial Psychology, 18,* 138–155.

Porras, J. I., & Robertson, P. J. (1992). Organizational development: Theory, practice, and research. In M. D. Dunnette & L. M. Hough (Eds.), *Handbook of industrial and organizational psychology* (Vol. 3, 2nd ed., pp. 719–822). Palo Alto, CA: Consulting Psychologists Press.

Porter, G. (1996). Organizational impact of workaholism: Suggestions for researching the negative outcomes of excessive work. *Journal of Occupational Health Psychology, 1,* 70–84.

Porter, G. (2001). Workaholic tendencies and the high potential for stress among co-workers. *International Journal of Stress Management, 8,* 147–164.

Porter, L. W., Allen, R. W., & Angle, H. L. (1981). The politics of upward influence in organizations. In B. Staw (Ed.), *Research in organizational behavior* (pp. 109–149). Greenwich, CT: JAI Press.

Porter, L. W., & Lawler, E. E. (1968). *Managerial attitudes and performance.* Homewood, IL: Irwin.

Porter, L. W., & Roberts, K. H. (1976). Communication in organizations. In M. D. Dunnette (Ed.), *Handbook of industrial and organizational psychology.* Skokie, IL: Rand McNally.

Porter, L. W., & Steers, R. M. (1973). Organizational, work, and personal factors in employee turnover and absenteeism. *Psychological Bulletin, 80,* 151–176.

Porter, L. W., Steers, R. M., Mowday, R. T., & Boulian, P. V. (1974). Organizational commitment, job satisfaction, and turnover among psychiatric technicians. *Journal of Applied Psychology, 59,* 603–609.

Post, J. M. (2011). Crimes of obedience: "Groupthink" at Abu Ghraib. *International Journal of Group Psychotherapy, 61(1),* 49–66.

Postmes, T., Spears, R., & Cihangir, S. (2001). Quality of decision making and group norms. *Journal of Personality and Social Psychology, 80,* 918–930.

Powell, G. N., & Butterfield, D. A. (1994). Investigating the "glass ceiling" phenomenon: An empirical study of actual promotions to top management. *Academy of Management Journal, 37,* 68–86.

Powell, G. N., & Butterfield, D. A. (1997). Effect of race on promotions to top management in a federal department. *Academy of Management Journal, 40,* 112–128.

Powell, K. S., & Yalcin, S. (2010). Managerial training effectiveness: A meta-analysis 1952–2002. *Personnel Review, 39,* 227–241.

Premack, S. L., & Wanous, J. P. (1985). A meta-analysis of realistic job preview experiments. *Journal of Applied Psychology, 70,* 706–719.

Primoff, E. (1975). *How to prepare and conduct job element examinations.* Personnel Research and Development Center, Washington, DC: U.S. Government Printing Office.

Pritchard, R. D., Dunnette, M. D., & Jorgenson, D. (1972). Effects of perceptions of equity on worker motivation and satisfaction. *Journal of Applied Psychology, 56,* 75–94.

Pritchard, R. D., Hollenback, J., & DeLeo, P. J. (1980). The effects of continuous and partial schedules of reinforcement on effort, performance, and satisfaction. *Organizational Behavior and Human Performance, 25,* 336–353.

Pritchard, R. D., Leonard, D. W., Von Bergen, C. W., & Kirk, R. J. (1976). The effects of varying schedules of reinforcement on human task performance. *Organizational Behavior and Human Performance, 16,* 205–230.

Probst, T. M. (2003). Exploring employee outcomes of organizational restructuring: A Solomon four-group study. *Group & Organization Management, 28,* 416–439.

Prussia, G. E., Fugate, M., & Kinicki, A. J. (2001). Explication of the coping goal construct: Implications for coping and reemployment. *Journal of Applied Psychology, 86,* 1179–1190.

Pulakos, E. D. (1984). A comparison of rater training programs: Error training and accuracy training. *Journal of Applied Psychology, 69,* 581–588.

Pulakos, E. D., Arad, S., Donovan, M. A., & Plamondon, K. E. (2000). Adaptability in the workplace: Development of a taxonomy of adaptive performance. *Journal of Applied Psychology, 85,* 612–624.

Quiñones, M. A. (1997). Contextual influences on training effectiveness. In M. A. Quiñones & A. Ehrenstein (Eds.), *Training for a rapidly changing workplace: Applications of psychological research* (pp. 177–199). Washington, DC: American Psychological Association.

Quiñones, M. A., Ford, J. K., & Teachout, M. S. (1995). The relationship between work experience and job performance: A conceptual and meta-analytic review. *Personnel Psychology, 48,* 887–910.

Rademacher, R., Simpson, D., & Marcdante, K. (2010). Critical incidents as a method for teaching professionalism. *Medical Teacher, 32,* 244–249.

Rafaeli, A., & Pratt, M. G. (Eds.). (2006). *Artifacts and organizations: Beyond mere symbolism.* Mahwah, NJ: Erlbaum.

Rafferty, A. E., & Griffin, M. A. (2006). Perceptions of organizational change: A stress and coping perspective. *Journal of Applied Psychology, 91,* 1154–1162.

Ragins, B. R. (1989). Barriers to mentoring: The female manager's dilemma. *Human Relations, 42,* 1–22.

Ragins, B. R. (1999). Gender and mentoring relationships: A review and research agenda for the next decade. In G. N. Powell

(Ed.), *Handbook of gender in organizations* (pp. 347–370). Thousand Oaks, CA: Sage.

Ragins, B. R., & Cotton, J. L. (1993). Gender and willingness to mentor in organizations. *Journal of Management, 19*, 97–116.

Ragins, B. R., & Cotton, J. L. (1999). Mentor functions and outcomes: A comparison of men and women in formal and informal mentoring relationships. *Journal of Applied Psychology, 84*, 529–550.

Ragins, B. R., Cotton, J. L., & Miller, J. S. (2000). Marginal mentoring: The effects of type of mentor, quality of relationship, and program design on work and career attitudes. *Academy of Management Journal, 43*, 1177–1194.

Ragins, B. R., & Scandura, T. A. (1993, April). *Expected costs and benefits of being a mentor.* Paper presented at 8th annual conference of the Society for Industrial/Organizational Psychology, San Francisco, CA.

Ralston, D. A. (1989). The benefits of flextime: Real or imagined? *Journal of Organizational Behavior, 10*, 369–373.

Randall, M. L., Cropanzano, R., Bormann, C. A., & Birjulin, A. (1999). Organizational politics and organizational support as predictors of work attitudes, job performance, and organizational citizenship behavior, *Journal of Organizational Behavior, 20*, 159–174.

Randolph, W. A., & Posner, B. Z. (1992). *Getting the job done: Managing project teams and task forces for success.* Englewood Cliffs, NJ: Prentice Hall.

Rantanen, M., Mauno, S., Kinnunen, U., & Rantanen, J. (2011). Do individual coping strategies help or harm in the work-family conflict situation? Examining coping as a moderator between work-family conflict and well-being. *International Journal of Stress Management, 18(1)*, 24–48.

Rao, V. S. (1995). Effects of teleconferencing technologies: An exploration of comprehension, feedback, satisfaction and role-related differences. *Group Decision and Negotiation, 4*, 251–272.

Rasmussen, K. G. (1984). Nonverbal behavior, verbal behavior, resume credentials, and selection interview outcomes. *Journal of Applied Psychology, 69*, 551–556.

Rauschenberger, J., Schmitt, N., & Hunter, J. E. (1980). A test of the need hierarchy concept by a Markov model of change in need strength. *Administrative Science Quarterly, 25*, 654–670.

Raven, B. H. (1992). A power/interaction model of interpersonal influence: French & Raven thirty years later. *Journal of Social Behavior and Personality, 7*, 217–244.

Raven, B. H., Schwarzwald, J., & Koslowsky, M. (1998). Conceptualizing and measuring a power/interaction model of interpersonal influence. *Journal of Applied Social Psychology, 28*, 307–322.

Raver, J. L., & Gelfand, M. J. (2005). Beyond the individual victim: Linking sexual harassment, team processes, and team performance. *Academy of Management Journal, 48(3)*, 387–400.

Raver, J. L., & Nishii, L. H. (2010). Once, twice, or three times as harmful? Ethnic harassment, gender harassment, and generalized workplace harassment. *Journal of Applied Psychology, 95(2)*, 236–254.

Reichers, A. E. (1987). An interactionist perspective on newcomer socialization rates. *Academy of Management Review, 12*, 278–287.

Reilly, R. R., & McGourty, J. (1998). Performance appraisal in team settings. In J. W. Smither (Ed.), *Performance appraisal: State of the art in practice* (pp. 244–277). San Francisco, CA: Jossey-Bass.

Reinsch, N. L., & Beswick, R. W. (1995). Preferences for sending word-processed versus handwritten messages: An exploratory study. *Journal of Business and Technical Communication, 9*, 45–62.

Rennesund, A. B., & Saksvik, P. O. (2010). Work performance norms and organizational efficacy as cross-level effects on the relationship between individual perceptions of self-efficacy, overcommitment, and work-related stress. *European Journal of Work and Organizational Psychology, 19(6)*, 629–653.

Rentsch, J. R., & Steel, R. P. (1998). Testing the durability of job characteristics as predictors of absenteeism over a six-year period. *Personnel Psychology, 51*, 165–190.

Rice, B. (1982). The Hawthorne defect: Persistence of a flawed theory. *Psychology Today, 16(2)*, 70–74.

Rice, R. W. (1978). Construct validity of the least preferred coworker (LPC) score. *Psychological Bulletin, 85*, 1199–1237.

Rice, R. W., Gentile, D. A., & McFarlin, D. B. (1991). Facet importance and job satisfaction. *Journal of Applied Psychology, 76*, 31–39.

Riggio, R. E. (1986). Assessment of basic social skills. *Journal of Personality and Social Psychology, 51*, 649–660.

Riggio, R. E. (1987). *The charisma quotient.* New York: Dodd-Mead.

Riggio, R. E. (2001). Interpersonal sensitivity research and organizational psychology: Theoretical and methodological applications. In J. A. Hall & F. Bernieri (Eds.), *Measurement of interpersonal sensitivity* (pp. 305–317). Mahwah, NJ: Erlbaum.

Riggio, R. E. (2005). Business applications of nonverbal communication. In R. E. Riggio & R. S. Feldman (Eds.), *Applications of nonverbal communication* (pp. 119–138). Mahwah, NJ: Erlbaum.

Riggio, R. E., Aguirre, M., Mayes, B. T., Belloli, C., & Kubiak, C. (1997). The use of assessment center methods for student outcome assessment. In R. E. Riggio & B. T. Mayes (Eds.), *Assessment centers: Research and applications* (pp. 273–278). Corte Madera, CA: Select Press.

Riggio, R. E., Chaleff, I., & Lipman-Blumen, J. (Eds.). (2008). *The art of followership.* San Francisco: Jossey-Bass.

Riggio, R. E., & Cole, E. J. (1992). Agreement between subordinate and superior ratings of supervisory performance and effects on self- and subordinate job satisfaction. *Journal of Occupational and Organizational Psychology, 65*, 151–158.

Riggio, R. E., & Cole, E. J. (1995, August). *Stress and coping processes in on-duty firefighters.* Paper presented at meeting of the American Psychological Association, Toronto, Canada.

Riggio, R. E., Mayes, B. T., & Schleicher, D. J. (2003). Using assessment center methods for outcome assessment. *Journal of Management Inquiry, 12*, 68–78.

Riggio, R. E., Murphy, S. E., & Pirozzolo, F. J. (Eds.). (2002). *Multiple intelligences and leadership.* Mahwah, NJ: Erlbaum.

Riggio, R. E., & Throckmorton, B. (1988). The relative effects of verbal and nonverbal behavior, appearance, and social skills on evaluations made in hiring interviews. *Journal of Applied Social Psychology, 18*, 331–348.

Riordan, C. A. (1989). Images of corporate success. In R. A. Giacalone & P. Rosenfeld (Eds.), *Impression management in the organization* (pp. 87–103). Hillsdale, NJ: Erlbaum.

Rioux, S. M., & Penner, L. A. (2001). The causes of organizational citizenship behavior: A motivational analysis. *Journal of Applied Psychology, 86*, 1306–1314.

Ritchie, R. J., & Moses, J. L. (1983). Assessment center correlates of women's advancement into middle management: A 7-year longitudinal analysis. *Journal of Applied Psychology, 68*, 227–231.

Robbins, S. P. (1974). *Managing organizational conflict: A nontraditional approach.* Englewood Cliffs, NJ: Prentice Hall.

Robbins, S. P. (1979). *Organizational behavior: Concepts and controversies.* Englewood Cliffs, NJ: Prentice Hall.

Robbins, T. L. (1995). Social loafing on cognitive tasks: An examination of the "sucker effect." *Journal of Business and Psychology, 9,* 337–342.

Robertson, I. T., Baron, H., Gibbons, P., MacIver, R., & Nyfield, G. (2000). Conscientiousness and managerial performance. *Journal of Occupational and Organizational Psychology, 73,* 171–180.

Robertson, I. T., & Kinder, A. (1993). Personality and job competencies: The criterion-related validity of some personality variables. *Journal of Occupational and Organizational Psychology, 66,* 225–244.

Roche, G. R. (1979). Much ado about mentors. *Harvard Business Review, 57,* 14–19.

Rodgers, R., & Hunter, J. E. (1991). Impact of management by objectives on organizational productivity. *Journal of Applied Psychology, 76,* 322–336.

Rodríguez-Bailón, R., Moya, M., & Yzerbyt, V. (2000). Why do superiors attend to negative stereotypic information about their subordinates? Effects of power legitimacy on social perception. *European Journal of Social Psychology, 30,* 651–671.

Roethlisberger, F. J., & Dickson, W. J. (1939). *Management and the worker.* Cambridge: Harvard University Press.

Rogelberg, S. G., & Rumery, S. M. (1996). Gender diversity, team decision quality, time on task, and interpersonal cohesion. *Small Group Research, 27,* 79–90.

Ronen, S. (1981). Arrival and departure patterns of public sector employees before and after implementation of flextime. *Personnel Psychology, 34,* 817–822.

Ronen, S. (1989). Training the international assignee. In I. L. Goldstein (Ed.), *Training and development in organizations.* San Francisco, CA: Jossey-Bass.

Ronen, S., & Primps, S. B. (1981). The compressed work week as organizational change: Behavioral and attitudinal outcomes. *Academy of Management Review, 6,* 61–74.

Rosa, R. R., Colligan, M. J., & Lewis, P. (1989). Extended workdays: Effects of 8-hour and 12-hour rotating shift schedules on performance, subjective alertness, sleep patterns, and psychosocial variables. *Work & Stress, 3,* 21–32.

Rose, R. M. (1987). Neuroendocrine effects of work stress. In J. C. Quick, R. S. Bhagat, J. E. Dalton, & J. D. Quick (Eds.), *Work stress: Health care systems in the workplace* (pp. 130–147). New York: Praeger.

Rosen, C., Case, J., & Staubus, M. (2005). *Equity: Why employee ownership is good for business.* Boston, MA: Harvard Business Press.

Rosen, C., Klein, K. J., & Young, K. M. (1986). *Employee ownership in America: The equity solution.* Lexington, MA: Lexington Books.

Rosen, C. C., Levy, P. E., & Hall, R. J. (2006). Placing perceptions of politics in the context of the feedback environment, employee attitudes, and job performance. *Journal of Applied Psychology, 91,* 211–220.

Rosenfeld, P., Giacalone, R. A., & Riordan, C. (2002). *Impression management: Building and enhancing reputations at work.* Stamford, CT: Thompson.

Rosenman, R. H. (1978). The interview method of assessment of the coronary-prone behavior pattern. In T. M. Dembroski, S. M. Weiss, J. L. Shields, S. G. Haynes, & M. Feinlib (Eds.), *Coronary-prone behavior* (pp. 55–69). New York: Springer-Verlag.

Rosenman, R. H., Friedman, M., Strauss, R., Warm, M., Kositchek, R., Hahn, W., & Werthessen, N. T. (1964). A predictive study of coronary heart disease: The Western Collaborative Group Study. *Journal of the American Medical Association, 189,* 15–22.

Rosenthal, R. (1991). *Meta-analytic procedures for the social sciences* (2nd ed.). Newbury Park, CA: Sage.

Rosenthal, R. (1994). Interpersonal expectancy effects: A 30-year perspective. *Current Directions in Psychological Science, 3,* 176–179.

Rosenthal, R., & Jacobson, L. (1968). *Pygmalion in the classroom: Teacher expectations and pupils' intellectual development.* New York: Holt, Rinehart and Winston.

Rospenda, K. M., Richman, J. A., Ehmke, J. L. Z., Zlatoper, K. W. (2005). Is workplace harassment hazardous to your health? *Journal of Business and Psychology, 20,* 95–110.

Rost-Roth, M. (2010). Intercultural training. In D. Matsumoto (Ed.), *APA handbook of intercultural communication* (pp. 293–315). Washington, DC: American Psychological Association.

Roth, P. L., BeVier, C. A., Switzer, F. S., & Schippmann, J. S. (1996). Meta-analyzing the relationship between grades and job performance. *Journal of Applied Psychology, 81,* 548–556.

Roth, P. L., Bobko, P., & McFarland, L. A. (2005). A meta-analysis of work sample test validity: Updating and integrating some classic literature. *Personnel Psychology, 58,* 1009–1037.

Roth, P. L., & Campion, J. E. (1992). An analysis of the predictive power of the panel interview and pre-employment tests. *Journal of Occupational and Organizational Psychology, 65,* 51–60.

Rothausen, T. J., Gonzalez, J. A., & Griffin, A. E. C. (2009). Are all the parts there everywhere? Facet job satisfaction in the United States and the Philippines. *Asia Pacific Journal of Management, 26(4),* 681–700.

Roznowski, M. (1989). Examination of the measurement properties of the Job Descriptive Index with experimental items. *Journal of Applied Psychology, 74,* 805–814.

Rubin, R. S., Tardino, V. M. S., Daus, C. S., & Munz, D. C. (2005). Toward understanding emotional management at work: A quantitative review of emotional labor research. In C. E. J. Härtel, W. J. Zerbe, & N. M. Ashkanasy (Eds.), *Emotions in organizational behavior* (pp. 189–211). Mahwah, NJ: Erlbaum.

Russell, J. S. (1984). A review of fair employment cases in the field of training. *Personnel Psychology, 37,* 261–276.

Russell, R. D., & Russell, C. J. (1992). An examination of the effects of organizational norms, organizational structure, and environmental uncertainty on entrepreneurial strategy. *Journal of Management, 18,* 639–656.

Rutledge, T., Stucky, E., Dollarhide, A., Shively, M., Jain, S., Wolfson, T., Weinger, M. B., & Dresselhaus, T. (2009). A real-time assessment of work stress in physicians and nurses. *Health Psychology, 28(2),* 194–200.

Ryan, A. M., & Sackett, P. R. (1987). Pre-employment honesty testing: Fakeability, reactions of test takers, and company image. *Journal of Business and Psychology, 1,* 248–256.

Rynes, S. L. (1989). The employment interview as a recruitment device. In R. W. Eder & G. R. Ferris (Eds.), *The employment interview: Theory, research, and practice* (pp. 127–141). Newbury Park, CA: Sage.

Rynes, S. L. (1993). When recruitment fails to attract: Individual expectations meet organizational realities in recruitment. In

H. Schuler, J. L. Farr, & M. Smith (Eds.), *Personnel selection and assessment: Individual and organizational perspectives* (pp. 27–40). Hillsdale, NJ: Erlbaum.

Sachau, D. A. (2007). Resurrecting the motivation-hygiene theory: Herzberg and the positive psychology movement. *Human Resource Development Review, 6(4),* 377–393.

Sackett, P. R., Borneman, M. J., & Connelly, B. S. (2008). High-stakes testing in higher education and employment: Appraising the evidence for validity and fairness. *American Psychologist, 63(4),* 215–227.

Sackett, P. R., & Mullen, E. J. (1993). Beyond formal experimental design: Towards an expanding view of the training evaluation process. *Personnel Psychology, 46,* 613–627.

Sackett, P. R., & Wanek, J. E. (1996). New developments in the use of measures of honesty, integrity, conscientiousness, dependability, trustworthiness, and reliability for personnel selection. *Personnel Psychology, 49,* 787–829.

Sadowski-Rasters, G., Duysters, G., & Sadowski, B. M. (2006). *Communication and cooperation in the virtual workplace: Teamwork in computer-mediated-communication.* Northampton, MA: Edward Elgar.

Sagie, A. (1998). Employee absenteeism, organizational commitment, and job satisfaction: Another look. *Journal of Vocational Behavior, 52,* 156–171.

Saks, A. M. (1994). A psychological process investigation of the effects of recruitment source and organization information on job survival. *Journal of Organizational Behavior, 15,* 225–244.

Saks, A. M. (1996). The relationship between the amount and helpfulness of entry training and work outcomes. *Human Relations, 49,* 429–451.

Saks, A. M. (2006). Antecedents and consequences of employee engagement. *Journal of Managerial Psychology, 21(7),* 600–619.

Saks, A. M., & Ashforth, B. E. (1997). Organizational socialization: Making sense of the past and present as a prologue for the future. *Journal of Vocational Behavior, 51,* 234–279.

Saks, A. M., & Cronshaw, S. F. (1990). A process investigation of realistic job previews: Mediating variables and channels of communication. *Journal of Organizational Behavior, 11,* 221–236.

Salancik, G. R., & Pfeffer, J. (1977). Who gets power and how they hold on to it: A strategic-contingency model of power. *Organizational Dynamics, 5,* 3–21.

Salas, E., & Cannon-Bowers, J. A. (2001). The science of training: A decade of progress. *Annual Review of Psychology, 52,* 471–499.

Salas, E., Rozell, D., Mullen, B., & Driskell, J. E. (1999). The effect of team building on performance: An integration. *Small Group Research, 30,* 309–329.

Salgado, J. F., Anderson, N., Moscoso, S., Bertua, C., & de Fruyt, F. (2003). International validity generalization of GMA and cognitive abilities: A European community meta-analysis. *Personnel Psychology, 56,* 573–605.

Salgado, J. F., Anderson, N., Moscoso, S., Bertua, C., de Fruyt, F., & Rolland, J. P. (2003). A meta-analytic study of general mental ability validity for different occupations in the European community. *Journal of Applied Psychology, 88,* 1068–1081.

Salgado, J. F., Moscoso, S., & Lado, M. (2003). Test-retest reliability of ratings of job performance dimensions in managers. *International Journal of Selection and Assessment, 11,* 98–101.

Salgado, J. F., Viswesvaran, C., & Ones, D. S. (2001). Predictors used for personnel selection: An overview of constructs, methods and techniques. In N. Anderson, D. S. Ones, H. K. Sinangil, & C. Viswesvaran (Eds.), *Handbook of industrial, work, & organizational psychology* (pp. 165–199). London, UK: Sage.

Salimaki, A., & Jamsen, S. (2010). Perceptions of politics and fairness in merit pay. *Journal of Managerial Psychology, 25(3),* 229–251.

Sallis, J. F., Johnson, C. C., Trevorrow, T. R., Hovell, M. F., & Kaplan, R. M. (1985, August). *Worksite stress management: Anything goes?* Paper presented at the meeting of the American Psychological Association, Los Angeles, CA.

Salovey, P., & Mayer, J. D. (1990). Emotional intelligence. *Imagination, Cognition, and Personality, 9,* 185–211.

Sanna, L. J., & Parks, C. D. (1997). Group research trends in social and organizational psychology: Whatever happened to intragroup research? *Psychological Science, 8,* 261–267.

Sauley, K. S., & Bedeian, A. G. (2000). Equity sensitivity: Construction of a measure and examination of its psychometric properties. *Journal of Management, 26,* 885–910.

Savicki, V., & Kelley, M. (2000). Computer mediated communication: Gender and group composition. *CyberPsychology & Behavior, 3,* 817–826,

Sawyer, J. E., Latham, W. R., Pritchard, R. D., & Bennett, Jr., W. R. (1999). Analysis of work group productivity in an applied setting: Application of a time series panel design. *Personnel Psychology, 52,* 927–947.

Scandura, T. A., & Graen, G. B. (1984). Moderating effects of initial leader-member exchange status on the effects of a leadership intervention. *Journal of Applied Psychology, 69,* 428–436.

Scandura, T. A., & Williams, E. A. (2001). An investigation of the moderating effects of gender on the relationships between mentorship initiation and protégé perceptions of mentoring functions. *Journal of Vocational Behavior, 59,* 342–363.

Scarpello, V., & Campbell, J. P. (1983). Job satisfaction: Are all the parts there? *Personnel Psychology, 36,* 577–600.

Scarpello, V., & Vandenberg, R. J. (1992). Generalizing the importance of occupational and career views to job satisfaction attitudes. *Journal of Organizational Behavior, 13,* 125–140.

Schachaf, P. (2008). Cultural diversity and information and communication technology impacts on global virtual teams: An exploratory study. *Information & Management, 45(2),* 131–142.

Schachter, S., & Burdick, H. (1955). A field experiment of rumor transmission and distortion. *Journal of Abnormal and Social Psychology, 50,* 363–371.

Schaubroeck, J., Ganster, D. C., Sime, W. E., & Ditman, D. (1993). A field experiment testing supervisory role clarification. *Personnel Psychology, 46,* 1–25.

Schaubroeck, J., Jones, J. R., & Xie, J. L. (2001). Individual differences in utilizing control to cope with job demands: Effects on susceptibility to infectious disease. *Journal of Applied Psychology, 86,* 265–278.

Schaufeli, W. B., Salanova, M., Gonzalez-Roma, V., & Bakker, A. B. (2002). The measurement of engagement and burnout: A two sample confirmatory factor analytic approach. *Journal of Happiness Studies, 3,* 71–92.

Schaufeli, W. B., & Van Dierendonck, D. (1993). The construct validity of two burnout measures. *Journal of Organizational Behavior, 14,* 631–647.

Schein, E. H. (1968). Organizational socialization and the profession of management. *Industrial Management Review, 34,* 171–176.

Schein, E. H. (1969). *Process consultation: Its role in organization development.* Reading, MA: Addison-Wesley.

Schein, E. H. (1992). *Organizational culture and leadership* (2nd ed.). San Francisco, CA: Jossey-Bass.

Schein, E. H. (1996). Culture: The missing concept in organization studies. *Administrative Science Quarterly, 41,* 229–240.

Schein, V. E. (1977). Individual power and political behaviors in organizations: An inadequately explored reality. *Academy of Management Review, 2,* 64–72.

Schippman, J. S., Prien, E. P., & Katz, J. A. (1990). Reliability and validity of in-basket performance measures. *Personnel Psychology, 43,* 837–859.

Schleicher, D. J., Day, D. V., Mayes, B. T., & Riggio, R. E. (2002). A new frame for frame of reference training: Enhancing the construct validity of assessment centers. *Journal of Applied Psychology, 87,* 735–746.

Schmidt, F. L. (1973). Implications of a measurement problem for expectancy theory research. *Organizational Behavior and Human Performance, 10,* 243–251.

Schmidt, F. L., & Hunter, J. E. (1977). Development of a general solution to the problem of validity generalization. *Journal of Applied Psychology, 62,* 529–540.

Schmidt, F. L., & Hunter, J. E. (1998). The validity and utility of selection methods in personnel psychology: Practical and theoretical implications of 85 years of research findings. *Psychological Bulletin, 124,* 262–274.

Schmidt, F. L., Hunter, J. E., McKenzie, R. C., & Muldrow, T. W. (1979). Impact of valid selection procedures on work-force productivity. *Journal of Applied Psychology, 64,* 609–626.

Schmidt, F. L., Hunter, J. E., Outerbridge, A. N., & Trattner, M. H. (1986). The economic impact of job selection methods on size, productivity, and payroll costs of the federal work force: An empirically based demonstration. *Personnel Psychology, 39,* 1–29.

Schmidt, F. L., Law, K., Hunter, J. E., Rothstein, H. R., Pearlman, K., & McDaniel, M. (1993). Refinements in validity generalization methods: Implications for the situational specificity hypothesis. *Journal of Applied Psychology, 78,* 3–13.

Schmidt, F. L., & Ones, D. S. (1992). Personnel selection. *Annual Review of Psychology, 43,* 627–670.

Schmidt, R. A., & Bjork, R. A. (1992). New conceptualizations of practice: Common principles in these paradigms suggest new concepts for training. *Psychological Science, 3,* 207–217.

Schmidt, S. M., & Kipnis, D. (1984). Managers' pursuit of individual and organizational goals. *Human Relations, 37,* 781–794.

Schminke, M. (1993). Consequences of power in a simulated job: Understanding the turnover decision. *Journal of Applied Social Psychology, 23,* 52–78.

Schminke, M., Ambrose, M. L., & Cropanzano, R. S. (2000). The effect of organizational structure on perceptions of procedural fairness. *Journal of Applied Psychology, 85,* 294–304.

Schnake, M. E. (1991). Organizational citizenship: A review, proposed model, and research agenda. *Human Relations, 44,* 735–759.

Schneider, B. (1985). Organizational behavior. *Annual Review of Psychology, 36,* 573–611.

Schneider, B., & Bowen, D. E. (1995). *Winning the service game.* Boston, MA: Harvard Business School Press.

Schneider, B., Brief, A. P., & Guzzo, R. A. (1996). Creating a climate and culture for sustainable organizational change. *Organizational Dynamics, 24,* 6–9.

Schneider, B., Erhart, M. G., & Macey, W. H. (2011). Perspectives on organizational climate and culture. In S. Zedeck (Ed.), *APA handbook of industrial and organizational psychology* (Vol. 1, pp. 373–414). Washington, DC: American Psychological Association.

Schneider, D. J., Hastorf, A. H., & Ellsworth, P. C. (1979). *Person perception.* Reading, MA: Addison-Wesley.

Schneider, J., & Locke, E. A. (1971). A critique of Herzberg's incident classification system and a suggested revision. *Organizational Behavior and Human Performance, 6,* 441–457.

Schonfeld, I. S. (1990). Coping with job-related stress: The case of teachers. *Journal of Occupational Psychology, 63,* 141–149.

Schrader, B. W., & Steiner, D. D. (1996). Common comparison standards: An approach to improving agreement between self and supervisory performance ratings. *Journal of Applied Psychology, 81,* 813–820.

Schriesheim, C. A., Bannister, B. D., & Money, W. H. (1979). Psychometric properties of the LPC scale: An extension of Rice's review. *Academy of Management Review, 4,* 287–290.

Schriesheim, C. A., & Hinkin, T. R. (1990). Influence tactics used by subordinates: A theoretical and empirical analysis and refinement of the Kipnis, Schmidt, and Wilkinsen subscales. *Journal of Applied Psychology, 75,* 246–257.

Schriesheim, C. A., Hinkin, T. R., & Podsakoff, P. M. (1991). Can ipsative and single-item measures produce erroneous results in field studies of French and Raven's (1959) five bases of power? An empirical investigation. *Journal of Applied Psychology, 76,* 106–114.

Schriesheim, C. A., & Kerr, S. (1974). Psychometric properties of the Ohio State leadership scales. *Psychological Bulletin, 81,* 756–765.

Schriesheim, C. A., & Kerr, S. (1977). Theories and measures of leadership: A critical appraisal of current and future directions. In J. G. Hunt & L. L. Larson (Eds.), *Leadership: The cutting edge* (pp. 9–45). Carbondale, IL: Southern Illinois University Press.

Schuler, R. S., & Sethi, A. S. (1984). Time management and leader communication behavior. In R. S. Schuler & A. S. Sethi (Eds.), *Handbook of organizational stress coping strategies* (pp. 69–87). Cambridge, MA: Ballinger.

Schultz, K. S., Riggs, M. L., & Kottke, J. L. (1999). The need for an evolving concept of validity in industrial and personnel psychology: Psychometric, legal, and emerging issues. *Current Psychology: Developmental Learning Personality Social, 17,* 265–286.

Schwab, D. P., Olian-Gottlieb, J. D., & Heneman, H. G. (1979). Between-subjects expectancy theory research: A statistical review of studies predicting effort and performance. *Psychological Bulletin, 86,* 139–147.

Schweiger, D. M., Sandberg, W. R., & Ragan, J. W. (1986). Group approaches for improving strategic decision making: A comparative analysis of dialectical inquiry, devil's advocacy, and consensus. *Academy of Management Journal, 29,* 51–71.

Scott, G., Leritz, L. E., & Mumford, M. D. (2004). The effectiveness of creativity training: A quantitative review. *Creativity Research Journal, 16,* 361–388.

Scott, K. D., & Taylor, G. S. (1985). An examination of conflicting findings on the relationship between job satisfaction and absenteeism: A meta-analysis. *Academy of Management Journal, 28,* 599–612.

Scott, W. D. (1908). *The psychology of advertising.* New York: Arno Press.

Scott, W. G., Mitchell, T. R., & Birnbaum, P. H. (1981). *Organizational theory: A structural and behavioral analysis.* Homewood, IL: Irwin.

Seibert, S. E., & Kraimer, M. L. (2001). The five-factor model of personality and career success. *Journal of Vocational Behavior, 58,* 1–21.

Selye, H. (1976). *The stress of life* (Rev. ed.). New York: McGraw-Hill.

Seo, M., Feldman Barrett, L., & Bartunek, J. M. (2004). The role of affective experience in work motivation. *Academy of Management Review, 29,* 423–439.

Sethi, A. S. (1984a). Meditation for coping with organizational stress. In A. S. Sethi & R. S. Schuler (Eds.), *Handbook of organizational stress coping strategies* (pp. 145–165). Cambridge, MA: Ballinger.

Sethi, A. S., & Schuler, R. S. (Eds.). (1984). *Handbook of organizational stress coping strategies.* Cambridge, MA: Ballinger.

Shahani, C., Weiner, R., & Streit, M. K. (1993). An investigation of the dispositional nature of the time management construct. *Anxiety, Stress, and Coping, 6,* 231–243.

Shaiken, H. (1984). *Work transformed: Automation and labor in the computer age.* New York: Holt, Rinehart and Winston.

Shaw, J. D., Gupta, N., Mitra, A., & Ledford, G. E. (2005). Success and survival of skill-based pay. *Journal of Management, 31,* 28–49.

Shaw, M. E. (1964). Communication networks. In L. Berkowitz (Ed.), *Advances in experimental social psychology* (Vol. 1, pp. 111–147). New York: Academic Press.

Shaw, M. E. (1978). Communication networks fourteen years later. In L. Berkowitz (Ed.), *Group processes* (pp. 351–362). New York: Academic Press.

Shaw, M. E. (1981). *Group dynamics: The psychology of small group behavior* (3rd ed.). New York: McGraw-Hill.

Shen, J. (2005). International training and management development: Theory and reality. *Journal of Management Development, 24(7),* 656–666.

Sheppard, B. H. (1974). Third party conflict intervention: A procedural framework. In B. M. Staw & L. L. Cummings (Eds.), *Research in organizational behavior* (Vol. 6, pp. 141–190). Greenwich, CT: JAI Press.

Sherif, M., Harvey, O. J., White, B. J., Hood, W. R., & Sherif, C. W. (1961). *Intergroup conflict and cooperation: The Robbers Cave experiment.* Norman, OK: Institute of Group Relations.

Shore, L. M., & Wayne, S. J. (1993). Commitment and employee behavior: Comparison of affective commitment and continuance commitment with perceived organizational support. *Journal of Applied Psychology, 78,* 774–780.

Shouksmith, G., & Burrough, S. (1988). Job stress factors for New Zealand and Canadian air traffic controllers. *Applied Psychology: An International Review, 37,* 263–270.

Sia, C., Tan, B. C. Y., & Wei, K. (2002). Group polarization and computer-mediated communication: Effects of communication cues, social presence, and anonymity. *Information Systems Research, 13(1),* 70–90.

Sias, P. M., & Jablin, F. M. (1995). Differential superior-subordinate relations, perceptions of fairness, and coworker communication. *Human Communication Research, 22,* 5–38.

Silverman, S. B., & Wexley, K. N. (1984). Reaction of employees to performance appraisal interviews as a function of their participation in rating scale development. *Personnel Psychology, 37,* 703–710.

Simmons, P. O. (1993). The Judd test for Lotus 1–2–3. *HR Magazine, 38,* 33–36.

Simon, S. J., & Werner, J. M. (1996). Computer training through behavior modeling, self-paced, and instructional approaches: A field experiment. *Journal of Applied Psychology, 81,* 648–659.

Sims, H. P., Szilagyi, A. D., & Keller, R. T. (1976). The measurement of job characteristics. *Academy of Management Journal, 19,* 195–212.

Sims, R. L., & Keenan, J. P. (1998). Predictors of external whistleblowing: Organizational and intrapersonal variables. *Journal of Business Ethics, 17,* 411–421.

Smith, B. N., Kerr, N. A., Markus, M. J., & Stasson, M. F. (2001). Individual differences in social loafing: Need for cognition as a motivator in collective performance. *Group Dynamics: Theory, Research, & Practice, 5,* 150–158.

Smith, C. A., Organ, D. W., & Near, J. P. (1983). Organizational citizenship behavior: Its nature and antecedents. *Journal of Applied Psychology, 68,* 653–663.

Smith, K. G., Locke, E. A., & Barry, D. (1990). Goal setting, planning, and organizational performance: An experimental simulation. *Organizational Behavior and Human Decision Processes, 46,* 118–134.

Smith, L., & Folkard, S. (1993). The impact of shiftwork on personnel at a nuclear power plant: An exploratory survey study. *Work & Stress, 7,* 341–350.

Smith, M. (1994). A theory of the validity of predictors in selection. *Journal of Occupational and Organizational Psychology, 67,* 13–31.

Smith, P. C. (1976). Behavior, results, and organizational effectiveness: The problem of criteria. In M. D. Dunnette (Ed.), *Handbook of industrial and organizational psychology* (pp. 745–766). Skokie, IL: Rand McNally.

Smith, P. C., & Kendall, L. M. (1963). Retranslation of expectations: An approach to the construction of unambiguous anchors for rating scales. *Journal of Applied Psychology, 47,* 149–155.

Smith, P. C., Kendall, L. M., & Hulin, C. L. (1969). *The measurement of satisfaction in work and retirement.* Chicago, IL: Rand McNally.

Smith, P. C., Kendall, L. M., & Hulin, C. L. (1987). The revised JDI: A facelift for an old friend. *The Industrial-Organizational Psychologist, 24(4),* 31–33.

Smith, T. W., & Pope, M. K. (1990). Cynical hostility as a health risk: Current status and future directions. *Journal of Social Behavior and Personality, 5,* 77–88.

Smither, J. W. (1998). Lessons learned: Research implications for performance appraisals and management practice. In J. W. Smither (Ed.), *Performance appraisal: State of the art in practice* (pp. 537–547). New York: Jossey-Bass.

Smither, J. W., Wohlers, A. J., & London, M. (1995). A field study of reactions to normative versus individualized upward feedback. *Group & Organization Management, 20,* 61–89.

Smith-Jentsch, K. A., Jentsch, F. G., Payne, S. C., & Salas, E. (1996). Can pretraining experiences explain individual differences in learning? *Journal of Applied Psychology, 81,* 110–116.

Snyder, R. A., & Morris, J. H. (1984). Organizational communication and performance. *Journal of Applied Psychology, 69,* 461–465.

Society for Industrial and Organizational Psychology (SIOP). (2003). *Principles for the validation and use of personnel selection procedures* (4th ed.). Bowling Green, OH: SIOP.

Solomon, R. L. (1949). An extension of control group design. *Psychological Bulletin, 46*, 137–150.

Somech, A., Desivilya, H. S., & Lidogoster, H. (2009). Team conflict management and team effectiveness. The effects of task interdependence and team identification. *Journal of Organizational Behavior, 30(3)*, 359–378.

Song, Z., Li, W., & Arvey, R. D. (2011). Associations between dopamine and serotonin genes and job satisfaction: Preliminary evidence from the Add Health Study. *Journal of Applied Psychology, 96(6)*, 1223–1233.

Sonnentag, S., Brodbeck, F. C., Heinbokel, T., & Stolte, W. (1994). Stressor-burnout relationship in software development teams. *Journal of Occupational and Organizational Psychology, 67*, 327–341.

Sonnentag, S., & Zijlstra, F. R. H. (2006). Job characteristics and off-job activities as predictors of need for recovery, well-being, and fatigue. *Journal of Applied Psychology, 91*, 330–350.

Sorensen, E. (1994). *Comparable worth: Is it a worthy policy?* Princeton, NJ: Princeton University Press.

Sosik, J. J., Avolio, B. J., & Kahai, S. S. (1997). Effects of leadership style and anonymity on group potency and effectiveness in a group decision support system environment. *Journal of Applied Psychology, 82*, 89–103.

Soucek, R., & Moser, K. Coping with information overload in email communication: Evaluation of a training intervention. *Computer in Human Behavior, 26(6)*, 1458–1466.

Spangler, W. (1992). Validity of questionnaire and TAT measures of achievement: Two meta-analyses. *Psychological Bulletin, 112*, 140–154.

Sparks, K., & Cooper, C. L. (1999). Occupational differences in the work-strain relationship: Towards the use of situation-specific models. *Journal of Occupational and Organizational Psychology, 72*, 219–229.

Spector, P. E. (1987). Interactive effects of perceived control and job stressors on affective reactions and health outcomes for clerical workers. *Work and Stress, 1*, 155–162.

Spector, P. E. (1992). A consideration of the validity and meaning of self-report measures of job conditions. In C. L. Cooper & I. T. Richardson (Eds.), *International review of industrial and organizational psychology* (Vol. 7, pp. 123–151). New York: Wiley.

Spector, P. E. (1997a). *Job satisfaction: Application, assessment, causes, and consequences.* Thousand Oaks, CA: Sage.

Spector, P. E. (1997b). The role of frustration in antisocial behavior at work. In R. A. Giacalone & J. Greenberg (Eds.), *Antisocial behavior in organizations* (pp. 1–17). Thousand Oaks, CA: Sage.

Spector, P. E. (2001). Counterproductive work behavior: The secret side of organizational life. *Psychological Science Agenda, 14*, 8–9.

Spector, P. E., Bauer, J. A., & Fox, S. (2010). Measurement artifacts in the assessment of counterproductive work behavior and organizational citizenship behavior: Do we know what we think we know? *Journal of Applied Psychology, 95(4)*, 781–790.

Spector, P. E., Chen, P. Y., & O'Connell, B. J. (2000). A longitudinal study of relations between job stressors and job strains while controlling for prior negative affectivity and strains. *Journal of Applied Psychology, 85*, 211–218,

Spector, P. E., Dwyer, D. J., & Jex, S. M. (1988). Relation of job stressors to affective, health and performance outcomes: A comparison of multiple data sources. *Journal of Applied Psychology, 73*, 11–19.

Spector, P. E., & Fox, S. (Eds.). (2005). *Counterproductive work behavior: Investigations of actors and targets.* Washington, DC: American Psychological Association.

Spector, P. E., & Jex, S. M. (1991). Relations of job characteristics from multiple data sources with employee affect, absence, turnover intentions and health. *Journal of Applied Psychology, 76*, 46–53.

Spence, J. T., & Helmreich, R. L. (1983). Achievement-related motives and behaviors. In J. T. Spence (Ed.), *Achievement and achievement motives: Psychological and sociological approaches* (pp. 7–74). San Francisco, CA: Freeman.

Spence, J. T., & Robbins, A. S. (1992). Workaholism: Definition, measurement, and preliminary results. *Journal of Personality Assessment, 58*, 160–178.

Spielberger, C. D., & Reheiser, E. C. (1994). The job stress survey: Measuring gender differences in occupational stress. *Journal of Social Behavior and Personality, 9*, 199–218.

Spreitzer, G. M. (1996). Social structural characteristics of psychological empowerment. *Academy of Management Journal, 39*, 483–504.

Spreitzer, G. M., Cohen, S. G., & Ledford, G. E., Jr. (1999). Developing effective self-managing work teams in service organizations. *Group & Organization Management, 24*, 340–366.

Stagl, K. C., Salas, E., & Burke, C. S. (2007). Best practices in team leadership: What team leaders do to facilitate team effectiveness. In J. A. Conger & R. E. Riggio (Eds.), *The practice of leadership* (pp. 172–198). San Francisco, CA: Jossey-Bass.

Stahelski, A. J., Frost, D. E., & Patch, M. E. (1989). Use of socially dependent bases of power: French and Raven's theory applied to workgroup leadership. *Journal of Applied Social Psychology, 19*, 283–297.

Stahl, M. J., & Harrell, A. (1981). Modeling effort decisions with behavioral decision theory: Toward an individual differences model of expectancy theory. *Organizational Behavior and Human Performance, 27*, 303–325.

Stamp, G. (1990). Tokens and glass ceilings: The real issue of minorities in organizations. *Equal Opportunities International, 9*, 9–15.

Stanton, J. M. (2000). Reactions to employee performance monitoring: Framework, review, and research directions. *Human Performance, 13*, 85–113.

Stanton, J. M., & Barnes-Farrell, J. L. (1996). Effects of electronic performance monitoring on personal control, task satisfaction, and task performance. *Journal of Applied Psychology, 81*, 738–745.

Stanton, J. M., & Julian, A. L. (2002). The impact of electronic monitoring on quality and quantity of performance. *Computers in Human Behavior, 18*, 85–101.

Stauffer, J. M., & Buckley, M. R. (2005). The existence and nature of racial bias in supervisory ratings. *Journal of Applied Psychology, 90*, 586–591.

Staw, B. M., & Ross, J. (1985). Stability in the midst of change: A dispositional approach to job attitudes. *Journal of Applied Psychology, 70*, 469–480.

Steers, R. M., & Braunstein, D. N. (1976). A behaviorally based measure of manifest needs in work settings. *Journal of Vocational Behavior, 9*, 251–266.

Steers, R. M., & Porter, L. W. (Eds.). (1991). *Motivation and work behavior* (5th ed.) New York: McGraw-Hill.

Stein, F. (2001). Occupational stress, relaxation therapies, exercise and biofeedback. *Work: Journal of Prevention, Assessment & Rehabilitation, 17(3),* 235–246.

Steiner, D. D., Lane, I. M., Dobbins, G. H., Schnur, A., & McConnell, S. (1991). A review of meta-analyses in organizational behavior and human resources management: An empirical assessment. *Educational and Psychological Measurement, 51(3),* 609–626.

Sternberg, R. J. (2002). Successful intelligence: A new approach to leadership. In R. E. Riggio, S. E. Murphy, & F. J. Pirozzolo (Eds.), *Multiple intelligences and leadership* (pp. 9–28). Mahwah, NJ: Erlbaum.

Stevens, C. K. (1997). Effects of preinterview beliefs on applicants' reactions to campus interviews. *Academy of Management Journal, 40,* 947–966.

Stevens, C. K. (1998). Antecedents of interview interactions, interviewers' ratings, and applicants' reactions. *Personnel Psychology, 51,* 55–85.

Stevens, M. J., & Campion, M. A. (1994). The knowledge, skill, and ability requirements for teamwork: Implications for human resource management. *Journal of Management, 20,* 503–530.

Stevens, M. J., & Campion, M. A. (1999). Staffing work teams: Development and validation of a selection test for teamwork settings. *Journal of Management, 25,* 207–228.

Stewart, G. L., & Barrick, M. R. (2000). Team structure and performance: Assessing the mediating role of intrateam process and the moderating role of task type. *Academy of Management Journal, 43,* 135–148.

Stewart, G. L., & Manz, C. C. (1995). Leadership for self-managing work teams: A typology and integrative model. *Human Relations, 48,* (747–770).

Stogdill, R. M. (1948). Personal factors associated with leadership: A survey of the literature. *Journal of Psychology, 25,* 35–71.

Stogdill, R. M., & Coons, A. E. (Eds.). (1957). *Leader behavior: Its description and measurement.* Columbus, OH: Ohio State University, Bureau of Business Research.

Stokes, G. S., Mumford, M. D., & Owens, W. (1994). *Biodata handbook.* Menlo Park, CA: Consulting Psychologists Press.

Stokes, G. S., Mumford, M. D., & Owens, W. A. (Eds.). (1994). *Biodata handbook: Theory, research and use of biographical information in selection and performance prediction.* Palo Alto, CA: Consulting Psychologists Press.

St-Onge, S. (2000). Variables influencing the perceived relationship between performance and pay in a merit pay environment. *Journal of Business and Psychology, 14,* 459–479.

Stork, D., & Richards, W. D. (1992). Nonrespondents in communication network studies. *Group and Organization Management, 17,* 193–209.

Streufert, S., Pogash, R., & Piasecki, M. (1988). Simulation-based assessment of managerial competence: Reliability and validity. *Personnel Psychology, 41,* 537–557.

Stroh, L. K., Black, J. S., Mendenhall, M. E., & Gregersen, H. B. (2005). *International assignments: An integration of strategy, research, and practice.* Mahwah, NJ: Lawrence Erlbaum.

Strube, M. J., & Garcia, J. E. (1981). A meta-analytic investigation of Fiedler's contingency model of leader effectiveness. *Psychological Bulletin, 90,* 307–321.

Struthers, C. W., Weiner, B., & Allred, K. (1998). Effects of casual attributions on personnel decision: A social motivation perspective. *Basic and Applied Social Psychology, 20,* 155–166.

Stumpf, S. A., & Hartman, K. (1984). Individual exploration to organizational commitment or withdrawal. *Academy of Management Journal, 27,* 308–329.

Sturman, M. C., Hannon, J. M., & Milkovich, G. T. (1996). Computerized decision aids for flexible benefits decisions: The effects of an expert system and decision support system on employee intentions and satisfaction with benefits. *Personnel Psychology, 49,* 883–908.

Suleiman, J., & Watson, R. T. (2008). Social loafing in technology-supported teams. *Computer Supported Cooperative Work (CSCW), 17,* 291–301.

Sundstrom, E., de Meuse, K. P., & Futrell, D. (1990). Work teams: Applications and effectiveness. *American Psychologist, 45,* 120–133.

Sutherland, L. F., Fogarty, G. J., & Pithers, R. T. (1995). Congruence as a predictor of occupational stress. *Journal of Vocational Behavior, 46,* 292–309.

Sutherland, V. J., & Cooper, C. L. (1988). Sources of work stress. In J. J. Hurrell, L. R. Murphy, S. L., Sauter, & C. L. Cooper (Eds.), *Occupational stress issues and developments in research* (pp. 3–40). Philadelphia, PA: Taylor & Francis.

Svyantek, D. J., Goodman, S. A., Benz, L. L., & Gard, J. A. (1999). The relationship between organizational characteristics and team building success. *Journal of Business and Psychology, 14,* 265–283.

Taber, T. D., & Taylor, E. (1990). A review and evaluation of the psychometric properties of the Job Diagnostic Survey. *Personnel Psychology, 43,* 467–500.

Takalkar, P., & Coovert, M. D. (1994). International replication note: The dimensionality of job satisfaction in India. *Applied Psychology: An International Review, 43,* 415–426.

Tan, H. H., & Tan, M. (2008). Organizational citizenship behavior and social loafing; The role of personality, motives, and contextual factors. *Journal of Psychology: Interdisciplinary and Applied, 142(1),* 89–108.

Tang, T. L., Tollison, P. S., & Whiteside, H. D. (1987). The effect of quality circle initiation on motivation to attend quality circle meetings and on task performance. *Personnel Psychology, 40,* 799–814.

Tang, T. L., Tollison, P. S., & Whiteside, H. D. (1991). Managers' attendance and the effectiveness of small work groups: The case of quality circles. *The Journal of Social Psychology, 131,* 335–344.

Tang, T. L., Tollison, P. S., & Whiteside, H. D. (1996). The case of active and inactive quality circles. *The Journal of Social Psychology, 136,* 57–67.

Tannenbaum, S., & Yukl, G. (1992). Training and development in work organizations. *Annual Review of Psychology, 76,* 759–769.

Taormina, R. J. (2009). Organizational socialization: The missing link between employee needs and organizational culture. *Journal of Managerial Psychology, 24(7),* 650–676.

Taris, T. W., Kalimo, R., & Schaufeli, W. B. (2002). Inequity at work: Its measurement and association with worker health. *Work & Stress, 16,* 287–301.

Tavakolian, H. R. (1993). Break on through to the other side of the glass ceiling. *Equal Opportunities International, 12,* 14–20.

Taylor, D., Block, C., & Berry, P. (1958). Does group participation when using brainstorming facilitate or inhibit creative thinking? *Administrative Science Quarterly, 3,* 23–47.

Taylor, F. W. (1911). *The principles of scientific management.* New York: Harper.

Taylor, M. S., & Giannantonio, C. M. (1993). Forming, adapting, and terminating the employment relationship: A review of the literature from individual, organizational, and interactionist perspectives. *Journal of Management, 19,* 461–515.

Taylor, P. J., Russ-Eft, D. F., & Chan, D. W. L. (2005). A meta-analytic review of behavior modeling training. *Journal of Applied Psychology, 90,* 692–709.

Taylor, P. J., & Small, B. (2002). Asking applicants what they would do versus what they did do: A meta-analytic comparison of situational and past behaviour employment interview questions. *Journal of Occupational and Organizational Psychology, 75,* 277–294.

Teagarden, M. B. (2007). Best practices in cross-cultural leadership. In J. A. Conger & R. E. Riggio (Eds.), *The practice of leadership* (pp. 300–330). San Francisco, CA: Jossey-Bass.

Teboul, J. (1991). *Managing quality dynamics.* Englewood Cliffs, NJ: Prentice Hall.

Tehrani, N., & Piper, N. (2011). Traumatic stress in the police service. In N. Tehrani (Ed.), *Managing trauma in the workplace: Supporting workers and organizations* (pp. 17–32). New York: Routledge.

Tepper, B. J., Duffy, M. K., & Shaw, J. D. (2001). Personality moderators of the relationship between abusive supervision and subordinates' resistance. *Journal of Applied Psychology, 86,* 974–983.

Tepper, B. J., Lockhart, D., & Hoobler, J. (2001). Justice, citizenship, and role definition effects. *Journal of Applied Psychology, 86,* 789–796.

Tepper, B. J., & Taylor, E. C. (2003). Relationships among supervisors' and subordinates' procedural justice perceptions and organizational citizenship behaviors. *Academy of Management Journal, 46,* 97–105.

Terjesen, S., & Singh, V. (2008). Female presence on corporate boards: A multi-country study of environmental context. *Journal of Business Ethics, 83,* 55–63.

Tesluk, P. E., & Jacobs, R. R. (1998). Toward an integrated model of work experience. *Personnel Psychology, 51,* 1–36.

Tesser, A., & Rosen, S. (1975). The reluctance to transmit bad news. *Advances in Experimental Social Psychology, 8,* 192–232.

Tett, R. P., Jackson, D. N., & Rothstein, M. (1991). Personality measures as predictors of job performance: A meta-analytic review. *Personnel Psychology, 44,* 703–742.

Thacker, R. A., & Wayne, S. (1995). An examination of the relationship between upward influence tactics and assessments of promotability. *Journal of Management, 21,* 739–756.

Tharenou, P. (1993). A test of reciprocal causality for absenteeism. *Journal of Organizational Behavior, 14,* 269–290.

Tharenou, P. (2001). The relationship of training motivation to participation in training and development. *Journal of Occupational and Organizational Psychology, 74,* 599–621.

Theorell, T., Westerlund, H., Alfredsson, L., & Oxenstierna, G. (2005). Coping with critical life events and lack of control – the exertion of control. *Psychneuroendocrinology, 30(10).* 1027–1032.

Thomas, K. W. (1976). Conflict and conflict management. In M. Dunnette (Ed.), *Handbook of industrial and organizational psychology* (pp. 889–936). Chicago, IL: Rand McNally.

Thomas, K. W. (1992). Conflict and negotiation processes in organizations. In M. D. Dunnette & L. M. Hough (Eds.), *Handbook*

of industrial and organizational psychology (2nd ed., Vol. 3, pp. 651–717). Palo Alto, CA: Consulting Psychologists Press.

Thornton, G. C., & Rupp, D. E. (2006). *Assessment centers in human resource management: Strategies for prediction, diagnosis, and development.* Mahwah, NJ: Erlbaum.

Tiegs, R. B., Tetrick, L. E., & Fried, Y. (1992). Growth need strength and context satisfactions as mediators of the relations of the job characteristics model. *Journal of Management, 18,* 575–593.

Tiffin, J. (1968). *Purdue pegboard.* West Lafayette, IN: Science Research Associates.

Tjosvold, D. (1984a). Effects of crisis orientation on managers' approach to controversy in decision making. *Academy of Management Journal, 27,* 130–138.

Tjosvold, D. (1984b). Effects of leader warmth and directiveness on subordinate performance on a subsequent task. *Journal of Applied Psychology, 69,* 222–232.

Tjosvold, D. (1988). Cooperative and competitive interdependence. *Group & Organization Studies, 13,* 274–289.

Tjosvold, D. (1998a). Cooperative and competitive goal approach to conflict: Accomplishments and challenges. *Applied Psychology: An International Review, 47,* 285–342.

Tjosvold, D. (1998b). Making employee involvement work: Cooperative goals and controversy to reduce costs. *Human Relations, 51,* 201–214.

Tjosvold, D., Morishima, M., & Belsheim, J. A. (1999). Complaint handling on the shop floor: Cooperative relationships and open-minded strategies. *The International Journal of Conflict Management, 10,* 45–68.

Tjosvold, D., XueHuang, Y., Johnson, D. W., & Johnson, R. T. (2008). Social interdependence and orientation toward life and work. *Journal of Applied Social Psychology, 38(2),* 409–435.

Tornow, W. W. (1993). Perceptions or reality: Is multiperspective measurement a means or an end? *Human Resource Management, 32,* 221–230.

Tosi, H., & Tosi, L. (1987). What managers need to know about knowledge-based pay. In D. B. Balkin & L. R. Gomez-Mejia (Eds.), *New perspectives on compensation* (pp. 43–48). Englewood Cliffs, NJ: Prentice Hall.

Towler, A. J., & Dipboye, R. L. (2001). Effects of trainer expressiveness, organization, and trainee goal orientation on training outcomes. *Journal of Applied Psychology, 86,* 664–673.

Tracey, J. B., Tannenbaum, S. I., & Kavanagh, M. J. (1995). Applying trained skills on the job: The importance of the work environment. *Journal of Applied Psychology, 80,* 239–252.

Trahan, W. A., & McAllister, H. A. (2002). Master's level training in industrial/organizational psychology: Does it meet the SIOP guidelines. *Journal of Business and Psychology, 16,* 457–465.

Trevino, L. K., & Webster, J. (1992). Flow in computer-mediated communication. *Communication Research, 19,* 539–573.

Trevor, C. O., Gerhart, B., & Boudreau, J. W. (1997). Voluntary turnover and job performance: Curvilinearity and the moderating influences of salary growth and promotions. *Journal of Applied Psychology, 82,* 44–61.

Trice, H. M., & Beyer, J. M. (1986). Charisma and its routinization in two social movement organizations. *Research in Organizational Behavior, 8,* 113–164.

Truxillo, D. M., Donahue, L. M., & Sulzer, J. L. (1996). Setting cutoff scores for personnel selection tests: Issues, illustrations, and recommendations. *Human Performance, 9,* 275–295.

Tsai, W. (2001). Determinants and consequences of employee displayed positive emotions. *Journal of Management, 27*, 497–512.

Tschan, F. (1995). Communication enhances small group performance if it conforms to task requirements: The concept of ideal communication cycles. *Basic and Applied Social Psychology, 17*, 371–393.

Tubbs, M. E. (1986). Goal setting: A meta-analytic examination of the empirical evidence. *Journal of Applied Psychology, 71*, 474–483.

Tubbs, M. E., Boehne, D. M., & Dahl, J. G. (1993). Expectancy, valence, and motivational force functions in goal-setting research: An empirical test. *Journal of Applied Psychology, 78*, 361–373.

Tucker, F. D. (1985). A study of the training needs of older workers: Implications for human resources development planning. *Public Personnel Management, 14*, 85–95.

Tung, R. L. (1997). International and intranational diversity. In C. S. Granrose & S. Oskamp (Eds.), *Cross-cultural work groups* (pp. 163–185). Thousand Oaks, CA: Sage.

Turban, D. B. (2001). Organizational attractiveness as an employer on college campuses: An examination of the applicant population. *Journal of Vocational Behavior, 58*, 293–312.

Turban, D. B., Forret, M. L., & Hendrickson, C. L. (1998). Applicant attraction to firms: Influences of organization reputation, job and organizational attributes, and recruiter behaviors. *Journal of Vocational Behavior, 52*, 24–44.

Tziner, A. (1982). Differential effects of group cohesiveness types: A clarifying overview. *Social Behavior and Personality, 10*, 227–239.

Tziner, A., Joanis, C., & Murphy, K. R. (2000). A comparison of three methods of performance appraisal with regard to goal properties, goal perception, and ratee satisfaction. *Group & Organization Management, 25*, 175–190.

Tziner, A., Kopelman, R., & Joanis, C. (1997). Investigation of raters' and ratees' reactions to three methods of performance appraisal: BOS, BARS, and GRS. *Canadian Journal of Administrative Sciences, 14*, 396–404.

Tziner, A., Ronen, S., & Hacohen, D. (1993). A four-year validation study of an assessment center in a financial corporation. *Journal of Organizational Behavior, 14*, 225–237.

Udechukwu, I. I. (2009). Correctional officer turnover: Of Maslow's needs hierarchy and Herzberg's motivation theory. *Public Personnel Management, 38(2)*, 69–82.

Uhl-Bien, M. (2004). Relationship development as a key ingredient for leadership development. In S. E. Murphy & R. E. Riggio (Eds.), *The future of leadership development* (pp. 129–147). Mahwah, NJ: Lawrence Erlbaum.

Unden, A. (1996). Social support at work and its relationship to absenteeism. *Work & Stress, 10*, 46–61.

Urch Druskat, V., Sala, F., & Mount, G. (Eds.). (2006). *Linking emotional intelligence and performance at work: Current research evidence with individuals and groups.* Mahwah, NJ: Erlbaum.

Ury, W., Brett, J., & Goldberg, S. (1988). *Getting disputes resolved: Designing systems to cut the costs of conflict.* San Francisco, CA: Jossey-Bass.

U.S. Department of Labor. (1991). *Dictionary of occupational titles* (4th ed.). Washington, DC: U.S. Government Printing Office.

U.S. Department of Labor. (2011). Employer compensation and benefit statistics. Retrieved from http://www.bls.gov/home.htm

Vale, C. D., & Prestwood, J. S. (1987). *Minnesota clerical assessment battery.* San Antonio, TX: The Psychological Corporation.

Valentine, S., & Fleischman, G. (2004). Ethics training and businesspersons' perceptions of organizational ethics. *Journal of Business Ethics, 52(4)*, 391–400.

van Beek, I., Taris, T. W., & Schaufeli, W. B. (2011). Workaholic and work engaged employees: Dead ringers or world's apart? *Journal of Occupational and Health Psychology, 16*, 468–482.

Vandenberg, R. J., & Lance, C. E. (1992). Examining the causal order of job satisfaction and organizational commitment. *Journal of Management, 18*, 153–167.

Van de Ven, A. H., & Delbecq, A. (1974). A task contingent model of work-unit structure. *Administrative Science Quarterly, 19*, 183–197.

van de Vliert, E., Euwema, M. C., & Huismans, S. E. (1995). Managing conflict with a subordinate or a superior: Effectiveness of conglomerated behavior. *Journal of Applied Psychology, 80*, 271–281.

van der Vegt, G., Emans, B., & van de Vliert, E. (1998). Motivating effects of task and outcome interdependence in work teams. *Group & Organization Management, 23*, 124–143.

Van Dyne, L., Graham, J. W., & Dienesch, R. M. (1994). Organizational citizenship behavior: Construct redefinition, measurement, and validation. *Academy of Management Journal, 37*, 765–802.

Van Eerde, W., & Thierry, H. (1996). Vroom's expectancy models and work-related criteria: A meta-analysis. *Journal of Applied Psychology, 81*, 575–586.

Van Iddekinge, C. H., Roth, P. L., Raymark, P. H., & Odle-Dusseau, H. N. (2011). The criterion-related validity of integrity tests: An updated meta-analysis. *Journal of Applied Psychology, 96*, 1167–1194.

van Knippenberg, D., De Dreu, C. K. W., & Homan, A. C. (2004). Work group diversity and group performance: An integrative model and research agenda. *Journal of Applied Psychology, 89*, 1008–1022.

Van Knippenberg, D., & Van Ginkel, W. P. (2010). The categorization-elaboration model of work group diversity: Wielding the double-edged sword. In R. J. Crisp (Ed.), *The psychology of social and cultural diversity* (pp. 257–280). Chichester, UK: Wiley-Blackwell.

Van Vianen, A. E. M. (2000). Person-organization fit: The match between newcomers' and recruiters' preferences for organizational cultures. *Personnel Psychology, 53*, 113–149.

Van Vianen, A. E. M., & Van Schie, E. C. M. (1995). Assessment of male and female behaviour in the employment interview. *Journal of Community and Applied Psychology, 5*, 243–257.

Van Yperen, N. W. (1998). Informational support, equity and burnout: The moderating effect of self-efficacy. *Journal of Occupational and Organizational Psychology, 71*, 29–33.

Van Yperen, N. W., Hagedoorn, M., & Geurts, S. A. E. (1996). Intent to leave and absenteeism as reactions to perceived inequity: The role of psychological and social constraints. *Journal of Occupational and Organizational Psychology, 69*, 367–372.

Vance, R. J., & Colella, A. (1990). Effects of two types of feedback on goal acceptance and personal goals. *Journal of Applied Psychology, 75*, 68–76.

Vance, R. J., MacCallum, R. C., Coovert, M. D., & Hedge, J. W. (1988). Construct validity of multiple job performance measures using confirmatory factor analysis. *Journal of Applied Psychology, 73*, 74–80.

Vandenberg, R. J., & Barnes-Nelson, J. (1999). Disaggregating the motives underlying turnover intentions: When do intentions predict turnover behavior? *Human Relations, 52,* 1313–1337.

Vanderslice, V. J. (1988). Separating leadership from leaders: An assessment of the effect of leader and follower roles in organizations. *Human Relations, 41,* 677–696.

Vecchio, R. P. (1977). An empirical examination of the validity of Fiedler's model of leadership effectiveness. *Organizational Behavior and Human Performance, 19,* 180–206.

Vecchio, R. P. (1982). A further test of leadership effects due to between-group and within-group variation. *Journal of Applied Psychology, 67,* 200–208.

Vecchio, R. P. (2000). Negative emotion in the workplace: Employee jealousy and envy. *International Journal of Stress Management, 7,* 161–179.

Vecchio, R. P. (2007). Situational leadership theory: An examination of a prescriptive theory. In R. P Vecchio (Ed.), *Leadership: Understanding the dynamics of power and influence in organizations* (2nd ed., pp. 318–334). Notre Dame, IN: University of Notre Dame Press.

Verbeke, W. (2000). A revision of Hofstede et al.'s (1990) organizational practices scale. *Journal of Organizational Behavior, 21,* 587–602.

Verquer, M. L., Beehr, T. A., & Wagner, S. H. (2003). A meta-analysis of relations between person-organization fit and work attitudes. *Journal of Vocational Behavior, 63,* 473–489.

Victor, B., & Blackburn, R. S. (1987). Interdependence: An alternative conceptualization. *Academy of Management Review, 12,* 486–498.

Vigoda, E. (2000). Organizational politics, job attitudes, and work outcomes: Exploration and implications for the public sector. *Journal of Vocational Behavior, 57,* 326–347.

Vigoda, E. (2001). Reactions to organizational politics: A cross-cultural examination in Israel and Britain. *Human Relations, 54,* 1483. 1518.

Vigoda-Gadot, E., & Angert, L. (2007). Goal setting theory, job feedback and OCB: Lessons from a longitudinal study. *Basic and Applied Social Psychology, 29(2),* 119–128.

Vinchur, A. J., & Koppes, L. L. (2011). A historical survey of research and practice in industrial and organizational psychology. In S. Zedeck (Ed.), *APA handbook of industrial and organizational psychology* (Vol. 1, pp. 3–36). Washington, DC: American Psychological Association.

Viswesvaran, C. (2001). Assessment of individual job performance: A review of the past century and a look ahead. In N. Anderson, D. S. Ones, H. K. Sinangil, & C. Viswesvaran (Eds.), *Handbook of industrial, work & organizational psychology* (Vol. 1, pp. 110–126). Thousand Oaks, CA: Sage.

Viswesvaran, C., & Ones, D. S. (2000). Perspectives on models of job performance. *International Journal of Selection and Assessment, 8,* 216–226.

Viswesvaran, C., Ones, D. S., & Schmidt, F. L. (1996). Comparative analysis of the reliability of job performance ratings. *Journal of Applied Psychology, 81,* 557–574.

Viswesvaran, C., Sanchez, J. I., & Fisher, J. (1999). The role of social support in the process of work stress: A meta-analysis. *Journal of Vocational Behavior, 54,* 314–334.

Viswesvaran, C., Schmidt, F. L., & Ones, D. S. (2005). Is there a general factor in ratings of job performance? A meta-analytic

framework for disentangling substantive and error influences. *Journal of Applied Psychology, 90,* 108–131.

Vodanovich, S. J. (2003). Psychometric measures of boredom: A review of the literature. *Journal of Psychology: Interdisciplinary and Applied, 137,* 569–595.

Voskuijl, O. F., & van Sliedregt, T. (2002). Determinants of interrater reliability of job analysis: A meta-analysis. *European Journal of Psychological Assessment, 18,* 52–62.

Vroom, V. H. (1964). *Work and motivation.* New York: Wiley.

Vroom, V. H., & Jago, A. G. (1978). On the validity of the Vroom-Yetton model. *Journal of Applied Psychology, 63,* 151–162.

Vroom, V. H., & Jago, A. G. (1988). *The new leadership: Managing participation in organizations.* Englewood Cliffs, NJ: Prentice Hall.

Vroom, V. H., & Jago, A. G. (1995). Situation effects and levels of analysis in the study of leader participation. *Leadership Quarterly, 6,* 169–181.

Vroom, V. H., & Yetton, P. W. (1973). *Leadership and decision-making.* Pittsburgh, PA: University of Pittsburgh Press.

Waclawski, J., & Church, A. H. (Eds.). (2002). *Organization development: A data-driven approach to organizational change.* San Francisco, CA: Jossey-Bass.

Wageman, R., & Baker, G. (1997). Incentives and cooperation: The joint effects of task and reward interdependence on group performance. *Journal of Organizational Behavior, 18,* 139–158.

Wahba, M. A., & Bridwell, L. T. (1976). Maslow reconsidered: A review of research on the need hierarchy theory. *Organizational Behavior and Human Performance, 15,* 212–240.

Wainer, H. (Ed.). (2000). *Computerized adaptive testing: A primer* (2nd ed.). Mahwah, NJ: Erlbaum.

Waldman, D. A. (1994). The contributions of total quality management to a theory of work performance. *Academy of Management Review, 19,* 510–536.

Waldman, D. A., Atwater, L. E., & Antonioni, D. (1998). Has 360-degree feedback gone amok? *Academy of Management Executive, 12,* 86–94.

Waldman, D. A., Bowen, D. E. (1998). The acceptability of 360-degree appraisals: A customer-supplier relationship perspective. *Human Resource Management, 37,* 117–129.

Waldman, D. A., & Korbar, T. (2004). Student assessment center performance in prediction of early career success. *Academy of Management Learning & Education, 3(2),* 151–167.

Walker, A. G., & Smither, J. W. (1999). A five-year study of upward feedback: What managers do with their results matter. *Personnel Psychology, 52,* 393–423.

Wallach, M. A., Kogan, N., & Bem, D. J. (1962). Group influence on individual risk taking. *Journal of Abnormal and Social Psychology, 65,* 75–86.

Walton, R. E. (1972). How to counter alienation in the plant. *Harvard Business Review, 50,* 22.

Walton, R. E., & Dutton, J. M. (1969). The management of interdepartmental conflict: A model and review. *Administrative Science Quarterly, 14,* 73–84.

Walumbwa, F. O., Wang, P., Lawler, J. J., & Shi, K. (2004). The role of collective efficacy in the relations between transformational leadership and work outcomes. *Journal of Occupational and Organizational Psychology, 77,* 515–530.

Walz, S. M., & Niehoff, B. P. (1996). Organizational citizenship behaviors and their effect on organizational effectiveness in limited-menu restaurants. In J. B. Keys & L. N. Dosier (Eds.),

Academy of Management best paper proceedings (pp. 307–311). Briarcliff Manor, NY: Academy of Management.

Wanberg, C. R., & Banas, J. T. (2000). Predictors and outcomes of openness to changes in a reorganizing workplace. *Journal of Applied Psychology, 85,* 132–142.

Wanek, J. E. (1999). Integrity and honesty testing: What do we know? How do we use it? *International Journal of Selection and Assessment, 7,* 183–195.

Wang, G., Oh, I., Courtright, S. H., & Colbert, A. E. (2011). Transformational leadership and performance across criteria and levels: A meta-analytic review of 25 years of research. *Group & Organization Management, 36(2),* 223–270.

Wang, S., Jiao, H., Young, M. J., Brooks, T., & Olson, J. (2007). Comparability of computer-based and paper-and-pencil testing in K-12 reading assessments: A meta-analysis of testing mode effects. *Educational and Psychological Measurement, 68(1),* 5–24.

Wang, S., Young, M. J., Brooks, T., & Olson, J. (2007). A meta-analysis of testing mode effects in grade K-12 mathematics tests. *Educational and Psychological Measurement, 67,* 219–238.

Wanous, J. P. (1989). Installing realistic job previews: Ten tough choices. *Personnel Psychology, 42,* 117–134.

Wanous, J. P. (1992). *Organizational entry: Recruitment, selection, and socialization of newcomers* (2nd ed.). Reading, MA: Addison-Wesley.

Wanous, J. P. (1993). Newcomer orientation programs that facilitate organizational entry. In H. Schuler, J. L. Farr, & M. Smith (Eds.), *Personnel selection and assessment: Individual and organizational perspectives* (pp. 125–139). Hillsdale, NJ: Erlbaum.

Wanous, J. P., Keon, T. L., & Latack, J. C. (1983). Expectancy theory and occupational/organizational choices: A review and test. *Organizational Behavior and Human Performance, 32,* 66–86.

Wanous, J. P., Poland, T. D., Premack, S. L., & Davis, K. S. (1992). The effects of met expectations on newcomer attitudes and behaviors: A review and meta-analysis. *Journal of Applied Psychology, 77,* 288–297.

Wanous, J. P., Reichers, A. E., & Hudy, M. J. (1997). Overall job satisfaction: How good are single-item measures? *Journal of Applied Psychology, 82,* 247–252.

Wanous, J. P., Reichers, A. E., & Malik, S. D. (1984). Organizational socialization and group development: Toward an integrative perspective. *Academy of Management Review, 9,* 670–683.

Wanous, J. P., Stumpf, S. A., & Bedrosian, H. (1979). Job survival of new employees. *Personnel Psychology, 32,* 651–662.

Warr, P., Allan, C., & Birdi, K. (1999). Predicting three levels of training outcome. *Journal of Occupational and Organizational Psychology, 72,* 351–375.

Warr, P., & Birdi, K. (1998). Employee age and voluntary development activity. *International Journal of Training and Development, 2,* 190–204.

Warr, P., & Bunce, D. (1995). Trainee characteristics and the outcomes of open learning. *Personnel Psychology, 48,* 347–375.

Wasik, B. (1984). *Teaching parents effective problem solving: A handbook for professionals.* Chapel Hill: University of North Carolina Press.

Watson, G. (1971). Resistance to change. *American Behavioral Scientist, 14,* 745–766.

Watson, W. E., Kumar, K., & Michaelsen, L. K. (1993). Cultural diversity's impact on interaction process and performance: Comparing homogeneous and diverse task groups. *Academy of Management Journal, 36,* 590–602.

Waung, M. (1995). The effects of self-regulatory coping orientation on newcomer adjustment and job survival. *Personnel Psychology, 48,* 633–650.

Wayne, S. J., & Ferris, G. R. (1990). Influence tactics, affect, and exchange quality in supervisor-subordinate interactions: A laboratory and a field study. *Journal of Applied Psychology, 75,* 487–499.

Weber, M. (1947). *The theory of social and economic organizations* (A. M. Henderson & T. Parsons, Trans.). New York: Free Press.

Webster, J., & Martocchio, J. J. (1993). Turning work into play: Implications for microcomputer software training. *Journal of Management, 19,* 127–146.

Webster, J., & Martocchio, J. J. (1995). The differential effects of software training previews on training outcomes. *Journal of Management, 21,* 757–787.

Wech, B. A., Mossholder, K. W., Steel, R. P., & Bennett, N. (1998). Does work group cohesiveness affect individuals' performance and organizational commitment? A cross-level examination. *Small Group Research, 29,* 472–494.

Wechsler, D. (1981). *Wechsler adult intelligence scale-revised.* New York: The Psychological Corporation.

Weekley, J. A., & Gier, J. A. (1987). Reliability and validity of the situational interview for a sales position. *Journal of Applied Psychology, 72,* 484–487.

Weekley, J. A., & Jones, C. (1997). Video-based situational testing. *Personnel Psychology, 50,* 25–49.

Weekley, J. A., & Jones, C. (1999). Further studies of situational tests. *Personnel Psychology, 52,* 679–700.

Weenig, M. W. H. (1999). Communication networks in the diffusion of an innovation in an organization. *Journal of Applied Social Psychology, 29,* 1072–1092.

Weierter, S. J. M. (1997). Who wants to play "follow the leader"? A theory of charismatic relationships based on routinized charisma and follower characteristics. *Leadership Quarterly, 8,* 171–193.

Weisband, S. P. (1992). Group discussion and first advocacy effects in computer-mediated and face-to-face decision-making groups. *Organizational Behavior and Human Decision Processes, 53,* 352–380.

Weisband, S. P., Schneider, S. K., & Connolly, T. (1995). Computer-mediated communication and social information: Status salience and status differences. *Academy of Management Journal, 38,* 1124–1151.

Weiss, D. J., Dawis, R. V., England, G. W., & Lofquist, L. H. (1967). Manual for the Minnesota Satisfaction Questionnaire. In *Minnesota Studies on Vocational Rehabilitation* (Vol. 22). Minneapolis, MN: University of Minnesota Industrial Relations Center.

Weiss, H. M., Ilgen, D. R., & Sharbaugh, M. E. (1982). Effects of life and job stress on information search behaviors of organizational members. *Journal of Applied Psychology, 67,* 60–66.

Weiss, H. M., Suckow, K., & Rakestraw, T. L., Jr. (1999). Influence of modeling on self-set goals: Direct and mediated effects. *Human Performance, 12,* 89–114.

Weiss, R. M. (1987). Writing under the influence: Science versus fiction in the analysis of corporate alcoholism programs. *Personnel Psychology, 40,* 341–356.

Welbourne, T. M. (1998). Untangling procedural and distributive justice: Their relative effects on gainsharing satisfaction. *Group & Organization Management, 23,* 325–346.

Welbourne, T. M., & Ferrante, C. J. (2008). To monitor or not to monitor: A study of individual outcomes from monitoring one's peers under gainsharing and merit pay. *Group & Organization Management, 33(2)*, 139–162.

Werbel, J. D., & Gilliland, S. W. (1999). Person-environment fit in the selection process. *Research in Personnel and Human Resources Management, 17*, 209–243.

Werner, S., & Ones, D. S. (2000). Determinants of perceived pay inequities: The effects of comparison other characteristics and pay-system communication. *Journal of Applied Social Psychology, 30*, 1281–1309.

Wesson, M. J., & Gogus, C. I. (2005). Shaking hands with a computer: An examination of two methods of organizational newcomer orientation. *Journal of Applied Psychology, 90*, 1018–1026.

Westman, M., & Eden, D. (1997). Effects of a respite from work on burnout: Vacation relief and fade-out. *Journal of Applied Psychology, 82*, 516–527.

Wexley, K. N. (1986). Appraisal interview. In R. A. Berk (Ed.), *Performance assessment: Methods and applications* (pp. 167–185). Baltimore, MD: The Johns Hopkins University Press.

Wexley, K. N., & Baldwin, T. T. (1986). Post-training strategies for facilitating positive transfer: An empirical exploration. *Academy of Management Journal, 29*, 503–520.

Wexley, K. N., & Latham, G. P. (1991). *Developing and training human resources in organizations* (2nd ed.). New York: Harper-Collins.

Wexley, K. N., & McCellin, D. G. (1987, August). *The effects of varying training task difficulty on training transfer.* Paper presented at the 95th annual convention of the American Psychological Association, New York.

Wexley, K. N., & Latham, G. P. (2001). *Developing and training human resources in organizations* (3rd ed.). Englewood Cliffs, NJ: Prentice-Hall.

Wexley, K. N., & Yukl, G. A. (1984). *Organizational behavior and personnel psychology* (Rev. ed.). Homewood, IL: Irwin.

Whalen, T., & Wright, D. (2000). *The business case for web-based training.* Boston, MA: Artech House.

Wheaton, G. R., & Whetzel, D. L. (1997). *Contexts for developing applied measurement instruments.* In D. L. Whetzel & G. R. Wheaton (Eds.), *Applied measurement methods in industrial psychology* (pp. 1–10). Palo Alto, CA: Davies-Black.

Wheeler, D. D., & Janis, I. L. (1980). *A practical guide for making decisions.* New York: Free Press.

Wichman, A. (1994). Occupational differences in involvement with ownership in an airline employee ownership program. *Human Relations, 47*, 829–846.

Wiesenfeld, B. M., Brockner, J., & Thibault, V. (2000). Procedural fairness, managers' self-esteem, and managerial behaviors following a layoff. *Organizational Behavior and Human Decision Processes, 83*, 1–32.

Wiesenfeld, B. M., Raghuram, S., & Garud, R. (2001). Organizational identification among virtual workers: The role of need for affiliation and perceived work-based social support. *Journal of Management, 27*, 213–229.

Wiesner, W. H., & Cronshaw, S. F. (1988). A meta-analytic investigation of interviewer format and degree of structure on the validity of the employment interview. *Journal of Occupational and Organizational Psychology, 61*, 275–290.

Wildman, J. L., Bedwell, W. L., Salas, E., & Smith-Jentsch, K. A. (2011). Performance measurement at work: A multilevel perspective. In S. Zedeck (Ed.), *APA handbook of industrial and organizational psychology, Vo.1: Building and developing the organization* (pp. 303–341). Washington, DC: American Psychological Association.

Williams, J. R., & Johnson, M. A. (2000). Self-supervisor agreement: The influence of feedback seeking on the relationship between self and supervisor ratings of performance. *Journal of Applied Social Psychology, 30*, 275–292.

Williams, J. R., & Levy, P. E. (1992). The effects of perceived system knowledge on the agreement between self-ratings and supervisor ratings. *Personnel Psychology, 45*, 835–847.

Williams, K. Y., & O'Reilly, C. A. (1998). Demography and diversity in organizations: A review of 40 years of research. *Research in Organizational Behavior, 20*, 77–140.

Williams, L. C., & Day, B. T. (2011). Medical cost savings for web-based wellness program participants from employees engaged in health promotion activities. *American Journal of Health Promotion, 25(4)*, 272–280.

Williams, L. J., & Hazer, J. T. (1986). Antecedents and consequences of satisfaction and commitment in turnover models: A reanalysis using latent variable structural equation methods. *Journal of Applied Psychology, 71*, 219–231.

Williams, S., & Taormina, R. J. (1992). Unanimous versus majority influences on group polarization in business decision making. *The Journal of Social Psychology, 133*, 199–205.

Williams, T. C., & Rains, J. (2007). Linking strategy to structure: The power of systematic organization design. *Organization Development Journal, 25(2)*, 163–170.

Williamson, L. G., Campion, J. E., Malos, S. B., Roehling, M. V., & Campion, M. A. (1997). Employment interview on trial: Linking interview structure with litigation outcomes. *Journal of Applied Psychology, 82*, 900–912.

Wilson, K. Y. (2010). An analysis of bias in supervisor narrative comments in performance appraisal. *Human Relations, 63(12)*, 1903–1933.

Winter, D. G. (1973). *The power motive.* New York: Free Press.

Winter, D. G. (2002). The motivational dimensions of leadership: Power, achievement, and affiliation. In R. E. Riggio, S. E. Murphy, & F. J. Pirozzolo (Eds.), *Multiple intelligences and leadership* (pp. 119–138). Mahwah, NJ: Erlbaum.

Winters, D., & Latham, G. P. (1996). The effect of learning versus outcome goals on a simple versus a complex task. *Group & Organization Management, 21*, 236–250.

Withey, M., Daft, R. L., & Cooper, W. H. (1983). Measures of Perrow's work unit technology: An empirical assessment and a new scale. *Academy of Management Journal, 26*, 45–63.

Witt, L. A. (1998). Enhancing organizational goal congruence: A solution to organizational politics. *Journal of Applied Psychology, 83*, 666–674.

Witt, L. A., & Nye, L. G. (1992). Gender and the relationship between perceived fairness of pay or promotion and job satisfaction. *Journal of Applied Psychology, 77*, 910–917.

Wittig, M. A., & Berman, S. L. (1992). Wage structure analysis: An empirical approach to pay equity in segregated jobs. *Social Justice Research, 5*, 291–317.

Woehr, D. J. (1992). Performance dimension accessibility: Implications for rating accuracy. *Journal of Organizational Behavior, 13*, 357–367.

Woehr, D. J. (1994). Rater training for performance appraisal: A quantitative review. *Journal of Occupational and Organizational Psychology, 67*, 221–229.

Woehr, D. J., & Arthur, W. (2003). The construct-related validity of assessment center ratings: A review and meta-analysis of the role of methodological factors. *Journal of Management, 29*, 231–258.

Woehr, D. J., & Huffcutt, A. I. (1994). Rater training for performance appraisal: A quantitative review. *Journal of Occupational and Organizational Psychology, 67*, 189–205.

Woehr, D. J., & Roch, S. G. (1996). Context effects in performance evaluation: The impact of rate sex and performance level on performance ratings and behavioral recall. *Organizational Behavior and Human Decision Processes, 66*, 31–41.

Wofford, J. C., Goodwin, V. L., & Premack, S. (1992). Meta-analysis of the antecedents of personal goal level and of the antecedents and consequences of goal commitment. *Journal of Management, 18(3)*, 595–615.

Wofford, J. C., & Liska, L. Z. (1993). Path-goal theories of leadership: A meta-analysis. *Journal of Management, 19*, 857–874.

Wohlers, A. J., Hall, M., & London, M. (1993). Subordinates rating managers: Organizational and demographic correlates of self-subordinate agreement. *Journal of Occupational and Organizational Psychology, 66*, 263–275.

Wohlers, A. J., & London, M. (1989). Ratings of managerial characteristics: Evaluation difficulty, coworker agreement, and self-awareness. *Personnel Psychology, 42*, 235–261.

Wolf, F. M. (1986). *Meta-analysis: Quantitative methods for research synthesis.* Beverly Hills, CA: Sage.

Wolf, S. G. (1986). Common and grave disorders identified with occupational stress. In S. G. Wolf & A. J. Finestone (Eds.), *Occupational stress: Health and performance at work* (pp. 47–53). Littleton, MA: PSG Publishing.

Wonderlic, E. F. (1983). *Wonderlic Personnel Test.* Northfield, IL: Wonderlic and Associates.

Wong, C., Hui, C., & Law, K. S. (1998) A longitudinal study of the job perception-job satisfaction relationship: A test of the three alternative specifications. *Journal of Occupational and Organizational Psychology, 71*, 127–146.

Woodman, R. W., & Pasmore, W. A. (Eds.). (1987). *Research in organizational change and development* (Vol. 1). Greenwich, CT: JAI Press.

Woodward, J. (1965). *Industrial organization: Theory and practice.* London, UK: Oxford University Press.

Wratcher, M. A., & Jones, R. D. (1986). A time management workshop for adult workers. *Journal of College Student Personnel, 27*, 566–567.

Wright, G. E., & Multon, K. D. (1995). Employer's perception of nonverbal communication in job interviews for persons with physical disabilities. *Journal of Vocational Behavior, 47*, 214–227.

Wright, P. M., Lichtenfels, P. A., & Pursell, E. D. (1989). The structured interview: Additional studies and a meta-analysis. *Journal of Occupational and Organizational Psychology, 62*, 191–199.

Wright, T. A., & Cropanzano, R. (1998). Emotional exhaustion as a predictor of job performance and voluntary turnover. *Journal of Applied Psychology, 83*, 486–493.

Xin, K. R., & Tsui, A. S. (1996). Different strokes for different folks? Influence tactics by Asian-American and Caucasian-American managers. *Leadership Quarterly, 17*, 109–132.

Yaffe, T., & Kark, R. (2011). Leading by example: The case of leader OCB. *Journal of Applied Psychology, 96(4)*, 806–826.

Yammarino, F. J., & Waldman, D. A. (1993). Performance in relation to job skill importance: A consideration of rater source. *Journal of Applied Psychology, 78*, 242–249.

Yang, J., & Mossholder, K. W. (2004). Decoupling task and relationship conflict: The role of intragroup emotional processing. *Journal of Organizational Behavior, 25*, 589–605.

Yang, L. Che, H., & Spector, P. E. (2008). Job stress and well-being: An examination from the view of person-environment fit. *Journal of Occupational and Organizational Psychology, 81(3)*, 567–587.

Yates, J., & Orlikowski, W. J. (1992). Genres of organizational communication: A structrational approach to studying communication and the media. *Academy of Management Review, 17*, 299–326.

Ybema, J. F., Smulders, P. G. W., & Bongers, P. M. (2010). Antecedents and consequences of employee absenteeism: A longitudinal perspective on the role of job satisfaction and burnout. *European Journal of Work and Organizational Psychology, 19(1)*, 102–124.

Yeager, S. J. (1981). Dimensionality of the job descriptive index. *Academy of Management Journal, 14*, 205–212.

Yen, H. R., & Niehoff, B. P. (2004). Organizational citizenship behaviors and organizational effectiveness: Examining relationships in Taiwanese banks. *Journal of Applied Social Psychology, 34*, 1617–1637.

Yetton, P. W., & Bottger, P. C. (1982). Individual versus group problem solving: An empirical test of a best-member strategy. *Organizational Behavior and Human Performance, 29*, 307–321.

Yoon, M. H., & Suh, J. (2003). Organizational citizenship behaviors and service quality as external effectiveness of contact employees. *Journal of Business Research, 56*, 597–611.

Yorks, L. (1979). *Job enrichment revisited.* New York: AMACOM.

Young, A. M., & Perrewé, P. L. (2000). What did you expect? An examination of career-related support and social support among mentors and protégés. *Journal of Management, 26*, 611–632.

Youngblood, S. A. (1984). Work, nonwork, and withdrawal. *Journal of Applied Psychology, 69*, 106–117.

Yukl, G. A. (1971). Toward a behavioral theory of leadership. *Organizational Behavior and Human Performance, 6*, 414–440.

Yukl, G. A. (1981). *Leadership in organizations.* Englewood Cliffs, NJ: Prentice Hall.

Yukl, G. A. (1989). *Leadership in organizations* (2nd ed.). Englewood Cliffs, NJ: Prentice Hall.

Yukl, G. A. (1998). *Leadership in organizations* (4th ed.). Englewood Cliffs, NJ: Prentice Hall.

Yukl, G. A. (2007). Best practices in the use of proactive influence practices by leaders. In J. A. Conger & R. E. Riggio (Eds.), *The practice of leadership* (pp. 109–128). San Francisco, CA: Jossey-Bass.

Yukl, G. A., & Falbe, C. M. (1990). Influence tactics and objectives in upward, downward, and lateral influence attempts. *Journal of Applied Psychology, 75*, 132–140.

Yukl, G. A., & Falbe, C. M. (1991). Importance of different power sources in downward and lateral relations. *Journal of Applied Psychology, 76*, 416–423.

Yukl, G. A., Guinan, P. J., & Sottolano, D. (1995). Influence tactics used for different objectives with subordinates, peers, and superiors. *Group & Organization Management, 20*, 272–296.

Yukl, G. A., & Tracey, J. B. (1992). Consequences of influence tactics used with subordinates, peers, and the boss. *Journal of Applied Psychology, 77*, 525–535.

Yukl, G. A., & VanFleet, D. D. (1992). Theory and research on leadership in organizations. In M. D. Dunnette & L. M. Hough (Eds.), *Handbook of industrial and organizational psychology* (Vol. 3, 2nd ed., pp. 147–197). Palo Alto, CA: Consulting Psychologists Press.

Zaccaro, S. J., & Banks, D. (2004). Leader visioning and adaptability: Bridging the gap between research and practice on developing the ability to manage change. *Human Resource Management, 43(4)*, 367–380.

Zaccaro, S. J., Foti, R. J., & Kenny, D. A. (1991). Self-monitoring and trait-based variance in leadership: An investigation of leader flexibility across multiple group situations. *Journal of Applied Psychology, 76*, 179–185.

Zahn, G. L. (1991). Face-to-face communication in an office setting. *Communication Research, 18*, 737–754.

Zander, A. (1950). Resistance to change—its analysis and prevention. *Advanced Management Journal, 15*, 9–11.

Zapf, D., Seifert, C., Schmutte, B., Mertini, H., & Holz, M. (2001). Emotion work and job stressors and their effects on burnout. *Psychology & Health, 16*, 527–545.

Zaremba, A. (1988, July). Communication: Working with the organizational grapevine. *Personnel Journal*, pp. 83–84.

Zedeck, S. (1977). An information processing model and approach to the study of motivation. *Organizational Behavior and Human Performance, 18*, 47–77.

Zeitlin, L. R. (1995). Organizational downsizing and stress-related illness. *International Journal of Stress Management, 2*, 207–219.

Zhou, J., & George, J. M. (2001). When job dissatisfaction leads to creativity: Encouraging the expression of voice. *Academy of Management Journal, 44*, 682–696.

Zweig, D., & Scott, K. (2007). When unfairness matters most: Supervisory violations of electronic monitoring practices. *Human Resource Management Journal, 17*, 227–247.

Zweig, D., & Webster, J. (2002). Where is the line between benign and invasive? An examination of psychological barriers to the acceptance of awareness monitoring systems. *Journal of Organizational Behavior, 23*, 605–633.

Zwerman, W. L. (1970). *New perspectives on organizational theory*. Westport, CT: Greenwood Press.

CREDITS

Text Credits

Page 10 Excerpt By permission of the Society for Industrial and Organizational Psychology.

Page 41 Excerpt Reprinted with permission from PSYCHOLOGY TODAY MAGAZINE, Copyright © 1982 Sussex Publishers, LLC.

Page 56 Table 3.1 Adapted from: Plachy, R. J., & Plachy, S. J. (1998). More results-oriented job descriptions. By permission of AMACOM.

Page 57 Figure 3.1 By permission of Jaisingh V. Ghorpade.

Page 63 Figure 3.2 Adapted from Flanagan, J. C. (1954). The Critical Incidents Technique. Psychological Bulletin, 51, 342.

Page 64 Figure 3.3 McCormick, E. J., Jeanneret, P. R., & Mecham, R. C. (1969). Position Analysis Questionnaire (p. 4). West Lafayette, IN: Occupational Research Center, Purdue University. By permission of the Purdue Research Foundation.

Page 66 Table 3.2 Adapted from Flanagan, J. C. (1954). The Critical Incidents Technique. Psychological Bulletin, 51, 342.

Page 69 Box 3.1 www.mynextmove.org.

Page 74 Figure 3.4 Terjesen, S., & Singh, V. (2008). Female presence on corporate boards: A multi-country study of environmental context. Journal of Business Ethics, 83, 55–63. By permission of Springer, Ltd.

Page 80 Excerpt Mulcahy 2010, PMP Exam Prep, 6/e. RMC Publications, Inc.

Page 84 Definition Gatewood, Feild, & Barrick (2008). Human Resources Selection, 6/e. By permission of Cengage Learning.

Page 87 Figure 4.2 Millsap & Kwok (2004).

Page 90 Figure 4.3 Cascio, Wayne E., APPLIED PSYCHOLOGY IN PERSONNEL MANAGEMENT, 3rd Ed., © 1987. Reprinted and Electronically reproduced by permission of Pearson Education, Inc., Upper Saddle River, New Jersey.

Page 110 Figure 5.3 Bennett Mechanical Comprehension Test (BMCT). Copyright © 1942, 1967–1970, 1980–1981 NCS Pearson, Inc. Reproduced with permission. All rights reserved. "Bennett Mechanical Comprehension Test" and "BMCT" are trademarks, in the US and/or other countries, of Pearson Education, Inc. or its affiliates(s).

Page 119 Figure 5.5 From Formative Years in Business: A Long-Term A.T.&T. Study of Managerial Lives, by D. W. Bray, Richard J. Campbell, and D. L. Grant, p. 24–25. Copyright © 1974. Reproduced with permission of John Wiley & Sons, Inc.

Page 131 Table 6.2 Table from The Measurement of work Performance: Methods, theory, and applications by F. J. Landy and J. L. Farr. Copyright 1983, Elsevier Science (USA), reproduced with permission from the publisher.

Page 140 Figure 6.2 Guion, R. M. Personnel Testing, 1965. By permission of the McGraw-Hill Companies.

Page 142 Figure 6.3 Berk, Ronald A. Performance Assessment: Methods and Applications. p. 93, figure 2.2 and p. 103, figure 3.2. © 1986 The Johns Hopkins University Press. Reprinted with permission of The Johns Hopkins University Press.

Page 143 Figure 6.4 Berk, Ronald A. Performance Assessment: Methods and Applications. p. 93, figure 2.2 and p. 103, figure 3.2. © 1986 The Johns Hopkins University Press. Reprinted with permission of The Johns Hopkins University Press.

Page 149 Table 6.3 Harris, T. E. (1993). Applied organizational communication: Perspectives, principles, and pragmatics. Hillsdale, NJ: Erlbaum. By permission of Taylor & Francis, Inc.;

Page 161 Table 7.1 Leibowitz, Z. B., Farren, C., & Kaye B. I. (1986). Designing Career Development Systems (p. 7). By permission of John Wiley & Sons, Inc.

Page 195 Excerpt By permission of M. M. Machlowitz.

Page 197 Excerpt From Komaki, Coombs, & Schepman, 1991. Motivational implications of reinforcement theory. Steers & Porter, eds. Motivation and work behavior, 5/e, NY: McGraw Hill, pp. 87–107.

Page 203 Figure 8.2 Hackman, J. R., & Oldham, G. R. (1976). Motivation through the design of work: Test of a theory. Organizational Behavior and Human Performance, 16, 256. By permission of Academic Press.

Page 223 Figure 9.1 Copyright 1967, Vocational Psychology Research, University of Minnesota. Reproduced by permission.

Page 224 Figure 9.2 Smith, P. C., Kendall, L. M., & Hulin, C. L. (1985). Job descriptive index. From The measurement of satisfaction in work and retirement (rev. ed.). Bowling Green, OH. By permission of Bowling Green State University.

Page 228 Figure 9.4 Mowday, R. T., Steers, R., & Porter, L. W. (1979). The measure of organizational commitment. Journal of Vocational Behavior, 14, 228. By permission of Elsevier, Ltd.

Page 242 Table 9.1 Podsakoff, P. M., MacKensie, S. B., Paine, J. B., & Bachrach, D. G. (2000). Organizational citizenship behaviors: A critical review of the theoretical and empirical literature and suggestions for future research. Journal of Management, 26, 513–563. By permission of Sage Publications, Ltd.

Page 258 Table 10.2 By permission of C. David Jenkins.

Page 258 Table 10.2 Haynes, Feinleib, Levine, Scotch, & Kannel, 1978, The relationship of psychosocial factors to coronary heart disease in the Framingham study. American Journal of Epidemiology, 107, 384-402. By permission of Oxford University Press.

Page 262 Table 10.3 By permission of Elsevier, Ltd.

Page 264 Figure 10.1 Adapted from Cohen, S. V. (1980). After-effects of stress on human behavior and social behavior: A review of research theory. Psychological Bulletin, 88, 85.

Page 266 Table 10.4 Reproduced by special permission of the Publisher, MIND GARDEN, Inc., www.mindgarden.com from the Maslach Burnout Inventory Human Services Survey by Christina Maslach & Susan E. Jackson. Copyright Copyright © 1986 by CPP, Inc. Further reproduction is prohibited without the Publisher's written consent.

Page 271 Excerpt Wasik, B. 1984. Teaching parents effective problem solving: A Handbook for professionals. Chapel Hill: University of North Carolina Press.

Page 274 Table 10.5 Bennett, R. J. & Robinson, S. L. (2000). Development of a measure of workplace deviance. Journal of Applied Psychology, 85, 349–360.

Page 282 Table 11.1 Organizational Communication: The Essence of Effective Management by Philip V. Lewis. By permission of John Wiley & Sons, Inc.

Page 311 Table 12.1 Benne K. D., & Sheats, P. (1948). Functional roles of group members. Journal of Social Issues, 4, 41–49. By permission of John Wiley & Sons, Inc.

Page 328 Excerpt Blake, Mouton, & Sloma, 1964, p. 189, An actual case history of resolving intergroup conflict. Blake, Shepard & Mouton, Managing intergroup conflict in industry. Houston, TX: Gulf.

Page 338 Table 12.4 Hackman, J. R. (1998). "Why teams don't work," Theory and Research On Small Groups, R. Scott Tindale et al. (eds.), with kind permission from Springer Science+Business Media B. V.

Page 349 Figure 13.1 Blake, R. R., & McCanse, A. A. (1991). Leadership dilemmas-grid solutions. Houston, TX: Gulf. By permission of Taylor & Francis Journals.

Page 351 Figure 13.2 Fiedler, F. E. (1967). A theory of Leadership effectiveness (pp. 40-41). By permission of the McGraw-Hill Companies.

Page 357 Table 13.1 The table "Five Decision-Making Strategies: The Model" originally appeared as Table 2.1, Decision Methods for Group and Individual Problems in LEADERSHIP AND DECISION-MAKING, by Victor H. Vroom and Philip W. Yetton, © 1973. Reprinted by permission of the University of Pittsburgh Press.

Page 376 Table 14.1 Kipnis, D., Schmidt, S. M., & Wilkinson, I. (1980). Intraorganizational influence tactics: Explorations in getting one's way. Journal of Applied Psychology, 65, 445–448.

Page 382 Table 14.2 Hinkin, T. R., & Schriesheim, C. A. (1989). Development and application of new scales to measure French and Raven (1959) bases of social power. Journal of Applied Psychology, 74, 561–567. (American Psychological Association).

Page 388 Figure 14.1 Robbins, S. P., ORGANIZATIONAL BEHAVIOR: CONCEPTS & CONTROVERSIES, 1st Ed., © 1979. Reprinted and Electronically reproduced by permission of Pearson Education, Inc., Upper Saddle River, New Jersey.

Page 398 Figure 14.3 Cobb, A. T. (1984). Academy of Management Review (Vol. 9, pp. 482–493). Reprinted by permission of the Academy of Management.

Photo Credits

Chapter 1
Page 5 Jacques Boyer/Roger-Viollet/The Image Works.
Page 7 John Lent/Associated Press.
Page 14 ARENA Creative/Shutterstock.

Chapter 2
Page 24 Juice Images109/Alamy.
Page 34 ArrowStudio, LLC/shutterstock.

Chapter 3
Page 59 Olaf Doering/Alamy Limited.
Page 68 Simone van den Berg/Shutterstock
Page 72 Copyright, Doug Marlette.

Chapter 4
Page 80 Nancy Kaszerman/ZUMA Press/Newscom.

Chapter 5
Page 105 Chris Cooper-Smith/Alamy.
Page 114 wavebreakmedia ltd/Shutterstock.
Page 120 Rido/Shutterstock.
Page 122 imageegami/Shutterstock.
Page 124 ScienceCartoonsPlus.com.

Chapter 6
Page 134 marcovarro/Shutterstock.
Page 145 image100 Business AC/image100/Alamy.

Chapter 7
Page 159 Alexander Raths/Shutterstock.
Page 173 Lisa S./Shutterstock.
Page 179 Steve Cole/Getty Images.
Page 184 Jim West/Alamy Limited.

Chapter 8
Page 197 Prodakszyn/Shutterstock.
Page 204 Blaj Gabriel/Shutterstock.

Page 213 Michael Runkel/Robert Harding World Imagery/Alamy.

Chapter 9
Page 237 Mim Friday/Alamy.
Page 242 wavebreakmedia ltd/Shutterstock.

Chapter 10
Page 252 Vincent Hazat/PhotoAlto/Alamy.
Page 255 Jetta Productions/Blend Images/Alamy.
Page 267 Shutterstock Images.
Page 274 David Urbina/PhotoEdit.

Chapter 11
Page 284 Idealink Photography/Alamy.
Page 287 Martin Shields/Alamy.
Page 295 Henry Martin/The New Yorker Collection/ www.cartoonbank.com.

Chapter 12
Page 310 Ton Koene/Age Fotostock.
Page 323 Alex Gallardo/Reuters.

Chapter 13
Page 343 Molly Riley/REUTERS.
Page 352 Zurijeta/Shutterstock.
Page 361 Jose Gil/Alamy.

Chapter 14
Page 381 kolvenbach/Alamy.
Page 396 Big Cheese Photo/Superstock.

Chapter 15
Page 416 Robert Landau/Alamy.
Page 420 piluhin/Alamy Limited.
Page 422 VIEW Pictures Ltd/Alamy.
Page 432 auremar/Shutterstock.

AUTHOR INDEX

Note: Locators in italics indicate tables or figures.

SUBJECT INDEX

Note: Locators in italics indicate tables or figures.